Teaching Students with Learning
and Behavior Problems

Teaching Students with Learning and Behavior Problems

Managing Mild-To-Moderate Difficulties in Resource and Inclusive Settings

Sixth Edition

Donald D. Hammill
Nettie R. Bartel

pro·ed

8700 Shoal Creek Boulevard
Austin, Texas 78757

pro·ed

© 1995 by PRO-ED, Inc.
8700 Shoal Creek Boulevard
Austin, Texas 78757-6897

Library of Congress Cataloging-in-Publication Data

Hammill, Donald D., 1934–
    Teaching students with learning and behavior problems : managing
mild-to-moderate difficulties in resource and inclusive settings /
Donald D. Hammill, Nettie R. Bartel. — 6th ed.
      p.   cm.
    Includes bibliographical references (p.   ) and indexes.
    ISBN 0-89079-610-6
    1. Learning disabilities.   2. Learning disabled children-
-Education—Canada   3. Learning disabled children—Education-
-United States.   I. Bartel, Nettie R.   II. Title.
LC4704.H35   1995
371.9—dc20   94-15554
                                       CIP

Production Manager: Alan Grimes
Art Director: Lori Kopp
Reprints Buyer: Alicia Woods
Editor: Debra Berman
Editorial Assistant: Claudette Landry

Printed in the United States of America

2   3   4   5   6   7   8   9   10   99 98 97 96

Contents

· ·

Preface

All teachers, whether they teach regular or exceptional students, frequently encounter youngsters at the elementary or secondary level who are not responsive to instruction or who are disruptive in class. These students may evidence problems in reading, arithmetic, language, or writing or in social adjustment or motivation. Most of them are probably the victims of poor teaching, insufficient background experience, and/or inadequate motivation. No students are immune to the debilitating effects of these three factors; bright or retarded, sound or crippled, stable or difficult students can be affected at one time or another.

Over the years, the schools have evolved numerous alternatives for handling below-average learners. Psychological services, special education classes, and remedial programs have been provided. With this proliferation of specialized educational services, teachers have become increasingly dependent upon noninstructional personnel to assist them in teaching students with school-related problems. Thus, educational assessment has become the responsibility of the school psychologist; slow learners are shunted off to the "retarded" class; poor readers are referred to the remedial reading specialist; and troublesome students eventually are placed in classes for the "emotionally disturbed." The great majority of difficult students, however, remain in the regular class under the supervision of the teacher, who is expected to meet their individual needs.

Many students presently enrolled in special education classes will likely be integrated into regular classes within the next few years. The trend toward isolating problem children, which was so prevalent during the past few decades, is being reversed as educators recognize that special class placements bring few benefits to mildly handicapped children. Educators and others find the special class solution philosophically objectionable in the 1990s. School systems are not likely to return these students to the educational mainstream without making some provisions on their behalf. These provisions will probably take the forms of resource rooms, consultants, tutors, and itinerant programs.

Teachers are currently responsible for the achievement of many students who are difficult to teach, and in the future they will probably be responsible for more of these students. Unfortunately, many teachers lack the information that would enable them to cope with these students. A number of elementary and secondary education teacher-training programs fail to sufficiently familiarize their students with basic assessment procedures, diagnostic and prescriptive teacher techniques, and remedial materials and methods. Yet knowledge of a wide variety of remedial and developmental instructional approaches and activities is necessary to accommodate the disparate educational needs of nonachieving pupils.

With these ideas in mind, we have written this book for teachers. Our intentions were (1) to succinctly review the roles and duties of teachers in the management of students with school-related problems; (2) to provide teachers with a series of discussions that focus on these school-related difficulties (e.g., reading, spelling, arithmetic, handwriting, and behavior); (3) to provide, along with these discussions, basic information regarding appropriate assessment techniques and instructional methods; and (4) to provide teachers with suggestions for specific materials and sources.

We do not presume to present and discuss all the possible evaluation and instructional methods that are available to teachers today. This would have been a monumental effort, and one that we have neither the energy nor the experience to undertake. Instead, we have shared with the reader those exceptional approaches and ideas with which we have had some direct personal experience.

We are not necessarily endorsing the materials or methods described here; rather, we have tried to provide information on representative techniques to enable teachers to choose materials appropriate for their students. Teachers are urged to evaluate the effectiveness of their selections in their own classrooms, as research on the efficacy of most programs is inadequate or nonexistent.

Some special comment should be made about this sixth edition. First, we have checked to make sure that all tests and methods referred to are still popular and available. Second, we have continued to focus on the school-age student.

Finally, we want to express our deep appreciation to the college instructors who over the years have continued to adopt our book for their classes, and to the teachers who have found our work useful and recommended it to their colleagues. It has been your loyal support, dear readers, that has made this sixth edition possible.

Chapter 1

Meeting the Special Needs of Students

DONALD D. HAMMILL AND NETTIE R. BARTEL

Most experienced teachers are able to recognize children and adolescents who seem bright but who fail to make expected gains in a particular skill after repeated exposure to training. If the skill is reading, the teacher may notice that the student reads aloud quite well but has great difficulty with comprehension during silent reading. Another student may become confused when directions are given orally but exhibit comparative superiority in reading and writing. A third youngster may have adequate listening and speech skills but manifest problems when he or she engages in math activities.

Some students evidence discrepancies of varying degrees between their estimated intellectual ability and their actual performance; others show marked divergence between the skills in which they excel and those in which they are inadequate or marginal; and others are merely slow in acquiring necessary school behaviors. To a large extent, these problems involve the understanding or the use of spoken or written language and are manifested in difficulty with reading, thinking, talking, listening, writing, spelling, or arithmetic. They may also include behavior problems. The problems range from mild to intense and are occasionally associated with blindness, deafness, psychosis, and/or severe mental defect. For the most part, however, the difficulties are found in mild to moderate degree in individuals who are otherwise "normal."

In the past, school personnel have been quick to confuse a student's school problem with a diagnostic label. Students who performed inadequately in the classroom tended to be labeled "retarded," "disturbed," "learning disabled," or "deprived," when their problems in fact were reading, writing, or mathematics. Although students exist for whom these labels are appropriate, teachers should be cautioned that labels have been applied to students in a rather indiscriminate fashion and that an uncounted number of students have been misdiagnosed and misplaced. Such terms have little use for the classroom teacher who must devise instructional techniques that are effective for individual students, especially those with mild to moderate problems.

In practice, a teacher must prepare an educational program in response to an individual student's educational needs and behaviors, not in response to a diagnostic label or definition the student may or may not satisfy. The nature of the program that is prepared will reflect in large part the teacher's (and the school's) philosophy and attitudes regarding a number of educational matters. In the remainder of this chapter, we delineate these factors and discuss issues that relate to them.

We have organized our thinking about these important factors in terms of an instructional model, which is presented in Figure 1.1. Although in practice the elements of the model are quite interrelated, for discussion purposes we have separated them arbitrarily into three basic parts: (1) the assumptions that influence instruction, (2) the components involved in instruction, and (3) the cycle used to implement instructional programs.

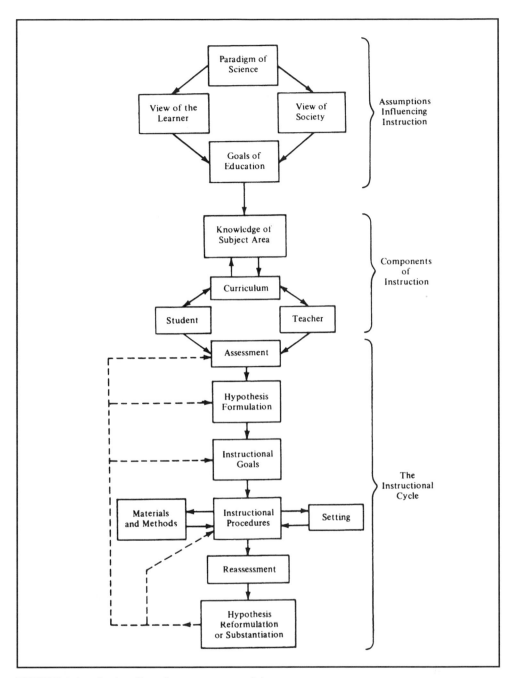

FIGURE 1.1.   Instructional sequence model.

Adapted from "Approaches for Alternative Programming" by N. R. Bartel, D. N. Bryen, and H. W. Bartel; in *Alternatives for Teaching Exceptional Children* (p. 354) by E. L. Meyen, G. A. Vergason, and R. J. Whelan (Eds.), 1975, Denver, CO: Love Publications.

ASSUMPTIONS INFLUENCING INSTRUCTION

The program that teachers elect for each student will necessarily reflect their assumptions and beliefs about the purpose of education, the nature of learning, and the role of the student, the teacher, and even society in the schooling process. These assumptions are rarely made explicit as far as teachers are concerned, yet they govern almost all the decisions that teachers make. These assumptions include the answers (implicit or explicit) to such questions as these: What are the schools for? What is this particular student supposed to get out of school? How is this student supposed to fit into society ultimately? What is the nature of the world and of the role of the student and the teacher within it? Let us briefly turn to this last question first.

A perusal of the many approaches to educating the student with learning and behavioral problems presented in this book will quickly lead the reader to the conclusion that the last question posed in the previous paragraph has not been answered. The various approaches are quite obviously based on differing, even inconsistent, assumptions about the nature of the world and of the student and the teacher within it. For example, among the approaches reviewed, one will see evidence of a world view that is highly mechanistic and predictable. For such a perspective, the machine is the most appropriate metaphor. Here, the student is seen as a relatively passive component in a setting that is arranged so that events (instructional happenings) impinge on him or her in such a way that fully predictable outcomes will come about. The teacher serves as the master technician who engineers the learning environment in such a way that the most desirable results will occur. The act of learning, then, is something that happens as a result of the application of predetermined forces. The ideal curriculum for such a viewpoint is "teacher-proof." That is, the program is packaged in such a way pedagogically and substantively that the teacher cannot interfere with the learning process. Similarly, the program is designed so that the probabilities are great that the learner will emit only the desired responses.

The contrasting position holds that the world is in continuous transition from one state to another by means of progressive differentiation. This view leads one to think of students, even students with learning and behavioral problems, as active individuals who not only make predetermined "correct" responses but also interact with, and change, their learning environment. Thus, learning is not merely the quantitative accumulation of objective facts but an active cognitive construction and transformation of reality.

That these issues have not been resolved in the education of students with learning problems is evident in the competing curricula. On the one hand, one sees widespread use of programmed materials, which promise precision, ease of measurement, and ready accountability. Clearly, the implicit assumption is that the curriculum developer has access to society's knowledge store and has arranged this knowledge in appropriate bits and sequences to which the learner need only be exposed following prescribed procedures. The behavior of both the teacher and the student is predictable. Seen from this orientation, the effective teacher is one who is able to move the learner quickly through the prescribed components of the curriculum with minimal obtrusion stemming from teacher or learner idiosyncracies.

On the other hand, the alternative world view is noted for its open-endedness and unpredictability. Here curriculum designers and implementers may follow some variation of the Piagetian notion of assimilation and accommodation. That is, they acknowledge that the learner is shaped repeatedly by the realities of the world and that he or she returns the favor by continuously moving to reshape those world realities. To them, education is not getting a learner to make predictable responses, but seeing to it that he or she is progressively being changed by and changing the environment. Clearly, these underlying assumptions have major implications for the choices that a teacher makes in instructional planning and implementation.

COMPONENTS OF INSTRUCTION

The choices that the teacher must make are further complicated by decisions that must be made concerning the components of instruction. As can be seen in Figure 1.1, the teacher's job is to bring the student and the learning task into some kind of proximity with each other. However, even this seemingly simple responsibility turns out to be complicated.

Educators assume that students and curricular materials cannot be randomly matched to each other. That is, if one is teaching social studies to a group of second graders, one cannot simply walk down to the school library and pull any text from the social studies section of the shelves and assume that it will meet the learners' needs. When selecting materials, the teacher should consider such factors as the children's age, overall developmental level, and interests. Conversely, just because a teacher is fond of a particular reading series or spelling book does not mean that it can be used effectively with the group of students being instructed.

This brings us to a most interesting question, one that will surface repeatedly throughout this book: What are the learner's characteristics that a teacher should take into account in selecting instructional materials? Conversely, what are the curricular characteristics that a teacher must reckon with in determining their potential effectiveness with a student? A perusal of the educational research literature quickly leads one to conclude that each of an almost infinite array of characteristics—ranging from whether the student went through a creeping stage to whether the student's father lives in the home—has been thought by someone to be a significant variable that should be taken into account by the teacher. By no means does everyone agree on what to look for. Obviously, if the teacher is ever going to have any time to do any teaching, he or she must select from an almost endless range of pupil behaviors those that have sufficient implications for instruction to be worth noting and reporting.

The situation with respect to variability among curricular approaches is similar. Thus, to use an example from beginning reading, serious claims have been made that picture words, words using a unique alphabet, or words printed in different colors, to name a few, should be considered by the classroom teacher for teaching reading to certain students. Is the teacher to assume that letter-color aptitude, for example, is a significant student characteristic that should be measured and related to the use of color in the curriculum?

When one considers the possible permutations in the infinite range of potential student characteristics that could be measured and matched to an almost infinite range of curriculum characteristics, the problem becomes staggering indeed. This book represents an effort to reduce the teacher's task to more manageable proportions. We have tried to indicate the most promising aspects of the student's functioning to consider in instructional planning. We have drawn heavily from developmental psychology, particularly the work of Piaget, Bruner, and Gagné.

On the curriculum side, some observations are also in order. We note that curricula may be placed on a continuum ranging from (1) broad-based systems represented in schoolwide adopted programs in reading, science, and other subjects intended for use with all students to (2) narrow and prescriptive approaches intended to meet the particular subject or skill needs of individual students.

Many of the newer approaches that have been found to be most successful with students who have learning and behavioral problems are found at the prescriptive end of the scale, and the reader will find such approaches heavily represented in the chapters of this book. One could probably make a case that the boys and girls for whom this book is written are precisely those for whom the more widely used school-adopted educational programs have been unsuccessful. The ideas, concepts, facts, and skills that other students pick up quickly from the traditional approaches have, for some reason, not been acquired by these students. Because of this, we have included many references to prescriptive teaching approaches throughout this book. However, we caution the reader that no instructional program has been devised to date that can anticipate all the learning possibilities that occur in the classroom. No program can preplan every possible utterance or action of the teacher or student.

When using any of the many structured approaches described in the subsequent pages, teachers should watch for those unique teaching–learning interactions that cannot be fully planned in advance. Furthermore, we caution teachers against making the presumptions that the only significant learning is that which the teacher has decided on ahead of time and that everything that is important can be reduced to a paper-and-pencil test or lesson. The highly structured approaches are at their best in teasing out the subelements of such complicated tasks as decoding words and sentences and arithmetic computation. They have been much less successful in helping teachers develop ways of teaching and measuring reading comprehension and arithmetic understanding. The problem that faces classroom teachers, however, is that they cannot sit still, letting time go by, while the theoreticians and the experts decide whether, for example, the reading act is a unitary phenomenon or can be validly broken into subelements.

The seeming inability of many learners to master content that is presented in the traditional way has led educators to present the content in a different format or medium or in the same format but in different-sized chunks. This breaking down of a body of content into its component parts or steps has become known as "task analysis," "learning hierarchies," or the "diagnostic approach." In each instance, the specific step presented to the student is based on what he or she has previously mastered and is "tailored" in such a way that he or she has a high likelihood of mastering the task. Although the specifics of the procedures recommended by the various proponents of task analysis vary, several general commonalities characterize the approach. All advocates of task analysis recommend the differentiation of tasks into micro units or subordinate subskills or lower level topics that the learner can master one step at a time. Only when the student has demonstrated success on one task is the next task in the hierarchy presented. The teacher does not have to undertake a complete task analysis for every bit of classroom instruction. Most curricular guides, if well organized and well differentiated, can be used as rough task analytic outlines. In fact, a good scope-and-sequence chart can serve many of the functions of a task analysis.

Having reviewed the assumptions influencing instruction and the components of instruction, we turn next to a consideration of the sequential nature of the instructional process itself.

THE INSTRUCTIONAL CYCLE (THE INDIVIDUALIZED EDUCATIONAL PLAN)

The various stages of the instructional cycle coincide to a great extent with what has become known as the Individualized Educational Plan (IEP). The IEP is a requirement of the federal Education of All Handicapped Children Act (P.L. 94-142), which mandates that every student who is disabled must have an individually planned and implemented educational program. Although, legally speaking, the IEP is required only for students with disabilities, it is equally appropriate for every student, handicapped or not, who has been singled out to receive special instruction or services. The elements of the IEP include the assessment of the student, the formulation of long-range goals and short-term objectives, a description of the proposed educational intervention with specification of type and duration of each aspect of instruction, and an evaluation of the effort. These elements are closely related to the steps specified in the instructional cycle of our model (Figure 1.1). Because the IEP will be required for all students having disabilities, no matter what their educational setting, and because the IEP concept is implicit in subsequent chapters of this book, we offer the following as a general overview, which is adaptable to each of the subsequent chapter contents.

Assessment

Before developing and implementing instructional plans for students, teachers must assemble a critical body of knowledge about each student's problem. This includes knowing the kind of problem manifested, the degree of its severity, the specific ability and subject matter strengths and weaknesses, the attitudes that the student has toward learning and self-worth, and the many other factors that may cause or contribute to the disability.

At one time or another, the teacher will need to know the answers to the following questions. These particular questions relate to reading, but similar ones can be formulated that pertain to writing, math, behavior, and so forth.

Does Susan read significantly below her peers?

At what level does she read?

After a semester of remedial reading, how much improvement did she make?

What is the average reading level of the students in her class or school?

Given her performance, does she qualify for placement in a special class?

Which of her particular skills are deficient?

Where should instruction begin?

What and how should she be taught?

To answer these and other equally important questions, teachers will have to interpret data drawn from many sources. Some information may help the teacher reach a diagnosis in terms of physical, emotional, social, and environmental conditions. Other information may help the teacher decide just what skills should be taught, the order of their presentation, and the best methods of instruction. In collecting this information, teachers will have to employ many diverse assessment techniques, to interpret results from several points of view, and to know when to use standardized or nonstandardized techniques.

Assessment Techniques

A variety of assessment techniques are available for teachers. Of these, the most frequently employed are testing, evaluating students' products, direct observation, interviewing, analytic teaching, and reviewing school records.

TESTING

A test is any instrument or systematic procedure that measures a sample of behavior. Tests are used to answer the question "How well does the individual perform, either in comparison with others or in comparison with a domain of performance skills?" Tests include all teacher-made tests, checklists, and rating scales.

PRODUCT EVALUATION

All procedures that are used to assess students' products are considered to be assessment tools. The products, such as speech and oral reading samples, essays, or math papers, can be checked for errors, rated on overall quality, or evaluated according to levels, with scope-and-sequence charts or developmental scales as guides.

DIRECT OBSERVATION

A considerable amount of useful information can be obtained from direct observation. Targeted students can be watched carefully in classrooms or at play and their behavior noted. Observation is a valuable tool when the teacher wants to verify the existence of behavioral problems.

INTERVIEWING

The interview is actually a conversation that is directed to a definite purpose other than satisfaction in the conversation itself. Much useful information can be obtained from interviewing parents, teachers, agemates, and the students themselves.

ANALYTIC TEACHING

Analytic teaching is accomplished through an ongoing process of teaching the student and evaluating his or her responses to dynamic instructional activities and tasks. Sometimes it is called prescriptive, diagnostic, or clinical teaching. For example, a teacher might use an analytic teaching procedure to assess the depth of John's knowledge about colors. To do this, the teacher must evaluate John's responses to a series of tasks that are specifically prepared to yield answers relating to the following questions:

1. Can John match the basic colors (place red chips together, blue chips together, etc.)? If not, what colors does he have difficulty in matching?

2. If asked to point to the red chip, then to the blue chip, and so forth, can John select the correct chip from among others of different colors?

3. If the teacher points to the red chip, then to the blue chip, and so forth, and says "What color is this?" does John answer correctly?

These three questions all relate to the general question of whether John can recognize colors, but they also provide different kinds of information about the level of his knowledge, the particular colors he does not know, and how to begin to teach him. First he learns to discriminate among the colors, then he learns the labels (receptive language), and finally he uses the labels in speech (expressive language).

REVIEW OF RECORDS

In a complete evaluation, one must not forget to review the cumulative records in the school office. They are a good source of background information about the student and his or her progress through school.

Methods of Interpreting Assessment Information

Regardless of which techniques are used to obtain assessment data, their results can be interpreted from a norm-, criterion-, or nonreferenced point of view.

NORM REFERENCING

In norm-referenced interpretations, a student's performance is compared with some average made by people who comprise a normative (referent) group. The interpretation may be applied to the findings of highly standardized tests and reported quantitatively, as in the example "Bill's IQ is 85, indicating an intellectual performance of one standard deviation below the mean of the population that is his age."

In cases where statistically prepared norms are available, the results are reported as percentiles, age or grade equivalents, standard scores, and quotients. All these normative statistics permit a person's performance to be described in terms of its discrepancy from the known average performance of people his or her age. This average is learned by administering the procedure to a large, representative sample, called the standardization population.

Norm-referenced interpretations can also be applied to assessment results derived from observation or other nontest procedures. Here, the examiner's experience serves as a substitute for statistically derived normative tables. Such interpretations appear to be relatively subjective, as in the example "Of all the kids her age I have ever known, she is without doubt the meanest." In short, norm-referenced interpretations deal with what a person does relative to other people and the criteria for the judgments are based on either statistical or experiential data.

CRITERION REFERENCING

In criterion-referenced interpretations, a student's performance is considered in terms of a particular domain of specified skills, and no reference is made to the relative performance of others. The interpretation can be reported quantitatively, as in "William can spell *carriage* 75% of the time in a test situation" or "Sally scored 20 points in the game and made the team." Criterion-referenced interpretation deals with what a person does without reference to the performance of others.

NONREFERENCING

In nonreferenced interpretation, no attempt is made to relate results to either the performance of others or any particular skill domain. Instead, nonreferenced interpretations are attempts to learn what strategies or systems students use to solve problems and reach answers. This type of interpretation leads to such statements as "James used the mnemonic device H-O-M-E-S to help recall the names of the Great Lakes" or "Because Mary tries to spell words just as she pronounces them, she misspells many words."

Standardized and Nonstandardized Techniques

Three elements comprise standardization: (1) set administration procedures, (2) objective scoring criteria, and (3) a specified preferred frame of reference for interpreting results. If these elements have been handled properly, a technique will pass the two "proofs" of adequate standardization—that is, its results will demonstrate reliability and validity. Techniques that have adequate reliability and validity are called standardized (formal); techniques that do not have these qualities are called nonstandardized (informal).

The advantages of standardized procedures are obvious. If procedures are followed properly, they yield objective results. The degree to which the examiner can have confidence in the results is known and documented by reliability and validity research. Also, guidelines are provided for the proper interpretation of the results. Because of these advantages, standardized procedures are often required by law or school policy, especially where diagnosis and placement into special education programs are the purposes of the assessment.

The advantage of nonstandardized procedures lies in their flexibility. For example, their administration and scoring can be adapted to meet the special requirements of individual students; answers can be probed to learn more about the nature of a student's problem or knowledge; and the procedures can be used to study areas for which standardized procedures are not available. However, the value of using such procedures is a function of the examiner's competence.

Assessment plays an important role in the education of problem learners, and considerable skill is required to assess students properly. Fortunately, several comprehensive sources are available to those readers who desire more information on this topic. In particular, we recommend the books by Hammill (1987), McLoughlin and Lewis (1994), Salvia and Ysseldyke (1991), and G. Wallace, Larsen, and Elksnin (1992).

A good source of test reviews is Conoley and Kramer's (1989) *The Tenth Mental Measurements Yearbook.* It is perhaps the most comprehensive listing of test reviews available today. Although most of the reviews are competently handled, many of them are subjective and contradictory. A source for objective ratings of norm-referenced tests is Hammill, Brown, and Bryant's (1992) *A Consumer's Guide to Tests in Print,* in which accepted standards relevant to the statistical properties of tests are applied to measures that are widely used today. As a result, each test is rated as A (highly recommended), B (recommended), or F (not recommended). This guide is a valuable resource for professionals responsible for selecting tests for school use.

Long-Range Goals and Short-Term Objectives

Once the teacher has analyzed a student's performance and has identified those areas of functioning that need strengthening, goals and objectives for that student can be developed. As noted previously, the specific goals that are established will be heavily affected by the teacher's assumptions concerning the nature of the student and by his or her beliefs about the overall goals of education. Thus, the teacher who states in the IEP that a long-range goal is for the student to become familiar with certain classic English poems is manifesting a belief that the job of the schools is to transmit culture. Similarly, the teacher who states that a long-range goal is for the student to attain a fifth-grade reading comprehension level is expressing a belief that a purpose of education is to help the student develop functional adult competencies. A third type of goal might be even more open-ended, in that the student may be expected to become a more creative citizen or in some way to positively affect his or her environment.

Short-range objectives are also required in the IEP and should be derived from the long-range goals. Objectives serve an important communication function in that, if well expressed, they convey a picture of the behaviors the student will perform after instruction is completed. Several additional criteria characterize well-written objectives. For example, the desired behavior should be stated in terms that are objective and measurable. Furthermore, the conditions under which the student is supposed to perform should be described. Additional information about objectives that relate to the various areas of pupil performance are addressed in the chapters that follow.

Instructional Materials, Procedures, and Settings

Once the objectives have been specified, the teacher is faced with the task of selecting appropriate instructional materials and methods. In addition, an educational setting that enhances the student's likelihood of meeting the objectives must be selected. These two considerations are addressed next.

Materials and Procedures

The selection and implementation of the most effective materials for a student are based directly on the observed abilities and problems that he or she manifests. For example, in the arithmetic area, Ronald's initial profile might appear as shown in Figure 1.2. His profile in this graph is interpreted to indicate that he is having a great deal of difficulty in multiplication (he has not yet been exposed to division), and a further weakness is apparent in his lack of understanding of place value.

The next task for the teacher is to explore further the student's trouble in multiplication and place value. To consider the multiplication example only, the teacher might probe as indicated in Figure 1.3. In the second level of this graph, immediately below the student's characteristics, is sketched the profile of a multiplication program that should be maximally effective with the student. Note, for example, that the program is very strong in presenting multiplication as an array of rows and columns (precisely where Ronald is weakest), pays little attention to multiplication as repeated addition (which he has already mastered), and emphasizes the

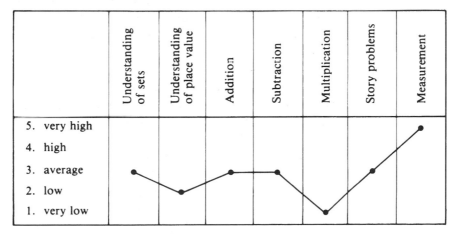

FIGURE 1.2. Graph of arithmetic ability.

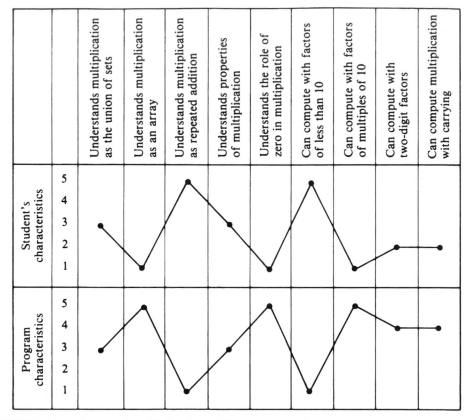

FIGURE 1.3. Graph of multiplication ability. 1 = very low; 2 = low; 3 = average; 4 = high; 5 = very high.

role of zero and multiplying by multiples of 10 (both areas in which he is very weak).

Teachers will not find ready-made programs for every profile of abilities and disabilities that might be discovered in the classroom. They will have to adapt, modify, and improvise. Sometimes the two profiles—learner characteristics and program characteristics—will not fit well. In that case, teachers still will need to sketch the interface, so that they will be cognizant of potential problems and be able to anticipate program failures. In some cases, teachers will be at a loss as to how to plan a program that fits a particular student's needs. In those cases, they should plot the student's profile in the area of difficulty and consult with the nearest regional instructional materials center and possibly acquire the appropriate materials there. A perusal of the many approaches suggested in the subsequent chapters of this book for arithmetic, reading, spelling, and writing should also provide ideas for the teacher who is faced with the difficult but crucial task of matching student variables to program variables.

The lengthy, time-consuming procedures spelled out here should *not* be used every time the teacher is faced with an instructional decision. They are best employed with those students who have pronounced difficulty in given subject areas. With these students, previous efforts at remediation usually have yielded little improvement. Ultimately, the time spent in detailed diagnosis and planning is time well spent for these students, and the pinpointing of areas of difficulty is well worth the extra effort involved.

To some extent, the selection of instructional materials reflects an individual teacher's subjective preferences in style, format, and response mode. However, an awareness of certain guidelines can facilitate intelligent curricular decision making. These guidelines have to do with three basic aspects involving material selection: design, method, and practicality.

DESIGN

Curriculum design is concerned with the overall organization of the school experiences of a student. Specific questions that might be posed as questions of design are the following:

1. Is the material organized into subject areas such as reading, arithmetic, and social studies, or is it organized in terms of "experiences" or "units" that cut across traditional subjects? Which approach makes the most sense for the student under consideration?

2. If organized in terms of subject areas, is the material ordered in hierarchical, sequential steps? Are there sequences related to known facts in child development (e.g., the Piagetian stages of cognitive development)? Is the order of sequences logically related to such order as exists within the subject area itself (e.g., in arithmetic, multiplication should be taught before division because multiplication skills are required in the operations of division)?

3. What criterion is required for the student to proceed from one step to the next? Is mastery of a preceding task a prerequisite to going on to a subsequent task? Is some kind of prerequisite external "readiness score" required before entry into the program or before going on to new units? If so, do these readiness scores bear a manifest relationship to the material they are supposed to make the learner ready for? In general, the closer the readiness task is to the actual required skill, the more effectively it predicts success. For example, ability to walk a balance beam has much less "face validity" as a reading readiness predictor than does, say, being able to distinguish d from b.

4. A further consideration underlying the design of materials has to do with its rationale. Is there any utilization of reinforcement (tangible rewards, social approval, or immediate feedback to the student)? Are basic skills incorporated as a basis for further learning? Is there any research evidence on soundness of the rationale (i.e., are there basic or applied studies supporting the approach)?

A well-designed program has clearly defined objectives for each program component. In any given lesson, the teacher should be able to state unequivocally what the purpose of the lesson is. How clear are the objectives for the materials under consideration? Are the objectives precise enough for the teacher to ascertain whether they have been reached? Are the objectives compatible with the learning experiences of the student in other subject areas (e.g., do they permit coordination between social studies and reading)?

METHOD

Questions of method are variations of the question "What do the teacher and the students have to do to successfully use the materials?" One set of these questions concerns the "who" of the instructional process. Can the students be instructed as one large group? If not, can provisions be made for occupying the other members of the class productively? Can the material be adapted for either a tutoring, small-group, or large-group situation? Must the teacher be actively involved in all phases of the instruction, or can the youngsters work on their own some or all of the time? To use the materials, what does the teacher have to do or say? Are the instructions too complicated? Is it physically possible for the teacher to do what is required (e.g., position figures on the flannelboard while reading verbatim instructions, and at the same time walk up and down the aisles to check each student's response)? Is there a balance between teacher-doing and pupil-doing, and between teacher-talk and pupil-talk? Are a variety of responses elicited from the pupils (e.g., oral and written responses, manipulation, painting, demonstrating)? Are several sensory modalities, either singly or in combination, involved? Is a student penalized when he or she cannot perform an expected response (e.g., because the student cannot use his or her hands or has difficulty in oral expression)? Are the required responses related to the desired learning (e.g., if the desired outcome is silent reading comprehension, is the student required to read silently and tested on mastery, or is he or she required to "word-call" orally)?

Does the material permit adaptations that facilitate learning? For example, can the student who has a sight problem still learn through listening and touch? Is there a way that students can serve as each other's tutors, to relieve pressure on the teacher? Can the material readily be broken into smaller steps or supplemented with other materials, for those students who have difficulty?

Can the material be individualized, both in terms of rate of presentation and in terms of intensity? That is, can the rapid learner move through the material quickly and the slow learner more deliberately? Are there provisions for the student who is making virtually no incorrect responses to skip unnecessary examples or pages? Conversely, does the material incorporate an opportunity for the student who is making many errors to relearn the material, perhaps through a different format or presentation?

Is the material sufficiently flexible to allow switching to another approach if that should appear desirable? Some programs are so unique that switching to another is impractical because of the material's limited ability to generalize to other areas. For example, if a teacher decides to use a reading program with a unique orthography, he or she must be aware of the fact that this is a long-term decision and difficult to change. One cannot switch orthographies every few months without seriously hampering a student's growth in reading. Similarly, certain programmed programs in reading and arithmetic are so unique that no alternatives exist to which the student can reasonably be switched if it becomes necessary to do so for reasons such as program failure.

PRACTICALITY

Finally, some practical considerations need to be taken into account in instructional material selection. First, how attractive is the material? Will a youngster want to use it because of its appeal, effective use of color, format, motivational devices, attractive visual arrangement, uniqueness, or variation in presentation? Are the materials practical and durable? Is the price reasonable? Are any hazardous elements present? Can the material be used independently, or does it require close supervision? Is the quality of drawings or photographs adequate? Can the materials be brought out, used, and reassembled for storage in a reasonable length of time? Are the materials reusable, or must new kits, sets, or workbooks be purchased for each additional student? Is use of materials or the grading of the students' responses unnecessarily boring or laborious for the teacher?

The teacher will quickly find that no one program, no matter how excellent, will work with all students, and some programs will not work with any students. For this reason, a teacher needs to have access to many approaches, involving a variety of different formats, strategies, and modalities. Based on knowledge of the needs of a particular learner, the teacher can make intelligent decisions regarding the how, what, and when of instruction. This knowledge is particularly imperative, because few products have been widely tested before they are offered to the public. The materials are beautifully packaged, widely advertised, and sold in large quantities, usually long before there is evidence to support their value. Efficacy research follows the release of commercial materials by 3 to 5 years, if ever. Therefore, teachers almost always are required to use unvalidated programs. No "consumer's report" for teachers exists, no book that can be consulted to point out shortcomings, limitations, or strengths of the various materials. It is strictly a "buyer, beware" market.

However, many of the teaching methods commonly used in the schools have existed for years, and a body of research has accumulated about many of them. The teacher, therefore, is well advised to undertake a library investigation of the particular method he or she wants to implement to see what success others have had with the program. *Educational Index, Dissertation Abstracts, Mental Retardation Abstracts,* and *Special Education Abstracts* are profitable initial sources of information. Many companies have assembled data on their programs and will provide it on request; of course, one should not expect anything critical from this source.

Use of a particular method should not necessarily be avoided because research on it does not exist. The teacher could use it on an experimental basis. For example, the teacher can test pupils in arithmetic, implement the unvalidated program for several months, and then retest the pupils to see if the program was indeed profitable. If the pupil performance could be compared with that of a control group, the results of the study would be made considerably more creditable.

Because of our recognition of the importance of instructional materials and methods to good educational practice, we have devoted a major part of each of the following chapters to descriptions of widely used programs, methods, and materials. Where information is available regarding the effectiveness of the approaches that are described, it too is presented. In addition, a lengthy section dealing specifically with selecting and analyzing methods has been included in the final chapter of this book.

The Educational Setting

Although this book does not purport to deal with the management difficulties of students who are profoundly retarded, psychotic, autistic, aphasic, dyslexic, or severely sensory impaired, the techniques presented can be adapted to ameliorate these students' school-related problems. For these students, the instructional setting is likely to continue to be the special class or the large or small residential facility. Actually, the number of students for whom such placements are appropriate is quite small. The overwhelming majority of students who evidence problems are in need of remedial education designed to enable them to function in the general class as soon as possible. Several models are employed in the schools to provide students with needed services.

THE GENERAL CLASSROOM

Most students who develop difficulties in school can be successfully managed by their regular teacher; their problems tend to be of a mild and easily corrected variety. The general classroom is by far the most desirable setting for students to receive remedial help, and the classroom teacher is usually the best person to direct the remedial lessons. In this way, the learner remains with peers and does not have to suffer the indignity of leaving the room to obtain corrective help elsewhere. However, often the teacher–pupil ratio is too high, the teacher lacks the experience, or the student's problem is too obdurate to be ameliorated in the general classroom setting. Alternatives must then be sought.

THE SPECIAL CLASS

Before 1950, the most frequently employed alternative for dealing with students with behavioral and/or educational problems was the self-contained special class. Many arguments set forth in defense of this placement are apparently reasonable. The argument is often made that students placed in these classes receive the benefits of specially trained teachers, special materials and methods, smaller classes, and individualized instruction. In fact, this is rarely the case. Until recently, untrained teachers were the rule rather than the exception; although the class enrollments were smaller than in general classes, there did not seem to be greater individualization of instruction; and the teachers used much the same approach toward classroom management and selection of materials that was used in the general class.

Research indicates that students placed in special classes achieve in schoolwork no better than, and often not as well as, similar students left in the general class. Findings regarding the effects of such placements on self-concept and adjustment are equivocal at the present time.

Special classes exist in assorted types and are restricted to students diagnosed as having a specific condition, such as mental retardation, emotional disturbances, or learning disability. For the most part, students placed in these settings are more similar to typical students than they are different from them. Although they may be poor readers or difficult to cope with, there is little justification for subjecting them to such a drastic measure as isolation from the general class.

Because of the added stigma that inherently goes with placement in a self-contained class, the segregation from peers, and the doubtful benefits to be derived, this alternative should be used with considerable caution and viewed as a last resort. For readers who are interested in additional references concerning the use of the special class for handling children with learning or behavior problems, the work of Dunn (1968), Christopolos and Renz (1969), and Iano (1972) is recommended.

THE SPECIAL SCHOOL

The special school for students with various learning problems is the natural extension of the self-contained class. Here the student not only is segregated from peers but also is removed completely from the regular school premises. The student may attend the special school and return home after classes or may be in residence at the school. The advantage of such a placement is the student's immersion in a total program. In addition to the expense involved, the pro and con arguments are basically the same as those advanced regarding the special class. This placement should be viewed as a last possible alternative for students who cannot be accommodated in any other setting.

THE RESOURCE ROOM

The resource room is a promising alternative to self-contained facilities. This model permits the student to receive instruction individually or in groups in a special room outfitted for that purpose. The emphasis is on teaching needed specific skills. At the end of the lesson, the learner returns to the regular classroom and continues his or her education there. In this way, the student is based in the regular class with peers and leaves only for periods of time during the school day. Several variations of the resource room model are available:

1. *The categorical resource room.* To qualify for placement in a categorical resource room, the student must satisfy a designated special education category or definition, such as retarded, disturbed, or learning disabled. Readers who are interested in implementing this variation of the resource room model are referred to the work of Glavin, Quay, Annesley, and Werry (1971) with emotionally disturbed children; of Sabatino (1971) with learning disabled children; and of Barksdale and Atkinson (1971) with mentally retarded children.

2. *The noncategorical resource room.* This noncategorical resource room is highly recommended. Students who are referred to the resource room are not labeled by category, and programs are designed for them on the basis of instructional, emotional, and behavioral need. Even "gifted" youngsters can be accommodated. In addition to the fact that the students involved remain in the regular classroom for most of the day, there are distinct advantages to this alternative. They include (a) students with handicaps do not have to be bused to the nearest school where there is an appropriate categorical class; (b) the number of students who can be seen daily is at least 2.5 times the number seen in the self-contained class; (c) the room serves all students in the school and is not limited to special education–type students; and (d) the close communication between resource room and regular teacher allows for cooperative handling of the student and his or her problem.

3. *The itinerant program.* The problems handled by the itinerant program may be either disability based or noncategorical. The program is constructed around mobile resource rooms, and the teacher is not "housed" in any one school. Its advantage lies in its mobility, but it has serious limitations. They include the following: (a) because the teacher is not attached to a particular school, it is difficult for him or her to become fully accepted in any of the schools in which he or she operates; (b) much teacher time is spent in transit; and (c) transportation of materials is a chronic problem.

Readers who desire a comprehensive account of the operation of resource programs are referred to *The Resource Program: Organization and Implementation* (Wiederholt, Hammill, & Brown, 1993) and *The Resource Teacher: A Guide to Effective Practices* (Wiederholt, Hammill, & Brown, 1983). In these volumes, the authors describe in detail the types of resource programs that can be implemented in the schools; define the role of the resource teacher relative to assessment, instruction, and consultation; and outline the procedures to be followed in setting up a program. In addition, they review the kinds of teacher activities that help students improve in reading, math, spoken language, spelling, handwriting, written expression, and behavior.

SCHOOL CONSULTATION

School consultation as a mode of service delivery is an option for providing educational support to students with mild handicaps within general school programs. A comprehensive review of the literature on school consultation from the fields of special education, school psychology, guidance and counseling, and organizational development may be found in the *Journal of Learning Disabilities* (Idol & West, 1987; West & Idol, 1987). Medway's (1982) literature review in educational psychology, as well as the meta-analysis research of Medway and Updyke (1985), also suggest that consultation is generally an effective form of intervention in applied settings. Textbooks on school consultation have been written in the fields of special education (DeBoer, 1986; Heron & Harris, 1993; Idol, 1993; Idol, Nevin, & Paolucci-Whitcomb, 1993).

Two primary alternatives employing consultation as a mode of special education service delivery are a consulting teacher program and a resource/consulting teacher program. A third alternative is collaborative consultation, the preferred model for delivery of indirect, consultative support to mildly handicapped and at-risk students in mainstream settings.

THE CONSULTING TEACHER MODEL

The consulting teacher program is the oldest of the three alternatives. Consulting teacher programs were being used in Vermont as early as the late 1960s. This model was developed through a cooperative effort of the Vermont State Department of Education and the University of Vermont. Consulting teachers in Vermont work as adjunct faculty to the university, providing training and assistance to classroom teachers (Christie, McKenzie, & Burdett, 1972; McKenzie, 1972). Subsequently, classroom teachers receive university credit for accepting handicapped students in their classrooms and working cooperatively with the consulting teacher in the development of teaching and behavior management programs. In the Vermont consulting teacher model, the consultation process begins when a student is referred by a classroom teacher for special education services (Fox et al.,

1973). To be eligible for the program, a student must have a significant need for consulting teacher services, and measured levels of language, arithmetic, and/or social behaviors must be deficient and deviate from minimum classroom standards.

THE RESOURCE/CONSULTING TEACHER MODEL

The resource/consulting teacher model was developed at the University of Illinois by Idol and colleagues in the late 1970s (Idol-Maestas, Lloyd, & Lilly, 1981). The model was designed to incorporate the roles and duties of resource teachers, who provide *direct* service to students with handicaps, and consulting teachers, who provide *indirect* service to these students by working cooperatively with their classroom teachers. Direct service is provided in the form of tutorial or small-group instruction, with emphasis on use of cross-age tutoring programs. The instruction is directly related to the curricula used in the general school program and is data based. Resource/consulting teachers monitor the daily progress of the students.

Indirect, or consultative, service is based on the Tharp–Wetzel triadic model of consultation (Tharp, 1975), with the classroom teacher serving as the mediator and working directly with the handicapped student. Consultative services are provided for special education students, although they are not the exclusive recipients of program benefits. Other special needs students, without special education labels, benefit from this service when resource/consulting and classroom teachers modify instruction to better accommodate them. Consultative efforts are directed primarily toward (1) transferring students' newly acquired skills from resource to classroom instruction; (2) modifying instructional strategies to resolve academic and study skill problems; (3) modifying classroom management strategies to accommodate students with behavior problems; (4) developing, with the cooperation of teachers and parents, home management and home tutorial programs that complement classroom efforts; and (5) sharing teaching and management strategies with other teachers via inservice training workshops.

COLLABORATIVE CONSULTATION MODEL

Whereas earlier special education consultative programs are based on a model in which the consultant serves as an expert, the collaborative consultation model focuses on using the expertise of both the classroom and the special education teacher, working together, to develop alternative solutions to classroom-related learning and behavior problems. Collaborative consultation can occur between two teachers, among members of a building-based team, or among a building administrator, a teacher, and a parent. Many combinations are possible.

The model recommends that collaborative consultation be practiced by following a series of steps in the problem-solving process:

1. Gain acceptance among team members.
2. Assess learning and behavior problems within the context of the classroom and the curriculum.
3. Develop goals and objectives based on the assessment outcomes.
4. Implement a cooperatively planned instructional and/or management program.
5. Evaluate the effects of the program.
6. Redesign the program depending on the type of change needed.

The content and intensity of instructional intervention and the responsibilities for implementing the instructional strategies are determined by the collaborating dyad or team and are dependent on each individual student's special needs. This decision-making process is greatly enhanced by use of the Levels of Intensity of Instruction decision-making framework described by Idol, West, and Lloyd (1988). A preservice and inservice training curriculum, *Collaboration in the Schools* (West, Idol, & Cannon, 1988), has been developed to aid school professionals in the development of collaborative problem-solving and communicative/interactive skills.

School consultation, in all of its various forms of service delivery and models, is having a positive influence on school reform and, in particular, the relationship between special education and general education. Researchers and teachers are currently experimenting with school consultation, prereferral systems, and teacher assistance teams as primary vehicles for preventing and remediating learning and behavioral problems as well as for coordinating instruction.

Reassessment and Hypothesis Reformulation

In the instruction model (Figure 1.1), the last stage pertains to the evaluation of student progress and its use in reformulating educational goals and objectives and/or in revising instructional procedures. This activity is also an important part of the IEP. The program evaluation should be continual, occurring periodically throughout the year, and the findings should be incorporated immediately into instructional action by accelerating, attenuating, modifying, or even discontinuing the student's program. Teachers and parents should understand that maximum accountability can be derived only from an evaluation plan that provides ongoing feedback. Students should not be evaluated only at the end of the year, when it is too late to do anything if objectives have not been met.

Naturally, the evaluation plan should be developed in such a way that permits the answering of the question "Were the long-term goals and short-term objectives for this student actually achieved?" Because at the present time no comprehensive test package exists that adequately tests students in all areas of functioning, the plan will have to have several dimensions, including the use of both standardized and informal assessment techniques. Also, direct observation of the student's performance may be used. If the objectives are precisely stated in such terms as "The student will be able to correctly read aloud the first 10 words of the Dolch Sight List with 90% accuracy in 3 minutes," the objective itself becomes the evaluation plan. There should be little question as to whether the student has achieved this particular objective; it can be easily established by direct observation.

The various elements of our instructional model, and of the IEP as well, are interrelated and depend on one another for consistency and for effectiveness. Each aspect of the teaching–learning process directly affects, and is affected by, every other aspect. The cyclical, interrelated nature of the elements is implicit in the model.

Chapter 2

Enhancing Speaking and Listening Skills

NETTIE R. BARTEL

Speaking and listening are the two most commonly used communication processes. Long before children can read, they hear and receive information about the world around them through listening. Students who listen well are at an enormous advantage in virtually every school task—in following directions, in understanding content, and in discerning the intentions of teachers and peers. Students who speak clearly and appropriately likewise are in a position to present themselves and what they know in the most favorable way.

Speaking and listening are skills that are frequently taken for granted in the classroom. Compared with teaching reading skills, relatively little attention is paid in most classrooms to helping students acquire good listening habits. Similarly, whereas all students are given formal instruction in learning to communicate through written language, few children are given help in learning to speak well.

By the time they have reached adolescence, most students have developed and use their speaking and listening skills rather well. Among the competencies most students have acquired by this time are the following:

1. Ability to express both positive and negative feelings, needs, desires, and ideas to others, and to understand these when expressed by others.

2. Ability to influence other people, and be influenced by them, and to negotiate their interests through language.

3. Ability to take the role of another person in both the speaking and the listening role—that is, to take into account the person's interests, experiences, comprehension ability, and affective state.

4. Ability to use complex referential communication (talk about objects, events, and ideas that are not present), and to understand these when listening to others.

5. Ability to use language to regulate thinking and problem solving.

Although most adolescents have these competencies, every teacher has had students in the classroom who do not speak and listen effectively. "He hears but doesn't understand," "She can't seem to express herself," or "I know he knows the answer, but he just can't say it," are descriptions of students that most teachers have encountered.

Some students with speaking and listening difficulties have problems in the actual production of speech—that is, they have trouble articulating speech sounds, or they have unusual qualities of voice pitch or intonation that make their speech difficult to understand. Other children have hesitations or repetitions in their speech that are characterized as stuttering. Many articulation problems tend to disappear as the students get older and as their speech-producing anatomical structures become mature. Those children who stutter, who have voice disorders, or whose articulation problems persist past age 8 or 9 will require the attention of a speech clinician. Such interventions are most effective when classroom teachers work closely with the speech–language specialists.

A much larger group of students do not acquire and use language normally. Their problems are usually complex, and involve cognitive, psychological, social, and linguistic aspects. Sometimes physiological factors are believed to contribute, also. These students may have difficulties in organizing their ideas, intentions, and feelings into verbal form. Often what they say is inappropriate. Many times they do not fully understand what is being said to them.

Terms such as "language disordered," "language impaired," "language delayed," or "language learning disabled" are often used to refer to this latter group of students. Their difficulties in language may appear to be part of pervasive disorders in thinking and in perceiving. They are not members of any homogeneous group, although some of them may also carry labels such as "learning disabled." In fact, approximately half of the students in today's schools who are labeled "learning disabled" have some sort of specific language impairment.

This chapter is about these children. It focuses on the nature of their speaking and listening problems and the relationship of these to overall language, cognitive, and social development. We consider how teachers can identify students with speaking or listening difficulties and how such students can be helped.

IMPORTANCE OF SPEAKING AND LISTENING

Most communication between people takes the form of speaking to others or listening to what others say. From the earliest ages on, children learn that they can affect the people around them by speaking, and that what those people say can in turn affect them. Later in life, speaking and listening proficiently are essential for success in school and for vocational fulfillment. Throughout life, speaking and listening connect individuals specifically to family and friends, and more generally to the surrounding world. Speaking and listening skills have implications at the cognitive, interpersonal, and vocational levels throughout the lifespan.

Importance for Cognition

At the cognitive level, how one "talks to oneself" contributes to the way the individual solves problems, the strategies employed in routine tasks, and the way the person regulates his or her own thinking and behavior. Increasingly, research is showing that such "self-talk" is instrumental in effective and efficient self-regulation of behavior in all aspects of life. The act of listening and comprehending is itself a cognitive act.

Listening is the primary learning modality throughout most peoples' lives. Listening is a process in which people fit incoming information into what they already know. Whereas a few years ago nobody knew about the dangers of AIDS or the upcoming political developments in the former Soviet states, today most people are well informed about both. Individuals developed these new understandings and concepts by *listening* to radio and television news, to advertisements, to conversations, and so on.

For students in school, self-talk may take the form of self-regulating such important processes as finding the main idea in paragraphs, going through the steps of long division, checking answers on tests, and so on. For students, as for adults, listening is the medium through which most learning occurs. Learning has a number of aspects, among them the ability to listen to large amounts of information, to sort out what is important, and to connect what is important with what one already knows, so it can later be retrieved and expressed. These are the steps of listening and speaking well. The student who cannot or will not listen with comprehension is at an enormous disadvantage in mastering new material. Likewise, the student who cannot speak with appropriateness and effectiveness about what is on his or her mind will likewise fail on many learning tasks.

Importance for Interpersonal Relationships

At the social-interpersonal and civic level, the importance of speaking and listening is self-evident. In fact, it is usually the interpersonal level that comes to mind when one thinks about speaking and listening. Every familial and social role—parent, child, spouse, friend, neighbor, citizen, and so on—is heavily impacted by how one speaks and listens. A person's success or failure in these roles is frequently a function of his or her speaking and listening skills.

Every classroom teacher has seen students who say socially inappropriate things. These students—often described as "weird" by their peers—do not quite "fit" in the way they talk to other students or to the teacher. Frequently, these same students misinterpret what others say to them, mistaking a friendly tease for an insult, or becoming confused or frustrated by others' verbalizations. The result is often social isolation or rejection, which in turn may lead to more extreme antisocial behavior.

Importance for Vocation

No matter in which occupation students eventually find themselves, their speaking and listening skills will continue to be largely responsible for their job satisfaction and success. In some vocational areas, this is readily apparent—the teacher, the waiter, the counselor, the secretary. However, virtually every job can be enhanced by effective speaking and listening skills. Indeed, it is not too much to say that without good speaking and listening skills, most persons will have limited success in whatever career or vocation they pursue.

COMMUNICATION AND LANGUAGE

To understand the nature of speaking and listening, one must consider some related concepts and definitions. The ways in which speaking and listening relate to communication and language are described in this section.

Communication

Human relationships are characterized by communication from one person to the other. In fact, if communication were absent, relationships could not exist. Communication is an active process in which a sender encodes or formulates an idea, intention, or feeling, which he or she transmits to a receiver. The receiver decodes or comprehends the message. Communication partners may choose to communicate in spoken, written, or manual signing form. Although messages may be received by any of the senses, in this chapter, we consider only the oral forms of communication—speaking and listening to spoken speech. A schematic representation of communication is presented in Figure 2.1.

As illustrated in Figure 2.1, the speaker and the listener each has a private cognitive world of ideas, intentions, and feelings. In any given communicative act, only a sample of this world can be communicated. Thus, the "shared world" is always only a fraction of what the speaker potentially could try to communicate. The more experiences (real or vicarious) the speaker and listener have in common, the greater the overlap in ideas, intentions, and feelings in their private worlds. (This is why a twin frequently "knows" what the other is going to say even before he or she says

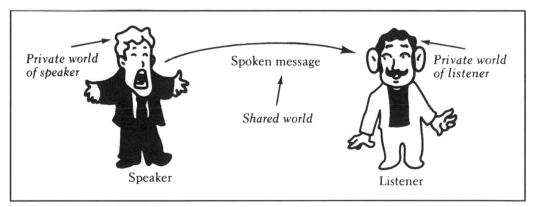

FIGURE 2.1. The act of communication—The intersection of the worlds of the speaker and the listener.

it.) Conversely, the fewer experiences (real or vicarious) the speaker and listener have in common, the less the overlap. (This is why people from very different cultures sometimes have difficulty understanding each other.)

In the listening part of the communication act, the listener receives the communication and attempts to make it fit into his or her own private cognitive world. The more differentiated and developed the listener's mental structures of ideas, intentions, and feelings are, the more likely he or she is to find a "niche" for (i.e., understand) the new information. This is why listeners find it easy to understand conversations about familiar topics and have trouble understanding speech about unfamiliar topics. Thus, a good experiential background that gives students the raw materials of ideas, intentions, and feelings is an essential prerequisite for learning to speak and listen effectively.

Language

Language is a symbol system or code through which ideas about the world are communicated through a conventional set of arbitrary signals. The symbolic nature of language means that languages involve representations of things that stand for other things—thus the word *cat* stands for a four-legged meowing animate object whether or not that object is present when the word is uttered. This representational quality of language enables a person to speak about objects, events, and experiences that are not present, that are hypothetical or even impossible, and yet to communicate meaning to the listener.

The beginning of language is an idea, intention, or feeling about some aspect of the world; language enables a person to code that idea, intention, or feeling, following specific rules. Those same rules enable the listener to decode the signal and understand what idea, intention, or feeling it was with which the speaker started. A person cannot talk about something of which he or she knows nothing (although some people try!). Similarly, for listeners to comprehend the communication, they must have some knowledge about the intended referent. The knowledge and feelings that people have about objects and events in the world comprise the content about which they communicate, and indeed form the cognitive basis of language.

Figure 2.2 presents a schematic representation of language processes. Although the focus here is on speaking and listening, similar linguistic processes take place when language is written and read or when it is signed and observed visually.

The process through which an idea, intention, or feeling becomes operationalized into a spoken series of speech sounds is heavily conceptual. The same is true of the process of hearing speech sounds and translating them into ideas, intentions, and feelings.

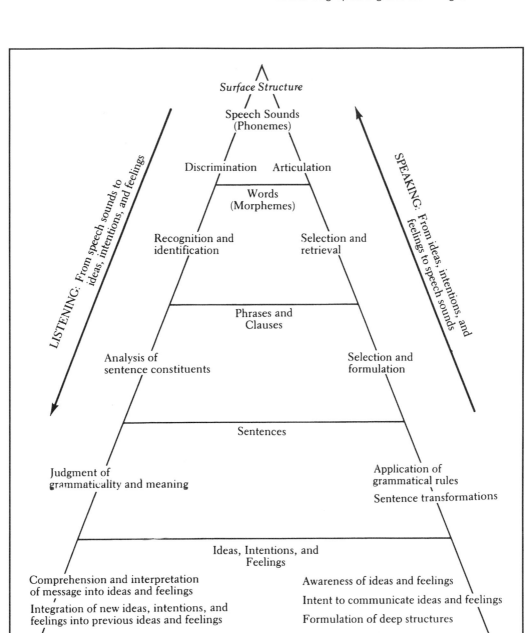

FIGURE 2.2. Language—the process of speaking and listening.

Speaking

Speech is verbal communication from the sender to the receiver. It involves a complex process of identifying ideas or feelings, formulating these into an appropriate and grammatical sequence of words and sentences, and finally

TABLE 2.1. Levels of Listening

TYPE OF LISTENING	DESCRIPTION	EVIDENCE OF DIFFICULTY
Passive listening	Awareness of auditory events but no responses (mental, verbal, or motor)	*Child may not be able to* pay attention distinguish information sounds from background noise
Factual listening	Attention to factual information; ability to answer literal comprehension questions	*Child may not* know the meanings of words or grammatical forms remember *who, when, where, what,* and *how* in what has been heard recall the sequence of events
Interpretive listening	Attention to several levels of meaning; listening "between the lines"; linking what is being heard to previous learning; identifying the sequence of ideas, main idea, and relationships among ideas	*Child may not be able to* state the main idea summarize predict outcomes fit new ideas with previously learned ideas solve new problems based on new learning generalize to new situations compare new learning with previous learning discern the motivation of the speaker
Evaluative listening	Attending to the truth, clarity, plausibility, completeness, consistency, and implications of what is heard	*Child may not be able to* recognize incompleteness or redundancy see bias or lack of internal consistency see implausibility in the "real world" distinguish between trivial and important
Metacognitive listening	Awareness of whether listening is complete; ability to judge own comprehension of material; ability to separate "what I'm sure about" from "what I'm not sure about" and "what I know I don't know"	*Child may not be able to* recognize own lack of comprehension predict ability to answer comprehension questions correctly detect what is not understood distinguish between material that is incomprehensible and own lack of comprehension

coordinating the speech-producing mechanisms of human anatomy to produce speech sounds, intonation, pitch, stress, and juncture (see Figure 2.2).

Successful speakers are able to use more than one level of speaking—ranging from the informal expressions used in day-to-day conversations with family members to more formal English used in work or classroom settings to the literary level that may be used in a presidential inaugural address or a poetry reading. A good speaker is able to judge a communicative situation in terms of the level of speaking that is appropriate. Using a level that is too low for the occasion makes the speaker appear ignorant; using a level that is too high marks the speaker as pretentious. The speaker's ability to judge what kind of speech is appropriate for a given situation is discussed further in the later section on language use.

Listening

Listening is much more than simply hearing. It includes complex processes that begin with the sensation of sound, but also includes the entire process of deriving meaning from the communication event.

Some listening events clearly require more attention and thinking than do others. For example, listening to the radio on the way to work may require relatively little active cognitive activity, compared with listening to someone give directions for how to get back on the freeway. The levels of listening are hierarchical, in that higher level listening skills build on the lower level skills; in fact, the higher level skills are not possible without the lower level skills.

An effective listener is able to gauge the requirements of the situation and expend the appropriate amount of energy and attention to what the circumstances demand. Table 2.1 describes five levels of listening, and provides some examples of difficulties students may have in listening at each of the levels.

COGNITIVE BASIS OF SPEAKING AND LISTENING

Although the reciprocal relationship between language and thought has been widely acknowledged, this relationship is not completely understood. Some research links cognitive development with speaking and listening skills in both normal students and those with disabilities. For this reason, we take the point of view that assessment and intervention in these areas must take cognitive development into account—a perspective we share with most widely used intervention programs.

The work of Piaget (1962) has been instrumental in shaping the way this relationship is currently perceived. Using the basic functions of *assimilation* (the tendency of the organism to incorporate environmental stimuli into a system of mental structures) and *accommodation* (adjusting to the environment), the child constantly searches for *equilibrium* (i.e., balance). Even very young children are problem solvers, attempting to reconcile events in the world around them with their present state of understanding while simultaneously changing their understanding in response to actions in their environment. People of all ages seek to make meaning of events in their environment, and this meaning is often coded in language.

Language is used by children to influence other people—to direct their attention, to request certain actions, and to respond to others' requests. As children grow in their abilities to influence their social environment, they also become able to influence their physical environment to attain their desired ends. Children are active, not passive, and interact with and transform their conceptions of events. Children are not merely responders to acts and situations, but are also initiators—a fact that shows up in all observations of children's language acquisition.

Piaget pointed out additional characteristics of young children's thinking. A number of these are summarized in Table 7.1 in Chapter 7, "Problems in Mathematics Achievement." While these cognitive abilities manifest themselves in children's functioning in mathematics, they also show up in how they speak and how they understand what is said to them.

Young children's thinking is characterized by an inability to see the world from a point of view other than their own. This quality, known as *egocentricity,* characterizes both language and thought in early childhood and manifests itself in speech that does not make allowances for the perspective of the listener. Thus, the child returning home from nursery school may relate events to his or her parents in a way that assumes they were there, experiencing the events too. At this age, the child's thinking and language are not yet able to take into account the fact that, because the parents were not present, a conversation about what happened must be preceded with some essential background. Only later does the child's thinking and language become nonegocentric—that is, go beyond the personal point of view.

Young children's thinking, and hence their speech, is further characterized by immature cognitive structures for understanding *classification* by function, color, size, shape, or several criteria simultaneously. This underlies the frequent overextensions (calling all four-legged animals "doggies") or underextensions (calling only the family's pet dog "doggie"). Lack of cognitive structures to understand *seriation* may express itself as difficulty both in narrating and in comprehending what comes first, what second, and so on, in a story. The lack of conservation ability, or *decentration,* concerns children's inability to disregard misleading or distracting visual or auditory stimuli, and keep their attention focused on the salient characteristic of the object or event in question. Thus, a child may see a ball of clay being rolled into a snake but still insist that the amount of clay in the roll is greater than that in the ball.

Other cognitive landmarks, such as knowing about means–end, causality, object permanence, and symbolic play, may be necessary but not sufficient conditions for language acquisition. Language and thought are unified processes, and thought cannot occur without language. As the child matures, his or her mental structures and speech become more internalized.

PREREQUISITES TO EFFECTIVE SPEAKING AND LISTENING

Before students can learn to speak and listen effectively, they must possess a number of skills. These prerequisites are found in the linguistic, cognitive, and social domains.

Linguistic Prerequisites

Clearly, speakers or listeners need some understanding and proficiency in language skills. Speakers need to know the meanings and usages of words (semantics and morphology), and how to put these words into grammatical sentences (syntax). They also need to know how to articulate the speech sounds clearly and correctly (phonology). Similarly, listeners need to know the meanings and usages of words and the grammatical rules for interpreting the meanings of sentences. They also must be able to discriminate among the speech sounds.

Cognitive Prerequisites

As described in the preceding section on the cognitive basis of speaking and listening, one cannot speak or listen with competence if one does not have the cognitive background to speak or to listen with comprehension. A student with severe mental retardation may have difficulty, even when motivated, in following simple directions or in articulating basic ideas. A third-grade student may understand the speech sounds, words, and grammar of each sentence spoken by the social studies teacher, but be unable to comprehend the content of a lecture on early American history because of a lack of knowledge or concepts to which to relate the new information. An intelligent adult may listen without comprehension to an advanced physics lecture even though most of the words and grammar are familiar, and be unable to grasp the main idea or to articulate appropriate questions on the material. Clearly, a general level of cognitive competence is necessary for rudimentary communicative competence; specialized conceptual competence may be needed for the comprehension of sophisticated or technical information.

Social Prerequisites

For communicative competence to exist, speakers and listeners also must have some sense of their social relationship to each other. Parents speak differently to their children than to other adults. Teachers present material differently to students who already have mastered most of the ideas than to those who are being introduced to the content. Effective communicators constantly adjust their speaking based on their judgments about the

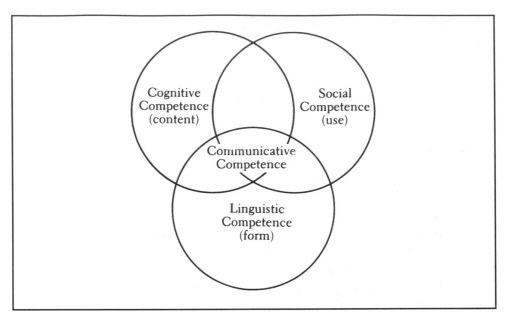

FIGURE 2.3. The three domains of communicative competence.

listeners' comprehension. They shift vocabulary level, restate main ideas, and give additional details as needed to enhance communication effectiveness.

In summary, effective communication is possible only when a person exercises some skills in at least three domains: linguistic, cognitive, and social. The person with communicative competence is able to say the right thing (cognitive competence) in the right way (linguistic competence) in a socially appropriate way (social competence). The person with fully developed communicative competence has some ideas or content to convey and understands how to transform those ideas into specific speech sounds that comprise words and sentences. The particular language used depends upon the context of communication and the person's purpose in speaking.

The three domains of prerequisites correspond to the three major dimensions of language. In each speaking and listening act, issues regarding content (cognitive competence), form (linguistic competence), and use (social competence) must be taken into account. The interaction of these domains is presented schematically in Figure 2.3. Each of these areas is discussed in greater detail in the following sections.

DIMENSIONS OF SPEAKING AND LISTENING

Speaking and listening are language production and language comprehension strategies. In the following sections, we describe in greater detail the

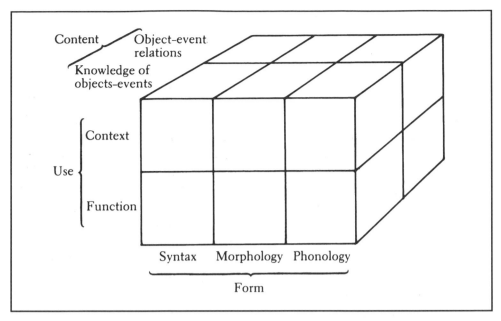

FIGURE 2.4. Dimensions of language.

language dimensions of content (semantics), form (syntax), and use (pragmatics). Figure 2.4 portrays the elements of each of these dimensions.

Language Content (Meaning or Semantics)

Language content (meaning or semantics) refers to the ideas, intentions, and feelings that speakers wish to communicate to others. Speakers express these ideas, intentions, and feelings through sentences, which may take the form of assertions, negations, commands, or questions. Ideas, intentions, and feelings grow out of speakers' perceptions of the world in which they live—the categories and qualities of the objects, persons, and events around them and the relationships among these. Until children have at least a rudimentary understanding of these objects, persons, and events, they have no referents for a semantic system.

Much has been written about the relationship between words and the concepts (objects, persons, and events) they represent. At first glance, children seem to learn about objects such as desks, flowers, cats, and balloons and then learn the corresponding words—*desk, flower, cat,* and *balloon*—which they then use every time they want to refer to the objects. However, the process of learning concepts and the appropriate labels for objects, persons, and events is not as simple as it seems.

Learning concepts is intimately tied to learning the meanings of words. Sometimes, of course, children (and adults!) use words for which they do not have the appropriate concept. In general, however, the concept must be acquired first, either through experience or through the use of other words or concepts (e.g., through looking up a word in the dictionary).

The first stage in concept learning is becoming aware of the concept as a unique class of objects, persons, or events. Once the concept has been identified as unique, it is labeled.

A problem commonly arises when a student is taught a label, such as *reptile,* for an object or class of objects. The student may apply the label correctly in the instructional situation but fail to do so later when called on to distinguish the reptile from other animals seen on a nature trip. This problem can be avoided by teaching language usage in a variety of situations in which the student is required to make a variety of distinctions. A major responsibility of the teacher is to provide sufficient experience in *concept generation.* This entails reliably distinguishing the referent in question in all settings and in all contexts; that is, a reptile is still a reptile whether it is seen in a zoo, in a pond, or as a picture in a book.

To facilitate this process, the concept's *critical attributes* can be identified and described. Comparisons with competing concepts (e.g., those with similar shapes, sizes, colors, and functions) are useful. This stage of concept learning concerns the application of the new concept label to as-yet-unidentified exemplars. Thus, having learned that a given item is appropriately referred to as "reptile," the student must learn to refer to other similar items as reptiles also. Furthermore, the child must refrain from referring to noninstances of reptiles, such as frogs and toads, as reptiles. *Generalization* to other classes of objects, persons, and events should be promoted.

From the earliest learning on, children need to be made aware that a referent does not go by only one name and that it may be referred to in many different ways, depending on the alternatives from which the listener must distinguish the object. For example, the term *book* is sufficient to distinguish a book from crayons, puzzles, and games, but if the same book is to be distinguished from several other books, it must be referred to as "The Three Bears book," "Goldilocks book," or "big book," or with some other term that distinguishes it from all other objects with which it might be confused.

Learning the name for an object is only the first step in semantic learning. The more interesting and more functional steps are learning to use the label appropriately in an unfamiliar context and learning to anticipate the problem faced by the listener and modify the description of the referent accordingly. Problem solving that utilizes the new concept in conjunction with its appropriate label, or *application,* is the final stage of semantic learning.

Linguistic Form (Syntax, Morphology, and Phonology)

Although all aspects of language derive ultimately from a communicative intent (either receptive or expressive) that is cognitive in nature, one can, for analytical purposes, deal separately with the language's formal, structured aspects. Accordingly, we direct our attention to that aspect of language that has to do with the arrangement of words into meaningful sequence—*syntax.* We also include brief sections on *morphology,* which deals with the smallest meaningful grammatical units of language, and *phonology,* which deals with speech sounds.

Syntax

The rules regarding acceptable sequences of words in a language are known as grammar or syntax. Every language has syntactic rules that regulate which strings of words are grammatical and which are not. Some of these rules have to do with word order—for example, it is acceptable in English to say "John threw the ball to Mary" or "Mary threw the ball to John" but not "Mary John to ball threw the." Note that in the first two examples the same words are used, but the meaning of the sentence changes because the word order changes. Other syntactic rules govern the relationships of subjects to objects, specify active–passive transformations, have to do with negation, and indicate verb relations.

A substantial amount of research has been conducted on young children's learning of syntactic rules. In general, it has been found that most children begin to use two-word sentences between 13 and 24 months of age. These early sentences mark children's beginning attempts to use rules to combine linguistic units. Contrary to earlier speculation, it is now known that these first sentences are neither memorized imitations of adult speech nor random sequences of words. Rather, these first attempts at sentence production are orderly and rule governed, showing that even at early ages children attempt to discern regularities in the speech that they hear and to use these regularities, or rules, in their own speech. According to Menyuk (1969), by age 3 the typical child has developed, in the following order, a number of sentence types:

1. Joining of elements to make sentences ("allgone lettuce")

2. Development of subject-plus-predicate sentences ("Bebe go")

3. Expansion of the verb phrase ("The cat ran up the tree.")

4. Embedding of an element within a sentence ("I found the doggie that was lost.")

5. Use of negative, declarative, and interrogative transformations ("I can't go," "I go!" "Can't I go?")

By the time children are in first grade, they are using even more complicated sentence structure. The mean length of an utterance is 5.7 words, and the mean number of different words in 50 utterances is over 130. The average first grader knows the meanings of over 13,000 words (although he or she speaks only about 2,000).

Carrow-Woolfolk (1985) studied the abilities of children of various ages to hear and understand different sentence types. She found that about

75% of children learn to comprehend the following sentence types, in approximately the order given, at between 3 and 7-plus years of age:

Active declarative—present progressive ("The cat is eating.")

Interrogative *who* ("Who hurt my dog?")

Interrogative *what* ("What is your name?")

Interrogative *when* ("When can we go?")

Simple imperative ("Come!")

Negative imperative ("No!")

Active declarative—past tense ("We went to the zoo.")

Passive ("The cat was hit by the car.")

Explicit negation ("We can't go.")

Active declarative—past participle ("She has finished.")

Implied negation ("It's a different color.")

Active declarative—future ("We will move to New York.")

Active declarative—perfective ("Mom has been baking a cake.")

Conjunction *if . . . then* ("If you're scared, then don't do it.")

Conjunction *neither . . . nor* ("Look for the ball that is neither red nor yellow.")

Morphology

Morphemes are the smallest meaningful units of language. There are two types of morphemes—bound and free. Free morphemes are units that stand alone (e.g., *run, book, particular*). Bound morphemes are always attached to other units; in English they serve as prefixes and suffixes (e.g., *–ed, –er, pre–,* and *un–*).

Morphemes are used in English in a number of ways. Some of the more important are in the regulation of verb tense (walk, walk*ed,* walk*ing*); in the distinction between singular and plural forms (cat, cat*s;* witch, witch*es*); in the agentive form (farm, farm*er;* dance, danc*er*); in comparative forms (small, small*er,* small*est;* quick, quick*er,* quick*est*); and in modification of different parts of speech (true, *un*true; test, *pre*test; appear, *re*appear; quick, quick*ly*).

Although the overall course of morphological learning is sequentially similar from one child to the next, considerable inconsistency can be seen in any one child's use of morphemes. It is not uncommon, for example, for children to vacillate between *comed* and *came* or among *bringed, brang,* and *brought.*

Morphological forms, or inflections, are particularly influenced by geographical locations and dialects. The spoken English of students in our inner cities, for examples, frequently differs in inflection from standard English. The following are a few examples from Bartel, Grill, and Bryen (1973):

Feature	Standard English	Nonstandard English
Past tense		
Omission of final *ed*	passed, loaned	pass, loan
Future tense		
Omission of final *l*	You'll, he'll	you, he
Present tense		
Omission of final sound	I'm, it's	I, it
Possessive		
Deletion of final *s*	50 cents, 3 birds	50 cent, 3 bird
Third-person singular		
Deletion of final *s*	she works here	she work here

Clearly, when a teacher is attempting to establish whether a student has mastered a given morphological form, account needs to be taken of whether the student's dialect requires the use of that particular form. Interestingly, it appears that students who use a nonstandard dialect in speaking have little difficulty in listening to and comprehending standard English. Conversely, the standard English–speaking teacher may have considerable difficulty understanding a spoken dialect. For this reason, it is recommended that teachers of dialect-speaking students familiarize themselves with the features of nonstandard English so that the potential barriers to communication can be surmounted.

Phonology

Phonemes are significant units of speech sound; a difference in meaning results when one phoneme is substituted for another. For example, /p/ and /b/ are phonemes in English because substituting one for the other in a word such as *big* or *pat* results in a change in meaning. Phonemes may be vowels or consonants; they may be simple (/t/ or /h/) or compound (/th/ or /au/). The written equivalent for a phoneme is a *grapheme*. The grapheme equivalent for the speech sound /k/ is either the letter *c* or the letter *k*. This example shows that the phoneme–grapheme correspondence in English is not one to one. Sometimes two or more graphemes represent only one phoneme; for example, the letters *s* and soft *c* both have the phoneme equivalent /s/. Conversely, every teacher who has ever tried to teach phonics to a first or second grader knows that the letter *a* has several phonemic variations, as in *cat, always, alone, bravo,* and *said.*

Phonemes are usually described in terms of binary features. Binary features are polar opposites; if a phoneme is a vowel, for example, it cannot act as a consonant. In addition to the *vowel–consonant* binary pair, there is the *nasal–oral* pair (*m, n, ng* are nasal phonemes; *a, b, c, t, v, o* are oral phonemes), with nasal phonemes having their primary resonance in the nasal, as opposed to the oral, cavities, and the *voiced–unvoiced* pair (*b* is voiced and *p* is unvoiced, although it is articulated the same way as *b;* similarly, the *th* in *think* is unvoiced), with the voiced phoneme being produced with a voiced component.

In general, children's ability to hear differences in phonemes precedes by several months their ability to produce those differences; that is, auditory discrimination of specific speech sounds takes place before articulation of those same speech sounds. On the average, girls are able to produce all phonemes by the time they are in first grade; a few second-grade boys will still be having trouble producing some of the more difficult compound phonemes, such as /str/.

In addition to the units of sound that are used in producing speech, phonology takes into account the variations in intonation and stress and the pauses that occur in spoken language. Each of these may contribute to the meaning of the sentence and help convey the intent of the speaker. In the sentences "I am going too!" and "I am going too?" the different communicative intents of the speaker are conveyed by intonation.

Language Use (Function and Context)

There has been an upsurge recently in the interest of researchers and clinicians in how students *use* language—that is, the effectiveness with which they speak and listen. The social basis for language is as important as the cognitive and linguistic bases of language. People talk not simply because they have an idea about the world and not merely because they know how to articulate that idea in phonological and syntactic form. They talk because they want to get an idea across to someone else. Stripped to its core, communication is a process of sharing intents.

There are two major aspects of language use. The first, which pertains to the function or purpose of the communication, is called *pragmatics*. The second is the *context* in which the language use occurs.

Functions of Speaking and Listening

Apparently, the development of communicative competence with respect to language function occurs somewhat separately from the mastery of language form and content. Thus, students may be able to formulate language content but be unable to speak in ways that communicate their intent to others or to listen so as to discern the intent of others' communications. The communicative environment is a complex one, and even adults sometimes have problems shifting their analyses of communicative intentions from person to person and from place to place. A person's reasons for speaking and listening change many times during the day as he or she interacts with different people in different situations.

A number of categorization systems have been developed to help understand the communication abilities and intents of students at various developmental levels. An example of such a classification scheme developed by Curtiss, Prutting, and Lowell (1979) is presented with examples in Table 2.2.

TABLE 2.2.   Description of Pragmatic Categories

PRAGMATIC CATEGORIES	*OPERATIONAL DEFINITION*
Demand	A request for an action or an object ("I want glue," "More juice")
Command	An imperative ("Look at me!" "Come here!")
Question	A request for information or elaboration ("Who?" "What?" "Huh?")
Labeling	Identification of a person, object, or action ("That's a chair," "Here's José")
Response to a question	An act directly following a question posed to the child (head shake, change of topic, answer to the question)
Response to a summons	An act directly following a summons for the child's attention (head turn, eye contact)
Response to a command	An act directly following an imperative or request issued to the child (child follows directions, child changes topics)
Imitation	An imitation of an act or utterance performed by someone else
Repetition	An imitation of a child's own act or utterance
Summons	A request or demand for attention (a wave, tap on the arm, calling out someone's name)
Description	An act describing an event, a person, or an object ("He's tall," "It fell down")
Protesting	An act expressing resistance ("No," vehement head shake, physical resistance)
Ritual	A greeting or other social ritual ("Hi," "Bye-bye")
Request for approval	An act requesting approval from another person ("Is it okay for me to do this?" "Was that all right?")
Request for confirmation or acknowledgment	An act requesting another to confirm or acknowledge the child's behavior ("Do you understand?" "Did you hear me?")
Acknowledgment	An act evidencing comprehension of a situation, event, or message

From "Pragmatic and Semantic Development in Young Children with Impaired Hearing" by S. Curtiss, C. A. Prutting, and E. L. Lowell, 1979, *Journal of Speech and Hearing Research, 22,* pp. 534–552.

A student's ability to use spoken language is affected by the degree to which he or she is able to take the following into account:

The *setting or situation* in which the communication takes place

The *characteristics of the participants* in the communication event, including their purposes and intentions

The *topic* of conversation, including how to maintain it or change it

The *norms* for interpersonal conversations, including those of

—*quantity:* participants must be brief enough to avoid being redundant and to avoid boring their listeners, but they must say enough to enable the listener to understand their message;

—*quality:* participants must be able to verify what they say; the communication must be true and plausible, and the speaker must have credibility on that topic;

—*relevance:* participants must "stick to the topic" and avoid irrelevant verbalizations;

—*manner:* participants must be clear, succinct, and avoid overstatement. (Grice, 1975)

Indications are that the pragmatic aspects of language use develop in a predictable order. This sequence of development, as it is reflected in the literature, is summarized in Table 2.3.

Context of Speaking and Listening

Context has both a general and a specific focus. In general, children learn at early ages that they speak differently when there is company in the house, when they are in church, and when they are shopping with their parents. Both content and form are affected by the general features of context.

More specifically, the immediate context for a speaker is the listener, who is a major influence on the speaker's selection of content and form. Children and adults alike learn that there are some things that one simply does not say to some people, either because of their personal characteristics (he has a terrible temper) or because of their social role (she is the school principal). With respect to listening, one learns to not take Aunt Mildred's complaints to heart (she is not happy unless she is complaining), to jump when Dad says "jump" (he means it!), and to not take seriously compliments or insults given by someone who has had three drinks at a party.

Full communicative competence requires that speakers perform a rather sophisticated analysis of their context before they speak and as they listen. This analysis takes into account such questions as "What is the age of the listener?" (the ways we speak to and interpret the conversation of adults differ from the ways we speak to and interpret the conversation of children); "What does the listener (or speaker) know about this topic?" (we may go into more detail when we believe the listener is uninformed; we may discount the statements of a speaker whom we believe to be uninformed); "What action do I want the listener to take or what action does the speaker want me to take as a result of this communication?" (we may desire a verbal response or some action on the part of the listener; we may decide the speaker is trying to manipulate us into feeling guilty); "What do I want the listener to think of me or what does the speaker want me to think of him or her as a result of this communication?" (we may need to decide whether it

TABLE 2.3. The Acquisition of Pragmatics

BIRTH–AGE 6	AGES 6–12	ADULT COMPETENCE
Pre-speech acts: 　looking 　crying 　smiling 　gurgling 　grasping 　sucking 　pointing 　showing	Self-oriented perspective: cannot take listener into account, even though aware of listener's characteristics Increasing sophistication in persuasive communication ability Increasing ability to assume another's perspective in role playing	Differentiated adaptation to listener's 　age or disability 　status 　values 　sensitivities and feelings 　background information 　perspective 　personality 　behavior
Turn taking		
Beginnings of discourse skills	Beginnings and further development of metalinguistic awareness, the ability to think about language and to comment on it	Ability to judge and use speech of appropriate 　quantity (not too little or 　　too much) 　quality (truthfulness, 　　plausibility) 　relevance 　organization 　clarity 　directness
Functions: 　instrumental 　regulatory 　interpersonal 　personal 　heuristic 　imaginative 　informative 　textual	Development of conversational skills: 　turn taking 　initiating topic 　maintaining topic 　changing topic Awareness of social register	
Intentions: 　gaining attention 　labeling 　responding 　requesting 　greeting 　protesting 　repeating 　describing 　acknowledging 　confirming	Increasing ability to express feelings appropriately Elaboration and greater sophistication in all functions and intentions previously learned	Knowledge of who can say what, in what way, where and when, by what means, and to whom Sophisticated metalinguistic ability

matters to us and, if so, how). Most people take for granted their pragmatic skill in discerning contexts and become aware of this skill only in its absence (e.g., when the speaker fails to consider that the listener has already heard the joke twice before).

Interaction of Context and Function

In actual communicative interactions, the speaker must take context and function into account simultaneously. The speaker starts out with a communicative intent—a purpose for speaking (ritualizing, informing, controlling, etc.)—and then must analyze the setting, the topic, and the listener for any special considerations that enter into how that purpose or intent should be expressed. Table 2.4 presents a matrix of the interactions between communicative function and communicative context.

TABLE 2.4. Interaction of Pragmatic Functions and Contexts

FUNCTION	CONTEXT			PURPOSE/TASK
	SETTING	TOPIC	LISTENER	
Ritualizing	Uses communication rituals appropriately in a variety of different settings (e.g., home, church)	Uses discourse rituals pertinent to a variety of communication topics (e.g., greetings, religious or patriotic rituals)	Adapts communication rituals to take into account listener characteristics (e.g., infants, handicapped)	Uses rituals for many purposes (e.g., regulate interactions, entertain, unify, confirm identity or status)
Informing	Regulates informing function to be appropriate to setting (e.g., school, playground)	Can inform on simple and complex topics (e.g., relate events, explain ideas, describe persons)	Adapts level and style of informing to accommodate listener's experience, knowledge, interest	Can inform to achieve a variety of purposes (e.g., give directions, use narrative, explain)
Controlling	Uses level of control appropriate to setting (e.g., caring for toddler, soliciting help in cleaning up)	Uses direct or indirect control tactics depending on topic (e.g., urging peer not to smoke, stopping a child from stepping into traffic)	Adopts control strategies appropriate to listener (e.g., peer, parent, teacher)	Can control through demanding, offering, warning, threatening, giving permission, using persuasion
Feeling	Verbalizes feeling appropriate to the setting (e.g., sporting event, church, school)	Expresses feeling on a variety of topics (e.g., joy, sorrow, fear)	Expresses feelings in a way appropriate to the listener (e.g., parent, peer)	Uses feelings to accomplish desired task or function (e.g., provokes, placates, soothes)
Imagining	Verbalizes imagination at a level appropriate to the setting (e.g., home, school, with peers)	Uses creative expression within a variety of topics (e.g., recreational, predicting outcomes)	Formulates imaginary images and scenarios based on knowledge of the listener (e.g., peer, teacher)	Uses verbal imagination in functional ways (e.g., to create images, to dramatize an idea, to invoke humor)

ASSESSMENT OF SPEAKING AND LISTENING ABILITIES

How can teachers tell which students need extra help in developing speaking and listening skills? For some students the need may be quite obvious, but for other students careful assessment procedures may be necessary to establish the nature of any speaking or listening problems. Before we turn to a consideration of specific assessment procedures, some general observations need to be made. These pertain to the distinction between competence and performance and to the goals or purposes of assessments one may wish to undertake.

General Considerations in Assessment

In the preceding chapter, we considered several issues that need to be taken into account in assessing a student's level of performance in any area of functioning. In this section, we address a few of the assessment issues that are unique to the areas of speaking and listening.

Competence and Performance

The ability to understand and produce novel, appropriate, and grammatical sentences is evidence of a child's linguistic competence. *Linguistic competence,* the underlying knowledge that an individual has of a given language, is distinguished from *linguistic performance,* the actual expression of that competence in the understanding or producing of well-formed sentences. A student's linguistic competence can be masked by a variety of performance variables such as poor memory, distractibility, or lack of interest. Thus, a child's failure to follow oral directions, for example, may be due to a variety of motivational or attentional problems that are separate from the child's linguistic competence.

Although it would be of great educational significance to be able to directly measure a student's linguistic competence, competence itself can never be directly observed. A teacher can only infer that it is or is not present on the basis of a sample of the student's listening and speaking behavior. This makes for a major challenge in assessing the student's language abilities. Educators would like to be able to measure speaking and listening competence, but all they can actually measure is listening or speaking performance in a specific situation.

Nonstandard Dialect

In the section of this chapter dealing with morphology, we provided some examples of variations in English language usage that characterize the speech of many American students from various cultures (e.g., inner cities). Nonstandard English usage is not limited to the area of morphology, however, but appears in aspects of syntax, semantics, and even pragmatics. The speech of some students contains so many nonstandard features that a standard English–speaking listener might have some difficulty understanding the student. Should such students be considered to have speaking problems that require further assessment? Also, when assessments are done, should nonstandard speakers be penalized for responses that might be correct within a nonstandard dialect but incorrect according to standard English usage?

In addressing these questions, it is essential to separate linguistic considerations from sociocultural considerations. From a *linguistic* point of view, all dialects are created equal; that is, one dialect is not intrinsically superior to, more advanced than, or more appropriate than another. All known dialects can communicate the ideas, intentions, and feelings of speakers to listeners. From a *sociocultural* point of view, however, there clearly are differences between dialects. The reality is that standard English is a prerequisite for many jobs and positions in American society. Students whose speech is limited to a nonstandard dialect may find that their opportunities for advancement in society are limited by that fact. Thus, as a practical matter, when conducting assessments, teachers will want to make *linguistic* allowances for nonstandard speakers. To enhance students' life chances, however, teachers must see that every student has the opportunity to learn standard English for use in certain situations or registers. (As a matter of professional competence, teachers of nonstandard-speaking students should gain skill in understanding the nonstandard dialect.)

Goals of Assessment

Before any assessment of a student's abilities is undertaken, the goals of the assessment should be established. Assessment of a student's speaking and listening abilities may address any of the following questions:

Can the student communicate (speak and listen) functionally and appropriately in a variety of contexts? (See, e.g., Table 2.4.) *If not, the goal of assessment is to delineate the functions and contexts that are problematic so that targeted intervention may take place.*

Can the student communicate (speak and listen) functionally and appropriately with different audiences so as not to call unwanted attention to herself or himself? *If not, the goal of the assessment is to specify which social registers are unfamiliar to the child so that experiences in these may be provided.*

Does the student's speaking and listening show evidence of metacommunicative skills—that is, provide indications of self-regulation, self-questioning, and relating of present circumstances to past learning? *If not, the goal of the assessment is to identify missing or poorly developed cognitive strategies so that they can be taught, thus strengthening the student's self-monitoring abilities.*

Types of Difficulties Seen in School-Age Children

The complexity of learning to speak and listen leads to a wide variety of potential difficulties, but some aspects of communication appear to cause problems more often than do others. Tables 2.5, 2.6, and 2.7 list some of the difficulties with language content and form most frequently seen by classroom teachers.

Identifying Students with Speaking and Listening Difficulties

As pointed out earlier, speaking and listening, compared with writing and reading (their written counterparts), are rarely taught as regular subjects

TABLE 2.5. Types of Semantic Speaking and Listening Difficulties

DIFFICULTY	*EXAMPLES*
Difficulty with the following types of semantic categories:	
Homonyms	*pear* and *pair; male* and *mail*
Words that have more than one meaning	*glasses* as eyeglasses or drinking glasses; *run* as action of a person or an engine or as a hole in a stocking
Idioms	"He blew his cool."
Metaphors	"as fast as greased lightning"
Proverbs	"A bird in the hand is worth two in the bush."
Qualified attributes	"spoke *proudly*"; "*light* green"; "*somewhat* cold"
Spatial/temporal prepositions	*under; upon; by*
Personal pronouns	*I* and *you; he, him,* and *his*
Proximal/distant pronouns	*this* and *that; here* and *there*
Indefinite pronouns	*somewhat; somewhere; everyone*
Difficulty in word finding, leading to	
Frequent or prolonged hesitations	
Repeated use of meaningless sounds or phrases	"umm"; "watchamacallit"; "you know"; "and then"
Round-about descriptions or circumlocutions	"something to wear"; "this cold junk"
Overuse and imprecise use of verbs and nouns	*got* to mean *bought, brought, caught,* etc.; *stuff* to mean almost any object
Redundancies or repetitions	"I feel sick, really ill, sick all over, I'm feeling sick."
Substitution of phonetically similar words	*specific : Pacific; tangerine : tambourine; commuter : computer*
Substitution of semantically similar words	*Sir Steak Restaurant : Mister Beef Restaurant; equity : equivalence*

TABLE 2.6.   Types of Syntactic Speaking and Listening Difficulties

DIFFICULTY	EXAMPLES
Inability to correctly speak and understand the following constructions:	
Passive sentences	"The boy was bitten by the dog" understood as "The boy bit the dog"
Ambiguous sentences	"They were flying planes" understood as "They were planes that could fly"
Negative sentences	"Do not swim in water that is not shallow" understood as "Do not swim in shallow water"
Interrogative sentences	"Has Grandma finished her knitting?" understood as "Grandma has finished her knitting"
Verb tense	"And then the horse will jump over the fence" stated as "And then the horse will jumped over the fence"
Direct/indirect objects	"The films showed the Marines the enemy" understood as "The films showed the Marines to the enemy"
Reflexive pronouns	"The soldiers shot themselves" stated as "The soldiers shot theirselves"
Relative pronouns	"The man who stole the ring ran away" stated as "The man which stole the ring ran away"
Conjunctions	"We won't ask Mary to come, since we don't like her" understood as "We don't like Mary"
Embedded phrases or clauses	"The raccoon with the sore paw fell into the river" understood as "The raccoon went in the river"
Omission of words, phrases, and sentence parts	

to school-age children. This means that on a day-to-day basis students are not called on to speak and listen in the same way as they are called on to write and read. This being the case, difficulty with the former may not be as readily apparent as difficulty with the latter. Nevertheless, problems in speaking and listening can impede learning as significantly as can problems in writing and reading. Thus, the burden of identifying students with difficulties in speaking and listening falls heavily on the classroom teacher.

How does a teacher decide when a student is having significant difficulty in speaking and listening? How does a teacher identify students who are in need of systematic evaluations of their speaking and/or listening abilities? In general, the teacher can be guided by a consideration of the following questions. If the answer to any of them is "yes," it is likely that further assessment is in order.

TABLE 2.7. Types of Morphological Difficulties in Speaking and Listening

DIFFICULTY	EXAMPLES
Inability to correctly speak and understand the following constructions:	
Noun plurals, especially irregular forms	child*ren*, box*es*
Possessives	girl*'s*, girls*'*
Past tense	*went*, walk*ed*, *ran; comed, builded*
Comparative and superlative adjectives	small*er*, small*est*
Agentive	danc*er*, farm*er*
Adverbial forms	quick*ly*, remarkab*ly*
Prefixes and suffixes	*post*test, *pre*test, *in*justice; green*ish*, good*ness*
Suffixes that are homonyms	dog*'s* ears; dogs*'* ears; dogs running, dog*'s* running

With Regard to Speaking

Does the student's speech or lack of speech call unwanted attention to itself or to the student?

Does the student appear to be self-conscious or embarrassed about his or her speech?

Are listeners unable to readily understand the student's speech?

Does the student speak inappropriately or insufficiently?

With Regard to Listening

Does the student show evidence of failing to understand directions?

Does the student show inability to comprehend factual or inferential knowledge from a lecture, audiotape, or other source of auditory information?

Tables 2.8 and 2.9, checklists of listening skills and speaking skills, respectively, are provided to further assist teachers in identifying students with speaking and listening problems.

Use of Standardized Tests

Once a student has been tentatively identified, based on teacher observation and teacher checklists, as having difficulties in speaking and listening, more detailed assessment is required to establish the degree and nature of the difficulties. A common and useful approach is to employ one of the standardized

TABLE 2.8.   Listening Checklist

Passive listening

1. Appears to be paying attention to others' speech	A R S N
2. Appears to distinguish information sounds from background noise	A R S N
3. Responds appropriately when attention is directed toward spoken material	A R S N
4. Can name sounds in the environment	A R S N
5. Can articulate all speech sounds	A R S N
6. Seldom mispronounces common words	A R S N
7. Can repeat digits, words, phrases, and sentences that are presented orally	A R S N

Factual listening

1. Knows the meaning of words in spoken language	A R S N
2. Knows the meaning of idioms in spoken language	A R S N
3. Knows the meaning of syntactic and morphological forms	A R S N
4. Can recall the sequence of events in a spoken narrative	A R S N
5. Can recall the ideas or concepts in spoken material	A R S N
6. Can remember the who, when, where, what, and how of what has been heard	A R S N
7. Can follow directions given verbally	A R S N

Interpretive listening

1. Is able to state the main idea of spoken material	A R S N
2. Is able to summarize spoken material	A R S N
3. Is able to predict outcomes or endings of spoken stories or essays	A R S N
4. Is able to generalize from material heard orally	A R S N
5. Is able to compare and contrast new oral material with previously learned material	A R S N
6. Is able to "read" feelings and intentions of peers	A R S N

Evaluative listening

1. Is able to identify redundant spoken material	A R S N
2. Is able to identify incomplete spoken material	A R S N
3. Can distinguish between trivial and important spoken material	A R S N
4. Can identify internal inconsistency in spoken material	A R S N
5. Can identify bias in spoken material	A R S N
6. Can recognize implausible or improbable actions, events, or ideas in spoken material	A R S N

Metacognitive listening

1. Can judge whether he or she understands spoken material	A R S N
2. Can predict whether he or she could answer questions correctly	A R S N
3. Can judge whether spoken material is comprehensible	A R S N
4. Can identify what part of spoken material he or she understands or doesn't understand	A R S N

A = always gives indicated response
R = rarely gives indicated response
S = sometimes gives indicated response
N = never gives indicated response

TABLE 2.9. Speaking Skills Checklist

COMMUNICATION ACTS	NEVER	SELDOM	SOMETIMES	OFTEN	ALWAYS	QUALITY
Ritualizing						
1. Greets others appropriately	1	2	3	4	5	
2. Introduces him/herself appropriately	1	2	3	4	5	
3. Introduces people to each other appropriately	1	2	3	4	5	
4. Greets others appropriately when telephoning	1	2	3	4	5	
5. Introduces him/herself appropriately when telephoning	1	2	3	4	5	
6. Asks for persons appropriately when telephoning	1	2	3	4	5	
7. Says farewell appropriately	1	2	3	4	5	
8. Asks others to repeat appropriately	1	2	3	4	5	
9. Gives name (first and last) on request	1	2	3	4	5	
10. Gives address (number, street, town, etc.) on request	1	2	3	4	5	
11. Gives telephone number on request	1	2	3	4	5	
Informing						
1. Asks others appropriately for name	1	2	3	4	5	
2. Asks others appropriately for address	1	2	3	4	5	
3. Asks others appropriately for telephone number	1	2	3	4	5	
4. Asks others appropriately for the location of belongings and necessities	1	2	3	4	5	
5. Asks others appropriately for the location of events	1	2	3	4	5	
6. Responds appropriately to requests for the location of events	1	2	3	4	5	
7. Asks others appropriately for the time of events	1	2	3	4	5	
8. Responds appropriately to requests for the time of events	1	2	3	4	5	
9. Asks others appropriately for preferences or wants	1	2	3	4	5	
10. Responds appropriately to requests for preferences or wants	1	2	3	4	5	
11. Tells others realistically about abilities	1	2	3	4	5	
12. Tells realistically about the levels of various abilities	1	2	3	4	5	
13. Asks appropriately for information by telephone	1	2	3	4	5	
14. Asks appropriately for permission to leave messages	1	2	3	4	5	
15. Tells appropriately whom a message is for	1	2	3	4	5	
16. Leaves appropriately expressed messages	1	2	3	4	5	

(continues)

TABLE 2.9.   *Continued*

COMMUNICATION ACTS	NEVER	SELDOM	SOMETIMES	OFTEN	ALWAYS	QUALITY
			RATINGS			
Controlling						
1. Suggests places for meetings appropriately	1	2	3	4	5	
2. Suggests times for meetings appropriately	1	2	3	4	5	
3. Asks appropriately for permission	1	2	3	4	5	
4. Asks appropriately for reasons	1	2	3	4	5	
5. Tells reasons appropriately	1	2	3	4	5	
6. Asks appropriately for favors	1	2	3	4	5	
7. Responds appropriately to requests for favors:						
a. Accepts and carries out	1	2	3	4	5	
b. Evades or delays	1	2	3	4	5	
c. Rejects	1	2	3	4	5	
8. Offers assistance appropriately	1	2	3	4	5	
9. Makes complaints appropriately	1	2	3	4	5	
10. Responds to complaints appropriately:						
a. Accepts blame and suggests action	1	2	3	4	5	
b. Evades or refers	1	2	3	4	5	
c. Rejects blame	1	2	3	4	5	
11. Asks for intentions appropriately	1	2	3	4	5	
12. Responds appropriately to requests for intentions	1	2	3	4	5	
13. Asks to discontinue actions appropriately	1	2	3	4	5	
14. Asks appropriately for terms of contract:						
a. Pay	1	2	3	4	5	
b. Work hours	1	2	3	4	5	
c. Vacations, etc.	1	2	3	4	5	
d. Other	1	2	3	4	5	
15. Asks appropriately for changes in contractual terms:						
a. Pay	1	2	3	4	5	
b. Work hours	1	2	3	4	5	
c. Vacations, etc.	1	2	3	4	5	
d. Other	1	2	3	4	5	

(continues)

TABLE 2.9. *Continued*

COMMUNICATION ACTS	NEVER	SELDOM	SOMETIMES	OFTEN	ALWAYS	QUALITY
Feelings						
1. Expresses appreciation appropriately	1	2	3	4	5	
2. Apologizes appropriately	1	2	3	4	5	
3. Expresses agreement appropriately	1	2	3	4	5	
4. Expresses disagreement appropriately	1	2	3	4	5	
5. Expresses support appropriately	1	2	3	4	5	
6. Compliments appropriately	1	2	3	4	5	
7. Expresses affection appropriately	1	2	3	4	5	
8. Expresses positive feelings and attitudes appropriately	1	2	3	4	5	
9. Expresses negative feelings and attitudes appropriately	1	2	3	4	5	

Circle 1   If the speaker *never* uses the communication function or speech act appropriately for expressing intent or politeness features (social register).

Circle 2   If the speaker *seldom* uses the communication function or speech act appropriately for expressing intent or politeness features (social register).

Circle 3   If the speaker *sometimes* uses the communication function or speech act appropriately for expressing intent or politeness features (social register).

Circle 4   If the speaker *often* but not *always* uses the communication function or speech act appropriately for expressing intent or politeness features (social register).

Circle 5   If the speaker *always* uses the communication function or speech act appropriately for expressing intent or politeness features (social register).

Quality of speech acts may be noted as (1) informal, (2) formal, (3) direct, or (4) indirect.

From *"Let's Talk" Inventory for Adolescents* by E. Wiig, 1982, San Antonio, TX: Psychological Corporation. Reprinted with permission.

tests of language currently available. Table 2.10 presents brief descriptions of the most popular of these tests. Clearly, test developers have given much more attention to tests that measure speaking than to tests that measure listening. Those tests that do measure listening tend to measure student listening ability at the passive or factual level.

Analysis of Speech Samples

At times, it is necessary or desirable to look closely at actual samples of utterances by a student in either a spontaneous situation or a more structured setting. In either case, the sample of speech must be taped with an audio (or audio–video) recorder and the utterances transcribed.

TABLE 2.10. Commercially Prepared Tests of Speaking and Listening

NAME (AUTHOR OF TEST)	ASPECT OF LANGUAGE MEASURED	TARGET POPULATION	PURPORTED PURPOSE
Bankson Language Test–2 (Bankson, 1990)	Semantic knowledge, morphological and syntactic rules, visual perception, and auditory perception	Ages 4–8	To screen language and visual skill areas
Carrow Elicited Language Inventory (Carrow-Woolfolk, 1974)	Expressive language in elicited situation (emphasis on syntax)	Ages 3–8	To assess a child's productive control of grammar
Clinical Evaluation of Language Fundamentals–Revised (Wiig & Semel, 1987)	Comprehensive test of language functions	Kindergarten through grade 12	To analyze understanding and use of language in functional ways
Comprehensive Receptive and Expressive Vocabulary Test (G. Wallace & Hammill, 1994)	Receptive and expressive vocabulary	Ages 4–18	To estimate vocabulary competence
Goldman–Fristoe Test of Articulation (Goldman & Fristoe, 1972)	Articulation	Above age 2	To assess speech sound production
"Let's Talk" Inventory for Adolescents (Wiig, 1982)	Language use: context and function	Age 9 to young adulthood	To probe speech-act formulation ability in relation to communication function and intent and to audience
Peabody Picture Vocabulary Test (Dunn & Dunn, 1981)	Receptive vocabulary of standard English	Mental ages 2 to adult	To derive an IQ score
Test for Auditory Comprehension of Language (Carrow-Woolfolk, 1985)	Word meanings, grammatical morphemes, and the understanding of complex sentence constructions	Ages 3–10	To evaluate receptive language

(continues)

TABLE 2.10. *Continued*

NAME (AUTHOR OF TEST)	ASPECT OF LANGUAGE MEASURED	TARGET POPULATION	PURPORTED PURPOSE
Test of Adolescent and Adult Language (Hammill, Brown, Larsen, & Wiederholt, 1993)	Receptive and expressive aspects of vocabulary and syntax	Ages 11–26	To give indication of strengths and weaknesses in each area tapped
Test of Early Language Development (Hresko, Reid, & Hammill, 1990)	Content and form in both receptive and expressive modes	Ages 3–7	To give indication of screening and documenting problem
Test of Language Development: Intermediate (Hammill & Newcomer, 1988)	Receptive and expressive aspects of vocabulary and syntax	Ages 8–13	To give indication of child's overall strengths and weaknesses in each area tapped
Token Test for Children (DiSimoni, 1978)	Teach perceptive research language	Ages 3–12	To screen for receptive language dysfunction or rule out language impairment
Utah Test of Language Development (Mecham, 1989)	Expressive and receptive language, aspects of conceptual development	Ages 2–15	To derive an overall picture of a child's language development compared with his or her peers'

Once transcribed, a sample of utterances may be analyzed and coded any number of ways, depending on the skills of the teacher and the perceived area of student difficulty. A complete phonetic or syntactic analysis is usually beyond the scope of a classroom teacher's training and time and is ordinarily best left to a speech–language specialist. Much useful information can be gained from a variety of speech analysis systems, however. For example, Damico (1980) has proposed discourse analysis categories based on the speech parameters of quantity, quality, relation, and manner. An overview of this analysis as adapted by Wiig and Semel (1984) is presented in Table 2.11.

Whether the speech sample is spontaneous or elicited, it is important that it be obtained in as natural a communicative interaction as possible. To the degree possible, avoid contriving a situation that is not representative of the child's actual day-to-day speech. J. F. Miller (1981) provided the following suggestions (with our adaptations) on how to optimize procedures for obtaining speech samples. Although these suggestions are given as

TABLE 2.11. Discourse Analysis Categories

PARAMETER	CATEGORY/QUALITY	UTTERANCE NUMBER/ NUMBER OF OCCURRENCES
Quantity	Insufficient information bits	_____
	Nonspecific vocabulary (e.g., "it," "this," "here," "there")	_____
	Information redundancy (e.g., paraphrases, repetitions, circumlocutions)	_____
	Need for repetition (e.g., "What?" "Say that again")	_____
Quality	Message inaccuracy	_____
Relation	Poor topic maintenance (e.g., shifts topic, does not return to topic)	_____
	Inappropriate responses (e.g., *non sequitur,* off topic)	_____
	Inability to ask relevant questions	_____
	Situational inappropriateness (e.g., violates taboos)	_____
	Inappropriate speech style/register (e.g., uses informal style when formal is required, uses slang, swears)	_____
Manner	Linguistic nonfluency (e.g., filled pauses, interjections)	_____
	Revision behavior	_____
	Delays before responding (5–10 sec. or more)	_____
	Inability to structure discourse	_____
	Difficulty with turn taking	_____
	Inefficient attention to and use of gaze (e.g., for turn taking, maintenance)	_____
	Inappropriate intonational contours (e.g., question vs. statement)	_____
Summary	Total utterances	_____
	Total discourse errors	_____
	Total utterances with errors	_____
	Percentage of utterances with errors	_____

From *Language Assessment and Intervention for the Learning Disabled* (2nd ed.) by E. H. Wiig and E. Semel, 1984, Columbus, OH: Charles E. Merrill. (Adapted by Wiig and Semel from Damico, 1980.)

guidelines for obtaining speech samples for analyses, they are equally useful in providing direction for day-to-day verbal interactions with students.

Listen to the student and follow his or her lead. Make this a genuine communicative interaction. Respond to the student as a "real" listener would—replying, adding new information, questioning, and commenting.

Be patient with the student. A long, quiet pause on the tape recorder does not hurt. Avoid making the student feel anxious or rushed by overwhelming him or her with your intensity. He or she will speak when ready.

Take the student's perspective. Think like the student; put yourself in his or her place. Address his or her interests and point of view.

Respect the student and insist that the student respect you. Be warm and friendly but not patronizing. Value what the student says, and insist that your comments be taken seriously as well. Avoid playing the fool.

Further details on procedures, content selection, and interpretation criteria for assessing free and elicited speech samples may be found in J. F. Miller (1981).

PLANNING AND IMPLEMENTING SPEAKING AND LISTENING INTERVENTIONS

Having considered some of the issues related to assessment and having implemented assessment procedures, the teacher is ready to turn to actual intervention with the student who is having difficulty. Before an intervention is implemented, however, attention should be paid to the development and articulation of the intervention goals.

Intervention Goals

The goals of an intervention in a student's speaking and listening skills should grow out of a number of factors, including those described in the following sections.

The Age and Developmental Status of the Student

An appropriate intervention for a teenager would be quite different from that planned for a preschool child or a child in the early elementary grades. In the case of handicapped students, overall developmental status and particular handicapping conditions (e.g., hearing loss, mental retardation, motor problems in speech formation) need to be considered in the development of appropriate intervention goals. With handicapped and "normal" students alike, however, the overall goal is to develop age-appropriate skills in the student. The intent is to make a student's speech and listening behavior as similar as possible to those of other students of the same age.

Assessment Results

No intervention should proceed until an appropriate assessment, as described previously, has been conducted. The results of the assessment should guide the development of appropriate intervention goals. Not all students will show the same profile of strengths and weaknesses. Students may have sufficient strengths that no intervention is required in some areas of functioning; however, identified areas of weakness should be directly targeted for intervention.

Dimensions and Levels of Intervention Goals

Given the wide range of skills that are employed in effective speaking and listening, a very long list of intervention goals could be drawn up. Rather than attempt to be exhaustive, we will present several alternative dimensions and levels of goals that could be considered for a given student.

DIMENSIONS OF CONTENT, FORM, AND USE

Although our major focus throughout this chapter has been on the *use* of language in speaking and listening, the dimensions of content and form cannot be ignored. Some students have syntactic or phonological problems that present a compelling need for intervention. Other students have major difficulties producing and understanding language content—meanings of words, phrases, idioms, homonyms, sentences, and conversational discourse in general. Such students will require an intervention that emphasizes the content, or semantic aspect, of language production and comprehension. Figure 2.5 presents a model for diagnosis and intervention that considers the three dimensions of content, form, and use.

DIMENSIONS OF INTENT AND FUNCTION

Central to effective speaking and listening are the abilities to express one's communicative intent and to comprehend another speaker's communicative intent or purpose. Table 2.12 lists some intervention goals and some examples that address these dimensions.

DIMENSION OF CONTEXT

For effective communication to occur, both speakers and listeners must be able to discern and take into account the context in which a communicative interaction occurs. Goals for various contexts and some examples are provided in Table 2.13.

LEVEL OF INTERVENTION

Intervention in any of the dimensions noted above should take place at the level of sophistication that is appropriate for the student. Younger or less sophisticated students may need instruction in the direct, factual aspects of speaking and listening, whereas more mature students will benefit from an intervention that promotes evaluative and metacognitive levels of speaking and listening. Table 2.14 lists some intervention goals at each of these levels.

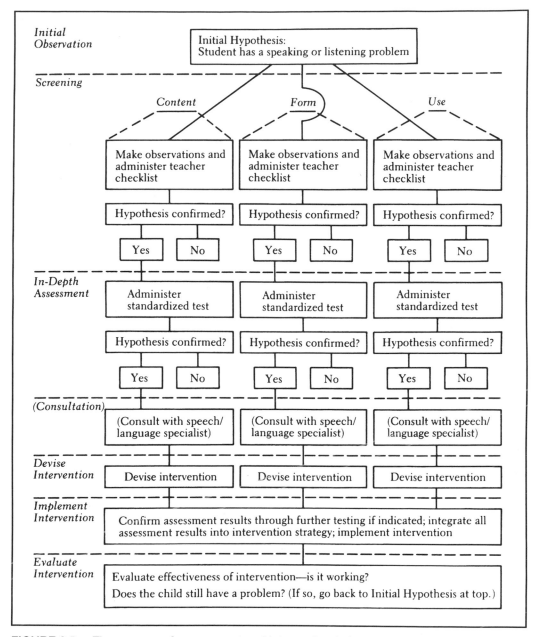

FIGURE 2.5. The process of assessment and intervention in language content, form, and use.

Principles of Intervention Based on Normal Development

Once the goals for intervention have been established, what does the teacher do next? A variety of approaches exist for teaching speaking and listening skills. What principles can guide teachers through the range of possible bases for interventions?

TABLE 2.12. Goals for Speaking and Understanding Communicative Intent

	SPEAKING		LISTENING	
	OBJECTIVES	EXAMPLES	OBJECTIVES	EXAMPLES
Ritualizing	Student is able to use rituals to regulate interactions, entertain, confirm identity or status, participate in religious or patriotic rituals	Participates in Pledge of Allegiance, participates in recitation of religious creed, gives greetings, begins and ends telephone conversations, makes introductions	Student can understand others' use of ritual, can detect the inappropriate use of rituals, can be entertained or made to feel part of a group through use of rituals	Knows the general and specific meaning of religious and socio-cultural rituals, discerns when rituals and conventions such as greetings are being used
Informing	Student can inform on simple and complex topics, relate events, explain ideas, describe persons, give directions, use narrative, give explanations	Tells stories and jokes, describes sporting events, recounts the plot of television dramas, summarizes news accounts, gives directions, explains reasons for decisions	Student can follow a narrated plot, understand oral directions, get the main idea of or summarize a spoken language account, comprehend the main points of a lecture	Follows a TV plot, gets the main idea of a political speech, judges the accuracy of a TV commentator, remembers the sequence of an oral story, remembers the important points of a lecture
Controlling	Student can control through demanding, offering, warning, threatening, giving permission, using persuasion	Persuades parent to let him or her use the car, warns someone about AIDS, gives permission to a peer to copy his or her drawing	Student can discern a speaker's intention in influencing him or her—warning, threatening, caing, persuading, negotiating	Discerns when being manipulated or exploited or when someone is trying to get him or her to do something, discerns a warning
Feeling	Student can verbalize feelings of self and evoke feelings in others through enraging, provoking, placating, soothing, comforting, encouraging, supporting, consoling	Comforts a peer whose dog was killed, taunts a sibling who "tattled," supports a classmate who lacks confidence, annoys a neighborhood vagrant, expresses anxiety about an upcoming exam	Student can discern others' feelings of joy, pity, fear, sorrow from what they say; is influenced to feel happy, guilty, sad, depressed, comforted, encouraged, by what others say to him or her	Accepts comforting from others, discerns others' feelings of empathy and support, discerns hostility or anger, makes judgment about the speaker's intent in general
Imagining	Student can use verbal imagination to create images, dramatize ideas, invoke humor, create moods, and evoke feelings	Creates an aura of mystery in a story, exaggerates an incident to make it more humorous, evokes pity when describing a hypothetical victim of hunger	Student can form mental images and moods based on others' descriptions of hypothetical images, sequences, moods, scenarios	Pictures events and moods being described in prose or poetry; gets the point of a joke, riddle, or pun; distinguishes fact from fantasy

TABLE 2.13. Goals for Speaking and Listening: Using Contexts Appropriately

CONTEXT	SPEAKING		LISTENING	
	OBJECTIVES	EXAMPLES	OBJECTIVES	EXAMPLES
Setting	Student can speak at appropriate level of formality, directness, politeness, dialect, given the social setting; can use appropriate social register	Lowers voice upon entering the school from the playground, speaks formally to French teacher during an oral exam, greets distant relatives politely at a family gathering	Student can understand the use of communication styles—formality, directness, politeness, dialect—appropriate to different settings	Is upset at persons whispering loudly in church, understands why some topics are not raised at dinner, knows why father "lets it all hang out" at the corner bar
Topic	Student can engage in a variety of topics effectively; can switch from one to another without confusion or discomfort	Uses sports jargon to discuss a baseball no-hitter, makes a formal oral presentation in history class, discusses feelings about a friend who has had an accident	Student can use levels of listening appropriate to a variety of topics	Uses passive listening level for lyrics of a popular song, factual level for a ball game on the radio, inferential level for a news special on Ethiopia, critical level for a political speech
Listener	Student can speak appropriately to listeners of different ages, abilities, classes, status, levels of authority and expertise	Uses short, simple sentences to his or her baby sister, addresses the town mayor as "Your Honor," uses profane language with friends until mother appears	Student can understand how speaker–listener characteristics such as authority, expertise, status, age, handicap, degree of intimacy regulate communication style	Is not disturbed when peer calls him or her a "fool" but is bothered when father does, knows why the parish priest is addressed as "Father," tells a peer not to talk back to the teacher
Purpose/Task	Student can use speech to accomplish many different tasks—regulation of self and others, informing, controlling, feeling, imagining, ritualizing	Offers his or her bike to a friend, requests a ride from another friend, describes an event at school to the family, teases a brother, says grace at the dinner table	Student can comprehend a variety of speech intents	Listens with comprehension to a lecture on rare fishes, step-by-step directions for making quiche, an argument in favor of capital punishment, an ad for pain tablets

TABLE 2.14. Speaking and Listening Goals for Different Levels of Intervention

LEVEL	SPEAKING GOALS	LISTENING GOALS
Passive	Student is able to state or repeat utterances that have no particular meaning for him or her.	Student is aware of auditory events and can distinguish information sounds from background noise.
Factual	Student is able to state factually accurate information, give correct directions, describe reality in literal terms, state correct sequences, and correctly use words, phrases, and sentences.	Student comprehends factual literal information including details and sequence and understands the meanings of words, phrases, and sentences.
Interpretive	Student is able to use metaphors, idioms, and inferences, state main ideas, summarize, solve new problems based on knowledge of principles, generalize, and compare and contrast.	Student can comprehend main ideas, summarize what has been said, predict outcomes, and understand metaphors, idioms, and inferences.
Evaluative	Student can speak without inconsistencies, redundancy, bias, or incompleteness, and avoids the trite and the trivial.	Student is able to judge the truth, clarity, plausibility, completeness, consistency, and implications of what is said.
Metacognitive	Student speaks with the comprehension of the listener in mind and adjusts his or her speech based on feedback from the listener.	Student is able to judge his or her own comprehension of spoken material and make adjustments in listening strategy to improve comprehension.

Most children learn to speak and listen without formal instruction or lessons, through everyday interactions with their parents. Such learning is remarkable in its effectiveness. Although this point of view is not unanimously held (especially with respect to students who are profoundly handicapped in language development), most speech–language specialists believe that early parent–child interaction can provide a useful instructional model for teachers working with children in whom, for one reason or another, the early learning did not "take." That is, to find clues as to what to do when some aspect of language has failed to develop on schedule, educators can examine what parents do naturally that teaches their children to speak and listen. Accordingly, we will briefly examine some of the characteristics of early parent–child communications that establish the foundation for good listening and speaking skills and that can be adapted by teachers for classroom instruction.

Establishing Mutuality and Line of Regard

From infancy onward, children and parents engage in mutual efforts to transmit feelings and intentions. Thus, the parent attending to a babbling infant may think or say, "What could Rebecca be trying to tell me? I wonder if she could be hungry again?" The 6-month-old child turns his head in response to hearing his name spoken as if to say, "What do you want me to do, Daddy?" These events and hundreds of similar ones represent early attempts by young children to make sense of the feelings, ideas, and intentions of the people around them—that is, to follow their "line of regard" (Bruner, 1975). From the earliest stages of infancy, children learn the routine "attend to, act upon." This paradigm sets the stage for their learning "if I listen (attend to), then something happens (act upon)." The act of listening becomes reinforced by consequent events. Paying attention, or listening, is a habit that is learned early in life by most children and provides a foundation for their later learning.

Children's first *listening* attempts involve hearing and attempting to understand. Reciprocally, parents try to interpret the initially crude and undifferentiated communication attempts of young children. Young children's talk is at first imprecise and limited, yet these first *speaking* efforts set the stage for a later period when their speech will be appropriate, sophisticated, and effective. The active listening and encouragement of parents is essential for this progress to occur.

As time goes on, both parents and children become more skillful in listening to each other and in understanding each other's intentions. Parents adjust their speaking to the children's level of listening ability, and children learn to speak ever more clearly and appropriately.

Establishing Intentions

Among the most important things a child learns is that other people have intentions, that they convey those intentions by speaking, and that the child can make life more pleasant by listening to those intentions. Later children learn that they too have intentions, that these can be communicated to others, and that others will act on what they have spoken. In school, a teacher can observe intent in a nonverbal child by noting the direction of the child's regard, by observing what satisfies the child (he or she stops whining when allowed to have a certain toy), by watching whether the child substitutes one strategy for another (if he or she does not get results by looking at the coat closet, he or she tries walking to the door to convey a desire to go outdoors), and, finally, by noting the child's persistence.

Awareness of a student's intentions is necessary for effective teaching of language, because the most effective teaching is that which helps the student make explicit what he or she already intends implicitly. For example, explicit instruction in a particular verb form is likely to be beneficial only when the student shows evidence of having grasped the meaning of the verb. Otherwise, the teacher is teaching nonsense words to the student.

Adjusting Communication to the Child's Level

Observations of mother–child interactions show that mothers regulate their verbalizations to fit their children's level of cognitive ability.

Thus, most mother-talk, or "motherese," directed toward young children is short, simple, and clear. Usually there is only one clause. The mother presents a limited number of words and semantic relationships. As children develop their ability to handle complexity, there is a corresponding change in the mother's responses to them. Effective caregivers adjust their linguistic demands on young children so that the children are challenged to develop their abilities to increasingly higher levels of differentiation and sophistication. Similarly, in the classroom, instruction in speaking and listening should take place at a level just above the students' ordinary level of functioning. Too easy instruction does not challenge students; too difficult instruction frustrates them.

Teaching Communication Rituals

Mothers develop routines that they use over and over again in interacting verbally with their young children. Repetition of words and actions, as in games like peek-a-boo or in waving bye-bye, helps children to learn sequences and to predict what will happen next in their environment. (Waving bye-bye is a child's first instruction in leave-taking competence.) Such routines and rituals form the basis for the highly ritualized nature of much adult communication—for example, "How are you?" "I'm fine, thanks. How are you?" Students with difficulties in the ordinary speaking and listening routines of day-to-day interactions with others need to practice these routines in low-pressure, even gamelike, settings.

Teaching Language Conventions

Increasing evidence indicates that caretakers have a controlling role in teaching children what is appropriate in terms of such conventions as how to start a conversation, how to make appropriate responses, and how to sustain and end discourse. Even such commonplace caretaker behavior as holding up an infant to wave bye-bye constitutes a lesson in how to appropriately end a social interchange.

Tables 2.15 and 2.16 summarize some of the rules and conventions governing language use that are learned by younger and older children. Much of this learning goes on in the home, in everyday social situations. In this section, we have highlighted only the most important of the processes underlying normal speech and listening skills acquisition.

Stages in Teaching Skills

As with all learning, the achievement of competence in speaking and listening can be separated into stages. Instruction is facilitated by clear distinctions among the stages of learning presented in Table 2.17.

In operationalizing the stages of speaking and listening learning, teachers often find that the *acquisition* stage requires the most heavily

TABLE 2.15. How Young Children Learn Appropriate Language Use

CATEGORY	EXAMPLES
Learning to be quiet	"Be quiet. Grandma's not feeling well." "Dad's upset about something else. Don't bother him now about your broken truck." "Shhh. Time to go to sleep."
Learning to be polite and considerate	"Don't interrupt while Auntie is talking." "Say 'thank you' to your cousin for the gift." "Let's call Uncle Joe and wish him a happy birthday."
Learning to take listener into account	"Don't say that when the pastor is here." "Don't talk back to the teacher." "Don't let Grandpa hear you saying those words." "Say goo-goo to the baby."
Learning to take setting into account	"Don't talk out loud in church; just whisper." "Don't say 'I wanna go wee-wee' so loudly in the store." "In the park you can play and shout as loudly as you want."
Learning to assert self	"Tell him you'll hit him back if he hits first." "Tell her it's your turn now to play with the train." "Don't let him call you bad names."
Learning discretion and social convention	"Don't tell her you don't like her. Tell her you can't come to her party because you have something else to do." "Susie has a new dress. Tell her she looks pretty." "Say 'I'm fine; how are you?' when he says 'How are you?'"
Learning to show concern for others	"Tell your cousin you're sorry he is sick." "Tell Jimmy you're sorry he lost his toy." "Let's call Grandma and ask her how she feels."
Learning to pay attention	"Listen carefully. The stove is too hot to touch." "Go to the closet in my room, and get my red purse. Bring it down to me, and I'll give you a quarter for the candy."
Learning about appropriate topics	"We don't talk about going to the bathroom in front of guests." "We don't tell everyone how much we paid for your bike."

teacher-directed preplanned activities. Ensuring sufficient practice at the *proficiency* stage of learning also requires specific preparation by the teacher. As learning moves to the stages of *maintenance* and *generalization,* the teacher may continue to provide preplanned lessons, but a decided opportunistic factor comes into play; that is, the teacher must remain vigilant throughout the day for opportunities for the child to practice the new

TABLE 2.16.   How Older Children Learn Appropriate Language Use

CATEGORY	EXAMPLES
Learning when not to say something	"When negotiating, don't give him your final offer first." "Dad's upset about something else. Don't bother him now about your math test."
Learning to be polite and considerate	"I think your Grandma would appreciate a call on her birthday." "Did you write a note thanking the hostess?"
Learning to take listener into account	"Tell us a different joke. We've already heard that one." "That's not a topic you discuss with your boyfriend." "I don't think your Polish friend appreciated that joke." "Read up on World War II; that's what your Grandpa likes to talk about."
Learning to take setting into account	"Keep your voice down in the funeral home." "When in Quebec, use whatever French you can muster." "People really let loose at a football game."
Learning to assert self	"Tell him you've had enough of his bullying." "You and your roommate will have to figure out a fair arrangement for cleaning your dorm room."
Learning discretion and social convention	"Don't tell her you don't like her. Just don't ask her out again." "Be sure to say something about how nice your date looks." "When in doubt, talk about the weather or politics."
Learning to show concern for others	"Have you called your cousin in the hospital?" "How do you think he feels about crashing his motorcycle?" "What could you do to make her feel better?" "Don't blame her. She couldn't have known . . ."
Learning to pay attention	"Listen carefully. The exit is the second one after the underpass. You turn left, go two lights, and then turn right."
Learning about appropriate topics	"We don't talk about Uncle Joe's drinking in front of guests." "We don't tell everyone how much we paid for the house."

TABLE 2.17. Stages of Learning

STAGE OF LEARNING	DESCRIPTION	POSSIBLE TEACHING APPROACHES	EXAMPLE (LEARNING TO USE APPROPRIATE GREETINGS AND FAREWELLS)
Acquisition	Initial learning of the new skill	Teacher *shows* (demonstrates skill) Teacher *says* (verbal instruction in producing skill) Teacher *elicits student response* with prompts and supervision	Discussion of different ways to greet and say farewell depending on listener and setting Teacher lists different settings on chalkboard Students role-play greetings and farewells in pairs
Proficiency	Achieving mastery of the skill with reduced prompting	Teacher reduces prompts while: Student *shows* (practices skill through motor behavior) Student *states* (practices skill through verbal behavior) Student *writes* (practices skill in written form) Student *simulates* (practices skill on computer)	Written exercises in which student matches appropriate greetings and farewells with situations (e.g., "Hi! I'm home at last!" and "Good morning, Miss Smith: I'm sorry I'm late" with a late arrival at home and at school, respectively) Comparison of results with others' (students working in pairs)
Maintenance	Demonstrating mastery of the skill over a period of time	Teacher *arranges learning maintenance opportunity* Student consolidates skills through workbook games peer exercises computer exercises Teacher *sees maintenance opportunity* in unrelated situation and requires that Student *states* the desired response orally Student *writes* the desired response Student *demonstrates* the response	(Two weeks later) Students use appropriate greetings in a social studies skit about George Washington at Valley Forge (greetings of commander to troops and vice versa, greetings of troops to civilians, etc.)

(continues)

TABLE 2.17. *Continued*

STAGE OF LEARNING	DESCRIPTION	POSSIBLE TEACHING APPROACHES	EXAMPLE (LEARNING TO USE APPROPRIATE GREETINGS AND FAREWELLS)
Generalization	Applying the skill to new situations in new contexts	Teacher *arranges generalization opportunity* through planned exercises application in other subjects Teaches *sees generalization opportunity* in unrelated situation and requires that student *generalize* to new verbal situation, new written situation, and new demonstration situation	Teacher observes student greetings on playground; reminds student about appropriate use and requests demonstration

skills or generalize them to new situations. These opportunities may present themselves in times and places (e.g., on the playground or during a mathematics lesson) that seem far removed from language teaching, but the ultimate test of speaking and listening competence is not whether the child can perform the skill but whether the child uses the skill in routine, day-to-day activities.

Teaching Speaking and Listening Skills

Commercial Materials for General Language Development

A wide variety of commercially produced materials for teaching speaking and listening skills are now available, especially for teaching younger children. A review of all of these materials is beyond the scope of this chapter. Because new materials are continually appearing, it is essential that the teacher be informed of and evaluate teaching approaches, language development kits, and other intervention materials as they become available. We have developed a set of criteria to assist the teacher in evaluating language intervention materials. These criteria are presented in Table 2.18. Along with the questions to be asked in evaluating speaking and listening instructional materials, we present what are currently thought to be the best instructional practices for addressing these questions.

Teacher-Developed Approaches

In general, children can best be taught to speak meaningfully and functionally in real-life situations involving "real" communication issues.

TABLE 2.18. Evaluation of Speaking and Listening Programs and Best Practices

EVALUATIVE QUESTION	BEST PRACTICE
Rationale	
Does the program attempt to provide instruction in speaking and listening in as naturalistic a way as possible?	Instruction in speaking and listening that is as natural and unobtrusive as possible has been found to be most effective for most students.
Does the program provide for both speaking and listening?	Real-life communication involves turn taking in speaking and listening—the most effective instruction does the same.
Does the program promote the speaking of "real" intentions, ideas, and feelings?	Wherever possible, especially at the proficiency and maintenance stages of instruction, student-initiated intentions should be used.
Does the program emphasize the functions of speaking and listening?	Speaking for speaking's sake and listening for listening's sake are rarely done in the "real" world. Learning to use these skills functionally ensures their use and reinforcement in day-to-day life.
Does the program promote integration into the rest of the school day and into other classroom activities?	The most desirable programs can be readily integrated into other parts of the school day and into other subject areas.
Does the program emphasize the learning of speaking and listening strategies or the learning of specific words and sentences?	Strategies can be used in many situations; specific words and sentences may never be used again.
Organization	
Does the program's activity arrangement follow what is known about the sequence of normal development of speaking and listening?	For students with mild to moderate speaking and listening problems, using normal development as a guide for sequencing is recommended. For severely handicapped students, other considerations enter in.
Does the program provide for preinstructional, instructional, and postinstructional, or follow-up, activities?	Using activities that "set the stage" (advance organizers) facilitates the acquisition and retention of learning strategies. Follow-up activities, or "boosters," aid in application and generalization of learned material.
Does the program specify entry behaviors or prerequisites?	Learning to speak and listen well is highly individualistic. The best learning takes place when instruction is at a level slightly more complex than the student's current level of functioning.
Does the program specify desired outcomes?	Evaluation of student progress requires knowing what outcomes are sought and being able to tell when they have been achieved.
Does the program use peers as part of the speaking and listening activities?	Use of peers has been found to facilitate speaking and listening to real communicative intentions. Peers help make the instructional program more naturalistic.

This means that commercially produced materials have limited application in teaching language use and that the most effective instruction is developed by the teacher as a result of joint teacher–student interactions.

Learning Activities

In this section, we present examples of approaches to teaching speaking and listening skills that can readily be used in most classrooms. In most cases, no particular materials other than those usually available in the classroom are required.

Factual and Interpretive Listening—Imagining Function

STAGE OF LEARNING

Acquisition

AGE OF STUDENTS

Grades 1 through 6

PURPOSE

To teach students to comprehend factual imaginary material and to interpret what is heard in the form of a drawing

MATERIALS REQUIRED

Large drawing paper folded into fourths (see below), crayons or magic markers

1	2
3	4

PROCEDURES

Introduce the lesson by saying, "Sometimes we hear things that are new to us. Someone may be talking about something that we've never seen before. When this happens, we have to listen extra hard to make a picture in our minds from what we hear.

"Today we're going to listen to a story about creatures we've never seen before. Your job is to listen to the story and picture in your mind what the creatures look like. Then draw the picture in your mind on the paper in front of you.

"Notice that the paper is divided into four parts, labeled 1, 2, 3, and 4. These numbers show that there are four scenes to the story. You will be drawing one picture for each scene." (For young students, use only one or two scenes, and simplify the scripts as appropriate. For older students, the scripts may be made more complicated.)

Scene 1

In a river far away lives a large monster. He is large and red and has sharp points all over his body. He has six legs and three black eyes. His two ears are large, green circles.

Scene 2

In the tall grass beside the river crawls a long, yellow, snakelike creature. This creature has a large blue bump on the end of his tail. His two red eyes are on the tip of his nose.

Scene 3

Flying overhead is a funny orange creature with no wings, only a propeller on his head. He has eight black legs like a spider. His body is covered with black dots, and he has three red horns that point straight ahead out of his body.

Scene 4

Now the crawling creature and the flying creature are attacking the monster. The crawling creature has circled himself around the monster and is squeezing him. The flying creature is sticking him from behind with his horns.

RESULTS

Examine each student's drawings carefully. What errors did the student make—are there patterns pertaining to size, color, shape, or position? Can the student handle more than one direction at a time? The results of your examination can be used as the basis for subsequent instruction.

Alternatively, have students exchange papers while you reread the scripts. Each must note the errors and omissions on the paper and explain why he or she thinks the student made those errors.

Taking the Listener into Account in Speaking and Following Spoken Directions in Listening—Informing Function

STAGE OF LEARNING

Acquisition

AGE OF STUDENTS

Grades 1 through 8

PURPOSE

To teach students to take the listener into account in informing speech; to teach students to follow verbal directions

MATERIALS REQUIRED

A table with two chairs facing each other on opposite sides of the table, an upright barrier on the table that prevents students from seeing each other's displays of blocks, two identical sets of blocks of different shapes and colors (for younger students) or Lego® brand or other more complicated building materials (for older students).

PROCEDURES

In this activity, students work in pairs—one student serves as speaker, one as listener.

The teacher builds a display with the blocks on the speaker's side of the table. The speaker describes to the listener what the teacher is doing, for example, "He is putting two red squares on top of the yellow rectangle." The listener, positioned so that he or she cannot see the teacher's display, must use the description given by the student speaker to build an identical display. Tape record the speaker's directions for later use.

Start with a simple display, especially with younger or handicapped students. In a later activity, students may work independently in pairs, without the teacher's assistance.

RESULTS

Compare the listener's display with the teacher's display. If there are any discrepancies, play the audiotape of the speaker's directions. Have the students figure out why the listener made a mistake—was the listener given faulty directions, or did he or she not listen carefully? Point out ways in which the speaker takes the listener into account (or fails to do so): giving the directions slowly; using accurate prepositions such as "beside," "above," or "under"; providing information in the correct sequence; and using words such as "it," "this one," or "the round one" only when the listener knows what the referent is.

Repeat the exercise with a very young listener to teach about how speakers adjust their informing function to take listener capabilities into account.

Using Speech to Affect the Behavior of Others and Analyzing Spoken Attempts to Change a Listener's Behavior—Controlling Function

STAGE OF LEARNING

Acquisition

AGE OF STUDENTS

Grades 1 through 8

PURPOSE

To teach students to use language effectively in situations where they wish to elicit a response from someone

MATERIALS REQUIRED

No special materials required

PROCEDURES

In this activity, students work in pairs—one student serves as the speaker who is trying to get the listener to do something, the other as the listener responding to the speaker.

The activities are in the form of role playing. Students select the role of speaker or responder in one of the following situations (other situations may be substituted for younger students):

1. Speaker (customer) is returning a defective appliance to the store. Speaker wants the responder (store representative) to refund the purchase price. Responder must try to implement the store policy, which is to make exchanges only.

2. Speaker wants the television set to a certain channel in order to watch a favorite show. Responder already has the TV set on another channel. The rule of the house is that whoever turns on the TV gets to choose the first program. Speaker must try to change the responder's mind.

3. Speaker has been grounded (cannot leave the house except for school) by his or her parents for a major infraction of rules. Speaker must try to convince responder (parent) to make an exception to the grounding for one night because of an important social event.

4. Speaker believes his or her examination has not been scored correctly. Speaker must try to convince responder (teacher) to give him or her some extra points on an essay question.

5. Speaker has a paper route. Responder (customer on route) has not paid for 2 months but still wants the paper delivered. Speaker must tell responder that he or she must pay up in order to receive more papers.

The role playing should be practiced in pairs, then demonstrated in front of the group. The group then should discuss the effectiveness and appropriateness of the speaker's attempt to affect the behavior of the responder, addressing issues such as the following:

a. Did the speaker clearly state the problem?

b. Did the speaker clearly make known what he or she wanted the responder to do?

c. Did the speaker take into account the status of the responder—clerk, peer, parent, teacher—in his or her style of communication?

d. Did the speaker avoid antagonizing the responder?

e. Did the speaker treat the responder with respect?

f. Did the speaker have hidden reasons for wanting the responder to act in a certain way?

g. Did the speaker show a willingness to negotiate?

h. Did the responder comprehend the speaker's problem?

i. Did the responder "listen to reason"?

j. Did the responder treat the speaker with respect?

RESULTS

After the discussion, repeat the exercise with the roles of speaker and responder reversed. Evaluate the extent to which speakers and responders incorporate the conclusions of the discussion.

Using Speech to Affect the Feelings of Others and Analyzing Spoken Attempts to Change a Listener's Feelings—Feeling Function

STAGE OF LEARNING

Acquisition

AGE OF STUDENTS

Grades 1 through 8

PURPOSE

To teach students to use language effectively in situations where they wish to affect the feelings of someone; to help students learn to respond to attempts by others to change their feelings

MATERIALS REQUIRED

No special materials required

PROCEDURES

In this activity, students first make a list of situations in which they might want to affect how someone else feels. Encourage students to draw on their own experiences, thinking of times when they felt the need to talk to someone about their feelings. After the list is developed, students work in pairs—one student serves as the speaker who is trying to change the listener's feelings, the other as the listener responding to the speaker.

The following list of situations may be used as a start (add other situations as suggested by students):

1. Responder's dog has been hit by a car. Speaker learns about this and wants to say something to respondent.

2. Responder is a new student at school and does not know anyone. Speaker wonders what to say to him or her.

3. Responder just gave a class report. Right after sitting down, responder noticed a big stain on the front of his or her shirt. Speaker wants to say something to responder.

4. Responder has a hard time learning history. A big history exam is coming up soon, and responder is worried. Speaker (who finds history easy) wants to talk to responder about the exam.

5. Responder has a habit of calling others names. Now responder has no friends, and he or she wonders why. Speaker wants to talk to responder about the situation.

6. Responder's father is seriously ill. Responder is the parent of the speaker. Speaker wants to talk to responder about the situation.

Before the role playing begins, students should spend time discussing exactly what feelings the responder has and how the speaker would know what feelings the responder has. The role playing itself should be practiced in pairs, then demonstrated in front of the group. The group then should discuss the effectiveness and appropriateness of the speaker's attempt to affect the feelings of the responder and the response of the responder, addressing issues such as the following:

a. Did the speaker clearly state his or her interest in the responder's feelings?

b. Did the speaker show empathy with the responder?

c. Did the speaker take into account the status of the responder— peer, parent, and so on—in his or her style of communication?

d. Did the speaker avoid antagonizing the responder?

e. Did the speaker treat the responder with respect?

f. Did the speaker show an ability to take the role of the responder?

g. Did the responder show a willingness to listen?

h. Did the responder treat the speaker with respect?

RESULTS

After the discussion, repeat the exercise with the roles of speaker and responder reversed. Evaluate the extent to which speakers and responders incorporate the conclusions of the discussion.

Using Speech to Inform Others—Informing Function (with the Listener as an Unseen Audience)

STAGE OF LEARNING

Generalization

AGE OF STUDENTS

Grades 1 through 8

PURPOSE

To teach students to use language effectively in situations where they do not know exactly what the listeners know

MATERIALS REQUIRED

No special materials required

PROCEDURES

In this activity students work in pairs—one student serves as a talk show host, the other as a person being interviewed on the talk show.

The activities are in the form of role playing an interview. Students select the role in which they want to be interviewed on the talk show. Students may invent their own roles or choose from the following:

1. Student is a national authority on a particular hobby (e.g., skate-boarding, riding horses, breeding dogs, collecting stamps).

2. Student has just done something unusual (e.g., flown the world's largest kite, made more money than anyone else playing Monopoly, been abducted by a UFO).

3. Student is a spokesperson for some cause at his or her school (e.g., cleaning up litter, allowing students to speak French at recess, freedom of press for the student newspaper).

4. Student has just starred in an imaginary movie or TV show.

Before the talk show begins, the host may assemble props—the book, kite, stamp collection, or whatever. Do not allow time for the host and the interviewee to practice, as this will be a "live" show. The talk show should take place in front of the group. The group then should discuss the effectiveness and appropriateness of the host's and the interviewee's speaking and listening behavior. The following questions should be discussed:

a. Did the host ask clear questions?

b. Did the host allow the speaker ample time to respond?

   c. Did the host bring the speaker back to the topic when the speaker got off the track?

   d. Did the host avoid antagonizing or embarrassing the speaker?

   e. Did the speaker and the host treat each other with respect?

   f. Did the speaker provide the audience with the background information they needed to understand what he or she was talking about?

   g. Did the speaker take the audience into account in other ways?

   h. Did the host follow up on his or her questions?

   i. Did the speaker answer the host's questions?

RESULTS

After the discussion, repeat the exercise with the roles of host and speaker reversed. Evaluate the extent to which hosts and speakers incorporate the conclusions of the discussion.

Using and Understanding Noun and Verb Phrases Effectively and Precisely—Syntax

STAGE OF LEARNING

Proficiency

AGE OF STUDENTS

Grades 1 through 5

PURPOSE

To teach students to use noun and verb phrases effectively; to teach listeners to use noun and verb phrases to get necessary information

MATERIALS REQUIRED

No special materials required

PROCEDURES

This activity is a variation of the children's game "I Spy." The format is gamelike in that a subject must identify an object (or person) in the room by describing it (this is the "clue"). Based on the subject's description, the other children must determine what object the subject has in mind. The subject collaborates with the teacher in selecting objects that require successively more complex descriptions. The following list of objects (or persons) illustrates what could be done:

Objects / persons selected	*Expanded noun or verb phrase*
1. Two books (one large and one small)	Size + noun
2. Three books (one large and red, one large and blue, one small and yellow)	Size + color + noun
3. Two posters (one with the Declaration of Independence on it, the other with the Constitution on it)	Noun + embedded noun phrase
4. Three students (one in the front, one in the back, one in the middle)	Expand verb phrase to verb + noun phrase
5. Two students working (one student working quickly, one student working slowly)	Expand verb phrase to verb + adverb

RESULTS

Discuss the use of expanded noun phrases and verb phrases in speaking precisely. Evaluate the extent to which listeners use these grammatical structures to comprehend the speaker's intent.

Taking Alternative Distinguishing Features into Account in Labeling Speech Acts—Semantics

STAGE OF LEARNING

Acquisition

AGE OF STUDENTS

Grades 1 through 5

PURPOSE

To teach students to label objects, persons, and events precisely and succinctly, taking into account the alternatives from which the object must be discriminated

MATERIALS REQUIRED

Arrays of objects or pictures suitable for the age of the students

PROCEDURES

Select arrays of objects or pictures suitable for the age and interests of the students. Sets of arrays should be designed to require students to attend to the different features distinguishing the items in each array, as in the examples in Figure 2.6. This exercise is best structured with students working in speaker–listener pairs—the listener evaluates the precision of the label used by the speaker. For young children, hiding an object such as

	Items Displayed	What the Student Says
Case 1		"...the rabbit"
Case 2		"...the animal"
Case 3		"...the black one"
Case 4		"...the large one"
Case 5		". . .the white one"
Case 6		". . .the round one"
Case 7		". . .the round, white one"
Case 8		". . . the round, white, wooden block that is about 2 inches across. . ."

FIGURE 2.6. Sample arrays for object-labeling activity.

a coin under the target object or person enhances interest and creates a gamelike situation. Other modifications may be made as appropriate.

In the first set of arrays shown in Figure 2.6, the speaker is asked to refer to a black rabbit. When presented with an array such as that depicted in Case 1 of Figure 2.6, the student might simply use "the rabbit" to refer to the animal. However, when presented with the alternatives in Case 2, where the student must distinguish the rabbit from a plant, an appropriate label might be "the animal." In the third case, where the distinction must be among rabbits of different colors, the label is not merely "rabbit," but "the black one," to distinguish it from the others. Finally, in Case 4, the label for the object is "the large one." Similar distinctions must be made in the second set of arrays of different shapes.

Point out to the students that in each instance the same object is being referred to—the black rabbit. However, different words must be used to refer to that object, depending on the alternatives from which it must be distinguished.

The listener must provide feedback to the speaker, pointing out whether and why the speaker's label makes it possible to distinguish the desired object from the alternatives in the array.

If students have difficulty with this exercise, explain that words are not simply names for things. Speakers must ask themselves, "What alternatives could confuse or distract the listener? What do I need to mention so that it is clear which alternative I am referring to?" Speakers must put themselves in the place of the listener and choose the particular words that will make clear to the listener their meaning, and hence the intended referent. The words chosen in one instance will be different from the words chosen in another instance, but in all cases the meaning is what is important. It is not enough to know that the word "rabbit" refers to a particular animate object; both speaker and listener must also know and communicate those features of the object in question that differentiate it from alternative objects.

RESULTS

After a discussion along the lines described above, reverse the roles of speaker and listener. Observe the degree to which students are able to speak and understand accurately the *meaning* of the labels used. Continue repeating the exercise with different arrays until students show evidence of the ability to use labels effectively to distinguish an object, person, or event from competing items.

Chapter 3

Teaching Students Who Have Reading Problems

NETTIE R. BARTEL

More time in the school day is devoted to the teaching of reading than to any other school subject, yet more students are characterized as having reading problems than any other kind of school difficulty. "Why Maria can't read" is a problem that has thus far eluded the best efforts of many individual teachers, concerned parents, local school districts, and even presidential commissions.

One reason that so many different people want to ensure that students learn to read is that reading is involved in every school subject, especially those in the upper grades. It becomes increasingly difficult for students to be successful in any subject area if their reading problems are not remedied.

Furthermore, inadequate reading skill can eventually interfere significantly with an individual's capacity for economic independence and with his or her general knowledge of the world. Although much information is communicated through television, print remains the medium through which most persons seek and find jobs, read maps and other documents, and engage in certain recreational activities. For most people, printed materials provide the only access to information that is available around-the-clock to the user. The importance of reading continues to hold with the increasing availability of computers as an information source. Virtually all commercial and home uses of computers (with the exception of computer games) require print literacy as a basic user skill. Thus, individuals who cannot read will find themselves at an even greater disadvantage in our increasingly computerized society.

This broad understanding of the importance of reading has led many educators to think in terms of *developing literacy* rather than in terms of *teaching reading*. Literacy reflects both the processes of learning (learning to read) and the products of learning (reading to learn). In addition, the acquisition of literacy includes an understanding of the importance of reading in leading an informed and successful life. Literacy is not simply reading and writing, but reasoning, constructing meaning, and problem solving with print. A growing awareness of the importance of literacy in this country, and elsewhere throughout the world, has brought about major changes in the purpose, content, and methodology of teaching reading. Increasingly, reading is perceived as a language process, and hence is best taught simultaneously with listening, spelling, and writing.

Many teachers, schools, and districts have moved to teaching literacy through materials and methods variously known as "whole language approaches," "literature-based approaches," or "integrated language approaches." Although some special educators have taken the position that a whole language approach is too unstructured for students having difficulty learning to read, many agree that it provides a useful balance to instructional approaches that had become too decontextualized, too fragmented, too focused on teaching decoding subskills, and too neglectful of attention to thinking, making meaning, and comprehension. Today, many students who have reading problems are being successfully taught in regular classrooms where literature-based instruction is becoming commonplace. Increasing numbers of these teachers, as well as remedial reading teachers and resource room teachers, are finding whole language teaching to be especially effective when cooperative learning or a buddy system is used. Where students have persistent difficulties, systematic direct instruction mini-lessons have been successfully used to help students to make meaning from text. (Teachers wanting additional information on this important issue are referred to Mather, 1992; Spiegel, 1992; and to the July/August 1993 issue of *Remedial and Special Education,* which is devoted to a fuller explication of this topic.)

Almost every classroom teacher has encountered students who cannot or do not read. Some of these students appear limited in ability; others appear confused, reluctant, or resistant. A significant number of such students are labeled as "learning disabled" or "dyslexic" or as having a "developmental reading disorder." Recent research has helped educators gain a firmer understanding of such students.

It is becoming clear that a cognitive-developmental perspective helps teachers understand why some students have unexpected difficulties learning to read. Most problem readers' difficulty is part of a mild but pervasive cognitive and linguistic "developmental lag." These students can attain reading fluency commensurate with their other cognitive and linguistic abilities if they are properly taught.

A smaller group of impaired students have more particular and severe reading difficulties. These students appear to have phonological problems that grow out of oral language processes. In particular, these students fail to learn how to segment spoken words into their constituent sounds at the critical time in the learning process (see the description of phonemic segmentation in the later section on the role of decoding skills in reading). Reading and spelling difficulties result.

We take the position that, regardless of the nature of the problem, virtually every student can learn to read if the difficulty is carefully diagnosed and an intervention is planned that is based on a firm understanding of what the reading act entails. This chapter is intended to help teachers design and implement needed procedures.

The first section of this chapter deals with the nature of reading, giving emphasis to current theories, recent developments in the areas of decoding and comprehension, and the types of problems encountered in the school. The second section deals with assessment techniques recommended for determining the appropriate level of individuals, as well as more effective instruction. The third section covers how to teach a student with a reading problem.

The information presented in this chapter should be regarded as a starting point. Teachers should take this initial information and, using their experiences, resources, and knowledge, continue to develop and refine materials to best suit the teaching situation. The teacher must be aware that unanticipated needs will arise that must be met. By careful planning and organization, the teacher can build a file of materials, both commercial and teacher made, that will be readily available for use when the need arises. Just as students grow in reading skill, teachers must grow in their acquisition of the skills for teaching reading and in their knowledge of the subject.

THE NATURE OF READING

To attempt to improve reading skills of students, one must first understand what reading is. Such an understanding is not easily acquired, for there are many competing conceptions about the nature of reading. The nature of reading becomes a significant issue in that a teacher's ideas about it have direct implications for the kind of instruction in reading he or she will undertake. Three topics are dealt with in this section: current theories about reading, the roles of decoding skills and comprehension in reading, and the types of reading problems encountered in the schools.

Current Theories About Reading

The major competing positions on the nature of reading can be characterized as "bottom-up" models, "top-down" models, and interactive models that combine the features of both. In general, the models that have been characterized as bottom-up emphasize that reading begins with letters on a page—letters that the reader must distinguish and organize as words, sentences, and, finally, meaningful paragraphs. On the other hand, the top-down models emphasize that the act of reading begins not with letter or word recognition, but with the mind of the reader already set to hypothesize, sample, and predict about the nature of what he or she is about to read. Interactive models hold that an efficient reader moves back and forth, or simultaneously attends to both what is in his or her mind (predicting or hypothesizing) and what is on the page (attending to specific letters and words).

Why do teachers need to have a clear sense of the nature of reading? The absence of a theory of reading leaves teachers vulnerable to parents who demand a specific reading approach for their child or to publishers who aggressively promote particular reading materials. Lack of an understanding of the nature of reading leads teachers to religiously follow lessons in a basal reader without knowing why they are engaging in certain instructional procedures; worse still, it deprives them of a perspective from which the progress or lack of progress of a particular student can be viewed.

Historically, most reading approaches developed for problem readers have taken the bottom-up orientation. This is somewhat understandable, insofar as this orientation has lent itself more readily to the differentiation of decoding subskills—subskills that seem to be more easily taught than the global comprehension strategies that seem to be identified with the top-down model.

The preoccupation with teaching subskills, particularly in word recognition, has led many to reject the bottom-up position, and to embrace the whole language approach referred to in the introduction. Our position is that an interactive model most adequately describes the reading process, particularly for the early stages of learning to read.

As the learner becomes more proficient in reading, he or she can give increasing attention to comprehension and relatively less attention to scrutinizing individual letters and words. (See Figure 3.1 for a graphic example

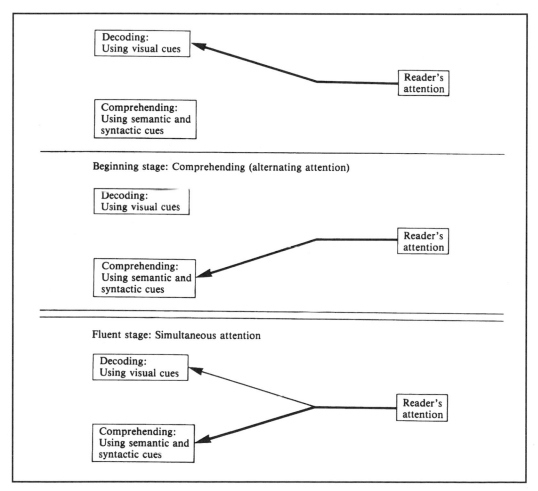

FIGURE 3.1. A developmental model of reading. Beginning stage shows attention alternating between decoding and comprehending. Fluent stage shows attention divided between decoding and comprehending, with both processes occurring simultaneously. The thin line indicates that only a small portion of attentional resources is allocated to decoding; the thick line indicates that a major portion of attentional resources is on comprehension.

Adapted from "Some Essentials of Decoding" by S. J. Samuels, 1981, *Exceptional Education Quarterly, 4,* p. 16.

of how the beginning reader must switch back and forth between decoding and comprehending while the fluent reader can simultaneously attend to both, with the emphasis on comprehension.)

Stanovich, Nathan, and Vala-Rossi (1987) described an *interactive-compensatory model* that is particularly useful for understanding the reading processes of students with cognitive-developmental reading delays or disorders. They proposed that poor readers who have slow, low-level decoding skills (bottom-up difficulties) make use of compensatory top-down knowledge-based processes. Learning to read for such students has meant learning to rely heavily on context in order to figure out new words. Fluent readers, on the other hand, have a high degree of automaticity in their decoding, which permits them to make facile and direct use of words on the printed page to acquire meaning. Because individuals are limited in their information processing capacity at any given time, persons who must use compensatory strategies are inevitably at a disadvantage in terms of their reading speed and accuracy.

The identification of words is a constructive act in which the output is greater than, and different from, the input. That is, the reader does not merely "transcribe" the written word into spoken form, but brings something quite apart from the printed page to the word identification act. That "something" is his or her own knowledge, ideas, experiences, and hypotheses. Because readers are culturally and individually unique, there is more than one "correct" interpretation of a text.

The recognition of multiple perspectives among readers is a natural outcome of viewing reading as a complex interaction among reader, text, and setting. Reading is an active process in which readers attempt to construct a meaning by calling on their prior knowledge about the topic, discerning what is on the printed page, and considering the social context of the reading event—for example, reading the newspaper, studying for an exam, reading a paragraph at the request of the teacher, or reading the instructions on the screen for a computer game. Not surprisingly, just as different listeners hearing the same speaker come to some variation in conclusions, so too do different readers construct somewhat different meanings based on unique prior experiences. Nevertheless, some common meaning is communicated and shared.

A good reader uses semantic, syntactic, and visual cues to recognize words and sentences and to get the "sense" of the passage. Word identification is constructive and integrative, with the reader melding together bits of visual, syntactic, and contextual information to derive meaning. In the fluent reader, the process is enormously efficient; the reader uses just enough visual cues to "fill in," that is, to confirm or disconfirm the ideas that he or she is developing about the passage. Let us take a hypothetical example to see how a reader uses visual, semantic, and syntactic cues. Let us suppose that a second grader, Tommy, is confronted with the following paragraph to read:

Little Fox and His Friends

Once there was a little fox who didn't like the dark. One morning, before the sun came up, Little Fox woke up all alone. His mother had gone hunting in the forest.

Simply by reading, or by being told what the story is about, Tommy can develop some expectancies about the content. He can, for example, expect to read about other animals. He can expect that the story will have words that refer to life in the forest. Particularly, if the teacher introduces the story carefully, using a directed reading activity format, the child will have some questions, expectancies, or hypotheses cued for him.

Tommy also has other information available to him. By second grade, he has had a lot of experience with his language (presumably English). This experience can help him as he begins to read the paragraph. If he has been exposed to stories such as fairy tales, he will know that the word right after the first word "Once" will probably be "upon" (for "Once upon a time . . .") or "there" (for "Once there was . . ."). Although the word "there" in isolation is frequently difficult for second graders, the cognitively and linguistically active child can be enormously helped in the reading task by, in this case, his prior knowledge of the way stories often begin and by his knowledge of the syntax of the English language.

The next word that may give Tommy difficulty is "didn't." The main cues that he can use here are syntactic and visual. By the second grade, Tommy's knowledge of English is such that he knows when he hears a sentence such as "Once there was a fox who . . ." that the next word will tell something about what the fox did or did not do. This knowledge, coupled with his understanding of the acoustic sound of /d/, the initial letter, may provide enough information for him to "guess" or "hypothesize" the correct word. If he guesses correctly, without too long a hesitation to break his train of thought, the next word, "like," will probably be easy for him. If he had to pause to ponder over "didn't," "like" will be more difficult, because he does not have the string of words "Once there was a little fox who didn't . . ." to help him figure out "like." We could continue our hypothetical analysis, showing how a wrong guess slows down the child and interferes with the cues of meaning and syntax.

According to many authorities, the best readers are those who can "guess" correctly most of the time, with a minimum use of cues. F. Smith (1982) discussed the significance of interaction and balance among the various types of cues—contextual, syntactic, and visual. Smith made the point that a very large number of cues are potentially available to the reader—if he or she had to use all of them, the reading act would be very slow indeed. However, because the cues are so redundant, the good reader selects and uses only a few. The effective use of contextual cues or of syntactic cues takes some of the interpretive load off the graphic cues so that, even if the beginning reader is not completely sure of all the distinctive features of a given letter or word, he or she needs only a little extra help to figure out the word. If the reader is uncertain, however, about each of the areas that could potentially help—contextual or semantic, syntactic, and graphic—he or she will slow down in the reading; and because of normal memory limitations, semantic and syntactic cues will fade rapidly. Although it is true that semantic and syntactic information can help with the visual, it is also true that, unless some visual cues are interpretable by the student, the semantic and syntactic help will quickly be lost. These processes of reading are highly interdependent. Accuracy and speed of decoding and word recognition have been found to be strongly related to reading comprehension.

The learning of individual words is thought to pass through three sequential stages (Ehri & Wilce, 1983). At first the word may be laboriously sounded out or read only with prompts from the teacher. *Accuracy* in word recognition is the first goal in learning words. As the student practices the word, accuracy becomes taken for granted and the focus shifts to the second stage, *automaticity*. That is, the entire word is recognized without deliberate processing of individual word parts. The third stage of word learning is increasing the *speed* of word identification. This takes place as the word becomes consolidated into and retrievable from memory. Only after all three stages of word learning have occurred can the reader fully concentrate on the meaning of the passage without the continual slowing distraction of required decoding procedures.

Little imagination is needed to see the potential reading problems that would be encountered by a student who was unfamiliar with the distinguishing features of the letters of the alphabet and who also was unsure of the content that he or she was supposed to read. When this situation is compounded with unfamiliarity with standard English syntax, as is the case with many students growing up in certain U.S. cultures, it is easy to see why many students have reading problems. Such learners are indeed triply handicapped, in that they cannot "trade" one type of information—semantic, syntactic, or graphic—for another, the way proficient readers do. It is ironic, indeed, that the process that will ultimately make it possible for the student to gain a knowledge of the world—reading—is in its initial stages itself heavily dependent on such knowledge.

Teachers who are not sure about the need to provide additional informational "prompting" for beginning readers are urged to consider their own reading behavior when confronted with reading material that is unfamiliar and perhaps highly technical. In such a situation, everybody slows down in rate, goes back over the material, and skips over words, hoping to make some sense out of them on the basis of the rest of the passage. One way or another, the reader tries to narrow down what the author is saying, to answer the questions in his or her mind.

Most current authorities in reading recognize the need for balanced instructional approaches that attend to the development of the various phonological, linguistic, and cognitive aspects of reading. As the understanding of the nature of decoding and the nature of comprehension has grown, teachers have become better able to teach these skills more effectively. In the next sections, we consider each of these areas in more detail.

The Role of Decoding Skills in Reading

The understanding of how children learn to recognize letters and words has undergone significant rethinking in the past few years. Educators now have a better picture of how learners acquire the ability to read.

Researchers, especially Ehri and colleagues (Ehri, 1988; Ehri & Wilce, 1985, 1987), have dealt directly with the question of how beginning readers learn to decode. Ehri's research shows that the earliest stages of reading (and also of spelling) progress as follows.

STAGE 1

At this stage, readers learn to "read" particular words on the basis of distinctive visual cues that are associated with those words. Thus, the student may know that at the corner service station the large red and white star with letters on it is "read" as "TEXACO." The student has learned the word *TEXACO* not on the basis of individual letters or sounds but on the basis of visual cues that accompany or are part of the word. It is believed that children learn the association between printed and spoken word in the same way as they learn and remember other visual events in their environment—through paired-associate learning.

Readers at this stage do not have decoding skills, but they are able to read some words, often relying heavily on semantic context. This is evidenced by substitutions such as that of "look" for "see." Readers at this stage often confuse words that are similar in configuration—for example, *boot* and *look* (two *o*s in the middle).

At this stage, children are able to "read" only a limited number of words. Their memorized associations are between particular written and spoken words, and they are not able to generalize to read unfamiliar, albeit similar, words. If more words are learned, they are again learned as straightforward associations between visual and verbal events or stimuli.

STAGE 2

A significant advance in reading ability occurs when children learn to recognize and use letter–sound relationships. As children acquire some knowledge of the relationships between letters and their sounds, they begin to use it in identifying specific words. Thus, a student may know only the letters and sounds of *T* and *X,* but be able to use this knowledge to read the word *TEXACO.* At the beginning of this stage, students pay attention to only a few letters in words; they are able to read some words by forming and remembering phonetic associations between graphemes and phonemes.

What marks this stage as a true departure from the previous stage is that students are beginning to "crack the code"; that is, they read words by remembering associations between letters in spellings and sounds in pronunciations. This rudimentary phonemic awareness marks the beginning of the ability to decode new words.

At first, students are able to apply their decoding skills only in simple left-to-right sequence. Typically, the only novel words that can be successfully decoded are of the CVC (consonant–vowel–consonant) form—for example, *dak, jit,* or *bot.* Only later can the student look ahead in the word to the silent *e* ending to correctly read novel words such as *dake, jite,* or *bote.*

What brings about this shift to phonemic awareness is not well understood. Some authorities believe that a child's learning that written letters make up the parts of a word is analogous to a child's learning that words are the constituent parts of a sentence. These people believe that children extract the underlying rules by themselves; others believe that the teaching of phonics is essential for this learning to take place.

STAGE 3

Once readers have mastered the letters of the alphabet and their sounds, they are positioned to learn more complex and comprehensive decoding skills. They know that sequences of letters represent pronunciation segments and that these must be blended with other pronunciation segments to make up complete words. They move from a purely phonetic understanding of reading and spelling to a morphemic understanding of words; that is, they no longer try to read *giraffe* as g-i-r-a-f-f-e or to spell it *geraf.* Advancing to a morphemic understanding permits students to recognize systematic spelling patterns in words and to make sense of many letters that previously seemed to be exceptions to the rules. This knowledge marks a new stage of reading capability.

Stage 3 readers are able to divide words into their constituent sounds or phonemes, a process called *phonemic segmentation.* Phonemic segmentation is involved in both reading and spelling. The reader at this stage is learning to automatically recognize units of words, or graphemic clusters. Thus, the student no longer struggles with individual letter-by-letter sounding out, but is able to tell at a glance that *–tion* and *–cian* have the same sound.

Phonemic segmentation ability seems to be both a prerequisite for and a consequence of learning to read and spell and is quite difficult for children younger than age 5 or 6. The research shows that phonemic awareness is most effectively taught concurrently with reading. As children learn phonemic segmentation, they become better readers and spellers. And as they learn the letters and their sounds as part of reading and spelling instruction, they usually improve in phonemic segmentation. According to most authorities, children enter this stage first for reading and then for spelling.

As indicated earlier, decoding skills are essential for comprehension. However, the ultimate goal of reading is gaining meaning from text. It is to comprehension that we next direct our attention.

The Role of Comprehension in Reading

What do we mean by "reading comprehension"? As described in the earlier section on the nature of reading, comprehension is an active process of hypothesis testing or schema building. As readers acquire additional information, they are able to confirm, refine, or disconfirm their hypotheses or expectations about the text. If the reader is unable to formulate or confirm hypotheses, comprehension is not taking place. Good readers ask themselves a series of questions pertaining to comprehension as they read. Although most of these questions are implicit in proficient reading, they may need to be made explicit for students who have comprehension difficulties. (See the later section on strategy training for further discussion of this point.) The following self-questions—ranging from the micro level of individual words to the macro level of the reader's store of information about the world—regulate readers' comprehension.

Do I know the words? "Knowing" words means both decoding the words (connecting to the reader's phonological knowledge) and understanding the meaning of the words (connecting to the reader's semantic knowledge). Comprehension failure at this level requires a corrective strategy such as rereading to invoke contextual clues, asking someone to pronounce the word or to state its meaning, or referring to a print authority, usually a dictionary.

Do the sentences make sense? Good readers keep track of the grammatical structure of the sentences. They continuously watch to see whether the text fits the grammatical rules they know implicitly. Thus, when they read "The boy away the far abut," they may recognize each of the individual words perfectly, but still slow down because a failure of comprehension is detected. The reader may conclude that the text is inaccurate, but only after checking his or her own knowledge of grammar to see whether there could possibly be a fit between what is on the page and his or her own grammatical knowledge.

These two comprehension checks—using knowledge of vocabulary and knowledge of grammar—are performed so efficiently by most readers that they are hardly aware of what they are doing. Only when they are reading very unfamiliar material or when they encounter difficulties do they realize that they "watch themselves" as they read.

How do these ideas relate to the ideas previously read? Good readers observe interconnections among the different parts of the text. Thus, when they encounter the sentence "She brushed her hair," they immediately know that "her hair" refers to the actor's own hair because of the content that has preceded that particular sentence. However, when the text states "She brushed *his* hair," readers sense that something unexpected is happening and may have to go back in the text to find to whom "his" could be referring. Proficient comprehenders keep in mind the many different strands of the text, weaving them together into a coherent and integrated tapestry as they read. They keep track of the "loose ends" that must be tied to the rest of the text as reading progresses. As long as the pieces are falling into place, reading proceeds smoothly and quickly—on "automatic pilot," some authorities have analogized. When the reader no longer can keep the various threads straight, reading slows down or stops, and the reader must resort to conscious, explicit strategies for correcting the comprehension failure.

How does the material "hang together"? Proficient readers continually monitor the new information that the text brings them as they read, and they make judgments about that information. In effect, they hold in their minds everything they have read to that point and evaluate each new sentence against the growing knowledge base. They continually ask themselves a series of questions: Is the new information consistent with what I've read before? Is this idea redundant? Is this information trivial or important? Is this information related to what I've read so far? Could this be true considering what I read in the last sentence or paragraph? What is the concept that all these instances are examples of? What inferences must I make to discover the author's main point?

How does this material fit into what I already know about the "real world"? Comprehending readers continually judge the truth, plausibility, and validity of what they read in the light of their prior knowledge and experiences. If they read about purple cows and flying dogs, they may conclude that they are not comprehending the text or that the author is trying for a special effect or that the world has changed mightily since they last experienced it. However, they must make some cognitive resolution of the information that does not fit the ideas they already have about reality. They will tend to understand and remember information that connects at many points to concepts and ideas that are already present in their minds. This is why a given passage of text seems easy to the reader who is already familiar with the general content but hard to the reader who does not have a background of experience or knowledge into which to fit the new information. For example, reading and understanding a paragraph on one of Henry VIII's many wives is much easier for someone who knows British history than for someone who has no knowledge of the political–religious difficulties of that era. The second reader may know all the words and may be able to understand the passage sentence by sentence, but will still lack a full comprehension of the material. The first reader may not know all the words and may even be confused by some unusual grammatical usage in one of the sentences, but will be able to get more out of the passage because of the differentiated cognitive schemas he or she already has about related information.

Is this material clear and complete? Finally, good readers have a sense of when the text has presented a clear and complete picture. Referring again to the metaphor of the tapestry, the proficient reader has a sense that he or she has been able to tuck in all the loose ends. No strands are left hanging, unconnected to the rest of the picture. A sense of cognitive closure and the satisfaction of completeness are present. All parts of the tapestry are discernible and in focus.

Good readers know when they have not understood; they experience a sense of incongruity or lack of fit or closure. They may choose to go back over the material and reread more carefully; they may probe nuances; they may analyze words, phrases, or sentences; they may try to visualize contexts or scenes; they may make inferences or deductions. Alternatively, they may decide to write off the material—that is, they may decide that it is not worth further effort. However, they will do so consciously, with the full awareness that their comprehension of the material was incomplete.

Poor readers, on the other hand, have difficulty detecting comprehension failures. They may forge ahead, failing to notice that their understanding and the text are moving further and further apart, and that each instance of comprehension failure in a passage makes subsequent parts of the passage more difficult to understand. Comprehension difficulties in a passage are cumulative because comprehension of subsequent material cannot be facilitated by correct understandings already acquired, as is the case when comprehension is occurring.

In recent years, materials have become available that assist teachers in developing these self-questioning and self-regulating comprehension skills. These approaches, sometimes known as "cognitive strategy training," "problem solving," or "reciprocal teaching," are described later in this chapter, but in general they teach the students how to summarize, how to predict endings, how to clarify material they do not understand, and how to ask relevant questions.

Types of Reading Problems

Ideally, students read at a level commensurate with their mental age, *not* their chronological age or grade placement. Unfortunately, many students for one reason or another do not read at their mental age level. Students with reading problems are often labeled as "developmental," "corrective," "retarded," or "remedial." Sometimes more complicated and threatening labels are attached—"strephosymbolic," "dyslexic," "brain injured," and so on. It should be pointed out that these words have no generally accepted meaning among professionals working in the field. For example, "developmental" may refer to a class (or to a student) taught using regular class methods; may be limited to students who are performing at a level commensurate with their ability; or may be used with students who are working far behind their expectancy but are still being taught by regular class methods. A "corrective" class may be one in which the students are functioning below expectancy but do not appear to have any associated learning problems (brain damage, specific learning disabilities, etc.); "corrective" may also refer to any student who is 1 to 2 years behind expectancy regardless of the presence or absence of any associated learning problems. To some professionals, "remedial" students have associated learning problems; to others, the term is applied to all students who are more than 2 years behind expectancy in reading. Because of this confusion, we rarely use any of these terms; however, if these terms are used in schools for any purpose, we recommend that teachers become familiar with their local definitions.

Although teachers should be familiar with these medical and psychological terms, and the conditions they represent, they should keep in mind that knowledge of the terms or the conditions is not particularly helpful in teaching students to read. In fact, most reading problems found in the classrooms are not of a highly clinical nature; rather, they have a relatively obvious cause.

The types of reading problems that a teacher identifies will be related to the view that the teacher holds about the nature of reading. If the teacher believes that reading consists of saying the word *look* in response to seeing the letters l-o-o-k, and nothing more, he or she will not identify as a problem the fact that the child may not understand what it means to "look."

Our interactive view of the nature of reading leads us to identify the reading problems listed in Table 3.1. Obviously, not every poor reader will exhibit *all* of the problems.

Some students may experience temporary lags in reading development due to external causes and a few may have serious word-learning problems. A student may fall behind in reading due to an extended absence from school, a temporary failure in vision (which can be corrected by appropriately prescribed glasses), a temporary failure in hearing (e.g., a tonsillectomy sometimes causes a temporary loss of hearing), a constant change in schools, a radical change in the reading program (from a basal approach to an augmental alphabet approach such as initial/teaching/ alphabet), or poor teaching. In such cases, nothing is wrong with the student's central nervous system; the student is neither mentally retarded nor emotionally disturbed. If appropriate steps are taken through the careful assessment of the student's needs and proper instruction is provided, the difficulty can usually be overcome by using appropriate materials designed for the student's instructional level. Most of these problems can be handled in the ongoing classroom situation.

A few students evidence severe reading problems and experience great difficulty in attaching meaning to word or wordlike symbols when taught by the usual visual–auditory techniques. Often these students need specialized word-learning techniques similar to those presented in the section of this chapter titled "Examples of Specific Remedial Techniques in Reading."

ASSESSING READING PROBLEMS

To effectively teach a student with reading problems, a teacher needs to learn more about the student's strengths and weaknesses in reading. First,

TABLE 3.1. Comparison Between Good and Poor Readers

WHAT THE GOOD READER DOES	WHAT THE POOR READER MAY DO
Notes the distinctive features in letters and words	Fails to notice distinctions between *b* and *d*, or *was* and *saw*, or *m* and *n*, or the configuration of other letters and words; focuses only on certain characteristics, such as beginnings of words
Predicts the endings of words (e.g., "righ__"), phrases (e.g., "once upon a _____"), or sentences (e.g., "the fire _____ed") with feasible hypothesis	Cannot predict reasonable or possible endings of words, phrases, or sentences
Expects what he or she reads to make sense in terms of his or her own background	Fails to relate reading content to his or her own background
Reads to identify meaning rather than to identify letters or words	Reads to identify individual letters or individual words, or reads because he or she has to
Shifts speed and approach to the type and purpose of reading	Approaches all reading tasks the same way
Formulates hypotheses or expectations about the way the passage will develop an idea	Cannot/does not develop expectations or predictions concerning the direction or main idea of a passage
Takes advantage of the graphic, syntactic, and semantic cues in a passage to speed reading and improve comprehension	Becomes bogged down in attempting to decipher the passage on a letter-by-letter or word-by-word basis
Is aware of a breakdown in comprehension and adjusts reading strategy accordingly	Is unaware of comprehension problems and hence does not adjust reading strategy

Portions of this table are adapted from "A Psycholinguistic View of the Fluent Reading Process" by C. R. Cooper and A. R. Petrosky, 1976, *Journal of Reading, 20,* pp. 184–207.

the teacher needs to obtain a general picture of the student's overall level of reading performance. Then, additional assessment must be done to explore the nature of the student's difficulties. A number of useful techniques are available for obtaining this information, many of which are described in this section. Their use by teachers will result in a precise picture of the level and nature of a student's reading performance.

A discussion of assessment must be introduced with a word of caution. Overtesting can be as undesirable as no testing at all. A full clinical evaluation of a student's reading problems may take as long as 2 days to complete; however, very few students need this kind of detailed work. A few teachers who have been exposed to some formal training in the evaluation of reading, as in a graduate course, may become overzealous and feel that every student needs to be given an informal reading inventory, an interest inventory, an attitude scale, an associative learning test, a test of memory span, and so on. Actually, all this testing can consume too many hours that could better be devoted to instruction. A good rule to follow is to test minimally to find out where to initiate instruction and to identify areas of strength and weakness. Then, through analytic or clinical teaching, the teacher can continue to uncover the student's needs and to meet them with appropriate instruction as they arise.

Establishing a Reading Level

Teachers often need to estimate quickly the reading level of a particular student or class of students. Two popular ways of doing this involve the use of informal oral reading and informal reading inventories.

Informal Oral Reading

Although today "round-robin" reading is generally condemned as a teaching method, the procedure does enable the teacher to quickly identify those students who need immediate attention. Each student is asked to read a short passage from a book to determine whether he or she can pronounce the words successfully. If the student has trouble with more than 5 words out of every 100, reads in a word-by-word manner, reads too slowly, or exhibits other difficulties, it is likely that the material is too difficult.

The oral reading should be carried out in a nonthreatening manner, and the teacher should note the more severe cases of reading failure without drawing embarrassing attention to the reader. The teacher can accomplish this in a small-group situation by prefacing the lesson by saying, "This is a new reading book; this morning I want to find out if it is the right book for this group." If this approach is not deemed advisable, then the teacher can call on each student to read on an individual basis while the rest of the group is engaged in some other activity. In cases where this approach does not give enough information to establish an individual's reading level, an informal reading inventory may be administered.

Informal Reading Inventory

A complete, informal reading inventory (IRI) is usually regarded as a clinical instrument used by reading specialists, but on occasion a teacher may want to use it. Although informal reading inventories are too time-consuming for classroom administration, they can provide precise and valuable information about an individual student's reading difficulty. In the event that a teacher desires a detailed evaluation, he or she should probably request that an informal reading inventory be administered by the reading specialist. Botel (1966), Newcomer (1986), and Silvaroli (1994) have developed informal reading inventories that are available commercially.

Analyzing Specific Reading Skills

A number of strategies are available to the teacher who wishes to probe specific skill levels in reading. Several of these are described in this section. First, the use of standardized, norm-referenced tests is discussed because they provide a quick objective way of documenting competence in a wide variety of reading skills, including vocabulary and passage comprehension, word recognition, phonics, alphabet knowledge, and oral reading rate. The discussion next turns to curriculum-based measurement, to teacher-made word-recognition tests, to teacher-made reading comprehension tests, to analysis of oral reading miscues, and to newer approaches for assessing literacy.

Standardized Norm-Referenced Reading Tests

A number of commercially prepared standardized norm-referenced reading tests are available. All of them assist the teacher in identifying difficulties in word attack; most of them also assess comprehension problems. The best known of these tests are summarized in Table 3.2. All of the listed tests are intended for individual administration.

TABLE 3.2. Standardized Norm-Referenced Reading Tests

TEST (AND PUBLISHER)	GRADE LEVELS	WHAT THE TEST MEASURES
Diagnostic Reading Scale (Spache, 1981)	1–8	Word recognition, phonics, and reading comprehension
Durrell Analysis of Reading Difficulty (Durrell & Catterson, 1980)	1–6	Word and letter recognition, blending, spelling, listening, and recall
Formal Reading Inventory (Wiederholt, 1985)	1–12	Silent reading comprehension and oral reading miscues
Gray Oral Reading Tests (Wiederholt & Bryant, 1992)	1–adult	Oral reading rate, accuracy, and comprehension
Stanford Diagnostic Reading Test (Karlsen, Madden, & Gardner, 1984)	1–adult	Vocabulary, auditory discrimination, phonics, syllabication, and comprehension
Test of Early Reading Ability (Reid, Hresko, & Hammill, 1989)	Pre–2	Alphabet knowledge, comprehension, and conventions of print
Test of Reading Comprehension (L. Brown, Hammill, & Wiederholt, 1995)	2–12	Vocabulary, paragraph comprehension; syntactic reading. Supplemental tests of "school language" and vocabularies of science, social studies, and math
Woodcock Reading Mastery Tests–Revised (Woodcock, 1988)	K–12	Word identification, attack, and comprehension; also passage comprehension

Pre = preschool; K = kindergarten.

Curriculum-Based Measurement

Curriculum-based measurement (CBM) refers to a set of standardized procedures that can be used by teachers to measure students' performance in reading, spelling, writing, and mathematics. In this section, we discuss CBM only as it applies to reading. CBM can be used as an alternative to standardized, norm-referenced reading tests in evaluating student progress. CBM materials are developed by the teacher, based on a long-range instructional goal for a particular student. The following is an example of a program developed for a fourth-grade student with some reading problems.

GOAL

Given a passage from the Level 4 Houghton Mifflin reader, Jimmy will read 50 words correctly per minute with no more than 5 errors.

MATERIALS

Randomly preselected pages from the Level 4 Houghton Mifflin reader—a copy for the student and a copy that can be marked for the teacher. Pages selected should be typical, that is, should not contain pictures or too much dialogue, poetry, or exercises.

MEASUREMENT PROCEDURES

Jimmy is asked to read one of the passages. He is timed for 1 minute (or for 2 minutes, if time permits, and the total is divided by 2). The performance is scored for numbers of correct words and errors. Measurement procedures are repeated weekly.

EVALUATION AND RECORD KEEPING

Jimmy's performance is recorded weekly, and records are kept from week to week to see how well teaching is helping to achieve the goal. A sample graph of Jimmy's performance is presented in Figure 3.2.

CBM has several advantages. The major advantage is that CBM connects testing with teaching. There is no question of the relevance of the test materials to the day-to-day reading instruction of the student. Teachers are able to graphically chart the progress that the student is making toward the long-range goal that was established. The use of the reader itself for the criterion reading task gives the measure face validity. Repeatedly measuring the same global reading task (reading aloud for 1 minute) ensures the reliability of the measure. Research has established that the reliability and validity of CBM are equal to those of most standardized norm-referenced tests.

Teacher-Made Word-Recognition Tests

Word-recognition tests are being used less widely today because they do not serve authentic communication purposes. However, they do have cer-

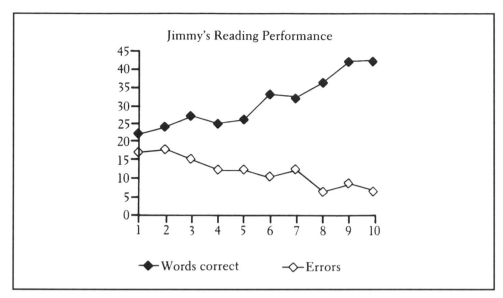

FIGURE 3.2. Sample graph of reading performance.

tain specific uses: (1) they serve as an indication of a student's sight vocabulary; (2) they give clues to the word-attack skills that the student uses to work out unfamiliar words; and (3) they give some indication of where to initiate reading instruction with the child. It must be remembered that they measure only a student's sight vocabulary and word-attack skills. This kind of test does not measure meaning or comprehension. Therefore, word-recognition tests, if used alone, may place the student above his or her true instructional level. This is because many students can "read" a passage glibly and then not be able to recall the most obvious literal information included in the text. "Oh, I read it; I didn't know that I was supposed to remember anything," has been said by more than one student to a puzzled teacher who cannot understand how a child can word-call so well but not understand or retain any of the thoughts expressed in the passage.

A number of commercially prepared word-recognition lists are available. Some of these are arranged by difficulty level by grade; others are compilations of words most typically found in basal readers. Teachers may also develop their own lists of words from the reading materials that they are using.

By carefully recording the student's responses, the teacher can assess weaknesses in word-attack skills. Of course, *every* error should not be treated as a significant problem. However, when the student has been administered vocabulary tests at several grade levels, patterns usually emerge. For example, if a fifth or sixth grader misses many words at the preprimer levels, he or she probably has not established a basic sight vocabulary. At levels beyond this, the student may miss initial consonants, final consonants, endings, or make other errors. A list of some of the common word-attack errors is given in Table 3.3.

TABLE 3.3.   Common Word Attack Errors

	EXAMPLE	
PROBLEM	TEXT SAYS	STUDENT READS
1. Omission of letters in a word	grown furniture	gown funiture
2. Insertion of letters into a word	sight chimney	slight chimaney
3. Substitution of consonants in a word (initial, medial, final)	nice fright lad	mice flight lab
4. Substitution of medial vowels	hat dog	hot dug
5. Reversal of letters in a word	saw there	was three
6. Addition of endings	sheep gave	sheeps gaved
7. Omission of endings	friends bark	friend bar
8. Syllable omission	visiting trying	visting trine

Teacher Assessment of Comprehension

As noted in the previous section on comprehension, much research has been conducted recently on questions of how readers understand what they read. As yet, no well-developed assessment devices exist that take into account the most recent research. However, teachers can supplement the more traditional approaches to measuring comprehension with informal assessments of various aspects of comprehension. Table 3.4 presents a summary of procedures that teachers can adapt for classroom use.

Analyzing Oral Reading Miscues[1]

The assessment procedures described to this point will provide teachers with a number of ideas for instruction. However, each classroom has within it a small number of boys and girls whose reading problems are so persistent that additional, more intensive analysis is required. This statement is based on the belief that students' errors or miscues are not random or capricious, except in the most unusual circumstances. On the contrary,

---

1. We use the term *miscue* rather than *error* for much the same reasons as those articulated by K. S. Goodman (1969); that is, the term miscue is less judgmental and avoids the implication that good reading cannot involve departures from the printed text (expected responses).

TABLE 3.4. Informal Assessment of Students' Comprehension Skills

TYPE OF ASSESSMENT	PURPOSE	PROCEDURES
Self-report		
Student rating of comprehension	To evaluate students' ability to accurately judge their own comprehension	Students are asked to silently read a series of short passages of the same length, graded from three levels below their instructional reading level to three levels above it. Time spent reading each passage is noted. More time should be spent on more difficult passages. After reading each passage, students indicate the degree to which they understood it—all of it, most of it, some of it, none of it. They then answer several performance questions on each passage. Actual performance is compared with predicted performance. *Variation:* Introduce confusing, inconsistent, out-of-sequence material or nonsense words into the passages. Repeat procedures.
Student prediction of success	Same as above	Students are asked to indicate when they are ready to be tested on written material they have been studying. After the test, they are asked to predict their score. Predictions are compared with actual performance.
Oral reading		
Oral reading of passage at instructional level	To obtain a measure of students' awareness of comprehension failure	Students are presented with a passage of text at their instructional level into which have been inserted some "errors"—nonsense words, ungrammatical usage, or semantic inconsistencies or anomalies. Note whether students hesitate, slow down, reread, or substitute something that makes sense.
Reading for different purposes	To evaluate students' ability to adjust their reading behavior to the purpose of reading	Students are asked to silently read a series of short passages of the same length, at their instructional level, for the following purposes: (1) to find the name of the main character, (2) to be able to state the main idea, and (3) to be able to "answer any question" about the passage. The length of time spent on each passage is noted. After each passage is read, the student is asked the criterion questions to see whether the passage has been comprehended at the appropriate level of scrutiny. Least time should be spent on Purpose 1; most time on Purpose 3.
Prediction of missing or incomplete material		
Missing words (cloze technique)	To evaluate students' ability to select or generate plausible words for those missing in text	Students are provided with a passage of text at their instructional level from which key words have been deleted. Either a blank or a set of multiple-choice options marks each deletion. The student reads the passage and generates or selects a word that "makes sense." Selection of appropriate options indicates reading comprehension.
Missing story endings or paragraph conclusions	To evaluate students' ability to select or generate plausible story endings or paragraph conclusions	Students read a short unfinished story or paragraph at their instructional level. They are asked to generate a plausible ending for the story or to select the best ending from several proposed alternatives. Better comprehenders generate or select more plausible endings.

(continues)

TABLE 3.4. *Continued*

TYPE OF ASSESSMENT	PURPOSE	PROCEDURES
Understanding and remembering main ideas		
Retelling a story or recounting major propositions	To evaluate the degree to which students can retell or recount the major developments or propositions in a story or paragraph	Students are asked to silently read a short passage at their instructional level that has discernible developments or arguments. They are then asked to state the main points of the passage or to retell the story. Performance is scored for number, sequence, and accuracy of stated propositions.
Summarizing a passage	To evaluate students' ability to identify or generate the main idea(s) of a passage	Students are presented with a passage at their instructional level and asked to perform each of the following five operations: (1) delete redundancy, (2) delete trivia, (3) provide superordinate sentence(s), (4) select topic sentence(s), and (5) generate topic sentence(s) if necessary. Each of these five operations is a summarizing subskill.
Identifying or formulating key questions	To evaluate students' ability to generate questions that are central to the meaning of the text and that can guide their comprehension efforts	Students are presented with a passage of text at their instructional level and are asked to generate or select questions that best capture the essence of the passage. They then must formulate or select the answers to their own questions. Good comprehenders are able to generate questions that go to the core of the meaning of the passage.
Clarifying understanding by verifying sentences related to text	To evaluate students' ability to identify the relationships of criterion sentences to material they have read	Students are asked to silently read a passage at their instructional level. A list of sentences is then presented to the students. They are asked to identify sentences of the following types: *originals* (sentences that are copied from the passage); *paraphrases* (sentences that have the same meaning as but contain different words than sentences in the text); *meaning-altered sentences* (those that contain many of the words in the passage but have altered meanings); and *distractors* (sentences that are on the same topic but have different words and different meanings). Good comprehenders are able to distinguish among these types of criterion sentences.
Activating related background knowledge	To assess the degree to which students relate information that they read to information that they have previously learned	Prior to silently reading a passage at their instructional level, students are given a set of purpose questions and asked to make predictions about the content of the upcoming passage. Students are encouraged to engage knowledge they already have on the topic. Performance on comprehension questions asked after reading is compared with performance on comprehension questions asked after reading of a similar passage for which no attempt was made to activate background knowledge.

such miscues occur in systematic patterns that can be identified by careful analysis of students' oral reading. A major goal of such qualitative miscue analysis is to derive ideas on what strategies the student is using that result in the obtained performance patterns. Once the teacher has detected the pattern of the miscues presented by the student, the teacher can develop hypotheses concerning the particular ineffective or inefficient strategies being utilized by the child and appropriate instructional efforts can follow.

The complete and comprehensive analysis of each oral reading miscue of a particular child would be too time-consuming for everyday classroom use. For example, the complete coding of the miscues of an average reader would call for approximately 2,000 separate decisions. Although such detailed analyses may be necessary for research purposes, a less detailed analysis can provide the classroom teacher with necessary and valuable insight. Teachers interested in the more comprehensive program for oral miscue analysis are referred to K. S. Goodman (1969), Y. M. Goodman (1972), and Weber (1968, 1970).

A word of caution on the use of miscue analytic procedures is appropriate. Good readers do not maximally utilize every cue presented on the printed page; that is, they do not make letter-by-letter discriminations, attending to each feature of each letter or even each word. In fact, some authorities (K. S. Goodman, 1969; F. Smith, 1982) have made strong cases that the really effective and efficient reader is one who is able to derive meaning from the printed page with a minimum use of cues. Thus, a good reader forms hypotheses about how the sentence, the paragraph, and the story will end. Subsequent reading behavior serves to confirm or disconfirm those hypotheses, which then become part of the "meaning" derived from the page, or become modified, respectively. Accordingly, teachers should not be overly concerned if, on occasion, a student emits a response that is at variance with the printed page. The teacher is properly concerned, however, when the miscues are of such a nature and frequency that the child's comprehension is impaired. Miscue analysis can help the teacher discover what faulty strategies and consistently misleading patterns or rules the student uses that interfere with the reading performance.

Table 3.5 presents the common miscue types. They are of interest to the teacher, but they provide insufficient detail as to the strategies that underlie their use. We suggest that teachers use Table 3.6 to further refine their examination of how the student responds to graphic symbols. In actual practice, teachers will find that the overwhelming number of miscues are substitutions of one kind or another. Hence, a closer look at substitution miscues (Table 3.6) is warranted.

Table 3.6 has been organized to indicate that most students' reading substitutions fall readily into graphic, syntactic, and semantic categories. These categories are, of course, not mutually exclusive. Any printed word has graphic, syntactic, and semantic characteristics, and a child may use faulty strategies that apply to these characteristics singly or in combination.

TABLE 3.5. Analysis of Oral Reading Miscues: Response Types

RESPONSE TYPE	DESCRIPTION	EXAMPLE[a]
Omission	The student omits a word or words.	the big red ball/the big ball
Insertion	The student adds a word or words.	the big ball/the big red ball
Sequence or order	The student makes a response that is expected elsewhere in the text—either immediately preceding or following (horizontal miscue) or immediately above or below (vertical miscue) the stimulus word	John and Harry found the dog/ John and Harry found the Harry
Substitution[b]	The student substitutes a word other than that in the text. (If the child makes a substitution on the first occurrence of the stimulus word, then on later occurrences makes the expected response, no further analysis is required—see self-correction below.)	The dog ran/The dog red
Sounding out	The student makes several tentative partial responses, voiced or unvoiced.	Patty will play/Patty will p——
Self-correction	The student makes any of the above response types, then spontaneously corrects the miscue.	That is good/What is—that is good
Dialect	The student makes any of the above, but in accordance with the rules of his or her dialect.	The boys were scared/ The boy be scared

[a]In each example, the printed text or expected response precedes the diagonal line; the student's miscue or the observed response follows.
[b]For more detailed analysis of substitutions, see Table 3.6.

An additional point about Table 3.6 is worth making. It is not accidental that the miscue characteristics are analogous to the aspects of language—phonology, syntactics, and semantics. We point this out again to underline the intimate relationship of the reading act to the student's language proficiency.

In performing a miscue analysis, teachers structure the situation much as they would in administering an informal reading inventory. In fact, if adequate protocols have been kept from a previous administration of an IRI, the teacher may be able to perform usable analyses without asking the student to read orally again. If no IRI protocols are available, the teacher asks the student to read several paragraphs at the instructional level, marking a double-spaced copy with an appropriate code. The miscues emitted by the student are then subjected to an analysis as follows. Using Table 3.5, the teacher categorizes the types of responses made by the student. Special note is made of the student's efforts at "sounding out" (these efforts are invaluable in helping the teacher derive hypotheses concerning

TABLE 3.6. Analysis of Substitution Miscues

TYPE OF SUBSTITUTION ANALYSIS[a]	EXAMPLE[b]	HYPOTHESIS OR "WHAT THE TEACHER DOES NEXT"
I. Graphic analysis		
a. No discernible similarity (no shared letters)	king/lady	Probe whether the student is guessing. Student may have virtually no word-attack skills (test further with commercial or teacher-made word-analysis test).
b. Words similar in overall configuration	leg/boy	Student may be utilizing configural clues—this is a strength that needs to be built on and supplemented with other word-analysis skills.
c. Reversal of single letter	bad/dad	Recheck student's ability to discriminate between *b* and *d,* also between other pairs, such as *p* and *q.* Provide left–right activities, also specific exercises for discrimination training. See also section on grammatical appropriateness.
d. Reversal of two or more letters	was/saw	Provide activities as indicated in I.c.
e. Beginning letters similar	play/plant	Student is correctly utilizing initial consonant blend cue. He or she needs to be encouraged to utilize middle and ending graphic cues, also to attend to context. Check other initial letters.
f. Middle letters similar	good/food	Same as I.e except with middle letters.
g. Ending letters similar	that/what	Same as I.e except with ending letters; also extra exercises with *wh* and *th* letters.
h. Single letter omission, insertion, or substitution	very/every	Student needs to be encouraged to look at entire word, also needs help on using syntactic and semantic cues.
i. Similar root word; suffix/prefix miscue	toys/toy	Check for presence of dialect; then use activities dealing with singular and plural; also encourage attention to word endings.
II. Syntactic analysis		
a. Beginning position in sentence	The boy . . ./ Who . . .	Check whether student can discriminate between these words when they occur later in the sentence; if so, he or she is relying heavily on syntactic cues (which is good), but needs more help on word-analysis skills.
b. Middle or ending position in sentence	Mary ran far/Mary ran fast	Student is using syntactic and semantic features of the sentence (good); needs help as in I.e.
c. Grammatical appropriateness (substituted word has same rate of occurrence as stimulus word? Sentence grammatical up to and including miscue?)	John found his pet/ John found his play	Student relying on initial letter cue (good), but is not showing grammatical awareness. Does student have mastery of oral language? If so, further testing and activities with cloze technique and "guess the end of the sentence" game might be used.

(continues)

TABLE 3.6. *Continued*

TYPE OF SUBSTITUTION ANALYSIS[a]	EXAMPLE[b]	HYPOTHESIS OR "WHAT THE TEACHER DOES NEXT"
III. Semantic analysis		
a. Stimulus word and child's response unrelated or only partially related	Peter could/ Peter cold	Student is using fairly sophisticated word-analysis skills (teacher can build on this), but needs sequential sentence speaking and reading opportunities. Other activities as in II.c.
b. Meaning of student's response acceptable in sentence, but not related to stimulus sentence or paragraph	Jerry went home/ Jerry went away	Student is thinking about the internal meaning of the sentence (good), but is not relating it to the meaning of the story. Student lacks word-analysis skills.

[a]Category types are not mutually exclusive.

[b]In each example, the printed text or expected response precedes the diagonal line; the child's miscue or the observed response follows.

the student's word-attack strategies; in fact, the student should be encouraged to "sound out" for this reason), self-correction (which similarly provides valuable insight into how the child monitors personal performance, and whether he or she utilizes feedback effectively), and dialect considerations. This latter issue will not be further explicated, except to say that the student's dialect will affect the interpretation given to graphic, syntactic, and semantic miscues; in fact, the presence or absence of a dialect will determine whether certain departures from the expected responses should be considered miscues at all.

Next, each miscue is analyzed according to its graphic, syntactic, and semantic characteristics. By noting the relative proportion of miscues in each category, the teacher can form a rough idea of whether the student's difficulty is more of the word-analysis type (mostly graphic miscues) or whether the child has linguistic or cognitive difficulty in forming hypotheses about the meaning of the material being read (such difficulty showing up more in syntactic and semantic miscues). We strongly urge teachers to attend closely to this latter miscue type, for it is our belief that linguistic and cognitive aspects of reading have been generally ignored by teachers.

After completing the miscue analysis, the teacher will find it useful to summarize the results on a record sheet such as the one presented in Table 3.7. The use of this record sheet should make it apparent at a glance where the student's faulty strategies seem to cluster. The teacher will then have a sound basis for beginning instruction designed to build on strengths and to redress weaknesses. The student's reading protocol should be readily available as instruction is planned.

TABLE 3.7. Sample Record Sheet for Oral Reading Miscues

Name _____ Age _____ Grade _____ Date _____

Sample of Reading Material on Which Analysis Is Based _____

Number of Words in Sample _____

Response Type/Number of Occurrences	*Response Type/Number of Occurrences*
Omission_____	Sounding Out _____
Insertion _____	Self-Correction _____
Sequence_____	Dialect _____
Substitution _____	

Substitution Analysis

Graphic analysis		*Syntactic analysis*	
a. No similarity	_____	a. Beginning position	_____
b. Configuration	_____	b. Middle or ending	
c. Single-letter reversal	_____	position	_____
d. Several letters reversed	_____	c. Grammatical	
e. Beginning letters similar	_____	appropriateness	_____
f. Middle letters similar	_____	Total syntactic miscues	_____
g. Ending letters similar	_____		
h. Single-letter miscue	_____	*Semantic analysis*	
i. Root word	_____	a. Meaning unrelated	_____
Total graphic miscues	_____	b. Story meaning distorted	_____
		Total semantic miscues	_____

Another technique for looking at students' miscues is provided by Wiederholt (1985) in the *Formal Reading Inventory: A Method for Assessing Silent Reading Comprehension and Oral Reading Miscues*. The test's standardization is extensive and includes numerous studies of reliability and validity. The norms are based on a large, nationally representative sample of students from Grades 1 through 12.

In using this test, the teacher first finds a student's silent reading comprehension level by having him or her read passages of increasing difficulty from a series of stories and answer literal, inferential, critical, and affective questions about their contents. The student's performance is reported as percentiles and standard scores. Next, three passages are selected from an equivalent form of the test. The student's silent reading comprehension level is used as a criterion; one of the selected passages is at the student's reading level, and the other two are easier and more difficult, respectively.

The three passages are read orally by the student, while the teacher records specific departures from the text. The types of departures noted are (1) meaning similarities, (2) function similarities, (3) graphic–phonemic similarities, and (4) self-corrections. The test's four forms allow teachers to pre- and posttest students on their silent reading comprehension and their oral reading miscues.

Newer Approaches to Assess Literacy

With the wider use of whole language or literacy-based reading programs, teachers have found that traditional approaches to assessment, especially standardized tests, do not yield the information that teachers need to know to carry on effective instruction. Many of these tests assess artificial skills in isolated and nonauthentic situations and fail to account for the prior knowledge and communicative intentions of students. Use of "real-life" reading strategies, such as asking for assistance or using a dictionary when confronting difficulties, are prohibited, and strategies of guessing or cheating often are rewarded. Anxiety is frequently heightened as the emphasis moves from understanding the text to getting the right multiple-choice answer—a reading situation that has no counterpart in real-life literacy. Furthermore, many traditional tests of reading lend themselves all too readily to misuse or misunderstanding.

No single approach has emerged as *the* solution for measuring students' literacy. In fact, given the multiple purposes of reading, it is unlikely that one test, no matter how well constructed, will ever fully measure all the complex, but essential interactions among reader, text, and setting. Given that a competent reader is *skilled* (decodes words and constructs meanings), *motivated* (reads voluntarily and purposefully), and *independent* (transfers literacy skills to real-life situations), assessment should address each of these characteristics. In the following section, we review some newer approaches to evaluating students' literacy. As always, the purpose of the assessment (student diagnosis, student placement, student instruction, reporting to parents, compliance with school or state policy) should determine testing format.

Literacy portfolios, one of the newer approaches, consist of formative (process) and summative (product) evaluations. As such, they may include anecdotal information based on classroom observations, lists of books read and to be read, records of difficult words or recurring problems, attitude or interest inventories, students' responses to the books they read, writing samples or students' journals, self-evaluations, and interviews of various kinds. Some of these data can be summarized on a profile sheet (see Figure 3.3).

Classroom observations can be made on 3-inch × 5-inch cards as events throughout the day warrant, and slipped into students' portfolios at the end of the day. Some students will have more than one observation on any particular day; others will have none. It is necessary to keep *records of*

Name: _____

Number of books read: _____

Types of books read (genre): _____

Level of books read: _____

Voluntary reading appropriateness: _____

Special difficulties: _____

_____

Other comments: _____

_____

FIGURE 3.3. Literacy profile sheet.

books read, both for assessment and instructional purposes. If a student has particularly enjoyed a book, similar books can be recommended. Where students have *recurring difficulties,* flash cards or word lists can be developed for their individual use. Where reading difficulties are similar to those of other students (e.g., difficulties in predicting endings), flexible group mini-lessons can be planned for remediation purposes. *Measures of attitude or interest* can be either formal or informal in nature, or they may be based on classroom comments or observations. Students' responses to the books they read may take the form of a traditional "book report," a critique of a character or plot, or completion of a story frame (see Figure 3.4). The literacy portfolio is a good place to keep reading or writing samples (if curriculum-based assessment is used, the results are filed here). *Self-evaluations* may be in the form of checklists, or be based on student comments in interviews. *Interviews* can often provide essential instructional insight into how the student can be helped to use more effective strategies.

TEACHING THE STUDENT WHO HAS A READING PROBLEM

Once the teacher has a clear picture of the student's reading problem, the task is to develop teaching strategies that are feasible and effective. Such strategies are to be implemented on a trial basis; if the student makes progress, the strategy should be continued. If discernible learning does not occur, however, it is appropriate to return to a previous point in the

Name of student: _____ Name of book: _____

Author: _____

The problem in the story is _____

_____

_____

_____

_____

_____

_____

The problem is solved when _____

_____

_____

_____

_____

_____

_____

At the end of the story _____

_____

_____

_____

_____

The author's message is that _____

_____

_____

The message makes me think that _____

_____

_____

Why I liked or did not like this story: _____

_____

_____

_____

FIGURE 3.4. Sample story frame.

instructional cycle (see Chapter 1)—that is, to retest the student with a view to generating an alternative hypothesis as to which approach might work with that student.

This may sound as if the teaching of reading is largely a matter of trial and error. Although research has not yet been able to show precisely which kind of reading approach works best with a student exhibiting certain learning styles or modality preference, a significant body of research and knowledge exists about useful overall instructional principles in reading, basal reading series intended for classroom use, and special remedial approaches intended for use with remedial or handicapped learners. It is to these topics that we turn next.

Instructional Principles in Teaching Reading

Even though much remains to be learned, the task of teachers is to use the knowledge that is available in their instructional procedures. The following sections are based on current literature on the nature of learning difficulties and on our present understanding of what constitutes effective teaching practices.

Maintain a Strong Academic Focus

It might appear to be self-evident that those students who are *taught* to read *learn* to read. However, the ready availability of computers, games, puzzles, and the ubiquitous workbooks and "seatwork" (all of which are frequently unrelated to the reading tasks at hand) has directed valuable classroom time away from actual teaching and learning of reading skills. In some classrooms, students rarely engage in actual reading activities and rarely are directly taught by the teacher in a sustained and organized way. The research is clear, however, that a task-oriented, businesslike atmosphere in the classroom is essential to steady student gains in reading. The research also shows that task-oriented, organized, academically focused teachers tend to be relaxed and friendly with the students and rank high in accepting students and promoting self-sufficiency.

What exactly is meant by maintaining a strong academic focus? The following characteristics have been found to be related to improved student achievement:

Prompt, specific feedback

Teacher monitoring of student responses

Clear, precise goal statements

Well-developed, systematic lessons

Few digressions from task

Efficient and systematic movement toward a goal

Well-developed follow-up activities

Precise use of student input

Buoyancy but not lightheartedness

Natural humor without sarcasm

High-achieving classrooms have significantly more monitored learning, structured learning activities, and paced curricular content. All of these activities point to active, teacher-directed instruction as opposed to a laissez-faire learning environment.

Teach Reading Strategies

The instructional principles discussed in this section are based on the view that many students with learning problems fail to deploy cognitive resources efficiently and effectively. This means that they are generally inattentive, inactive, and unable to generate appropriate learning strategies without outside help. Their difficulties are as much in the executive or monitoring (metacognitive) functions as in the performance (cognitive) functions. Although they use different terminology—for example, "academic strategy training," "cognitive behavior modification," "self-monitoring," or "metacognitive training"—a growing number of theorists and researchers are now coming to this point of view. Strategy training has been found to be effective with a wide range of learning problems.

ELEMENTS OF STRATEGY TRAINING

Strategy training has a number of different emphases. In general, researchers and practitioners agree that cognitive strategy training must include the following elements: skills training, self-regulatory training, and awareness training.

Skills Training

The emphasis in skills training is on helping students acquire proficiency in strategies that are specific to effective reading. Examples of skills that might be taught include strategies for decoding, such as using a dictionary, or for reading comprehension, such as discerning the main idea or summarizing a text passage. Many authorities believe that this type of specific strategy training is a prerequisite to other strategy emphases.

The general sequence is to teach the student task-specific strategies in isolation, then have the student practice those strategies in controlled or assisted situations, and finally have the student apply the strategies in a new learning situation.

Initially, a comprehensive diagnostic assessment of the student's reading abilities is undertaken to establish levels of functioning in areas of weakness requiring intervention (see the previous section on assessment).

Once these levels have been established, the cognitive behavior modification, or strategy training, is begun. The following stages are implemented:

Stage 1. The teacher demonstrates the technique, verbalizing the self-instructional strategy and reading the passage out loud.

Stage 2. The teacher and the student together utilize the strategy, overtly verbalizing each stage and orally reading the passage in question.

Stage 3. The student verbalizes the strategy and reads silently the next reading passage.

Stage 4. The student whispers the strategy and reads silently the next reading passage.

Stage 5. The student overtly uses the strategy and reads the passage silently.

If at any point the student has less than 90% comprehension on questions asked after the reading, he or she goes back to an earlier stage of instruction until that criterion is reached. If after three attempts the criterion has not been reached, the student is placed at a lower reading level.

Self-Regulatory Training

Once students have demonstrated mastery of the various reading skills, they must be taught how to use those skills appropriately. That is, they must be taught a set of superordinate, or general, strategies that help them flag situations in which a particular specific strategy might be helpful. For example, to use a specific strategy for reading comprehension, students must first determine when they need to use it; students must be trained to monitor themselves in such a way that they can tell whether they do or do not understand a particular passage.

Self-regulatory strategy training helps students to monitor their own reading by asking themselves questions such as "Do I know what this passage is about?" or "Do I understand these words?" (See also the preceding section on reading comprehension.) When students detect a problem in comprehension, they then must invoke one of the strategies learned in skills training to help them resolve the difficulty (e.g., use the dictionary, reread, summarize, find the main idea, ask the teacher).

Awareness Training

In addition to being trained in specific reading strategies and in strategies for monitoring and regulating themselves, students also must be taught information regarding the importance of strategy use. The research on strategy training clearly shows that performance is enhanced when students understand the significance and scope of such training. Feedback showing the beneficial effects of strategy use should be given to students.

Some students have learned faulty or incomplete reading strategies (e.g., use of the first sentence in a paragraph as the main idea of that paragraph) that may work some of the time. It is particularly difficult for students to relinquish strategies that sometimes lead to the correct answer; only explicit instruction in the usefulness of proper strategies will lead to their consistent use.

SUBJECTS OF STRATEGY TRAINING

From their review of comprehension strategy research, A. L. Brown, Palincsar, and Armbruster (1988) concluded that readers need the following strategies for successful comprehension.

Understanding the Purpose of Reading

Students need self-regulatory training in order to learn when to use a particular strategy—for example, skimming, reading for detail, or reading for the main idea. Only when students understand *why* they are reading a passage can they utilize the appropriate strategy. Before asking students to read a passage, be sure they know the purpose for reading. First provide explicit instruction; then have the students state the strategies they will use to achieve the purpose for reading that particular passage.

Foregrounding Relevant Background Information

Self-regulatory training is needed to assist some students in activating related knowledge that they have already acquired. Many problem learners do not automatically connect material being learned with material that has previously been mastered. Use prereading exercises that identify the topic and genre of material to be read. Require students to search their memories for related material. Set the stage for new reading material by previewing the material and using advance organizers. Teach students to try to bring related, previously learned information into the foreground of their awareness through self-questioning.

Directing Attention to Relevant Information

Not all information in a given reading passage is of equal importance. This is difficult for many problem readers to understand. Both successful decoding and successful comprehension require the reader to know what to pay attention to. Given human beings' finite memory capacity, not everything is worth attending to. Reading and remembering successfully means allowing yourself to ignore some aspects of letters, words, sentences, and longer passages. Explicitly teach students not to try to remember everything. Use a step-by-step sequence to help students sort out and evaluate bits of information in a reading passage and discard the redundant, the trivial, and the distracting. Use summarization techniques to help students learn to zero in on what is important and relevant.

Critically Evaluating the Internal Consistency of the Reading Passage

Good readers evaluate text for internal consistency during reading. That is, they consider previously stated propositions when they encounter new ones, and they compare them for compatibility. However, young children and problem learners seem to have difficulty doing this, even when the inconsistencies are within the same paragraph. The evidence points to a need for direct teaching of cognitive strategies to detect inconsistencies. Teach students to be vigilant for text inconsistencies. Assure them that simply because a fact is written down does not mean it is correct. Teach students to ask "Could *y* be true if *x* is true?" Children as young as 5 years of age have been shown to benefit from such direct instruction if it is simple and explicit.

Self-Monitoring to Detect Comprehension Breakdown

Baker (1985) suggested that readers use different kinds of standards to evaluate their understanding of text. These standards include the following:

Lexical standards. Can I recognize this word? Do I know the meaning of this word?

Syntactic standards. Does this sentence make grammatical sense? Who is the subject of this action? What is the object?

Semantic standards. What is the meaning of this sentence? What is the meaning of this text as a whole? Semantic standards have the following elements:

1. *Propositional cohesiveness.* Can a given proposition be successfully integrated into previous propositions?

2. *Structural cohesiveness.* Are the various ideas expressed related to a common theme?

3. *External consistency.* Are the ideas in the text consistent with the reader's previous knowledge and experience?

4. *Internal consistency.* Are the ideas in the passage consistent with one another?

5. *Informational clarity and completeness.* Does the passage give enough information to clearly achieve its purposes?

Increase students' awareness of the need to know when they understand and do not understand what they are reading. Have students predict how they will perform on comprehension questions; then provide information on actual performance and discuss the reasons for any discrepancies. Depending on the ages of the students, provide practice in detecting comprehension failure in the lexical, syntactic, and semantic areas by presenting passages with contrived problems of the various types in the text.

Deriving and Testing Inferences

Understandings that are not direct or literal are both the most important and the most difficult to derive from text. A variety of techniques can be used to strengthen students' ability to derive and evaluate inferences from a passage. Ask students to retell the story or to recount the major points or propositions of a passage they have just read. The students' performance should be discussed in terms of the number, sequence, and accuracy of stated propositions. Have students fill in missing words or phrases (cloze technique) or predict plausible story endings. Help students generate questions about the important points in a reading passage. Provide students with the opportunity to recognize or verify sentences related to text sentences. Give students practice in summarizing passages and using summarization subskills. The five subskills believed to underlie summarizing ability are the abilities to (1) delete redundancy, (2) delete trivia, (3) provide superordinate sentences, (4) select topic sentences, and (5) generate topic sentences if necessary.

Use Reciprocal Teaching in Teaching Reading Comprehension

Cognitive strategy training has been found to be most effective when teachers and students are intensely engaged with one another in a systematic way. The term *reciprocal teaching* has come to be used to describe a procedure in which teachers and students take turns leading a dialogue concerning a particular reading passage (A. L. Brown et al., 1988). Reciprocal teaching takes place in groups of 2 to 15 persons. The general procedure is for everyone in the group to silently read a segment of text selected by the teacher. First the teacher models; then a student is assigned to model and lead a discussion of what has been read. The activities focused on are summarizing, questioning, clarifying, and predicting. The teacher or students summarize the segment, ask several questions central to the meaning of the segment, discuss and clarify any difficulties experienced by group members, and finally predict what will follow in subsequent text segments. Initially, students need prompting and cuing by the teacher in order to take the leadership role in summarizing, questioning, clarifying, and predicting. The teacher provides feedback to the student leaders, increasing the demands on them as they become more proficient. The students' behavior becomes more and more like that of the teacher, while the teacher's behavior becomes less and less directive. Eventually, the teacher acts only as a supportive audience.

The characteristics of reciprocal teaching are the following:

> *Use of dialogue to model and explain cognitive processes.* The process of an expert's giving support to a novice is derived from Vygotzky (1978) and is called *scaffolding*. The prototype for the interaction between expert and novice (teacher and student) is that of the parent–child

dyad. The parent initially provides much support to the dependent child, but gradually increases demands and reduces support as the child becomes proficient and independent. The mechanism of this change is scaffolding—making underlying processes overt, explicit, and concrete (A.L. Brown & Palincsar, 1985).

Fading of the role of the teacher as a model. As reciprocal teaching progresses, the role of the teacher changes from that of model to that of consultant. The students take increasing responsibility for their own learning.

Active involvement in learning by students. The fact that students take the leadership role in reciprocal teaching ensures that learning becomes active. The quality of their participation increases dramatically as time goes on.

Provision of feedback to the learner. Initially, the teacher nudges the students to make appropriate summaries, questions, clarifications, and predictions. In the process, students learn when particular strategies are appropriate, and they also learn why. Student leaders are put in the position of evaluating the utility of strategies used by other students and hence learn generalization and transfer.

Since reciprocal teaching was first reported in 1984 by Palincsar and Brown, it has been found to be a highly successful way of improving reading comprehension in students with comprehension difficulties. Furthermore, effects of the training have been found to generalize to comprehending texts in subject areas such as social studies and science. Most encouraging of all, improvements have been found to hold up for months after initial training.

Use Task Analysis to Organize and Sequence Instruction

Frequently, the teacher will find that a student is deficient in a word-analysis or comprehension skill that had been previously taught. In such cases, it is helpful to analyze the skill in question to determine if it can be broken into component parts that can be separately and successfully taught to the student. Such an approach is called *task analysis*. In undertaking a task analysis of a given reading skill, the first step is to state clearly the objective of the task. This objective then needs to be scrutinized on the basis of the following criteria:

1. *Significance.* How important is it for the student to master this skill? Is it basic or trivial? Is it necessary?

2. *Relevance.* How relevant is this skill to the other things the student needs to learn or has learned?

Having determined that the task to be taught is a significant and relevant one, the teacher then identifies the subskills that are necessary for performing the target task. Once the subskills have been delineated, the teacher asks, "What does the student have to be able to do to perform each of the subskills?" The answer to this question leads to the development of sub-subskills. This procedure is repeated until the teacher arrives at a subskill level where the student is able to perform the tasks. (Figure 3.5 presents an example of a comprehension task analysis.)

COMPREHENSION TASK ANALYSIS

In Figure 3.5, the objective is to get the student to the point where he or she will be able to use temporal sequence clues to determine the logical order of a series of events in a story. A descending task analysis has been developed to show the levels of prerequisite tasks necessary to successfully perform the target task.

Some comments are necessary to provide perspective for this task analysis. First, sequence "clue words" have been categorized as "exact" and "nonexact." The categorizing of these clue words should help the student draw conclusions about the use of the clue words in determining sequence, because exact words (*first, last*) require a slightly different approach than do nonexact words (*next, later*).

Furthermore, the model presented in Figure 3.5 focuses only on the exact words (except at the target task level, which draws both categories together). The approach to teaching for the two categories is virtually the same. The main difference lies in the need for elaborate use of context clues when dealing with nonexact words. This technique does become evident in target task–level procedures.

Additionally, at the sub-subskill level, only one subgroup of exact words is illustrated (again because it is the same basic procedure for all subgroups). Numerical clue words, such as *first* and *second,* are the focus of the procedures. Although most students come to school already familiar with the concept behind these words, it is necessary to review them in relation to the reading and sequencing task.

Finally, teachers should note that interpretive skills, background experience, and semantic knowledge are necessary in utilizing both the exact and the nonexact words. Therefore, the developmental level of the student should be considered before a target skill such as this one is presented.

Teach Specific Reading Skills Directly

The term *direct instruction* has been used in a number of different ways—to denote a specific instructional program as well as to describe a teacher–student orientation that is characterized by a precise goal-oriented focus; careful sequencing of content; high pupil engagement; and teacher modeling, explanation, monitoring, and specific corrective feedback to students. Such an instructional style puts a heavy demand on the teacher—the teacher actually teaches, as opposed to merely arranging the

Target Skill Level

> When I meet any clue words or phrases that tell me *when*, I can use them to determine sequence.

Known words about which Level 2 *generalizations have been made*

    Baseline words—"exact" and "nonexact" clues

Observations necessary

    All words or phrases tell me *when*.
    Some words are "exact" clue words and some are "nonexact."

Subskill Level

> When I meet any "exact" clue words or phrases that tell me *when*, I can use them to determine sequence.

> When I meet any "nonexact" clue words or phrases that tell me *when*, I can use them to determine sequence.

Known words about which Level 1 *generalizations have been made*

    Baseline words—"exact" clues

Known words about which Level 1 *generalizations have been made*

    Baseline words—"nonexact" clues

Observations necessary

    All are words or phrases that tell *when*.
    All are "exact" clue words or phrases.

Observations necessary

    All are words or phrases that tell *when*.
    All are "nonexact" clue words or phrases.

Sub-Subskill Level

> When I meet ... I know they tell me *when*, and I can use them to determine time order.

> When I meet ... I know they tell me *when*, and I can use them to determine time order.

> When I meet ... I know they tell me *when*, and I can use them to determine time order.

> When I meet ... I know they tell me *when*, and I can use them to determine time order.

> When I meet ... I know they tell me *when*, and I can use them to determine time order.

Known words

first
second
third
fourth
fifth
etc.

Known words

today   last
tomorrow   finally
yesterday   etc.

Known words

next   before
then   later
after   etc.
now

Known phrases (words)

in the beginning
day before yesterday
at the end
next to last
etc.

Known phrases

by then
last week
later that day
etc.

Level at which child can perform all tasks and make all required generalizations

		Known words		
Monday	January	noon	first	1978	6:00
Tuesday	February	midnight	second	etc.	6:15
Wednesday	March		third		7:30
Thursday	April		fourth		etc.
Friday	May		fifth		
Saturday	June		etc.		
Sunday	July				
	August				
	September				
	October				
	November				
	December				

FIGURE 3.5. Example of comprehension task analysis.

Adapted from S. Tobia, B. Elliot, and C. Rubenstone, unpublished manuscript developed under the direction of M. S. Johnson at Temple University Laboratory School, Psychology of Reading Department, Philadelphia, 1978.

learning environment, or monitoring seatwork, or correcting seatwork or other assignments. In direct instruction, the teacher explains, models, demonstrates, and leads. Direct instruction means the teacher is centrally involved in the act of teaching and directly in command of, and responsible for, instructional activities.

Direct instruction of reading skills requires that the teacher have objectives for a lesson clearly in mind before starting a lesson (see Chapter 1 for points to keep in mind in formulating objectives). The precise delineation of objectives and subobjectives requires that the learning task be broken down into constituent parts so that instruction toward each objective can proceed in an orderly and sequential fashion. For this reason, direct instruction almost always requires the use of task analysis (which was described in the preceding section). In this section, we consider how the teacher actually directly teaches the skills and subskills identified in the task analysis.

The research on direct instruction has been generally supportive of its use. It has been most widely used for teaching word-analysis skills. More recently, whole language and systematic direct instruction have been successfully taught together.

In general, direct instruction follows a number of steps that are adaptable to the particular lesson being taught. These steps are

1. *Introduction.* The teacher reviews prior relevant learning, checks knowledge of prerequisite skills, activates prior knowledge, and states the purpose of the lesson.

2. *Direct instruction.* The teacher does the actual teaching—states, manipulates, explains, requests, and demonstrates. Best practices in direct instruction with problem learners include the following:

   Proceed in small steps.

   Provide many examples.

   Use questions to check students' understanding.

3. *Guided practice.* The students do several examples under the direct guidance of the teacher. The examples may be limited, cued, prompted, or otherwise modified at first to ensure student success. Best practices in teacher-directed applications include the following:

   Have students describe what they are doing.

   Focus directly on the material.

   Provide feedback on each step of the example at first.

   Follow correct responses with brief affirmative feedback.

   Follow incorrect responses with hints, simple questions, examples, or reteaching of the task element.

   Hold to a high mastery criterion (at least 80%).

4. *Independent practice.* The students work individually or in groups to reinforce, consolidate, and generalize their skills. Best practices at this stage include the following:

Actively monitor the students' performance.

Practice until automaticity is achieved (no hesitation).

Practice until a high rate of accuracy is achieved.

Practice until a high response rate is achieved (speed).

We provide a detailed example from Baumann (1984) to demonstrate each of the stages of direct instruction.

Sample Lesson Employing a Direct Instruction Paradigm[2]
(Lesson 2: Main Ideas and Details in Paragraphs—Implicit)

Introduction: "Remember last time when we learned how to find main idea sentences right in paragraphs? We called these main idea sentences *topic sentences.* Today you will learn how to find main ideas in paragraphs that do not have topic sentences; that is, paragraphs which actually do have main ideas in them, but paragraphs in which the main ideas are not stated. You will learn how to figure out these unstated main ideas by looking at the details in the paragraph and determining what all these details are talking about, and that will be the main idea. This is an important reading skill because many paragraphs have unstated main ideas, and if you can figure out what these main ideas are, you will understand and remember the most important information in the material you read."

Example: "Look at the example I have on this transparency."

My father can cook bacon and eggs real well. He can also bake cakes that taste wonderful. He cooks excellent popcorn and pizza. The thing he cooks best of all, however, is hamburgers barbecued on the grill.

"Follow along with me silently as I read the paragraph aloud." (Teacher reads paragraph.) "Notice that there is no single sentence that states the main idea; that is, there is no topic sentence. Rather, the entire paragraph consists of a series of details. That does not mean that there is not a main idea in this paragraph, however, for there is. What we will learn how to do today is to inspect paragraphs like this one that contain an unstated main idea and then figure out what that main idea is."

Direct Instruction: "Let's examine this same paragraph on the transparency and see if we can determine its main idea. Remember in our last lesson, we learned to figure out the topic of a paragraph—the one or two words that tell what a paragraph is about? What would be the topic of this paragraph? Would it be 'father cooking'?" (Student response.) "All right, the topic of the paragraph is 'father cooking.' Now let's list on the board all the ideas that tell about father cooking. Who can help us begin?" (Students respond by stating the four detail sentences in the paragraph, and the teacher writes them on the board in a numbered list.) "Very good. These are the ideas that tell us about father cooking, and we learned already that we can call these ideas *supporting details.* If supporting details go with a main idea, let's inspect these details and see if we

2. From "The Effectiveness of a Direct Instruction Paradigm for Teaching Main Idea Comprehension" by J. F. Baumann, 1984, *Reading Research Quarterly, 20,* pp. 93–115. Reprinted with permission of James Baumann and the International Reading Association.

can figure out what the main idea of this paragraph is." (Teacher rereads the supporting details on the board.) "Now what would be a main idea sentence we could come up with that goes with all these details?" (Teacher writes student responses on the board.) "Yes, there are several different ways of saying what the main idea is: 'Father can cook many different things' or 'Father is a good cook.' But the main idea tells us about all the details in the paragraph; that is, the biggest, most important, idea in the paragraph."

"Now look at this transparency. Who can tell me what it is?" (Student response.) "Yes, it is a table. Let's use this table to help us understand how main ideas and details go together. Just as a table is supported by its legs, so too, a main idea is supported by details. So let's put the main idea on the table and the supporting details on each of the legs. Who can help us get going? Let's start with the details on the legs." (Students respond and teacher writes details on table legs.) "Now let's put the main idea on the top of the table." (Teacher writes main idea on table top.) "Just as the legs of this table support the table top, so too, the details in this paragraph support the main idea of the paragraph. When you try to figure out the main idea of a paragraph, think of a table and legs to help you understand how supporting details and main ideas relate to one another, or go together." (Teacher then works through a second example paragraph in a similar fashion.)

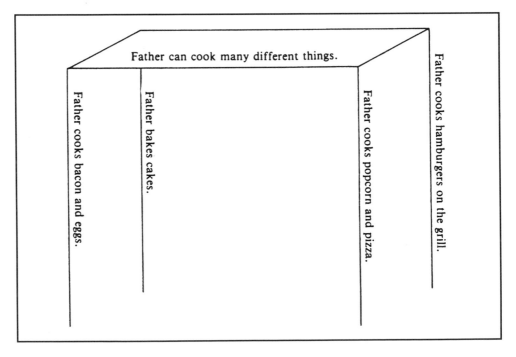

Teacher Directed Application: "I have a work paper we will complete together." (Teacher distributes work paper.) "Look at the paragraph after Number 1. Read this paragraph to yourself silently, and see if you can figure out the main idea. There is no topic sentence in this paragraph, so you will have to use the supporting details to determine what the main idea is. Then darken the letter that goes with the sentence you think best states the main idea of this paragraph." (Students complete exercise.) "All right, how did you do? Who can tell us what the main idea is?" (Student response.) "Correct, answer choice c, 'Animals help people in many different ways' is the main idea. Who can tell us

---

UNSTATED MAIN IDEAS AND DETAILS IN PARAGRAPHS
GROUP EXERCISE

1. Horses can carry people. Mules pull heavy loads. Dogs lead blind people across streets. Sheep give us wool, and cows give people milk to drink.
   (a) Animals give us many different foods to eat.
   (b) Horses and mules do heavy work for people.
   (c) Animals help people in many different ways.
   (d) Dogs and cats are good companions for people.

2. Mother likes to read mystery stories. Dad enjoys reading science fiction. My sister Kim likes to read joke books, and my little brother Thomas only likes to read comic books. But I enjoy reading nature books about wild animals.

   _____

3. Eohippus, the ancestor of the modern horse, lived fifty million years ago. Because the eohippus grazed on foliage, its teeth were very different from the teeth of the modern horse, which are adapted to eating grass. This "dawn horse" also had four toes on each of its front feet and three toes on each of its hind feet. Horses of today, however, have only one highly developed toe, covered by a hoof, on each foot.

   _____

4. Modern treasure hunting began in the northwestern United States in the late 1960s. Today, nearly one million people participate in this exciting hobby. Armed with metal detectors, these present-day adventurers track through old dumps, beaches, and schoolyards in search of lost "treasure." About 3,000 small businesses cater to the amateur treasure hunter, selling an estimated 600,000 metal detectors each year.

   _____

---

what the supporting details are for this main idea?" (Student response.) "Good, now let's try Exercise 2. Read this paragraph to yourself silently and then write what you think the main idea of the paragraph is on the line below the paragraph. Think of the table and legs idea to help you." (Students complete exercise.) "Who can tell us what the main idea is . . ." (Teacher and students proceed through the remaining exercises in a similar manner. If students have difficulty with the exercises, the teacher provides additional instruction.)

Independent Practice: "The final thing you will do in this lesson is to complete a work paper on your own." (Teacher distributes exercise.) "On this paper are some paragraphs for which you must figure out the main ideas, since there are no topic sentences in any of the paragraphs. For Number 1, the directions tell you simply to circle the statement that is the best main idea, and for Number 2, to write a main idea sentence for each paragraph. When completing these exercises, try to remember how to figure out the main idea by thinking of a statement that tells about the details in the paragraph; you also might want to use the table and legs idea to help you. Work carefully and do your best."

Name_____

UNSTATED MAIN IDEAS AND DETAILS IN PARAGRAPHS
INDEPENDENT PRACTICE

1. Read the following paragraphs and circle the letter of the statement that best tells the main idea for each paragraph.

Some dinosaurs were huge animals that were much larger than elephants. Some dinosaurs were small animals no larger than a chicken. Many dinosaurs, however, were middle-sized and about as big as a cow or horse.
(a) Some dinosaurs were chickens.
(b) All dinosaurs were huge, large animals.
(c) Dinosaurs were of different sizes.
(d) Dinosaurs were fearful, large animals.

Many dogs guard peoples' houses and stores. Some dogs are seeing-eye dogs and help blind people move around safely. Some dogs with keen noses are used to hunt criminals. But most dogs are just good friends for people.
(a) Dogs help blind people.
(b) Dogs help people in different ways.
(c) Dogs are good friends.
(d) Dogs hunt people and guard houses.

Many people are aware that the giraffe is the tallest animal on earth, but few realize that despite its long neck, the giraffe has the same number of neck bones that humans have—only seven. Also, many people think that giraffes have no voice. This is not true. Although giraffes rarely use their voice, they have vocal cords and are quite capable of making noises when they choose to. The "horns" that grow on their heads are not really horns at all. Instead, they are simply bumplike growths covered by skin and hair. Some giraffes even have three or four of these "horns," not the two most people think they have.
(a) Giraffes are tall animals with a real voice and bumplike horns.
(b) Giraffes can make sounds, even though people think they cannot.
(c) Giraffes and humans are alike in several ways.
(d) Giraffes are strange and surprising animals.

2. Each of the following paragraphs have unstated main ideas. Read each paragraph and try to figure out what a good main idea statement would be. Then write this statement on the line below each paragraph.

My mother wore bedroom slippers this morning. Then she put on running shoes for jogging. After jogging, she put on her old shoes to work in the garden. After lunch, she put on her new sneakers to play tennis. This evening she wore fancy high heels when she and Dad went out to dinner.

_____

Pumpkins, of course, can be made into pies. But pumpkins can also be used to make soup and cake. Some people roast pumpkin seeds and eat them. Probably most people use pumpkins to make Jack-o-Lanterns for Halloween.

_____

(continues)

A person with a metal detector will usually find things like bottle caps, tin cans, or perhaps a nickle or dime. But sometimes a person with a metal detector, if he or she is lucky, will find an old silver dollar or a valuable ring or piece of jewelry. Some people have found old coins worth very much money, perhaps $100 or $200. And a few lucky persons have found an entire treasure chest filled with gold and jewels.

We owe the word "sandwich" to the person who invented it—John Montague, the Earl of Sandwich. Louis Braille, who was blinded at the age of three, had to learn to read, from large, clumsy letters. He found these difficult to use, so he invented a system of raised dots which later became known as "braille." The German engineer Rudolf Diesel invented an internal combustion engine that would run on cheap crude fuel. Of course, now this engine is known as a "diesel" engine.

Teach Comprehension by Asking Appropriate Questions

As mentioned earlier, merely being able to recognize words is insufficient for receiving communication from the printed page. Understanding what the words, sentences, and paragraphs mean is the main purpose of reading. It follows, then, that the teaching of comprehension skills is a major objective for every teacher.

The use of questions to improve comprehension can help students understand and remember what they read. Asking the student questions *before* he or she reads a passage, as in a directed reading activity, helps the student focus attention on the information in the text that will help him or her answer the questions. However, this approach can direct the student's attention away from those parts of the narrative that do not contain information needed to answer questions. If, on the other hand, the student is told that he or she will be questioned *after* reading a passage, the student may try to remember as much as possible about all of the passage. The teacher must ascertain whether the student can attend to the passage without the need for specific guidance.

Ruddell (1976) developed a model of teacher questioning that facilitates moving the pupil's thinking from the literal or factual memory level toward the higher cognitive processes. These sequential steps were summarized by Singer (1978), as shown in Table 3.8.

Student responses to inferential, as opposed to factual, questions tend to be longer and more complex and utilize the higher cognitive processes. Furthermore, the quality of pupil responses can be improved by encouraging the student to delay the response for a few seconds, to take some "think-time" before trying to answer the teacher's questions.

TABLE 3.8. Teacher–Student Interaction in Questioning Strategy

Teacher–Student Interaction

Who Talks	*Function*
Teacher	Question
Student	Response

Questioning Strategy

Type	*Purpose*	*Question*
Focusing	Initiate discussion or refocus on the issue.	What did you like best about the story?
		What was the question we started to answer?
Controlling	Direct or dominate the discussion.	First, would you review the plot?
Ignoring or rejecting	Maintain current trend in discussion. Disregard a student's interest.	Would you mind if we don't go into that now
Extending	Obtain more information at a particular level of discussion.	What other information do we have about the hero?
Clarifying	Obtain a more adequate explanation. Draw out a student.	Would you explain what you mean?
Raising	Have discussion move from factual to interpretative, inferential, or abstraction and generalization level.	We now have enough examples. What do they have in common? (Abstract) Was it always true for his behavior? (Generalization)

Response Level

Factual or literal (what the author said)
Interpretative (integration of ideas of inference)
Applied (transfer of ideas or judgment that idea is subsumed under broader generalization)
Evaluative (using cognitive or affective criteria for judging issue)

From "Active Comprehension: From Answering to Asking Questions" by H. Singer, May 1978, *The Reading Teacher,* p. 903. Reprinted with permission of the author and the International Reading Association.

Teacher-posed questions serve a valuable purpose in focusing the student's attention on the material and in helping the student learn the type of questions to ask about a reading passage. The ultimate goal in reading for comprehension is not to read to answer someone else's questions, but to learn to ask appropriate questions for oneself as one reads. As noted in an earlier part of this chapter, the good reader develops hypotheses or questions as he or she reads, then reads on to see if the questions are answered the way he or she thinks they will be. This process occurs before, during, and after reading. Getting students to develop self-questioning skills has been found to be particularly helpful to students of low verbal ability. This approach is consistent with the section of this chapter that deals with teaching reading strategies.

Teaching students to generate their own questions entails the following procedures:

1. The teacher provides models of good questions.

2. The teacher phases out the questioning and, depending on the ages of the pupils, uses a picture, a title, an introductory paragraph, or another device to encourage the students to begin asking questions.

3. The questions generated by the students are used to set the purposes for reading and to encourage speculation about the main idea of the passage or story.

4. The students read the text to a point where their initial speculation is answered or intensified. At this point, the teacher encourages further questioning by the students. Depending on the passage, these questions may concern generalizations, concepts, predictions of plot resolution, interpretation, character development, or making inferences.

The last two steps are repeated until the passage is completed. Throughout, the teacher's role is one of eliciting student questions, encouraging students to recognize answers to their own questions, and guiding students to ask higher level questions.

Teach Fluency Through Sustained Silent Reading and Repeated Reading

One goal of reading instruction is to develop students' desire to read. Frequently, however, reading instruction is so intensive, so structured, and so "hard" that students have little or no opportunity to read material of their choice. To encourage students to develop a desire to read, as well as to consolidate learned reading skills, many teachers have relied on techniques involved in sustained silent reading and repeated reading.

SUSTAINED SILENT READING

Many teachers incorporate a period of sustained silent reading (SSR) into each school day. The method for doing this is summarized below and is based on the work of Cline and Kretke (1980), Gambrell (1978), McCracken and McCracken (1978), Minton (1980), and Moore, Jones, and Miller (1980). In large part, the success of an SSR program depends on the following procedures, which should be performed *before* the program is implemented.

1. Advertise and promote SSR well before attempting to implement it. Use bulletin boards, book displays, and letters to parents, as well as

reading aloud to the class and sharing thoughts about good books with pupils.

2. Assemble reading materials of many different topics, types, and difficulty levels. Include books, news magazines, newspapers, or other appropriate reading material.

3. Develop the rules for implementing SSR. This includes deciding what time of day it should take place and where students may engage in SSR (at desks, on mats, in reading nook, in library, etc.). For very young children, the SSR period might be only 5 minutes in length; older pupils enjoy reading for 15 to 20 minutes. The rules for SSR should make clear that material selection occurs *before* the actual reading time begins.

A few precautions will enhance the probability of success for an SSR program.

1. Ensure that *everyone,* especially the teacher (no grading of tests!), reads silently and without interruption during SSR.

2. Do not allow changes of reading material during the period.

3. Reluctant or resistant readers may sit quietly at their desks; they may not walk around the room or otherwise interrupt the readers.

4. There are no book reports, questions to answer, or other follow-up activities to SSR.

5. There should be a means of sharing what has been read with the teacher or other pupils for those who wish to do so. Bulletin boards, informal commenting, or a special weekly time for promoting books may be used.

6. If possible, invite parents or other school personnel to participate in SSR when possible.

In general, SSR promotes students' reading skills and improves their attitudes toward reading. These findings are most consistent when the teacher unfailingly participates in SSR and when a good selection of reading materials is available.

REPEATED READING

Repeated reading is another technique that has been promoted as a way of improving the performance of students in oral reading fluency and in comprehension. Most often, the technique takes the form of having the student repeatedly read orally a selection of approximately 200 words while simultaneously listening to a taped version of the same material. Sometimes, before the actual oral reading, students listen to the tape or the teacher, with or without "following along" in the printed text. The procedures are repeated, with the student working independently in a corner of the room, until some criterion of speed and accuracy is reached. At this point, the teacher listens to the student read orally; if the criterion (usually 85 words per minute) has been reached, new and slightly more difficult materials are prescribed.

Sometimes this technique is combined with other techniques. For example, repeated reading has been used together with the neurological impress method (a technique in which teacher and student read aloud together, with the teacher sitting behind the student and reading slightly faster and louder than the student), with improvement in word recognition and comprehension. Repeated readings (three and seven times) combined with comprehension cues have been found to be effective in increasing normal and learning disabled students' fluency and comprehension.

Teach Text Structure to Improve Reading Comprehension

As students progress through school, an increasing amount of the material to be learned is presented in content-area textbooks. Very large numbers of students have difficulty comprehending and remembering the material they read in their science, health, and social studies texts. Even if they can read all the words, they have difficulty deciding which ideas are important and how to extract the main idea from expository text. It has been found that one source of difficulty for these students is their unawareness of the structure of the text they are reading--description, sequence (narrative), cause and effect, compare/contrast, and problem solution.

Several approaches have been developed to help students become more aware of text structure and to use that awareness to facilitate their understanding of the material they are reading. Among the approaches that can be used are the following:

1. Directly teach text structure. Students are presented with examples of the different types of text structure, and the teacher leads a discussion on how knowledge of text structure can help understanding of the text.

2. Make visual representations of the way the material in the text is organized. Examples of such representations are presented below.

DESCRIPTION

Visual representations of descriptions are sometimes called semantic maps. Initially the teacher demonstrates the process of semantic mapping; then the students work independently. The passage is first read by everyone, and a discussion ensues as to what constitutes the main idea or concept. When this is decided on, a circle is made in the middle of the chalkboard, or paper, and the idea or concept is written down. Then the material is reread; as related characteristics or relationships to other concepts are encountered, these are represented with lines and additional circles

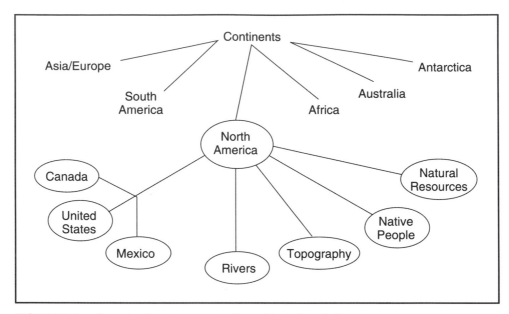

FIGURE 3.6. Sample visual representation of text description.

appropriately labeled. (See Figure 3.6 for an example of a visual representation of a text describing North America.)

SEQUENCE OF NARRATION

For a visual representation of sequence in a narrative, the teacher makes a long horizontal line on the chalkboard and inserts chapter subheadings along the line. This format can be adapted so that students can use it with paper-and-pencil at their desks. This approach is often helpful for understanding historical or biographical material. (See Figure 3.7 for an example from a history book.)

CAUSE AND EFFECT

In visual representations of cause and effect, either forward or reverse representations can be made. In the former case, the precipitating or

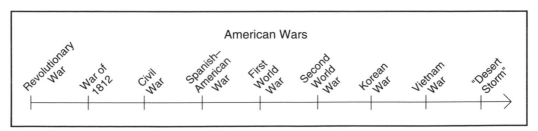

FIGURE 3.7. Sample sequence line.

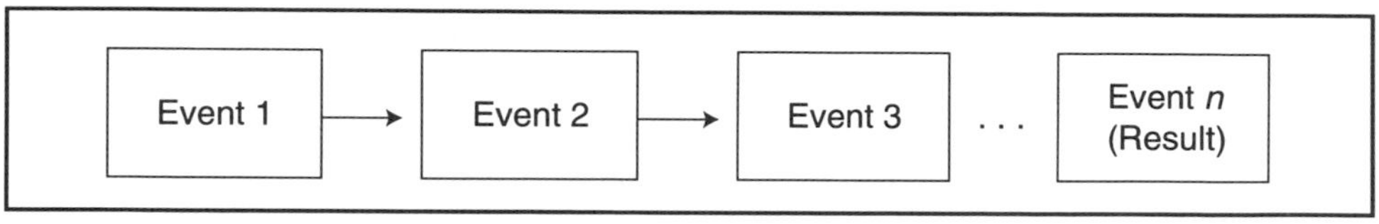

FIGURE 3.8. Sample visual representation of cause–effect text.

causal factors are identified first, and written down in the schematic representation; then the passage is reread to identify the outcome or effect, which is also written down (see Figure 3.8).

COMPARE/CONTRAST

A simple way to have students gain awareness of a compare/contrast text structure is to have them fold a piece of paper in half lengthwise, and label each side with the concepts or events that are being compared. Key comparison criteria can be written at one side, and then the passage is read. When information on one criterion is read, it is summarized in written form at the appropriate point on the paper. (See Figure 3.9 for an example.)

PROBLEM/SOLUTION

In a visual representation of a text presenting a problem and solution, a fill-in-the-blank format may be used. The students are presented with

	Spiders	Insects
Number of Body Parts		
Number of Legs		
Food		
Habitat		

FIGURE 3.9. Sample visual representation of compare/contrast text.

papers that contain partial sentences that they must complete as they read the materials. The general format is as follows:

_____had a problem because_____
_____.
Because of the problem, this happened: _____
_____.
As a result of this action, _____
_____.

Teaching students about text structure has been found to assist reading comprehension and retention of material. It also helps students with organizing their thoughts for writing compositions and essay questions.

Promote Literacy, Rather than Merely Teaching Reading

Literacy is functional and, like oral language learning, is best learned in authentic settings where written language is used as the basis of real and meaningful communication between writers and readers. Literacy socialization involves children's experiencing of literacy artifacts (e.g., alphabet blocks, books, newspapers, slogans on T-shirts) and literacy events (e.g., having stories read to them). Literacy experiences help children learn factual information ("what?"), reason information ("why?"), and affective information (motivation, feelings). Such exposure sets the stage for much subsequent learning required in later school years.

A literacy approach emphasizes these student processes and outcomes:

1. *Ownership.* Students value and take pride in their own ability to read and write, even if the results are not perfect.

2. *Communication.* Students see themselves as part of a community of persons who share ideas, intentions, and feelings through reading and writing.

3. *Risk taking.* Students explore literacy by experimenting with reading and writing activities.

4. *Voluntary communication.* Students have an active role in the selection of topics and materials about which to read or write, and the times they wish to read or write.

A literacy approach contains these curricular components:

1. *Reading comprehension.* This is a dynamic process involving interaction among the reader, the text, and the social setting in which the reading occurs. The purpose of reading is to construct a message based in part on each of these.

2. *Reading and writing to communicate.* Reading and writing are authentic processes through which ideas, intentions, and feelings can

be communicated, and which can contribute to meanings constructed by readers. Readers must take authors into account as they construct meanings from the text, and authors must take readers into account as they compose the text. These processes are similar to those engaged in by speakers and listeners (see Chapter 2 on speaking and listening).

3. *Linguistic knowledge.* Both reading and writing require a working knowledge of word representation and meaning, and of the structures of sentences, paragraphs, and larger units of text.

At any given time, whole literacy classrooms utilize any one of the following three organizational patterns:

1. The teacher (or district) selects one book or passage, which everyone in the group or the classroom reads. This could be a trade book, or one of the new literature-based basals. The teacher, or a student, leads a discussion on the text, emphasizing individual students' responses to the text, knowledge of story themes and elements, unanswered questions and clarifications, predictions, and summaries. Story frames or semantic maps may be used to illustrate or summarize the text. Students file any reports, summaries, or story frames in their individual portfolios. The teacher may keep a file of key words and sentences.

2. The teacher and students jointly select a book of text for reading, or a small group of students jointly selects reading material for their group, or students are paired as "buddies"—either self-selected or assigned. Group discussions follow the reading of the material, as above. Periodically, "reading workshops" or "writing workshops" are conducted. Small groups or pairs of children talk or write about books they have read, how the books affected them, and what they would like to read or write about next. Written materials are kept in individual or group portfolios, or they may be bound into a "book." Other forms of creative expression are encouraged—for example, illustrations, poems, songs, choral reading, dramatic vignettes, anagrams, clipboards, posters, and bulletin boards.

3. Students independently select materials to read. Classroom time is spent for sustained silent reading (see previous section on SSR), while the teacher meets with individual students to review decoding and comprehension and to identify and remediate problem areas. Students keep individual reading logs, noting the title and author of books read, as well as the date. Teachers periodically review the reading logs to note students' preferences, to see if they are reading widely and appropriately, and to make suggestions (not mandates) for further reading.

Classroom Approaches to Reading Instruction

The most common reading approach for regular education and mainstreamed students is the use of a basal reading series. As can be seen in

Table 3.9, basal readers come in several varieties—some are based on phonics, others are "linguistic," some have special remedial features (usually extra drill-and-practice), and some even present themselves as "literature-based" or "whole language–based." The use of basals has been severely criticized recently by professional organizations and in the professional journals. The criticisms have been directed at both the materials themselves (they make it more difficult for children to learn to read because the writing is stilted, monotonous, and unlike "real" communication from an author to a reader) and the teachers who use them (teachers become controlled, fragmented, "deskilled" automatons who use the basals in a mindless, rigid manner that is unresponsive to the interests and intentions of prospective readers). Nevertheless, basals continue to be used for reading instruction and, optimally, should be considered merely one more possible resource for teaching reading, along with trade books, periodicals, and other print media.

Table 3.9 summarizes the various approaches to the teaching of reading that are used often in regular classroom settings. In a later section, we address reading approaches that are more commonly used in resource rooms or other more intensive, clinical-type settings. Classroom approaches are used for regular developmental reading programs. They can also be adapted for the amelioration of specific reading problems in one student or a group of students with similar difficulties. A point to keep in mind with these classroom approaches is that, used by themselves, they rarely permit a teacher to utilize the best practices described in the previous section. For this reason, teachers will not want to use commercially prepared materials "as is," but view them as resources to be used and adapted as needed.

Special Remedial Approaches

The following teaching techniques are often used in schools or classes that specialize in children with reading disabilities. A regular classroom teacher would not usually be expected to use any of these clinical approaches in their entirety. However, they can be modified and adapted to meet the needs of specific children. (See also Chapter 11 on technology for computer and videodisc applications to reading.)

The Fernald (VAKT) Approach

If a child has a severe word-learning difficulty, and visual–auditory approaches have been unsuccessful, a modification of the Fernald (1988) Word Learning Technique is recommended. Although several authors refer to Fernald's remedial technique for teaching disabled readers as a kinesthetic method, the system is actually multisensory, involving four modalities simultaneously—visual, auditory, kinesthetic, and tactile (or VAKT). The approach is cognitive, for the words learned always originate with the reader and have contextual or meaningful association.

TABLE 3.9.   Classroom Reading Approaches

TYPE OF APPROACH	WHERE AVAILABLE	ADVANTAGES/ DISADVANTAGES/ SPECIAL COMMENTS
Complete Basals. These usually consist of reading texts, teacher's manual, and supplementary materials such as workbooks. They are often sequenced in a series from K to Grade 6 or 8. The instructional approach is one of introducing a controlled sight vocabulary coupled with an analytic phonics emphasis.	Reading: An American Tradition (Scott, Foresman) Connections (Macmillan) Holt Basic Reading (Holt, Rinehart & Winston) Houghton Mifflin Reading Series [also available in Spanish] (Houghton Mifflin) Reading Today and Tomorrow [emphasizes literature] (Holt, Rinehart & Winston) World of Reading (Silver Burdett & Ginn)	1. Basals lend themselves well to the three–reading-group arrangement; less well to individualizing 2. Content usually designed for the "typical" child; often not appealing to inner-city or rural children 3. Basals are generally well sequenced and comprehensive; attend to most aspects of developmental reading 4. Most have complete pupil packets of supplementary materials, saving teacher searching time 5. Basals are sufficiently detailed and integrated that successful use is possible for a teacher lacking in confidence or experience
Complete Basals with Extra Remedial Features. Same as above except material is presented in smaller units and more repetition is provided.	Focus: Reading for Success (Scott, Foresman) Reading Express (Macmillan) Merrill Skill-Text Series, Grades K–6; 7–12 (Merrill)	Attempts to accommodate the special needs of students with reading problems.
Synthetic Phonics Basals. Similar to above in some ways, but emphasis is on mastering component phonics skills, then putting together into words.	Lippincott's Reading Basics Plus (Macmillan) Scribner Reading Series (Macmillan) Reading Mastery: Distar 1–6 (SRA) Corrective Reading, Grades 4–12 (SRA) Open Court Headway Series (Open Court)	1. Same as above 2. Evidence is that a synthetic approach to word attack is rarely utilized by good readers
Linguistic Phonemic Approaches. Vocabulary that is used is highly controlled and conforms to the sound patterns of English (e.g., Nan, Dan, man, fan, ran, etc.). Most programs contain children's texts, teacher's manual, and supplementary materials.	Merrill Linguistic Readers (Merrill) Palo Alto Program (Harcourt Brace Jovanovich) SRA Basic Reading Series (SRA)	1. Content and usage in stories (especially early ones) sometimes contrived because of controlled vocabulary 2. Same as for Complete Basals

(continues)

TABLE 3.9. *Continued*

TYPE OF APPROACH	WHERE AVAILABLE	ADVANTAGES/ DISADVANTAGES/ SPECIAL COMMENTS
Integrated Language Basals. Emphasis is on teaching reading as part of a total language arts program, including listening, spelling, and writing.	Impressions (Holt, Rinehart & Winston) Open Court Reading and Writing (Open Court) HBJ Reading Laureate (Harcourt Brace Jovanovich)	This form of basal represents a fairly new development in the reading field. The effectiveness of this approach is not yet known.
Individualized Reading. Each child reads materials of own choice and at own rate. Word recognition and comprehension skills are taught as individual children need them. Monitoring of progress is done through individual teacher conferences. Careful record keeping is necessary.	Trade books of many different types, topics, and levels	1. Children are interested in content 2. Individualized reading promotes good habits of selection of reading materials 3. An extensive collection of books is needed for students to make choices 4. Teacher needs comprehensive knowledge of reading skills to make sure all are covered 5. Required record keeping can be cumbersome
Language Experience Approach. This approach is based on teacher's recording of child's narrated experiences. These stories become basis for reading. May be based on level of group or individual child. Stories are collected and made into a "book."	Teacher-made materials	1. Relationship to child's experience is explicit 2. Approach firmly establishes reading as a language/communicative act 3. Approach provides no systematic skill development (left up to the teacher to improvise) 4. Approach can reinforce only at child's existing level, rather than pushing him or her on 5. Usage is highly adaptable to pupils with unique needs and backgrounds

Fernald, who opened a clinic school at UCLA in 1920, was concerned with the emotional components of failure to learn. She felt that the child who fails in his or her school work is always an emotional problem. The circular aspect of this dilemma was approached in two ways: by analyzing the problem and by reconditioning the student. Both are positive approaches to remediation that call the learner's attention to what he or she has already learned and assure the student that one can learn any words that one wants to learn. To maintain a positive learning climate, the teacher avoids the following: (1) emotionally laden situations, (2) the use of methods associated with previous failure, (3) embarrassing situations, and (4) references to the learner's problems. Poor readers are divided into two groups: total or extreme disability, and partial disability. The VAKT method is used with children from both groups when the disability is failure to recognize words.

Perception of the word as a whole is basic to the Fernald method. For example, Sara begins remediation by story writing, initially about anything of interest, and later concerning her various school subjects. Sara "asks" for any word she does not know. It is written for her, learned by her, and used immediately in her story. What she has written is typed so that she may read it while its content is still fresh in her mind. For children with extreme disability, almost every word is necessarily taught.

Stage I uses a multisensory approach. When Sara requests a word, it is written or printed for her with black crayon in blackboard-size script on a piece of heavy paper. She traces the word with firm, two-finger contact (tactile–kinesthetic), and says the word aloud in syllables (auditory) as she traces. She sees the word while she is tracing (visual), and hears it as she says it (auditory). She repeats the process until she can write the word correctly twice, without looking at the sample. When tracing or writing, she always writes the word as a unit, without stopping. If she errs, Sara begins again with the first step. Copying a word by alternately looking at the sample and writing a few letters is forbidden. After the lesson, the words are filed alphabetically, to provide a record or source of the words learned.

After a period of tracing, the tactile phase is discontinued and Stage II is begun. Here Sara learns a new word by following the looking, saying, and writing steps of Stage I. Vocabulary is still learned in context and involves VAKT. There is no arbitrary time limit for the tracing period, and usually the student tends to drop tracing of his or her own accord.

Stage III dispenses with the kinesthetic mode, and Sara learns a new word merely by looking at the sample and saying it to herself.

Stage IV is achieved when Sara has the ability to recognize new words by their similarity to words or to parts of words that she has already learned (i.e., when she can generalize her reading skills). Teaching phonics is not considered necessary, for this generalizing process presumably occurs without phonetic analysis. At this stage, the student reads to satisfy her curiosity.

The amount of reading necessary before discontinuing remediation and returning the student to the regular classroom reading situation depends on the educational level he or she must reach. Older students spend more time in Stage IV, and they do not return to the regular instructional setting until they are able to read well enough to make progress at their own instructional level.

In addition to those already stated, the Fernald method maintains several principles:

1. Students are never read to; they must do their own reading.

2. The student never sounds out words, unless he or she does it while scanning a paragraph for unknown words before beginning to read that paragraph.

3. At any stage, material must be suited to the child's age and intelligence.

Careful scheduling is important, as the teacher cannot plan to work with one child unless all of the other children are involved in some purposeful activity. The student's resentment at being taken away from gym or art also might outweigh any positive accomplishment. It should be emphasized that the Fernald approach (VAKT) is basically a word-learning technique, and the child should have directed reading instruction in a group, or individually, to develop comprehension skills. Although this approach has found wide use, research on multisensory reading methods has been mixed.

The Gillingham (Orton) Phonics Approach

This remedial, phonics-oriented reading program (Gillingham & Stillman, 1970) is based on the theoretical work of Orton (1989). The systematic approaches to reading, spelling, and writing are adapted to all levels from age 6 through high school. This "alphabetic system" is based on the premise that children who fail to read by group methods do so because group programs rely on visual-receptive strength. In contrast, Gillingham's training system stresses auditory discrimination abilities with supplementary emphasis on kinesthetic and tactile modalities. Although phonetic methods help the child to synthesize what he or she sees with what he or she hears, visual perception is used minimally.

Gillingham's synthetic approach is essentially a formal skill-building program. Teachers are encouraged to follow the manual to attain success. The entire program is built on eight basic linkages that form the association of auditory, visual, and kinesthetic stimuli. Once the student has mastered basic sound production, he or she is introduced to phonograms (one letter or a group of letters that represents a phonetic sound). Once the phonograms have been mastered, they are used in drill procedures.

The teaching procedure begins with the introduction of the short "a" sound plus several specified consonant sounds. When these have been learned by the method above, blending is begun. Several phonogram cards are placed side by side. Individual sounds are produced in succession and with increasing speed until a fluid rate is achieved. The day following the initiation of the blending procedure, word analysis begins. This is achieved on an auditory level with the teacher sounding the word, and the student identifying the letters he or she hears. This process leads directly to the simultaneous oral spelling process, in which the teacher says the word, the student says the word, names the letters, then writes the letters as he or she names them. This procedure is always used in the production of phonetically pure words.

One of the stipulations of the early program is that the student is given no other printed materials. If the student remains in a regular class while receiving remedial help, all other subject material must be presented auditorially. After blending has been established with all of the phonetic sounds, a reader or primer may be introduced. Books are carefully screened to ensure that all words included are phonetic and thus suitable for blending. The student is then introduced to basic phonetic rules, including syllabication and accent (all of which are included in the manual). When the student is able to synthesize and analyze any combination of phonetic syllables, nonphonetic syllables are introduced and memorized as whole syllables.

Gillingham's program for developing skills combines the use of phonetic study as well as experiences and language stories. Tracing, copying, and dictation are used simultaneously to achieve different purposes. Tracing is useful in learning the formation of letters and establishing a letter sequence for spelling. Copying develops visual memory; after practicing, the students must produce a model that has been removed from sight. The purpose of dictation is to lengthen the auditory attention span and promote the association between auditory stimuli and visual imagery.

Initially, Gillingham felt that students who were capable of learning by visual methods should do so. However, in "Correspondence" (1958), she noted the difficulties students have with spelling and concluded that the kinesthetic and auditory stimuli provided in her program would prevent such difficulties. Therefore, she advised that all students be exposed to the "Alphabetic System."

The success of this system seems dependent on its use with children whose auditory discrimination is unimpaired. It is essential that the student's strengths as well as weaknesses be diagnosed. To extend its effectiveness, meaningful interpretations and activities must be introduced despite the admonitions of Gillingham.

Criticisms of this approach center on the lack of meaningful activities, the rigidity of the teaching procedures, and the tendency to develop labored reading. If valid, these points would certainly limit the usefulness of the system as a total reading program. Even though this approach had been used for many years, little if any comparative research on it has been published.

Reading Mastery Program

The *Reading Mastery Program* (1988), formerly known as DISTAR, comprises six levels, each of which is appropriate for a different grade level between 1 and 6. Each level has different authors. The program is highly structured and was originally developed for young culturally disadvantaged children. It has since been revised and reorganized so as to be suitable for handicapped students from beginning to more advanced reading levels (six levels in all).

The program consists of lessons based on carefully sequenced skill hierarchies that entail the following:

1. The teacher uses games, flash cards, chalkboard, wall charts, and so forth, to present a fully scripted lesson.

2. The students (individually and in unison as a group) provide the desired response.

3. Correct responses are immediately reinforced by the teacher.

4. Additional skill practice is provided.

5. The teacher evaluates the degree of mastery of individuals and the group on criterion-referenced tasks and tests.

6. Children are regrouped as necessary, depending on their performance.

The companion *Corrective Reading Program* is designed for older students who have not yet learned to read. It consists of two strands: decoding, which follows the regular Reading Mastery format, and comprehension, which presents real-life situations for adolescents.

Direct Instruction: Reading (Carnine & Silbert, 1990) has been more intensively researched than most curricular approaches. Where desired outcomes involve specific skills, this approach has been found to be successful, particularly with low-ability students. *Direct Instruction* has not been as successful where desired outcomes were of a more complex nature.

The Edmark Reading Program

The Edmark program (Bijou, 1993) was designed especially for lower functioning handicapped students for whom full adult literacy might not be a reasonable goal. It is designed to teach a survival sight vocabulary of 150 functional words. The program consists of several hundred lessons that use stories and student activities. The emphasis is on word recognition and word comprehension rather than on sentences. Readers who want a complete description of the program are referred to V. L. Brown's (1984a) comprehensive review.

Examples of Specific Remedial Techniques in Reading

The following list of remedial techniques can aid the teacher in helping certain students overcome specific difficulties in reading. The teacher should carefully file remedial activities so that they can be used again and again. In a few years, it is possible to collect a significant number of specific exercises that can be used for individual follow-up to a group reading lesson.

Problems with General Word Recognition (Basic Sight Vocabulary)

1. *The picture dictionary.* The student makes a scrapbook that is indexed with the letters of the alphabet. Pictures can be drawn or cut out of magazines. As the student learns a word, he or she pastes a picture on the page that has that letter. For example, the word *car* would go on the C page. This has advantages over commercial picture dictionaries because it contains the words that the student is learning and because the student makes it. It is most useful with nouns.

2. *Picture cards and tracing.* On one side of the card, a picture is placed with a word underneath it; on the other side, the word is printed (see example below). The teacher presents the card with the word and picture side up and pronounces the word. Next the student pronounces the word. Then the student pronounces and traces the word until he or she can recognize the word without seeing the picture. The words can be reviewed from time to time and used as an independent drill. This procedure is most useful with nouns.

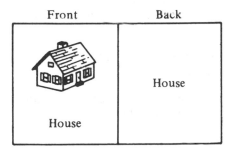

3. *Matching words with pictures.* This exercise can be used with words other than nouns. For example, a clear picture of a child running can be used to help teach the word *run*. On the back of the card, the picture is reproduced. The student is given three words and must match the word and the picture.

4. *Labeling.* Labels can be attached to the door, closet, window, pictures, bulletin board, and other things in the room so that the student will begin to associate the written symbol with the object.

5. *Tachistoscope.* To make a tachistoscope, the teacher can cut a piece of oaktag or cardboard to a 5-inch × 8-inch size. The top and bottom are folded down about $\frac{1}{2}$ inch to hold the word cards. A window is cut in the center to expose the word and a shutter is attached to the outside. Word cards can be made with basic sight vocabulary words on them. These can be flashed by quickly opening the shutter. If the student misses a word, it can be reexposed so that the student will be able to apply word-attack skills.

6. *Phrase cards.* Short phrases, then longer phrases should be introduced. These can be used in the tachistoscope exercise.

Problems with Word Reversals

1. The word is printed on a 5-inch × 8-inch card in crayon. The pupil is asked to say the word, trace it, and say it again. The student should do this a number of times and then be given an opportunity to read it in a sentence.

2. The teacher can hold up a card that is covered with a sheet of paper. The sheet of paper is then moved to the right so that the letters are exposed in the proper sequence.

3. The teacher can use a card with the word printed on it and the first letter lightly colored.

4. The teacher can place some design (e.g., a diamond) to call the student's attention to the first letter.

Problems with Letter Reversals

1. The letter should be placed on a 3-inch × 5-inch card. The student should first trace it until he or she is ready to write it correctly, and then practice writing it. This can also be done at the chalkboard.

2. Pictures can be used to illustrate words that begin with the letters the child reverses. For example, for the letters *b* and *d,* pictures of a boat and a duck can be used. The picture of the duck would be placed to the left of the *d.* The picture of the boat would be placed next to the lower part of the *b* and to the right of it.

3. Stories may be used to differentiate letters frequently reversed:

This is *b*

b is on the line

b is tall like a building

b looks to the right.

Problems with Initial Sounds

Note: Teacher's manuals of readiness and primary-level reading books may have more suggestions.

1. The teacher can dictate a series of three or four words that begin with the same sound. The student writes the letter that represents the initial sound.

2. On 3-inch × 5-inch index cards, the teacher places a letter on the left side and three or four phonograms on the right. The student is asked to give the initial sound and then the whole word.

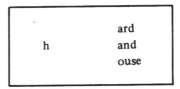

3. *Picture dictionary.* See Item 1 under "Problems with General Word Recognition."

4. *Rotating wheel.* Two cardboard circles, one smaller than the other, can be fastened together so that they rotate freely. Common phonographs are placed on the larger wheel; initial consonants are placed on the smaller one. As the larger circle is rotated, initial consonants can be combined with phonograms.

Problems with Final Sounds

Note: Teacher's manuals from linguistically based reading series have many suggestions for developing this skill.

1. A rhyming book can be made to illustrate word families.

2. The teacher asks the student to give a rhyming word for the one the teacher has just pronounced. These can be placed on the chalkboard and the parts that sound alike can be underlined.

3. Cards can be made with an initial consonant on the left and an ending on the right. The student blends the initial sound with the ending to make new words.

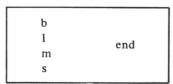

Problems with Medial Vowel Sounds

1. Practice exercises should be developed to make the student focus attention on the medial vowel sound in the word. For example:

   a. The cat sat on a (rig, rog, rug).

   b. The cat sat on a r__g.

2. Key cards can be made with the vowel colored to call attention to the sound

   b*a*t   b*e*t   b*i*t   b*o*t   b*u*t

   (Because "bot" is a nonsense word, the student may remember it for its uniqueness.)

Problems with Endings

Three columns of words can be placed on cards (or the chalkboard), and the student asked to select the one that has a different ending from the other two.

Problems with Context Clues

1. This teaches the student to anticipate meanings. If a new word, such as *toys,* is to be introduced, the teacher writes a sentence such as "Jim saw many _____ in the window of the store." The student is asked what Jim might have seen that starts with a *t*. (The teacher should read the sentence and have the student simply respond with the word *toys.*)

2. The teacher writes a sentence on the chalkboard containing only one word that the student does not recognize but can infer through the context.

   We ride to school on a (bus).

   At night I go to (bed).

   The student is asked to read the sentence silently. When the student has read it, the teacher asks if he or she knows what the last word is. If the student is having difficulty, further questions can be structured until he or she can infer the right word.

3. Sentences can be constructed with a number of choices. The student underlines the correct one to complete the sentence.

   Mary is wearing a new

   dress.

bless.

class.

4. The teacher or the students make up riddles. These can be put on spirit-duplicating masters or on the chalkboard. The students must infer each answer from the context.

I carry my home. I like to live in water. I am in this room. What am I?

Problems with Letter Discrimination

The teacher places a list of words on the chalkboard and the student underlines the words that begin with the same letter as the first one.

put	*hat*
porch	hold
ball	hot
pot	pot
doll	fat
pass	have

Problems with Phonemic and Word Discrimination

1. The teacher says that he or she is going to read a list of words. Most of them will begin alike (e.g., *bat, boat*). Every time the student hears a word that does not begin like boat, he or she should clap hands.

2. The student is told to shut his or her eyes. Pairs of words are read, and the student must tell if they sound exactly alike or are different.

3. Step 2 is followed with exercises on beginning sounds.

4. Step 2 is followed with exercises on final sounds.

5. The teacher pronounces a word and its beginning sound. The student is asked to give some more words that begin with the same beginning sound.

6. Step 5 is followed with exercises on ending sounds.

Problems with Compound Words

1. The student is given a list of compound words to separate.

2. The teacher gives the student two lists of words and asks him or her to draw lines from the left column to the right to make compound words.

Problems with Root Words

1. The teacher presents a list of words with variant endings and the student circles each root word.

2. The teacher presents the student with a list of words and a list of endings. The student is asked to make up as many *real* words as he or she can using the endings.

Problems with Suffixes

The teacher writes a sentence on the chalkboard with a derived form of a word in it. The student finds the root word and then explains how the suffix alters the meaning of the root word or what the meaning of the suffix is.

1. The teacher should start with words that do not change their spelling when a suffix is added.

2. Spelling variations can be introduced one at a time, with practice provided before another one is added.

Problems with Prefixes

1. The teacher writes sentences on the chalkboard that contain words with prefixes. The student is asked to locate each root word. The student then explains what each new word means.

2. The teacher writes sentences on the chalkboard. Each sentence is written twice, but in the second one space is left for a prefix on one word. The student is asked to think of a prefix that can be added to make the sentence mean the opposite.

> Jim locked the door.
>
> Jim ___locked the door.

Problems with Vocabulary Development

1. The teacher should use any opportunities to introduce new words in discussion and call attention to them—for example, "The sign over the main door of the school says 'exit.' What do you think it means?"

2. A modified crossword puzzle can be developed. For early grades, the first letter should be given.

3. Students can develop their own crossword puzzles.

4. The students can be asked to give words that they associate with the stimulus word (e.g., *volcano:* hot, lava, mountain, etc.). The relationships among the words given are then discussed.

Problems with Classification

1. The teacher prepares a list of words that can be separated into general classifications and asks the student to group them, e.g., *vegeta-*

bles—house—transportation: carrot, floor, car, airplane, tomato, helicopter, door, potato, train.

2. Lists of three or more words can be prepared. The student crosses out the one that does not belong.

Problems with Sequence

1. The teacher can cut up or draw a series of pictures that make a complete story when arranged in the proper sequence. The student arranges the pictures.

2. Strips of paper can be made with a single sentence on each. The student arranges them to tell a complete story.

3. The teacher writes out directions for making something in a scrambled order. The student numbers the steps in the order in which they should happen.

4. Comic strips can be cut apart; the student puts them back together in appropriate sequence.

Problems with Following Directions

1. The student is given a picture with specific directions as to how it should be colored and then completes it.

2. The teacher gives a student a series of oral directions and asks him or her to carry them out in the order in which they were given. Directions should be simple at the start and gradually become more complex.

Problems with Main Ideas

1. After reading the students a short story, the teacher writes a list of phrases on the chalkboard. Students are asked to choose the one that best tells the main idea. (In some cases, the phrases must be read to the students.)

2. The teacher reads a story to the students and asks them to make up a title and tell why it is a good one.

3. Exercises similar to 1 and 2 above can be done but with the student reading the story and completing the exercise independently.

4. Older students may be asked to choose details from the story that support the main idea. Diagrams may be used to represent this:

    Main Idea
    Early humans discovered fire in different forms.

    Supporting Details

lightning	hot lava of volcanoes	spark from stones rubbed together

Problems with Cause–Effect

1. The teacher performs actions, such as turning the light switch off. Students are asked what happened and why to establish the cause–effect relationship.

2. As part of a story activity, the teacher reads a causal statement and asks the students to give the effect.

3. The student is asked to match causes with effects.

Problems with Comparison/Contrast

1. After a student is shown two pictures that have some similarities to each other, he or she tells how they are alike and different.

2. The teacher can explain how two characters in a story are alike or different.

3. Older students may make a comparison/contrast chart.

Chapter 4

Problems in Written Composition

DONALD D. HAMMILL

Writing is a highly complex method of expression involving the integration of eye–hand, linguistic, and conceptual abilities. Because of its complexity, it is one of the highest forms of communication and hence is usually the last to be mastered. As an expressive form of a graphic symbol system used for conveying thoughts, ideas, and feelings, writing may be considered "the other side of the coin" from reading, which is the receptive form of that system.

The term *writing* refers to a variety of interrelated graphic skills, including (1) *composition,* or the ability to generate ideas and to express them in an acceptable grammar, while adhering to certain stylistic conventions; (2) *spelling,* or the ability to use letters to construct words in accordance with accepted usage; and (3) *handwriting,* or the ability to execute physically the graphic marks necessary to produce legible compositions or messages. For convenience, in this book we have arbitrarily divided the material on writing into three chapters. The first of these chapters deals with problems relating to composition; the next chapter handles spelling difficulties; and the third chapter discusses the problems of legibility. The present chapter, then, discusses the major elements that comprise written composition, the stages involved in the writing act, means by which composition can be assessed, and instructional considerations and practices for improving ability in this important skill.

THE MAJOR ELEMENTS IN WRITTEN COMPOSITION

Written composition includes at least three interrelated elements: a cognitive component, a linguistic component, and a stylistic component. When these are combined with two additional elements, handwriting and spelling, the result is the comprehensive concept of the entire writing process. A brief description of each of the components involved in composition follows.

Cognitive Component

The cognitive component refers to the ability to generate logical, coherent, and sequenced written products. The actual piece may be a creative story, a personal or professional letter, an essay, or a factual accounting of events; however, regardless of its content, the passage must be formulated in such a way that it is readily understandable to a reader. Maturity in a written product is usually signaled by the use of titles, paragraphs, definite endings, character development, dialogue, or humor, or the expression of some philosophical or moral theme. The cognitive component is not as easily defined as are the other components, but a product that is immature in its development of expression is frequently "sloppy" in the presentation of ideas, disjointed in thought sequence, lacking in theme, or simply difficult to understand. Because the cognitive aspects of writing are often vague and subjective, teachers have tended to overlook this aspect of writing. This is regrettable, for if a person does not write conceptually, effective written communication is virtually impossible.

Linguistic Component

The linguistic component refers to the use of serviceable syntactic and semantic structures. The selection of suitable words, tenses, plurals, subject–verb correspondences, and cases is essential to good writing. Particular vocabulary items and grammatical forms will vary somewhat from person to person, social class to social class, geographical area to geographical area, and ethnic group to ethnic group. In most cases, the particular grammars and vocabularies employed by different individuals are equally efficient in conveying a writer's meaning. For example, one person may write "I grew a lot this year," while another might write "I growed a lot this year." Even though the two individuals are using different grammatical rules in expressing the past tense of "grow," the sentences that are generated convey identical thoughts. Linguistically speaking, neither rule is right or wrong. If some people consider one form to be "better" than another, the reasons are likely to be rooted in sociological factors and personal preference. However, if writers wish to be "accepted" by the majority of readers who encounter their passages, some standards of linguistic usage must be maintained.

Relative to this point, Otto and Smith (1980) identified five levels of English usage: the illiterate, the homely, the informal standard, the formal standard, and the literary. Illiterate usage, characteristic of individuals out of the cultural mainstream, is rarely accepted in the classroom and is targeted for correction (e.g., "he done," "didn't have no," "them books"). The homely level is more acceptable to most people than the illiterate but is not quite as acceptable as standard forms of English. These homely forms, often regional in nature, are usually tolerated but rarely sanctioned by the school (e.g., confusion between *lie* and *lay,* and *like* and *as if*). Informal standard English is the level of colloquial speech and writing used by most educated persons. It is employed in conversations and correspondence with friends and relatives but generally not with strangers or in formal situations. The grammatical forms characteristic of this level are intended for everyday use and are considered by most individuals to be both functional and acceptable. Otto and Smith suggested that this level should be the language of the classroom and the goal for most elementary students. The final two levels, formal standard English and the literary, are reserved for special occasions and purposes. Both are characterized by the absence of colloquial expressions, more than usual attention to the tone of the words, and agreement in number, tense, and case (e.g., "I *shall* be there"). The structure used at the literary level raises the use of the English language to an art form (e.g., "Fourscore and seven years ago . . ." [literary form] for "Eighty-seven years ago . . ." [informal standard form]).

Stylistic Component

The stylistic component refers to the use of "accepted" fashions or rules established for punctuation and capitalization. The rules governing punc-

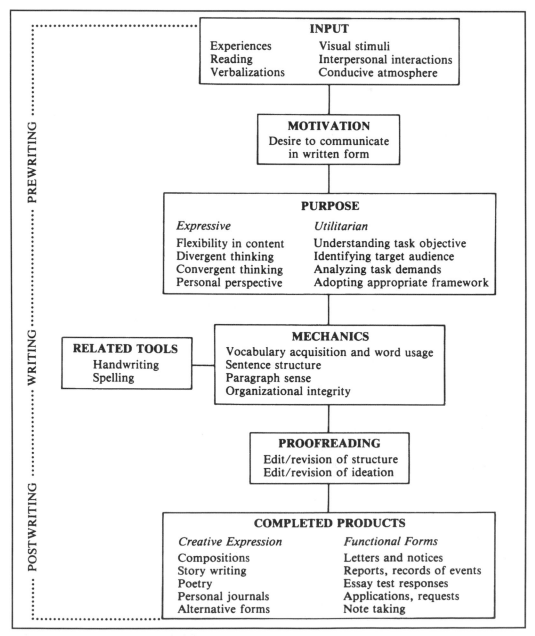

FIGURE 4.1. A model of written language.

From "Written Language for Mildly Handicapped Students" by E. A. Polloway, J. R. Patton, and S. B. Cohen, 1981, *Focus on Exceptional Children, 14*(3), p. 4.

tuation and capitalization must be learned by students before they can write effectively. In most instances, students quickly recognize that capital letters are used to give stress to words of special significance and that commas separate thoughts within a sentence.

Many of the rules governing the use of style are arbitrary in nature, based in tradition, and do not necessarily facilitate meaning. Consider, for example, the placement of the period in relation to the quotation marks in the following sentence: Mary said, "I saw the boy." Whether the period is placed inside or outside of the quotation marks does not affect the meaning of the sentence. Other rules, however, are essential to understanding the sense of sentences and passages. For example, the meaning of the sentence "In reading, comprehension will be impaired greatly by poor vocabulary development" is altered considerably if the comma is omitted. Without the comma between "reading" and "comprehension," the reader may mistakenly perceive "In reading comprehension" to be an introductory prepositional phrase and, as a consequence, stumble through the sentence.

Obviously, efficient and consistent use of the rules of punctuation and capitalization enhances the quality of a written product. In some instances, it is an absolute necessity for conveying the meaning of written communications.

Polloway, Patton, and Cohen (1981) positioned writing within a personal and social context. In their model (see Figure 4.1), the cognitive, linguistic, and stylistic elements are called *mechanics* and are but one aspect of a multifaceted writing experience involving prewriting and postwriting stages, as well as the writing act itself. This model has value for teachers because it focuses attention on the importance of considering the following factors before planning remedial programs: (1) the student's prior experiences, motivations, and needs; (2) the status of the student's current writing skills; and (3) the creative and functional products that are possible.

THE WRITING STAGES

In producing a written composition, individuals typically pass through several stages. These stages have been termed (a) *prewriting,* (b) *writing,* and (c) *postwriting* by Graves (1975) and Blake and Spennato (1980). This section, which discusses the stages of writing from the perspective of how the activities associated with each contribute to the completion of a written product, was originally included in Larsen's (1987) *Assessing the Writing Abilities and Instructional Needs of Students* (pp. 38–40).

Prewriting

During the prewriting stage, the writer selects a topic for the written piece, obtains information about the topic, and outlines information that will be discussed. The author also carefully considers the audience for which the writing is intended. A writer must imagine how another person will read and react to his or her piece as one step toward fully understanding how the message should be constructed.

Several activities help an individual in the prewriting stage. Blake and Spennato (1980) suggested that, once a topic is selected, relevant questions may be developed. For example, if Robert wishes to write about a football team, he might ask before he writes: (a) Who are the team's best players? (b) How many games have they won or lost? (c) What have been the most exciting episodes of the season? (d) Do any players have unusual habits or interesting "quirks"? and (e) Do they have a chance to win a championship? Having developed a list of questions, the writer can determine those having the greatest interest to the intended audience and those that will be included in the written product. Sequencing of the topics in a logical manner also greatly aids the readability of the written piece. Such activities are the heart of the prewriting phase and serve to facilitate the writing and postwriting phases.

Writing

During the writing stage, an author should be concerned primarily with meaning. In all likelihood, this stage will have many pauses—periods of rereading what has been written, interactions with others (verbal discussion of what is being written), consultations with additional resources such as encyclopedias, talking with oneself regarding the viability of what has been written and what is to be written, and reformulations of the ideas and organization of the topic under consideration.

As writers write, they begin to fully understand what must be written. During this phase, teachers must be willing to tolerate (and, in fact, encourage) crossed out words and sentences; incorrect spelling, punctuation, and capitalization; sentence fragments; and less than perfect handwriting. These characteristics of writing in progress are to be encouraged because they demonstrate that the student is actively reconceptualizing certain portions of the content and is willing to experiment with its form. Once the ideas have been adequately stated, supported, and organized, the piece can be polished and made to conform to literary standards.

Postwriting

Postwriting entails editing and revising a written product. During this stage, the completed passage is read by the writer, and the gaps within the presentation are identified. Where additional facts, details, or examples are needed, they are added. The main ideas of the composition, as well as those of individual passages, are clarified and relationships among them strengthened. Transitional phrases between paragraphs and sentences are added to aid readability. The writer should delete irrelevant material and correct errors in capitalization, punctuation, grammar, and spelling. This facet of the postwriting phase is called *copyediting*. Copyediting also involves rewriting awkward sentences and watching for inconsistencies.

Writers should solicit corrective feedback from others. In most cases, the individual providing the feedback will be a teacher, a parent, or an older student. Sometimes, the feedback will involve a few suggested corrections; in other cases, a complete rewriting of the piece will be recommended. The author should be helped to handle criticism objectively without feeling unduly shamed or frustrated. Suggestions for improvement should accompany feedback whenever possible.

Next, care is given to the handwriting or typewriting to effect a finished product. At the conclusion of the postwriting stage, the written piece is given to the intended reader.

Examples of the kinds of abilities that are associated with each writing stage are provided by G. Wallace, Cohen, and Polloway (1987) in Table 4.1. Study of the skills listed will help you to understand what is meant by the terms prewriting, writing, and postwriting.

TABLE 4.1. Abilities Associated with the Writing Stages

Prewriting

- Possesses the requisite experiential background
- Possesses the requisite oral receptive and expressive abilities
- Possesses the necessary rudimentary reading skills
- Writes (handwriting) legibly (or has developed requisite skill in alternative means)
- Has the desire to communicate in written form

Writing

- Writes simple phrases
- Writes simple sentences
- Writes compound and complex sentences
- Begins sentences with a capital letter
- Uses capital letters appropriately according to other rules
- Ends sentences with appropriate punctuation
- Uses punctuation marks appropriately according to other rules
- Demonstrates simple rules for sentences
- Demonstrates complex rules for sentences
- Identifies parts of speech
- Uses descriptive and varied vocabulary
- Writes complete paragraphs
- Writes notes and letters
- Expresses creative ideas in writing
- Takes effective lecture notes
- Responds accurately to essay exam questions

Postwriting

- Edits and revises for capitalization
- Edits and revises for punctuation
- Edits and revises for sentence structure
- Edits and revises for word usage
- Edits and revises for content and ideation
- Edits and revises for overall organization

From *Language Arts: Teaching Exceptional Students* (p. 307) by G. Wallace, S. B. Cohen, and E. A. Polloway, 1987, Austin, TX: PRO-ED. Copyright 1987 by PRO-ED, Inc. Reprinted with permission.

ASSESSING DIFFICULTIES IN WRITTEN COMPOSITION

Two important goals of assessment in written composition are to (1) identify individuals who are unable to write well enough to meet the minimum standards required for their personal daily needs and (2) inventory their specific instructional needs. To accomplish these goals, teachers must have mastered the informal and standardized techniques required to do an instructionally relevant evaluation. This section is devoted to discussion of these important topics.

Informal Assessment of Writing Skills

The teacher begins the written composition assessment by deciding which skills are to be evaluated and in what order they are to be assessed. Teachers will find these decisions easier to make if they have a scope-and-sequence chart such as the one in Table 4.2.

In this chart, the scope is represented by capitalization, punctuation, vocabulary, word usage, grammar, sentence construction, and paragraph construction. These are the major aspects in the writing curriculum. The specific skills and the order in which they are to be assessed (or taught) are covered in the sequence. In this case, the skills in the sequence are grouped according to grade levels.

The entries in the chart suggest the breadth of skills that can be assessed by the teacher but do not indicate the precise evaluation procedures to be used. For performing evaluations, teachers must rely on subjective interpretation of students' written work samples, on criterion-referenced tests that they have constructed for their own use, and on teacher-made checklists.

Consider the case of a second grader suspected of having a writing problem involving composition. If the individual conducting the evaluation were interested in the student's mastery of capitalization, he or she would first consult the chart to identify the capitalization forms that are characteristically taught in school between kindergarten and the end of the second grade. Examples of the student's written work could then be evaluated in terms of which forms have been acquired by the student, which forms have been insecurely mastered, and which forms are missing altogether. The main problem with the analysis of work samples is that the samples selected for evaluation may not adequately represent the student's writing weaknesses and strengths. For example, in executing spontaneous written products, such as essays or stories, some children write only sentences that contain the grammatical forms that they know how to use. Therefore, error analysis of their work may result in a distorted view of the skills that they have and have not acquired. Put another way, if error analysis is to work well, the writing assignments that are to be evaluated must include adequate opportunities for all types of errors to occur and to be observed. Because errors may or may not appear in spontaneously written products, the teacher may want to use additional procedures.

The teacher could generate a sentence that contains the particular element being evaluated (e.g., the capitalization of proper names, the use of a colon to separate the hour from minutes, the use of a comma to set off introductory clauses). Presumably, one or two sentences would be developed to correspond with each item on the chart. Next, the sentences would be typed so that the specific elements being tested were left unpunctuated (or punctuated incorrectly). The student would be asked to correct any errors that he or she recognized in the sentences. Example sentences might include the following:

1. The boy's name was bill.
2. School is out at 3 30.
3. After the movie was over Mary went to the store.

In the first sentence, students who strike out the "b" and replace it with a "B" are telling the teacher that they understand the capitalization rule that pertains to first names. Those who insert a semicolon after "Mary" on the third sentence, who see nothing wrong with the sentence, or who place a comma after "movie" are showing that they do not know how to apply the rule governing the punctuation of introductory clauses. The educational implications of the students' performance here are obvious—the students need to be taught the forms that they do not know and then given ample, meaningful opportunities to practice their newly acquired knowledge.

If this approach is attempted, the teacher needs to make sure that the vocabulary used in the sentences is well known to the students being evaluated. Students who do not understand the meaning of a written sentence certainly cannot be expected to punctuate it properly. If the teacher has any reason to suspect that students cannot read the sentence, the students should be asked to tell in their own words what the sentence means. If they are unable to do this, the sentence should be reworded using an appropriate vocabulary.

The teacher also will want to adhere very closely to the developmental sequence found in Table 4.2, for it indicates the order in which grammatical forms are usually taught in the schools. For example, with respect to the three sentences above, the table indicates that it is (1) during kindergarten and first grade that students learn that the first and last names of a person are capitalized, (2) during fifth grade that students learn that colons separate hours from minutes, and (3) between fourth and sixth grades that students learn that commas are used to set off an introductory clause. This information has relevance for teachers who must prepare special programs for individual students because it enables them to sequence both the goals that underlie training and the activities that are to be used to ameliorate deficiencies in the most desirable way.

TABLE 4.2. Scope and Sequence of Composition Skills

	GRADE 1	GRADE 2	GRADE 3
Capitalization	The first word of a sentence The child's first and last names The name of the teacher, school, town, street The word *I*	The date First and important words of titles of books Proper names Titles of compositions Titles: Mr., Ms., Miss	Proper names First word in a line of verse First and important words in titles of books, stories, etc. First word of salutation, such as *Dear* First word of closing, such as *Yours*
Punctuation	Period at the end of a sentence Period after numbers in any kind of list	Question mark Comma after salutation Comma after closing of a friendly note or letter Comma between the day of the month and the year Comma between the name of city and state	Period after abbreviations Period after an initial Use of an apostrophe in contractions such as *isn't, aren't* Commas in a list
Vocabulary	New words learned Choosing words that describe accurately Choosing words that make you see, hear, feel	Words with similar meanings; with opposite meanings Alphabetical order	Extending discussion of words for precise meanings Using synonyms Distinguishing meanings and spellings of homonyms Using the prefix *un* and the suffix *less*
Word Usage	*Generally in oral expression* Naming yourself last Eliminating unnecessary words (my father he) Using *well* and *good* Verb forms in sentences: 　is, are 　did, done 　was, were 　see, saw, seen 　ate, eaten 　etc.	*Generally in oral expression* Avoiding double negatives Using *a* and *an; may* and *can; teach* and *learn* Eliminating unnecessary words (this here) Verb forms in sentences: 　rode, ridden 　took, taken 　grow, grew, grown 　know, knew, known 　etc.	Using *there is* and *there are; any* and *no* Using *let* and *leave; don't* and *doesn't* Verb forms in sentences: 　throw, threw, thrown 　drive, drove, driven 　wrote, written 　tore, torn 　chose, chosen 　etc.

TABLE 4.2. *Continued*

GRADE 4	GRADE 5	GRADES 6, 7, AND 8
Names of cities and states Names of organizations, such as Boy Scouts, Grade Four, etc. Mother, Father, when used in place of the name Local geographical names	Names of streets Names of places, persons, countries, oceans, etc. Capitalization used in outlining Titles when used with names, such as President Lincoln Commercial trade names	First word of a quoted sentence Proper adjectives showing race, nationality, etc. Abbreviations of proper nouns and titles
Apostrophe to show possession Hyphen separating parts of a word divided at end of a line Period following a command Exclamation point Comma setting off an appositive Colon after the salutation of a business letter Quotation marks before and after a direct quotation Comma between explanatory words and a quotation	Colon in writing time Quotation marks around booklet title, pamphlet title, book chapter, and poem or story title Underlining book title Period after outline Roman numeral	Comma to set off nouns in direct address Hyphen in compound numbers Colon to set off a list Comma in sentences to aid in making meaning clear Comma after introductory clauses
Dividing words into syllables Using the accent mark Using exact words that appeal to the senses Using exact words in explanation Keeping individual lists of new words and meanings	Using antonyms Prefixes and suffixes Exactness in choice of words Dictionary work Contractions Rhyme and rhythm Classification of words by parts of speech Roots and words related to them Adjectives, nouns, verbs	Extending meanings In writing and speaking, selecting accurate words Selecting words for effectiveness and appropriateness Selecting words for courtesy Editing a paragraph to improve word choice
Agreement of subject and verb Using *she, he, I, we,* and *they* as subjects Using *bring* and *take* Verb forms in sentences: blow, blew, blown drink, drank, drunk lie, lay, lain take, took, taken rise, rose, risen teach, taught, taught etc.	Avoiding unnecessary pronouns (the boy he) Linking verbs and predicate nominatives Conjugation of verbs, to note changes in tense, person, number Transitive and intransitive verbs Verb forms in sentences: am, was, been say, said, said fall, fell, fallen etc.	Homonyms: *its, it's; their, there, they're; there's, theirs* Using parallel structure for parallel ideas, as in outlines Verb forms in sentences: beat, beat, beaten learn, learned, learned leave, left, left light, lit, lit forgot, forgotten etc.

(continues)

TABLE 4.2. *Continued*

GRADE 1	GRADE 2	GRADE 3
Grammar		
Not applicable	Not applicable	Nouns: recognition of singular, plural, and possessive Verbs: recognition
Sentences		
Writing simple sentences	Recognizing sentences, statement, and questions Composing correct and interesting sentences Avoiding running sentences together with *and*	Exclamatory sentences Using a variety of sentences Combining short, choppy sentences into longer ones Using interesting beginning and ending sentences Avoiding run-on sentences Proofreading sentences
Paragraphs		
Not applicable	Not applicable	Keeping to one idea Keeping sentences in order Deleting sentences that do not belong Indenting

TABLE 4.2. *Continued*

GRADE 4	GRADE 5	GRADES 6, 7, AND 8
Noun: common and proper; in complete subject Verb: in complete predicate Adjective: recognition Adverb: recognition (telling how, when, where); modifying verbs, adjectives, other adverbs Pronoun: recognition of singular and plural	Noun: possessive; object of preposition; predicate noun Verb: tense; agreement with subject; verbs of action and state of being Adjective: comparison; predicate adjective; proper adjective Adverb: comparison; words telling how, when, where, how much; modifying verbs, adjectives, adverbs Pronoun: possessive; object of preposition Preposition: recognition; prepositional phrases Conjunction: recognition Interjection: recognition	Noun: clauses; common and proper; indirect object Verb: conjugating to note changes in person, number, tense Adjective: clauses; demonstrative; descriptive; numerals; phrases Adverb: clauses; comparison; descriptive; *ly* ending; modification of adverbs Pronoun: antecedents; declension chart—person, gender, case; demonstrative; indefinite; interrogative; personal; relative Preposition: phrases Conjunction: in compound subjects and predicates; in subordinate and coordinate clauses Interjection: placement of in quotations
Using command sentences Complete and simple subject; complete and simple predicate Recognizing adjectives and adverbs; pronouns introduced Avoiding sentence fragments and a comma in place of a period Improving sentences in a paragraph	Using interesting sentences: declarative, interrogative, exclamatory, and imperative (*you* the subject) Agreement of subject and verb Compound subjects and predicates	Developing concise statements Indirect object and predicate nominative Complex sentences Clear thinking and expression
Selecting main topic Choosing title to express main idea Making simple outline with main idea Developing an interesting paragraph	Composing paragraphs Improving skill in writing a paragraph of several sentences Selecting subheads as well as main topic for an outline Courtesy in all communications Recognizing topic sentences Keeping to the topic as expressed in title and topic sentence Using more than one paragraph Developing a four-point outline Writing paragraphs from outline Using new paragraphs for new speakers in written conversation Keeping a list of books (authors and titles) used for reference	Analyzing a paragraph to note method of development Developing a paragraph in different ways (e.g., with details, reasons, or examples) Checking for accurate statements Using a fresh approach in expressing ideas Using transition words to connect ideas Using topic sentences Improving skill in complete composition—introduction, development, conclusion Checking for good reasoning Using bibliography in reports

Adapted from *Corrective and Remedial Teaching* by W. Otto and R. J. Smith, 1980, Boston: Houghton Mifflin, and from *Developing Language Skills in the Elementary School* by H. Greene and W. Petty, 1967, Boston: Allyn & Bacon.

The assessment of the content of a composition is more difficult, although the problems are hardly unsurmountable. The experienced teacher can probably read an essay and score it properly according to the criteria specified in the *Carlson Analytical Originality Scale* (Carlson, 1979) (see Table 4.3). This scale requires that the teacher rate the written content on five dimensions—story structure, novelty, emotion, individuality, and style.

TABLE 4.3. *Carlson Analytical Originality Scale* Scoring Key for Scoring Original Stories

Name of child _____   Name of teacher _____

Story type _____   Total score on scale _____

Scale Division A—Story Structure

1. Unusual title — 0 1 2 3 4 5
2. Unusual beginning — 0 1 2 3 4 5
3. Unusual dialogue — 0 1 2 3 4 5
4. Unusual ending — 0 1 2 3 4 5
5. Unusual plot — 0 1 2 3 4 5

Scale Division B—Novelty

6. Novelty of names — 0 1 2 3 4 5
7. Novelty of locale — 0 1 2 3 4 5
8. Unique punctuation and expressional devices — 0 1 2 3 4 5
9. New words — 0 1 2 3 4 5
10. Novelty of ideas — 0 1 2 3 4 5
11. Novel devices — 0 1 2 3 4 5
12. Novel theme — 0 1 2 3 4 5
13. Quantitative thinking — 0 1 2 3 4 5
14. New objects created — 0 1 2 3 4 5
15. Ingenuity in solving situations — 0 1 2 3 4 5
16. Recombination of ideas in unusual relationships — 0 1 2 3 4 5
17. Picturesque speech — 0 1 2 3 4 5
18. Humor — 0 1 2 3 4 5
19. Novelty of form — 0 1 2 3 4 5
20. Inclusion of readers — 0 1 2 3 4 5
21. Unusual related thinking — 0 1 2 3 4 5

Scale Division C—Emotion

22. Unusual ability to express emotional depth — 0 1 2 3 4 5
23. Unusual sincerity in expressing personal problems — 0 1 2 3 4 5
24. Unusual ability to identify self with feelings of others — 0 1 2 3 4 5
25. Unusual horror theme — 0 1 2 3 4 5

Scale Division D—Individuality

26. Unusual perceptive sensitivity (social and physical environment) — 0 1 2 3 4 5
27. Unique philosophical thinking — 0 1 2 3 4 5
28. Facility in beautiful writing — 0 1 2 3 4 5
29. Unusual personal experience — 0 1 2 3 4 5

Scale Division E—Style of Stories

30. Exaggerated tall tale — 0 1 2 3 4 5
31. Fairy tale type — 0 1 2 3 4 5
32. Fantasy-turnabout of characters — 0 1 2 3 4 5
33. Highly fantastic central idea of theme — 0 1 2 3 4 5
34. Fantastic creatures, objects, or persons — 0 1 2 3 4 5
35. Personal experience — 0 1 2 3 4 5
36. Individual story style — 0 1 2 3 4 5

From *Sparkling Words: Two Hundred Practical and Creative Writing Ideas* by R. K. Carlson, 1976, Geneva, IL: Paladin House Publishers.

Of course, because the ratings are subjective, they are only as good as the talent and experience of the individual doing the evaluation. Therefore, a few precautions should be taken to minimize the evaluator's subjectivity and to increase his or her reliability. Whoever is designated to evaluate the quality of the ideas expressed in students' written work should possess a set of "internalized norms." This can be done by standardizing the topics of the written pieces that are to be assessed. For example, if the examiner is called upon most often to assess the work of students in Grades 3 through 6, he or she should select three topics (e.g., "My Favorite Television Show," "The Place I'd Most Like to Visit," "The Person I Admire Most") and have a sample of 10 to 20 representative students at each grade level write a short composition on each topic. Reading approximately 60 essays all on the same topic will usually equip the examiner with a better-than-intuitive knowledge of what constitutes average, below-average, and above-average quality with regard to a given topic and will probably enable the examiner to complete Carlson's scale items with greater accuracy.

Norm-Referenced Tests of Writing

In addition to informal procedures, teachers can use standardized tests to measure written composition. Almost all achievement test batteries commonly used in the schools today include at least one subtest that measures some aspect of composition (e.g., *Comprehensive Test of Basic Skills,* 1990; *California Achievement Tests,* 1992; *Metropolitan Achievement Test,* 1992). These tests are helpful in screening but have limited diagnostic or instructional value. For the most part, they test only word usage ability (grammar) and do this using contrived (unnatural) testing formats. They do not involve the analysis of students' spontaneously composed stories.

The *Test of Written Language, Second Edition* (TOWL-2) (Hammill & Larsen, 1988) can be used to document the presence or absence of appreciable writing problems in students, determine the conditions under which they write better and worse, and identify gross areas of difficulty. The TOWL-2 was normed on a 16-state sample of 2,216 school-age students attending Grades 2 through 12. Normative data are available for students between the ages of 7-6 and 17-11.

The battery's 10 subtests are grouped into two parts: contrived subtests and spontaneous subtests. The contrived subtests measure writing within traditional test formats. The scores for the spontaneous subtests are derived by evaluating samples of students' writing done in response to one of two pictures. (See Figure 4.2 for a sample Profile/Story Scoring Form.)

A description of each TOWL-2 subtest is given below. With the exception of Subtests 2 and 9, which measure spelling, all the subtests measure various aspects of composition.

Subtest 1: Vocabulary.   The student writes a sentence that incorporates a stimulus word. Example: *ran* is the stimulus for "I ran to the store."

TOWL-2

Test of Written Language

Form A ☑ B ☐

PROFILE/STORY SCORING FORM

Donald D. Hammill & Stephen C. Larsen

IDENTIFYING INFORMATION

Name Floyd   Male ✓ Female _____

	Year	Month	Day
Date Tested	88	9	25
Date of Birth	74	3	4
Age	14	6	21

School Harris   Grade 8th

Examiner's name M. Cronin

Examiner's title Educ. Diagnostician

SECTION I RECORD OF SUBTEST SCORES

Subtests	Raw Scores	%iles	Std. Scores
I Vocabulary	7	5	5
II Spelling	3	2	4
III Style	2	2	4
IV Logical Sentences	2	2	4
V Sentence Combining	0	9	6
VI Thematic Maturity	6	25	8
VII Contextual Vocabulary	11	16	7
VIII Syntactic Maturity	110	25	8
IX Contextual Spelling	71	5	5
X Contextual Style	3	9	6

SECTION II RECORD OF OTHER TEST SCORES

Name	Date	Std. Score	TOWL-2 Equiv.
1 Slosson Int. Test	8-88	86	86
2 Test of Non Verb Int	88-6	94	94
3 Reading CTBS		3	85
4 Language CTBS		2	77
5 Math CTBS		4	92
6			
7			
8			
9			
10			

SECTION III COMPUTATION OF COMPOSITE SCORES

TOWL-2 COMPOSITES	STANDARD SCORES										SUM OF STD. SCORES	QUOTIENTS
	VO	SP	ST	LS	SC	TM	CV	SM	CSp	CSt		
Contrived Writing	5	4	4	4	6						= 23	(63)
Spontaneous Writing						8	7	8	5	6	= 34	(78)
Overall Written Language	5	4	4	4	6	8	7	8	5	6	= 57	(69)

FIGURE 4.2. A Sample *Test of Written Language–2* Profile/Story Scoring Form.

From *The Test of Written Language–2* by D. D. Hammill and S. Larsen, 1988, Austin, TX: PRO-ED. Reprinted with permission.

Subtest 2: Spelling. The student writes sentences from dictation, taking particular care to make proper use of spelling rules.

Subtest 3: Style. The student writes sentences from dictation, taking particular care to make proper use of punctuation and capitalization rules.

Subtest 4: Logical Sentences. The student rewrites an illogical sentence so that it makes better sense. Example: "John blinked his nose" is rewritten as "John blinked his eye."

Subtest 5: Sentence Combining. The student integrates the meanings of several short sentences into one grammatically correct written sentence. Example: "John drives fast" and "John has a red car" are combined into the single sentence "John drives his red car fast."

Subtest 6: Thematic Maturity. The student writes a story in response to one of two stimulus pictures. Points are earned for each instance in which the student mentions a predetermined element in the story content.

Subtest 7: Contextual Vocabulary. The vocabulary level of the student's story is evaluated by applying the long unduplicated word method.

Subtest 8: Syntactic Maturity. The Syntactic Maturity score is the number of words used in the composition to form grammatically acceptable sentences.

Subtest 9: Contextual Spelling. The score for this subtest is the number of correctly spelled words in the story.

Subtest 10: Contextual Style. The student's story is scored for the number of instances in which different punctuation and capitalization rules are used.

Readers who desire a comprehensive discussion of writing assessment are referred to two prime sources: Hall's (1988) *Evaluating and Improving Written Expression: A Practical Guide for Teachers* and Larsen's (1987) *Assessing the Writing Abilities and Instructional Needs of Students.* These volumes together provide the reader with answers to theoretical questions relating to writing assessment and with good current practices in standardized and informal evaluation.

TEACHING WRITTEN COMPOSITION

This four-part section focuses on how problem learners are taught writing. The first part provides the reader with important general considerations in teaching composition; the second part describes the language-experience approach; the third part outlines the kinds of remedial activities that can be used; and the fourth part describes commercially available teaching packages.

Considerations for Composition Instruction

Composition refers to the syntactic and semantic aspects of a student's written product. Skill in composition is manifested in the ability to capitalize and punctuate, to use vocabulary and grammatical forms, and to construct sentences and paragraphs. Obviously, a certain level of competence in all these abilities is essential if a student is to use writing as a means of self-expression. Before attempting to remedy problems in any of these areas, teachers must first be aware of (1) the goals of individualized instruction in writing, (2) the best time to begin teaching composition, (3) the scope and sequence of the specific skills to be taught, and (4) a framework for developing writing programs.

Goals of Individualized Instruction

The goals of instruction in composition are threefold. The first goal is to teach students the minimum competencies needed to succeed in the school curriculum. The second goal is to instruct them in those forms of writing required for success outside the school (letter writing, completion of forms, note taking, etc.). The third goal is to teach them to express their creativity in writing poetry, fantasies, and stories. Each of these goals is important, and the teacher should keep them all in mind when planning an intervention program for a particular student.

The Start of Instruction in Writing

Barenbaum (1983) overviewed a continuing controversy about when writing instruction should begin. In this dispute, the conventional wisdom and the research literature are at odds. Most school programs in language arts are based on the idea that listening and speaking abilities are taught first, reading next, and writing last. Emig (1977), however, pointed out that this sequence is not necessary and perhaps not even desirable.

The notion that writing should follow reading is challenged strongly by numerous researchers, including Britton (1978), Graves (1978), and Moffett (1973). Chomsky (1971) even suggested that writing naturally precedes reading. Given the state of the literature on this matter, it seems safe to conclude that writing should be taught simultaneously with reading, from the beginning of a student's school experience.

Scope and Sequence for Skills in Written Composition

In teaching written expression, the teacher must understand the theoretical basis and the specific sequence of skills that make up the instructional program to be used. The teacher can use this information as a guide for assessing a student's strengths and weaknesses in that program and also as a framework for planning short- and long-term objectives. The easiest way to obtain the needed knowledge about a particular approach is to prepare and study a scope-and-sequence chart in which the skills and conceptual ideas incorporated in the program are depicted. Fortunately, the authors of many programs provide teachers with scope-and-sequence data for their materials.

The theoretical constructs (i.e., the major aspects of the curriculum) are represented in the scope of the chart, and the skills of a particular construct and the order in which they are to be taught are displayed in the sequence. An example of a scope-and-sequence chart that is useful for assessment and remedial purposes in writing was presented in Table 4.2. This chart serves as a guide for identifying the skills that need to be taught, for deciding the order in which the skills are to be introduced, for recording an individual's progress, and for facilitating systematic instruction. The procedures for using a scope-and-sequence chart to assess skills in writing have already been described.

A Framework for Developing Writing Programs

Although important, knowledge of appropriate goals, starting points, and the scope and sequence of skills is an insufficient basis for planning instructional programs in writing. One must also have a conceptual framework around which to build goals, content, exercises, strategies, and other curricular activities.

Graham and Harris (1988) made 10 recommendations that should be considered in developing writing programs for students who have special needs. They asserted that these recommendations "are based on recent conceptualizations of the process of writing, principles of effective writing instruction, and current knowledge of exceptional students' writing abilities" (p. 506). Be this as it may, the recommendations do have a ring of common sense about them and provide the necessary framework for individualized composition instruction programs. They are listed below.

1. *Allocate time for writing instruction.* Have students write at least four times a week. Take care to provide sufficient motivation and guidance.

2. *Expose students to a broad range of writing tasks.* Vary tasks so that students have opportunities to persuade, inform, and entertain their readers. Emphasize purposeful writing.

3. *Create a social climate conducive to writing development.* Establish and maintain a classroom environment that is supportive, pleasant, and nonthreatening. Where possible, students should write collaboratively (e.g., a class newspaper).

4. *Integrate writing with other academic subjects.* If an essay is to be written on a topic, prior discussions and selected readings related to that topic can enhance the quality of the essay.

5. *Help students develop the processes that are central to effective writing.* Teach students the basic ideas behind the above-mentioned prewriting, writing, and postwriting stages, which are so popular in today's composition classes.

6. *Automatize skills for getting language onto paper.* Often weaknesses in spelling, style (capitalization and punctuation), and sentence construction inhibit a student's desire to write. Circumvent the problem by instructing the student to disregard such elements during writing.

7. *Help students develop explicit knowledge about the characteristics of good writing.* Teach students to evaluate the quality of their written work.

8. *Help students develop the skills to carry out more sophisticated composing processes.* The purpose here is to extend students' abilities. This can be accomplished by teacher–student content conferencing, outlining of basic ideas, and so forth.

9. *Assist students in the development of goals for improving their written products.* After each writing task is completed, have students evaluate their work and set goals for improvement.

10. *Avoid instructional practices that do not improve students' writing performance.* Pinpoint only a few errors at a time for correction. Emphasize those errors that obstruct a reader's comprehension of the text.

The Language-Experience Approach to Teaching Composition

In general, teachers usually use a variation of the language-experience approach to teach conceptual writing. With this technique, the teacher's knowledge of a particular youngster's background and interests serves as the basis of instruction. The teacher begins by recording a student's verbal description of objects and events on a chart or board. Contents of the chart are discussed with the student, and his or her attention is directed to the various mechanical and compositional aspects of written expression, as well as to the relationships existing between the student's experiences and both oral and written language. Gradually, the student assumes more and more responsibility for the writing of personal expressions. At first, the student is asked to write only those words that the teacher knows are well within his or her speaking vocabulary. Eventually, the student is asked to write complete compositions reflecting thoughts about some interesting topic or experience. The theme of these essays can be provided by the teacher or, as is more often the case, by the student.

At all times, the student is encouraged to write creatively; the emphasis of instruction is always on the quality of ideas expressed and on motivation for writing. In time, the more mechanical and rule-governed aspects of writing are introduced, but care is taken to make sure that the increased curricular focus on these skills does not interfere with the student's desire to write creatively. This approach to the teaching of conceptual writing is most effective when it is integrated with the teaching of other areas in the language arts curriculum (reading, spelling, penmanship, etc.).

Proofreading, the reading of a written product for the purpose of identifying errors, is an integral part of all approaches to teaching composition, including the language-experience method. Students are usually taught to proofread soon after they begin to read and write original compositions. Students can proofread their own work, the work of other pupils, or special pieces containing selected errors that have been composed by the teacher. Regardless of the material to be proofread, students will find the following questions designed by P. C. Burns and Broman (1983, p. 232) to be helpful guides to developing proofreading ability.[1]

1. As the teacher (or another pupil) reads the sentence, listen and look at each group of words to be sure it is a good sentence. Make sure that you have no run-on sentences.

2. Listen and look for mistakes in punctuation. Be sure that you have put in punctuation marks only where they are needed. Did you end sentences with the mark required?

3. Listen and look for mistakes in word usage. Be sure that you have said what you mean and that each word is used correctly. Is there any incorrect verb or pronoun usage?

4. Look for mistakes in capitalization. Did you capitalize the first word and all important words in the title? Did you begin each sentence with a capital letter?

5. Look for misspelled words. Use the dictionary to check the spelling of any word about which you are not sure.

6. Check legibility of writing and items such as margins, title, indents, and so on.

Specific Remedial Activities in Writing

Once a suitable scope-and-sequence chart has been developed and a student's skill deficiencies have been identified, the teacher is ready to choose instructional activities that are appropriate to the student's needs and situation. The activities described in this section are examples of those used to teach punctuation, capitalization, vocabulary, word usage, grammar, and sentence and paragraph construction. When applied to students with problems in writing, these activities should be used in conjunction with the language-experience approach discussed earlier.

Punctuation and Capitalization

The strategies for teaching punctuation and capitalization are basically similar. For example, to teach skills in either area, the teacher (1) uses the language-experience approach to collect passages of the student's

---

1. From *The Language Arts in Childhood Education* (5th ed., p. 232) by P. C. Burns and B. L. Broman, 1983, Boston: Houghton Mifflin. Copyright 1983 by Houghton Mifflin Company.

written work, (2) calls attention to each place in the essay where punctuation or capitalization is required, (3) discusses the need to use the skill to enhance meaning, (4) shows how to use the required skill properly, (5) provides activities for practice, and (6) arranges an opportunity for the student to demonstrate competence in spontaneous writing. To facilitate instruction in punctuation and capitalization, the teacher may want to use variations of the following activities. For example, students can

1. Match items on a list of punctuation marks with possible functions (stop, yield, etc.). *Examples:* period = stop; comma = yield.

2. Punctuate and/or capitalize written passages. *Example:* billys cat was lost but it was found quickly.

3. Proofread the work of their classmates and underline possible errors. The papers can be returned to the classmates for correction, or the students who did the proofreading may correct the errors.

4. Write passages dictated by the teacher. The sentences dictated should involve various examples of punctuation and capitalization.

5. Be taught to listen for drops in the teacher's voice when he or she is dictating. These drops indicate the end of a sentence or the need for a comma. Young students can clap their hands when they recognize a point where a punctuation mark should be placed.

6. Be asked to write sentences demonstrating a particular kind of form. *Example:* Write a sentence as if you were talking to Mr. Smith (quotation marks).

Vocabulary, Word Usage, and Grammar

The related areas of vocabulary, word usage, and grammar are often taught simultaneously. A student's vocabulary is the supply of words that he or she comprehends and uses in speaking and writing. The goal of vocabulary-development activities is to increase this supply of words in number and complexity. Word usage refers to the appropriateness of the student's selection of vocabulary in terms of accepted standards. Finally, grammar is the way in which words are structured or organized to form a complete thought. The following example illustrates these differentiations more clearly:

I am not going to school.	(The basic sentence)
I am not *attending* school.	(Improvement due to vocabulary)
I *ain't* going to school.	(Unacceptable usage—ain't)
I am going *not* to school.	(Incorrect organization of words—grammatical error)

When remediating vocabulary, word usage, and grammar, the teacher must account for the student's oral language and past experiences. In no instance should the teacher expect a student's written composition to reflect a vocabulary, a usage pattern, or a grammar that the child does not use in speaking. Therefore, the teacher must deal with these aspects of written expression to allow the student to use those forms with which he or she is familiar. For example, when experience charts are prepared, the student's own words and structure should be recorded. An attempt to remedy problems in written language must be preceded and accompanied by remediation in oral language.

The following list is an accumulation of suggested activities to increase *vocabulary* skills. They are drawn from P. C. Burns and Broman (1983), Otto and Smith (1980), and our own experience.

1. List on the board new words encountered in classroom and out-of-school activities.

2. Read stories, descriptions, poems, and other materials aloud to the students and follow up with group discussions.

3. Have a student go on "word hunts" outside the classroom. Most students will enjoy collecting words from billboards, warning signs, traffic signs, and so on. These words may be used as the student's weekly spelling list.

4. Discuss and use words appearing in reading material.

5. Let the student keep a list of words that he or she likes or wants to use. As an alternative, the student can write new words on an index card and file them with others in a "word box."

6. Make lists or charts of special-interest words, such as those related to football, television, and cooking.

7. Build words from root words by adding prefixes, suffixes, and so on.

8. List words that rhyme with others and discuss their meanings.

9. Suggest topics for written expression whereby students must employ the new vocabulary items.

10. Utilize word games, such as Scrabble.

11. Find synonyms and antonyms for new words.

12. Have students take turns bringing in new words for the day.

13. Use dictionary drills and emphasize proper use of reference books.

Teachers who want to remedy word-usage problems should attack only a few items at one time. The following list by Pooley (1960) includes word usage items that the teacher may target for remediation[2]:

1. The elimination of all baby-talk and "cute" expressions.

2. The correct uses in speech and writing of *I, me, he, him, she, her.*

---

2. From "Dare Schools Set a Standard in English Usage?" by R.C. Pooley, 1960, *English Journal, 49*, pp. 179-180. Copyright 1960 by the National Council of Teachers of English. Reprinted by permission of the publisher.

3. The correct uses of *is, are, was, were* with respect to number and tense.

4. Correct past tenses of common irregular verbs such as *saw, gave, took, brought, bought, stuck.*

5. Correct use of past participles of the same verbs and similar verbs after auxiliaries.

6. Elimination of the double negative: *we don't have no apples,* etc.

7. Elimination of analogical forms: *ain't, hisn, hern, ourn, theirselves,* etc.

8. Correct use of possessive pronouns: *my, mine, his, hers, theirs, ours.*

9. Mastery of the distinction between *its,* possessive pronoun, and *it's,* contraction of *it is.*

10. Placement of *have,* or its phonetic reduction to *v,* between *I* and a past participle.

11. Elimination of *them* as a demonstrative pronoun.

12. Elimination of *this here* and *that there.*

13. Mastery of use of *a* and *an* articles.

14. Correct use of personal pronouns in compound constructions: as subject (*Mary and I*), as object (*Mary and me*), as object of preposition (to *Mary and me*).

15. The use of *we* before an appositional noun when subject; *us* when object.

16. Correct number agreement with the phrases *there is, there are, there was, there were.*

17. Elimination of *he don't, she don't, it don't.*

18. Elimination of *learn* for *teach, leave* for *let.*

19. Elimination of pleonastic subjects: *my brother he; my mother she; that fellow he.*

20. Proper agreement in number with antecedent pronouns *one* and *anyone, everyone, each, no one.* With *everybody* and *none,* some tolerance of number seems acceptable now.

21. The use of *who* and *whom* as reference to persons (but note, *Who did he give it to?* is tolerated in all but very formal situations; in the latter, *To whom did he give it?* is preferable).

22. Accurate use of *said* in reporting the words of a speaker in the past.

23. Correction of *lay down* to *lie down.*

24. The distinction between *good* as adjective and *well* as adverb, e.g., *He spoke well.*

25. Elimination of *can't hardly, all the farther* (for *as far as*), and *Where is he (she, it) at?*

The teacher can utilize this list in targeting the particular usages to be attacked.

The most important factor in correcting word usage and grammatical errors is to provide ample opportunity for the student to utilize the correct forms in oral expression. The following list provides some suggested activities to increase efficiency in word usage:

1. Provide frequent opportunities for practice. Repetition should be emphasized.

2. Utilize the tape recorder in oral language activities.

3. Provide usage activities throughout the day, not only during a language time.

4. Rephrase students' incorrect usage in situations where correction will not prove embarrassing.

5. Have students clap or otherwise indicate when they hear a usage error in a selection.

6. Give students opportunities to mark incorrect usage in written expressive tasks.

7. Play games involving substitution of correct usage for incorrect usage in sentences.

8. Dramatize characters in plays utilizing different usage forms.

9. Attend primarily to those usage forms that are most socially unaccepted.

Grammar can be enhanced through most of the approaches mentioned for vocabulary and word usage. Initial instruction in the various grammatical structures is best provided through oral and written examples and repetition. After giving instruction in the simple sentences and questions using noun + verb, noun + verb + noun, and other simple constructions, the teacher will want to include instruction, group activities, and games that involve experimentation with noun and verb phrases and, later, clauses. For example,

The dog ran.

The big dog ran.

The big gray dog ran.

The big gray and white dog with a red collar . . .

. . . ran over the hill.

. . . ran over the green hill toward them.

Exercises such as these can be extended by incorporating new vocabulary.

P. C. Burns, Broman, and Wantling (1971, p. 21) provided the following 12 examples of how a student can be helped to manipulate grammatical structures and patterns to create sentence variations.[3] They are a useful guide in sequencing of instruction.

1. Elements (as adverbs) can be reordered:
   Marie stood by quietly. Quietly Marie stood by.

2. Indirect objects can be rearranged:
   He gave a ball to John. He gave John a ball.

3. The use of "there" provides an alternative:
   A visitor was upstairs. There was a visitor upstairs.

4. Adjectives can be used:
   The cat is dirty. The dirty cat . . . (or The cat that is dirty . . .)

5. Possessives can be formed:
   Bill has a dog. The dog is gentle.
   Bill's dog is gentle.

6. Comparisons can be made:
   John is strong. Tom is stronger.
   Tom is stronger than John.

7. Relatives (such as *that, which, who, whom*) can be utilized:
   The girl played the piano. The girl is my sister.
   The girl who played the piano is my sister.

8. Appositives can be employed:
   Clara is my youngest sister. She went to California.
   Clara, my youngest sister, went to California.

9. Noun phrase complements may consist of a "that" clause; infinitive clause ("for . . . to"); or gerundive clause (genetive or possessive form):
   That Bill arrived late bothered Sue.
   For Bill to arrive late bothered Sue.
   Bill's having arrived late bothered Sue.

10. Coordination:
    The phone rang. No one answered it.
    The phone rang, but no one answered it.

11. Subordination:
    The man was strong. He was tall. He was handsome.
    The man was strong, tall, and handsome.
    The wind was strong. The leaves fell to the ground.
    The leaves fell to the ground because (as, since, when) the wind was strong.

---

3. From *The Language Arts in Childhood Education* (p. 21) by P. C. Burns, B. L. Broman, and A. L. L. Wantling, 1971, Boston: Houghton Mifflin. Copyright 1971 by Houghton Mifflin Company. Reprinted with permission.

12. Sentence connection:
I am not going to the movie. I am going to the dance.
I am not going to the movie; however, I am going to the dance.

Activities employed to help students with learning problems develop grammatical skills will primarily be oral. Some examples of suggested activities are listed below:

1. Repeat and expand or elaborate student's utterances to form more complete or complex sentences.
2. Give students ample opportunities to participate orally in class:
—describing objects or events
—retelling a story
—discussing an experience or activity.

In the list of P. C. Burns et al. (1971), Items 5 through 8 and 10 through 12 involve some type of sentence combining. When used as an instructional technique, sentence combining has been shown to be extremely effective in enhancing students' ability to write syntactically (Phelps-Gunn & Phelps-Terasaki, 1982; G. Wallace et al., 1987), as well as to read with comprehension (Combs, 1977).

The sentence-combining technique is easy to use, especially with older students, who find it motivating. In part this is because there is no one correct way to combine sentences; many combinations are equally acceptable.

A resource for all who would plan sentence-combining activities is the *Sentence Combining: A Composing Book* by Strong (1983). The following examples of the technique are from his work.[4]

Main Drag, Saturday Night

1. The cars come cruising up Broadway.

2. The cars are glittering.

3. The paint is harsh.

4. The paint is metallic.

5. The paint is highly waxed.

The student is told:

1. As you combine sentences, listen to them; say them aloud in several ways; experiment with new structures.

2. In the beginning, at least, write out all the transformations you can think of for each cluster; then choose the one you like best.

3. In a special notebook, write out the final transforms for each string; use the notebook daily.

---

4. From *Sentence Combining: A Composing Book* (pp. x, 7) by W. Strong, 1983, New York: Random House. Copyright 1983 by Random House.

4. Compare your transforms with those of the other students; discuss which transformations sound best; try to figure out why.

5. Look for the patterns that show up over and over as you make your combinations; you'll also see patterns of spelling and punctuation as you work.

6. Go beyond the lists that are given in the text by following the Suggestions; in other words, *keep writing.*

Examples of how students may combine the first five sentences in the "Main Drag, Saturday Night" series into two sentences follow. The emphasis is on forming transformations, not on combining the sentences into a single correct way.

Transformation 1
The glittering cars come cruising up Broadway. Their paint is harsh, metallic, and highly waxed. . . .

Transformation 2
The cars that glitter come cruising up Broadway. Their metallic paint is harsh and highly waxed. . . .

Sentence and Paragraph Construction

To be competent in forming written sentences and paragraphs, students have to coordinate all the skills involved in punctuation, capitalization, vocabulary, word usage, and grammar. In addition, they must organize content. Problems commonly associated with students' sentence construction include fragments, run-on sentences, comma splices, sentences that are too simple or too complex, misplaced or dangling modifiers, pronouns without proper referents, lack of variety in sentence structure, pronoun–antecedent and subject–verb disagreement, overuse of expletives and passive voice, and tense-sequence problems. The teacher should attend to these errors individually by applying and/or adjusting instructional activities such as those that follow.

1. Ask students to arrange a string of written words to form a sentence.
   Examples:

fast	the	dog	black	ran
The	black	dog	ran	fast

2. Ask students to mark errors in given sentences or mark, correct, and rewrite the incorrect portions.

3. Ask students to complete partially written sentences.
   Examples:
   Mary went to the store to buy _____.
   Mary went to the store to buy _____, _____, _____, and _____.
   Mary went _____.

4. Do much group work in composing (e.g., preparing experience charts, writing letters to classmates, etc.).

5. Begin conceptual writing instruction with one-word composition, progress to simple sentences, and gradually increase the number and complexity of the sentences used in the exercises.

6. Encourage and provide opportunities for students to dictate letters and stories.

7. Utilize dictation and proofreading exercises in the writing program.

8. Give students a group of written statements comprising both complete sentences and fragments; ask them to select those that are fragments.

9. Ask students to underline subject and verb as clues to finding complete sentences and fragments.

10. Have students match predicate and verb phrases.

11. Give students an outline or form for a sentence to be constructed.
    Examples:

Noun	*Verb*	*Noun*	*Noun*
John	gave	Bill	the ball

12. Have students practice using connectives, such as *and, but, for, which, when,* and *because.*
    Examples:
    Willie was tired, _____ he got up early this morning.
    Susie ran well, _____ Judy won the race.

Once a student can compose complete sentences, the teacher should begin instruction on paragraph formation. Four major points should be stressed in teaching students to write paragraphs: the content to be expressed, the topic sentence, the order and flow of sentences and ideas within the paragraph, and the concluding sentence. Activities for each are provided below.

1. Collect statements made by students during a discussion, write them on the board, and ask the students to select those that go together.

2. Let students order the statements selected above.

3. Give students paragraph selections in which they must locate inappropriate sentences.

4. Give students paragraphs that contain appropriate but poorly sequenced sentences; have the students rearrange the sentences into a more meaningful order. Before assigning this task, the teacher may want to first check whether the young pupil can tell an experience in sequence or arrange comic strips and tell a story from the frames.

5. Provide opportunities, such as class or school newspapers, to motivate students to compose.

6. Employ dictation and proofreading activities.

7. Introduce students to the concept of outlining.

In conclusion, when using any of the activities described in this chapter, teachers should ensure that students are required to perform only those tasks in which they can experience some degree of success. As the student succeeds, the complexity of the tasks can be increased gradually until he or she has mastered the targeted skills or areas completely.

We conclude this section by referring the reader once again to *Evaluating and Improving Written Expression: A Practical Guide for Teachers* (Hall, 1988). This guide is advertised as "a step-by-step approach to analyzing and building writing skills, from idea to finished composition." Teachers and others who assess and teach written composition—as well as handwriting and spelling—will not be disappointed in this work. The book is filled with activities for developing creative and practical writing, organizational skill, sentence structure, and mature vocabulary.

Commercially Available Programs

In recent years, interest in written composition has increased markedly. Because of this increased interest, several comprehensive programs for training abilities in expressive writing have become available commercially. In general, these programs include sequenced lessons, systematic activities, teacher manuals, and student workbooks. To a considerable extent, they incorporate many of the informal activities described in the previous section. Three of the programs are discussed here as examples of the kinds of programs that are now available. The first program is intended as a developmental approach to teaching writing to beginning learners; the other programs are intended for remedial use. This section also includes a brief discussion of the role of computers in composition instruction.

Expressive Writing 1 and 2

Engelmann and Silbert's (1983) *Expressive Writing* program was designed for beginning writers who read at or above the third-grade level. The core of the program is fifty 45-minute lessons, each of which provides for practice in mechanics (punctuation and capitalization), sentence writing, paragraph writing, and editing. The teacher presents a lesson using instructions found in the Teacher Presentation Book (a teacher's manual); the students execute the lesson in space provided in their Student Workbook.

Consider Lesson 29 as an example. The lesson has four parts, each dealing with a different skill:

1. Editing run-ons. Students are given a series of run-on sentences to correct (e.g., "A girl bought an old bike from a friend and the bike had

rust on its handlebars and wheels and the girl and her friend fixed up the bike.")

2. Changing *was* to *did*. Students are asked to rewrite a passage so that all the sentences tell what a person or thing did, not what a person or thing was doing. For example, "One boy was falling down" is changed to "One boy fell down."

3. Introducing sequence in paragraphs. Students are shown a series of related pictures that depict a story. A paragraph accompanying the pictures tells the story depicted. Each element in the story is read aloud in sequence and associated with the picture.

4. Writing a paragraph that reports an event. Students are shown four story-related pictures about a rodeo and a box containing 14 printed words related to the rodeo theme. Students are asked to write a paragraph that reports what happened. They are directed in composing their paragraph—for example, they are told to indent, to start with "The cowboy," to tell what he did in the picture, and so forth.

At the end of the lesson, students are given the opportunity to self-evaluate aspects of their work. Other lessons vary in content but are similar in format to this one.

Basic Writing Skills

Gleason and Stults (1983a, 1983b) produced two sets of remedial activities. One set is for developing the sentence skills of students who read and spell at or above the third-grade level and who have problems in this area. The other set is for teaching style to students in Grades 7 through 12 who use little capitalization or punctuation in their daily writing. Both programs have a teacher's manual and a series of reproducible student worksheets.

The *Sentence Development* program (Gleason & Stults, 1983a) has 31 lessons that follow a consistent format. Lesson 8, for example, begins with the teacher's writing six statements on the board. One of them is a complete sentence that has been punctuated properly; the others either are fragments or have stylistic errors in them. The student is asked to answer three questions about each statement: Is it a sentence? Does it begin with a capital? Does it end with a correct end mark? Next, the students write five sentences about a picture depicted on their worksheet (see Figure 4.3). Students check each sentence by answering the questions at the bottom of the worksheet. Then a second picture is shown to the students, who respond by writing sentences. Afterwards, they proof their sentences for errors.

The *Capitalization and Punctuation* program (Gleason & Stults, 1983b) has 40 lessons. Each lesson deals with a different element and follows a fairly consistent format. For example, Lesson 15 deals with putting commas in the date. First, a series of sentences is read from the worksheet. Each sentence contains a punctuation error involving dates (e.g., "You will get paid on Friday June 3."). The proper punctuation of each sentence is

Lesson 8

Name _____

Date _____

Part A

1. _____
   _____
2. _____
   _____
3. _____
   _____
4. _____
   _____
5. _____
   _____

Proof your sentences.	1	2	3	4	5
1. Is it a sentence?	——	——	——	——	——
2. Does it begin with a capital?	——	——	——	——	——
3. Does it end with a period?	——	——	——	——	——

(continues)

FIGURE 4.3.   Sample *Sentence Development* Lesson.

From *Basic Writing Skills: Sentence Development* (pp. 149–150) by M. Gleason and C. Stults, 1983, Chicago: Science Research Associates.

Lesson 8

Name _____

Date _____

Part B: Mastery Quiz

Directions: Look at the picture. Write five interesting sentences about what's happening in the picture. Proof your sentences.

1. _____
   _____

2. _____
   _____

3. _____
   _____

4. _____
   _____

5. _____
   _____

FIGURE 4.3. *Continued*

discussed. Second, a set of unpunctuated sentences is provided (e.g., "will grandpa arrive by monday january 26"), and the student rewrites them, putting in the proper punctuation. Third, students are given the opportunity to generate five sentences that contain dates and proof their own work.

Needless to say, these commercial programs are highly sequenced, organized, and instructionally efficient. However, teachers must monitor student writing that is not integral to the special program to ensure that the skills being taught are being used in everyday writing and in other school-related writing.

Teaching Competence in Written Language

The authors of the *Teaching Competence in Written Language* program, Phelps-Terasaki and Phelps-Gunn (1988), recommended that their approach be used with students in remedial, resource, or speech–language therapy situations; students who require extra help in the regular classroom; adults in remedial or basic classes; and aphasic populations. The program comprises a Teacher's Guide, a student writing workbook (called a Student Tablet), and a Student Lesson Book.

Three major theoretical elements are integrated into the program. The first is an adaptation of the enormously successful Fitzgerald Key (Fitzgerald, 1966), which has been used for years to teach language structure to hearing impaired children. The second is an interactive teacher–student structure recommended by Lee, Koenigsknecht, and Mulhern (1975). The third is a heavy emphasis on pragmatic uses of writing. These three elements are incorporated into each of the 44 lessons in the program.

The program is systematic, individualized, and highly structured. It begins with the basic sentence, integrates the sentence into a paragraph, and concludes by focusing the paragraph around a purpose.

Lesson 10 serves as an example. Procedures for introducing the lesson are found on pages 19 and 20 of the Teacher's Guide. Students are directed to look at the picture opposite the lesson in the Student Lesson Book. After discussing the picture, students are asked to turn to the Sentence Guide for Lesson 10 in their Student Tablet. They are told that all of the sentences in the guide can be improved and that they are to correct the sentences. All the material pertaining to Lesson 10 is reproduced in Figure 4.4.

The commercial programs briefly discussed in this section are meant to serve as examples; most educational companies offer a variety of proficient, comprehensive remedial writing programs and supplemental materials that are every bit as good as those reviewed here. Teachers would do well to seek out these other programs, for each approaches writing in a slightly different way, is appropriate for a different age group, and uses a different theoretical frame of reference. Teachers may begin with the *Fokes Written Language Program* (Fokes, 1982), an approach for young writers, and with the 10-volume series by Verner and Minturn (1985) entitled *Critical Steps to Effective Reading and Writing*. The latter series is made up of

Description Picture: Lesson 10

(continues)

FIGURE 4.4. Lesson 10 from *Teaching Competence in Written Language.*

From *Teaching Competence in Written Language* by D. Phelps-Terasaki and T. Phelps-Gunn, 1988, Austin, TX: PRO-ED. Reprinted with permission.

LESSON 10: Review and Practice I

The Sentence Guide for Lesson 10 has ten sentences. These are not good sentences. Each sentence has one of the following mistakes:

1. The Who/What? column is blank.
2. The Doing What? column is blank.
3. The time is wrong.
4. The sentence does not paint a clear mind picture.

Look at the picture to the left. Use this picture to help you correct the mistakes in the sentences.

LESSON 10: REVIEW AND PRACTICE I

Goals

The purpose of this lesson is to provide you with a sample of each student's work so that you can monitor the students' progress up to this point in the program. Should you feel that the students do not exhibit adequate understanding and familiarity with the material presented thus far, Lesson 10 can be followed by extra practice and reinforcement of the earlier lessons. Before moving on, the students should have mastered the material up to this point.

Procedures

1. Ask the students to look at the picture opposite the lesson in the Student Lesson Book. Discuss the various things happening in the picture. Questions such as "And what else do you think is happening?" and "What about the boy (or dog or cat, etc.) over here in this corner?" are helpful ways to include more students in the discussion and also cover the picture.

2. After the students have discussed the picture, ask them to turn to the Sentence Guide for Lesson 10 in their tablets. Point out that there are 10 sentences on the Sentence Guide. Tell the students that each sentence needs to be corrected and improved.

3. Read the lesson aloud. Discuss the four possible mistakes in the sentences. Write each "problem" on the board, explain it, and give an example. The following is an example of a teacher explaining a missing subject to a class.

> The first problem that you must look for in the 10 sentences is a missing Who/What? column. That means that there is nothing in the column marked Who/What? When that happens, we don't know some important things about our sentence. Can anyone tell me why we need to fill in the Who/What? column? (Discuss the students' responses.) Here's an example of a sentence without the Who/What? column. (Write a sample on the board, such as "_____ ran down the street.") Who can correct this sentence? (Discuss the students' responses and write several on the board.) Some of the sentences on your Sentence Guide might have this problem.

Following this discussion, tell the students that only one thing is wrong with each sentence. Then ask them to correct the sentences on their Sentence Guide. Spot check to see that they are using capital letters and periods.

4. When the students are done, ask them to put their pencils or pens away. Correct each sentence on the board using the ideas of several students so that the students will learn that there are many ways to correct sentences, rather than just one right way. Have the students explain the corrections. This is a good time to look at each student's work and determine who needs more practice.

(continues)

FIGURE 4.4. *Continued*

Sentence Guide

LESSON 10

CONNECTORS And First Second Next Then Last	WHO/WHAT? Which? What kind of? How much? How many?	DOING WHAT?	DETAILS Why? (because, since, so that) What? When? Where? How?
	The black and white dog	is putting out	the fire with a firehose.
	The fire	started	tomorrow.
	It	is hanging	on the fire truck.
		is climbing	up the ladder.
	A boy and a girl		
	The fire truck	came	next week.
	He	is carrying	an ax.
	The orange cat	is parked	by the house.

FIGURE 4.4. *Continued*

10 volumes of blackline masters. Each master presents a lesson addressing some aspect of writing.

Computer Programs

The role of computers in composition instruction has been expanding. Several software packages have been developed for use at the elementary and middle school levels, the purpose of which is to assist students in acquiring desirable composition skills. Chief among these are *The Banks Street Writer* (1982, Scholastic), *Quill* (1984, Heath), *Story Maker* (1981, Bolt, Beranek, & Newman), and *Story Tree* (1984, Scholastic). These programs engage students in creative story-writing exercises; teach them to take notes, express ideas, and organize material; and imitate many of the prewriting activities employed by teachers. H. L. Burns (1984, p. 22) summarizes what computer writing programs can do as follows:

1. A program can ask the question.
2. A program can clarify the question.
3. Good software can define the dimensions of the question.
4. The software can call attention to the essay's purpose.
5. It can purposefully distract (for incubation's sake).
6. It can rephrase the question.
7. It can create random metaphors.
8. Invention programs can offer research questions.
9. A program can print a copy of the dialogue so a student can later evaluate the answers.

Readers who are interested in the potential of computers for writing instruction are referred to the cogent discussions of S. K. Miller (1985). In a two-part article published in *Direct Instruction News,* Miller traces the history of the microcomputer era, describes the writing software then available, and summarizes research in the area.

We conclude this section on teaching composition by paraphrasing Elizabeth Addison's seven writing techniques. Addison is a partner at The Write Impression, Inc., Atlanta, Georgia. Her techniques are discussed in detail by Buffington (1988) in his article "Paper Chases."

1. Know the mind of your intended reader. Write with the reader in mind. Anticipate and answer his or her questions.
2. Plan before you begin to write. Make notes and an outline. Order your ideas logically. Think before you write.
3. State your point quickly. Grab the reader's interest and hold it.

4. Be brief and to the point. Long, rambling, unfocused letters and essays evoke a negative opinion of the writer.

5. Keep your emotions in check. Emotionally laden thoughts rarely come across well in writing. When you are tempted to express ideas that involve strong emotion and language, it is always best to "sleep on" the ideas before putting them into written form. Emotion has its place in writing but should be expressed with caution and restraint.

6. Proofread all material that you write. Proofread once, twice, and then again. Stylistic, semantic, and grammatical errors can be embarrassing.

7. Finally, having written the piece with care, hang on to it. An alarming number of compositions are lost or misplaced before they reach the hands of their intended reader.

Writers of all ages, and especially those who have difficulty in composition, should practice Addison's techniques. Their use will go far toward helping a student master the skills necessary for good writing.

Chapter 5

······················ Spelling Skills ··················

Improving Spelling Skills

DONALD D. HAMMILL

Spelling is the forming of words from letters according to acceptable usage. Although words can be spelled orally, as in the traditional spelling bee, their written form is by far the more important because students use it when writing essays for teachers, notes to friends, correspondence to relatives, or grocery lists for themselves.

Although highly prized, proficient spelling is often an unattained outcome of language arts instruction. Most students are taught by means of a schoolwide program and readily become fluent spellers. However, many others, with comparable mental ability and interest, do not learn to spell adequately. When deficiencies are first observed, the teacher should immediately take steps to help the student overcome the problem. As a first step, the teacher should find the answers to several pertinent questions:

1. Does the student have sufficient mental ability to learn to spell?

2. Are the student's hearing, speech, and vision adequate?

3. What is the student's general level of spelling ability?

4. Does the student have any specific weaknesses in spelling?

5. What systems, techniques, or activities might be used to remedy difficulties?

Answers to the first two questions relate to a student's "readiness" or "capacity" for spelling. If teachers are unsure about the status of a student's intellectual or sensory abilities, a referral to the school psychologist or nurse may be in order. Procedures for answering the other three questions are provided in the remainder of this chapter. This chapter is designed to help teachers to better understand spelling skills and to acquire information about appropriate assessment techniques and various developmental and remedial teaching programs directed toward improvement in spelling.

ASSESSING SPELLING SKILLS

Four types of assessment techniques are discussed—tests with norms, tests with criterion-referenced items, informal spelling inventories, and other procedures. Tests with norms are superior by far when the teacher is asking the question "What is the general level of spelling ability?" For inventorying a student's spelling errors and patterns and for getting information needed to plan an individual remedial program, tests designed for criterion-referenced interpretation and other less standardized (informal) procedures are unsurpassed.

Norm-Referenced Spelling Tests

Most teachers are familiar with normed tests of spelling because all popular group-administered achievement batteries used in schoolwide testing programs include a spelling subtest (e.g., the *Metropolitan Achievement Test,* 1992). Teachers who work in special education are aware that all popular individually administered achievement batteries used to qualify students for special services also include a spelling subtest (e.g., the *Diagnostic Achievement Battery,* Newcomer, 1990; the *Wide Range Achievement Test,* Wilkinson, 1994; the *Peabody Individual Achievement Test–Revised,* Markwardt, 1989).

These tests have limited value, however, in that they yield a single score. A single score may be useful for documenting whether a student has a spelling problem, but it does not give the teacher information about the nature of the problem or the areas of spelling that may be deficient. The following two tests provide more interesting results for teachers and diagnosticians.

The Test of Written Spelling

Now in its third edition, the *Test of Written Spelling* (TWS) (Larsen & Hammill, 1994) is composed of 100 words that were chosen because they appear in each of the 10 spelling series that are used most often in the schools. Fifty of these words are "predictable" in that their spelling is consistent with certain phonological (i.e., phoneme–grapheme correspondence) rules or generalizations (e.g., *had, spring, pile, salute, legal*), and 50 words are "unpredictable" in that their spelling conforms to no useful phonological or morphological rules (e.g., *people, knew, eight, fountain, community*). Test results are interpreted in terms of the student's mastery of the predictable words, the unpredictable words, or the total number of words.

The test is normed on a nationwide sample of students who share the national characteristics relative to geographic location, sex, and urban–rural residence. Studies indicate that the TWS is reliable (i.e., internally consistent) at all grade levels between 1 and 12 (coefficients in the .80s and .90s), and that its results correlate strongly with other tests of spelling.

The Diagnostic Spelling Potential Test

The *Diagnostic Spelling Potential Test* (Arena, 1982) is designed for use with students aged 7 through adult. The entire test can be given in 25 to 40 minutes. Results are reported as standard scores, percentiles, and grade ratings.

The test has four subtests and two parallel forms. The names of the subtests and the abilities measured are as follows:

1. *Spelling* measures the ability to spell words from dictation.

2. *Word Recognition* assesses reading decoding skills.

3. *Visual Recognition* measures the ability to recognize the correctly spelled form of a word without the aid of an auditory stimulus.

4. *Auditory-Visual Recognition* taps the ability to recognize the correctly spelled form of a word when the word is pronounced.

This test has good reliability and validity. Its only shortcoming is that it was normed on a restricted sample of students (i.e., children living in California). When the test is used in conjunction with the TWS, the results can provide a valid picture of a student's spelling performance and lead to educational planning.

In general, the normed tests with the most complete standardizations are useful mainly for telling examiners who the poor spellers are. Unfortunately, they offer little information that a teacher can use to plan individual programs. On the other hand, the tests that provide a more complete analysis of an individual's spelling ability tend to have inadequate standardizations. The teacher, therefore, has to choose between using a test that has a sound research base but offers little instructionally relevant information and using a test that taps more components of spelling but has no reported reliability.

The teacher should be selective in the type of tests used and should consider the following three suggestions:

1. Know what the test measures and what its limitations are before giving it to the student; for example, know the types of students used for the standardization and norms and the reported reliability and validity of the test.

2. Be prepared to supplement the test where possible with other less standardized measures.

3. Use other evaluation techniques whenever specific information about the student's spelling abilities is required, and as a guide to planning a remediation program.

Criterion-Referenced Spelling Tests

Normed tests such as those just mentioned are built to be relatively short, highly reliable measurement devices. Tests built with criterion referencing in mind include a broad spectrum of items, reflecting most, if not all, of the elements that make up the skill being measured. The purpose of criterion referencing in educational practice is not to determine where the student stands relative to other students but to identify those components of the ability being assessed in which the student needs training.

This type of assessment helps the teacher to determine a student's instructional level and also measures progress toward the task goal. Tests designed for criterion referencing

1. Indicate the skills the student has and those the student needs.

2. Provide an objective measure of progress as the student moves from task to task.

3. Are based upon what content is to be taught.

The teacher can choose from many criterion-referenced tests. Two of these are presented in this book: Kottmeyer's (1959) *Diagnostic Spelling Test* and Greenbaum's (1987) *Spellmaster Assessment and Teaching System.*

The Diagnostic Spelling Test

The *Diagnostic Spelling Test,* which is presented in Table 5.1, is administered using a dictation format; for example, the examiner says to the students, "Not. He is *not* here," after which they write the word "not." After the student has completed the test, the number of correct spellings is totaled and first interpreted in a norm-referenced fashion using the data offered just below the table heading "Directions for Diagnostic Spelling Test." The results are next interpreted in a criterion-referenced manner. For example, the student who misspelled "not" probably has not yet mastered the phonological rule governing the short vowel /o/. Analysis of the student's errors on the test should result in the development of a relatively data-based remedial program.

Spellmaster

A second criterion-referenced approach, Spellmaster, was designed by Greenbaum (1987). Spellmaster is used to identify the elements that students need to learn. This is accomplished by administering grade-sequenced tests in which the elements within each word, rather than the whole word, are scored right or wrong. Regular words, irregular words, and homonyms are assessed.

An example of how the tests are scored and interpreted is provided in Figure 5.1. Regular Word Test 4 has been given to Pat M. This test measures proficiency in using vowels (*u-e*), digraphs and diphthongs ($\overline{oo}$, *oi, ou, ow, aw*), "r" control (*ar, er, ur,* etc.), "l" control (*all*), prefixes (*in–, re–,* etc.), and suffixes (*–er, –est,* etc.). Pat misspelled Items 1, 2, 6, 7, 10, 12, 20, 24–26, 30, 32, 35, and 39. On Item 1, she wrote *fearfull* instead of *fearful;* this error suggests difficulty with "l" control. In like manner, each misspelled word can be probed to identify the type or class of error being made.

TABLE 5.1. Kottmeyer's *Diagnostic Spelling Test*

DIRECTIONS FOR DIAGNOSTIC SPELLING TEST

Give List 1 to second or third graders.

Give List 2 to any pupil who is above Grade 3.

Grade Scoring, List 1:

   Below 15 correct: Below second grade

   15–22 correct: Second grade

   23–29 correct: Third grade

Give List 2 Test to pupils who score above 29.

Grade Scoring, List 2:

   Below 9 correct: Below third grade

   9–19 correct: Third grade

   20–25 correct: Fourth grade

   26–29 correct: Fifth grade

   Over 29 correct: Sixth grade or better

Give List 1 Test to pupils who score below 9.

LIST 1		LIST 2	
Word	**Illustrative Sentence**	**Word**	**Illustrative Sentence**
1. not	He is *not* here.	1. flower	A rose is a *flower.*
2. but	Mary is here, *but* Joe is not.	2. mouth	Open your *mouth.*
3. get	*Get* the wagon, John.	3. shoot	John wants to *shoot* his new gun.
4. sit	*Sit* down, please.	4. stood	We *stood* under the roof.
5. man	Father is a tall *man.*	5. while	We sang *while* we marched.
6. boat	We sailed our *boat* on the lake.	6. third	We are in the *third* grade.
7. train	Tom has a new toy *train.*	7. each	*Each* child has a pencil.
8. time	It is *time* to come home.	8. class	Our *class* is reading.
9. like	We *like* ice cream.	9. jump	We like to *jump* rope.
10. found	We *found* our lost ball.	10. jumps	Mary *jumps* rope.
11. down	Do not fall *down.*	11. jumped	We *jumped* rope yesterday.
12. soon	Our teacher will *soon* be here.	12. jumping	The girls are *jumping* rope now.
13. good	He is a *good* boy.	13. hit	*Hit* the ball hard.
14. very	We are *very* happy to be here.	14. hitting	John is *hitting* the ball.
15. happy	Jane is a *happy* girl.	15. bite	Our dog does not *bite.*
16. kept	We *kept* our shoes dry.	16. biting	The dog is *biting* on the bone.
17. come	*Come* to our party.	17. study	*Study* your lesson.
18. what	*What* is your name?	18. studies	He *studies* each day.
19. those	*Those* are our toys.	19. dark	The sky is *dark* and cloudy.
20. show	*Show* us the way.	20. darker	This color is *darker* than that one.
21. much	I feel *much* better.	21. darkest	This color is *darkest* of the three.
22. sing	We will *sing* a new song.	22. afternoon	We may play this *afternoon.*
23. will	Who *will* help us?	23. grandmother	Our *grandmother* will visit us.
24. doll	Make a dress for the *doll.*	24. can't	We *can't* go with you.
25. after	We play *after* school.	25. doesn't	Mary *doesn't* like to play.
26. sister	My *sister* is older than I.	26. night	We read to Mother last *night.*
27. toy	I have a new *toy* train.	27. brought	Joe *brought* his lunch to school.
28. say	*Say* your name clearly.	28. apple	An *apple* fell from the tree.
29. little	Tom is a *little* boy.	29. again	We must come back *again.*
30. one	I have only *one* book.	30. laugh	Do not *laugh* at other children.
31. would	*Would* you come with us?	31. because	We cannot play *because* of the rain.
32. pretty	She is a *pretty* girl.	32. through	We ran *through* the yard.

(continues)

TABLE 5.1. *Continued*

LIST 1		LIST 2	
Word	*Element Tested*	*Word*	*Element Tested*
1. not 2. but 3. get 4. sit 5. man	Short vowels	1. flower 2. mouth	*ow–ou* spellings of *ou* sound, *er* ending, *th* spelling
6. boat 7. train	Two vowels together	3. shoot 4. stood	Long and short *oo*, *sh* spelling
8. time 9. like	Vowel-consonant–*e*	5. while	*wh* spelling, vowel–consonant
10. found 11. down	*ow–ou* spelling of *ou* sound	6. third	*th* spelling, vowel before *r*
12. soon 13. good	Long and short *oo*	7. each	*ch* spelling, two vowels together
14. very 15. happy	Final *y* as short *i*	8. class	Double final consonant, *c* spelling of *k* sound
16. kept 17. come	*c* and *k* spellings of the *k* sound	9. jump 10. jumps 11. jumped 12. jumping	Addition of *s*, *ed*, *ing*; *j* spelling of soft *g* sound
18. what 19. those 20. show 21. much 22. sing	*wh, th, sh, ch*, and *ng* spellings and *ow* spelling of long *o*	13. hit 14. hitting	Doubling final consonant before adding *ing*
23. will 24. doll	Doubled final consonants	15. bite 16. biting	Dropping final *e* before *ing*
25. after 26. sister	*er* spelling	17. study 18. studies	Changing final *y* to *i* before ending
27. toy	*oy* spelling of *oi* sound	19. dark 20. darker 21. darkest	*er, est* endings
28. say	*ay* spelling of long *a* sound	22. afternoon 23. grandmother	Compound words
29. little	*le* ending	24. can't 25. doesn't	Contractions
30. one 31. would 32. pretty	Nonphonetic spellings	26. night 27. brought	Silent *gh*
		28. apple	*le* ending
		29. again 30. laugh 31. because 32. through	Nonphonetic spellings

From *Teacher's Guide for Remedial Reading* by William Kottmeyer, 1959, New York: McGraw-Hill. Coryright 1959 by Webster/McGraw-Hill, Inc. Reprinted with permission.

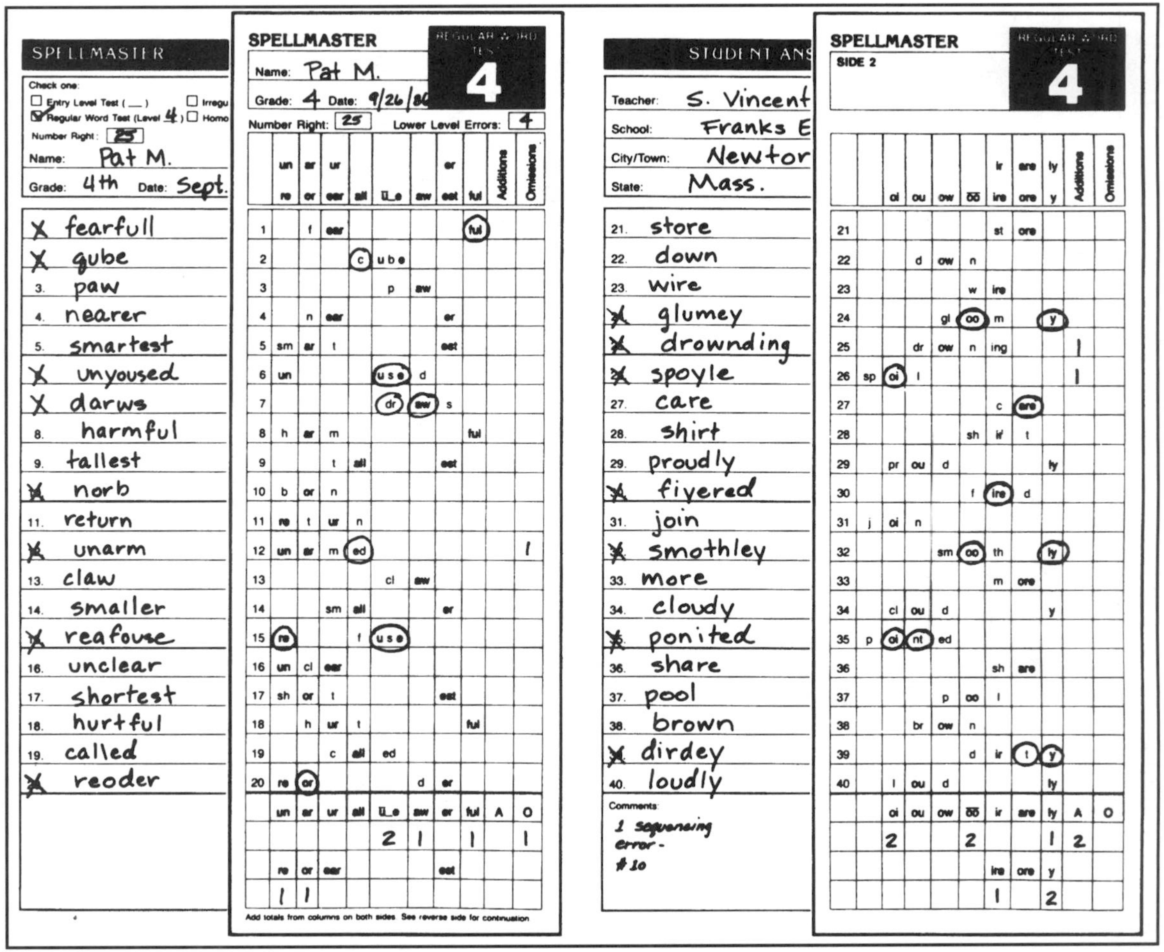

FIGURE 5.1. Pat M's performance on Spellmaster's Regular Word Test 4.

From *The Spellmaster Assessment and Teaching System* by C. R. Greenbaum, 1987, Austin, TX: PRO-ED. Copyright 1987 by PRO-ED, Inc. Reprinted with permission.

Informal Spelling Inventory

The informal spelling inventory (ISI) approach is a useful alternative to the standardized techniques just described. It is particularly valuable in that a teacher can construct the inventory to include the words that students must spell in order to pass his or her class.

G. Wallace and McLoughlin (1988) pointed out that the purposes of the ISI are to determine a general spelling level and to note particular error patterns. They recommend that teachers, in building an ISI, select 15 to 20 words from each basal spelling book in a given series. If the series has six levels, the ISI will have between 90 and 120 words divided into six lists, each having 15 to 20 words. The words on each list are dictated to a student, beginning with the first list. Testing stops when the student misses six consecutive words. The student's achievement level is determined by finding the highest level at which a score of at least 90% is obtained. The teaching level is the highest level at which a score of 75% to 89% is reached. Each word that is misspelled should be studied to identify the source of the error. Techniques described in the next section of this chapter are useful for this purpose.

Other Assessment Procedures

Information gleaned by assessing a student's actual spelling behavior will be of considerable value to teachers planning individualized programs of study. This evaluation is based primarily on the teacher's direct observation of a student's behavior in a variety of spelling situations and on an analysis of many samples of spelling work. In short, assessment is directed, structured, and/or analytic observation.

Brueckner and Bond (1967) systematized informal observations by suggesting the following guidelines for teachers to use[1]:

1. Analysis of Written Work, including Test Papers

   a. Legibility of handwriting

   b. Defects in letter forms, spacing, alignment, size

   c. Classification of errors in written work, letters, or tests

   d. Range of vocabulary used

   e. Evidence of lack of knowledge of conventions and rules

2. Analysis of Oral Responses

   a. Comparison of errors in oral and written spellings

   b. Pronunciation of words spelled incorrectly

---

1. From "The Diagnosis and Treatment of Learning Difficulties" by L. J. Brueckner and G. L. Bond, in *Educating Children with Learning Disabilities* by E. C. Frierson and W. B. Barbe (Eds.), 1967, New York: Appleton-Century-Crofts. Reprinted with permission.

  c. Articulation and enunciation

  d. Slovenliness of speech

  e. Dialect and colloquial forms of speech

  f. Way of spelling words orally:

   (1) Spells words as units

   (2) Spells letter by letter

   (3) Spells by digraphs

   (4) Spells by syllables

  g. Rhythmic pattern in oral spelling

  h. Blending ability

  i. Giving letters for sounds or sounds for letters

  j. Technique of word analysis used

  k. Quality and error made in oral reading

  l. Oral responses on tests or word analysis

  m. Analysis of pupil's comments as he states orally his thought process while studying new words

3. Interview with Pupil and Others

  a. Questioning pupil about methods of study

  b. Questioning pupil about spelling rules

  c. Questioning pupil about errors in convention

  d. Securing evidence as to attitude towards spelling

4. Questionnaire

  a. Applying checklist of methods of study

  b. Having pupil rank spelling according to interest

  c. Surveying use of written language

5. Free Observation in Course of Daily Work

  a. Securing evidence as to attitudes towards spelling

  b. Evidence of improvement in the study of new words

  c. Observing extent of use of dictionary

  d. Extent of error in regular written work

  e. Study habits and methods of work

  f. Social acceptability of the learner

  g. Evidences of emotional and social maladjustment

  h. Evidences of possible physical handicaps

6. Controlled Observation of Work on Set Tasks

    a. Looking up the meanings of given words in dictionary

    b. Giving pronunciation of words in dictionary

    c. Writing plural forms and derivatives of given words

    d. Observing responses on informal tests

    e. Estimating pupil scores when using a variety of methods studying selected words

For each student with a spelling problem, a careful analysis of errors should be made to discern whether a pattern of errors exists. For analysis and error tabulation, the teacher should use lists of spelling words written from dictation as well as uncorrected continuous prose, such as a story a student has made up. Edgington provided a sample of types of errors that exist in students' spelling work[2]:

Addition of unneeded letters (*dresses*)

Omissions of needed letters (*hom* for *home*)

Reflections of child's mispronunciations (*pin* for *pen*)

Reflections of dialectical speech patterns (*Cuber* for *Cuba*)

Reversals of whole words (*eno* for *one*)

Reversals of vowels (*braed* for *bread*)

Reversals of consonant order (*lback* for *black*)

Reversals of consonant or vowel directionality (*brithday* for *birthday*)

Reversals of syllables (*telho* for *hotel*)

Phonetic spelling of nonphonetic words or parts thereof (*cawt* for *caught*)

Wrong associations of a sound with a given set of letters (*u* has been learned as *ou* in *you*)

"Neographisms," or letters put in a word which bear no discernible relationship with the word dictated

Varying degrees and combinations of these or other possible patterns

Teachers should also know which words the student cannot spell. Therefore, each student who has difficulty in spelling should have his or her own list of frequently misspelled words. Because some words are more likely to be misspelled than others, the teacher should at some time assess the student's performance on the following list of 100 demons, or commonly misspelled words.[3] Teachers should select words from the list that correspond to the student's grade level.

---

2. From "But He Spelled Them Right this Morning" by R. Edgington, 1967, *Academic Therapy Quarterly, 3,* pp. 58–59. Copyright 1967 by PRO-ED, Inc. Reprinted with permission.

3. From *Spelling in Language Arts 6* by A. Kuska, E. J. D. Webster, and G. Elford, 1964, Ontario, Canada: Thomas Nelson & Sons (Canada) Ltd. Copyright 1964 by Thomas Nelson & Sons (Canada) Limited. Reprinted

ache	enemy	minute	rotten
afraid	families	neighbor	safety
against	fasten	neither	said
all right	fault	nickel	sandwich
although	February	niece	scratch
angry	forgotten	ninety	sense
answered	friendly	ninth	separate
asks	good-bye	onion	shining
beautiful	guessed	passed	silence
because	happened	peaceful	since
beginning	happily	perfectly	soldier
boy's	here's	piano	squirrel
buried	holiday	picnic	stepped
busily	hungry	picture	straight
carrying	husband	piece	studying
certain	its	pitcher	success
choose	it's	pleasant	taught
Christmas	kitchen	potato	their
clothes	knives	practice	there's
climbed	language	prettiest	through
course	lettuce	pumpkin	valentine
double	listening	purpose	whose
easier	lose	quietly	worst
eighth	marriage	rapidly	writing
either	meant	receive	yours

In addition to knowing which demons a student cannot spell, the teacher should know which of the most commonly used words a student cannot spell. Horn (1926) found that 100 words comprise 65% of all the words written by adults and that only 10 words (*I, the, and, to, a, you, of, in, we,* and *for*) account for 25% of the words used. Doubtlessly, many students are considered poor spellers because they cannot spell correctly the words on Horn's list. Poor spellers can improve noticeably and quickly if they are taught systematically the words on the list that they cannot spell. Horn's list is provided below, in order of frequency.[4]

1. I	21. at	41. do	61. up	81. think
2. the	22. this	42. been	62. day	82. say
3. and	23. with	43. letter	63. much	83. please
4. to	24. but	44. can	64. out	84. him
5. a	25. on	45. would	65. her	85. his
6. you	26. if	46. she	66. order	86. got
7. of	27. all	47. when	67. yours	87. over
8. in	28. so	48. about	68. now	88. make
9. we	29. me	49. they	69. well	89. may
10. for	30. was	50. any	70. an	90. received
11. it	31. very	51. which	71. here	91. before
12. that	32. my	52. some	72. them	92. two
13. is	33. had	53. has	73. see	93. send
14. your	34. our	54. or	74. go	94. after
15. have	35. from	55. there	75. what	95. work
16. will	36. am	56. us	76. come	96. could
17. be	37. one	57. good	77. were	97. dear
18. are	38. time	58. know	78. no	98. made
19. not	39. he	59. just	79. how	99. glad
20. as	40. get	60. by	80. did	100. like

4. From *A Basic Writing Vocabulary: 10,000 Words Most Commonly Used in Writing* by E. A. Horn, 1926, University of Iowa Monographs in Education, First Series, No. 4, Iowa City, Iowa.

Knowing how to spell the demons and the most commonly used words in the English language is a desirable outcome of instruction. In addition, Shinn (1982) suggested that students, especially those at the secondary level, should master the spelling of functional words. By functional words, he meant the words and phrases used in want ads, job application forms, home maintenance, and other everyday activities. Shinn's sample functional vocabulary lists are found in Table 5.2.

A teacher should assess problem students' spelling of these words and identify those words that students cannot spell correctly. The identified words should be systematically taught to the students. The ability to spell the vocabulary that is encountered frequently in everyday life will be of much value to students once they leave school.

TEACHING STUDENTS TO SPELL

Because students vary considerably in intellectual capacity and specific areas of weakness, spelling programs and remedial techniques should also vary with regard to level, theoretical orientation, vocabulary, manner of presentation, and format. The teacher cannot expect that a single spelling series will be suitable for all students. Therefore, he or she should have knowledge of an assortment of instructional alternatives. This section reviews briefly several developmental methods, remedial systems, and software programs, as well as a few game activities that can facilitate spelling competence if employed effectively.

Developmental Methods

A long-standing and sometimes confusing controversy exists among authorities regarding the teaching of spelling. Simply put, the conflict centers on the relative merits of using rules to enhance spelling competence. Some educators recommend the teaching of spelling rules that utilize a phonetic or sound–letter approach (Hanna & Moore, 1953; Hodges & Rudorf, 1965). They have found support in the work of Hanna, Hanna, Hodges, and Rudorf (1966), who programmed a computer with rules and then made it "spell" 17,000 words, which it did with remarkable accuracy. It spelled 50% of the words correctly; 37% were spelled with only a single error. A review of this project is in Hanna, Hodges, and Hanna (1971).

Other educators point out that English spelling forms are linguistically so irregular that spelling should be taught using almost no rules whatsoever. Still others suggest the limited use of teaching of rules. Spelling instruction, following this latter view, should involve a gradual accumulation of necessary and practiced words and include the introduction of rules whenever warranted.

TABLE 5.2. Shinn's Sample Functional Vocabulary Lists

WANT AD VOCABULARY

ability	domestic	necessary
ad	education	neighborhood
advance	employment	newspaper
advancement	errand	office
advertisement	excellent	opportunity
age	factory	overtime
agency	full-time	part-time
ambitious	future	permanent
apply	general	per week
assist	helper	position
beginner	hour	preferred
classified	inexperienced	raise
clerical	learn	reference
consider	light	steady
delivery		

JOB APPLICATION VOCABULARY

employer	physical	male
employed	type	birthplace
employment	widowed	degree
present	Social Security number	discharge
phone	(Soc. Sec. no.)	seasonal
application	position	wage
month (mo.)	relationship	former
rate	separated	emergency
relatives	middle	foreign
applied	signature	add
previous	course	previously
completed	department (dept.)	references
divorced	education	veteran
year (yr.)	experience	supervisor
business	military	entry
single	occupation	information
number (no.)	service	apprenticeship
zone	training	active
college	citizen	described
height	defect	duty
list	nature	discharged
weight	record	graduated
applicant	attend	handicaps
dependents	female	including
location	alien	referred
monthly	disability	vehicle
maiden	additional	vocational
notify	sex	sales
naturalized	subjects	attach
personal	accidents	authorization
remarks	classification	registration
status	earnings	percentage
trade	compensation	profession
salary (sal.)	draft	companies
rank	data	citizenship
persons	disabilities	principal
unemployed	factory	character

(continues)

TABLE 5.2. *Continued*

JOB APPLICATION VOCABULARY

certificate	fume	doctors
descent	graduation (grad.)	serial
details	government (gov't.)	stationary
item	hobbies	suggestion
length	issue	summarize
arrested	identification	example
complete	interviewers	mailing
disposition	insurance	written
graduate	injury	retirement
grammar	legal	Post Office (P.O.)
health	marriage	county
marital	nationality	telephone number (tel.
offense	photograph	no.)
traffic	postal	typewriter
university	qualification	administration
violation	recommended	

FUNCTIONAL WORD/PHRASE VOCABULARY

Adults Only	Closed	Do Not Block Walk
Air Raid Shelter	C.O.D.	Do Not Cross
Ask Attendant for Key	Credit	Do Not Enter
All Cars (Trucks) Stop	Danger	Do Not Push
Bank	Dangerous Curve	Do Not Use Near Flame
Beware of Dog	Dead End	Do Not Use Near Heat
Bridge Out	Deep Water	Do Not Refreeze
Bus Station	Deer Crossing	Do Not Stand Up
Caution	Dentist	Do Not Touch
Construction Zone	Detour	Doctor
Curve	Dim Lights	Don't Walk
City Hall	Dip	Down
Drugs	In	No Parking
Dynamite	Inspection Station	No Right Turn
Do Not Enter	Inflammable	No Passing
Drive Slowly	Information	No Right Turn On Red
Electrical Rail	Instruction	Light
Elevator	Keep Away	No Turns
Employee	Keep Moving	No "U" Turn
Employment Agency	Keep Out	Not A Through Street
Emergency Exit	Keep Off	One Way Do Not Enter
Enter	Keep Closed At All Times	One Way Street
External Use Only	Keep To The Right	Office
Explosive	Knock Before Entering	Open
Emergency Vehicle	Ladies	Out
Emergency	Left Lane Must Turn Left	Out Of Order
End 45	Last Chance For Gas	Pavement EndsEnd Con-
struction	Lane Ends	Ped Xing
Entrance	Live Wires	Play Ground
Exit Speed 30	Listen	Proceed At Your Own
Fallout Shelter	Look Out For Cars	Risk
Fare	Loitering Not Permitted	Private Road
Fire Escape	Loading Zone	Put On Chairs
Fire Extinguisher	Look Out	Pay As You Enter
First Aid	Lost And Found	Police

(continues)

TABLE 5.2. *Continued*

FUNCTIONAL WORD/PHRASE VOCABULARY

Flammable	Left Turn O.K.	Poison
For Sale	Men	Polluted
For Rent	Next Window	Private
Found	Merge Left	Public Telephone
Falling Rocks	Mechanic On Duty	Pull
Flooded	No Admittance	Push
Floods When Raining	No Checks Cashed	Quiet
Four Way Stop	No Credit	Noxious
Freeway	No Driving	Nurse
Freezer	No Dogs Allowed	Pedestrians Prohibited
Fresh Paint	No Dumping	Post No Bills
Gentlemen	No Fires	Post Office
Garage	No Left Turn	Posted
Gate	No Loitering	Private Property
Go Slow	No Fishing	Railroad Crossing
Gasoline	No Hunting	Rest Room
Glass	No Minors	R.R.
Handle With Care	No Smoking	Resume Speed
Hands Off	No Swimming	Right Lane Must Turn
Help Wanted	No Spitting	Right
Help Voltage	No Touching	Right Turn Only
Hospital	No Trespassing	Road Closed
Hunting Not Allowed	Not Responsible	Road Ends
Shelter	Shallow Water	Use Low Gear
School Zone	Shelter	Use Other Door
School Stop	Smoking Prohibited	Wait For Flagman
Slide Area	Step Down (Up)	Watch For Low Flying
Slippery When Wet	Three Way Light	Aircraft
Slow Down	Truck Route	Winding Road
Slow Traffic Keep Right	Take One	Walk
Speed Checked By Radar	Terms Cash	Wait
Steep Grade	Ticket Office	Watch Your Step
Stop	Thin Ice	Wet Paint
Stop Ahead	Third Rail	Women
Stop for Pedestrians	This Way Out	Yield
Stop Motor	This Side Up	Yield Right of Way
Safety First	Unloading Zone	

DRESSING/GROOMING VOCABULARY

arm	leg	gloves
face	mouth	button
hand	neck	buckle
nose	tongue	comb
foot	ear	brush
head	shoulder	soap
teeth	back	dress
finger	ankle	boots
knew	washcloth	sock
cheek	toilet paper	suit
chest	shampoo	shirt
wrist	belt	shoe
toe	shirt	zipper
toothbrush	hat	mitten

(continues)

TABLE 5.2. *Continued*

DRESSING/GROOMING VOCABULARY

nail clipper	pants	pocket
lotion	sweater	snap
chin	coat	zip
elbow	underwear	toothpaste
eye	bow	Kleenex
fingernail	pajamas	towel
hair		

HOME MAINTENANCE VOCABULARY

bed	dinner	drink
bathroom	knife	eat
broom	glass	cook
bucket	grandmother	flush
can	corn	rake
candle	grape	paint
closet	lettuce	crochet
lamp	salad	grapefruit
letter	tomato	lemon
pan	tea	milk
pillow	fish	sugar
pin	pea	coffee
pot	grandfather	cake
purse	cookie	soda pop
radio	apple	drum
room	banana	plant
rug	beans	sweep
sink	butter	wash
bathtub	cabbage	wipe
clothesline	saucer	work
record player	lunch	mother
stove	bowl	father
television	dish	sister
mirror	fork	baby
jar	plate	brother
yard	spoon	uncle
sheet	cereal	aunt
vase	fruit	carrot
refrigerator	juice	cheese
stamp	melon	rice
hose	squash	potato
telephone	watermelon	salt
toilet	hot dog	pepper
bottle	pancakes	egg
house	piano	ice cream
gate	bush	meat
blanket	fence	soup
oven	flower	vegetable
shelf	garden	hamburger
mailbox	grass	toast
cup	tree	honey
napkin	yard	record
breakfast		

Whatever the merits of the arguments may be, most of the developmental spelling series in common use seem to adhere to the idea that American English spelling is sufficiently rule governed that a basic linguistic approach, to be discussed shortly, can be used. Justification for this statement is based on the detailed survey of spelling instructional methodologies reported by Hammill, Larsen, and McNutt (1977). They found that three basal spelling series were used by approximately 60% of the 100 teachers surveyed in 22 states. The authors of these three spelling series all maintain that their method of teaching spelling is based on "linguistic theory."

Linguistics, the study of language, may be subdivided into four discrete but related topics: (1) phonology, the study of speech sounds; (2) morphology, the study of the meaningful units of speech; (3) syntax, the study of the rules that govern sentence formation or word order; and (4) semantics, the study of the process by which a global understanding is gained from the presented language. Although linguistic theories usually encompass all four areas of study, when they are applied to teaching spelling, two elements appear to receive a majority of the emphasis: phonology and morphology. A more specific explanation of these two areas follows.

The term *phonology* is derived from the word *phoneme,* which means a group of sounds so similar that they are considered equivalent. Although there may be slight variations in the production of a phoneme, for all intents and purposes, it is a single speech sound represented by various letters or groups of letters. There are approximately 36 phonemes in American English. A *grapheme* is the letter or combination of letters that represents a phoneme. For example, the phoneme /k/ may be represented by the grapheme "k," "c," or "ck."

The term *morphology* is derived from the word *morpheme,* which refers to the smallest units of meaningful speech. A morpheme may be a word (e.g., *boy,* because it cannot be broken into smaller units that yield meaning) or even a single letter (e.g., the plural marker /z/ in *boys*). Morphology includes the study of the inflections and changes in words that alter their meanings (e.g., prefixes and suffixes).

Although each of the three most used basal spelling series incorporates aspects of linguistic theory, the series are not identical. A brief description of the three spelling series follows.

The words for each unit in the *Silver Burdett Spelling* (1986) series are divided into basic lists and enrichment lists that are topical or thematic in organization. The basic words constitute approximately 90% of the words most students use in their daily writing, with each group or list focusing on one particular spelling pattern. The patterns generally are phonological (e.g., short *a* words) or morphological (e.g., prefixes that mean "not") in nature. In addition to providing general spelling lessons, *Silver Burdett Spelling* integrates many skills from a language arts curriculum (e.g., dictionary skills) and contains various enrichment or extension activities for the more able student.

Basic Goals in Spelling (Kottmeyer & Claus, 1988) also presents basic word lists and word lists for enrichment. The basic words were chosen because research revealed that they are commonly used in the writing vocabulary of students at each level. Although morphological relationships are included, the stress according to the series authors is on sound–symbol relationships, indicating the importance of phonology. The authors of the programs stress the importance of allowing the students to observe similarities of sound and spelling in words and to formulate generalizations, or rules, on their own, rather than stating spelling rules for the students to memorize.

E. E. Wallace, Taylor, Fay, Kucera, and Gonzalez (1988) reported that in the *Riverside Spelling* program presented words are grouped according to their particular spelling patterns: rhyming patterns (*bit, fit, hit*), non-rhyming patterns (*did, dig, dip*), and vowel-changing patterns (*pat, pet, put*). The words of the core vocabulary comprise 80% of the spelling needed by an elementary student, and the upper levels stress words that are important to adult living. Emphasis is placed on integrating various communication skills (e.g., speaking and listening skills, dictionary investigation, and composition).

Remedial Techniques for Spelling

Many students exposed to the traditional, classroom-based spelling programs reviewed in the previous section do not reach expected levels of achievement. With these students, the teacher may decide to try a remedial approach. With students who are targeted for remedial training, the teacher may find it useful to consider the general suggestions offered by Petty and Jensen (1980). In addition to encouraging the development of favorable attitudes toward spelling and good study habits, they recommended the following activities for teaching the "slow speller":

1. Emphasize the importance of the words the student is to learn. Teach a minimum list and make certain that the words on it are as useful as possible.

2. Teach no more words than the pupil can successfully learn to spell. Success is a motivating influence, and the poor speller has probably had much experience with failure in learning to spell the words in the weekly lessons.

3. Give more than the usual amount of time to oral discussion of the words to be learned. In addition to making certain the children know the meanings of the words, ask questions about structural aspects of the words.

4. Pay particular attention to pronunciation. Make certain the pupil can pronounce each word properly and naturally.

5. Strengthen pupils' images of words by having them trace the forms with their index fingers as you write them on the board.

6. Note bad study habits. Show how the habit is harmful and may prevent success in spelling.

7. Check and perhaps modify the child's method of individual study.

8. Provide a wide variety of writing activities that necessitate using the words learned. (pp. 456–457)

Remedial programs differ considerably from the developmentally oriented classroom basal series in that the student is taught on a one-to-one basis or in small groups. Also, multisensory, particularly kinesthetic, elements are frequently incorporated into the training activities. The four programs described in the following sections are suitable for students of all ages, including adolescents and adults.

Fernald's Multisensory Approach

Fernald's (1988) multisensory approach is reported to be highly successful with some students. The student traces the letters (tactile–kinesthetic), sees the tracing (visual), says the letters aloud (vocal), and hears what he or she says (auditory). For this reason, the approach is often referred to as the VAKT (visual–auditory–kinesthetic–tactile) technique.

Fernald's techniques are usually reserved for clinical use with students who have serious problems in spelling. This is unfortunate for, although the activities are highly individualized, they can easily be adapted to work in a regular classroom as well as in a remedial group. Fernald recommended that, when teaching remedial spelling, teachers adhere strictly to the following procedures:

1. The word to be learned is written on the blackboard or on paper by the teacher.

2. The teacher pronounces the word very clearly and distinctly. The students pronounce the words.

3. Time is allowed for each student to study the word.

4. When every student is sure of the word, it is erased or covered and the student writes it from memory.

5. The paper is turned over and the word is written a second time.

6. Arrangements are made so that it is natural for the student to make frequent use, in written expression, of the word he or she has learned.

7. The student is allowed to get the correct form of the word at any time when he or she is doubtful of its spelling.

8. If spelling matches (spelling "bees") are used, they are written instead of oral.

In her book, Fernald described in detail exactly how each of these steps is to be carried out, what verbal instructions are given to the student, and how spelling vocabulary lists are used to select the "foundation" words that should be taught first. Of all the approaches to the remedial teaching of spelling, this one is perhaps the most popular.

Slingerland's Alphabetic Approach

The original alphabetic approach to spelling was developed by Gillingham and Stillman (1970) and is known by several names, including the Gillingham, the Orton–Gillingham, and the Gillingham–Stillman method. The technique stresses the building of sounds into words through the application of visual, auditory, and kinesthetic associations. Students link a sound with a letter, establish a visual memory pattern for a particular word, and then reinforce that pattern by writing the word. This linkage is accomplished by a four-step cover-and-write procedure:

1. Students see a word and say it out loud.

2. They write the word twice (more often if necessary) while looking at it.

3. They cover the word and write it once again.

4. They check the correctness of their spelling by looking at it.

Beth Slingerland's adaptation of this method is particularly useful in remediating moderate to severe cases of spelling difficulty commonly found in school situations. Aho's (1967) description of the adaptation is reproduced below.[5]

> The children should be shown each letter as it is being taught or reviewed, given the name, the sound as *heard* and *felt* in a key word, and then in isolation, the teacher listening for individual weaknesses or errors as *each* child repeats.
>
> The children then trace a correctly formed large-sized pattern of the letter, using the first two fingers or the wrong end of a pencil and naming the letter as it is traced.
>
> After the "feeling" of the letter form is fairly secure, the children copy it and continue tracing lightly with a relaxed hand so the whole arm motion can be felt from the shoulder, the teacher giving help with correct letter forms if needed.
>
> The children are then taught the letter's sound. . . .

---

5. From "Teaching Spelling to Children with Specific Language Disability" by M. S. Aho, 1967, *Academic Therapy, 3* (1), pp. 46–50. Reprinted by permission of PRO-ED, Inc., Austin, TX.

When all have mastered the letter form and sound, the children should (1) name the letter as it is being formed, *h;* (2) give the key word *house;* and (3) give the sound /*h*/.

Large key cards should be placed on the wall for the child's quick and easy reference when he is in doubt or before he makes a "guessing mistake."

The letters may be grouped for similar movement patterns:

Manuscript:

b	f	h	k	l	t	p				
a	c	d	g	o	qu	s	e			
i	j	m	n	r	u	y	v	w	x	z

Cursive:

b	f	h	k	l	e		
a	e	d	g	o	qu		
i	j	p	r	s	t	u	w	(y)
m	n	v	x	y	z	(w)	

Spelling should now begin with letters as single elements of sound.

The teacher may ask: "What consonant says /*h*/?" One child answers: "H (forming the letter in the air as he names it), *house,* /*h*/." The children repeat, then write the letter on paper. Later the response may be simply, "*H,* /*h*/."

To further develop automatic response, say: "Make *b,*" "Make *a,*" "Make /*f*/," the children writing, naming, tracing, and making the next letter as directed. A rhythm should be kept in directing, leaving no lapses of time between directions.

Patterns should be made for tracing and practicing difficult letter connections, such as *br, os, wr,* etc. The large-spaced paper used to begin with may be reduced to smaller spaces after the children gain the "feel" of the sequential movement pattern necessary for the automatic formation of letters.

This adaptation classifies all words into three kinds for spelling. Children should become aware of these approaches to enable them to determine the method for study which gives them self-confidence.

Green-Flag Words are short vowel, purely phonetic words that can be spelled as soon as the letters and sounds of the letters required have been taught. However, unless a child speaks correctly (and this means teacher awareness, control, and direction of speech practice) even these will not be accurately phonetic for him. Unstudied Green-Flag words may be written from dictation following the pattern which is learned in the primary grades:

- Child repeats the word named by the teacher.
- Child hears and gives the vowel sound.
- Child names the vowel, forming the letter in the air as he names it.
- Child spells the word orally, writing each letter in the air as he names it.
- Child writes the word on paper. At times he retraces if needed.

Red-Flag Words are non-phonetic or irregular and must be "learned as wholes" because every sound cannot be heard. (While giving practice, the words are listed on the board accordingly as Red-Flag or Green-Flag words.) The phonetic parts should be noted and the difficult parts are underlined or stressed. In *laugh,* only the *l* is easy. The *augh* has to be learned as a whole. In *could, would,* and *should,* the beginning and ending sounds can be heard, but the *oul* must be learned, so the entire word is learned by this procedure:

- Child copies the word.
- The teacher checks for correct spelling and letter forms.

- Child traces over the letter lightly, naming each letter as it is formed.
- When he feels he has learned the word, he closes his eyes and tries writing the word in the air. He is encouraged to realize that if his hand stops, his brain is no longer directing his hand, so he hasn't learned the word and must do more tracing. He may also try writing the word and checking it with the correct pattern.
- The teacher may give the final checkup by dictating as words, in phrases, or as part of the dictation lesson.

Yellow-Flag Words, or ambiguous words, can be spelled in more than one way as far as the vowel or consonant sound is concerned. Spelling of these words begins after the vowel digraphs, diphthongs, and phonograms are introduced. (They will have been used for reading a considerable time before they are introduced for spelling unless given as "learned words.") From now on, spelling becomes more complicated.

Children in the third and fourth grades, having had training in this way, should acquire the ability to recall all the ways of spelling a given vowel or consonant sound that they have been taught:

/ā/	/ē/	/ī/	/ō/	/ū/	/oo/	/ĕ/	/ou/
a	e	i	o	u	u	e	ou
a-e	a-e	i-e	o-e	u-e	u-e	ca	ow
ai	ee	igh	oa	ew	ew		
ay	ea	ie	ow				
eigh	ie						
ea	y	y					

/c/	/au/	/i/	/oi/		/ch/	/j/
c	au	i	oi	er	ch	j
k	aw	y	oy	ir	tch	dge
ck				ur		

Practice should be given, in studying, in how to listen for or take note of the vowel sound and then to make a selection.

- Child repeats the word given by the teacher. (*Grain.*)
- Child hears and gives the vowel sound, /ā/. After working with the different ways that spell /ā/, the children will discover that /ā/ followed by a consonant sound could be *ai, a-e,* or *eigh;* that *ay* usually occurs at the end of a word or syllable, and that *ea* is found in only a few words.
- After generalizing, the child makes a selection and asks the teacher, "Is it *a-e?*" The teacher answers: "It would make the correct sound but it is not used in this word." The child thinks again and asks: "Is it *ai?*" The reply is: "Yes, in this case it is."
- Child repeats the word.
- Child spells the word, naming each letter as he writes it in the air.

In this way, the teacher serves as the dictionary while the children get the practice which precedes intelligent dictionary technique.

- Children repeat and write *grain* on paper.
- Children trace for study.

Additional related words may be given for further practice; for example, *trail, grave, snake, gray,* etc. Mixed groups of words with the vowel sound of

/ā/ may be given to be worked out and placed under the correct heading (for example, *chain, tray,* etc.) either as independent seat work or as the teacher dictates for organizational practice on paper.

Words for spelling should begin with simple three-letter phonetic short vowel words, progressing in difficulty as the children gain skill; for example, *lap, cast, pack, lash, chat, grasp, branch,* etc. After the "vowel concept" of short *a* is well understood, short *i* will be another sound to open the throat. (The secret of success is in very thorough teaching and the opportunity to "over-learn" the *a,* the *i,* and then discrimination.) Then the other vowels may be included. Continue with the following as the children are ready:

- Words with letter combinations, such as *ink, ank, ing, ong,* etc.
- Adding suffixes or endings and their meanings to words (no rules), for example, *ing, s* or *es, er, est, ed, less, ness, ly, y,* etc.
- Words where the short vowel sound is made long as in vowel–consonant–e words, such as *pan, pane, rip, ripe,* etc.
- Words containing vowel digraphs, diphthongs, and phonograms.
- Words of two or more syllables (over-emphasizing each syllable when pronouncing them). For example, *poppin, butter, fragment, lumber, fiddle, bumble, title, rifle, pavement, dictate,* etc.
- Words doubling the final *f, l, s;* words doubling the final consonant before adding an ending; and words dropping the silent *e* (which requires special teaching not included in this paper).

Phrase writing carried into sentences should begin early.

- Use phonetic words in simple phrases; for example, *grab* the *bat,* etc.
- Begin with a root word, carry it into phrases, and then into simple sentences. This should be dictated by the teacher. Put underlined words on the board to be copied if they haven't been taught:

Camp
camping   camps   camped   camper
to *go* camping   to camp *out*   camped and camped
I like to camp.   I like to go camping.   Do you like to go camping?

- Use any non-phonetic word, repeating it in different phrasing:

Laugh
laughing at that
a laughable matter
laughed and laughed

- The teacher should ask questions to give meaning:

List
What *did* Mother do? Listed the toys.
What *does* she do? Lists the toys.
What is she *doing?* Listing the toys.

- Use root words, dropping the silent *e* or doubling the final consonant, after the procedure for this more difficult spelling has been well structured.
- Write answers to questions. For a one-part question, the teacher should write: "Have you been to the zoo?" The child copies the question and writes: "Yes, I have been to the zoo."

For a two-part question, the teacher should write: "What city do you live in? In what state is it?" The child writes: "I live in Renton. Renton is in the state of Washington." Or, "I live in the city of Renton which is in the state of Washington."

Through structured dictation lessons, these children gain feeling for form, arrangement, sentence construction, continuity, and organization of thoughts which is carried over into individual creative writing. The material used should be made by the teacher and children, but with teacher-controlled guidance to insure the right words for their level of learning, organization, and overall planning.

After the teacher writes the story in cursive on a large sheet of paper so it can be seen about the room, the children copy it, the teacher checking before study to prevent incorrect practice. Any errors made in copying are bracketed to discourage erasing and untidy papers and to encourage the children to "stop and think" before writing.

Words that are too hard to be learned at this time are underlined. These will be written where they can be seen when the final dictation is given. (These may be used for extra work for those able to learn them, too.) The children should note the Green-Flag, Red-Flag, and Yellow-Flag words to determine the method of study.

The teacher should guide directed study in various ways:

- Special practice in writing phonetic words in and related to the story.
- Learning non-phonetic words.
- Adding suffixes and prefixes and their meanings. (Using rules.)
- Writing ambiguous words from the story and giving additional related words under correct headings as far as vowel sounds are concerned.
- Giving phrases from the story for a check.
- Playing games using ambiguous words with the teacher serving as the dictionary.
- Spelldown—requiring the correct response used for oral spelling.

When the weekly study is over, all evidences of study are removed and the teacher dictates the story sentence-by-sentence and phrase-by-phrase. (pp. 46–50)

Proff-Witt's Tutorial Program

The *Speed Spelling 1* and *Speed Spelling 2* programs by Proff-Witt (1978, 1979) incorporate multisensory elements found in the Fernald and Slingerland approaches. These elements are organized into a systematic, highly sequenced, and linguistically oriented tutorial program for use with students in Grades 1 through 12.

The carefully ordered daily lessons, each of which is designed to teach a specific aspect of spelling, form the core of the program. As an example, Lesson 14.4, Prefixes—dis-, mis-, is shown in Figure 5.2. All lessons take about 20 minutes to complete and consist of three parts: word reading, word writing, and sentence writing.

Students who can read the words listed in the lesson but who misspell some of them when writing are taught the misspelled words according to a five-point study plan that is described in the student booklet that accom-

14.4 Prefixes — dis-, mis-

OBJECTIVE	WHAT TUTOR SAYS	WHAT STUDENT DOES	WHAT TUTOR SAYS/DOES IF STUDENT IS RIGHT	WHAT TUTOR SAYS/DOES IF STUDENT IS WRONG
Given a list of words, student (S) says 20 words per minute with 2 errors or less.	A. Read these words. B. I am going to time you for 1 minute. Keep reading the words until the minute is over. Ready, read.	A. Reads words. B. Reads words.	A. **Good reading!** B. Count and chart the number of words right and wrong in 1 minute on Word Reading graph.	A. (1) **Listen** (say sounds of the word) (2) **Sound it out with me** (say sounds together) (3) **Sound it out by yourself** (student says sounds) (4) **What word?** (student says word)
When tutor says words, S writes 12 words in 1 minute with 2 errors or less.* Grades 1-3: write 10 words with 1 error or less.*	A. Write these words as I say them. B. I am going to time you for 1 minute. Keep writing the words as I say them until the minute is over. Ready....	A. Writes words. B. Writes words.	A. **Good spelling!** B. Count and chart the number of words right and wrong in 1 minute on Word Writing graph.* Write words missed on the Tutor Record Sheet.	A. See "How to Study" in the SPEED SPELLING *Student Book*
When tutor reads 2 sentences, S writes the words of the sentences with no spelling errors.	A. Write this sentence... (Choose 2 sentences. Read each 2 times slowly as S writes.)	A. Writes sentence.	A. **Good writing!** Count and chart the number of sentences with no spelling errors on the Sentence Writing graph.	A. Have S write the sentence the right way 1 time.

Word List

disband	misfire	displease	distaste	4
distrust	dislike	misdeal	misuse	8
mistake	misspell	disown	mislead	12
disobey	misprint	misconduct	disorder	16

* When the S passes (writes 12 words in 1 minute with 2 or less errors), write the date on the Skills Checklist in the *Student Book.* Have teacher give *Cycling Test 13.0a.*

Dictation Sentences**

The group must disband.
Tom showed disrespect for his father.
That mistake is a misprint.
Our gun will misfire.
Did she disobey the order?
They dislike a mismatched outfit.

FIGURE 5.2. Example lesson from *Speed Spelling 1.*

From *Speed Spelling 1* by J. Proff-Witt, 1978, Austin, TX: PRO-ED. Copyright 1978 by PRO-ED, Inc. Reprinted with permission.

panies the lessons. Students are told to do the following (Proff-Witt, 1978):

1. Copy the word.

2. Say each letter sound as you trace the letters. Then say the whole word. Do this three times.

3. Say each letter sound as you use your finger to write the letters in your hand. Then say the whole word. Do this three times.

4. Say each letter sound as you write the letters on paper with your eyes closed. Then say the whole word. Do this three times.

5. Test yourself to see if you can write the word the right way.

Shaw's Self-Teaching Approach

Shaw (1971) formulated a teaching system for the self-motivated older student or the adult who wishes to improve his or her spelling ability. He reduced spelling remediation to six basic methods:

1. Mentally see words as well as hear them.

2. Pronounce words correctly and carefully.

3. Use a dictionary.

4. Learn a few simple rules of spelling.

5. Use memory devices.

6. Spell carefully to avoid errors.

The relevance of these six strategies is described in detail in his book, along with numerous related training activities.

We conclude this section on remedial systems by referring the reader to Hansen's (1978) chapter in *The Fourth R: Research in the Classroom*. In this work, she reviews the research relating to three categories of behaviorally oriented methods for remedying spelling problems. Although all of these direct teaching procedures are useful, only one is described here because of the limits of space. The "cover–copy–compare" tactic comprises four steps:

> First, the student analyzes a word and notes its distinctive features; then, he or she writes the word while saying each letter silently; next, he or she covers the word and writes it once again from memory; finally, the student compares the written word to the original to see if it is spelled correctly. The pupil repeats the process until he or she spells each word correctly without referring to the model. (pp. 108–109)

Computer Software Spelling Programs

In recent years, a number of software packages designed specifically to facilitate spelling have become available. The advantages of these programs are obvious (e.g., they enhance independent study and their content is systematically presented). Mercer (1987) described some of the more popular programs available, two of which are reviewed briefly below.

The Spelling System

Produced by Milliken, *The Spelling System* teaches the major spelling patterns of English words, as well as many irregular words. In all, 1,400 words are taught to students in Grades 4 to 8. Posttesting is provided. The program includes four diskettes and a reproducible activity book, and it is designed to be used with the Apple II computer system.

Spelling Wiz

Produced by Science Research Associates, *Spelling Wiz* teaches 300 words commonly misspelled in Grades 1 to 6. A wizard character uses his magic wand to zap missing letters into words. The game has speed and difficulty options. Additional activities are provided on 24 blackline masters. This program may be used with the Apple II, IBM PC/PCjr, Commodore 64, Tandy 1000, and Atari systems.

Game Supplements for Spelling Instruction

Games are useful supplements to a spelling program. Although games provide for diversification in the method of presentation and help to foster interest in the teaching effort, the experienced teacher knows that they are intended as supplements and not as substitutes for a spelling program. Several examples of spelling games follow.

Tongue Twisters

The objective of Tongue Twisters is awareness of initial consonants.

DIRECTIONS

Students think of a sentence in which most of the words start with the same letter, such as "Funny father."

Examples
Funny father fed five foxes. Polly Page put a potato in her pocket.

VARIATION

The teacher writes each student's twister on the board.

Directions

The teacher asks, "How are many of these words similar? Draw a line under the similar parts." The teacher then helps the students to see that most of the words start with the same sound and letter.

Bingo

Bingo is a group game for Grades 3 to 6.

DIRECTIONS

Each student folds a paper into 16 squares. In turn, students are asked to give a word. A scribe writes the word on the board or challenges the donor to spell the word. The students each write the correctly spelled word on any 1 of the 16 squares. When all the squares are filled, a student is selected to come forward. With his or her back to the board, the student spells any one of the words a selected caller gives. Each correctly spelled word enables the students to place a marker on the corresponding Bingo square. The first student to complete a row or a diagonal calls "Bingo" and wins the game. The teacher keeps a list of the words called and checks off the winner. These Bingo squares may be kept for repeated playing.

Treasure Hunt

Treasure Hunt is a team game for Grades 2 to 6.

DIRECTIONS

The teacher selects teams, sets a time limit of 2 minutes, and writes a base word on the board at the head of each team's column. Each student can write only one word, a new one or a corrected one. At a given sign, the first student from each team races to the board and writes any word that can be made with letters in the base word. Each student races back, hands the chalk to the next student, and goes to the end of the line. The game continues until the teacher calls time. The group with the longest correct list in a specified limit is the winner.

Example

For the given base word *tame,* students might write:

tam

am

me

Anagrams

Students can make anagram or Scrabble games for independent activities.

VARIATION 1

Words can be made by adding a letter in vertical or horizontal order.

Example

Cat

   over

      e

      r

      y

VARIATION 2

Students start with a common word and change one letter each time the word is spelled. Winners are those who can complete the greatest numbers of correctly spelled words. Teachers act as final judges of correct spelling.

Example

dime—dome—home—hope

Word Search

Word Search is suitable for students of all ages and ability levels.

DIRECTIONS

A letter grid is prepared. The student is to identify as many words in the grid as he or she can. Points can be awarded based on the number of letters in the words identified. The game can be adapted for individual or group activity.

VARIATION

The difficulty of the game can be changed by using mature or easy words or by arranging the words in left to right, right to left, top to bottom, bottom to top, or diagonal order. An all-purpose letter grid is shown below.

C	L	E	A	N	I	N	G
L	A	O	M	R	Q	K	Z
X	C	T	E	A	M	B	E
B	O	U	C	J	O	U	T
H	O	E	D	Y	U	L	E
S	P	A	N	Z	S	E	E
S	U	C	A	K	E	L	M
M	T	E	B	G	T	I	Y

Telegraph

The objectives of Telegraph are quick thinking and correct spelling. It is a team game for Grade 5.

DIRECTIONS

A goal of 6 or 10 points is established for winning the game, and a time limit is set at four slow counts or 4 seconds for the hesitant speller. Each student is given one or two letters of the alphabet. The teacher pronounces a word to team one. The letters of the telegraph begin to respond in proper order. If the response is correct, the team gets 1 point and another word to transmit. The opposing side gets a word when

1. A member of the team fails to give a letter in the 4-second time limit or by four counts.

2. The completed word is misspelled.

3. Someone on the team "helps" to spell the word.

VARIATION

For primary grades, letters used or needed for the spelling of the teacher's list may be printed on 2-inch × 6-inch cards. Each child receives a card. When the teacher pronounces a word, the telegraph letters take their places in the proper order at the front of the room (alternatively, letters may be placed in a chart holder or on the blackboard ledge).

CONCLUSIONS

Several final observations about teaching and remediating spelling seem in order. For the most part, these conclusions pertain to the nature of spelling and its relationship to language arts instruction.

Spelling should not be taught apart from reading and writing. To be sure, some phoneme–grapheme correspondences, linguistic rules, and a considerable number of different words can be taught in isolation. However, no programs are complete enough, no time periods long enough, and no teachers tenacious enough to teach students all of the words they need to know how to spell in life. Therefore, no spelling program by itself is likely to acquaint the student with all the regularities, patterns, and rules that make up English spelling. A spelling curriculum can set the stage and point the direction for the student, but ultimately good spelling is a consequence of interaction with written language, especially writing.

This idea has the support of F. Smith (1983), who suggested that reading, as well as writing, is important to learning to spell. He mentioned that people can actually spell more words than they ever were taught to spell and more than they are ever called upon to use in writing. He suggested that people learned these words through reading. To him, spelling competence is a natural by-product of learning to read. He wrote,

> I am not asserting that anyone who reads will become a speller because that is not the case. But anyone who is a speller must be a reader. Reading is the only possible source of all the spelling information you have in your head. (1983, p. 193)

If F. Smith is correct, the traditional practices in remedial and developmental education of waiting until the student has mastered reading before introducing spelling and of teaching spelling largely in isolation should be avoided. Instead, reading and writing instruction should begin at the same time, and spelling should be introduced as soon as the student is capable of forming letters. Besides being taught through workbooks, sequenced lessons, and skill exercises, spelling should be integrated into a general language arts program as much as possible. Word recognition, reading comprehension, handwriting, punctuation and capitalization style, and spelling go hand in hand. These are all aspects of written language; they necessarily complement and reinforce one another.

Chapter 6

Correcting Handwriting Deficiencies

DONALD D. HAMMILL

N o matter how well conceived a composition may be, it is useless if it is so illegible that it cannot be read. At one time or another, we have all had the experience of hastily jotting down a good idea and later being unable to decipher the writing. If we frequently cannot read our own handwriting, consider the dismay of those individuals who occasionally have to read what we write. The frustration that teachers encounter as a result of attempting to read the all-too-often unreadable compositions of students is but another reason why good handwriting is desirable. Care must be taken in the physical preparation of compositions if they are to be understood. Also, legible handwriting is simply good manners, a courtesy that readers have the right to expect.

This discussion on correcting handwriting deficiencies is divided into two major parts. The first part describes procedures for measuring handwriting and determining specific deficiencies. The second part is devoted to describing activities and programs that are helpful in remedying poor handwriting.

MEASURING HANDWRITING

The discussion pertaining to the measurement of handwriting has three sections: (1) assessing handwriting readiness, (2) assessing general handwriting competence, and (3) assessing specific errors in handwriting.

Assessing Handwriting Readiness

We do not agree with the concept of "handwriting readiness" as traditionally defined and applied. We doubt, for example, that copying geometric shapes or developing laterality (handedness), ocular control, and visual perception of forms not involving words or letters has much to do with proficiency in handwriting. Much research supports this suspicion (T. L. Harris & Herrick, 1963; Niedermeyer, 1973; Wiederholt, 1971). All the so-called prerequisite readiness skills can probably be developed naturally without any specific instruction as a consequence of learning to write letters, words, and phrases directly. Because we do not believe these readiness skills need to be developed, we prefer a more direct approach to handwriting assessment, one that can be used to identify young students who are likely to become poor writers later in their school life and to pinpoint the specific areas of writing readiness in which training is needed. To achieve these purposes, the teacher can use the Writing subscale of the *Basic School Skills Inventory—Diagnostic* (BSSI) (Hammill & Leigh, 1983).

The BSSI was developed to measure fundamental school-related skills in young students aged 4-0 through 6-11. It was constructed primarily on the basis of the results of extensive interviews with kindergarten and first-grade teachers. In these interviews, the teachers were asked to describe the actual behaviors that seem to distinguish children who are "ready" for school from those who are not. The behaviors that related to writing were singled out and used to form the Writing subscale of the BSSI.

The BSSI can be used either in a norm-referenced fashion (i.e., to identify children who are "low in writing readiness" and therefore need special help) or in a criterion-referenced fashion (i.e., to decide what skills are to be taught and in what order). To use the scale, the teacher selects a particular student to be assessed, reads each item carefully, and then, using personal knowledge about the student's classroom performance relative to the item, decides whether he or she can do the task. The student is not taken aside and "tested" unless the teacher lacks sufficient familiarity with the student's writing behavior to answer the scale items. The items that comprise the subscale are reproduced below.[1]

Writing

Materials: primary pencil
                lined primary writing paper
                card containing a common word
                chalkboard

The items on this subtest measure the child's proficiency in using a pencil and paper for written expression. The items focus on those abilities and skills directly involved in writing letters, words, and sentences. The child may use either manuscript or cursive writing for each of the items.

1. *Does the child write from left to right?*
   To earn a pass on this item, a child should demonstrate some consistent knowledge of left–right progression in writing. Letters or words may be illegible, poorly formed, misspelled, or otherwise inadequate and still be recorded as a pass if, in the execution of her written efforts, the child proceeds in a left-to-right sequence. This sequence does not even have to be on a straight line; diagonal writing is permissible, as long as it is basically left to right.

2. *Can the child write his first name?*
   The intention of this item is to determine whether the child can write (manuscript or cursive) her first name on command. The letters do not have to be properly formed nor does spelling have to be exactly correct. The result must, however, be recognizable as being the child's actual name. Writing one's name from a model is not acceptable here.

3. *When given a common word on a card, can the child copy the word correctly on his own paper?*
   Place a card containing a common word with at least three letters on the child's desk. The pupil must copy the example correctly to receive

───────────

1. From *Basic School Skills Inventory–Diagnostic* by D. D. Hammill and J. Leigh, 1983, Austin, TX: PRO-ED. Reprinted with permission of authors and publisher.

credit for the item. The letters in the word must be recognizable and in proper order.

4. *When a common word is written on the chalkboard, can the child copy it correctly on her own paper?*
   Copying from the chalkboard is an activity required of pupils throughout the school years. Write a common word containing at least three letters on the chalkboard in the size and the type of print you would typically use. While sitting at his usual location in the room, the child must copy the word correctly. The copied word must be correctly spelled, although quality of handwriting is not a consideration on this item.

5. *Can the child write letters upon request by the teacher?*
   Ask the child to write each of the following letters as you say them: *a, b, e, h, m, t.* While the letters do not have to be perfectly formed, all six letters must be clearly legible in order for the child to receive credit.

6. *Can the child write her last name?*
   To receive credit for this item, a child should make a solid attempt at writing his last name. The name may be misspelled and some of the letters may be reversed or poorly formed. The child receives credit for producing a recognizable version of her last name without copying from a model.

7. *When writing, can the child stay on the line?*
   This is a relatively difficult task for many children. In scoring the item, you are concerned with the child's skill at organizing and spacing the letters squarely on the line, not with the legibility or quality of the letters themselves.

8. *When sentences or instructions are written on the chalkboard, can the child copy them correctly on his own paper?*
   Write the following sentence, using the size and type of print you would typically use on the chalkboard: *The dog is brown.* The child must copy the sentence as it appears on the board. Spelling, capitalization, punctuation, and word order must be correct. The child should receive credit even though the letters may be poorly formed and spaced, if the sentence has been properly copied otherwise.

9. *Can the child write simple words dictated by the teacher?*
   Select three simple words that are definitely in the child's vocabulary. Ask the child to write each word after it is dictated. You may repeat words or use the words in context if necessary. To pass the item, the child's effort must yield a recognizable version of each of the three words. However, the words do not have to be correctly spelled, nor do the letters have to be perfectly formed or spaced.

10. *Can the child write simple sentences dictated by the teacher?*
    Create a simple sentence containing no more than four words that are in the child's vocabulary. Ask the child to write the sentence after you say it in a natural, conversational manner. Do not pause between words to enable the child to write each word after it is presented. You may repeat the sentence if the child does not appear to understand or remember it. To receive credit, the child must write each of the words in the correct sequence from left to right. Spelling, capitalization, punctuation, and penmanship should not be considered in scoring the item.

11. *Can the child spell simple words correctly?*
Ask the child to write each of the following words: *in, cat, make.* Say each word to the child, use the word in a simple sentence, and then repeat the word (for example, "*in,* The boy is *in* the house, *in*"). Although the quality of formation of letters is not important, the child must produce clearly recognizable letters in the correct sequences for all three words to pass the item.

12. *Can the child write a complete sentence consisting of at least four words?*
This item pertains to the child's ability to compose a grammatically and syntactically correct sentence. Ask the child to write a story containing at least four sentences. To receive credit, the child must write at least one complete sentence in which at least four words are used with correct grammar and sentence structure. Spelling, penmanship, capitalization, and punctuation do not have to be correct. However, the child's response must clearly include at least four words used properly as a complete unit containing a subject–predicate relationship.

13. *Does the child share information or ideas with others through meaningful and purposeful writing?*
To receive credit on this item, the child must demonstrate the ability to use writing skills independently and spontaneously, regardless of level, to communicate with other people. The child may do this, for example, by writing letters to other children, writing stories for family members, writing notes to the teacher or other students, or in any other manner in which the writing activity is self-initiated and self-directed. Writing letters or stories in fulfillment of class assignments should not be counted.

14. *Can the child write a simple story consisting of at least three sentences?*
To pass this item, the child must be able to independently compose a story that contains a minimum of three sentences. Although the sentences do not have to be grammatically or syntactically perfect, they must be related to some extent in theme or topic. Credit should be awarded even if the relationship among the sentences is minimal (for example, "Tom is my brother. He is big. He likes ice cream."—In this story, all three sentences relate to the topic of Tom). Spelling, capitalization, punctuation, and handwriting quality do not affect scoring on this item.

15. *Does the child use correct capitalization and punctuation in writing?*
Ask the child to write the following two sentences as you dictate them: *I have a ball. The ball is red.* Since the purpose of this item is to determine if the child possesses beginning skills pertaining to capitalization and punctuation, you may repeat the sentences, pausing between words if necessary, to enable the child to write each word as you say it. The child passes the item if he capitalizes the first word in each sentence and places a period at the end of both sentences. Scoring of the item is not affected by the child's spelling or quality of handwriting.

Four-year-olds who score zero on this scale, 5-year-olds who score 2 points or less, and students older than 5 years old who score 6 points or less should be studied further. Possibly a program of special early writing activities should be provided.

Assessing General Handwriting Competence

The experienced teacher has no difficulty in identifying students whose handwriting is below average for their age. However, new teachers or teachers who wish to quantify their observations will find the following techniques helpful.

A popular informal device for assessing the cursive and manuscript handwriting of students in Grades 1 through 8 is Zaner-Bloser's *Evaluation Scale* (1984). To administer this test, the teacher writes a particular sample sentence on the chalkboard. After several practice efforts, the students copy the example on a piece of paper. They are allowed 2 minutes to complete the task. Each paper is then compared with a series of five specimen sentences that are appropriate to the student's grade placement. Each of the sentences represents a different quality of penmanship, ranging from "excellent for grade" to "poor for grade." The use of the specimen sentences permits teachers to make rough estimates about the adequacy of a student's penmanship compared with that of other youngsters in the same grade. Also, space is provided for checking areas that are satisfactory and those that are in need of improvement. Areas checked are letter formation, slant, spacing, alignment/proportion, and line quality. Two examples of Zaner-Bloser's evaluation sentence charts, one for manuscript and one for cursive writing, are provided in Figure 6.1.

Use of these measures will permit only the grossest evaluation of a student's handwriting. For example, they allow the examiner to determine if the student's penmanship skills are seriously behind, level with, or appreciably above those of peers, but they do not yield the kinds of specific information about the child's handwriting that can be used to formulate a remedial program. To derive maximum value from this procedure, teachers must subject the student's written products to a thorough analysis of errors.

Assessing Specific Errors in Handwriting

Having determined, through direct observation or through the use of one of the scales just mentioned, that a problem does exist, the teacher can use Ruedy's (1983) checklist as an initial guide to error analysis (see Table 6.1). While the student is actively engaged in some writing activity, the teacher observes any problematic habits that might affect the quality of the handwriting (e.g., posture, pencil grip); these are noted on the checklist. Later, the writing sample is evaluated for errors involving letter formation and slant, fluency, spacing, and so forth; these too are noted on the checklist.

Although checklists will provide the teacher with some valuable information, they yield no data about the particular letters that are illegible. Therefore, when engaged in a complete analysis of the errors in a student's handwriting, the teacher should keep in mind the work of Newland (1932),

FIGURE 6.1. Evaluation scale for manuscript (first grade) and cursive writing (fifth grade).

From *Evaluation Scale* by Zaner-Blaser staff, 1984, Columbus, OH: Zaner-Bloser, Inc. Copyright 1984 by Zaner-Bloser, Inc. Reprinted with permission.

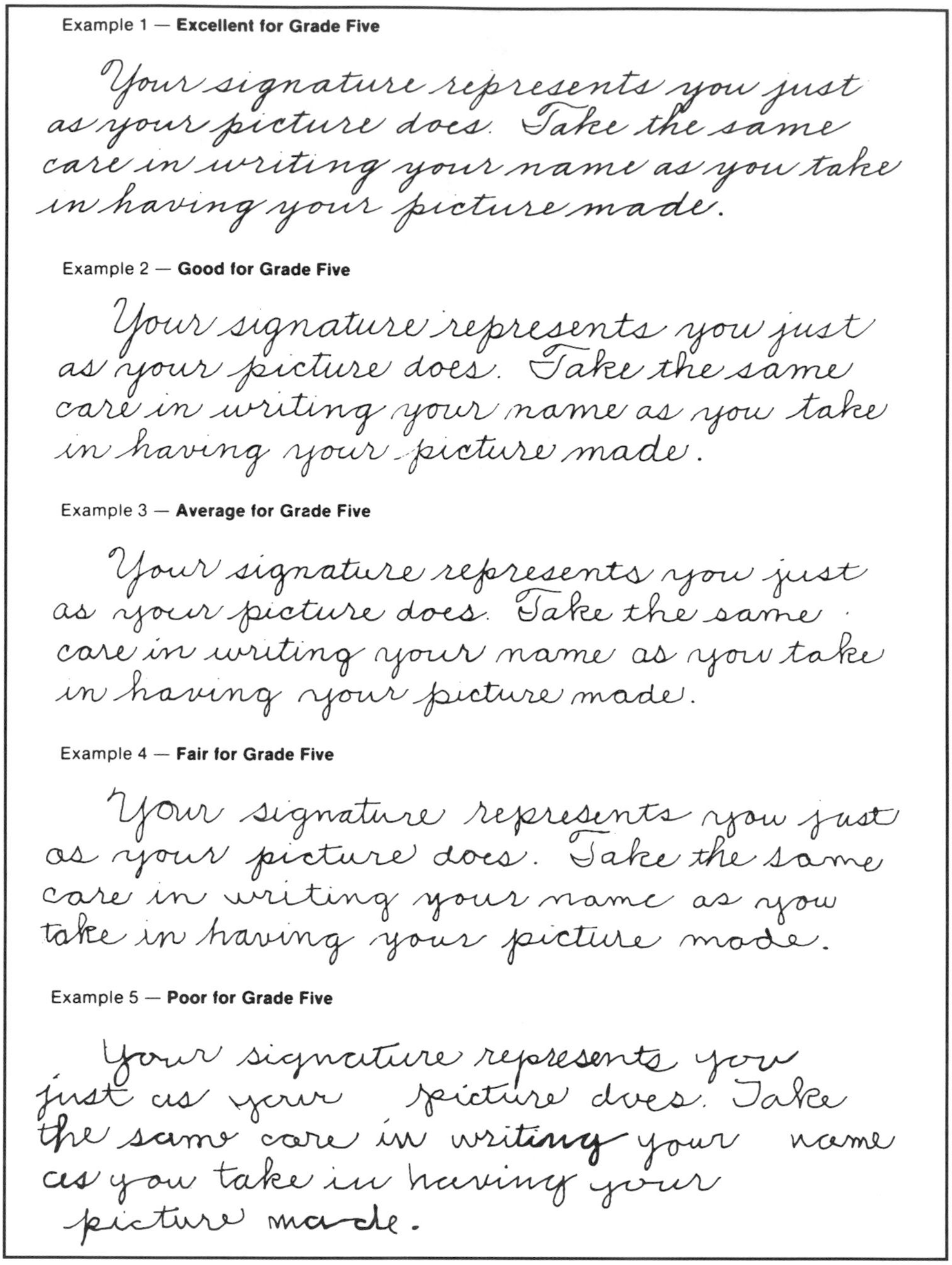

Example 1 — **Excellent for Grade Five**

Your signature represents you just as your picture does. Take the same care in writing your name as you take in having your picture made.

Example 2 — **Good for Grade Five**

Your signature represents you just as your picture does. Take the same care in writing your name as you take in having your picture made.

Example 3 — **Average for Grade Five**

Your signature represents you just as your picture does. Take the same care in writing your name as you take in having your picture made.

Example 4 — **Fair for Grade Five**

Your signature represents you just as your picture does. Take the same care in writing your name as you take in having your picture made.

Example 5 — **Poor for Grade Five**

Your signature represents you just as your picture does. Take the same care in writing your name as you take in having your picture made.

FIGURE 6.1. *Continued*

who studied the handwriting of 2,381 people and analyzed the errors they made. He identified the most common illegibilities in cursive handwriting by elementary-school students and classified the errors into 26 major groups. Surprisingly, almost half of the illegibilities were associated with the letters *a, e, r,* and *t.* If teachers are familiar with these common errors,

TABLE 6.1. Student Handwriting Evaluation Sheet

	O.K.	NEEDS REVIEW
1. Performance observation.		
a. pen or pencil is held properly	☐	☐
b. paper is positioned at a "normal" slant	☐	☐
c. writing posture is acceptable	☐	☐
d. writing speed is acceptable	☐	☐
2. Correct letter formation.		
a. closed letters are closed	☐	☐
b. looped letters are looped	☐	☐
c. stick letters are not loops	☐	☐
d. i's and j's are dotted directly above	☐	☐
e. x's and t's are crossed accurately	☐	☐
f. m's and n's have the correct number of humps	☐	☐
g. all lowercase letters begin on the line (unless they follow b, o, v, or w)	☐	☐
h. b, o, v, and w end above the line	☐	☐
i. all lowercase letters end on the line	☐	☐
j. v's and u's are clearly differentiated	☐	☐
k. connecting strokes of v and y are clearly not rv and ry	☐	☐
l. uppercase letters are correctly and acceptably formed	☐	☐
m. numbers are correctly formed	☐	☐
3. Fluency.		
a. writing is smooth, not choppy	☐	☐
b. pencil pressure appears even	☐	☐
c. words appear to be written as complete units	☐	☐
d. letter connection is smooth	☐	☐
4. Letter size, slant, and spacing.		
a. lowercase letters are uniform size	☐	☐
b. uppercase letters are clearly larger than lowercase letters	☐	☐
c. uppercase letters are uniform in size	☐	☐
d. tail lengths are consistent and do not interfere with letters on the line below	☐	☐
e. tall letters are a consistent height and are clearly taller than other letters	☐	☐
f. writing is not too small or too large	☐	☐
g. slant of letters is acceptable	☐	☐
h. slant of letters is consistent	☐	☐
i. spacing of letters and words is consistent	☐	☐
5. Student attitude toward writing.		
a. student's opinion of his writing skills	☐	☐
b. "writing is hard"	☐	☐
c. writes too slowly	☐	☐
d. feels good about writing	☐	☐
6. Overall teacher evaluation.	☐	☐

(continues)

TABLE 6.1. *Continued*

Teacher Recommendation:

☐ You appear to write smoothly and easily. Your letters are formed correctly. Letter size, slant, and spacing are good. Your writing is neat and legible. It is *not* necessary for you to complete the handwriting exercises.

☐ You appear to write smoothly and easily. You have developed your own writing style which is acceptable, neat and legible. It is *not* necessary for you to complete the handwriting exercises.

☐ You appear to write smoothly and easily. However, your letter formation, neatness, and legibility need some work. Please complete the handwriting exercises.

☐ Writing seems to be difficult for you. You need practice in handwriting skills. Please complete the handwriting exercises.

From "Handwriting Instruction: It Can Be Part of the High School Curriculum" by L. R. Ruedy, 1983, *Academic Therapy, 18*(4), pp. 427–428. Copyright 1983 by PRO-ED, Inc. Reprinted with permission.

they will recognize them in their students' written work. The 10 most common errors were as follows[2]:

1. Failure to close letters (e.g., *a, b, f*) accounted for 24% of all errors.

2. Top loops closed (*l* like *t, e* like *i*) accounted for 13%.

3. Looping nonlooped strokes (*i* like *e*) accounted for 12%.

4. Using straight-up strokes rather than rounded strokes (*n* like *u, c* like *i*) accounted for 11%.

5. End-stroke difficulty (not brought up, not brought down, not left horizontal) accounted for 11%.

6. Top short (*b, d, h, k*): 6%.

7. Difficulty crossing *t*: 5%.

8. Letters too small: 4%.

9. Closing *c, h, u, w*: 4%.

10. Part of letter omitted: 4%.

Newland's (1932) research concerning common errors can easily be incorporated into a simple criterion-referenced assessment procedure that can be used to identify the letters that are illegible in a student's writing and to estimate the particular kinds of errors being made in the formation of those letters. The first step is to obtain a sample of the student's ability to write the letters that are most likely to be illegible. To do this, the teacher might have the student write 5 to 10 *a*'s in a row in cursive, then

2. From "An Analytical Study of the Development of Illegibilities in Handwriting from the Lower Grades to Adulthood" by T. E. Newland, 1932, *Journal of Educational Research, 26*, 249–258.

an equal number of *b*'s, *e*'s, *h*'s, *m*'s, *n*'s, *o*'s, *r*'s, and *t*'s. These particular letters are selected because the research suggests that they are the ones that are most often produced in a defective, unreadable fashion. The student's paper might look like the following:

a h d a h
l h b t b, etc.

An alternative to Step 1 might be to take an example of the student's spontaneous or elicited written work and circle the *a*'s, *b*'s, *e*'s, *h*'s, and so on. The next step is to evaluate the way a pupil forms letters according to the criteria listed in Figure 6.2. If the manner in which the student forms the

		Wrong	*Right*
1.	*a* like *o*	*o*	*a*
2.	*a* like *u*	*u*	*a*
3.	*a* like *ci*	*ci*	*a*
4.	*b* like *li*	*li*	*b*
5.	*d* like *cl*	*cl*	*d*
6.	*e* closed	*e*	*e*
7.	*h* like *li*	*li*	*h*
8.	*i* like *e* with no dot	*e*	*i*
9.	*m* like *w*	*w*	*m*
10.	*n* like *u*	*u*	*n*
11.	*o* like *a*	*a*	*o*
12.	*r* like *i*	*i*	*r*
13.	*r* like *n*	*n*	*r*
14.	*t* like *l*	*l*	*t*
15.	*t* with cross above	*t*	*t*

FIGURE 6.2. Evaluating formation of letters.

letters differs from that suggested in the column marked "right," one can assume that illegibility will be increased. The handwriting examples under the "wrong" column indicate the most common errors made in the formation of the eight letters. These particular errors are often referred to in the language arts literature as the 15 handwriting demons and are purported to cause or contribute to most of the illegibilities in cursive writing.

For teachers who desire a more structured approach to the informal assessment of handwriting errors, we recommend the checklist of Gueron and Maier (1983). This checklist (reproduced in Table 6.2) can be applied to any handwriting sample. Its use will direct the teacher's attention to all major errors that contribute to illegible handwriting.

The procedures outlined in this section will enable teachers to identify (1) the students who need help in handwriting, (2) the general areas requiring attention (slanting, spacing, etc.), (3) the individual letters being misformed, and (4) the specific kinds of errors causing the illegibilities. Teachers need this kind of information to individualize remedial programs.

TABLE 6.2. Analysis of Handwriting Errors

Directions: Analysis of handwriting should be made from a sample of the student's written work, not from a carefully produced sample. Evaluate each task and mark in the appropriate column. Score each task "satisfactory" (1) or "unsatisfactory" (2).

I. Letter formation

   A. Capitals (score each letter 1 or 2)

A ___	G ___	M ___	S ___	Y ___
B ___	H ___	N ___	T ___	Z ___
C ___	I ___	O ___	U ___	
D ___	J ___	P ___	V ___	
E ___	K ___	Q ___	W ___	
F ___	L ___	R ___	X ___	

Total ___

B. Lowercase (score by groups)

Score (1 or 2)

   1. Round letters
     a. Counterclockwise
      a, c, d, g, o, q   ___
     b. Clockwise
      k, p   ___
   2. Looped letters
     a. Above line
      b, d, e, f, h, k, l   ___
     b. Below line
      f, g, j, p, q, y   ___
   3. Retraced letters
    i, u, t, u, w, y   ___
   4. Humped letters
    h, m, n, v, x, z   ___
   5. Others
    r, s, b   ___

(continues)

TABLE 6.2. **Continued**

C. Numerals (score each number 1 or 2)

1 ____	4 ____	7 ____	10–20 ____
2 ____	5 ____	8 ____	21–99 ____
3 ____	6 ____	9 ____	100–1,000 ____
			Total ____

Score
(1 or 2)

II. Spatial relationships

A. Alignment (letters on line) ____
B. Uniform slant ____
C. Size of letters
  1. To each other ____
  2. To available space ____
D. Space between letters ____
E. Space between words ____
F. Anticipation of end of line (hyphenates, moves to next line) ____

Total ____

Score
(1 or 2)

III. Rate of writing (letters per minute)

Grade 1: 20
2: 30
3: 35
4: 45
5: 55
6: 65
7 and above: 75 ____

Scoring	Satisfactory	Questionable	Poor
I. *Letter formation*			
A. Capitals	26	39	40+
B. Lowercase	7	10	11+
C. Numerals	12	18	19+
II. *Spatial relationships*	7	10	11+
III. *Rate of writing*	1	2	6

From *Informal Assessment in Education* by G. R. Gueron and A. S. Maier, 1983, Palo Alto, CA: Mayfield. Reprinted with permission.

REMEDYING PROBLEMS IN HANDWRITING

The remainder of this chapter is devoted to discussing how handwriting can be taught to students who exhibit difficulty in developing proficiency in the skill. Specifically, five topics are dealt with. These are (1) background information, (2) description of a remedial program, (3) correction of common handwriting difficulties, (4) classroom approaches for use with normal learners and writers with mild problems, and (5) supplemental teaching materials.

Background Information Concerning Handwriting Instruction

Before we describe selected procedures for teaching handwriting, several important points should be made. These points pertain to the management of left-handed writers, the current ideas about cursive and manuscript writing forms, the role of readiness in teaching, a scope-and-sequence guide to writing objectives and instruction, and principles for effective programs.

Left-Handed Writers

Teaching handwriting to left-handed students presents a few special problems, although in general the techniques used with right-handed students will suffice with slight adjustment. Some of the adjustments are depicted later in this chapter in Figure 6.7. Readers are referred to the work of Petty and Jensen (1980) or Polloway and Smith (1992) for thorough discussions of modifications for left-handed learners. Current thinking dictates that a student who is definitely left-handed should be allowed to write with the preferred hand. Forcing the student to use the right hand is not recommended.

Cursive or Manuscript

Often teachers are unsure whether to teach manuscript or cursive initially. Arguments for starting with cursive writing are that it reduces spatial judgment problems for students and that there is a rhythmic continuity and completeness that is not present in manuscript writing. Also, reversals are virtually eliminated with cursive writing. When cursive is taught initially, the need to transfer from one form to the other is avoided. Many problem writers have difficulty transferring to cursive after learning manuscript writing.

An advantage of manuscript writing is that it is supposed to be easier to learn because it consists of only circles and straight lines (Voorhis, 1931). Also, manuscript letters are closer to the printed form used in reading than are cursive letters. Some educators (Plattor & Woestehoff, 1971) believe that students do not have to transfer to cursive writing at all since the manuscript form is readable and just as rapid.

Overall, the research suggests that in most cases either style can be taught. The common practice, however, is to begin with manuscript and to introduce cursive at about the third-grade level.

The Role of Writing Readiness in Teaching

The concept of handwriting readiness should be considered carefully before planning an instructional program for any student. Most students are "ready" to begin to write before they reach their sixth birthday and enter school. In point of fact, children usually start reading and writing during the preschool years as a natural consequence of daily interaction with the print that is omnipresent in their environment. Children must be able to see, to grasp a pencil, and to think of an idea before they can learn to write, and, of course, they must want to write. When these abilities are present, formal instruction in writing can begin with every likelihood of success. When these basic abilities are lacking, they will unlikely be developed by a traditional school "readiness" program.

We feel that the most efficient way to teach students to write is directly, with a straightforward approach. Practice in writing is the best way for students to learn to write in a left-to-right direction, to discriminate one letter from another, and to use a pencil to form legible letters. Perceptual–motor training, tracing of geometric shapes, walking board exercises, and activities that do not involve letters are off-task and should be avoided—unless they are being done for their own sake, to improve general eye–hand coordination or to amuse the children. Fortunately, some readiness programs that are available commercially do emphasize the skills of early writing; these should be sought out and used.

A Scope-and-Sequence Chart for Handwriting Instruction

In teaching handwriting, the teacher needs a scope and sequence of skills. The scope-and-sequence chart enables the teacher to identify skills to be taught and their order of presentation. Graham and Miller (1980) presented an eight-level handwriting scope-and-sequence chart. In this chart (presented as Figure 6.3), each level represents approximately one school year. The authors pointed out that, "depending upon the student's characteristics and the severity of the handicapping condition, the rate of progression through the curriculum may be either decelerated or accelerated" (p. 5).

Principles for Effective Programs

We conclude this section with a listing of the principles and conditions that are vital to the preparation of effective programs for poor writers. The items in this list are drawn from the work of Graham and Miller (1980, pp. 5–6), who recommended that handwriting instruction be

1. Taught directly, rather than incidentally.
2. Individualized to each student's needs.
3. Planned, monitored, and modified according to assessment information.
4. Flexible in its use of different techniques.
5. Taught in a short daily period.
6. Done in meaningful contexts when possible.
7. Unaccepting of slovenly work.

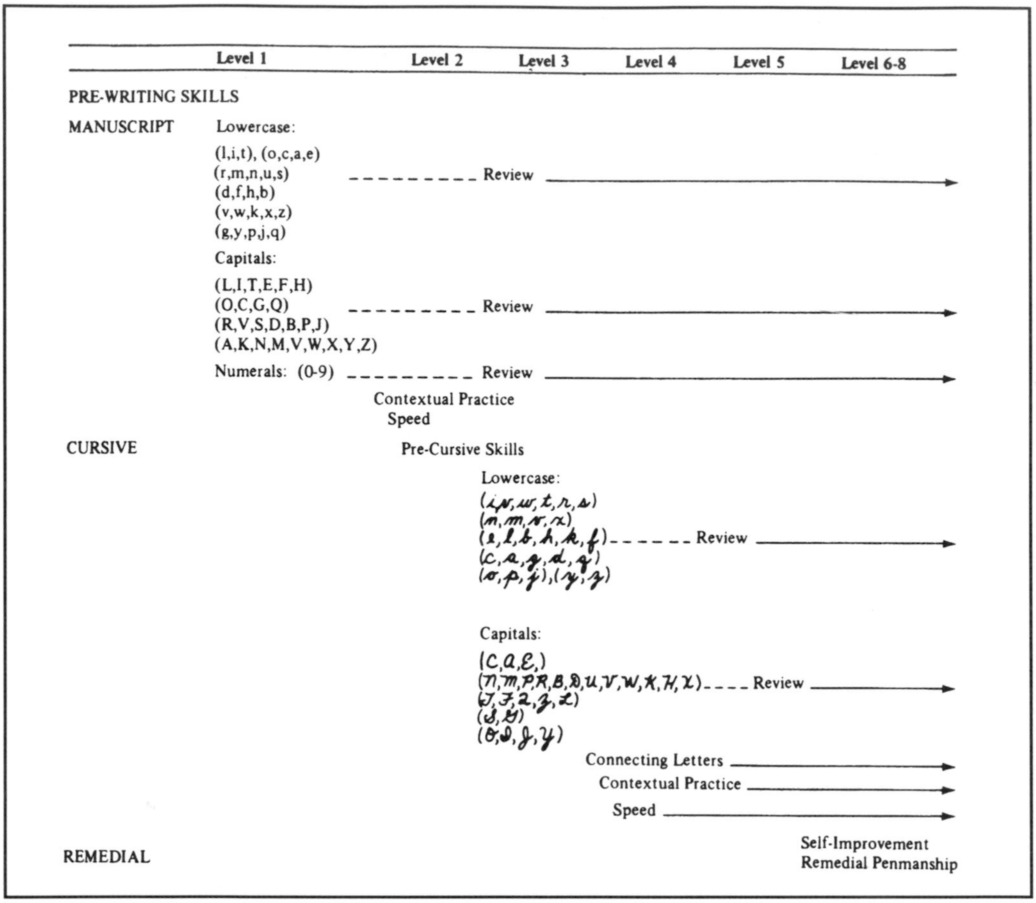

	Level 1	Level 2	Level 3	Level 4	Level 5	Level 6-8

PRE-WRITING SKILLS

MANUSCRIPT — Lowercase:

(l,i,t), (o,c,a,e)
(r,m,n,u,s) ────────── Review ─────────────────────────►
(d,f,h,b)
(v,w,k,x,z)
(g,y,p,j,q)

Capitals:

(L,I,T,E,F,H)
(O,C,G,Q) ────────── Review ─────────────────────────►
(R,V,S,D,B,P,J)
(A,K,N,M,V,W,X,Y,Z)

Numerals: (0-9) ────────── Review ─────────────────────►

Contextual Practice
Speed

CURSIVE — Pre-Cursive Skills

Lowercase:

(i,v,w,t,r,s)
(n,m,v,x)
(e,l,b,h,k,f) ────── Review ─────────────────────►
(c,a,g,d,q)
(o,p,j),(y,z)

Capitals:

(C,a,E,)
(n,m,P,R,B,D,U,V,W,X,H,L) ──── Review ───────────►
(J,J,2,z,z)
(S,H)
(O,D,J,Y)

Connecting Letters ───────────────────────►
Contextual Practice ──────────────────────►
Speed ────────────────────────────────────►

REMEDIAL — Self-Improvement
Remedial Penmanship

FIGURE 6.3. Handwriting scope and sequence.

From "Handwriting Research and Practice" by S. Graham and L. Miller, 1980, *Focus on Exceptional Children, 13*, p. 6.

8. Dependent on attitudes of student and teacher.

9. Undertaken in a conducive atmosphere.

10. Taught by teachers who can write legibly.

11. Accompanied by self-evaluation.

12. Encouraging a consistent, legible style.

A Specific Remedial Program

After targeting a level and a letter for training, the teacher is ready to intervene. The procedures for teaching handwriting skills necessary for legible writing are subdivided by Reger, Schroeder, and Uschold (1968, pp. 220–224) into four developmental levels.[3] The teacher should begin with

---

[3]Material in this section was drawn from *Special Education: Children with Learning Problems* by R. Reger, W. Schroeder, and K. Uschold, 1968, New York: Oxford University Press. Copyright 1968 by Oxford University Press, Inc. Used with permission.

Level I and move gradually to Level IV as the pupil masters the skills. Although this sequence could be used as a program for all pupils, it is intended for use with students who experience difficulty in handwriting. Most students will respond adequately to one of the developmental systems described later in this chapter.

Level I—Introductory Movements

Using the chalkboard as a prop, the teacher discusses how the movements of writing are made; for example, "First we go up and then we go down." The teacher demonstrates on the board. Or he or she says, "We go away from our body and then toward our body." The students make the movement at the board, looking at the teacher's model rather than the board as they draw. They say "up" when they are going up and "down" when they are going down. The movements should be rhythmic and free flowing. The students should stand at least 6 inches from the board.

After the student has had several days of practicing the movement on the board following the procedure above, the auditory clue is eliminated. The student makes the movement on the board in silence, still looking at the model rather than his or her hands. Then the outlined procedures are repeated, this time on paper or large newsprint, using crayon. Reger et al. (1968, p. 221) suggested the movements shown in Figure 6.4.

The teacher will also want to keep in mind Spalding and Spalding's (1986) observation that only the six different pencil strokes shown in Figure 6.5 are necessary for making lowercase manuscript letters. One or two

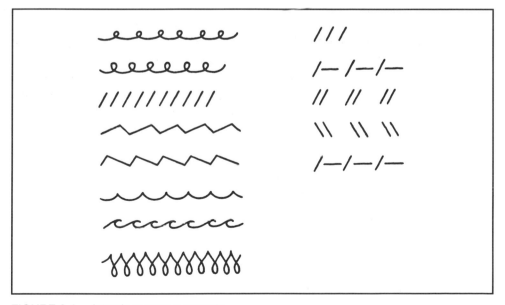

FIGURE 6.4.   Introductory movements.
From *Special Education: Children with Learning Problems* by R. Reger, W. Schroeder, and K. Uschold, 1968, New York: Oxford University Press.

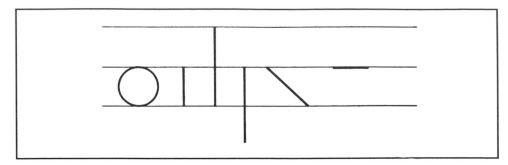

FIGURE 6.5. Pencil strokes needed for lowercase letters.
From *The Writing Road to Reading* (3rd ed., p. 67) by R. B. Spalding and W. T. Spalding, 1986, New York: William Morrow. Reprinted with permission of the authors and publisher.

of these movements can be introduced each week in conjunction with Reger's exercises. If a student has difficulty with any of the movements, additional practice should be given as often as possible. Before a new movement is introduced, the previous ones should be reviewed.

Level II—Introductory Movements on Paper

In Level II, the procedures from Level I are repeated, but the student is allowed to look at the paper. The teacher should keep in mind that (1) the student should have correct posture when performing the movements; (2) the slant of the paper should be correct, and dependent on the hand used; and (3) the hand position should be proper. Teachers can usually find detailed descriptions of the proper positions for writing in the teacher's manuals that accompany the various commercially available writing programs.

The paper used for the first movements on paper should have 1-inch spaces. The letters should be three spaces high initially, then two spaces high, and finally one space high. The teacher can line the paper with felt-tipped markers, using blue for the top line, green for the middle line, and red for the bottom line. This helps the children stay on and within the lines. Serio (1968) is a source of information regarding writing materials, especially pencils and paper with colored lines.

Level III—Movements for Cursive Writing

In Level III, the procedures set forth under Level I are followed, using Spalding and Spalding's (1986) movements shown in Figure 6.6. According to Spalding and Spalding, cursive writing is an adaptation of manuscript and it is only necessary to teach five connecting strokes. Students begin on the chalkboard and eventually progress to newsprint, using crayon or marker.

FIGURE 6.6. Cursive writing.

From *The Writing Road to Reading* (3rd ed., p. 83–84) by R. B. Spalding and W. T. Spalding, 1986, New York: William Morrow. Reprinted with permission of the authors and publisher.

Level IV—Movements for Cursive Writing on Paper

In writing letters, students progress from the chalkboard (repeating the procedures stipulated under Level I), to 1-inch–lined paper where three lines have been drawn with red, green, and blue markers, and finally to regular-lined paper. Materials for Level IV include overlays on which each letter has been made with felt-tipped marker, blank overlays, and an overhead projector.

In general, the following sequence is appropriate for teaching at this level:

1. The teacher names the letter.

2. The teacher discusses the form of the letter while the student looks at it.

3. The teacher makes the letter for the student on a blank overlay. The different parts of the letter are made with different-colored markers to show the various movements.

4. To show the direction of the letters, such as *s, z,* and others, cinematic materials are used. A Polaroid filter mounted on a motorized clear plastic wheel is placed over the transparency. The teacher can thus move the letters from left to right, or right to left, to show the student the direction of the letter.

5. Kinesthetic feel for the form of letters is developed by having students use sunken and raised script letterboards.

6. The student makes the letter while looking at the model.

7. The student keeps his or her eyes on the model, not on the hand.

8. The teacher helps the student compare his or her work with the model.

9. To help the student who has difficulty with the letter, the teacher may give oral clues or hold the student's hand as he or she makes the letter. Some students may need to write the letter in salt or sand (on a salt tray).

10. The student writes the letter on the chalkboard without the model.

11. The student writes the letter on newsprint without a model, eyes averted.

12. The student writes on paper with eyes on the paper.

In this sequence, 1-inch–lined paper should be used, with the writing space divided into three parts (by colored markers). The teacher puts a model of the letter on the student's paper, and the letter form and direction are discussed. If the top line is always blue, the middle line green, and the bottom line red, the teacher can say to the child "Start on the red line, go up to the blue line, come down to the red line." The lines should be dark and heavy so that the student will be able to stay within them.

When the student traces the model of the letter and makes a row of letters, the teacher should watch the student carefully. In this way, the teacher can evaluate the student's success with the letter and decide where he or she needs help. The student is then taught to write within the 2-inch–lined area, next within 1-inch lines, and finally on regular primary paper.

Before each writing assignment, correct habits for writing should be reviewed. The teacher should demonstrate proper positioning of the paper and then check each paper for positioning. Masking tape or marks on the desk can be used to show the student how he or she should position the paper. Writing posture also should be discussed and demonstrated: elbow on the desk, nonwriting hand holding the paper, fingers on the pencil correctly, feet on the floor, head properly tilted.

Because paper positions, body positions, and pencil grips are different for left- and right-handed writers, teachers have to be aware of these differences and help their students to adopt an effective stance. Postures, grips, and positions for left- and right-handed persons are pictured in Figure 6.7.

When the student has succeeded in writing the letters accurately, he or she should be taught to connect letters and then to write simple words. As the student progresses, he or she should be asked to copy simple sentences and then gradually encouraged to attempt to write without copying. At this point, handwriting becomes an expressive language ability. The time of the writing period will vary from class to class and from student to student. If one student can tolerate writing only one line, he or she should write only that much. If another student can write a whole page, he or she should be allowed to do so.

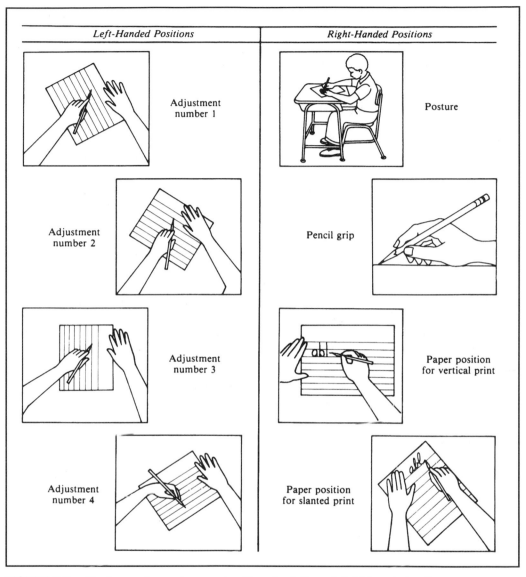

FIGURE 6.7. Posture, grip, and paper positions for left- and right-handed writers.
From "Handwriting Research and Practice: A Unified Approach" by S. Graham and L. Miller, 1980, *Focus on Exceptional Children, 13,* pp. 2, 9, and 12.

The "applied behavioral analysis" (ABA) technique is particularly productive when specific errors in handwriting have been noted and selected for improvement. For example, the teacher may have decided as a result of observation or testing that the student's difficulty is centered in letter illegibility, improper spacing, sloppiness, slowness, and/or unacceptable slanting. One of these problems, probably the one that is the most annoying to the teacher, can be chosen as the target for retraining and the principles of ABA implemented. The dynamics of managing an ABA program are based on the ideas expressed in the behavior modification section in Chapter 8. Individuals interested in this approach should read the section mentioned, as well as Lovitt's (1975) description of how the technique has been used to help improve students' handwriting skills.

Correcting Common Problems

Wasylyk and Milone (1984) pointed out that the correction of poor habits in older students is perhaps the most neglected aspect of handwriting instruction. They went on to discuss ways of correcting these habits by focusing on the most commonly encountered problems. Common handwriting problems and techniques that may be used to ameliorate them are listed in Table 6.3.

Classroom Approaches to Handwriting Instruction

The experienced teacher will recognize readily that the procedures just outlined cannot be used with all the students in a regular class. They are best reserved for use in special remedial classes with an enrollment of 6 to 10 students or with those students in the regular class who are developing problems in writing. Although this book is concerned primarily with the management of students with problems, an overview of the "developmental" teaching systems is included because such systems can often be used in their entirety or in adapted form with remedial cases.

Three classroom systems are described briefly in this section. The first, *Handwriting: Basic Skills and Application,* is among the most popular in use today. The other two, *D'Nealian Handwriting* and *Cursive Writing Program,* contain elements that make their use with remedial cases highly attractive.

Handwriting: Basic Skills and Application

Handwriting: Basic Skills and Application (Barbe, Lucas, Wasylyk, Hackney, & Braun, 1987) comprises a series of nine student workbooks and teacher's editions covering kindergarten through Grade 8. Throughout, the teacher is given instructions regarding management of the left-handed student, correct ways of holding the pencil, and proper positions for the paper.

The program teaches the most widely used alphabets, introduces letters in a logical sequence, provides specific instruction in letter formation and ample opportunities for practice, maintains manuscript skills through continual review, emphasizes handwriting in a variety of practical situations, and provides supportive materials such as handwriting awards, special pencils, practice paper, and chalkboard activities. These ideas are incorporated into the lessons that make up the program.

TABLE 6.3. **Common Handwriting Problems and Corrective Techniques**

Handwriting is so small that it cannot be read easily.

- Use ruled paper on which a midline appears, or rule a midline on standard writing paper. Explain that minimum letters touch the midline.
- Practice large writing at the chalkboard.
- Give correct models of words, have the student copy them, then evaluate for size.
- Identify the problem so the student is aware of what must be corrected.

When two maximum undercurves are joined (ll, fl), letter formation suffers.

- Emphasize that the basic undercurve stroke must be made correctly.
- Make a wide undercurve to allow room for the loop that follows.
- Make slant strokes parallel to each other.

The height of the lowercase letters is not consistent.

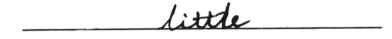

- Use paper that has a midline and a descender space, or rule a midline on standard paper.
- Have the student identify maximum, intermediate, and minimum letters.
- Evaluate writing for alignment by drawing a horizontal line across the tops of the letters that are supposed to be of the same size.
- Shift paper as the writing progresses.

The maximum letters (b, t, h, k, l) are made without loops.

- Demonstrate and explain proper formation of the undercurve that begins the loop of the letter.
- Demonstrate and explain proper formation of the slant stroke.
- Point out that the top of the letter is rounded and determines the width of the loop.

The slant of the writing is irregular.

- Check for correct paper position.
- Pull strokes in the proper direction.
- Shift paper as writing progresses.
- Shift hand to the right as writing progresses.
- Evaluate slant by drawing lines through letters to show the angle at which they are made.

(continues)

TABLE 6.3. *Continued*

When an undercurve joins an overcurve (in, um), the letters are poorly written.

instrument

- Show how the undercurve to overcurve is a smooth, flowing stroke.
- Explain that the undercurve ending continues up and then quickly overcurves into the downward slant stroke.

The quality of the writing changes within a single word.

laboratory

- Shift both the paper and the hand as the writing progresses. The paper moves toward the student, and the hand moves away.
- Write in the same area of the paper, roughly a 6-inch–diameter circle that is located at the midpoint of the body about 10 inches from the edge of the desk.
- Do not reach out to write or write very close to the body.

The letters a, d, g, o, and q are not closed.

bout amount

- Stress proper beginning strokes.
- Write correctly formed model letters on the student's paper, explaining the strokes while the student watches.

Nonlooped letters such as t, p, i, u, and w are looped and become difficult to read.

little

- Demonstrate that there is a pause at the top of these letters.
- Encourage the student to write more slowly, as speed causes the loops in the letters.
- Pause before making the slant stroke in the letters a, d, g, i, j, p, q, t, u, w, and y.
- Emphasize the retrace in these strokes.

Checkstroke joinings (for example br, we) are poorly made.

break weather

- Demonstrate the letters b, v, o, and w, and explain the strokes as you form them.
- Use the auditory stroke description "retrace and swing right" as students practice b, v, o, and w.
- Demonstrate correct joinings in which the first letter has a checkstroke.
- Point out the letter forms that change when they are preceded by a checkstroke: br, os.

Handwriting is so slow that there is no smoothness in the individual letters.

Intermediate

- Encourage students to write letters with smooth and complete motions.
- Engage in relaxation exercises before practicing writing. Excessive muscle tension is the cause of slow writing.
- Emphasize rhythm rather than alignment or slant. These qualities can be developed later.

(continues)

TABLE 6.3. *Continued*

Joinings involving overcurves, such as ga and jo, are not well made.

baggage   job

- Show how all overcurve connections cross at the baseline, not above or below it.
- Make the overcurve motion continuous. Do not change its direction in midstroke.
- Check letter formation.

From "Corrective Techniques in Handwriting: Cursive" by T. M. Wasylyk and M. N. Milone, in *Handwriting: Basic Skills for Effective Communication* (pp. 334–338) by W. B. Barbe, V. H. Lucas, and T. M. Wasylyk (Eds.), 1984, Columbus, OH: Zaner-Bloser. Reprinted with permission.

The lessons are organized according to the types of strokes required to form particular letters—for example, undercurve letters (*i, j*), cane stem letters (*u, y*), and cursive joinings (*li, bl*). Each lesson begins with a discussion of the letter being taught. Next, the teacher demonstrates (slowly) the letter form and verbalizes the strokes while writing the letter on the chalkboard. The student then traces or writes the strokes and letters. Kinesthetic–tactile reinforcement through motioning the letter in the air and tracing the letter with the finger or pencil is also incorporated into the teaching steps. Next, goals are set and supplemental materials are chosen. There follows a discussion of teaching steps and activities. After the student has completed the lesson, his or her progress is evaluated.

D'Nealian Handwriting

The *D'Nealian Handwriting* system (Thurber, 1981) provides the teacher with an alternative to the traditional methods in which the manuscript–cursive choice is accepted as an instructional necessity. In this system, the lowercase manuscript letters closely resemble the corresponding cursive letters. The D'Nealian letter forms are depicted in Figure 6.8. It is obvious that except for *b, f, r, s, v,* and *z* the manuscript letters can be easily changed to cursive simply by adding the joining uphill (⌣) and overhill (⌒) strokes. Recommendations are included regarding letter size, spacing and slant, rhythm, and evaluation. Evaluation is unique in that it stresses general legibility, rather than strict adherence to particular letter formations, model perfection, and so forth. Because the materials provided are not essential, the program is cost effective. For many remedial cases, the D'Nealian approach may well work and should be tried. V. L. Brown (1984b) provided a detailed description of this program emphasizing its use with special and remedial students.

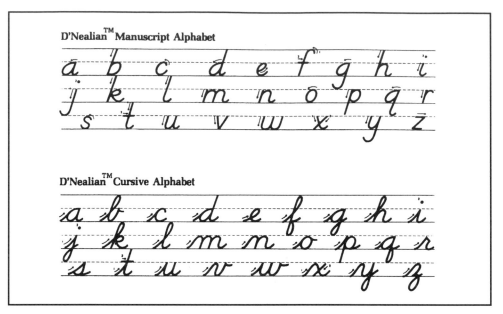

FIGURE 6.8. D'Nealian handwriting.

From *D'Nealian™ Handwriting* by D. N. Thurber, 1981, Glenview, IL: Scott, Foresman. Copyright 1981 by Scott, Foresman and Company. Reprinted with permission.

The Cursive Writing Program

The *Cursive Writing Program* (S. K. Miller & Engelmann, 1980) was designed to teach cursive writing to students who have already mastered manuscript writing. The program teaches how to form letters, construct words, transcribe sentences, and write fast and accurately. There are 140 twenty-minute developmentally sequenced lessons in the program. Materials consist of a teacher's manual and a student workbook containing practice pages. The lessons follow a consistent format—a series of exercises followed by an awarding of points for successful work. An entry test allows for individualization and makes the program suitable for classroom or remedial use.

Supplemental Teaching Materials

In addition to the commercial programs, a multitude of supplemental teaching materials exist that are useful in remediating writing problems. Exactly which of these materials is appropriate depends entirely on the needs of the individual children being taught. Examples of the kinds of materials that are used from time to time are discussed below. Because, as a rule, teaching materials do not have authors, the name of the publishing company from which the material is available appears in parentheses after the material's title.

Motor Coordination Chalkboards

The kind of eye–hand coordination involved in using writing implements is essential to the development of proper handwriting skills. The *Motor Coordination Chalkboards* (PRO-ED) were designed to develop such abilities. The materials are particularly helpful for working with students with aphasia, orthopedic disabilities, and learning disabilities. This therapy tool consists of eight different boards that progress from simple to complex manual-motor patterns. A unique feature of the boards is the raised lines, which provide tactile–kinesthetic feedback.

Right-Line Paper

Right-Line Paper (PRO-ED) is designed to be used by learning disabled, physically handicapped, partially sighted, and adult rehabilitation students who have difficulty staying on the lines of regular writing paper. This paper has a raised line superimposed on the printed line. The raised line enables the writer to feel as well as see the base line. The printed line is green so that it can be easily distinguished from pencil or pen marks. The paper comes in narrow or wide rule. The wide-rule paper has a dashed line between each raised line to serve as a guide for letter formation.

Pencil Grips

The simple and practical pencil grips that are available from many companies can improve penmanship by reducing hand and finger stress. Use of a grip gives the writer a more efficient, comfortable hold on a pencil or pen. The grips are especially useful for young writers, motor handicapped students, and remedial cases.

Write On–Wipe Off (WOWO) Boards

The Write On–Wipe Off Boards (Palmer) are durable white plastic boards imprinted with a permanent Palmer Method alphabet for extra letter practice. The boards are available with either a manuscript or a cursive alphabet. Each board comes with a water-based marker for easy cleaning—simply wipe off.

Chapter 7

Problems in
Mathematics
Achievement

NETTIE R. BARTEL

Mathematics proficiency is a necessary skill for success in school and in life. Nevertheless, many American children have difficulty in understanding mathematics, a conclusion documented by numerous educational reports. In children with learning disabilities, about two out of three require remediation in mathematics (McLeod & Armstrong, 1982). These facts have given rise to repeated calls to improve the teaching of mathematics to American students.

How can this be accomplished? In this chapter, we first consider the goals of mathematics teaching, and review the necessary cognitive prerequisites for students to benefit from such teaching. Then we discuss the assessment of difficulties in mathematics, and consider instructional approaches that are particularly appropriate for students with difficulties in this subject. We conclude with a section on verbal problem solving—an area of great importance, but of particular difficulty for many students.

ESTABLISHING GOALS IN MATHEMATICS INSTRUCTION

Any instruction should be undertaken only if it is responsive to some goal that has been established for a particular child or for a group of children. Teachers will find many sources that will help to articulate the goals of a mathematics program: curriculum guides, professional publications, and scope-and-sequence charts accompanying commercial materials. However, many older mathematics curricula, especially those designed for special education students, emphasize computational routines and memorization of basic facts (Mastropieri, Scruggs, & Shiah, 1991). Verbal problem solving and "thinking mathematically" have often been dismissed as being "too hard" for such children. Because the explicit application of mathematics to everyday life is more urgent for students with learning problems than for those students who are able to generalize on their own, we strongly support mathematics goals that feature the teaching of cognitive strategies and reasoning, and their application to real-life problems.

The National Council of Teachers of Mathematics has taken the lead in pressing for deeper mathematical understandings. In 1989, they published standards for what it means for students to be "mathematically literate":

1. *To learn to value mathematics* (to understand and respect the pervasive presence of mathematics in all areas of life)

2. *To learn to reason mathematically* (to describe, prove, justify, and elaborate on thinking)

3. *To learn to communicate mathematically* (to effectively use diagrams, models, maps, charts, drawings, sketches, and other representations of mathematical ideas and principles)

4. *To become confident of their mathematical ability* (to feel self-efficacious in using mathematical reasoning and calculations in addressing problems)

5. *To become mathematics problem solvers* (to learn when, where, and how to use mathematical principles and reasoning to solve problems)

For our purposes, we have developed the following set of broad mathematical goals:

1. Development of problem-solving ability, including ability to think convergently, divergently, logically, and creatively and to use computers for problem solving.

2. Development of understanding of basic mathematical concepts and terms.

3. Development of the ability to understand and perform measurements of distance, weight, temperature, quantity, area, speed, volume, and money with conventional and metric units, where appropriate.

4. Development of the ability to perform basic mathematical computations using calculators or computers as appropriate.

5. Development of an understanding of how mathematics computation and concepts are utilized in real-life situations.

This last goal is included in recognition of the fact that, for most persons, mathematics will serve as a tool in daily living. For example, in a study conducted by the author with graduate students in special education, newspapers and radio and television news programs were analyzed for prerequisite mathematical understandings. It was found that, to fully comprehend such material, individuals needed to understand the following:

1. Money relationships (including large sums)

2. Measurements—temperature, speed, distance, weight or quantity, and area (listed in order of frequency)

3. Time—past, present, future; hour, day, week, month, season, year, and decade

4. Computations with whole numbers, fractions, decimals, and percentages, including ratios

COGNITIVE PREREQUISITES

A number of cognitive abilities are needed to learn mathematics. The most basic of these are prerequisite to the acquisition of the most fundamental mathematical understandings; the higher order cognitive abilities are

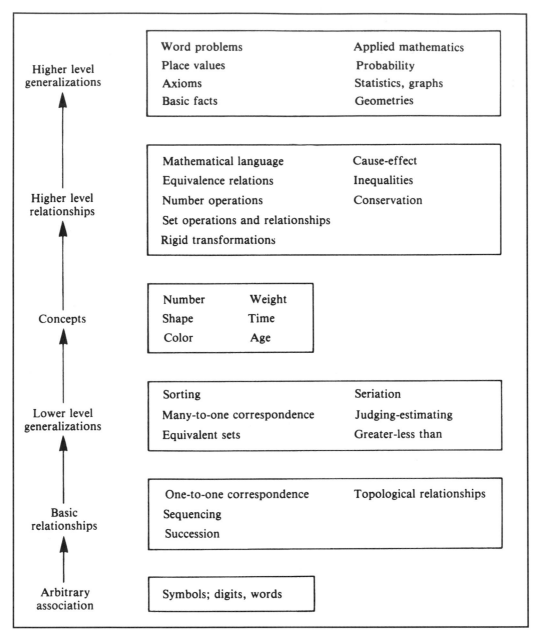

FIGURE 7.1. Cognitive factors and their relationship to mathematics understanding.

From *Teaching Mathematics to Children with Special Needs* by F. K. Reisman and S. H. Kauffman, 1980, Columbus, OH: Charles E. Merrill. Copyright 1980 by Charles E. Merrill Publishing Co. Reprinted with permission.

required before students can master more complex or more abstract mathematical concepts. Reisman and Kauffman (1980) described the importance of cognitive factors in mathematics learning and schematically portrayed their relationship to mathematic understandings. Their schema are reproduced in Figure 7.1.

Figure 7.1 makes it clear that continued and progressive cognitive growth is needed for a student to make progress in mathematics. The three most elementary kinds of cognitive factors—ability to remember arbitrary associations, ability to understand basic relationships, and ability to make lower level generalizations—may be thought of as the basis for formal mathematics instruction. If these abilities are not present, students will not understand the mathematics that is being taught to them. Table 7.1 provides examples of how children demonstrate the presence of these cognitive abilities.

Once the student has demonstrated basic readiness for mathematical thinking, higher level mathematical understandings can be introduced. To do this successfully, the teacher must consider both the student's general intellectual capability and the kinds of mathematical understanding he or

TABLE 7.1. Prerequisite Cognitive Abilities for Basic Mathematics

COGNITIVE ABILITY	EXAMPLES OF HOW CHILD DEMONSTRATES ABILITY		
	ORALLY STATES	DEMONSTRATES WITH OBJECT	MATCHES/ SELECTS/OTHER
Classification by function	Can child state why a toy car does not belong in an array of toy furniture?	Can child arrange groups of objects by function, e.g., all transportation by air, land, water?	Can child match pictures of items that "go with" other items by function, e.g., mitten with hand, boot with foot?
by color	Can child state why red block does not belong with blue blocks?	Can child group objects by color?	Can child match objects by color?
by size	Can child state why large flag does not belong in group of small flags?	Can child arrange objects into groups by size?	Can child select "large" or "small" object in group?
by shape	Can child state why circles do not belong in group of squares?	Can child group objects by shape?	Can child identify several circular shaped or rectangular shaped objects in the room?
by several criteria simultaneously	Can child state differences among prearranged groups of blue squares, red squares; blue squares, red circles?	Can child sort objects on basis of simultaneous criteria of size and function, size and shape, color and shape, etc.?	Can child select which one "does not belong" in array employing two criteria at once?
Seriation linear	Can child state basis of linear serial array based on increasing size?	Can child arrange objects in order of increasingly intense color?	Can child select item missing in a serial array?

(continues)

TABLE 7.1. *Continued*

	EXAMPLES OF HOW CHILD DEMONSTRATES ABILITY		
COGNITIVE ABILITY	*ORALLY STATES*	*DEMONSTRATES WITH OBJECT*	*MATCHES/ SELECTS/OTHER*
unit	Can child state relationships between sets of 1, 2, 3, 4, etc.?	Can child develop sequence of objects or numerals, based on units in each?	Can child count to 10 or 20? Can child tell which numeral contains more—4 or 6, 3 or 8, etc.?
temporal	Can child state what he or she did first in a simple task, what last?	Can child follow simple directions, e.g., "First put the block in the box; next put the penny beside the tray"?	Is there informal evidence of child's developing temporal sense—e.g., does child know which task is done after recess without being told?
one-to-one correspondence	Can child state the number of pencils that will be required for a group of three children?	Can child "order" milk for the class lunch based on the number in attendance? Does he or she know how to distribute the milk when it is received?	Can child pair boots or mittens with the owner?
understanding of spatial relations	Can child state which object is over, under, in, or beside with respect to another object?	Can child match geometric objects to openings into which they fit?	Can child distinguish between right and left?
Conservation of shape	Can child state if, and why, a ball of clay has the same mass whether rolled into a ball or into a rope?	Can child show that a ball of clay can be made into a rope and back into a ball again?	Can child (a) break clay into smaller pieces and then put it back into a ball and (b) flatten clay like a pancake and then put back into ball?
of liquid	Can child state which glass contains more water?	Can child demonstrate equality by pouring water into a glass?	Can child demonstrate equality by pouring water from one glass into several smaller ones?
of number	Can child state which row has more blocks?	Can child make equal numbers in these rows?	Can child recognize that the number of pencils is the same whether they are packed in a box or scattered on a desk?

she has already acquired. Whether one is dealing with initial mathematics instruction or with the introduction of a more advanced topic, the teacher's effectiveness and efficiency are enhanced by introducing the topic that the students are ready to learn. The real test of readiness for a given mathematical topic is not whether that topic comes next in the workbook but whether the pupils have mastered the prerequisite skills and the cognitive operations underlying the topic to be introduced.

ESTABLISHING CAUSES FOR DIFFICULTY IN MATHEMATICS

When a student demonstrates difficulty in mathematics performance, the teacher will want to undertake a preliminary appraisal of possible reasons for the problem. This initial appraisal is usually informal in nature and highly subjective. At this point, the teacher is attempting to generate hypotheses about the possible reasons for the difficulty; he or she will then try to confirm these initial hypotheses using more objective means. Depending on what is discovered, the teacher may refine, reformulate, or implement an intervention based on that first hypothesis. Descriptions of some of the more general reasons underlying mathematics difficulty are presented below.

1. *Ineffective instruction* probably accounts for more cases of problems in arithmetic than any other factor. Students who are the victims of poor teaching can frequently be identified by their relatively good performance in arithmetic concepts that are usually acquired incidentally (size relationships or value of coins) compared with their performance in areas that are usually understood as the result of specific instruction ("carrying" in addition or long division). Remediation is usually effective if it is planned on the basis of a diagnosis of specific deficits.

2. *Difficulties in abstract or symbolic thinking* will interfere with the student's ability to conceptualize the relationship between numerals and objects that they represent, the structure of the number system (base of 10), and relationships between units of measurement. Teachers of students with these difficulties frequently turn in frustration from attempting to get the child to master concepts to emphasizing the rote manipulation of numerals. This may create a facade of arithmetic competence when in fact the student does not understand what he or she is doing.

3. *Reading problems* frequently are responsible for the difficulties of those students who perform well on tests of computation or on oral story problems, but who do poorly in typical workbook or standardized

test situations in which they must be able to read the problem to understand which mathematical process to perform.

4. *Poor attitudes or anxiety* about mathematics may inhibit the performance of some students. Careful observation on the part of the teacher may provide the first indication that this is at the root of the child's problem. Does the student avoid mathematics? Does the student "play sick" when it is time for mathematical activities?

5. *Use of organized strategies and rules that are badly applied or distorted to some degree* is a problem for other students. Ginsburg (1989) concluded that the mistaken rules used by students often have sensible origins, and are derived from faulty observations or instructions; that is, these students have imperfectly learned rules, such as "always subtract a smaller number from a larger number," and inappropriately apply that rule in a subtraction problem that requires regrouping.

6. *Failure to use "common sense" in mathematics* is another cause of difficulty. Ginsburg (1989) noted that frequently students correctly use understandings such as one-to-one correspondence in everyday activities, but do not apply this knowledge in mathematical problems. Such students often see mathematics as separate from the knowledge that they correctly know and practice in other activities.

ASSESSING MATHEMATICS PERFORMANCE

To engage in appropriate and efficient instruction, the teacher must first employ a set of assessment procedures that permit him or her to have a detailed picture of each student's strengths and weaknesses in mathematics. Most teachers discover quickly that the standardized survey type of mathematics achievement tests yields little information. The teacher needs to study in depth the areas of difficulty pointed out by the survey test. For example, the student who is shown to be having computational difficulties is given a much more detailed inventory of computational problems. The teacher appraises the student's performance on the various computation tasks to determine the types of errors that trouble the student. Further probing of the student's errors is done through intensive analysis of written work and/or through an oral interview in which the student "thinks out loud" while solving problems.

The entire assessment process can be conceived of as a search on the part of the teacher for the faulty concepts and strategies being used by the student. Initial testing is gross and provides only the most general clues to the teacher. Successive assessment efforts, based on clues obtained from previous testing, help the teacher to zero in on the child's difficulty. Having discovered the problem, the teacher then plans an intervention to correct the difficulty. If the student shows improvement, the teacher may conclude that the problem was correctly identified and followed by appropriate instruction. Continued failure by the student indicates a need for reexamination of the assessment process and/or of the subsequent instruction.

This section provides some details on the assessment of a student's performance in mathematics. The utilization of commercially produced tests as well as teacher-made inventories is considered. Procedures for conducting an oral clinical interview and for analyzing a student's errors in mathematics also are described.

Commercially Available Tests

A teacher could establish a student's overall performance level by having him or her "try out" in various mathematics tests, programs, or instructional systems. We believe, however, that it is much more efficient and reliable to administer commercially available standardized tests. These tests will give the teacher a general idea of students' functional level in mathematics and some idea of their performance in mathematical subareas.

One readily accessible body of test information is the results of the group-administered survey tests usually given systematically during the school year. All of these tests (e.g., the *Metropolitan Achievement Test,* 1992; the *California Achievement Tests,* 1992) include at least one subtest dealing with mathematics. This is also true of the individually administered achievement survey tests (e.g., the *Diagnostic Achievement Battery,* Newcomer, 1990; the *Wide Range Achievement Test,* Wilkinson, 1994; the *Peabody Individual Achievement Test–Revised,* Markwardt, 1989). Regrettably, the results of these survey tests have limited utility for the teacher in that they yield only information about students' general level of proficiency.

Of considerably more value to the teacher are the results of individually administered multifaceted test batteries that are designed to produce information about a variety of discrete mathematical skills and competencies (see Table 7.2). These results can be used to inventory a youngster's strengths and weaknesses in mathematical skills and concepts and point the way to areas that should be probed in depth through comprehensive informal analysis.

The authors of a few mathematics programs provide their own placement tests to help teachers establish the student's entry level into the program. Of course, such tests are usually applicable only to that program.

Even for students whose test performance indicates grade-level or near–grade-level functioning, we recommend that the teacher check the errors made by the pupil to see whether the student's performance is reasonably even across the various types of mathematics problems; by

TABLE 7.2. **Multifaceted Tests of Mathematics Performance**

TEST	SKILLS MEASURED	GRADE LEVEL	SPECIAL FEATURES
Diagnosis: An Instructional Aid: Mathematics (Troutman, 1980)	Middle- and upper-elementary mathematical skills	Grades 3–8	Contains survey test for global assessment Has criterion-referenced "probes" for further testing in identified areas of weakness
Hudson Education Skills Inventory (Hudson & Colson, 1988)	All mathematical areas	Grades K–12	Criterion referenced Curriculum based A testing-for-teaching approach
Key Math: Revised (Connolly, 1988)	1. Content 2. Operations 3. Applications	Grades K–6	Convenient and attractive to administer Requires almost no reading or writing
Sequential Assessment in Mathematics Inventory (Reisman, 1984)	Eight areas of mathematics	Grades K–8	Organized by topic Available in computer form
Stanford Diagnostic Mathematics Test, 3rd ed. (Beatty, Madden, Gardner, & Karlsen, 1984)	1. Number system and numeration 2. Computation 3. Application	Grades 1.5–12	Four separate levels Group administered Norm referenced Can be used in a limited way as a criterion-referenced test Patterns of performance or strengths and weaknesses can be identified
Test of Early Mathematics Ability (Ginsburg & Baroody, 1990)	Both formal and informal aspects of math	Ages 4–9	Norm referenced Measures basic math prerequisites at preschool level
Test of Mathematical Abilities (V.L. Brown, Cronin, & McEntire 1994)	1. Vocabulary 2. Computation 3. Information 4. Story problems 5. Attitudes	Grades 3–12	Norm referenced Includes attitudes

excelling in one area, say addition, one can obtain a fairly average score even if performance in another area, say multiplication, is very poor. The analysis of errors and error patterns has been found to be particularly helpful for pupils who are new to the teacher.

Curriculum-Based Assessment and Teacher-Made Assessment Inventories

Curriculum-Based Assessment

In recent years, much dissatisfaction has been expressed by teachers who have found that standardized tests often do not reflect the content that has been taught in their particular classrooms. Such tests are often seen as unrelated to the actual curriculum in use. This dissatisfaction has resulted in the widespread use of curriculum-based assessment, which is assessment based on the specific instructional program in use in a given class. Actual test items are drawn directly from the textbook, workbook, or computer program that the students are using. Typically, curriculum-based assessment is conducted at regular intervals (e.g., weekly or monthly) using comparable types of test items. In this way, comparisons can be made of student progress from one interval to the next. For example, the curriculum may deal with multiplication problems of increasing complexity over a 2-month instructional period. The teacher could design curriculum-based multiplication tests, administered semi-weekly, each with 30 items drawn from the mathematics text in the section being studied at that time. The student's number correct at each interval could be plotted on a graph, thus providing direct visual representation of the student's progress or lack thereof.

Teacher-Made Inventories

For students with recurring or pervasive difficulties, more extensive assessment in the form of a teacher-made inventory is required. The teacher's first step in developing an inventory is to choose the content to be assessed. For most children, this will not be difficult, as a quick perusal of their standardized or curriculum-based tests or their day-to-day classroom performance will provide information on areas of weakness. For example, a student may correctly perform most of the addition problems for his or her grade placement, but be unsuccessful on most of the subtraction problems.

The next step is to establish whether the student has the necessary underlying concepts and capacities required for the subtraction tasks. For help with this task, the teacher is referred to Figure 7.2, which outlines the general hierarchical interrelationships between and among various areas of mathematical functioning. In each case, the source of an arrow may be considered to be a necessary prerequisite for full mastery of the capability to which the arrow is pointing. Thus, in the subtraction example, the student would need to have evidenced readiness capabilities and mastery of basic mathematical concepts and vocabulary. An alternative approach is to conduct a task analysis and/or concept analysis of each of the terminal skills desired in the subtraction area.

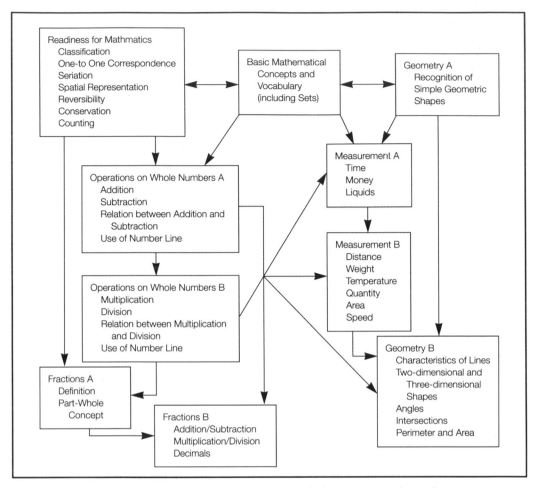

FIGURE 7.2. Summary scope and sequence in typical elementary mathematics.

The final step in determining what should go into the inventory is to decide in what form and under what conditions the child is supposed to be able to perform the task. Objectives should be stated in *precise, observable* terms. (See Chapter 1 for a fuller discussion of the stating of objectives.)

Now the teacher is ready to begin to write the actual items. They may be adapted from commercial texts or workbooks, or the teacher may create them. An example of a subtraction inventory, adapted from P. C. Burns (1965) and limited to the vertical format, is presented in Table 7.3.

To further probe the student's understanding of concepts underlying subtraction proficiency and to assess ability to perform subtraction problems in a variety of formats and contexts, Burns (1965) suggested a series of follow-up exercises, presented in Table 7.4. These are examples of the types of questions that a teacher could ask a student to gain further knowledge about the student's thinking processes. Because it is well known that

TABLE 7.3. Sample Analytical Inventory: Subtraction

PROBLEM TYPE	EXERCISES FOR CHILD TO COMPLETE			
Basic subtraction facts without zero	1. 4 −2	2. 8 −1	3. 17 −3	4. 15 −6
Basic subtraction facts involving zero	5. 7 −7	6. 9 −0		
Higher-decade subtraction fact requiring no regrouping	7. 79 −6			
Higher-decade subtraction fact requiring regrouping	8. 75 −9			
Higher-decade subtraction fact, with difference in ones' place	9. 25 −23			
Higher-decade subtraction fact; zero in ones' place in minuend	10. 20 −3			
Subtraction of ones and tens with no regrouping required	11. 47 −24			
Three-digit minuend minus two-digit subtrahend; no regrouping	12. 169 −45			
Subtraction of ones, tens, hundreds; no regrouping	13. 436 −215			
Two-digit minuend minus two-digit subtrahend; regrouping tens and ones in minuend required	14. 46 −38	15. 72 −34		
Three-digit minuend minus two-digit subtrahend; regrouping tens and ones in minuend required (zero in difference)	16. 272 −64			
Three-digit minuend minus two-digit subtrahend; regrouping hundreds and tens of minuend required	17. 528 −54			
Subtraction of ones, tens, hundreds; regrouping tens and ones in minuend required	18. 742 −208	19. 750 −374		
Subtraction of ones, tens, hundreds; regrouping hundreds and tens in minuend required	20. 724 −183	21. 307 −121		
Subtraction of ones, tens, hundreds; regrouping entire minuend required	22. 531 −173			
Four-digit minuend minus three-digit subtrahend; regrouping entire minuend required	23. 1076 −247	24. 5254 −968	25. 5805 −978	

(continues)

TABLE 7.3 *Continued*

PROBLEM TYPE	EXERCISES FOR CHILD TO COMPLETE
Subtraction of ones, tens, hundreds, thousands; regrouping hundreds, tens, and ones of minuend required	26. $\begin{array}{r} 4553 \\ -1258 \\ \hline \end{array}$
Subtraction of ones, tens, hundreds, thousands; regrouping entire minuend required	27. $\begin{array}{r} 9563 \\ -2687 \\ \hline \end{array}$
Five-digit minuend minus four-digit subtrahend; regrouping entire minuend required	28. $\begin{array}{r} 23238 \\ -3879 \\ \hline \end{array}$
Five-digit minuend minus four-digit subtrahend; regrouping entire minuend (involving zeros) required	29. $\begin{array}{r} 10000 \\ -7192 \\ \hline \end{array}$
Five-digit minuend minus five-digit subtrahend; regrouping entire minuend required	30. $\begin{array}{r} 30503 \\ -19765 \\ \hline \end{array}$

Adapted from "Analytical Testing and Follow-up Exercises in Elementary School Mathematics" by P. C. Burns, 1965, *School Science and Mathematics, 65,* pp. 34–38.

students' mistakes in mathematics are often based on their faulty understanding or faulty application of mathematical rules, such further probing by the teacher can lead directly to correcting the students' understanding. The teacher's careful questioning and observing of the student is often called a clinical mathematics interview, which is described next.

The Oral Interview (Clinical Mathematics Interview)

The oral interview is a procedure through which a teacher attempts to gain an understanding of the underlying thinking processes, the "reasoning," that students use as they attempt to solve mathematical problems. Regardless of whether the problem to be solved is a "simple" problem in calculation or a multistage verbal problem, the solution requires students to make use of a set of assumptions, strategies, or rules. The basic procedure in the oral interview is to get the student to "think out loud," thus sharing with the teacher those underlying assumptions, strategies, and rules. When these underlying assumptions, strategies, or rules are faulty, misapplied, distorted, or just plain wrong, the teacher can specifically correct or redirect the student's thinking. In this way, the student subsequently can use correct procedures for entire classes of similar problems.

TABLE 7.4. **Follow-Up Exercises for the Analytical Test of Subtraction**

1. Make a dot drawing to represent the fact that 17 take away 8 leaves 9.
2. What subtraction fact does this drawing illustrate?

12 cookies in all

⟨ 000000000000 ⟩

left   eaten

3. Show on the number line how the answer to 31 minus 12 might be found.
4. Start at 57 and count down by 5's to the first number in the thirties. To do this, say, "57, 52, 47," and so on.
5. Write three different ways to read the number statement 24−8=16 (as "8 from 24 leaves 16").
6. What is the result when zero is subtracted from a number?
7. What is the result when a number is subtracted from itself?
8. What pairs of one-digit numbers would make each a true sentence?
   $\square + \square = 9$ $\square + \square = 11$ $\square + \square = 13$
9. What basic subtraction fact helps you to subtract 6 from 53?
10. Start with 13, subtract 6, add 3, subtract 4, subtract 3. Where are you?
11. There is a two-digit minuend and a one-digit subtrahend whose difference is 9. What might they be?
12. Think the answers to the following questions. Then write the answers.
    a. 7 from 18 leaves how many?
    b. 68 and how many more equals 72?
    c. The difference between 77 and 24 equals what number?
    d. Is 19 minus 12 equal to 7?
    e. When 203 is taken from 526, what is left?
    f. Is 60 from 388 equal to 328?
    g. Does 65 minus 9 equal 56?
    h. If you take 36 from 64, what do you get?
    i. How many are left if 19 is subtracted from 52?
    j. 525 is how much less than 3478?
13. In subtracting 1 ft 3 in. from 3 ft 1 in., to what name would you change one of the measures?
14. When 16 is subtracted from 51, to what number name is the 51 changed?
15. Do the following subtractions, using numerals and words.
    a. 20 = 2 tens 0 ones =   b. 31 = 3 tens 1 one   =
        −3 = _____ 3 ones =   −17 = 1 ten 7 ones =

    c. 500 = 5 hundreds 0 tens 0 ones =
        −125 = 1 hundred 2 tens 5 ones =

16. Use the words hundreds, tens, and ones to show the renaming of 413 in subtracting 187 from 413.
17. What do the digits at the top of the work mean?

		9 1̶0̶
3 13	6 12	4 10
a. 4̶3̶	b. 7̶2̶4	c. 5̶0̶0̶
−18	−183	−125
25		

18. Write the number sentence for this word problem. There are 527 pupils in the Madison School, of whom 283 are boys. How many girls are there?
19. How can an equivalent addition question be written for the subtraction question 42 − 26 = *n*?
20. Does *n* + 17 = 42 represent an addition or a subtraction situation? Does *n* − 17 = 25 represent a subtraction situation?

(continues)

TABLE 7.4. *Continued*

21. For each addition statement, write the subtraction statement that "undoes" it. The first one is done for you.

   6 + 4 =   36 + 7 =   58 + 17 =
   10 − 6 = 4
     or
   10 − 4 = 6

22. Write the missing numeral for each of the following statements:

   19 − ▢ = 7   ▢ − 47 = 24   36 − 28 = ▢

23. Subtract $6.98 from $10.00.

24. Subtract. Check your answers by subtracting the difference from the minuend. Check again by adding the difference and the subtrahend.

162	806	1422	8461
75	436	766	7298

From "Analytical Testing and Follow-up Exercises in Elementary School Mathematics," by P. C. Burns, 1965, *School Science and Mathematics, 65,* pp. 34–38. Reprinted with permission.

When the oral interview is used for students who have been taught with traditional approaches, the process is likely to be time-consuming because the student must first be taught the technique of thinking aloud. In this case, for reasons of time, the teacher will probably confine the use of the oral interview to only those students with the most entrenched or perplexing difficulties.

However, when mathematics instruction in the classroom emphasizes thinking and cognitive strategies are taught as a means for solving mathematical problems, the oral interview will become a natural part of ongoing classroom activity. Students will routinely think out loud to both the teacher and their classmates, thus sharing on an ongoing basis their underlying assumptions, strategies, and rules. By requiring students to describe and justify their mathematical thinking as a regular, expected classroom activity, the teacher will have fairly extensive knowledge about the thought processes that individual children use to solve problems. Then the oral interview as a discrete formal procedure will need to be used less often. In cases where a particular student is having persistent or subtle difficulties, the teacher can still set aside special time for additional probing of underlying assumptions, strategies, and rules. In this case, the time spent in the activity is likely to be more efficiently used, because the student will be familiar with the procedure of thinking out loud.

Table 7.5 outlines the basic procedures of an oral interview (clinical mathematics interview). During and after the oral interview, the teacher is actively considering the reasoning that the child uses in solving the problems. Some of the incorrect strategies can be corrected "on the spot." Others will require more extensive reinstruction, either to one student or to a group of students having similar difficulties. In some instances, the teacher may assign a "buddy" who can work with the child in joint thinking-out-loud problem-solving activities.

TABLE 7.5. **The Clinical Mathematics Interview**

STAGE	*GOALS*	*PROCEDURES*
Before the interview	1. To select the problem areas to be analyzed	1. *Identify the general areas of student difficulty by* a. observing the student in the classroom b. noting the student's classroom performance c. noting the student's performance on tests 2. *Develop a hypothesis as to why the student is having difficulty.* Try to structure the problem in a format that will clearly show the strategy used by the student in solving the problem. 3. Using the information from 1 and 2 above, *choose problems in the order in which they appear in the task analysis in Figure 7.2.* (For example, if the student is having difficulty in both addition and multiplication, addition problems should be cleared up first. Once this has been accomplished, the student will need to be retested on written multiplication before oral probing in that area. It may be that correction of the faulty addition strategy will modify the difficulty in multiplication.) 4. For the first interview, and until you and the student are comfortable with the process, a. *choose problems from an existing test or inventory* (later devise your own); b. *choose an "easy," uncomplicated problem* (to the degree possible without violating 3 above); c. *begin slowly and on a small scale* (expand later if necessary); and d. *plan to keep the interview short.*
	2. To establish rapport with the student	1. *Choose a quiet place without distractions.* 2. *Try to make the student comfortable.* Spend time with the student before the interview. It may be helpful to bring in a peer and have the students work in pairs. 3. *Explain the purpose of the interview honestly* (e.g., "I want to learn more about how you do mathematics. Then we can work together to help you do better."). 4. *Plan to keep a written or taped record of the student's responses.* If the interview is to be taped, the student should be told.
During the interview	1. To observe the student's strategies in solving problems 2. To discern the student's cognitive strategies 3. To describe the student's use of strategies	1. *Present the student with the problem you have selected.* 2. *Ask the student to solve the problem in written form and to explain orally what he or she is doing.* (Remember, this is a diagnostic exercise, not an instructional lesson.) 3. If the student begins to write without explaining what he or she is doing, ask "Why did you do that?" or "How did you get that answer?" Initially, *keep your query very general.*

(continues)

TABLE 7.5 *Continued*

STAGE	GOALS	PROCEDURES
		4. *Leave the student free to solve the problem in his or her own way* without any hint that he or she is doing something wrong. Avoid giving clues or asking leading questions. If the student directly asks whether the answers are correct, say "Today we are mostly interested in how you are solving the problem. Tell me in your own words what you are doing." Don't put words in the student's mouth.
		5. *Encourage the student.* Smile, nod, wait, say "Yes-s-s" or whatever to keep the student talking; repeat the student's last response if he or she seems to get stuck (e.g. "So then you carried the 3 to the tens' column . . . ," ask the question another way, or ask the student to describe what he or she has done another way.
		6. If the student does not provide enough detail, *follow up on his or her strategy* (e.g., "Can you tell me why you put that number 1 up there?").
		7. *Avoid criticizing or pushing too hard,* especially on the first interview. Take a break or shorten the interview if the student becomes distracted or too discouraged.
After the interview	1. To summarize your observations of the student's performance	1. After observing and analyzing the student's responses for a sufficient period of time, *formulate a tentative summary of the student's strengths and weaknesses in that problem area.*
	2. To formulate a more refined hypothesis of the student's problem-solving strategies	2. *Specify precisely what the student is doing wrong. Specify what the student is doing right.*
		3. Taking 2 above into account, *decide what the next instructional steps should be.*
	3. To develop an intervention that corrects faulty student strategies and provides an effective alternative	4. *Devise an instructional plan that corrects the student's faulty strategies.*
		5. *Implement the instructional plan.*
		6. *Reassess the student.*
		7. *Modify the instructional plan if necessary.*
		8. *Reteach as necessary.*
		9. *Repeat the entire process for the next problem area.*

In his analysis of the mathematics assumptions, strategies, and rules mistakenly used by many children, and discovered by teachers as a result of oral interviewing, Ginsburg (1989) concluded the following:

1. Most mistakes made by students in mathematical problem solving are not random. Many mistakes result from organized strategies and rules that are inappropriately applied or distorted to some degree. For example, one student solved the following problem as indicated:

$$\frac{3}{8} \quad + \quad \frac{1}{8} \quad = \quad \frac{4}{16}$$

Clearly this student was using rules to solve the problem, but needed further instruction on the *appropriate* application of addition rules when adding fractions.

2. The rules used by the students may have sensible origins, having been derived from classroom instruction, but misapplied, or from faulty observation. Often such information can be useful to a teacher who learns that the instruction that he or she thought he or she was giving is being perceived very differently by some of the students. In other words, the students may be learning something that the teacher did not know was being taught. For example, one teacher taught the following problems in introducing students to "carrying" in adding two-digit numbers:

(1)	(1)	(1)	(1)
16	26	17	38
+8	+7	+4	+9
24	33	21	47

Later, a student solved the following problems in this way:

(1)	(1)	(1)	(1)
24	35	27	52
38	29	77	46
97	18	56	38
159	72	150	138

This student's problem was initially perplexing to the teacher, because the first and the fourth problems were solved correctly. Only through the oral interview did the teacher discover that the student had learned that one should *always carry a 1* to the ten's column if the sum of the one's column is more than 9. By uncovering the student's underlying rule, the teacher could immediately correct the student's thinking.

3. Students may not use "common sense" in their mathematics performance. Remediation in this case consists of helping the child to trust his or her intuitive knowledge of everyday events, and to see the relationships of logic used in nonschool problem solving to the logic that can be used for classroom problem solving.

Analysis of Errors

The identification and interpretation of a student's errors, whether evidenced in written work or in the oral interview, provide the basis on which the teacher develops an appropriate instructional program. Error analysis is not a one-time event, but an ongoing, integral aspect of student evaluation and student instruction. An analysis of the errors that students are making also provides feedback to the teacher on the effectiveness of the teacher's instruction. It tells the teacher whether the students are "getting it" from the teaching techniques that are being used, or whether something else should be tried. For all these reasons, it is important for the teacher to be proficient in the analysis of student errors.

This section identifies some of the common types of errors made by pupils (see Table 7.6) and provides some examples of error analyses. Errors made in verbal problem solving are dealt with in the next section.

An examination of Table 7.6 shows that student errors can be classified under four headings: problems in knowing facts (declarative knowledge), problems in knowing procedures (procedural knowledge), problems in knowing when or where to use certain facts or procedures (conditional knowledge), and random errors of carelessness or inattentiveness. Persistent errors in these various categories of knowledge call for different interventions, as indicated in Table 7.7.

A step-by-step approach designed to help teachers analyze errors and plan instruction to remediate these faulty strategies is presented in Table 7.7. Both the student's written work and the student's "thinking out loud" are used as sources of diagnostic information for the teacher. In each case, what the student does and what the student says lead the teacher to a tentative hypothesis concerning the source of computational difficulty. After identifying the problem, the teacher can make a good guess as to what instructional procedures will be effective with the child. Possible teaching strategies for each instance are listed in the column labeled "What the Teacher Does Next."

TEACHING MATHEMATICS

Effective instruction is the ultimate goal of every teacher's efforts. We begin this topic with a set of principles that have been found to characterize most effective instruction in mathematics. This discussion is followed by descriptions of several instructional approaches and adaptations for students having particular difficulty in mathematics. We conclude with a section on how to best teach verbal problem solving—an area of great difficulty for many students.

Important Principles for Effective Instruction in Mathematics

Sufficient research has been conducted on effective instruction in mathematics that some guiding principles can be stated. The following are summaries of what is currently known about how to best teach mathematics:

1. Use a wide range of "tools" for exploring, representing, and communicating mathematical ideas. These include manipulatives, charts,

TABLE 7.6. Failure Strategies Used in Mathematics Computation

TYPE OF FAILURE STRATEGY	EXAMPLE		CORRECTIVE TEACHING STRATEGIES
	PROBLEM	PUPIL RESPONSE	
Declarative Knowledge Obvious computational error	42 × 3	42 × 3 146	Use manipulatives, flashcards, or worksheets as appropriate to develop a high rate of correct responses. Use different formats to encourage mastery—e.g., 3 + 2 = ?; 3 + ? = 5. Chart student progress, showing rate and percentage correct.
Procedural Knowledge Defective operation Regrouping incorrectly	24 + 39	24 + 39 513	Reteach place value with manipulatives— bundles of straws, chips, cards, etc. Use actual pennies, dimes, and dollars for practicing calculations. Use column paper to emphasize keeping ones in the ones' place, and so on. Use magic marker of different colors to emphasize place value.
Wrong order of steps in computation process	21 × 32	21 × 32 63 42 483	Reteach place value, emphasizing working with the one's place first. Demonstrate right-to-left sequence. Use magic marker and color grids to emphasize correct sequence.
Omitting steps	367 × 25	367 × 25 1535 614 7675	Have student describe the procedures used. Point out that the multiplication of the tens' place cannot be omitted. Practice on simpler problems first. Use a colored grid for practice problems.
Format problems	432 × 55	432 × 55 2160 2160 4320	Use column or graph paper to help the student maintain the correct format. Or use stick pins with colored heads to help "hold" the place.
Conditional Knowledge Wrong operation	38 − 11	38 − 11 49	Probe to see if the student understands the meaning of the computation signs; have student point to the sign in each problem and state the operation orally; have student outline the sign in crayon before calculating the answer.
Random Responses	432 × 55	432 × 55 123	Use the oral interview technique to see what the student was thinking. Reteach the basic processes required. Motivational and attentional factors may need to be addressed.

TABLE 7.7. Sample Inventory of Subtraction of Whole Numbers: Error Analysis[a]

PROBLEM PRESENTED	WHAT THE CHILD WRITES	WHAT THE CHILD SAYS (ORAL INTERVIEW)	ERROR ANALYSIS— TEACHER'S HYPOTHESES	WHAT THE TEACHER DOES NEXT
7 −3	7 −3 2	7 take away 3 = 2.	Doesn't know number fact.	Presents same problem in another form (to rule out random error). Checks other subtraction facts. Provides practice with physical objects, worksheets, number line, flashcards, games, etc. Retests before going to more difficult subtraction.
15 −6	15 −6 11	6 take away 5 is 1; 1 stays the same.	Faulty algorithm; doesn't understand integrity of minuend and subtrahend; doesn't know number fact.	Checks further to see if child always subtracts smaller number from larger. Reviews addition and subtraction with one-digit numbers, then two-digit. Has child respond orally before returning to written form.
85 −3	85 −3 52	3 from 8 is 5; 3 from 5 is 2.	Subtraction problem worked left to right; problem with place value (subtracting ones from tens).	Reviews place value at the enactive, iconic, and symbolic levels; provides practice with subtraction algorithm in simpler two-digit problems.
85 −9	85 −9 86	The 8 goes down here; then you have to change the 5 to 15, then subtract 9 from 15.	Subtraction problem worked left to right; doesn't understand effect on tens of regrouping ones.	Provides experience with place value—manipulating bundles of straws (1s, 10s, 100s), pocket chart, or Stern materials; then provides workbook pictorial practice. Finally, reworks symbolic problem.

(continues)

Problem	Error analysis	Child's explanation	Corrective procedure
$\begin{array}{r}91\\-83\\\hline 1\end{array}$	Problem in regrouping; possible problem in number fact.	Since you can't take 3 from 1, the answer is 1; also because 8 from 9 is 1.	Reviews place value (tens and ones); performs several problems of this type on the pocket chart, or with Cuisenaire rods. Provides successful experience on problems of this type before returning to numerical form.
$\begin{array}{r}523\\-284\\\hline 249\end{array}$	Sequence is the problem here. The child performed all the steps correctly but in the wrong order.	This 2 (in tens place) should be 12, that makes this 5 a 4. Now 12 – 8 = 4 and 4 – 2 = 2. To take 4 away over here (ones column) you make the 3 to a 13; 13 – 4 = 9; change 12 to 11.	Provides practice with right-to-left sequence in problems not involving regrouping. Uses place-value box or chart to show why sequence affects results.
$\begin{array}{r}300\\-157\\\hline 053\end{array}$	Relationship of empty sets of ones to tens to hundreds a problem. Child doesn't understand conversion from one unity to another.	You have to get ones from the three because there aren't any here (pointing to 0s); 3 take away 2 makes the 3 a 1. Now we have 10 ones, and 10 tens, and we can subtract.	Provides child with experience in converting tens to ones and hundreds to ones. (It might be very effective to use dollars, dimes, and pennies first, and then the paper-and-pencil mode.) First provides practice using only tens and ones together, then hundreds and tens together, then hundreds and ones together, finally conversions involving all three units in one problem.

aFor an excellent discussion and numerous examples of error analysis, the reader is referred to *Error Patterns in Computation: A Semi-Programmed Approach* (4th ed.) by R. B. Ashlock, 1986, Columbus, OH: Charles E. Merrill.

graphs, maps, pictures, drawings, sketches, "doodles," models, calculators, computers, and other representations. Then link concrete and symbolic representations (National Council of Teachers of Mathematics, 1991).

2. Emphasize the thinking that lies behind solving the problem (the strategies). Model the thought processes required for problem solution by "thinking out loud." While doing this, occasionally make "mistakes" so that students can see how faulty strategies lead to incorrect solutions. Through thinking out loud, require students to describe and justify their mathematical thinking. Encourage classroom discussion on alternative ways to solve problems. Accept more than one way of arriving at the correct solution; where possible, accept more than one correct answer. Using the chalkboard for students to write out the steps in the problem solution while they state their reasoning for each step is often effective.

3. Introduce mathematics topics and problems from the context of real-life situations faced by the students. Encourage students to express intuitions and "common sense" as to how a problem should be solved. Focus on helping students fully understand all facets of a few problems that have meaning for them, as opposed to working a lot of non-meaningful problems, even if this means working only one or two problems during an entire class period. This is particularly important during the acquisition stage of instruction (see subsequent section).

4. Be prepared to alter the lesson plan if it becomes apparent that the students lack prerequisite knowledge or have failed to acquire underlying understandings. Slow down the curriculum timeline, if necessary, to enable students to fully understand the material being presented. Pay particular attention to what students are revealing about their underlying assumptions, rules, and understandings when they think out loud. This information should directly find its way into the instructional decisions the teacher makes. Instruction is much more effective if it is reciprocally related to assessment because both are ongoing. Stay with a topic, reteaching it from a different point of view if necessary, until the students have reached an 80% to 90% mastery level.

5. Use curricular materials flexibly. There is no "perfect" set of materials. While mathematics textbooks, "kits," workbooks, and computer programs abound, their usefulness lies in how they are used. Select materials that provide for learning from direct experience, from observation, and from manipulation of symbol systems. Personalize the formal curriculum by using analogous problems experienced by the students in the class. Such problems can be devised by the students themselves.

6. Pay attention to the stages of learning—acquisition, proficiency, maintenance, and generalization. These stages are depicted in Table 7.8.

TABLE 7.8. Stages of Learning in Mathematics

STAGE OF LEARNING	DESCRIPTION	TYPICAL TEACHING APPROACHES	EXAMPLE: LEARNING TO DO LONG DIVISION
Acquisition	Initial learning of the new skill	Teacher *shows* (demonstrates skill) Teacher *says* (verbal instruction in producing skill) Teacher *elicits student response* with prompts and supervision	Teacher or a student demonstrates examples on the chalkboard Teacher explains each of the steps on the chalkboard or with overhead transparencies Students do examples on the chalkboard or at their desks under teacher supervision
Proficiency	Achieving mastery of the skill with reduced prompting	Teacher reduces prompts while Student *shows* (practices skill through motor behavior) Student *states* (practices skill through verbal behavior) Student *writes* (practices skill in written form) Student *simulates* (practices skill on computer)	Students solve written exercises in long division using a variety of formats— e.g., paper and pencil, drill and practice on the computer, homework exercises Students work in pairs to solve student-generated problems involving long division
Maintenance	Demonstrating mastery of the skill over a period of time	Teacher *arranges maintenance opportunity* Student *consolidates* skills through workbook games peer exercises computer exercises Teacher *sees maintenance opportunity* in unrelated situation and requires that Student *state* the desired response orally Student *write* the desired response Student *demonstrate* the response	Teacher provides one or two review problems each day for several weeks (Two weeks later) Students solve several long division problems on a chapter test, do a review page of problems, make up problems for one another to solve

(continues)

TABLE 7.8. *Continued*

STAGE OF LEARNING	DESCRIPTION	TYPICAL TEACHING APPROACHES	EXAMPLE: LEARNING TO DO LONG DIVISION
Generalization	Applying the skill to new situations in new contexts	Teacher arranges generalization *opportunity* through planned exercises application in other subjects Teacher *sees generalization opportunity* in unrelated situation and requires that Students *generalize* to new verbal situation, new written situation, and new demonstration situation	Teacher identifies opportunities in other subjects for use of long division skills—e.g., social studies, science, homeroom activities Students identify situations in which long division is required, formulate the problems, and solve them

7. Modify the instructional approach to accommodate students with particular learning difficulties. A summary of the possible adaptations of mathematics instruction is presented in Table 7.9. (For further ideas, the teacher is referred to Bley & Thornton, 1989; Cawley, Baker-Kroczynski, & Urban, 1992; Giordano, 1993; Rivera & Bryant, 1992.)

Approaches to Teaching Mathematics

As stated in the introductory section to this chapter, teachers have a great number of instructional mathematics materials from which to choose. This section briefly describes some of the approaches that might be used with students with problems in mathematics achievement.

Basal Math Texts

For many years, the use of basal texts has been the most common way of teaching mathematics. Generally the materials consist of student texts, student workbooks, and teacher's manuals. Sometimes additional supplementary materials are available, such as spirit duplicator masters, charts for recording student progress, or quizzes or tests to establish whether a student is ready to begin a new section. Examples of elementary basal math series are

Essentials of Math (Ginn)

Harper and Row Mathematics

Holt Math 1000 (Holt, Rinehart & Winston)

Holt School Mathematics (Holt, Rinehart & Winston)

TABLE 7.9. Modification of Instruction in Mathematics for Learning Disabled Students

INSTRUCTIONAL MODIFICATION (STAGE OF LEARNING)	DESCRIPTION	EXAMPLES
Modify the content (acquisition)	Alter the type or amount of information presented to a student; substitute content.	A unit on rate–time–distance algebraic problems is not taught to a seventh-grade student; instead the student is given extra practice learning how to balance a checkbook. A third-grade student is provided with the correct answers to a set of story problems—the student's task is only to describe how the correct answer was obtained.
Modify the nature of teacher input (acquisition and generalization)	Alter the input from the teacher (e.g., manipulate, display, say, write); repeat or simplify instructions; read the questions to the student (rather than telling the student to read).	Before having a second-grade student begin work on a page of subtraction and addition problems, the teacher requires the student to point to the operation sign of each problem and orally state whether the problem requires addition or subtraction.
Adjust the instructional pace or sequence (acquisition, proficiency, and generalization)	Alter the length or frequency of instructional periods; slow down the rate of presentation; defer the introduction of certain content; provide more frequent reviews.	The teacher plans two 15-minute math periods each day rather than one 30-minute period. Worksheets are kept to a maximum of six problems each.
Use alternative teaching techniques (all stages)	Change some aspect of verbal instruction, demonstration, modeling, rehearsal, drill and practice, prompts and cues, feedback, reinforcement, or error contingencies.	The teacher provides step-by-step direct supervision for each of three long division questions during the acquisition stage of instruction; feedback is given on each step of the process.
Alter the demands of the task (all stages)	Allow use of a calculator; allow the student to make pointing rather than oral responses or oral rather than written responses.	The teacher allows a third-grade student to use counting beads as an adjunct to completing a worksheet. The teacher works orally for a few minutes each day with a first-grade student who has difficulty writing.
Change the instructional delivery system (all stages)	Change the *primary instructional personnel* (use peer tutors, classroom aides, or itinerant or consultant teachers); change the *instructional format* (use computer-assisted instruction or programmed instruction); change the *instructional context* (use small-group instruction or one-to-one instruction).	The teacher assigns a peer to play a number game and to use multiplication flashcards with a student for 3 days before any independent written work is required. For a review of making change with money, a small group of third-grade students are permitted to "play store." As a reward for completing an assignment, a student is permitted to use the computer for a game-format drill and practice on division facts.

McGraw-Hill Mathematics

Math for Individual Achievement (Houghton Mifflin)

Scott, Foresman Mathematics

SRA Mathematics Program (Science Research Associates)

Math Kits

Many publishers produce mathematics instructional programs in the form of kits or packages with various components. Usually these consist of activity cards for daily lessons, teacher's guides, and materials for student activities. Most of these kits are designed to supplement text- and workbook-based mathematics programs.

Special Approaches

A few educational approaches have been developed for children who require a more concrete, less abstract approach to mathematics—the Cuisenaire-Gattegno approach, the *Direct Instruction Mathematics* program, and the *Key Math Early Steps Program*. Each of these is described briefly.

CUISENAIRE-GATTEGNO RODS

Invented by George Cuisenaire in 1953, and further developed by Caleb Gattegno, the Cuisenaire rods are instructional aids that seem particularly relevant to a modern mathematics curriculum. They are capable of generating student interest and enthusiasm while promoting a dialogue between learner and teacher. The rods are based on a definition of mathematics as a process of observation and discovery of relationships. They were designed for the purpose of teaching conceptual knowledge of the basic structure of mathematics, rather than simply the manipulative skills. The teacher's role in the setting provided by the rods is to observe and ask questions about what the students are discovering for themselves, rather than to instruct or explain. A student who works out facts and ideas for himself or herself seem to learn and retain them better. Through the use of rods, a kindergartner is introduced to algebraic equations and a basic appreciation of place value and the number system.

The 291 wooden Cuisenaire rods vary in length and color. The rods use both color and length to embody algebraic principles and number relationships. They are 1 centimeter square in cross section and from 1 to 10 centimeters long. The red rods represent the quantities of 2, 4, and 8; the blue-green rods, 3, 6, and 9; the yellow rods, 5 and 10; the black rod, 7; and the white cube, 1. Since the rods have no numerals on them, students who have not yet developed an adequate number background can use the materials to explore relationships between quantities. Students who possess basic number awareness can work with the rods in terms of the principles identified with particular operations.

Training Techniques and Program Organization

Introduction of the rods at any given grade level is done in the following four stages:

1. Independent exploration, in which the student is permitted to "play" with the rods.

2. Independent exploration and hands-on activities with the rods, in which relationships are observed and discussed without the use of mathematical notation. The following aspects of mathematics are explored at this point: equivalence, trains (sequences), patterns, greater than and less than, staircase (seriation), complements, trains of one color, transformations, and odds and evens.

3. Directed activities in which mathematical notation is introduced and used without assigning number value to the rods. Opportunities for independent exploration are still needed.

4. Directed activities in which the use of mathematical notation is extended and number values are assigned to the rods. Independent exploration will go beyond the directed activities.

The rods should only be used for the purpose of discovery and verification. The method is valueless if students are unable to do sums without the help of the rods. As soon as the student understands the process, he or she must be encouraged to work it out mentally.

Four booklets that accompany the rods treat such topics as cardinality, ordinality, factors, equivalence, permutations, transformations, complements, various forms of measurement, inequalities, proportions, basic whole numbers and rational number operations, and number properties. The booklets are concerned with various aspects of basic mathematics; however, they cannot be considered a complete program.

Although these materials can be used in grades kindergarten through 6, they are usually emphasized through grade 3. They may be used with an entire class, a small group, or an individual student. They have been successfully utilized with students possessing a varied range of abilities—the deaf, mentally retarded, gifted, and emotionally disturbed—as well as with other students who need visual and tactile reinforcement for effective learning.

Evaluation

Research on the Cuisenaire-Gattegno materials has not been conclusive. Some research (e.g., Aurich, 1963; Crowder, 1965) found that the rods were more effective for first-graders than traditional approaches were. Other research (e.g., Haynes, 1963; Nasca, 1966) found that students in later elementary grades performed no better on standardized achievement tests when the Cuisenaire-Gattegno rods had been used than when a traditional program had been used. Overall, the research shows that the rods are at least as effective as more traditional mathematics programs. In addition, these materials minimize drill and rote learning and promote discovery and understanding by the individual child according to his or her own developmental level. Student interest and enthusiasm is usually high. The concreteness of the materials and their suitability for manipulation by a tactile modality make them particularly useful for children with whom a traditional mathematics program has been unsuccessful.

The Cuisenaire rods have been criticized on the grounds that some students become too dependent on them and are unable to function at a symbolic, abstract level without them. However, used judiciously in conjunction with other models and approaches, the Cuisenaire rods have a place as supplemental materials in a modern mathematics curriculum for children with learning problems.

DIRECT INSTRUCTION MATHEMATICS

The *Direct Instruction Mathematics* (Silbert, Carnine, & Stein, 1981) approach is based on the belief that teachers are responsible for a number of the variables that affect mathematics learning, including program design, presentation techniques, and organization of instruction. The explicit purpose of Direct Instruction is to provide the teacher with a set of direct prescriptions to bring about student acquisition, retention, and generalization in mathematics.

Training Techniques and Program Organization

Direct Instruction Mathematics comes in book form. It can be thought of as a comprehensive outline of a mathematics program with numerous examples and models. It offers suggestions in eight areas of teacher instruction—specifying objectives, devising problem-solving strategies, determining necessary preskills, sequencing preskills and skills, selecting a teaching procedure, designing formats (such as criteria for acceptable student responses or procedures for correction of errors), selecting specific examples, and providing for practice and review.

Presentation techniques are provided as well, to ensure student attention and encourage teachers to teach to a criterion of mastery rather than to just the end of the lesson.

The program also deals with considerations involved in selecting materials, modifying commercial programs, and placing and grouping students. Finally, it provides a coherent plan to assist the teacher through a unit of instruction.

Evaluation

Direct Instruction Mathematics has its own criterion-referenced evaluation procedures which facilitate evaluation. The program has a great deal of structure and teacher control and requires specific responses from students, in contrast to other approaches, which allow greater teacher and student variation. Its emphasis on public, observable teacher behavior makes this program more easily supervised and evaluated than some others.

The design of the program provides a framework for analyzing a student's performance in order to separate student problems due to faulty teaching from student problems arising from deficiencies within the student. This latter feature makes the program especially useful in remedial settings. A more detailed evaluation of this program is provided by V. L. Brown (1985).

Direct Instruction is one of the few instructional approaches that have been shown through research to lead to measurable academic gains. Gersten (1985) and Gersten, Woodward, and Darch (1986) reported favorable results with special education students.

KEY MATH EARLY STEPS PROGRAM

The *Key Math* (Connolly, 1985) mathematics program for kindergartners, first graders, and students with handicaps is designed to combine the advantages of both textbook-oriented and activity-oriented methods. It is presented as a systematic, consistent program that fosters the development of cognitive skills and promotes content application. Provisions are made for differentiating among average, slow, and fast learners.

Training Techniques and Program Organization

Early Steps is organized into stages that address 55 broad instructional objectives. Each stage is an extended lesson that includes, in order: (1) presentation activities, (2) small-group exploration, (3) teacher-led integration, (4) seatwork, and (5) optional practice and enrichment activities.

Program materials consist of a variety of concrete, pictorial, and symbolic materials, including the following: teacher's guide, instructional manual, 300 Key Math cubes, 60 attribute blocks, 180 math chips, 12 tumblers, 4 deck cards, 28 numeral cards, 2 math boards, 5 math trays, 8 meter ropes, 20 activity cards, 10 resource folders, 200 blackline masters, and a scope-and-sequence chart.

At the end of each stage, one or more worksheets are used to evaluate each student's understanding of that stage. Criteria for rating students at the mastery, partial mastery, and awareness levels are included.

Evaluation

The teacher's guide notes that the program was field tested in 26 schools, but the results of the field test are not presented. Other research on the program has not yet appeared.

Adapting Existing Curricula to the Needs of Students

The previous sections have described a number of potentially useful approaches to instructing students who are having difficulty in mathematics. Unquestionably there are many classroom situations in which the use of these approaches will be quite satisfactory for many students.

Teachers sometimes find themselves in situations, however, where commercially prepared materials are not available or are not appropriate for the students they are teaching in mathematics. In such cases teachers must either develop their own materials (a difficult and time-consuming undertaking) or adapt existing materials or approaches so that they better meet the needs of the students in the classroom.

A number of the instructional dimensions can be altered to improve the quality and effectiveness of mathematics instruction for some students. Because of the highly individualistic nature of the difficulties that students can have in mathematics, the adaptation of instructional content, methods, and context remains heavily dependent on good teacher judgment. By taking into account what the student knows in mathematics and how he or she uses that knowledge and by taking into account the characteristics of the mathematics curriculum, the teacher can modify the curricular side of the equation so that a better match can be obtained between student and instruction. Table 7.9 summarizes the dimensions that can be considered in such adaptation.

Verbal Problem Solving

Probably no area of mathematics performance causes students more difficulty than verbal problem solving. Although all the causes of poor problem-solving ability are not known, they almost certainly include the following:

1. *Lack of practice.* Some teachers do not fully recognize the complexity of problem solving and fail to teach it in a systematic way. Considerable time must be allotted for the successful development of problem-solving skills.

2. *Inadequate development of underlying capabilities.* Task analysis and research have indicated that the following are related to ability to solve mathematical problems:

   a. *Ability to perform required computations.* An understanding of the four fundamental operations (addition, subtraction, multiplication, division) is vital for problem solving.

   b. *Ability to read with understanding.* It is apparent that students with reading problems are at a disadvantage in mathematics. Such students will have difficulty reading and understanding directions and explanations in the mathematics book. They will have particular trouble with story problems, even if they know the required computations and procedures. Reading mathematical problems is further complicated by the fact that many words have a different meaning in mathematical context than in everyday life (e.g., "set," "order," "power," "root").

c. *Ability to estimate answers.* Checking the "reasonableness" of an obtained answer requires the ability to estimate. Poor problem solvers tend not to be proficient in the skill of estimating.

d. *Acquisition of prerequisite concepts and cognitive structures.* There is reason to believe that the capacities described in the section on "Readiness" are necessary for children to solve mathematical problems. For example, Steffe (1968) reported that ability to conserve was related to problem-solving performance.

e. *Ability to organize required problem-solving steps in sequence.* Although the evidence is mixed as to the necessity for teaching specific problem-solving steps to most children, we advocate the use of such procedures for children who are having inordinate difficulty. The problem-solving procedure followed is outlined in Table 7.10.

A large number of mathematics instructors and researchers have given thought to the elements and strategies involved in successful verbal problem solving. Clearly, students' abilities to read, analyze, explore alternatives, represent the problem visually, implement, and verify are all involved. Successful problem solving involves a series of steps, which we have represented in Table 7.10. Table 7.11 draws attention to some of the aspects of problem solving that are particularly difficult for students with learning problems and suggests some best practices that may be implemented to assist the students.

TABLE 7.10. Suggested Procedures and Strategies in Verbal Problem Solving

PROCEDURES	STRATEGIES USED	PROBLEM A: Mary has 3 apples. Betty has 2 pears. Peter has 4 apples. How many pieces of fruit do the girls have?	PROBLEM B: Bill has 5 quarters, 3 dimes, and 4 pennies. How much money will he have left if he spends 45 cents for candy?
	Conceptualize the Problem		
A. Preview: Read the problem			
1. Identify unknown words.	Reading	"pieces"	None
2. Identify words with unusual usages.	Reading	None	None
3. Identify any cue words, e.g., "total," "in all," "how many were left."	Reading	None	"How much . . . have left"
4. Ask "Is this problem like any problem I've done before?" Look for patterns.	Analyzing (comparing with analogous problems)	"This is like the problems we had about marbles."	"This is like the money problems we did yesterday."
B. Rereading: Information processing			
1. Identify what is given.	Analyzing		
a. Is renaming required?			
i. unit conversion?		No	Quarters and dimes to cents
		Apples and pears to fruit	No
ii. categorization? (superordinate, subordinate categories)		Yes "Peter has 4 apples."	Yes
b. Is sufficient information given?		Yes	Yes
c. Is irrelevant or distracting information given?		No	No
2. Identify what is asked for; formulate hypothesis.	Analyzing		
a. What process is required? (comparing, combining, etc.)		Combining	Converting, combining, separating
b. What unit or category is required? (minutes, inches, apples, dollars, etc.)		Fruit	Dollars and cents

(continues)

TABLE 7.10. *Continued*

PROCEDURES	STRATEGIES USED	PROBLEM A: Mary has 3 apples. Betty has 2 pears. Peter has 4 apples. How many pieces of fruit do the girls have?	PROBLEM B: Bill has 5 quarters, 3 dimes, and 4 pennies. How much money will he have left if he spends 45 cents for candy?
	Visualize the Structure of the Problem		
1. Use manipulatives (tangible objects).	Analyzing Exploring		
2. Use fingers or other counting representation.	Analyzing Exploring		25, 50, 75, 100, 125 10, 20, 30 1, 2, 3, 4
3. Use a number line or "doodles" drawn on paper—Cross out what is not needed; circle what is needed to solve the problem.	Analyzing Exploring	xx ✓✓ xxxx	

(continues)

TABLE 7.10. *Continued*

PROCEDURES	STRATEGIES USED	PROBLEM A: Mary has 3 apples. Betty has 2 pears. Peter has 4 apples. How many pieces of fruit do the girls have?	PROBLEM B: Bill has 5 quarters, 3 dimes, and 4 pennies. How much money will he have left if he spends 45 cents for candy?
Select and Implement the Procedure			
A. Refine hypothesis: Operation analysis 1. Decide the problem type: *Change:* An exchange occurs that changes the size of a given set of objects. *Combine:* Two quantities must be considered in combination. *Compare:* Two quantities must be compared and their differences quantified.	Analyzing	This is a *combining* problem, because two quantities are considered together.	This is a *comparing* problem, because two quantities of money are compared, and the difference calculated.
2. Write the mathematical sentence using easier numbers.	Planning	Not applicable	Bill has 10 cents. How much money will he have left if he spends 5 cents for candy? Solution pattern: Comparing. Subtract money spent from original amount of money: original money − money spent = required answer. 10 − 5 = 5 cents.
3. Write the actual mathematical sentence.	Implementing	3 + 2 + 4 = required answer	$5 \times .25 = a$ $3 \times .10 = b$ $4 \times .01 = c$ $a + b + c = d$ $d - .45 =$ required answer
4. Perform the operation.	Implementing	3 + 2 = 5	$5 \times .25 = 1.25$ $3 \times .10 = .30$ $4 \times .01 = .04$ $1.25 + .30 + .04 = 1.59$ $1.59 - .45 = 1.14$

(continues)

TABLE 7.10. *Continued*

PROCEDURES	STRATEGIES USED	PROBLEM A: Mary has 3 apples. Betty has 2 pears. Peter has 4 apples. How many pieces of fruit do the girls have?	PROBLEM B: Bill has 5 quarters, 3 dimes, and 4 pennies. How much money will he have left if he spends 45 cents for candy?
		Check and State the Answer	
A. Reread the problem and recheck visualization of problem.	Verifying	Repeat steps above.	Repeat steps above.
B. Recheck calculations.	Verifying	Repeat calculations (with a different approach if possible).	Repeat calculations (with a different approach if possible).
C. Estimate the answer.	Verifying	Students use the visualization to help estimate the answer.	Students use the visualization to help estimate the answer.
D. Compare estimate to obtained answer.	Verifying	Student decides whether estimated answer confirms calculations.	Student decides whether estimated answer confirms calculations.
E. State the answer in full sentence format.	Verifying	The girls have 5 pieces of fruit.	Bill will have $1.14 left.

TABLE 7.11   Aspects of Verbal Problem Solving

ASPECT	BEST PRACTICE	EXAMPLES	
Difficulty of vocabulary	Vocabulary level should be keyed to students' reading ability.	Compare:	Mother made 3 pies. Then she made 2 more. How many pies did she make in all? The theoretical mathematician performed 3 calculations. Then she performed 2 more. How many calculations did she perform in all?
Difficulty of grammar: active/ passive voice	Provide students with problems using active voice first; use passive voice later.	Compare:	Mary gave 4 apples to Sue. Sue gave 3 apples to Debra. How many more apples did Mary give away than Sue? Sue was given 4 apples by Mary. Debra was given 3 apples by Sue. How many more apples were received by Sue than by Debra?
Negation	Provide students with strategies for dealing with negation in verbal problems—they should think of the statement in its positive meaning, then reverse for the negative.	Compare:	Betty lit 5 of the 12 candles in the dining room. Nancy lit 1 of the 5 candles in the living room. How many candles did the girls light? Betty did not light 7 of the 12 candles in the dining room. Nancy did not light 4 of the 5 candles in the living room. How many candles did the girls light?
		Or:	Betty did not light 7 of the 12 candles in the dining room. Nancy lit 1 of the 5 candles in the living room. How many candles did the girls light?
Simple/ complex sentences	Assist students in developing strategies for restating complex sentences in simpler forms.	Compare:	Mother made 3 pies. Then she made 2 more pies. How many pies in all did she make? Mother made 3 pies from the apples she bought at the store. Then she made 2 pies with the cherries that the girls had picked. How many pies in all did she make?
Classification	Provide students with experience in detecting superordinate and subordinate classifications of both subjects and verbs.	Compare:	Mother made 3 pies. Then she made 2 more. How many pies did she make in all? A *boy* made 3 pies. A *girl* made 2 pies. How many pies did the *children* make? Mother *baked* 3 pies. Then she *prepared* 2 more. How many pies did she *make in all*?

(continues)

TABLE 7.11. *Continued*

ASPECT	BEST PRACTICE	EXAMPLES	
Extraneous or missing information	Assist students in developing procedures for checking problems for extraneous or missing information of a quantitative or qualitative nature.	*Compare:*	Mary gave 4 apples to Janet. Sue gave 3 apples to Debra. How many more apples did Mary give away than Sue? Mary gave 4 apples to Janet. Sue gave 3 apples to Debra. Lisa gave 2 apples to Betty. How many more apples did Mary give away than Sue?
		Or:	Mary gave 4 apples to Janet. She gave a few apples to Sue. How many apples did Mary give away? Which information is missing? a) the name of Mary's friend b) the number of apples Mary had at first c) the number of apples Mary gave to Sue d) the number of apples Mary gave to Janet
Use of cue words	Avoid the use of words that cue a student to use a particular operation such as addition or subtraction without analyzing the nature of the problem (e.g., "in all" or "were left"). Restate the problem so that cue words are avoided.	*Compare:*	Betty lit 7 candles in the dining room. Then she lit 5 candles in the living room. How many candles did she light *in all*? Betty lit 7 candles in the dining room. Then she lit 5 candles in the living room. How many candles were now lit?
		Or:	Betty lit 7 candles in the dining room. Then she lit 5 candles in the living room. How many candles were lit by Betty?
Use of reverse questions	Vary the type of question asked to ensure students' careful analysis of the problems presented.	*Compare:*	Mother had made 3 pies. Then she made 4 more pies. How many pies did she make? Mother had 3 pies yesterday. Now she has 7 pies. How many pies did she make today?
		Or:	The butcher sold 20 pounds of meat. He received $3.00 per pound. How much money did he receive? The butcher sold 20 pounds of meat. He received $60.00. How much did he receive per pound of meat?
Use of cloze technique	Provide students with problems for which they must supply the appropriate word to make the problem's calculations accurate.	*Compare:*	Mother made 3 pies. Then she made 2 pies. How many pies in all did she make? Mother made 3 pies. Then she (ate, made, sold) 2 pies. Now she has 5 pies.
		Or:	Mother made 3 pies. Then she _____ 2 pies. Now she has 5 pies.

(continues)

TABLE 7.11. *Continued*

ASPECT	BEST PRACTICE	EXAMPLES	
Problems in which students identify "true," "false," or "can't tell" statements	Provide students with problems for which they must designate follow-up statements as "true," "false," or "can't tell" based on the information given.	*Problem:*	The coach gave 3 basketballs to the boys on the A Team. The coach gave 4 basketballs to the boys on the B Team. The coach gave 2 baseballs to the girls on the A Team. The coach gave 6 baseballs to the girls on the B Team. Describe the following statements as True, False, or Can't Tell. a) The girls got more balls than the boys. b) The A Team got more balls than the B Team. c) There are more girls on the A Team than on the B Team. d) There are more girls than boys. e) The coach had more baseballs than basketballs. f) The coach has 4 balls left.

The ideas in this table have been adapted from the author's experience and from *Mathematics for the Mildly Handicapped: A Guide to Curriculum and Instruction* by J. F. Cawley, A. M. Fitzmaurice-Hayes, and R. A. Shaw, 1988, Boston: Allyn & Bacon.

Chapter 8

Evaluating and Managing Classroom Behavior

LINDA BROWN

Teachers are expected to manage the motley assortment of behaviors that occur daily in their classrooms. They are expected to control and redirect the less desirable behaviors and to encourage and strengthen the desirable behaviors. This book is concerned principally with the management of problem behaviors, but most of the techniques presented can be used equally well to promote positive behaviors.

Of the problem behaviors that arise in classrooms, aggressive behaviors are the most apparent: fighting, stealing, destroying property. Self-destructive behaviors, such as substance abuse, self-injurious behaviors, or even suicide, also are quite visible. These behaviors obviously are harmful to the students involved, and some of them are harmful to innocent bystanders. All of them certainly disrupt the ongoing educational program in the classroom.

Passive behaviors, by definition, are less obvious problems. Still, they prevent the affected student from participating fully in the academic and social activities of the school community. This category includes such behaviors as withdrawing from interaction, refusing to speak, and crying.

Some of these problems are more serious than others, but dealing with them—passive and aggressive behaviors alike—consumes a great deal of the teacher's time and attention. A tremendous amount of time is also devoted to a variety of minor but aggravating problems such as talking without permission, swearing, poking classmates, and running through the corridors. Unfortunately, dealing with problem behaviors leaves the teacher very little time to deal with the positive behaviors that one would hope to strengthen and encourage: effective social skills, such as making and keeping friends or dealing with peer pressure; self-regulatory behaviors, such as beginning and completing work on time, working independently, or dealing with angry feelings; and conduct or habits that are indicative of a healthy self-concept, such as taking pride in oneself and feeling good about one's accomplishments.

This chapter presents a variety of strategies that teachers can use to manage and improve the behavior of their students. The assessment techniques described emphasize an ecological model that encourages teachers to approach a target behavior directly and to pay special attention to the situational and environmental influences that may contribute to or aggravate a problem behavior or that may inhibit a desirable behavior. The eclectic selection of management techniques presented will help the teacher to manage the behavior patterns observed in a classroom and to alter ecological variables determined to be important aspects of such behaviors.

ASSESSING PROBLEM BEHAVIORS

The evaluation of school-based problems is a responsibility that usually is shared by classroom teachers and appraisal personnel. In some instances, such evaluations are the sole responsibility of teachers, especially during the initial stages. The assessment unit of this chapter has been designed to assist classroom teachers in this process. In the first part of this section, we describe a rationale for ecological assessment, a model that is well suited to behavioral evaluations in school settings. In the second part, we describe seven specific assessment strategies for teachers to use in measuring problem behaviors.

An Ecological Framework for Assessing Problem Behaviors

Teachers often observe behaviors that interfere with a student's school learning or that are symptomatic of emotional distress. For example, Jim cries every morning while on the school bus, unusual behavior for a fourth-grade student; Mary cuts high school English repeatedly but attends her other classes regularly; Willie is given to spitting on other people and pulling out patches of his hair; Nellie is friendless, is frequently involved in fighting and teasing episodes, and is verbally abusive to her classmates; Sarah constantly talks out in class and almost never is in her seat; and David is abnormally reticent and withdrawn.

When a student is suspected of being emotionally or behaviorally disordered or of exhibiting behavioral problems related to a learning difficulty, school personnel will need considerable information about the problem before they can make placement, diagnostic, or educational decisions. When the situation is thought to be serious, the teacher will want to prepare a written description detailing the precise behaviors that are of concern and the situations in which these behaviors occur. The teacher will need to document through objective means the presence and severity of the observed problems and then to probe the areas of difficulty more fully and systematically. Such documentation may be necessary to qualify a youngster for special services, to help the teacher set priorities for those behaviors requiring immediate attention, or to demonstrate that behavioral change has occurred as a result of treatment.

This information must be gathered within an ecological frame of reference. Ecological assessment allows an examiner to evaluate a student's status in the various ecologies or environments in which the student functions. This type of evaluation is rapidly gaining popularity in the public schools, and many states now require that students identified as emotionally disturbed be evaluated in an ecological manner.

Rhodes and Tracy (1972), in the first volume of *A Study of Child Variance,* established rules that allowed them to sift through vast amounts of theoretical information in order to generate theory clusters to explain disturbed or deviant behavior. One of the clusters that emerged was ecological in nature. Obviously the terms *ecology, ecosystem,* and even *ecological assessment* have been borrowed from the biological and botanical sciences; however, they carry very specific definitions in education and psychology.

Rhodes and Paul (1978, p. 191) called ecological theories "holistic phenomena" that explained how the various "social, physical, and psychic processes [of an ecosystem] . . . become a disability . . . [and] are transformed into deviance." The theory obviously posits that deviance may result from disturbed relationships between an organism and its environment (i.e., between a student and the classroom or the home). Therefore, the observed relationships and the environment deserve as much time under the diagnostic microscope as the organism itself. In other words, teachers should pay as much attention to such things as the classroom structure, the curriculum, school rules and regulations, and friendships and cliques among students as they do to individual students who may be experiencing difficulty.

Ecological assessment avoids at least two of the pitfalls inherent in more traditional behavioral evaluations. First, ecological assessment obviously provides a much broader and more natural picture of the target child than do conventional evaluations that typically remove students from the classroom and evaluate them in an isolated, sterile environment such as a testing room or the school psychologist's office. Ecological assessment also differs radically in its assumptions about the nature of behavioral difficulties. Whereas traditional evaluations assume that the child is or has the problem, ecological assessment assumes that many factors other than student-centered ones may cause or aggravate behavioral problems.

No behavior occurs in a vacuum. A so-called problem behavior may be an entirely normal reaction to a difficult or bizarre situation. It also is possible that the behavior is, in fact, "normal," but that a particular perception of that behavior is deviant. For instance, a teacher who is unfamiliar with 6-year-olds may perceive normally busy first graders as hyperactive and make referrals on that basis. We know, for instance, that teachers' evaluations of behavior can affect their subsequent academic evaluations and that estimates of academic competence can affect behavioral evaluations. Students of average or above-average academic ability seem to be given greater behavioral latitude than their less academically competent peers. It also is possible for elements of the school environment to exacerbate problem behaviors. A classic example is provided by the student (or teacher!) who becomes restless and troublesome in a hot, noisy classroom. Obviously, the source of the problem may lie within the environment and not within the child. Only through ecological assessment can any of these suppositions be validated.

Several environments may be tapped during ecological assessment. Among these are the school, the home, and the community, as well as the student's interpersonal environment and the aspects of personality and self-esteem that make up an individual's internal ecology. Within the school setting, which is the environment we are most concerned with in this chapter, a teacher can assume that students change ecologies each time they change classes, teachers, or academic content or format within the same classroom. An example of the latter might be moving from a supervised reading group to an art interest center or even to independent reading activities. Presumably the requirements for success vary in each of these ecologies. One environment may require a great deal of verbalization (a language-experience reading group) whereas another requires silence (the library); one may require independence and creativity (an exploratory interest center) whereas another requires strict conformity and adherence to established rules and regulations (a chemistry lab or woodworking shop). A student is usually required to function in all of these very different environments during a typical school day.

Ecologies also may be discerned on the basis of the perceptions being recorded. The activities taking place in a reading group no doubt look very different through the teacher's eyes than through the students' eyes. Most teachers who undertake ecological assessment will want to seek the perceptions of the target student and that student's teacher(s), parent(s), and peers. If the student in question is participating in a work-study program, the teacher also may want to gather information from supervisors or co-workers in that environment.

In the *Behavior Rating Profile, Second Edition* (BRP-2), an ecological assessment battery that is described in detail later, L. Brown and Hammill (1990) propose a two-dimensional model that includes a variety of perceptions that are evaluated within several environments or ecologies. Using this model, which is presented graphically in Table 8.1, the teacher decides which ecologies should be assessed and whose perceptions should be sought. Data then are gathered from these sources and assembled into an ecological profile.

TABLE 8.1. Relationship of *Behavior Rating Profile, Second Edition* Components to Type of Respondent and Ecology

COMPONENT	RESPONDENT				ECOLOGY		
	Student	*Teacher(s)*	*Parent(s)*	*Peers*	*Home*	*School*	*Social Life*
Student Rating Scale: Home	X				X		
Student Rating Scale: School	X					X	
Student Rating Scale: Peer	X						X
Teacher Rating Scale		X				X	
Parent Rating Scale			X		X		
Sociogram				X			X

From *Behavior Rating Profile, Second Edition* by L. L. Brown and D. D. Hammill, 1990, Austin, TX: PRO-ED. Reprinted with permission of the authors and the publisher.

Seven General Techniques for Assessing Problem Behaviors

Seven general techniques that classroom teachers can use to evaluate problem behaviors are described in this section. These include (1) direct observation, (2) behavioral checklists and inventories, (3) Q-sorts, (4) interviews, (5) examination of teacher–pupil interaction in the classroom, (6) sociometrics, and (7) standardized tests of personality. By taking care to note the people from whom information is gathered and the environments that they seem to evaluate, teachers can tailor ecological assessment plans to satisfy their particular assessment needs.

Direct Observation

The most convenient way to measure a behavior is to observe it directly in the classroom. Three direct observation techniques are described here: (1) automatic recording, (2) analysis of permanent products, and (3) observational recording.

AUTOMATIC RECORDING

Automatic recording involves the measurement of behavior by machines. For instance, in biofeedback such behaviors as pulse, heart rate, blood pressure, and galvanic skin response are measured by sensitive mechanical devices. In laboratories where animal research is conducted, machines are used frequently to record the movements or responses of the laboratory animals. These machines are costly to purchase and to maintain, and they are rigid in their functioning, usually incapable of being adapted to measure more than a single behavior or set of behaviors. For these reasons, automatic recording devices are rarely used in school settings. They are mentioned here only to familiarize teachers with their existence.

ANALYSIS OF PERMANENT PRODUCTS

The product-analysis technique is infinitely more useful to teachers. In fact, a good deal of teaching, particularly diagnostic teaching, involves the regular use of this technique, in which a teacher evaluates the tangible result of a student's behavior rather than the behavior itself. For example, a student's spelling paper is the "permanent product" of taking a spelling test. The number of correctly spelled words (or correctly worked algebra problems, complete sentences written, etc.) can be counted and verified easily. Although often used by teachers to measure pupil status or progress in academics, the technique is seldom employed to assess affective behaviors because they do not usually result in permanent products.

OBSERVATIONAL RECORDING

Observational recording of classroom behaviors is another useful technique for educators. Seven observational methods are described briefly

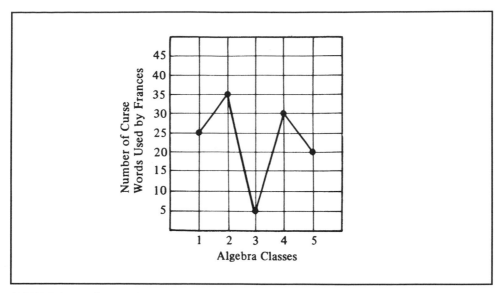

FIGURE 8.1. Graph of Frances's swearing behavior during algebra class.

here: (1) anecdotal recording, (2) event recording, (3) duration recording, (4) interval recording, (5) time sampling, (6) latency recording, and (7) planned activity check. The data generated by the last six of these various techniques are recorded in a systematic way so that they can be interpreted quickly and easily. Anecdotal records, of course, usually are presented in narrative form. The most common way of recording data gathered through the other techniques is by graphing, as in Figure 8.1. The teacher can easily glance at a graph to note trends or to see when the rate or duration of a behavior begins to increase or decrease.

1. *Anecdotal records* provide an account of everything that is done to, with, for, by, or around the target student. Obviously, no individual teacher can take the time to gather all the anecdotal data that are required for a comprehensive record. Occasionally, other personnel such as trained volunteers, aides, or student teachers can be assigned some responsibility for gathering these data. Ideally, a videotape recording of the student's entire school day should be available for analysis, but, of course, this is not practical in most situations.

   A coding system or some form of shorthand may be devised to permit the observer to record as much information as possible in a short amount of time and space. The shorthand is transcribed later into narrative form that can be understood by individuals who are unfamiliar with the coding system. A coded entry in an anecdotal record might look like this: "1025—sci ctr—X pokes SL—SL cries, X pokes more—M, SR, PR also in ctr—M calls Δ, others tell X to quit—Δ comes to ctr." Translated, this means that at 10:25 in the science interest center, the target child (X) poked at Susan Lily (SL) until she cried, after which he continued poking her. The other children in the science center (M, SR, and PR) told the target child to quit poking, and M called the teacher (Δ), who then came to the science center.

Anecdotal records are especially useful when a teacher is unable to identify the pattern of the student's problem. By analyzing a continuous recording of the student's behavior over a period of time, the teacher may learn that the behavior occurs only in certain situations or at certain time periods in the day or that every occurrence of the problem behavior is followed by a positive reward, perhaps by increased teacher attention and interest. In some instances, the classroom teacher can identify these variables using continuous interval recording, a more time-efficient measurement device.

2. *Event recording* is a frequently used direct observation technique. It is simply a record of the number of times a defined behavior occurs; in other words, it is a behavioral frequency count. Using this technique, a teacher learns that Frances used 26 curse words during the 30-minute algebra class on Monday, 33 on Tuesday, 7 on Wednesday, 28 on Thursday, and 19 on Friday. These data are recorded in the form of a conventional graph in Figure 8.1.

3. *Duration recording* is used when a teacher is more concerned with how long a behavior lasts than with the frequency of occurrence. A record of the duration of a child's temper tantrum, for instance, may occasionally be more important than a record of the number of outbursts occurring during a given time period. Consider the case of Linda, who has difficulty attending to the task at hand. She exhibited only one instance of off-task behavior during the independent work period; however, that one instance lasted for 20 minutes.

4. *Interval recording* combines the two previously described techniques, giving the teacher a measure of both the frequency and the duration of a behavior. An observation period is divided into equal, usually short, time periods. For instance, the 5 minutes after recess may be divided into thirty 10-second intervals. The teacher observes continuously during the 5-minute session and notes whether the defined behavior occurs during each of the shorter intervals. For instance, if Pat talked without permission during twenty-five of the thirty 10-second intervals, the results would be reported as 83% of the time spent talking out. The record of Pat's talking (T) would probably look something like this:

T_1	T_2	T_3	T_4	T_5	T_6
T_7	T_8	T_9	T_{10}	11	12
13	T_{14}	T_{15}	T_{16}	T_{17}	T_{18}
T_{19}	T_{20}	T_{21}	T_{22}	T_{23}	T_{24}
T_{25}	T_{26}	T_{27}	T_{28}	29	30

The duration of the talking can be calculated easily: Pat was talking during twenty-five 10-second intervals, or for 4 minutes and 10 seconds. Event data also can be extracted: Pat talked out twice, from the 1st through the 10th 10-second interval and again from the 14th through the 28th interval. Data for a period of days could be graphed in any of the three ways shown in Figure 8.2.

5. *Time sampling* is very similar to interval recording, but it is sometimes more useful for longer periods of observation because it does not require the teacher to observe continuously. The observation period again is divided into equal, but usually longer, time periods. For instance, Mr. Nixon, the world history teacher, may divide his 50-minute class period into five 10-minute intervals. He then conducts a time sampling of Henry's behavior while Henry is supposed to be answering the questions at the end of Chapter 14 in the world history textbook. At the end of (not throughout) each 10-minute interval, Mr. Nixon observes to see if Henry is answering the questions. If Henry were working (W) four of the five times that Mr. Nixon

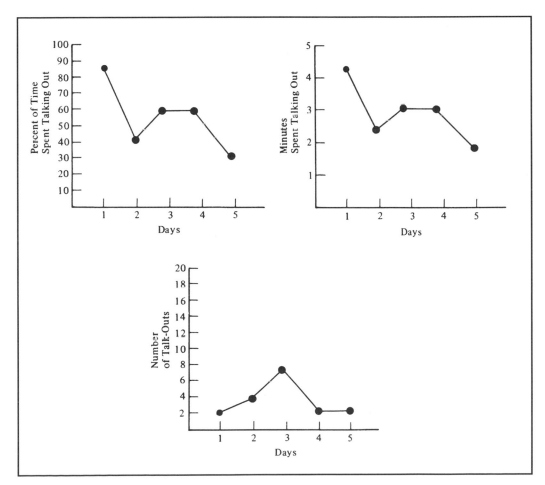

FIGURE 8.2. Methods of graphing data.

observed him, he would be recorded as working 80% of the time. Mr. Nixon's time sampling record might look like the following:

W	W	W	W	

The mechanical advantages of this technique are obvious. It requires only 2 or 3 seconds to glance at a particular student and then make a check on a record sheet. In addition, the disruption of instruction or other class activities is minimal. The disadvantage is that the individual recording Henry's work behavior does not know that Henry worked throughout each 10-minute interval, only that Henry was working at the instant of observation. The more observation periods that are recorded, the higher the probability of accurate measurement: Henry would unlikely be sufficiently prescient to stop and start his work at precise intervals—unless, of course, Mr. Nixon gave himself away and unwittingly provided Henry with a cue.

6. *Latency recording* provides information that frequently is of concern to teachers and parents alike, namely the amount of time it takes a student to respond. In other words, the point of interest is not whether a student can perform a particular task but whether the student will respond within a reasonable period of time. This technique is similar to duration recording, in that it is a time measure. The period being measured, the latency period, is the time between a command and a response. For instance, if Mark is asked to begin writing an essay and dawdles for 10 minutes before putting pencil to paper, the latency recording is 10 minutes; or, if Cara is asked to return to her seat and wanders around the room for 2.5 minutes before doing so, the latency record is 2.5 minutes. In both instances, the assumption is made that the students are fully capable of exhibiting the requested behavior: Mark can write an essay and Cara can sit at her desk. The behavior being measured is the quickness of their responses. Latency intervals can be recorded conventionally or graphed.

7. *Planned activity check,* sometimes called "placheck," is used to measure the behaviors of groups of children. Teachers using this technique are interested in the percentage of students engaged in a defined behavior. Perhaps a teacher wants to do a placheck of the children working on an assignment in an independent interest center. The teacher first would count the number of students working and then would count the number of students actually in the interest center. If 10 students were in the center and only 4 were engaged in the assignment, the placheck record would be 40%. Placheck records often are taken on a time sampling basis. For example, Mr. Nixon, the world history teacher, might do placheck every 10 minutes during his 50-minute class period. If 25 students were in the class and 24 were working at the first check, 20 at the second check, 25 at the

third and fourth checks, and 5 at the final check, the placheck records would be 96%, 80%, 100%, 100%, and 20%, respectively. Mr. Nixon might conclude that studying behavior dropped off during the final 10 minutes of his class, or that students were working diligently but required only 40 minutes rather than the allotted 50 minutes, particularly if this pattern continued over a period of time. He might adjust his planning to make better use of the final 10 minutes.

Behavioral Checklists and Rating Scales

Teachers, diagnosticians, and mental health professionals often turn to behavioral checklists and rating scales when they are evaluating the presence and severity of problem behaviors. These instruments have a number of advantages. First, they tend to be concise and time efficient. Second, they are behaviorally oriented, and therefore are more specific and objective than many other measures of affect. They can be used with a single student or with groups of students and can be adapted to a variety of respondents. Finally, they are equally sensitive to acting-out as well as acting-in behaviors, helping the evaluator to focus on passive or withdrawn behaviors that may otherwise go unnoticed in a busy classroom. In this section, we are concerned with standardized, norm-referenced checklists, as well as with informal checklists that teachers may develop themselves.

NORM-REFERENCED CHECKLISTS

Until recently, most published behavioral checklists and inventories had no clear-cut superiority over informally devised checklists. They frequently had only rough criteria for interpretation and lacked adequate reliability or validity. However, that condition has changed: Well-built, psychometrically sound instruments are now available for use.

Virtually all norm-referenced behavioral checklists and rating scales are of the paper-and-pencil variety. The person completing the checklist reads a list of items and marks a response on an answer sheet. Some points to be considered when using and interpreting rating scales and checklists are the content of the items, the type of response that is given, and the person who is completing the checklist.

Item Content

Checklist items may include a mixture of normal and problem behaviors, or they may be limited solely to problem behaviors. Some examiners believe that concentrating on problem behaviors in the limited time available for evaluation is the most efficient practice. Others believe that using a mixture of items prevents a subject from responding in a set manner, making it more difficult to dissemble or give the expected answer; however, subjects who want to manipulate their responses are remarkably good at doing so, regardless of the content of the items.

Response Format

Two response patterns are commonly employed on checklists. The first is concerned primarily with the presence or absence of a behavior rather than with its frequency or severity. In this instance, the response is usually dichotomized:

Breaks class rules	True—False
Has nervous tics	Present—Absent
Is shy	Yes—No
Cries when frustrated	Observed—Not Observed

Where severity and frequency are also of interest, a Likert-type response is employed:

Breaks class rules	Five or more times per class—Three or four times per class—One or two times per class—Zero times per class
Has nervous tics	Very much like the student—Like the student—Not like the student—Not at all like the student
Is shy	Usually—Sometimes—Rarely
Cries when frustrated	Daily—Weekly—Never

Respondent

The respondent who provides information on the checklist can be the target student, a classmate or peer, a parent, a teacher, or a sibling. An important point is that most behavior checklists are actually measuring perceptions of behaviors, rather than actual instances of behaviors.

For example, the teacher may be responding to the item "Breaks class rules." The response choices are *frequently, sometimes,* and *rarely.* The teacher's response reflects the teacher's perception of the frequency of that student's rule-breaking behavior; it is not necessarily fact.

Gender bias is an excellent example of this phenomenon. The teacher may be more tolerant of, or inured to, rule breaking by boys than by girls. Therefore, the behavior of a male student who failed to follow class rules four times during an hour class period might earn a response of "Sometimes," whereas the behavior of a female student with the same number of rule-breaking incidents during that class period might be rated "Frequently."

Some checklists use this phenomenon to their advantage. An example is the *Behavior Rating Profile, 2nd Edition* (BRP-2) (L. Brown & Hammill, 1990). The BRP-2 is ecological in nature. Each of its six components is completed by a different set of respondents, and at least two perceptions are solicited of the home, school, and interpersonal environments occupied by the student being evaluated. Table 8.1 earlier in this chapter demonstrated these relationships. Using the BRP-2, an examiner can determine how the school environment is perceived by the teacher, by the student, or by the student's classmates. Differences among teachers and classes can be documented. Likewise, perceptions of the student at home are offered by the parents, the child, and perhaps by brothers and sisters or other adults in the home. Interpersonal relationships are evaluated from the perspective of the student and his or her classmates and peers.

This information can be valuable to an examiner seeking to understand the nature of the problems being reported. For example, James is a student whose behavior is viewed as deviant by his fifth-grade teacher. Do James's other teachers—the art teacher, the physical education instructor, the band director, the special education teacher—view him similarly or do their responses on a behavioral checklist reveal markedly different perceptions? If the latter, is this because his behavior actually differs in each of these settings (something that could be determined through direct observation) or is it because the teachers' requirements and expectations differ (something that could be determined through an interview)? Likewise, if James views his class as a negative experience, is this perception shared by his classmates? Do they also find the class to be negative or is James's perception unique?

Similarly, the examiner may want to ask a student's parents to complete behavioral checklists on all of their children rather than only on the target child. Do the parents view their children similarly? Do mother and father express similar feelings or does each parent express different perceptions? The same axiom may be applied to inventories completed by the target student: Do brothers and sisters concur with that child's perceptions of the home ecology?

We emphasize that, even though investigations of this scope are consistent with the principles of ecological assessment, they should be undertaken only when the need is warranted. The process can be quite time consuming and should not be lengthened unnecessarily. We suggest these variations as a means of stimulating the formation of alternative hypotheses regarding problem behaviors. A low score on a behavioral measure should not be interpreted flatly as a sign of deviance on the part of the child. It is the profile or pattern of scores that is important.

INFORMAL BEHAVIORAL CHECKLISTS

Teachers and diagnosticians may find that in some instances an informal checklist or rating scale based upon a particular classroom, a specific student, or an identified set of behaviors is helpful. When care is given to its construction, use, and interpretation, the specificity of an informal instrument may prove more valuable than the psychometric superiority of a norm-referenced instrument.

Teachers who want to build their own checklists and rating scales should keep in mind the same criteria for standardization that authors of published tests follow. For instance, there should be specific criteria for administering, scoring, and interpreting the test. This ensures a certain amount of objectivity in the test: Each user will employ the same materials, allow the same amount of time, and count the same items as right or wrong (or present/absent, serious/minor, very much like/somewhat like/somewhat unlike/very much unlike the student, depending on the scoring instructions). Teachers who make up their own tests should take the time to write down specific, detailed instructions that another professional could use to administer and score the test. Suggestions for interpreting the results according to some frame of reference also should be provided. Following these simple procedures ensures that the teacher-made test will be useful not only to the teacher who built it but also to another professional or on another occasion.

Q-Sorts

Q-sorting is uniquely suited to ecological assessment because it is a technique that can be used by teachers to compare two interpretations of a single set of behaviors. For example, a teacher might describe behaviors associated with reading (e.g., reads well, doesn't like to read, reads at home) or even social attributes (e.g., dates a lot, can't dance, has friends). The teacher, counselor, or diagnostician then would compare how a student viewed the various items from both realistic and idealistic points of view (e.g., this is how I behave; this is how I wish I behaved). Directions for constructing a Q-sort and suggestions for its use are presented in this section.

The first step in using the Q-sort is to devise or obtain a list of descriptor statements, called a Q-deck. Probably the most widely used Q-decks within the special education community are those developed by Kroth (1973). Minner and Beane (1985) also developed a Q-deck specifically for special education teachers. Here are Kroth's (1973) descriptors:

Parent Q-Sort Items[1]

1. Does assigned chores.
2. Does homework on time.
3. Goes to bed without problems.
4. Comes home when he or she should.
5. Argues with parents.
6. Has friends.
7. Likes school.
8. Cries or sulks when he or she doesn't get own way.
9. Throws temper tantrums.
10. Likes to watch TV.
11. Likes to read.
12. Plays alone.
13. Eats between meals.

---

1. From "The Behavioral Q-Sort as a Diagnostic Tool" by R. Kroth, 1973, *Academic Therapy, 8,* p. 327. Copyright 1973 by PRO-ED, Inc. Reprinted with permission of the author and publisher.

14. Is overweight.

15. Is destructive of property.

16. Gets ready for school on time.

17. Makes own decisions.

18. Chooses own clothes.

19. Is unhealthy.

20. Fights with brothers and sisters.

21. Has a messy room.

22. Responds to rewards.

23. Does acceptable schoolwork.

24. Is a restless sleeper.

25. Stretches the truth.

The items in a Q-deck can be drawn from any setting deemed to be important or of interest: home, school, nonacademic classroom activities, interpersonal relationships, and so on. Q-sorts can contain any number of items per deck, although most range from 25 to 100 items. With children or subjects of limited attention, decks of 25 and 36 items are most common. Whatever the total number of items, the number must be a perfect square so that the items can be sorted into a pyramid, as in Figure 8.3.

A Q-deck is constructed with each item or descriptor statement written on an individual card. These items are then read by the student completing the Q-sort. Each card from the deck is placed on the formboard in the column deemed most descriptive by the respondent ("most like me," "very much like me," etc.). All the squares on the pyramid must be used: None may be left blank and none may be used twice, although students may rearrange the items until they are satisfied with their responses. Students sort the items twice. On the first sort, they place the items into categories that reflect how they believe they really are; this is called the *real sort*. The second time, the students sort the items into the categories as they wish they were; this is called the *ideal sort*.

Students' responses are marked on a record form, such as that shown in Figure 8.4, and a simple correlation is calculated between the two sorts. For example, if a student sorted Item 1 as "a little like me" on the real sort, a 4 would be recorded in the first column (S-1). If the student rated the same item as "unlike me" on the ideal sort, a 7 would be recorded in the second column (S-2). The difference between the sorts is 3, and this value is recorded in the D column. The difference squared (D^2) is 9. The D^2 column is summed, and the total (ΣD^2) is substituted into the formula beside the chart. This formula will yield a correlation coefficient; it will not be larger than +1.00 or smaller than −1.00. The further the correlation is from $r = .00$, the greater the agreement between the real and the ideal sorts. A positive correlation means that the relationship between the real and the ideal sorts is positive: The more Juan says "Does assigned chores" is really like

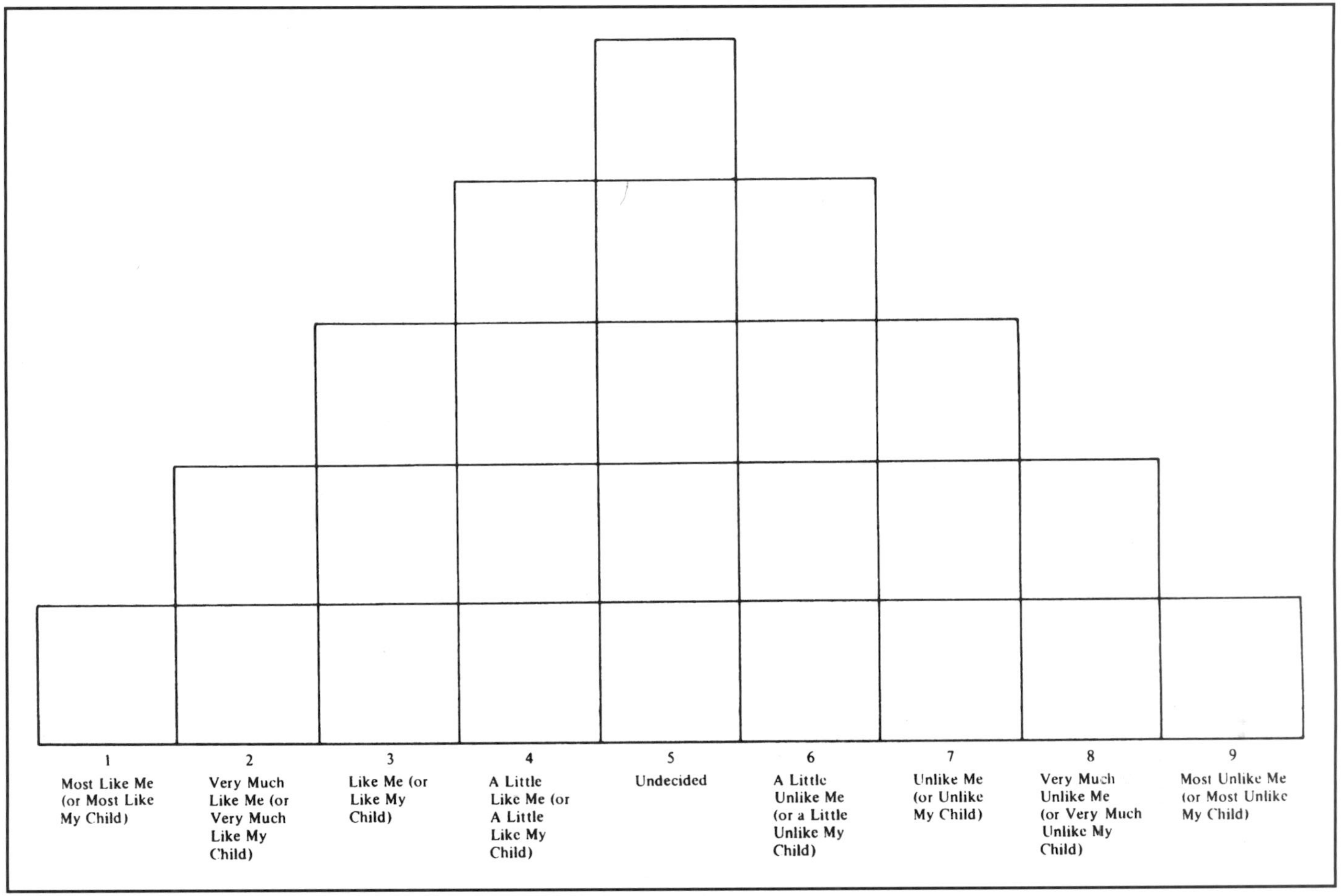

FIGURE 8.3. Q-Sort formboard.

From "The Behavioral Q-Sort as a Diagnostic Tool" by R. Kroth, 1973, *Academic Therapy, 8*, p. 327. Copyright 1973 by PRO-ED, Inc. Reprinted with permission of the author and the publisher.

The column labels of the formboard are:

1. Most Like Me (or Most Like My Child)
2. Very Much Like Me (or Very Much Like My Child)
3. Like Me (or Like My Child)
4. A Little Like Me (or A Little Like My Child)
5. Undecided
6. A Little Unlike Me (or a Little Unlike My Child)
7. Unlike Me (or Unlike My Child)
8. Very Much Unlike Me (or Very Much Unlike My Child)
9. Most Unlike Me (or Most Unlike My Child)

Q-Sort Record Form

School _____ Teacher _____ Grade ____ Age _____

Name of Examiner _____ Relationship to Child _____

Card No.	Column S-1	Column S-2	D	D²	
1					$n = 1 - \dfrac{\Sigma D^2}{200}$
2					
3					
4					
5					
6					
7					
8					
9					
10					
11					
12					
13					
14					
15					
16					
17					
18					
19					
20					
21					
22					
23					
24					
25					
			Σ =		

FIGURE 8.4.   Q-Sort Record Form.

From "The Behavioral Q-sort as a Diagnostic Tool," by R. Kroth, 1973, *Academic Therapy, 8,* p. 327. Copyright 1973 by PRO-ED, Inc. Reprinted with permission of the author and the publisher.

him, the more he wishes it could be characteristic of his ideal self. The opposite is true for a negative correlation: The more Juan reports "Does assigned chores" is really like him, the more he wishes it were not like him ideally.

In most instances, the teacher will be less interested in the correlation between the two sorts than in those individual items that have large discrepancies between them. Items with great discrepancies between the sorts probably describe target behaviors for intervention. If the student rates an item such as "Likes to read" as "like me" on the ideal sort but as "very unlike me" on the real sort, the teacher may have identified an area in which the student is ready to begin work for improvement.

Kroth (1973) wrote an excellent article on the uses of the behavioral Q-sort, and interested teachers are advised to read it. He suggested that Q-sorts could be administered to students' parents and teachers, with the real sort representing the way they believe their children behave and the ideal sort representing the way they wished their children would behave. This use of the technique would permit analysis of various combinations of Q-sort responses, such as the child's ideal sort compared with the parent's ideal sort, the regular classroom teacher's real sort compared with the resource teacher's real sort, the child's real sort compared with the teacher's real sort, and so on. Again, particular discrepancies may be more important than the actual correlation between the sorts. If the child's regular class teacher rates "Likes to read" as "a little unlike my child" and the special education teacher rates this same item as "like my child," an important discrepancy *may* have been identified.

Q-sort items can be read to nonreaders, although this approach has not been particularly successful. Children who cannot read the items have great difficulty manipulating the cards, especially when only a few slots are left on the formboard and some rearranging is necessary. Students who are easily frustrated also have difficulty with the Q-sort because they are forced to limit their choices within each category to a specific number of items. Most students, however, enjoy the activity and can complete it independently after brief instructions have been given.

Interviews

Interviewing is a useful and versatile assessment technique. Interviews can be extremely formal procedures following a specific protocol, or they can be more informal, relying on the skill and instinct of the interviewer for structure.

Regardless of its formality, objectives should be established before an interview is undertaken. Interviews usually are conducted to obtain information, such as a health history from a medical professional, a reason for referral from a teacher, or a statement of a parent's goals and expectations for a child. They also can be used as a vehicle to provide information to students, parents, and other professionals about the nature of a problem or condition, about educational and treatment options, or about the assessment process itself. Interviews also are used to confirm or verify information previously obtained, although unnecessary requests for information already provided in writing or in another interview can be especially vexing, demonstrating a lack of preparation or sensitivity on the part of the interviewer.

When conducting an interview, the interviewer should consider the following points:

1. Have a goal for the interview (obtaining specific information, getting to know one another, eliciting cooperation, etc.).

2. If necessary, write down or outline the questions to be asked and the information to be conveyed.

3. Take a moment to appraise the physical surroundings of the interview through the other person's eyes.

4. Use probe or guide questions to move the interview into appropriate areas or into new areas when a topic is dead or unfruitful.

5. Be alert to sensitive or touchy topics.

6. Monitor yourself for defensive behaviors or responses.

7. Indicate a willingness to cooperate and a desire to work together.

8. Encourage the interviewee to participate actively in the interview and to contribute information.

9. Complete the interview on an upbeat tone that will put future interactions on a positive footing.

10. If you do not take notes during the interview, make a few notes as soon after the interview as possible.

11. If possible, videotape yourself in interview and then evaluate your performance or ask others to do so. Role-playing interview or specific situations that you find difficult during interviews may be helpful, too.

Examination of Teacher–Pupil Interaction in the Classroom

Obviously, many of the problems in classrooms do not spring from a single cause. Rather, they are products of the interaction of two or more variables. This section examines techniques used to measure the type and quality of teacher–child interaction.

Even though a number of interaction analysis instruments are available today, we describe only one, the *Flanders Interaction Analysis System* (Flanders, 1970). This system does not focus on any one student's interactions with the teacher. Instead, it codes and analyzes the verbal interactions between the teacher and all of the students in a class. It is more valuable for teachers who wish to modify their own behavior in the classroom than for teachers who are interested in describing the behavior of those few students who are exhibiting problems. Flanders identifies 10 behaviors, which are recorded in 4-second intervals. The 10 behaviors include seven teacher responses and initiations, two student behaviors, and a no-behavior or silence category. The teacher responses are (1) accepting students' feelings, (2) praising or encouraging students, and (3) accepting/using students' ideas. Teacher initiations are (4) asking questions, (5) lecturing, (6) giving directions, and (7) criticizing. The two student behaviors are (8) responding to the teacher and (9) initiating talk or conversation. The final category is (10) silence or confusion. Observational periods should be short, perhaps a maximum of 30 minutes at a time, and data should be taken for several days.

Because Flanders's system is more effective at focusing on the teacher than on specific students, an abbreviated form of the system was developed by R. M. Smith, Neisworth, and Greer (1978) to identify the major type of verbal interaction occurring within a classroom. This not only reduces the coding that is required, but also eliminates the need for an observer, because the analysis is derived from the teacher's review of a videotape or audiotape of classroom instruction.

Sociometrics

The sociometric nominating technique was originally developed by Moreno (1934). It was widely used in the 1950s and reemerged as a major diagnostic and research tool in the 1980s. Sociometrics may be used to determine each student's position within the class by analyzing peer choices made by each student in the group and appraising the role of the student within that group.

In applying this technique to the classroom situation, the teacher typically asks each student to choose one, two, or three students with whom he or she would like to engage in the activity specified in the stimulus question (e.g., inviting to a party, bringing home after school, doing homework). This information can aid the teacher in understanding the social structure within the group. Nominations on a sociogram may be mapped as illustrated in Figure 8.5. In this example, 10 students were asked to choose two classmates with whom they would like to work on an art project. A schematic such as this clearly indicates which children are isolates (i.e., neither choosing nor being chosen by other students), which are desired partners, which are ignored, and so on. In addition, specific friendships or attachments can be identified.

After the teacher has determined which student is isolated or without friends, he or she can begin to seek out the causes. Frequently, the explanations are quite simple, such as being new to the class, living outside the community, being older than the other children, or having poor personal hygiene. The teacher can then structure situations in which the isolate can interact with others. Sometimes the causes are more complicated, but only if they are understood can the teacher help the student develop the social,

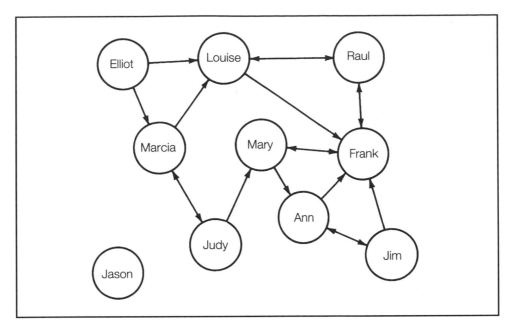

FIGURE 8.5. Sociometric map.

athletic, or academic skills necessary to enter into the mainstream of the group's social system. Isolation also may be the result of attitudes toward handicapped students, minority-group members, or same-sex peers. In that case, the teacher should focus on *group* attitudinal and behavioral changes instead of changes within the isolated member.

Another use of sociometrics, infrequently practiced, is to provide feedback on the teacher's behavior. Often the teacher consciously or unconsciously praises or rebukes the same student. This habit could be corroborated or disproved by asking the class to "Write the name of the class member whom Ms. Jones likes best" or "Write the name of the class member whom Ms. Jones does not like." If teachers receive a variety of names in response to these questions, they probably are not isolating the same children. If only one or two names are reported by the class, teachers actually may be betraying personal preferences, causing the certain class members to feel rejected or anonymous.

Sociograms can be scored as well as mapped. Scores are based on a combination of negative nominations (i.e., nominations in response to a question such as "Whom would you least like to work with on a project at school?") and positive nominations (i.e., nominations in response to a question such as "Whom would you most like to work with on a project at school?"). Sometimes negative and positive nominations are combined; sometimes only negative or only positive nominations are considered. By using various combinations of negative and positive nominations, it is possible to identify particular types of social status, such as students who are popular (those with a high number of positive nominations and a low number of negative nominations), rejected (those with a high number of negative nominations and a low number of positive nominations), controversial (those with high numbers of negative and positive nominations), or neglected (those with no nominations at all).

One can also generate standard scores for raw sociometric data. For instance, the sociogram for the *Behavior Rating Profile, Second Edition* (BRP-2) (L. Brown & Hammill, 1990) subtracts negative nominations from positive nominations, rank orders students on the basis of this raw score, and then converts the raw score to a standard score with a mean of 10 and a standard deviation of 3. Many researchers use a rank-order procedure to arrive at T-scores or z-scores. The BRP-2 authors suggest that sociograms are most efficient with classes of at least 20 students. They also emphasize that students participating in the sociogram should have been in the class for at least 6 weeks, in order to permit the formation of the relationships measured by the sociogram.

Gronlund and Linn (1990) and some other appraisal authorities believe that responses to one pair of stimulus questions should not be generalized to anticipated responses from another pair of questions. For instance, a set of questions related to cooperating on schoolwork presumably would attract different responses than a set of questions related to playing together on a kickball team. This may not be the case, however. Schwarzwald, Laor, and Hoffman (1986) pointed out that the format employed in sociometric peer-nominating techniques forces the exclusion of some children, thereby drawing attention away from the activity specified in the stimulus question and focusing it instead on such variables as personal preferences, gender, race, or ethnicity.

Sociograms appear to be a dependable rating technique that can be a valuable tool for measuring the status of an individual student, the status of a group of students, and the status or effectiveness of a behavioral intervention.

Standardized Tests of Personality

Standardized tests of personality are rarely administered to students exhibiting the sort of mild and moderate behavioral difficulties that are the focus of this book. Although other professionals often use standardized personality measures to evaluate seriously involved students, personality tests are rarely, if ever, given by classroom teachers. Occasionally, however, teachers are provided with the results of these tests and, for this reason, they should have some basic information about commonly used personality measures.

Self-report devices, such as sentence-completion tests or adjective checklists completed by the subjects themselves, constitute one broad category of personality tests. For instance, a subject may be asked to complete a sentence stem such as "The thing I like most about school is . . ." or "My mother . . ." or "I am afraid when . . . ." Another self-report format presents the subject with a series of statements ("I am happy," "People usually like me") or questions ("Are you frequently ill?" "Do you like to go to parties?") to which the subject responds "yes" or "no," "true" or "false," and so on. Another common self-report format asks the subject to choose between a pair of statements the one that is most descriptive ("I like to play team sports" or "I like to play games by myself").

Self-report measures have several inherent weaknesses. Predominant among these is the ease with which the individual completing the instrument can hide or disguise feelings. Some instruments have built-in "lie scales" to offset the effects of such dissemblance. Other tests avoid the problem through careful standardization and normative procedures, viewing the dissemblance itself as an important personality trait or characteristic to be considered. Still other tests adopt a projective format to avoid dissemblance.

Projective tests constitute another major type of personality measure. In projective testing, the subject is presented with a neutral stimulus, such as an ink blot, a drawing, or a picture, and asked to describe what is seen or to tell a story about it. The respondent presumably projects his or her feelings onto the neutral stimulus. Another type of projective personality testing involves the analysis of students' drawings. Subjects are asked to draw pictures of themselves, people in general, family members, their homes, and so on. Projective personality tests obviously are far more subjective than self-report personality tests. Interpretation, therefore, is highly dependent on the competence and experience of the examiner.

Among the better built tests available for use with school-age students are the *Children's Apperceptive Storytelling Test,* the *Depression and Anxiety in Youth Scale,* the *Index of Personality Characteristics,* the *Reynolds Adolescent Depression Scale,* and the *Self-Esteem Index.* These tests are listed and described briefly below.

1. The *Children's Apperceptive Storytelling Test* (Schneider, 1989) is an individually administered, broad-based personality measure appropriate for use with children 6 through 13 years of age. The child is asked to tell a story about a picture. The test takes 30 to 45 minutes to administer.

2. The *Depression and Anxiety in Youth Scale* (DAYS) (Newcomer, Barenbaum, & Bryant, 1994) is a paper-and-pencil self-report instrument designed to identify major depressive and overanxious disorders in students 6 through 19 years of age. DAYS includes student, teacher, and parent rating scales and requires approximately 20 minutes for administration and 5 minutes for scoring.

3. The *Index of Personality Characteristics* (L. Brown & Coleman, 1988) is a multiple-trait personality inventory that employs a paper-and-pencil format. It is appropriate for use with students 8 to 18 years of age. In addition to the Total Test score, it has eight scores arranged in four pairs: the Academic and Nonacademic scales, the Perception of Self and Perception of Others scales, the Acting In and Acting Out scales, and the Internal Locus of Control and External Locus of Control scales.

4. The *Reynolds Adolescent Depression Scale* (W. M. Reynolds, 1987) is useful for students in Grades 7 through 12. It is a quickly administered paper-and-pencil test that yields a Total score.

5. The *Self-Esteem Index* (SEI) (L. Brown & Alexander, 1991) spans the school-age range from 8 to 19 years of age. It is a paper-and-pencil instrument that generates five measures of self-esteem: a global Self-Esteem Quotient, and measures of Familial Acceptance, Academic Competence, Peer Popularity, and Personal Security.

MANAGING PROBLEM BEHAVIORS

Most intervention strategies presented in this section are strongly associated with specific schools of thought. For instance, the various behavior modification strategies were developed and are used primarily by individuals holding a behavioral point of view, and techniques such as life-space interviewing evolved from the work of analytically oriented professionals. We believe that each of the techniques described in this section has value in some situations and that the use of all of them is well within the professional educator's ability.

The first step in devising an intervention plan—establishing a goal for behavioral improvement and assessing the current level of the behavior problem—has already been discussed. In this section, eight methods for managing behavior are described: behavior modification; behavioral self-control; contracting; Long and Newman's techniques for managing surface behaviors; Trieschman's strategy for managing temper tantrums; life-space interviewing; projective techniques, such as role playing, puppetry, play therapy, and art and music therapy; and cognitive therapies. Commercially available programs that purport to assist in the development of students' affective domains also are reviewed. Biochemical interventions, such as the use of diet and drugs to control behavior, are neither initiated nor carried out by the teacher, but they are used so frequently with school-age children that we discuss them briefly.

Behavior Modification

Rationale

Classroom management, consequence management, or behavior modification has its roots with the behavioral learning theorists such as Thorndike, Pavlov, Watson, and Jones. Clinical experimentation with individual children and adults brought this approach into the foreground in the 1960s, with the renewed interest in the interaction between people and their environment. Behavior modification is a systematic, highly structured approach to altering behavior. Its use will have the effect of strengthening, weakening, or maintaining target behaviors.

Procedures

A plan to modify a target behavior comprises three phases: (1) obtaining baseline data, (2) selecting and implementing a particular modification technique, and (3) verifying the results of a particular intervention.

TAKING BASELINE DATA

The selection of any intervention technique is predicated upon the assumption that the teacher has defined the target behavior and has taken baseline data regarding its frequency or duration. The direct observation techniques described earlier in this chapter are often employed in gathering baseline information. To ensure a representative sample of a student's behavior, five measurement periods usually are devoted to collecting baseline data. The effects of intervention strategies then can be determined objectively by comparing the behaviors during the baseline period with subsequent increases or decreases in the targeted behaviors.

SELECTING A TREATMENT

Reinforcement and punishment are the two basic treatments in behavior modification. Extinction, differential reinforcement, shaping, discrimination training, generalization, modeling, and token economies are other popular techniques.

Reinforcement

A reinforcer is any event that occurs after a behavior and that increases the frequency or duration of the behavior and/or increases the likelihood that the behavior will recur. A graph depicting the frequency of a behavior that is being reinforced successfully will show an upward trend. Teachers may assume that being smiled at, receiving an A grade, or being given 5 minutes of free time is a reinforcing event, at least to most students; however, this conclusion is justified only when there is an observed increase in the behaviors that these events follow. In fact, the teacher will quickly discover that many students who exhibit problem behaviors are not reinforced by the "usual" things.

Some behaviorists refine this definition of reinforcement by describing its negative and positive instances. For instance, the reader may have encountered the terms *negative reinforcement* (a reinforcement procedure in which something aversive or negative is removed from the environment) and *positive reinforcement* (a reinforcement procedure in which something pleasant or positive is added to the environment). These refined definitions can be quite confusing. The important consideration is whether the behavior has been strengthened, in which case one can say it has been reinforced.

Observation of students will generally give the teacher ample ideas of things that are likely to be rewarding for them. Additional information can be obtained by asking individual students to complete an interest inventory or by directly asking students what they like to do. The teacher can select a potential reinforcer from the lists that have been developed or ask the student to do so. If the event proves to be reinforcing—that is, if the target behavior increases—the teacher will continue to use the reinforcer, alternating it occasionally with other reinforcers to prevent the pupil from becoming tired of "the same old thing." Overuse of a reinforcer eventually will result in satiation and in the loss of reinforcement power. If the event does not prove to be reinforcing (i.e., if the target behavior does not increase), the teacher must select another potential reinforcer from the student's reinforcement menu.

Reinforcers may be primary or secondary. Examples of primary reinforcers are food, money, a drink of water, lavatory privileges, playing ball in the gym, drawing paper, crayons, chewing gum, and similar tangible items. Secondary reinforcers usually are social rather than tangible or physical, and often gain their power from being associated with a primary reinforcer. Several examples of secondary reinforcers are a star or an A on a paper, moving one's seat close to the teacher, verbal praise, a praising note sent home to parents, a pat on the shoulder, and a hug. A primary goal of behavior modification is to encourage a student or class of students to work for social reinforcement. Thus, whenever food or toys are given as a consequence, they must be accompanied by social reinforcement—verbal praise, a smile, or a hug—so that the primary reinforcement becomes associated with social approval. Eventually, the social reinforcement will have the same effect as a tangible item.

Reinforcement can be delivered on either a ratio or an interval schedule, and in either case the arrangement or reinforcement can be fixed or variable. With *ratio* schedules, the number of responses a student makes is important. The rate of reinforcement on ratio schedules is largely self-controlled, because the more behaviors the students produce, the more reinforcement they will receive. For this reason, ratio schedules usually yield fairly high rates of responding. *Interval* schedules deliver reinforcement after a specified amount of time has elapsed, rather than after a particular number of behaviors have been performed. Reinforcement on interval schedules is controlled by the teacher, not by the student; a set amount of time must pass before reinforcement can be delivered, regardless of the number of behaviors produced. Consequently, interval schedules tend to yield low rates of responding.

On a *fixed* schedule, reinforcement occurs at a regular interval or after a set number of responses. Fixed schedules are characterized by pauses in responding after reinforcement, because the students know when reinforcement will occur again. Reinforcement in *variable* schedules occurs at irregular intervals or after varying numbers of responses. Variable schedules therefore are characterized by fairly steady rates of responding, because the students are uncertain when reinforcement will be delivered.

Thus, reinforcement can be of four varieties: fixed ratio, variable ratio, fixed interval, and variable interval. *Fixed ratio* schedules result in high rates of behavior with pauses. *Variable ratio* schedules produce high steady rates of responding. *Fixed interval* schedules yield low rates of responding with pauses. *Variable interval* schedules result in low steady rates of responding. Cumulative graphs of typical behavior patterns on each of these schedules are shown in Figure 8.6.

On a continuous fixed ratio (CFR) schedule, every behavior or response is reinforced. This schedule is valuable for stimulating behaviors that may not occur frequently. On the other hand, it is an inefficient means of maintaining behaviors, because the acquired behavior disappears rapidly if reinforcement ever is withdrawn. The behaviors that we exhibit in using vending machines are frequently cited as examples of those maintained on a CFR schedule. The insertion of 50 cents into a pop machine almost always is rewarded with a can of soda. This is a CFR schedule: Every behavior is reinforced. If the machine is broken, however, the insertion of the correct number of coins will not be reinforced by the appearance

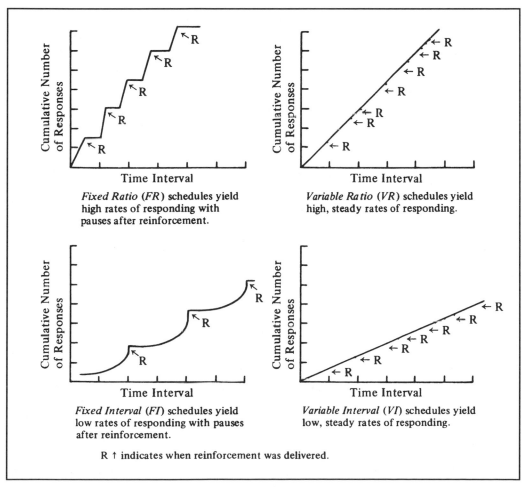

FIGURE 8.6.   Cumulative graphs of behaviors maintained on different schedules of reinforcement.

of a can of soda. One might insert another quarter, but an individual would unlikely continue to put money into a nonreinforcing machine. Therefore, one of the intermittent schedules described below is preferred for maintaining a behavior after it has been acquired on a CFR schedule.

On a fixed ratio (FR) schedule, reinforcement follows a fixed number of responses. For example, a behavior that is reinforced on an FR-3 schedule would be reinforced after every third response (i.e., after the 3rd, 6th, 9th, 12th, etc., behaviors). In fact, CFR could be called an FR-1 schedule. Piecework is an example of behavior that is maintained on an FR schedule. Fruit pickers who are paid by the basket are reinforced on an FR schedule, as are students who receive free time after completing a set amount of work. An FR schedule results in high rates of behavior with pauses following reinforcement. For instance, a student who completes a page of problems in a math workbook and then is reinforced (by receiving a star, a smile, or an "attaboy" from the teacher) is likely to rest or take a breather before beginning the next page.

On a variable ratio (VR) schedule, reinforcement follows an average number of responses. On a VR-3 schedule, reinforcement might follow any number of behaviors, as long as the average number of responses per reinforcement is 3. Gambling on slot machines is an example of behavior that is maintained on a VR schedule. The machines are calibrated to provide reinforcement (a jackpot) after an average number of coins has been inserted. A VR schedule results in a high, steady rate of responding. Such response patterns might be seen in classes where the teacher constantly moves around the room reinforcing the students after they have completed varying amounts of work.

On a fixed interval (FI) schedule, reinforcement follows the first behavior to occur after a fixed period of time has elapsed. FI-2 minutes means that reinforcement will follow the first behavior to occur after 2 minutes, after 4 minutes, after 6 minutes, and so on. It does not matter whether the student emits 1 behavior or 100 behaviors during the 2-minute interval; reinforcement will not occur until the allotted time has passed. The FI schedule yields a low response rate with pauses after reinforcement. Students who know that their math workbooks will be checked every morning at 11:00 (FI-24 hours) are likely to work with increasing speed until that time and to stop working until the interval is about to close the next morning, again working at faster rates as 11:00 approaches. On a variable interval (VI) schedule, reinforcement follows the first behavior to occur after an average amount of time has passed. This schedule yields low steady rates of behavior.

Take, for example, David, who has 15 math problems to complete during the 20-minute math period. On an FR-5 schedule, David would receive reinforcement after completing each group of five problems (e.g., after the 5th, 10th, and 15th problems were completed). The teacher would expect David to work fairly quickly in order to receive his reinforcement faster, but also would expect him to take a break after receiving each reinforcement and before starting the next block of five problems.

If David were receiving reinforcement on a VR-5 schedule, however, he would be reinforced after an average of every five problems completed (e.g., after the 2nd, 9th, and 15th problems). On this schedule, the teacher would expect David to work relatively quickly, because he controls his own rate of reinforcement, and also to work without pauses or breaks, because he does not know exactly when reinforcement will be forthcoming.

On an FI-5 minute schedule, the teacher would reinforce David for the first problem completed after every 5-minute interval (e.g., at 5-, 10-, 15-, and 20-minute intervals) during the math period. The teacher would expect David to work more slowly than he did under ratio reinforcement, because his work rate will not affect the amount of reinforcement. David also would be expected to pause after each reinforcement was delivered.

Finally, on a VI-5 minute reinforcement schedule, David would be reinforced for the first problem completed after an average of 5 minutes had passed (e.g., after 4, 11, 14, and 20 minutes). The teacher would expect the same lower rate of responding associated with the fixed interval schedule, but would expect steady work because David cannot anticipate when reinforcement will occur on a variable schedule.

Regardless of the reinforcement schedule that a teacher elects to employ, it is imperative that the teacher deliver reinforcement as quickly as possible to avoid reinforcing the wrong behavior. The student should know why reinforcement is delivered. It helps if the teacher verbalizes the reason as the points, tokens, or praise are delivered: "Good, Billie! You worked quietly for two minutes. Here is your token." It also is important to remember that the reinforcement must be delivered *only* as a consequence of the desired behavior. If free time is the reinforcer that is being used, then free time should not be available at any other time in the regular daily schedule.

Reinforcing incompatible responses involves rewarding action that is incompatible with the bothersome behavior. For example, suppose a student talks out loud most of the morning. Instead of punishing the student for talking without permission, the teacher decides to reward the child for completing 10 arithmetic problems. To accomplish this task and obtain the reward, the child works hard, becoming too busy to talk. The desired behavior is incompatible with talking aloud. Not only does this approach reduce disturbing behavior, but it also increases desirable academic performance. Reinforcing incompatible responses is an easily applied and effective procedure for classroom use.

Punishment

A *punisher* is any event that follows a behavior and that decreases the frequency or duration of the behavior and/or decreases the likelihood that the behavior will recur. The frequency graph of a behavior that is being punished will show a downward trend. Again, the assumption that such things as expulsion from school, low grades, or standing in the hall are punishing must be proved. For example, Brett swears in class and his teacher decides to punish this behavior by sending him to the principal's office. If Brett's swearing increases, the teacher must assume that going to the principal's office, or perhaps leaving the classroom, is, in fact, reinforcing for Brett, not punishing. Expulsion and suspension are classic examples of presumed punishers that usually are not punishing, which is why "repeat offenders" are frequently seen in detention hall or placed on suspension.

Negative and positive reinforcements were discussed earlier. The reader also may encounter descriptions of two punishment procedures: Punishment can be achieved by adding something aversive to the environment or by removing some pleasurable consequence. Again, the important thing for the teacher to note is whether the target behavior decreases.

The teacher will select a punishment procedure if the goal is to decrease a behavior and if this goal cannot be achieved by reinforcing an incompatible behavior. Obviously, precise definition of the target behavior is crucial. For instance, a teacher could elect to reinforce a student for talking only with permission, to punish the same student for talking without permission, or to do both. In the vast majority of instances, it is more desirable to reinforce than to punish. Whenever punishment is used, it should be accompanied by reinforcement if at all possible. Punishing a behavior merely tells the student that the behavior is unacceptable; it does not in any way indicate alternative behaviors that are considered appropriate.

Punishment has the effect of arresting or suppressing behavior without eliminating or extinguishing it. It is beneficial only when applied to specific acts (running out into the street) rather than to generalized situations (being naughty). Momentarily stopping an undesirable behavior has positive effects when it is accompanied by the demonstration and reinforcement of alternative responses. Effective ways to use reprimands, a common form of punishment in the school setting, are outlined by Van Houton (1980).

The effectiveness of a punisher is governed by many of the same variables that affect reinforcers. Punishers will be more powerful if they are delivered immediately, if the student knows why they are delivered, and if delivery of punishment is contingent upon a specific behavior. In addition, both punishers and reinforcers are most effective when they are not overused.

The teacher must be aware of the possible negative effects of using punishment. The emotional side effects, such as guilt, fear, withdrawal, and frustration, may lead to other maladaptive behaviors. In addition, the punishing teacher may serve as a negative, aggressive model for other students or may become a conditioned punisher so that, even after the behavior has been eliminated, the teacher still is viewed as a punishing agent rather than as a positive, reinforcing presence.

Kohn's (1993) recent book, *Punished by Rewards,* is an engaging and controversial look at rewards and punishments as they are used in American society. Some readers will be outraged by Kohn's iconoclastic views, but all will find significant points to consider before setting up their next intervention.

Extinction

Extinction occurs when a reinforcing event is withdrawn and the behavior that it used to follow subsequently decreases. For example, Carolee had a tendency to talk without permission. After she was corrected by the teacher, Carolee's talking without permission increased, so the teacher's corrections apparently reinforced the unwanted behavior. Extinction has occurred if Carolee's talking-out behavior decreases after the teacher withdraws the apparent reinforcement (the corrections) by ignoring the talking out. Teachers often unwittingly reinforce undesirable behaviors, as Carolee's teacher did. Extinction, then, is a tool that can be invaluable.

Unfortunately, extinction is difficult to implement because many troublesome behaviors cannot be ignored or extinguished. Violent or destructive behaviors obviously cannot be ignored. Similarly, behaviors that continually disrupt the educational program are not good candidates for extinction; sanctions from the teacher or from classmates usually must be applied. Contagious behaviors, such as false hiccoughing or perhaps swearing, also do not lend themselves well to extinction. Finally, teachers should not attempt to ignore or extinguish behaviors that are outside their own personal tolerance levels. Some teachers, for instance, can ignore swearing, thereby robbing it of its shock or annoyance value and extinguishing it. However, teachers who find that they cannot tolerate swearing (or other behaviors) should not attempt to extinguish the behaviors but should look instead for alternative management techniques. We all have behaviors that "pull our chains"; having recognized what they are, we should not expect ourselves to exhibit the superhuman effort needed to ignore or extinguish them!

Differential Reinforcement

Differential reinforcement involves two or more different responses: One response is reinforced and the other(s) is/are extinguished. For example, Marty frequently made self-deprecatory remarks (one response), only rarely noting something that he did well (a second, different response). His teacher ignored the negative remarks (extinction) and reinforced the positive remarks (by attending to them). Eventually, Marty spoke more highly of himself as a result of differential reinforcement. Differential reinforcement is valuable because its use reduces or eliminates undesirable behaviors while simultaneously encouraging behaviors considered to be appropriate.

Shaping

Shaping is the differential reinforcement of successive approximations of a behavior. For example, Karen, a first grader, is out of her seat 60% of the time during the reading period. Using differential reinforcement, the teacher can extinguish Karen's out-of-seat behavior (by ignoring it) and reinforce her in-seat behavior (by praising it). The goal for Karen is to be in her seat throughout the reading period. Successive approximations of this goal would be increasing percentages of time she must spend in her seat before receiving reinforcement, perhaps 50%, then 55%, and so on. The final goal (i.e., for her to be in seat during the entire reading period) would be achieved through a shaping process. In fact, education itself is primarily a process of shaping.

Discrimination Training

Discrimination training involves a single behavior that is reinforced in the presence of one stimulus and is extinguished in the presence of other stimuli. For instance, Matt is reinforced for responding "two" when he is asked to supply the answer to "1 + 1 = _____." However, that same response ("two") is extinguished when Matt is asked to supply the answer to other questions, such as "2 + 3 = _____" and "1 + 2 = _____." Discrimination training has also occurred with the students who learn that they can be late for Mr. Penny's English I class but that they must be on time for Ms. Schroeder's algebra class. Discrimination training also might be used to teach an adolescent with mental retardation that kissing is acceptable with some people (e.g., with relatives) but that it is not acceptable with other people (e.g., with strangers, co-workers, or supervisors).

Generalization

Generalization is the occurrence of a response learned through discrimination training in the presence of a novel or unknown stimulus. For example, Matt has learned through discrimination training to respond "red" when he sees red circles and red squares and to refrain from making that response when he sees blue circles or green squares. Generalization has occurred if Matt responds "red" when presented with novel stimuli such as red triangles and does not respond "red" when presented with blue, green, or yellow triangles. Generalization is the desired outcome of any intervention plan, regardless of the methodology employed. Students must be able to generalize what is learned, or they will be doomed to treat every situation they encounter as a new one. The following steps will facilitate the generalization of a student's behavior from one school situation to another or from school to home.

1. Place the behavior on an intermittent reinforcement schedule where every behavior is *not* reinforced.

2. Fade the reinforcer from primary to social, perhaps by beginning with food, then giving tokens to exchange for food, and finally giving only grades or praise.

3. Have another adult such as a parent or student volunteer participate in the intervention or behavioral training.

4. Have an extinction period, gradually withdrawing reinforcement and returning to no treatment.

5. Contract with the student to monitor his or her own behavior by keeping a record and turning it in at the end of the week for reinforcement, gradually thinning the reinforcement schedule.

6. Use tokens to bridge the gap between primary and social reinforcement and to encourage delay in gratification. Delay in gratification should occur under natural circumstances and should not become an exercise to its own end. It is doubtful that any teacher reading this book would wait a week to pick up a paycheck, merely to demonstrate the self-discipline to delay gratification!

The time requirements for this technique are great. The steps are essential, however, for successful application. Once this procedure has been practiced, its time efficiency increases markedly.

Modeling

In modeling, verbal instructions or imitation is used to teach a student a new behavior. Instructional training, a form of modeling, involves three steps: a verbal description of the desired behavior, a demonstration by the learner of the described behavior, and reinforcement following the demonstration of the behavior. Imitation training, another form of modeling, also consists of three stages: demonstration by the teacher of the target behavior, an imitation by the learner of the demonstrated behavior, and reinforcement of the imitation. Instructional training is said to take place when, for instance, the teacher says, "Please sit at your desk"; the student complies; and the teacher smiles and says, "Thank you." Imitation training occurs when the teacher makes the *s* sound; the student imitates it; and the teacher says, "Good."

Modeling also occurs when the student observes that another student who is engaging in instructional or imitation learning is being reinforced (or punished) for complying (or not complying). The student who observes that Mark is permitted to go to recess as soon as he has complied with the teacher's instructions to clear off his desk is quite likely to follow suit and clear off her desk, too (if recess is reinforcing). Likewise, the same behavior will result if she sees that the recess privilege is withdrawn from a student who failed to comply with this request.

Token Economies

Reinforcers may be delivered in *token economies,* settings in which the students receive tokens with which they can later buy tangible items or privileges. In a token economy, the student has a task (his or her "job"), such as correctly working five arithmetic problems or sitting quietly in the reading circle, and is paid with a token upon completion of the job. Poker chips, pieces of paper, and stars are examples of items that can be used as tokens. Tokens (like money) are then exchanged in the economy for things the student wants: 5 tokens may buy a piece of gum, 10 may buy a luncheon date with the teacher or some free time, 50 may buy a field trip, and 500 may buy a day off from school. Reinforcement in a classroom token economy can be determined by students as well as by teachers.

A token economy system has many advantages. The problem of satiation is avoided because the "store" where tokens are exchanged provides a wide variety of reinforcers on the "menu." The system also eases the problem of thinning the reinforcement schedule, because a student eventually must do more work for each token; that is, inflation occurs! Whereas 5 minutes of independent work may be needed to earn one token today, a month later it may take 6 or 7 minutes of independent work to earn a token. Token systems demand that the students exercise some delay of gratification while providing immediate, tangible reinforcement. They are also very natural. Students can see a variety of token systems functioning in the "real world" around them.

VERIFYING RESULTS

Most teachers will readily recognize the effects of an intervention and will not see the need to verify the results experimentally. In some instances, however, it is important to demonstrate formally that the changes achieved through a behavior modification plan are not the result of other happenings. For instance, Sandy's teacher may have instigated a behavior modification program to reduce the girl's aggressive behavior and the behavior may have disappeared, but there is no proof that the change in behavior was a result of the program that the teacher instigated rather than a visit by Sandy's grandmother or some other variables at home. A reversal or return to baseline is one form of verification. This involves a brief interruption of the intervention program to see if the target behavior begins to approximate its previous baseline level. The program is then reinstituted, and the results are verified if the behavior again changes.

Many teachers object to using the reversal procedure because they believe they are pulling the rug out from under a pupil by reinforcing a particular behavior and then momentarily withdrawing the reinforcement. Multiple baseline is a verification procedure that avoids this problem. This procedure involves the use of the same intervention program initiated at staggered intervals for several students exhibiting similar behavior problems or for one student exhibiting a variety of behavior problems (e.g., cursing for Sally, Susie, and Sara, or cursing, spitting, and fighting for Sally). If similar results are achieved on each of the multiple baselines after the same intervention has been initiated, verification has taken place. Although the classroom teacher may find these procedures to be too cumbersome and time consuming to implement on a regular basis, certainly behavior modification results of an experimental or research nature should be verified through these or other means.

Behavioral Self-Control

Rationale

Behavioral self-control is a technique in which students themselves implement programs to change their own behaviors. Self-control can be implemented as a first effort to change behavior, or it can be used to maintain behaviors when externally implemented behavior modification programs are phased out. Behavioral self-control programs are an ideal way to help students assume responsibility for their own behavior. A tangential benefit is that they relieve school personnel or parents of the time requirements associated with more traditional behavior modification methods.

Procedures

Self-control techniques can be taught to most school-age children. In this section, we describe four specific techniques: self-assessment, self-observation, self-reinforcement, and self-punishment.

Self-assessment, or self-evaluation, techniques require students to appraise their own behavior. Teachers can help students do this by having them (1) complete a rating scale or checklist, (2) prompt or cue appropriate behaviors verbally (e.g., "Now I am going to . . ."), or (3) discuss orally or in writing a specific rule infraction or disruptive behavior they have committed. Obviously, this technique requires some verbal competence and is not appropriate for language-disordered students, extremely concrete thinkers, or very young children.

Self-observation, or self-monitoring, is simply observing and recording one's own behavior in a consistent, systematic way. Awareness of one's behavior frequently is sufficient impetus to improve or change it. For instance, keeping a calorie count or a weight chart is often helpful in maintaining desired weight. In the classroom, students can be taught to record such behaviors as talking without permission or completing assigned work, or teachers who want to alter their own classroom behavior can record the number of positive (or negative) comments they make in the course of a school day. A simple recording technique, such as a tally sheet or graph, will be easy to use and will provide a visual indication of behavioral improvement (or deterioration). Self-observations can be made on a frequency or duration basis.

Self-reinforcement occurs when individuals reward themselves for good or appropriate behaviors. Students decide what the reinforcer will be and establish the reinforcement/behavior ratio. Self-reinforcement is often implemented as a token economy where students reward themselves initially with stars, checkmarks, or tokens that are later exchanged for tangible rewards or privileges at school and home. Workman (1982) described the use of fantasies as self-reinforcers. Obviously, self-reinforcement must be preceded by self-observation.

Self-punishment is used less frequently than the other techniques for the same reasons that punishment is used less frequently than reinforcement in traditional behavior modification programs. In addition, it requires great fortitude to consciously inflict punishment on oneself! People who are trying to quit smoking and burn a dollar bill for each cigarette they smoke are practicing self-punishment. In school, students may be trained to remove points from their total for such infractions as being tardy or failing to complete assignments. Self-punishment works most effectively when combined with self-reinforcement of competing or alternative behaviors.

Other self-control techniques the reader may encounter include self-instruction (which involves rehearsal, prompting, and verbal mediation strategies), alternative response training (which involves learning to substitute a new behavior for a less appropriate one), and stimulus control (which involves arranging the environment to avoid stimuli that are known to elicit inappropriate or unwanted behaviors). All of these techniques, however, involve some form of self-assessment, self-observation, self-reinforcement, or self-punishment.

Contracting

Contracting for behavioral change is a popular and effective method for giving students some responsibility for changing their own behavior. A contract is a *two-way* agreement. The child agrees to behave in a certain fashion or to do a certain task at or within a given period of time. The teacher (or parent or other school personnel) agrees to deliver specific kinds of support during the contract and a particular payoff when the contract has been fulfilled. Sample behavioral contracts are shown in Figures 8.7 and 8.8.

Long and Newman's Techniques for Managing Surface Behaviors

Rationale

Perhaps the most succinct discussion of the management of surface behaviors is offered by Long and Newman (1980). Their techniques are intended for use as "stop-gap" devices to prevent escalation of behavior problems or to avoid negative contagion. If necessary, the behaviors may be explored in depth (clinical exploitation) at a later time.

Procedures

Twelve interference techniques are described: planned ignoring, signal interference, proximity control, interest boosting, hurdle lessons, restructuring of the classroom program, support from routine, direct appeal to value areas, removal of seductive objects, antiseptic bouncing, tension decontamination through humor, and physical restraint.

Date: SEPT. 5, 1977

STUDENT: I agree to follow these rules to student behavior: 1) when my teacher is giving instructions, I will look at her and listen 2) I will complete my workbook assignments in reading

Signed: Albert Johnson

TEACHER: I agree to help Albert by: 1) calling him by name when I am giving instructions 2) Giving him short workbook assignments he will be able to finish. I will give him a check at the end of each hour for following each rule and I will send his checklist home every Friday

Signed: Mrs J. Rhoads

PRINCIPAL: I agree to help Albert by: Having a 10 minute conference with him every Friday to discuss his progress

Signed: Pete Principle

PARENTS: I/We agree to help Albert by: Purchasing Sullivan workbooks for him. 2) He will earn 2¢ of his allowance for each check he brings home on Friday

Signed: Albert Johnson, Sr
Mary G. Johnson

FIGURE 8.7. Formal contract.

From *The Resource Room: Access to Excellence* by P. Hawisher, 1975, Lancaster, SC: Region V Education Service Center. Reprinted with permission of the author and the publisher.

Planned ignoring closely resembles the extinction technique described in the behavior modification section of this chapter. The basic assumption is that many behaviors will lose steam and disappear if they are ignored. If the teacher attempts to intervene, that attention may add fuel to the fire and increase or prolong the behavior. A teacher must care-

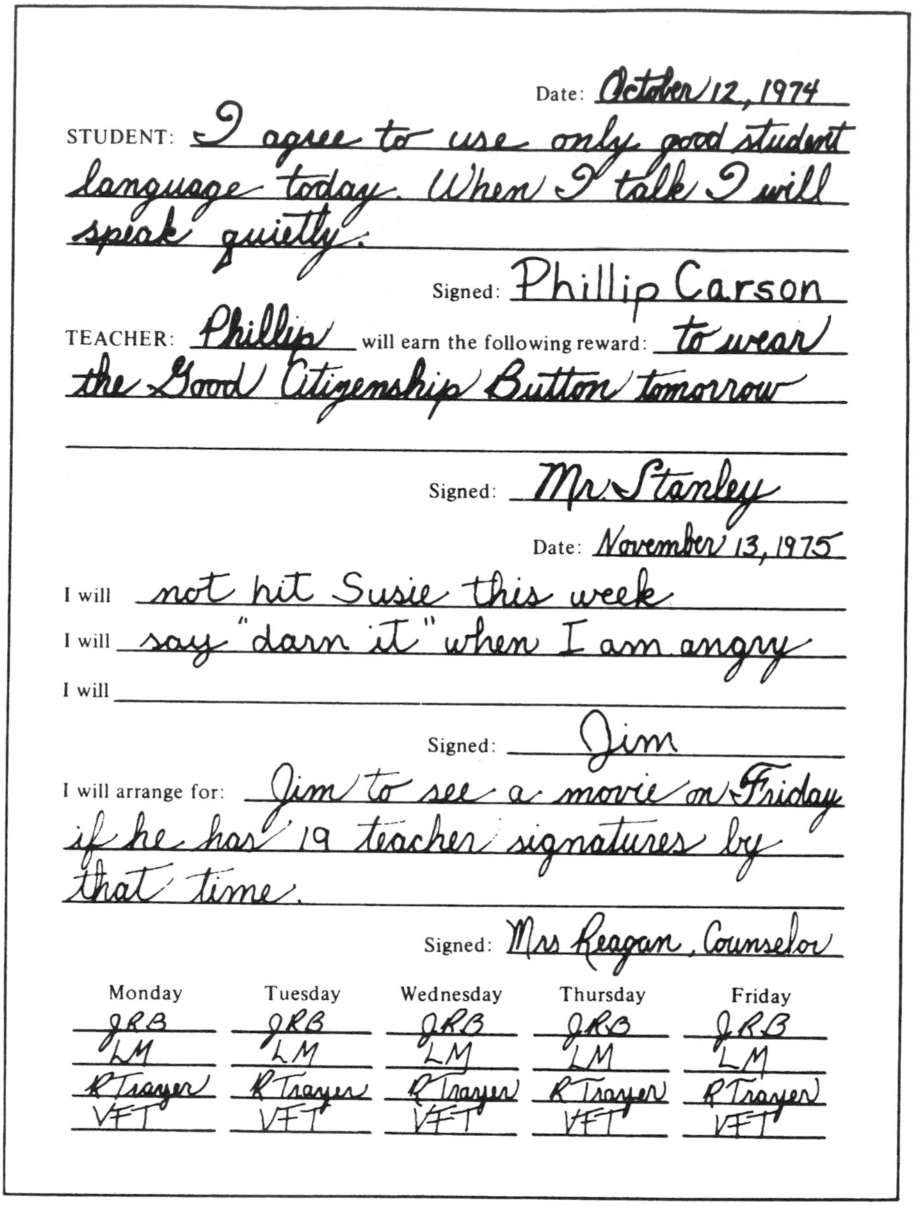

Date: *October 12, 1974*

STUDENT: *I agree to use only good student language today. When I talk I will speak quietly.*

Signed: *Phillip Carson*

TEACHER: *Phillip* will earn the following reward: *to wear the Good Citizenship Button tomorrow*

Signed: *Mr Stanley*

Date: *November 13, 1975*

I will *not hit Susie this week.*

I will *say "darn it" when I am angry.*

I will _____

Signed: *Jim*

I will arrange for: *Jim to see a movie on Friday if he has 19 teacher signatures by that time.*

Signed: *Mrs Reagan, Counselor*

Monday	Tuesday	Wednesday	Thursday	Friday
JRB	*JRB*	*JRB*	*JRB*	*JRB*
LM	*LM*	*LM*	*LM*	*LM*
R Trayer	*R Trayer*	*R Trayer*	*R Trayer*	*R Trayer*
VFT	*VFT*	*VFT*	*VFT*	*VFT*

FIGURE 8.8. Informal contract.

From *The Resource Room: Access to Excellence* by P. Hawisher, 1975, Lancaster, SC: Region V Education Service Center. Reprinted with permission of the author and the publisher.

---

fully judge his or her own tolerance level for the behavior in question and the excitement level of the class before electing to use planned ignoring.

Signal interference involves the use of a cue to let the student know that a particular behavior should be abandoned. Early in a behavior, a stern "school marm" stare, eye contact, or a hand gesture may stop a problem before it develops. Sometimes the signal will be part of a contract between the teacher and the student. For instance, the teacher and student may be working on new ways to express anger; when the student becomes angry, the teacher signals that this is the time to try the new procedure.

Proximity control is a time-honored technique. The teacher's presence in a potential trouble spot is usually sufficient to stop many disruptive surface behaviors such as whispering or passing notes. This technique also can be effective with children who are working on a particularly troublesome academic task—or who are having difficulty controlling their impulses—and gain strength from the teacher's presence.

Interest boosting and *hurdle lessons* are very similar techniques. In the former, the teacher displays interest in the student as an individual; this interest may help the student rekindle waning interest or even come to view the teacher as a positive force. The latter involves individual attention, too, usually in the form of academic assistance or on-the-spot tutoring to help the student get past momentary frustration.

Restructuring the classroom program and *support from routine* are opposite techniques. Both require the teacher to be sensitive to the tenor of the classroom: Do the students need a fresh outlook or a change of pace, or will a familiar, predictable, no-surprises approach be more supportive? Perhaps a student has just lost control of himself and left the classroom in tears. Obviously, this will be upsetting to the other students. The teacher must decide whether it is better to pick up the lesson where it was stopped or to initiate a complete change of activity.

Direct appeal to value areas is a way to get students to think about a situation in terms of the values they have internalized. For instance, the teacher might point out the consequences of behavior (If the students do not finish the current task, there will not be time for a highly desired task) or try to elicit peer pressure (What will the other kids think if you do this?). The trick is to learn to say no without being angry and to say yes without feeling guilty.

Removal of seductive objects is often preferable to trying to manage the behaviors they elicit. The relief map of the Rocky Mountains that students are building in geography has not lost its seductive powers simply because the arithmetic period has begun. Removing, or at least covering, the map will prevent many problems.

Antiseptic bouncing is used to remove a student from the classroom without any punitive overtones. This technique is useful for preventing the spread of contagious behaviors, such as giggling, hiccoughing, or making animal noises. It also gives embarrassed or angry students an opportunity to cool down and gain control. Antiseptic bouncing might take the form of sending a student out to determine the status of the softball diamond, sending the student to the office with a message, or simply allowing the student to get a drink of water.

Tension decontamination through humor reflects the power of good humor. Many tense situations can be relieved or defused by a single good-natured or humorous remark from the teacher. The key is to ensure that the joke is not at the expense of a student.

The final management technique, *physical restraint,* is used on those occasions when a student has lost control completely. Physical restraint is intended to prevent the student from injuring himself or herself or others and to communicate the teacher's willingness to provide external control.

Most teachers already use many, if not all, of these management techniques. Their power as intervention strategies will be increased if teachers use them consciously and on a planned basis.

Trieschman's Strategy for Managing Temper Tantrums

Rationale

Tantrums are quite common among young children and students with emotional problems. Trieschman (1969) hypothesized that a temper tantrum is not a single behavior but a series of events with definite stages. He identified six stages, which were given descriptive names: the Rumbling and Grumbling stage, the Help-Help stage, the Either-Or stage, the No-No stage, the Leave Me Alone stage, and the Hangover stage. Tantrums are managed by dealing with the behaviors in each stage. If the early stages are managed appropriately, according to Trieschman, tantrums may occur less frequently or may possibly be prevented from occurring at all.

Procedures

During the Rumbling and Grumbling stage, the student is generally grumpy. He or she appears to be dribbling (as opposed to gushing) hostility. The student is seeking the focal issue for the tantrum he or she has already decided to have. In many instances, the issue that the student selects is one that lacks a satisfactory solution. For instance, a child may demand that an irreparably broken toy be mended immediately. Management is aided by identifying the pattern of Rumbling and Grumbling. Frequently, tantrums will have a similar time and place (e.g., right before lunch or only in the physical education class) or will be kicked off by the same focal issue. The teacher who recognizes the pattern sometimes can help the student to verbalize the problem rather than to act out the front issue for the problem. This is usually accomplished through life-space interviewing, a technique that is discussed later.

The Help-Help stage is the first really loud, noisy stage of the tantrum. The student "has found his issue and is now signaling his need for help. The signal he uses is usually a very visible and deliberate rule-breaking act" (Trieschman, 1969, p. 179), which is designed to attract adult attention. The child senses that he or she is losing internal control and is demanding that an authority figure intervene and impose external control.

Management primarily involves teaching the student to signal a need for help in a more appropriate manner by substituting an appropriate signal for the inappropriate rule-breaking signal. It may be necessary at this point for the teacher to utilize the physical restraint technique described by Long and Newman while verbalizing to the student a desire to help the student control his or her behavior. It is best, according to Trieschman, to avoid pointing out that the student broke a rule: The student knows he or she broke the rule and did it deliberately.

The Either-Or stage represents the student's attempt to show that he or she still can control the situation by setting out alternatives. The student often tries to insult the adult or authority figure who is attempting to help by making fun of the adult's personal or sexual characteristics. The most important part of the management at this stage is to model appropriate anger for the student. "Helpfully modeling reasonable anger is something a child could imitate more easily than boundless patience and complete passivity in the face of fury" (Trieschman, 1969, p. 186). Any either-or proposition that can be accepted should be promoted by the adult, and additional alternatives also may be proposed.

The No-No stage is the one in which the student will respond negatively to any suggestion or statement by the adult. It is frequently impossible to manage a tantrum that has reached this stage, although sometimes the tantrum can be pushed back to the previous (Either-Or) stage. If good rapport exists between the student and the teacher, it may even be possible to point out the foolishness of the No-No stage by stating questions in such a way that the student actually complies with the teacher's wishes by saying no. This technique can certainly backfire, however, and should be used with extreme caution so that the student does not come to believe that he or she is being made fun of or is once again "the goat." The noisy part of the tantrum usually dies down at the end of this stage.

The Leave Me Alone stage is relatively quiet and is often mistaken for a return to normal behavior. It is not. The noise is gone and the student may be more amenable to assistance from the adult, but the student is not ready to resume interaction with the world and should not be expected to do so. The student's desire to be left alone should be respected, although the adult should remain within eyeshot or earshot to assure the student that external control is still available if it becomes necessary again. As little conversation as possible is advisable at this stage.

During the Hangover stage, two states of affairs may arise. Some students experience a "clean drunk" after their tantrums. They have no painful memories of the tantrum and appear to have returned to normal. Other students experience a hangover and feel quite guilty and embarrassed about the incident. The memory is painful. The latter condition is more desirable. If a student experiences a clean drunk, it may be possible to induce a hangover that can be exploited, probably through life-space interviewing. Signal words can be devised, as can other alternative behaviors that are more acceptable than tantruming. "Reviewing the sequence of events . . . and learning alternative coping skills is constructive" (Triesch-man, 1969, p. 192) use of the student's hangover.

Life-Space Interviewing

Rationale

Life-space interviewing (LSI) is a psychoeducationally oriented technique aimed at dealing with the everyday interactional problems that occur in the classroom. Originally designed for use by teachers assigned to cope with crisis situations, LSI can be used effectively within the classroom. Rational and semidirectional in its approach, LSI attempts to structure a situation so that students can work out their own problems. The teacher's role is one of listener and facilitator in the decision making enacted by the students involved. The technique is nonjudgmental and presents immediate concrete consequences to the students without the typical value appeals that adults frequently make in reaction to behavioral outbursts. Teachers must have supervised training to learn to use LSI effectively.

Procedure

Describing the way LSI might be used to deal with an actual incident is perhaps the most effective way of explaining the approach. Consider the following incident: In the middle of a handwriting lesson, Johnny and David suddenly broke into a violent fight—cursing, yelling, and hitting each other; the teacher told the rest of the class to continue working and asked the two boys to come up and talk privately about what just happened.

The LSI approach would proceed in the following manner:

Step 1. The teacher asks Johnny what happened, telling David that he will have equal time to explain as soon as Johnny finishes. The aim of this step is to determine each child's *perception* of what happened. The facts are not important, but rather each child's understanding of the incident. At this point, the teacher simply listens.

Step 2. Through objective questioning, the teacher tries to determine if the boys' explanations for fighting really constitute the crux of the problem. Are they fighting over the ownership of a pencil, or is this the manifestation of a deeper worry? Frequently, students bring to school arguments or hostilities that have developed at home, on the school bus, or at recess. Questioning by the teacher is an attempt to discover how extensive the problem is, without making any interpretations.

Step 3. After the boys have had a chance to express thoroughly their feelings about the fight and why they think it happened, they are asked what they feel they *can* (not *should*) do about it. By asking this, the teacher brings the values of the children to the surface. If their suggestions for a remedy are acceptable to all three involved, the interview is terminated here. A note of caution to the teacher: Do not ververbalize. Given a structured and guided opportunity to deal with their problems, students often can reach an acceptable solution without extensive suggestions by the teacher.

Step 4. If the problem is not resolved at this point, the teacher takes a more direct role, pointing out the reality factors of the situation and the consequences of the behavior if it occurs again. Once more, value judgments are minimized. The teacher should not moralize about the impropriety of cursing and fighting, but simply say that the rules of the school prohibit fighting in class and explain the consequences.

Step 5. By talking with the boys, the teacher can explore their motivation for change. If there is no discernible remedy for the situation, the teacher can make suggestions, such as breaking the pencil in half or flipping a coin.

Step 6. The final step is to develop a follow-through plan with the boys that includes discussing alternative procedures should the problem arise in the future. Consequences are once again clearly described by the teacher.

The effectiveness of the LSI approach is dependent on the attitudes and behavior of the teacher. Consciously structuring responses will facilitate positive outcomes. During the interview, a casual and polite atmosphere should be maintained; this reduces the defensive and hostile feelings of the students. The teacher should sit close to the students and avoid towering above them, appearing as much as possible to be neutral and approachable.

If the teacher knows something about the incident, he or she should confront the students with this knowledge. This frequently places the problem in its proper perspective and saves time by eliminating the need for each student to give a detailed description of the event. The students will readily add their own perceptions of what occurred. The teacher should avoid asking "why" questions, because many young or disturbed students lack the insight or verbal ability to explain their actions. By calmly stating that situations like this sometimes do occur, or that no real harm has been done, the teacher reassures the student that the teacher is not such a terrible person, enabling the student to "open up" to the teacher. Most important, the students should be listened to, helped to plan for future incidents, and given a chance to ask questions.

This approach has many advantages. It demonstrates to students that they have alternative ways of dealing with their problems. At the same time, students are encouraged to see the consequences of their behavior in an actual life experience without being subjected to moralizing and punishment. Through neutral and supportive communication between student and teacher, hostilities, frustrations, and guilt are relieved. This can help to avoid explosive outbursts later that same day. Because the intervention is immediate, the student's desire for help and motivation for change are greatly increased. Life-space interviewing frequently leads to as much growth in the teacher as in the pupils. This is particularly true when teachers and pupils come from different cultural backgrounds. Careful listening on the part of the teacher can lead to insights into the reasons underlying students' behavior.

LSI also has a few limitations that must be described. First, in a class of perhaps 20 to 30 students, the immediate, time-consuming interview may not be feasible. However, if the teacher has confidence in the rationale of LSI, there is no reason why the teacher–pupil interaction cannot be delayed until recess or after school. Second, LSI requires expert emotional control and sensitivity on the part of the teacher. If the teacher becomes involved in the emotionalism of the problem, effectiveness is sacrificed and the technique becomes useless. A third, more subtle limitation to LSI is that, by removing the student from a 30-to-1 classroom situation to a 2-to-1 personal interaction, the teacher may be reinforcing the negative behavior instead of changing it.

LSI should not be attempted without supervised training and practice in the use of the technique. An excellent resource is Wood and Long's (1991) *Life Space Intervention,* which provides practical and detailed descriptions of LSI procedures in applied settings.

Projective Techniques

Rationale

Projective techniques frequently utilize supportive media, such as puppets, dramatic play, toys, books, art materials, and music, as stimuli to encourage students to express ("project") feelings that they might not reveal in conversation or interviews. Therapies based on projective theory have been developed largely in clinical practice and are used primarily by specially trained professionals. Most have a decided neo-Freudian orientation. However, some of these techniques may be used by classroom teachers to highlight a specific problem area or to explore it in depth. In particular, role playing and puppetry are used by classroom teachers, as well as some aspects of art and music therapy. Some projective techniques will be used by members of the professional support team working with seriously disturbed children who are receiving help or therapy outside the classroom.

Role Playing

Role playing is a form of "let's pretend." The children act out situations that involve problems of getting along together. A distinctive version of role playing, called psychodrama, has been developed by Moreno (1946).

Psychodrama is usually employed with a severely disturbed individual, who is asked to come up on a stage and express real or fantasized feelings and problems. There is no criticism in psychodrama, only "controlled confrontation." Participation is voluntary. Some of Moreno's psychodramatic techniques include role reversal (where individuals exchange roles), soliloquy, double (where a "helper" participates in the play), mirror (where one participant "apes" the actions of another), behind the back (where other participants talk about the target individual), empty chair (where the student addresses an empty chair), magic shop (where goals and aspirations are expressed), and ideal other (where the student acts out his or her ideal alter ego). Psychodrama requires the presence of a trained therapist because of its explosive nature; therefore, it is not recommended for use in the classroom. However, role playing as a technique for learning new behaviors and skills can be appropriately adapted to the classroom.

Interpersonal problems often find solution through acceptance of criticism or other forms of perceived punishment or rejection. Students can learn how to cope with these experiences by exploring various responses and reactions. One student might portray the role of an angry member of the class, and another student might play himself or herself entering into a potential fight with that student. Through suggestions from the teacher and class members, the student can learn to respond to anger more skillfully and without losing face. This technique can also help physically or mentally handicapped students face real or imagined social reactions without reverting to excessive emotional outbursts.

Wood (1981) suggested a variety of useful and creative activities involving role playing, puppetry, and other "fantasy" activities. Carpenter and Sandberg (1985) examined psychodrama techniques with delinquent and aggressive adolescents.

Puppetry

Theories that utilize the construct of the "unconscious" as a potent motivator in human behavior recognize the need for bringing unconscious feelings to the level of consciousness. An effective way of doing this is through the use of puppetry, another form of psychodrama. The puppets have specific meaning to each student, who is able to project hate, anger, fears, and desires onto them in a neutral, fantasylike manner. Many of these feelings ordinarily remain suppressed because expression of them in actual life situations is often too threatening to the student or is socially unacceptable. However, as Woltmann (1971) stated, "Puppetry carries with it the reassurance that everything on the stage is only a make-believe affair" (p. 226). To kill the bad guy is acceptable. Not only does he always come to life during the next show, but with each "killing" comes the release of suppressed rage, which otherwise is often inappropriately released during instructional time.

All that puppetry requires is commercial or homemade puppets and a structure that can serve as a stage. Often the students themselves can create the needed equipment. The puppet characters should combine both fantastic and realistic factors, so that the student can enter easily into the activity and identify with the characters and their problems. Woltmann suggested the use of the following types of puppet actors: (1) the hero; (2) a bad mother, often appearing as a witch; (3) a bad father, appearing as a giant; (4) a boy or girl representing the student's idealized self; and (5) an animal. Other personalities can be added as the students begin to interact in this problem-solving world of fantasy.

Initially, an adult should act as the puppeteer, following the commands of the audience. Some students may yell out "Kill the witch! Kill her!" while others shrink away in fear. It frequently is helpful to bring a fearful student behind the stage while the acting is going to assure him or her that it is only make-believe. During the show, all student commands should be accepted, but afterward alternative solutions to the problems revealed in the fantasy play can be discussed and acted out. Puppetry can dispel intense feelings and contribute to learning alternatives to stereotypic behaviors. The teacher should be careful to resolve any problems broached in the play so that the students have a "clean slate" and are relaxed for the next activity.

Play Therapy

The use of play therapy in school differs in some ways from play as a psychotherapeutic technique. A primary goal in school is to increase the individual's understanding of himself or herself by creating a free situation (play) in which the student is given the opportunity to self-actualize. According to Axline (1964), an acknowledged authority on the technique of play therapy, "the child must first learn self-respect and a sense of dignity that grows out of his increasing self-understanding before he can learn to respect the personalities and rights and differences of others" (p. 67). In psychotherapy the aim is to discover unconscious motivations by interpretive techniques. Both educational and psychotherapeutic play share several views: (1) the relationship between therapist (or teacher) and the student is the key to emotional growth, and (2) the selection and use of various play activities express personal and social needs. The play situation is usually the most comfortable one for the student and the most conducive to self-expression.

Play materials are provided for the student, but their use should not be contrived by the therapist. Recommended materials are

sandbox	basin filled with water
doll house	toy dishes
toy soldiers	toy police and fire trucks
crayons	toy animals
scissors	hammer

Ginott (1961), another early proponent of play therapy, suggested that young children who are "socially hungry" are the best candidates for play therapy. The technique seems to lose its effectiveness after about age 8, according to Ginott, who also pointed out that play therapy probably is counterindicated for children who are aggressive or have deviant sexual drives, children who suffer from intense sibling rivalries or extreme hostility, children who tend to steal, children who are prone to have unusually strong stress reactions, and children who engage in sociopathic behaviors.

Although there are no clear-cut procedures for play therapy, Kessler (1966, pp. 376–377) restated Axline's eight basic principles[2]:

1. The therapist must develop a warm, friendly relationship with the child.

2. The therapist accepts the child exactly as he is.

3. The therapist establishes a feeling of permissiveness in the relationship.

4. The therapist is alert to recognize the feelings [of the child] and to reflect the feelings back to the child so that she gains insight into her behavior.

5. The therapist maintains a deep respect for the child's ability to solve his own problems.

6. The child leads the way; the therapist follows.

7. The therapist does not attempt to hurry the therapy along.

8. The therapist establishes only those limitations that are necessary to anchor the therapy to the world of reality and to make the child aware of his responsibility in the relationship.

The effects of play therapy have been equivocal. The decision whether to use play therapy depends on more than reports of efficacy studies, however; the time required for the process and the size of the class are practical determinants. As Newcomer (1993) wrote in her book, *Understanding and Teaching Emotionally Disturbed Children and Adolescents,*

> It seems most likely that play therapy, while not a panacea (it certainly is not the best means of remediating serious reading or speech problems, as Axline suggested), is a valuable avenue for reaching young children. If a teacher's goals . . . pertain to helping children develop increasingly mature and adaptive social skills, establishing a nonthreatening relationship . . . , and/or providing opportunities . . . to model better adjusted peers, it should prove to be a helpful technique. (p. 482)

---

2. From *Psychopathology of Childhood* by J. W. Kessler, 1966, Englewood Cliffs, NJ: Prentice-Hall. Copyright 1966 by Prentice-Hall, Inc. Reprinted by permission.

Art and Music Therapy

The goals of art and music therapy parallel those previously expressed for play therapy, puppetry, and role playing: encouraging students to express themselves freely and without fear. Music and various art media such as paint and clay may elicit expressions of feelings that would not surface otherwise. Art and music therapy provide nonthreatening situations in which students can share their feelings and release inner tensions.

For art therapy, a wide variety of media should be available in the classroom or therapy room. Freestyle activities such as finger painting, clay sculpting, and drawing provide unstructured avenues for expression. Denny (1977) suggested a number of goals for art therapy in the schools. Among these are encouraging spontaneous expression, building rapport by encouraging interaction with other participants, facilitating the expression of inner feelings, and exploring self-perceptions. It is not unusual for teachers to detect some of the problems that students are experiencing by examining their art work. Usually, however, this merely confirms problems that already have been identified. Teachers are cautioned *not* to use art therapy as a diagnostic tool unless they have had specific training in this area.

Music is often cited as a universal language, and it plays an important role in the social life of many adolescents. Music can have a quieting effect on unusually active students and can promote concentration, because it helps to shut out noises that might otherwise be distracting. Aggressive behaviors can be vented through such music activities as dancing; playing drums, rhythm sticks, or sandpaper blocks; and singing action songs. In addition to engaging in traditional therapeutic activities of singing, dancing, or playing musical instruments, students can talk or write about the feelings elicited by certain types of music or about musical content, such as historical information on certain pieces of music, composers' biographies, and so on.

Cognitive Interventions

Cognitive behavior modification and other so-called rational approaches to behavioral control and improvement have gained increasing recognition and widespread acceptance since the early 1960s. Three major cognitive intervention strategies are discussed in this section: Glasser's reality therapy (RT), Ellis's rational-emotive therapy (RET), and Meichenbaum's cognitive behavior management (CBM). Although CBM is the most widely used in American schools, all of these approaches can be applied, at least in part, by classroom teachers, as well as by therapists, counselors, psychologists, and other mental health professionals.

Rationale

Cognitive intervention programs require a life-style change for the students who are involved in them. Students are not placed into prefabricated intervention programs; they are expected to assume responsibility for their own behavior and to help develop and guide their own therapy. Students learn that they are responsible for the course of their own lives, with no excuses made. They are constantly called on to make value judgments regarding their behavior and to commit themselves to change and improvement. Several courses of action may be attempted before the student falls into a behavioral pattern that is both personally comfortable and socially acceptable. In the course of RT, RET, or CBM, students become increasingly aware of the "reality of the world around them" (Glasser, 1965, p. 6) and are able to identify and let go of the many irrational beliefs that may have motivated their behavior previously, such as the "idea that it is a dire necessity for an adult human to be loved or approved by virtually every significant other person in his life" (Ellis, 1962, p. 153).

Procedures

Each of these cognitive interventions sports a full-blown therapy program to which we cannot do justice in the space allowed. Interested readers should consult the authors' original works for more detail. Glasser outlined an overall approach to reality therapy (1965) and later described its application in the school setting (1969). Ellis looked at the principles of rational-emotive therapy as they operate in a therapeutic setting (1962, 1970, 1974) and in overall life choices (Ellis & Harper, 1977). He also developed a handbook for the approach (Ellis & Grieger, 1977). RET was adapted for use by elementary school teachers (Knause, 1974) and learning disabilities specialists (Knause & McKeever, 1977). Roush (1984) provided guidelines for counselors using RET with children and youth. The best descriptions provided by Meichenbaum for his cognitive behavior management strategies are in his 1977 text and his 1983 monograph. K. R. Harris, Wong, and Keogh (1985) edited a special issue of the *Journal of Abnormal Child Psychology* devoted to CBM; Wong's (1985) article in that issue is particularly noteworthy for its attention to school-related issues. We summarize the basic tenets of these three cognitively based therapies in the remainder of this section.

Ellis (1974) discussed several premises that he considered basic to *rational-emotive therapy.* Probably the most important tenet is that change must be effected in the inner language that people use to talk to themselves about their behavior, their values, and their reasons for acting in a particular way. Ellis believed that such a language change will facilitate behavior change by allowing clients to clarify their reasoning through the formation and use of hypotheses. Ellis emphasized that the burden for the success of any intervention must be assumed by the client, although he stressed that no blame should be attached to failure and that the therapist can "sell" or market behavioral change in much the same way that one might sell laundry detergent or diet soda. Ellis stressed that the causes of one's problems are found only in the present, and there is little, if any, exploration of past behaviors, previous life experiences, or previous situations in RET. He insisted on practice and homework for clients. In general, this therapy is highly verbal and thus may not be appropriate for students who have language or general reasoning difficulties. Zionts (1985) devoted two chapters of his text to practical ways of implementing RET in a school.

According to Coleman (1986), *reality therapy* comprises three general stages: establishing an involvement, forcing a value judgment, and finding alternative ways of behaving. Within this framework, Glasser's (1969) "3Rs"—responsibility, reality, and right and wrong—are emphasized. Responsibility is required for people to meet their own personal needs without infringing on the rights of others in the process; irresponsibility, in Glasser's view, leads to disturbance. Reality requires that people accept the world around them, including societal canon law and, most important, the true relationship between their behavior and its consequences. Right–wrong requires a value judgment whereby people recognize that deviant behavior is wrong because it is harmful to oneself and to others. Glasser discussed ways that teachers can implement reality therapy in the classroom. He said that the teacher should continually ask three questions of the student: "What are you doing?" "Is your behavior helping you or those around you?" "What could you do differently?" He advocated a more behavioristic approach than did Ellis, and for this reason Newcomer (1993) suggested that reality therapy may be more useful with young children or with students whose verbal reasoning powers are limited or impaired.

Meichenbaum's (1975) approach is even more behavioral. His *cognitive behavior modification* methods are essentially values clarification combined with social skills training. He suggested the use of basic modeling principles to help students acquire self-control over their behaviors. In general, he suggested the need to identify problem areas through discussion or role playing. Skills to be acquired are broken down into subcomponents, and their verbal aspects are studied carefully. The teaching process begins after a concise explanation of why a particular skill needs to be learned. The steps of the skill are defined; modeled by the teacher, therapist, or a peer; practiced by the target student through role playing and real-life situations; and altered or reinforced through feedback and praise. Meichenbaum proposed that many of these steps can be accomplished in group sessions, because many students lack the same (or similar) basic social skills.

In reviewing cognitive behavior management strategies, Lloyd (1980) identified several characteristics that most approaches have in common:

1. Cognitive behavior modification is a self-imposed treatment, similar to the self-control strategies presented earlier in this chapter.

2. Self-talk or other verbalization strategies are taught, principally through modeling or imitation.

3. Problem solving is the primary goal, and a basic strategy is to help children consider several possible alternative behaviors before acting or responding.

Commercially Available Programs

Rationale

A number of affective education programs and curricula are available commercially. They attempt to enrich the child's socioemotional experience, particularly the development of self-esteem, the acquisition of social and interpersonal skills, and the expression of feelings and emotions. Most of these programs teach students to be open to new experiences, to label and express feelings, and to identify and clarify values. For instruction, they depend heavily upon the use of puppetry, role playing, sociodrama, and discussion.

Programs

Several programs are discussed in this section: *My Friends and Me; Developing Understanding of Self and Others–Revised; Toward Affective Development; Adventures of the Lollipop Dragon; Walker Social Skills Curriculum; Talking, Listening, Communicating;* and values clarification.

My Friends and Me (Davis, 1977) was written for a preschool or low-functioning audience. Through the use of discussion, puppetry, role playing, and drawing, students go through the process of self-identification and recognition of group rights and responsibilities. There are eight units: Social Identity, Emotional Identity, Physical Identity, Intellectual and Creative Identity, Cooperation, Consideration for Others, Ownership and Sharing, and Dependence and Help.

The *Developing Understanding of Self and Others–Revised* (DUSO-R) (Dinkmeyer, 1982) kits are designed for use from kindergarten through second grade (D-I) and for third and fourth grades (D-II). D-I stresses the inquiry method of learning. Stories, puppetry, music, and discussion are used to promote the eight unit themes: (1) Understanding and Accepting Self; (2) Understanding Feelings; (3) Understanding Others; (4) Understanding Independence; (5) Understanding Goals and Purposeful Behavior; (6) Understanding Mastery, Competence, and Resourcefulness; (7) Understanding Emotional Maturity; and (8) Understanding Choices and Consequences. Daily lesson plans for DUSO activities are presented in the manual. Role playing, puppetry, and listening are the primary activities used to develop the eight themes in D-II. Stimulus posters and situation cards are provided to assist the teacher in initiating discussion around these themes: (1) Towards Self-Identity: Developing Self-Awareness and a Positive Self-Concept; (2) Towards Friendship: Understanding Peers; (3) Towards Responsible Interdependence: Understanding Growth from Self-Centeredness to Social Interest; (4) Towards Self-Reliance: Understanding Personal Responsibility; (5) Towards Resourcefulness and Purposefulness: Understanding Personal Motivation; (6) Towards Competence: Understanding Accomplishments; (7) Towards Emotional Stability: Understanding Stress; and (8) Towards Responsible Choice Making: Understanding Values.

Toward Affective Development (TAD) (DuPont, Gardner, & Brody, 1974) is a popular, widely used affective curriculum. It was designed for "normal" children in Grades 3 through 6, but is also appropriate for guidance or remedial work as well as for gifted populations. Lessons are organized into five major units that use a student's real or vicarious experiences as the basis for growing and learning. These units include Reaching In and Reaching Out; Your Feelings and Mine; Working Together; Me: Today and Tomorrow; and Feeling, Thinking, Doing. Most of the activities are verbal: brainstorming, role playing, and discussion groups. TAD's 190 activities are accompanied by manuals; shapes, pictures, print blocks, and pens to create stories and scenes; "alter ego" dolls named Willdoo and Candoo; records and cassettes; and spirit masters describing family activities that support the TAD program.

The *Adventures of the Lollipop Dragon* (1970) was designed for students in the primary grades. Six filmstrips are included in the kit. They depict stories that emphasize personal relationships and interdependency (e.g., taking turns, sharing with others, and working in groups). The "hero" of the series is the Lollipop Dragon, who inhabits a small kingdom where the economy is based on the production of lollipops. The filmstrips are accompanied by records and cassettes of the stories and by a coloring book, "How the Lollipop Dragon Got His Name."

The *Walker Social Skills Curriculum* has two components: the ACCEPTS Program (Walker et al., 1983) and the ACCESS Program (Walker, Todis, Holmes, & Horton, 1988). ACCEPTS is a complete social skills curriculum designed for use with handicapped and nonhandicapped students in kindergarten through Grade 6. It utilizes direct instruction principles to teach specific social skills: classroom skills, basic interaction skills, getting along skills, making friends skills, and coping skills. The kit includes scripts for teaching these skills, suggested behavior management techniques, a screening device, and guidelines for selecting children for the program. Procedures for training teachers to use the curriculum are also included. Two optional videotapes are available—one demonstrates appropriate and inappropriate examples of the skills being taught, and the other, for parent and teacher groups, demonstrates the program's application.

ACCESS is for middle school and high school students. It teaches peer-to-peer skills, skills for relating to adults, and self-management skills. The kit includes 30 teaching scripts, an eight-step instructional procedure, a student study guide, and suggestions for grouping students. The guidelines include strategies for behavior management, motivation, and generalization.

TLC is an acronym for *Talking, Listening, Communicating* (Bormaster & Treat, 1994), a curriculum guide that outlines 156 activities to help students build interpersonal relationships. The activities require 30 minutes or less and include paper-and-pencil as well as interactive activities. The book is sequenced and addresses such topics as Sharing Self, Sharing Values, Improving Interpersonal Communications, Relating to Others,

Developing Creativity, Decision Making by Consensus, and Solving Problems as a Group. Particular attention is given to the skills required for effective group functioning.

Values clarification is an affective education process, although it is not packaged as a kit. The reader is referred to two excellent books, *Values Clarification* (Simon, Howe, & Kirschenbaum, 1978) and *Developing Values with Exceptional Children* (Simon & O'Rourke, 1977), which describe the technique of values clarification and offer specific activities for a classroom teacher to use in helping students through the process. These activities help students to examine their particular value and belief systems, including their attitudes, interests, and feelings, so that they can ultimately make intelligent choices about their behavior. Table 8.2, from Abrams's (1992) article, summarizes three different perspectives of the values clarification process.

Biochemical Interventions

In some cases, a biochemical intervention may be employed to alter or control a child's behavior. Possible interventions include prescribing medication, eliminating food additives, controlling allergies, regulating the sugar content of the blood, and prescribing large doses of vitamins and minerals. Most prominent among these approaches are stimulant drug therapy and diet therapy, both of which are discussed briefly here.

We should reiterate that teachers do *not* prescribe or implement biochemical interventions. However, they may be called upon to participate in the therapy by reporting any observed changes in a student's behavior or any side effects of the therapy. Most teachers who have students with behavioral problems in their classes will eventually have a student who is undergoing diet or drug therapy. For these reasons, we include the present discussion.

Two excellent reviews of the literature concerning diet and drug therapy have been written for educators. The first is a monograph by Sieben (1983), and the second is an article by Silver (1987). Interested readers are encouraged to consult these two sources; they are scholarly and quite readable.

Psychotropic (mood altering) drugs have been used successfully with severely disturbed, usually institutionalized patients. Major tranquilizers and antipsychotic drugs (e.g., phenothiazines) are used to treat serious conditions such as personality disorders or psychoses, where they have proved to be palliative and to relieve delusions and hallucinations in adult and adolescent patients. Antidepressants have proved more effective with adults than with children.

Stimulant drug therapy involves the prescription of psychostimulants (e.g., Ritalin, Cylert, or Dexedrine), major and minor tranquilizers, antidepressants, anticonvulsants, lithium, or even caffeine for children to control their behavior, usually hyperactivity. Silver (1987) reported

TABLE 8.2. Three Views of Values Clarification: Skills Involved in the Valuing Process

1. The Valuing Process: Criteria for a Full Value
   - A. Choosing
     1. Freely
     2. From alternatives
     3. After thoughtful consideration of the consequences of each alternative
   - B. Prizing
     1. Cherishing, being happy with choice
     2. Willing to affirm choice publicly
   - C. Acting
     1. Acting upon the choice
     2. Acting repeatedly with a pattern or consistency

2. The Valuing Process
   - A. Feeling
     1. Being open to one's inner experience
        - (a) Awareness of one's inner experience
        - (b) Acceptance of one's inner experience
   - B. Thinking
     1. Thinking on all seven levels (memory, translation, application, interpretation, analysis, synthesis, and evaluation)
     2. Employing critical thinking skills
        - (a) Distinguishing fact from opinion
        - (b) Distinguishing supported from unsupported arguments
        - (c) Analyzing propaganda, stereotypes, etc.
     3. Employing logical thinking (logic)
     4. Employing creative thinking
     5. Employing fundamental cognitive skills
        - (a) Language use
        - (b) Mathematical skills
        - (c) Research skills
   - C. Communicating (verbally and nonverbally)
     1. Sending clear messages
     2. Listening empathetically
     3. Drawing out
     4. Asking clarifying questions
     5. Giving and receiving feedback
     6. Engaging in conflict resolution
   - D. Choosing
     1. Generating and considering alternatives
     2. Thoughtfully considering consequences, pros and cons
     3. Choosing strategically
        - (a) Setting goals
        - (b) Gathering data
        - (c) Solving problems
        - (d) Planning
     4. Choosing freely
   - E. Acting
     1. Acting with repetition
     2. Acting with a pattern and consistency
     3. Acting skillfully, competently

3. Values Clarification as Development of Student Interaction Skills
   - A. Communicating
   - B. Empathizing
   - C. Problem Solving
   - D. Assenting and Dissenting
   - E. Decision Making
   - F. Personal Consistency

From "Values Clarification for Students with Emotional Disabilities" by B. J. Abrams, 1992 (Spring), *Teaching Exceptional Children*, p. 31. Reprinted with permission.

research showing that 0.5% of children are treated with psychostimulants, down from 5% to 10% about two decades previously.

Ritalin (methylphenidate), Cylert (pemoline), and Dexedrine (dextroamphetamine) can improve the behavior of hyperactive children (Wolraich, 1977). Sieben (1983) noted, however, that "their demonstrated effectiveness does not condone their indiscriminate use. They are not a replacement for special education or a cure-all for emotional problems because their long-term benefits and effects on academic performance and intelligence have not been established" (p. 158). There is no evidence that stimulant drug therapy is any more effective than behavior modification or many of the other interventions described in this chapter (Sroufe, 1975). Sieben went on to note that there is no evidence that major tranquilizers, minor tranquilizers (e.g., Valium or Librium), lithium, antidepressants, or anticonvulsants affect hyperactive behavior. Caffeine is similarly ineffective.

The psychostimulants appear to provide symptomatic relief of hyperactive behaviors, but they do not cure the condition. They are considered to be nonaddictive, because they can be withdrawn abruptly without any symptoms. The side effects of these drugs include loss of appetite, headaches, upset stomach, insomnia, and high blood pressure.

The success of diets that eliminate food additives is less clear. The Feingold, or Kaiser–Permanente, diet (Feingold, 1975) is the most well known of these diets. Feingold claims (but offers no empirical evidence) that 40% of hyperactive children will improve if their diet is free of salicylates, artificial colors and flavors, and preservatives. The diet eliminates almonds, apples, apricots, berries, cherries, grapes, oranges, peaches, plums, tomatoes, cucumbers, lunch meats, colored cheeses, most breads, cereals, bakery goods, desserts, candies, beverages, mustard, catsup, margarine, most butters, toothpaste, mouthwash, cough drops, antacids, pediatric vitamins, perfume, and most over-the-counter medications.

Despite Feingold's unsupported claims, only a very small percentage of hyperactive children (less than 1%) show any improvement in behavior when on his diet. When blind dietary crossover designs were used (neither the subject nor the researcher knew whether the subject was on the diet at first and then went off it, or was off the diet at first and then went on it), there was a small change in subjects who experienced the control condition first and the diet second; there was no change in subjects who experienced the diet first and then the control condition. Similarly, only minimal reactions were elicited when challenge designs were used (the subject was on the diet and was periodically "challenged" with a prohibited food).

In summary, the Feingold diet produces limited positive results. Researchers cannot yet identify good candidates for the diet by means of any *a priori* criteria. Nor can they identify the chemical basis for eliminating the specified foods; their chemical structures are not similar. Furthermore, the diet probably does not meet the long-term nutritional needs of children who are on it and the diet is an arduous one to adhere to.

Chapter 9

Teaching Study Skills to Students

JOHN J. HOOVER

Through study skills education, students acquire important skills necessary to succeed with a variety of daily tasks. For many learners, the difference between success and failure in school may be found in deficient study skills knowledge and usage as well as in the inability to apply acquired study skills to different educational tasks. As students develop efficient study skills usage, they are, in effect, learning how to learn. Study skills assist students to succeed in various learning situations more efficiently and effectively as new information is acquired, retained, and applied to other learning situations (Langone, 1990). Although study skills are considered important in learning, Woolfolk (1990) observed that regular instruction in study skills does not typically occur in school. Johnson, Schneider, and German (1983) pointed out that, because study skills are not an integral part of the curriculum, teachers need to stress "the importance of study skills and to address the use of methods and materials that can initiate independent learning" (p. 263). In addition, teachers must stimulate the use of study strategies by building them into daily classroom activities (Good & Brophy, 1990).

This chapter was written to show teachers how to help students in any grade acquire and maintain effective study skills. The first section discusses the nature of study skills, specifically emphasizing what study skills are and why they are important to students in the learning process. The second section deals with methods for assessing study skills and highlights the importance of informal assessment in identifying students' specific strengths and weaknesses. The third section describes several student strategies, numerous teaching activities, and parent strategies for assisting students to acquire and maintain study skills. The chapter concludes with several activities for students to apply their knowledge of study skills.

THE NATURE OF STUDY SKILLS

To improve student usage of study skills, one must understand the importance of study skills and recognize the different types of study skills available to students. Although poor student performance in daily educational tasks may result from many factors, lack of effective study skills is a major contributing factor for many students with learning and behavioral problems. To fully understand why ineffective study skills contribute to poor classroom performance, one must first know what study skills are and why they are important to daily instruction. This section discusses a definition of study skills, the different types of study skills, the importance of study skills, and the relevance of study skills for students with special needs.

A Definition of Study Skills

Study skills have been defined as "tools" students use in the classroom and as "competencies" necessary for effective learning to occur. As defined by Lock (1981), study skills are "tools students use to absorb the material they are to learn" (p. 3). They are necessary to progress successfully through the subject areas emphasized in school (Choate et al., 1987). Study skills include the many techniques or strategies that students employ in order to cope with daily educational tasks and requirements. The complex task of studying, which must be mastered by students if they are to succeed in school, requires skills such as effective use of reading rates; time management; test-taking, note-taking, and outlining skills; reference material use; and self-management of behavior.

Devine (1987) defined study skills as "those competencies associated with acquiring, recording, organizing, synthesizing, remembering, and using information and ideas found in school" (p. 5). Seven learning components identified from the literature that are affected by the use of study skills are illustrated in Figure 9.1. These components are acquisition, recording, location, organization, synthesis, and memorization, as well as the integration of these components. The circular figure depicts not only each individual learning component but also the continuous interrelationships among the areas. The dotted line that separates the individual components from the integration component emphasizes the importance of the combined use of study skills in the overall learning process.

One or more of these learning components are emphasized as students undertake each educational task. Study skills are techniques and strategies that assist the learner in completing adequately and efficiently the educational tasks associated with the learning components (Hoover, 1993b). Thus, proficiency in the use of a variety of study skills (e.g., test taking, report writing, outlining, library use) facilitates effective mastery of the learning components encountered on a daily basis in school.

Types of Study Skills

A variety of study skills associated with the different learning components exist. These skills include effective use of reading rate, listening, note taking, report writing, oral presentation, use of graphic aids, test taking, library use, and time management. Given its importance and close association with note taking, outlining has been included to form the study skill of note taking/outlining. In addition, reference material/dictionary use and self-management of behavior are important tools necessary for efficient and effective learning. Table 9.1 lists each study skill addressed in this chapter and gives a summary of its significance to learning.

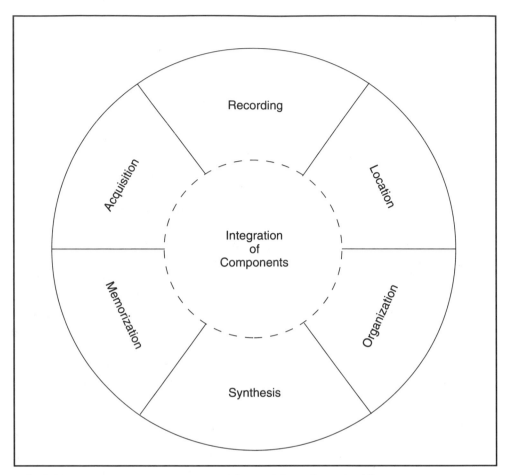

FIGURE 9.1. Learning components addressed through study skills.

From *Teaching Study Skills to Students with Learning Problems* (p. 4) by J. J. Hoover, 1993, Boulder, CO: Hamilton Publications.

The following subsections explore these 11 study skills in greater detail, highlighting specific techniques associated with their effective use and presenting suggestions for helping students to master them. Numerous best practices for teaching each study skill are also provided. These are based upon my experiences and several sources, including Devine (1987), Harris and Sipay (1990), Hoover (1993b), Mercer and Mercer (1993), and G. Wallace and Kauffman (1986). The reader is referred to these sources for additional practices. Specific teaching activities to enhance study skills are presented later in this chapter.

Effective Use of Reading Rate

Although most, if not all, aspects of reading are related either directly or indirectly to all study skills, flexibility in the use of different reading rates is particularly important (Harris & Sipay, 1990). Thus, rates of reading should be emphasized in teaching study skills to students, especially

TABLE 9.1. Study Skills: Tools for Learning

STUDY SKILL	SIGNIFICANCE FOR LEARNING
Effective use of reading rate	Reading rates should vary with the type and length of the reading assignment.
Listening	Listening skills are necessary to complete most educational tasks or requirements.
Note taking/outlining	Effective note-taking/outlining skills allow students to document key points of topics for future study.
Report writing	Report writing is a widely used method for documenting information and expressing ideas.
Oral presentation	Oral presentation provides students with an alternative method for expressing themselves and reporting information.
Use of graphic aids	By using graphic aids, students can depict complex or cumbersome material in a meaningful format.
Test taking	Effective test-taking skills help to ensure that students' abilities are accurately assessed.
Library use	Skill at library use facilitates access to much information.
Reference material/dictionary use	Independent learning may be greatly improved through effective use of reference materials and dictionaries.
Time management	Time management can reduce the number of unfinished assignments and permit more effective use of time.
Self-management of behavior	Self-management assists students in assuming responsibility for their own behaviors.

From *Teaching Study Skills to Students with Learning Problems* (p. 18) by J. J. Hoover, 1993, Boulder, CO: Hamilton Publications.

as students move through the grades (Heilman, Blair, & Rupley, 1981). Although several terms are used in the literature to describe different reading rates, the most common are skimming, scanning, rapid reading, normal reading, and careful or study-type reading.

Skimming is a fast-paced reading rate and should be used when the student is only trying to grasp the general idea of the material. When skimming is used, different sections of material are purposely glossed over. *Scanning* is also a fast-paced reading rate, but it is used when the reader is looking for a specific item or piece of information. Scanning is used, for example, when one searches for a telephone number, a name in a story, or the name of a state in an alphabetical list. *Rapid reading* is used to grasp only the main ideas of material or to review familiar material. Some details may be identified through rapid reading, especially if the information is being acquired for temporary use only. *Normal reading* is the rate of reading used for identifying details or relationships, problem solving, or finding the answer to a specific question. *Careful or study-type reading* involves a slow rate of reading and is used to master details, retain material, evaluate information, follow directions, or perform other activities for which careful, detailed reading is required.

Evans, Evans, and Mercer (1986) maintained that the appropriate reading rate depends both on the purpose of the reading and on the nature of the material being read. In many situations, two or more rates are used to complete a task. For example, a student may scan several paragraphs to locate a name. Once the name has been identified, normal or study-type reading may be necessary to determine what that person was doing at that particular point in the story. Effective use of reading rate is a necessary study skill for special students and requires guided instruction.

Best practices for teaching effective use of reading rate include

1. Ensuring that proper reading rates are used for different types of activities
2. Establishing clear purposes for reading assignments
3. Ensuring that each student understands when and how to use each type of reading rate
4. Encouraging students to reread sections of material—at the proper reading rate—when comprehension is poor
5. Providing opportunities to practice each reading rate

Listening

Listening, like effective use of reading rate, is important in many different educational activities. According to Gearheart, Weishahn, and Gearheart (1992), the majority of a student's school day is spent in listening-related activities. This finding is supported by Devine (1987), who wrote that listening is the primary mechanism by which information is acquired by students. According to Lerner (1993), however, educators have neglected the important skill of listening.

Listening refers both to *hearing* someone speak and to *comprehending* the verbal message. Listening includes receiving the information, applying meaning, and providing some evidence of understanding what was heard. Effective listening is required in many different situations, including formal presentations, conversations, and exposure to either auditory environmental stimuli or audiovisual material. When students engage in activities where listening is required, teachers must ensure that classroom conditions facilitate effective listening. Devine (1987) indicated that listening skills can be improved through appropriate teaching and continued practice and stated that "teachers must teach students how to listen" (p. 32).

Best practices for teaching listening skills include

1. Minimizing distractions and quickly dealing with classroom disruptions
2. Ensuring that the locations of all students in the classroom are such that they are able to hear verbal interactions

3. Encouraging students to speak loudly enough that all can hear

4. Repeating important items and emphasizing important content in the verbal message

5. Beginning lectures at a point familiar to all students and gradually bridging to new material

6. Assisting students to realize the importance of the material being presented

7. Providing frequent summaries at strategic points in the verbal message

8. Using visual materials to support oral presentations

Note Taking/Outlining

The combined areas of note taking and outlining provide students with skills that can enhance performance in various areas of learning. These include listening, reading, vocabulary, and thinking. Note taking requires the student to classify and synthesize information as it must reflect both the organization and the purpose of the presented material. Essentially, note taking/outlining requires students to document major ideas and the most important topics for later use. According to Ekwall and Shanker (1985), the skill of note taking becomes easier once effective outlining skills have been developed. In reference to special learners, these students often do not learn note taking/outlining skills as quickly as other students. However, they are capable of acquiring these skills if given sufficient practice and systematic instruction. Instruction in note taking is particularly appropriate for students with learning problems.

Best practices in teaching note taking/outlining skills include

1. Ensuring that students follow a consistent format when outlining or taking notes

2. Assisting students to identify key topics and ideas

3. Discussing the uses and advantages of note taking/outlining

4. Modeling various note taking/outlining formats when presentations are made to students

5. Beginning with simple note taking/outlining activities and gradually increasing to more complex activities

Report Writing

As pointed out by Devine (1987), report writing involves the skills necessary to organize one's ideas and present them, on paper, in a meaningful and appropriate way. These skills include the ability to organize, use proper spelling and punctuation, outline, take notes, select topics, locate information in dictionaries and other reference materials, and use a library. Thus, report writing is similar to reading and listening in that it encompasses a variety of study skills. Teachers of special students should provide careful and consistent direction in each area associated with written reports to ensure satisfactory progress and growth in this study skill area.

Best practices in teaching report writing include

1. Clarifying the specific purpose for the written assignment
2. Assisting students to organize their ideas
3. Beginning with simple, less complex written assignments
4. Ensuring that students proofread their written work
5. Encouraging the use of a dictionary and other reference materials when necessary
6. Working with students as they progress through different stages of writing assignments (e.g., structuring sentences and paragraphs, outlining, formulating ideas)
7. Providing periodic review and encouragement as written reports are completed

Oral Presentation

Many of the skills necessary for report writing are also important for oral presentations. Oral presentations may supplement a written report or may be used as a separate information reporting method. Activities such as interviews, debates, group discussions, and individual/group presentations fall within the scope of oral presentation. Some students who are experiencing difficulty with written assignments may benefit from various forms of oral presentation. To minimize the anxiety often associated with speaking in front of groups of people, however, this study skill should be introduced thoughtfully and in a nonthreatening manner.

Best practices in teaching oral presentation include

1. Allowing extra time for preparation of oral presentations, in addition to the time allotted for completion of the written report
2. Providing a nonthreatening environment for oral presentation in order to reduce peer criticism
3. Being flexible in structuring the conditions under which students make oral presentations (e.g., seated at or standing by their desks, in front of a small group, in front of the whole class)
4. Ensuring that students know the purpose of their oral presentations

Use of Graphic Aids

Another popular technique for facilitating effective learning is the use of graphic aids, which include charts, graphs, maps, models, pictures, and photographs. Wallace and Kauffman (1986) identified several reasons for presenting information in graphic form: (1) complex material may be comprehended more easily in visual form; (2) graphic illustrations facilitate the presentation of large abstractions in small, more manageable pieces; and (3) similarities within and differences among cultural, geographic, and economic situations can be depicted visually and studied via graphic aids. Thus, a variety of important concepts and events may be learned effectively through visual material. However, some students, especially those with learning disabilities, experience difficulty with discrimination of visual materials. These students must be taught what to look for and attend to while reading and interpreting visual material. Some learners require direct teaching to learn to use graphic aids accurately.

Best practices in teaching the use of graphic aids include

1. Periodically allowing graphic presentations as an alternative to oral or written reports

2. Discussing with students why material is presented graphically

3. Strategically incorporating visuals into oral presentations made to students

4. Assisting students via leading questions to focus on key features of the graphic material

5. Allowing students sufficient time to read and interpret graphic aids as they are being presented

Test Taking

One fact few educators dispute is that tests are an integral part of the educational system. Almost from the day they enter school, students are subjected to various forms of assessment and evaluation, and tests are one of the primary assessment tools used in schools. However, as Good and Brophy (1990) pointed out, most students do not possess sufficient test-taking abilities. In addition to learning and remembering the information, students must be able to apply their knowledge in different test-taking situations. Otherwise, test results may reflect the students' lack of knowledge concerning test-taking skills rather than their knowledge of the material or processes being assessed.

Test-taking skills are the abilities needed to prepare and study for tests, take tests, and review test results. Test-taking skills address several test-related areas: reading directions, organizing answers, and proofreading and checking responses, as well as thinking through questions prior to documenting answers. Although special students are frequently subjected to testing situations, teachers should not assume that these students are familiar with test-taking skills. Test-taking abilities can be learned through instruction and practice. Specifically, research (e.g., Ritter & Idol-Maestas, 1986) suggests that students with poor reading comprehension can benefit from instruction in test-taking skills. In turn, such instruction will assist educators in obtaining more accurate information and more meaningful test results.

Best practices in teaching test taking include

1. Showing students how to take different types of tests

2. Explaining different methods of study and types of materials necessary to study for objective and essay tests

3. Exploring with students the purposes for taking tests

4. Reviewing completed tests with students, highlighting test-taking errors

5. Ensuring that students know how much time is allotted for completion of a test

6. Exploring test-making procedures with students, explaining different types of questions

Library Use

Students at all grade levels are periodically required to use the library. The study skill of library use is concerned with the abilities needed to locate materials in a library. According to Wesson and Keefe (1989), this study skill involves familiarity with the catalog system, especially computerized systems; the location of films, filmstrips, resource guides, and curriculum materials; and the general layout and organization of the library. In addition, students need to know about the critical role the media specialist plays in the library and the support he or she can provide to students and teachers. By allowing students many opportunities to use the library facilities with guided instruction, teachers can help students to develop this important skill gradually and systematically. Mastropieri and Scruggs (1994) cautioned, however, that library facilities may appear unstructured and distracting to students accustomed to a highly structured classroom setting. Teachers must assist these students to become aware of the purpose of libraries prior to library assignments or visits.

Best practices in teaching library use include

1. Emphasizing the use and importance of the library within the overall educational program

2. Familiarizing students with the functions and organization of the school and classroom libraries

3. Periodically requiring the use of library materials in assigned tasks

4. Ensuring that the students are aware of the specific purpose of using the library when they are assigned a library activity

5. Encouraging students to use the media specialists and other library personnel as necessary

Reference Material/Dictionary Use

Two more study skills become important once specific material has been located in the classroom or school library. These pertain to using materials one has located—specifically, using a dictionary and other reference materials in connection with library research, report writing, and oral presentation. Harris and Sipay (1990) suggested four skills required to use these materials properly. These include understanding (1) the purposes of the table of contents and index; (2) alphabetical order; (3) the use of chapter headings as a quick reference; and (4) the way content is arranged within dictionaries, encyclopedias, and other reference materials. This study skill also includes knowledge of the functions of various reference materials. Special students will require practice in order to effectively master and maintain this study skill.

Best practices in teaching reference material/dictionary use include

1. Ensuring that all students have a dictionary readily available for their use

2. Providing assignments that require use of reference materials

3. Ensuring that each student possesses the reference material/dictionary use skills necessary to complete assigned tasks

4. Creating situations that teach students the use of these materials through direct application

5. Discussing the components of reference materials and dictionaries prior to their use for assignments

Time Management

Some students have difficulty organizing and managing their time, which may lead to incorrect or unfinished assignments. The study skill of time management involves allocating time effectively to facilitate completion of daily assignments and responsibilities. As students progress into the secondary level of education, work loads tend to increase, and effective time management becomes progressively more essential. As this occurs, teachers of special learners should structure learning situations in ways that assist students to manage their time effectively.

Best practices in teaching time management include

1. Rewarding students for effective use of time

2. Periodically creating situations in which students are required to budget their own time

3. Verbally encouraging on-task behaviors, especially during independent work times

4. Ensuring that students know the time allotted for completion of each activity

5. Providing sufficient time for students to manage their time as well as to complete assigned tasks

Self-Management of Behavior

In addition to managing time, many students must learn to manage their own behavior, especially during independent work time. Inappropriate behaviors can interfere seriously with task completion, even among students who possess sufficient study skills in other areas. Reiter, Mabee, and McLaughlin (1985) found that self-monitoring is an effective technique for reducing the time required for task completion and increasing time-on-task behaviors. Chapter 8 in this text provides a more detailed discussion of self-management, emphasizing the notion that self-management and control of behavior assist students to assume responsibility for their own behaviors. Effective self-management allows students to monitor their own behavior and change those behaviors that interfere with completion of assigned tasks. Programs concerned with self-control and self-management of behavior are described by Fagen, Long, and Stevens (1975) and Workman (1982). Such programs can help students with task completion as well as overall management of their own classroom behaviors.

Best practices in teaching self-management of behavior include

1. Ensuring that students are aware of specific behavioral expectations when they are completing specific tasks

2. Monitoring self-management programs and progress with students

3. Assisting students to set realistic goals in their self-management programs

4. Being consistent in the implementation of behavioral expectations

5. Allowing sufficient time (which will vary across students) for a self-management program to be implemented and effects tested

The Importance of Study Skills in Learning

Our quest as educators is to assist students in acquiring accurate and meaningful information. We also must ensure that accurate information is obtained from students to determine mastery. To be competent educators of students with learning and behavior disorders, we must be able to ascertain the difference between students' genuine lack of knowledge and an apparent lack of knowledge resulting from their inability to accurately record, demonstrate, or produce knowledge they possess. The accuracy with which students acquire and demonstrate knowledge is directly related to the study skills that they employ or fail to employ during the instruction and evaluation process.

According to Pauk (1984), effective usage of study skills represents efficient use of one's time and mind. Lock (1981) succinctly summarized the importance of study skills: "Successful students know how to study" (p. 3). Students must possess and make effective use of study skills in order to meet the daily demands placed upon them, especially during activities that are not highly teacher directed. These include independent research or library use, test preparation, completion of homework, transition between classes or rooms, and on-time completion of various assignments spanning as much as 1 or 2 months in time. Effective use of study skills in connection with these and similar tasks not only assists students to more easily and accurately complete assigned work but also reduces dependence on teachers. Students also may become better able to deal effectively with anxiety related to learning, as their approach to tasks such as note taking, outlining, listening, test taking, time management, and remembering information becomes more systematic. Specifically, students must develop and use study skills in order to

1. Complete assignments efficiently and effectively

2. Minimize wasted time in school

3. Complete work on time

4. Get the most out of any particular assignment

5. Complete tasks independently

6. Take charge of their own learning

7. Be responsible for their own learning

8. Proofread and review work carefully prior to submission to the instructor

9. Plan and carry out daily, weekly, or monthly schedules effectively

10. Make complex assignments less cumbersome and more manageable

11. Complete homework

12. Work with other classmates

A major goal of education is to teach students the skills they will need to lead independent and productive lives. An emphasis on the effective use of study skills may assist students with learning and behavior problems to acquire greater independence on completion of school. Although the discussion of study skills in this chapter primarily emphasizes their application in educational settings, use of these skills may facilitate learning in situations other than the school.

The Relevance of Study Skills Instruction for Students with Special Needs

Gearheart et al. (1992) found that students who exhibit learning problems frequently do not possess sufficient study skills to work proficiently in regular classes. In particular, Alley and Deshler (1979) observed that learning disabled adolescent students generally are not taught study skills at the elementary level. Other researchers have also documented the deficiency of study skills in students with special learning needs (Alley, Deshler, & Warner, 1979; Hoover & Collier, 1992; Salend, 1990; Schumaker, Sheldon-Wildgen, & Sherman, 1980).

Specifically, Mandlebaum and Wilson (1989) noted deficient note-taking, listening, test-taking, and scanning skills in learning disabled (LD) high school students. Link (1980) reported that secondary LD students have problems with several study skills, including note taking and skimming. T.E.C. Smith and Dowdy (1989) found that LD adolescents often experience difficulty organizing information.

Mercer and Mercer (1989) documented deficient test-taking skills among mildly handicapped students. Their research found that these learners may experience difficulty adapting to the format and tasks associated with standardized achievement tests. In support, Taylor and Scruggs (1983) noted that behavior disordered and learning disabled elementary students experience test-taking problems associated with format and distractors.

In the broader context of independent living, Stodden and Boone (1987) determined that many students with handicaps do not possess the skills needed to lead independent lives after they leave formal schooling. R. G. McKenzie (1991) noted that these widespread deficiencies in study skills among students with special learning problems suggest that an increased emphasis on the development and maintenance of effective study skills is needed in programs for special students at the elementary and secondary levels.

ASSESSING STUDY SKILLS

The primary goal of assessing the use of study skills is to determine which skills students use effectively to master the various elements of instruction. Meaningful study skill assessment provides answers to questions such as these:

1. Does the student adjust his or her reading rate appropriately when reading a selection?

2. How and in what ways does the student manage time?

3. Does the student possess and employ test-taking strategies?

4. Is the student able to record brief and accurate notes during a lecture or similar note-taking situation?

5. Does the student monitor and accept responsibility for his or her own behaviors?

The assessment of study skills should determine both what the student's status is relative to study skills and how the student employs particular study strategies. Students, for example, may be quite familiar with the procedures associated with a particular study skill strategy but fail to employ them effectively in actual classroom situations. Therefore, a meaningful assessment must include the collection and documentation of data on the use of study skills, based on observation and completion of assessment devices that reflect specific study skills necessary to successfully complete classroom-specific instructional tasks. Although a variety of both formal and informal devices exist for assessing study skills, many teachers find the informal devices and procedures to be of the most use as they implement ongoing study skills programs in their classrooms. However, an understanding of the strengths and potential weaknesses associated with norm- and criterion-referenced commercial devices will assist teachers in making informed decisions concerning the best method for assessing study skill proficiency among their students.

Norm-Referenced Instruments

The norm-referenced general achievement tests typically used in schools (e.g., *California Achievement Tests,* 1992; *Comprehensive Tests of Basic Skills,* 1990) devote at least one section or subtest to study skills. Although specific titles of study skills subtests vary among tests (e.g., Reference Skills, Study Skills, Reference Materials), the subtests are structured in similar ways, reflecting a narrow range of similar study skills. For example, the *California Achievement Tests* contain a subtest titled Reference Skills, which purports to assess the study skill areas of dictionary and reference material usage, map reading, use of catalog system, and reading and interpreting of tables and diagrams. As few as five questions are designed to assess each of these subareas. This type of general achievement instrument allows for comparison of students' performances and typically possesses adequate reliability and validity. However, given the limited scope and range of the study skill assessed, this type of instrument provides little information on actual use of study skills at the classroom level. Thus, this type of testing is of limited value for ongoing study skills programs in the classroom.

The use of norm-referenced general achievement tests to assess skills in lower achieving students requires special considerations. McLoughlin and Lewis (1990) noted that these measures often produce a low estimate of the performance of students with special needs. In addition, they say that group-administered tests frequently are timed, require answers to be recorded by the student, and assume that students have sufficient independent work skills, are capable of monitoring their time and behaviors, and are able to sustain attention to the tasks presented by the test. G. Wallace and Kauffman (1986) pointed out that these tests often include only a small number of items assessing study skills, and thus may not provide sufficient information for an adequate assessment. Although group tests may be used as screening devices to identify students who may require further assistance, care should be taken to interpret the results realistically in light of these potential problems.

In addition to norm-referenced general achievement instruments, other standardized measures have been developed for the specific purpose of assessing study skills. *The Study Skills Counseling Evaluation* (Demos, 1976) is a questionnaire that contains norms for secondary and postsecondary learners. This 50-item device assesses the study skill areas of (1) study-time distribution, (2) study conditions, (3) note taking, (4) test taking, and (5) other habits and attitudes associated with study skills. Another published standardized study skills instrument, the *Study Habits Checklist* (Preston & Botel, 1967), is designed for students in Grades 9 to 14 and assesses a variety of study skill areas. The checklist provides scores on 37 study skills and habits. Because this type of standardized instrument focuses exclusively on study skills, it may provide additional information beyond that generated by the typical norm-referenced general achievement test batteries. As a result, a study skills–specific device may be more useful for general screening and for making student comparisons. However, like the general achievement tests, this type of measure may lack the depth, scope, and relevance necessary to make classroom decisions concerning an ongoing study skills program.

Criterion-Referenced Instruments

Criterion-referenced tests can be used to measure mastery levels of particular skills. These tests should be used when the purpose of testing is to assist classroom teachers plan programs. Criterion-referenced tests identify specific study skills that students have mastered, as well as those that require additional attention, without regard for a student's standing relative to other learners of similar age and grade level.

A variety of criterion-referenced instruments are also available for assessing study skills. These tests typically provide a more complete assessment of various study skills than do the general achievement tests. However, criterion-referenced devices may also be limited with respect to the types of study skills covered. For example, *BRIGANCE Prescriptive Study Skills: Strategies and Practices* (Brigance, 1988) is devoted exclusively to the following types of study skills:

Outlining

Reading and interpreting maps and graphs

Reference material and dictionary use

Understanding and using parts of a book

Alphabetizing

Use of library catalog cards

Although a fairly thorough assessment of each of these areas is achieved through use of the BRIGANCE device, many other study skills often used by students are not covered. Thus, this device is appropriate for a complete assessment of selected reference skills and graph and map use, should these be the study skills targeted for assessment. For classroom application decisions that relate to other study skill areas, teachers may want to use criterion-referenced devices that focus on the specific study skills used by the students. However, one concern with published commercial devices, whether they are norm- or criterion-referenced instruments, is that they often contain items not of immediate importance to the teacher and they may exclude items of immediate relevance to a specific study skills program. As a result, informal assessment and use of teacher-made devices may be the best choices for conducting periodic assessment of student progress in ongoing study skills programs.

Informal and Teacher-Made Checklists

According to Gueron and Maier (1983), informal assessment relies on observations and interviews as well as tests to gather necessary information for immediate classroom application. This includes the use of teacher-made devices to assess specific study skill areas. Several informal inventories and checklists currently exist. *The Reading Difficulty Checklist* (Ekwall, 1992) covers effective use of reading rate and dictionary use. *The Study Skills Checklist* (Estes & Vaughan, 1985) assesses test taking, use of graphic aids, note taking, and outlining. The *Checklist of Reading Abilities* (Maier, 1980) also includes items associated with effective use of reading rate, use of graphic aids, reference material/dictionary use, library use, and note taking/outlining. The *Study Habits Inventory* (Devine, 1987) assesses time management, note taking/outlining, use of graphic aids, effective use of reading rate, library use, reference material/dictionary use, and report writing.

Many teachers of special students develop their own checklists. McLoughlin and Lewis (1990) suggested that teacher-made devices provide a quick and efficient way to gather information and to identify areas in which students require further assistance. According to Estes and Vaughan (1985), "informal analysis of students' study skills may be the easiest aspect of diagnosis for . . . helping students improve their learning abilities" (p. 120).

When study skills are assessed informally, teachers should follow steps such as those in Figure 9.2. This figure, generated from information documented by Hoover (1993b) and Estes and Vaughan (1985), illustrates several steps to follow to informally assess study skills:

1. Identify those study skills necessary to complete the assigned tasks or courses of study.

2. Construct a teacher's checklist based on the items identified. (As noted earlier, one concern with published devices is that they often contain items not of immediate importance to the teacher.)

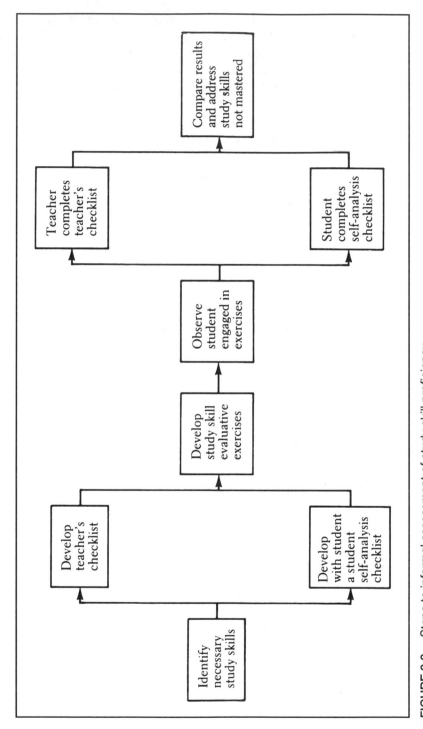

FIGURE 9.2. Steps to informal assessment of study skill proficiency.

Adapted from *Teaching Study Skills to Students with Learning Problems* (p. 47) by J. J. Hoover, 1993, Boulder, CO: Hamilton Publications.

Study Skills Inventory

Name: _____

Date (Pre): _____   Date (Post): _____

Study Skills	Pre	Post
Reading rate Scanning		
Skimming		
Normal rate		
Rapid reading		
Careful reading		
Listening Attends to listening tasks		
Applies meaning to verbal messages		
Filters out auditory distractions		
Notetaking/outlining Uses headings appropriately		
Takes brief and clear notes		
Records important information		
Uses for report writing		
Uses during lectures		
Constructs well organized outlines		
Has organized note card format		
Report writing Organizes thoughts		
Uses proper punctuation		
Uses proper spelling, grammar		
Oral presentation Participates freely		
Organizes presentation		
Uses gestures		
Speaks clearly		
Graphic aids Attends to relevant elements		
Understands purposes		
Incorporates in presentations		
Develops own visuals		

Study Skills	Pre	Post
Test taking Organizes answers		
Proofreads		
Reads and understands directions		
Identifies clue words		
Properly records responses		
Answers difficult questions last		
Narrows possible correct answers		
Corrects previous test-taking errors		
Library use Uses card catalog		
Can locate materials		
Understands organization of library		
Understands role of media specialist		
Reference/dictionary use Identifies components		
Uses guide words		
Understands uses of each		
Uses for written assignments		
Identifies different reference materials		
Time management Organizes daily activities		
Organizes weekly/monthly schedules		
Understands time management		
Reorganizes time when necessary		
Prioritizes activities		
Self-management of behavior Monitors own behavior		
Changes own behavior		
Thinks before acting		
Takes responsibility for own behavior		

Rating scale: 1 = not mastered; 2 = partial mastery/needs improvement; 3 = mastered.

FIGURE 9.3. Study Skills Inventory.

From *Teaching Study Skills to Students with Learning Problems* (p. 49) by J. J. Hoover, 1993, Boulder, CO: Hamilton Publications.

3. Construct a self-analysis checklist (similar to Item 2) to be completed by the students.

4. Develop and implement evaluative activities that require use of the desired study skills.

5. Observe the students during these activities, record results, and have students complete their self-analysis form.

6. Compare results obtained from the teacher's and students' completion of the checklists.

Adhering to these steps ensures that the informal assessment of study skills covers the elements important in determining students' proficiency at study skills and provides a systematic way for gathering data relevant to improving a study skills program in the classroom. Teachers can develop their own inventory, such as the one provided in Figure 9.3, if commercial study skill instruments are inappropriate for a particular situation. This instrument may be used along with the steps outlined for informal assessment of study skills.

TEACHING STUDY SKILLS

The first two sections of this chapter have provided various suggestions and ideas to help teachers assist students in acquiring and maintaining study skills. This final section presents various study strategies for students, as well as numerous teaching activities that facilitate improvement of study skills. This is not a comprehensive list of instructional strategies and activities, and not every method will be appropriate for all students with learning or behavioral problems. Individual needs and abilities must be considered when selecting strategies and activities for use with special learners. For additional information, the reader is referred to the specific sources cited.

Student Strategies

Study strategies are methods and procedures that students employ to complete learning activities. Fourteen established strategies are explored in this section. Strategies that pertain to reading are described first, followed by those for improving other study skill areas. Some of these strategies are presented in the literature within a learning-strategies model or format. Ritter and Idol-Maestas (1986) stated that "a learning-strategies model offers a problem-solving approach that is not restricted to applications specific to the context in which the strategy is taught" (p. 351). In the following discussions, however, each strategy is presented relative to specific study skills (e.g., effective use of reading rate, note taking, report writing, test taking). Table 9.2 lists the major skill areas emphasized by each student strategy.

TABLE 9.2. Study Strategies and Major Skill Areas Emphasized

STRATEGY	SKILL AREAS EMPHASIZED
SQ3R	Reading
PQ4R	Reading
OARWET	Reading
OK5R	Reading
Panorama	Reading
REAP	Reading, writing, thinking
ReQuest	Reading, questioning strategies
RARE	Reading
TQLR	Listening
GLP	Note taking
COPS	Written assignments
TOWER	Report writing
SCORER	Test taking
SQRQCQ	Word math problems

From *Teaching Study Skills to Students with Learning Problems* (p. 55) by J. J. Hoover, 1993, Boulder, CO: Hamilton Publications.

SQ3R

SQ3R is a popular study strategy in reading. It encompasses five procedural steps—*survey, question, read, recite,* and *review*—used to comprehend reading material. When using this method, students first survey the introductory statement, various headings, and summaries in an attempt to grasp the main idea of the reading selection or assignment. Surveying also includes paying specific attention to graphic aids. The students then formulate questions about the reading selection in an effort to identify the purpose for reading the material. These include who, what, where, why, and how questions. The third step involves reading the material and attending specifically to the questions generated. Upon completion of the reading, students attempt to answer the questions without direct reference to the selection. Finally, the readers review the material and any notes compiled during the reading to verify the answers.

In regard to students with special learning needs, several suggestions should be considered. A slight variation in the SQ3R procedures was suggested by Ekwall and Shanker (1985), who proposed that some students document the answers to the questions as soon as the answers are encountered, rather than waiting until the entire selection has been read. Also, Alley and Deshler (1979) suggested that SQ3R should be individualized for special students, whereas Wallace and Kauffman (1986) noted that this strategy requires practice and that it is best used relative to specific content material being read. If SQ3R is implemented appropriately based on learning needs, Mercer and Mercer (1989) suggested that this strategy may provide a systematic approach to improve study skills.

PQ4R

PQ4R is a variation of the SQ3R method designed to assist the learner to become a more discriminating and systematic reader. This strategy contains the elements of *preview, question, read, reflection, recite,* and *review.* The process is similar to the SQ3R method except that a reflection stage is added. During the reflection stage of PQ4R, the student rereads various parts of the selection that were unclear initially. This step aids students in organizing their thoughts as they seek answers to the questions. Woolfolk (1990) wrote that this strategy helps students to make connections between old and new information and is appropriate for use with older students.

OARWET and OK5R

Two other variations of the SQ3R strategy are OARWET, which refers to *overview, achieve, read, write, evaluate,* and *test,* and OK5R, which refers to *overview, key idea, read, record, recite, review,* and *reflect.* These strategies are similar to the SQ3R method, with selected elements added or further delineated. Pauk (1984) suggested that these alternatives may prove useful with students who have difficulty with the SQ3R approach.

Panorama

Devised by Edwards (1973), *Panorama* includes three stages. In the first stage (preparatory stage), the purpose for reading the material is determined, the most appropriate reading rate is selected, and questions about the material are formulated based on the headings. In the second, or intermediate stage, the material is surveyed to determine the organizational format of the selection; then the material is read, and notes are taken relative to the formulated questions. The last stage (concluding stage) involves memorizing the material with the aid of outlines and summaries; an evaluation component determines retention.

REAP

The REAP strategy is designed to improve reading, thinking, and writing skills. Developed by Eanet and Manzo (1976), REAP refers to *read, encode, annotate,* and *ponder.* Initially, the students read the material and then write the author's message in their own words (encode). During the annotate stage, the reader must "differential the author's ideas, translate them into his own language, and then summarize the results in writing" (Wallace & Kauffman, 1986, p. 295). This is accomplished through use of one or more annotations (i.e., summary, question, critique, motivation, heuristic, thesis, intention). Through this approach, the author's main ideas are summarized and relationships among various aspects of the author's message are determined. The author's purpose and motives are explored, along with significant questions addressed by the author. In addition, the readers' reactions to the author's thesis are considered. The final stage in this strategy provides students with the opportunity to think and engage in discussions about the author's message.

ReQuest

ReQuest (Manzo, 1985) assists students in relating previously learned knowledge to new learning. ReQuest refers to *reciprocal questioning*. It encourages learners to question prior to reading and to base the reading activity on anticipated questions. The teacher and students take turns asking questions about the initial sentence(s) in a selection. The questions generated by the teacher should help students realize the knowledge they already possess relative to the topic, as well as serve as a model for the types of questions the students may ask when it is their turn. The person who responds to a question does so with his or her book closed. As the teacher and students take turns asking each other questions about additional sentences in the first few paragraphs, the teacher provides feedback on the quality of questions asked by the students. This procedure is continued until the students are capable of projecting answers to questions such as "What do you think you will find out in the rest of the selection?" (Estes & Vaughan, 1985, p. 149). This strategy is best used in individual or small-group situations and, according to Harris and Sipay (1990), requires students to possess sufficient word-recognition skills.

RARE

RARE is a reading comprehension strategy discussed by Gearheart, DeRuiter, and Sileo (1986). RARE refers to *reviewing* the questions at the end of the reading selection, *answering* any questions one can, carefully *reading* the selection, and *expressing* answers to the questions one was unable to answer initially. Students may already possess enough knowledge about the topic of a passage to answer one or more of the comprehension questions, or they may be able to gain sufficient knowledge through skimming the material. They then read the material carefully (study-type reading) to obtain answers to the rest of the questions. Thus, like other study strategies designed to improve reading performance, RARE emphasizes reading for a specific purpose (i.e., to answer comprehension questions related to the reading selection).

TQLR

Developed by Tonjes and Zintz (1981), the TQLR strategy is designed to help students become better listeners. It comprises *tuning in, questioning, listening,* and *reviewing.* The strategy requires initially that listeners be ready for the verbal communication. Listeners should attempt to identify the position the speaker will take and then listen for the actual position taken. As the verbal communication continues, listeners should generate questions about the topic, and, upon completion of the talk, mental review should occur to ensure that the important points are remembered.

GLP

GLP, which stands for *Guided Lecture Procedure* (Kelly & Holmes, 1979), is a strategy to facilitate effective note taking during lecture situations. Prior to the lecture, students are told the purposes and objectives of the lecture and allotted time to write them down. During the initial part of the lecture, the lecturer stops and students are given time to write, in shortened form, all the information they can recall from the lecture. After the remaining portion of the lecture has been completed, students discuss the entire lecture in small groups with teacher guidance, taking notes as information is shared. The actual lecture notes are developed during this time. After the small-group activity, the lecture content and the GLP process are reflected upon by the students, and the main points of the lecture are summarized (in narrative form) without benefit of the notes developed previously. In addition to improving note-taking skills, the GLP strategy motivates students by involving them actively in the lecture situation.

COPS and TOWER

COPS is a strategy for monitoring errors in written assignments (Schumaker et al., 1981). It employs four questions that pertain to important aspects of a written assignment: "Have I *capitalized* all words requiring capitalization?" "How is the *overall appearance* of the work?" (This includes spacing, indentation, sentence structure, and legibility.) "Have I used *punctuation* appropriately?" "Have I used correct *spelling* throughout the written material?" (Mercer & Mercer, 1989).

TOWER is a strategy that may be employed prior to and during the actual writing assignment (e.g., reports, themes). TOWER refers to *think, order ideas, write, edit,* and *rewrite.* COPS and TOWER may be used together to encompass the outlining, drafting, and editing of a written work (Mercer & Mercer, 1989).

SCORER

SCORER is a strategy designed to assist learners with test taking (Carman & Adams, 1972). The acronym refers to *schedule* time, look for *clue words, omit* difficult questions, *read* carefully, *estimate* answers, and *review* the work. Students begin by planning how they will use the time allotted for taking the test; they review the entire test to identify easy and difficult items, varying point values assigned to items, and the number of items. Students then search for clue words, such as "usually," "never," or "sometimes." In true–false items, the words "usually" and "sometimes" often indicate a true statement, whereas the words "never" and "always" frequently signal false items.

Students work through the test, leaving the more difficult items until last; these should be marked for easy identification (e.g., by placing a check mark in the margin next to any item that is not answered initially). Careful reading of the test questions and directions is always necessary. For those items that require calculations, the students estimate the answers before doing the actual calculations in order to eliminate obviously wrong answers and reduce careless errors. Once the test has been completed, each answer is reviewed carefully.

In their discussion of the use of SCORER with students with poor reading comprehension, Ritter and Idol-Maestas (1986) wrote that these learners "could benefit from instruction in a test-taking approach" (p. 355).

SQRQCQ

The SQRQCQ strategy, developed by Fay (1965), assists students with word problems in math. It involves six steps: *surveying* the word problem, deciding what *question* is being asked, *reading* the problem more carefully, *questioning* the processes required to obtain the answer, *computing* the answer, and *questioning* again to ascertain whether the problem was answered correctly and logically.

Teaching Activities

The remainder of this section lists a variety of activities teachers can use to aid students in the acquisition and maintenance of study skills, along with suggestions for parents to help their children at home. Activities are presented for each major study skill area discussed in this chapter. These activities, which emphasize practice in the use of study skills via planned learning activities, are drawn from my experience and the work of Devine (1987), Harris and Sipay (1990), Mercer and Mercer (1989), and Wallace and Kauffman (1986).

Effective Use of Reading Rate

1. Instruct students to examine reading material prior to reading it, in order to determine approximate level of difficulty.

2. Give students a written passage from which selected key words have been omitted. Instruct students to provide the missing words after reading the passage at different reading rates. Discuss the effects of different rates on their ability to determine the missing words.

3. Instruct students to scan several paragraphs to find a particular name, and then ask for a specific contextual detail given at that point in the story.

4. Instruct students to review the index of a book in order to find specific selected topics and state the numbers of the pages on which these topics are discussed.

5. Encourage students to select a reading passage and then generate questions that would be answered using different reading rates.

6. After presenting new words to students, instruct them to scan the story and find the first time each word is used.

7. Give students the opportunity to employ various reading rates in the same situation by requesting answers to general and specific-detail questions.

Listening

1. Prior to lecturing, write an outline of the lecture on the board. At strategic points in the lecture, stop and ask students to identify on the outline the next point to be discussed.

2. Upon completion of a lecture, instruct students to outline its important points.

3. At strategic points during a lecture, ask students to summarize the material just presented and to predict the next topic to be covered.

4. Instruct students to identify various sounds they hear during the day. Discuss potential problems that may arise if these sounds occur during a lecture situation.

5. Have students listen for special sequencing words or phrases (e.g., "first," "second," "in summary").

6. Instruct one student to interview a second student about a specific topic while a third student observes the interview. Upon completion of the interview, each student summarizes what was said. Interpretations of the interviews are then compared.

7. Ask students to paraphrase directions for various assignments (e.g., homework, independent work, spelling assignment).

8. Instruct students to generate a list of "good listener" guidelines (e.g., looking at the person speaking, remaining quiet) and post them in a strategic position in the room.

9. At the start of a lecture, inform students that it contains one or more factual errors. Instruct students to be prepared to identify the error(s) when the lecture is over.

10. Prior to a lecture, list on the board several questions that will be addressed in the lecture. Discuss the questions after the lecture has been completed.

11. Prior to a lecture, list on the board, out of sequence, the most important topics of the lecture. Upon completion of the lecture, instruct students to arrange the topics in the order of their presentation.

Note taking / Outlining

1. Place an outline of a reading selection on the blackboard, read the material with the students, and review and discuss the outline.

2. Ask students to outline a major topic or story covered on a radio or television news program.

3. Have students take notes on a brief lecture you present, and then ask them to compare their notes.

4. Write a skeleton outline of a reading selection on the board, but fill in only the main headings. Instruct students to read the selection and complete the outline.

5. Provide students with a skeleton outline and a list of words on a topic. Instruct them to complete the outline, using the list of words to generate main ideas, subheadings, and specific details.

6. Present students with note cards that contain sufficient information to write a brief paragraph on the topic. Have them write a paragraph, summarizing the contents of the note cards.

7. Give students a series of note cards that describe events pertaining to a familiar topic. Scramble the note cards, and instruct students to arrange the cards in proper sequence.

8. Provide students with note cards that contain everything except topic headings. Instruct them to read each card and generate possible topic headings.

9. Have students read a passage and complete note cards on it.

10. Assign peers to review other students' notes with them after a lecture or other note-taking activity so as to ensure that the essential information was documented.

Report Writing / Oral Presentation

1. Review rules of punctuation and capitalization prior to beginning a written assignment.

2. Instruct students to prepare both a written and an oral report on the same topic and discuss advantages and disadvantages of each.

3. Provide students with a paragraph in which no capital letters have been used. Instruct them to edit the paragraph and capitalize appropriate words.

4. Have students make oral presentations in different situations (e.g., one-to-one, small group, whole class).

5. Help students develop a monthly newspaper, ensuring that each student makes some contribution.

6. Give students assignments for which they must summarize lengthy material.

7. Provide students with an outline of a topic. Instruct them to generate a written or oral narrative summary of the ideas covered in the outline.

8. Have students write and share letters similar to those found in newspaper columns.

9. Instruct students to record notes for a research paper on index cards and then sort them into proper sequence.

10. Give students a paragraph containing both complete and incomplete sentences. Ask them to identify the sentences of each type.

11. Provide students with opportunities to gather or share information orally through various means (e.g., debates, interviews, investigative reporting).

Use of Graphic Aids

1. Ask students to bring maps of their community to school, and challenge them to find the shortest routes to various places.

2. Provide students with a graphic aid, and ask questions that can be answered only by studying the visual.

3. Instruct students to review only the picture within a reading selection and then write what they believe to be the main ideas in the material.

4. Have students find examples of and explain different types of graphs (e.g., picture, circle, pie, bar, line).

5. Provide students with different types of maps (e.g., road, political, weather), and have them identify similarities and differences among them.

6. Have students practice making and labeling their own graphic aids.

7. Provide students with some written material, and ask them to develop graphic aids for it.

Test Taking

1. Provide students with sample questions from various tests (e.g., multiple choice, true–false, essay), and discuss how they might approach each type of question to determine the answer.

2. Identify and discuss vocabulary terms often found in test directions (e.g., *compare, contrast, match, evaluate*).

3. Instruct students to write on the test form any facts or formulas that they memorized previously, as well as ideas that may pertain to specific questions.

4. Present and discuss the following test-taking guidelines for completing multiple-choice items: know the number and kind of answers to select, remember the question, narrow the possibilities

by eliminating obviously wrong answers, and record each answer carefully.

5. Have students indicate how they obtained the answers to sample test questions and identify possible clues in the questions.

6. Instruct students to outline reading material to be covered in an exam and anticipate potential essay, true–false, or multiple-choice questions.

7. Review previous tests with students and discuss ways their performances might be improved through the use of test-taking hints.

8. Have students generate different types of test questions from the same material. Discuss similarities and differences in the types of information required to answer the various questions.

9. Familiarize students with general test-taking guidelines: review the entire test, know the time allotted for completion of the test, know the point values of different test items, read and reread the directions and questions, identify clue words in questions, and respond to more difficult items after the easier questions have been answered.

Library Use

1. Have students make visual displays that show how to use the catalog system and reference materials and how to check out library material.

2. Give each student a different card or printout from the catalog system and have the student identify all types of information shown.

3. Have students complete subject and author cards for a selection from the school library and then compare their cards with the actual catalog cards or computerized system.

4. Allow students to develop their own classroom library, complete with a catalog system.

5. Give students a library assignment and instruct them to identify the locations in the library of the materials they use to complete the assignment.

6. Explain the computer printout resulting from a computer search, and ask each student to find an article or document listed on the printout.

7. Have students make a graphic display of the organization of their school library, with the locations of different types of resources and materials highlighted.

Reference Material / Dictionary Use

1. Ask each student to provide his or her own definition of a word and compare it with the dictionary definition.

2. Give students the name of a place, and ask them to identify the different types of information about the place that various reference materials (e.g., atlas, encyclopedia) supply.

3. Instruct students to identify the dictionary's guide words for a selected word.

4. Provide students with some information about a specific topic within a reading selection. Have them identify the index entry word(s) most appropriate for gaining further information about the topic.

5. Supply students with various questions, and ask them to identify the reference materials they might consult to answer the questions.

6. Give a small group of students an assignment that requires the use of various reference materials. Assign each student in the group a different task for which different reference materials are needed. Have the students discuss the types of information gathered from their respective reference materials.

Time Management

1. Assign a group of students a task, and tell them to discuss how they will budget their time to complete the task.

2. Instruct students to estimate the amount of time needed to complete a task and then compare the estimate with the actual amount of time required.

3. Ask students to record how they spend their time outside of school. Discuss the distribution of time with them.

4. Instruct students to keep a notebook in which they record daily assignments and due dates.

5. Have students construct a semester calendar on which are marked dates for tests, papers, and events.

6. Provide students with a timer that they set prior to beginning a series of assigned tasks. Have them record the number of tasks completed within the time they allotted, as well as the actual time required to complete all the tasks. The timer may also be used to time the completion of one specific task.

7. Instruct students to list their daily or weekly activities in the order of importance, list them again in the order in which they are actually completed, and compare the two lists.

8. Allow students opportunities to share their time management procedures with their classmates.

Self-Management of Behavior

1. Instruct each student to develop a self-monitoring chart for a selected behavior and to enter a check mark on it each time he or

she exhibits the behavior. Review each student's results with him or her.

2. Provide students with an alternative place in the classroom in which to complete their work. Allow students the freedom to choose their work place.

3. Lead students in activities that relate to evaluating consequences prior to taking action (e.g., "What might happen if . . . ?").

4. Role-play problem situations that have several possible solutions. Discuss the implications of each solution.

5. Prior to beginning an assignment, discuss options available to students if assigned work is completed and if it is not completed.

6. Provide students with opportunities to distinguish thoughts from actions. For example, allow students to respond to the question "Have you ever thought of doing something but decided not to?" Explore reasons why it was a good idea not to engage in the activity.

Encouraging Parental Support of Study Skills Development

Ongoing study skills programs help students to acquire and maintain study skill proficiency throughout school. Just as a program in school should be developed and followed, so should a home-based program. Teachers can and should encourage study skill usage at school, and parents may provide valuable support at home to the efforts provided by educators. The emphasis on study skills development at home serves several important purposes in students' overall education. These include

1. Ongoing parental involvement with children's progress in school

2. Reinforcement at home of study skills learned and used in school

3. Parent understanding of potential problems encountered by children through examination of their study habits related to different assignments

4. Parent opportunity to help children learn from previous errors as study skill abilities are practiced and developed at home

5. Improvement in children's ability to complete homework or other tasks in a timely and efficient manner

Involvement with study skills development provides rewarding experiences for both parents and children. Teachers should discuss their study skills programs with parents and encourage their support at home. By providing parents with suggestions for helping study skill development at home, the overall education process is strengthened. The following types of activities for developing study skills at home should be shared with parents and supported by teachers:

1. Discuss different study skills with children to help them see their importance in learning and in completing assigned tasks.

2. Discuss with children how they approach different learning tasks and explore their use of different study skills.

3. Demonstrate the proper use of needed study skills during homework or other related tasks.

4. Identify a specific time and place for after-school studying at home.

5. Discuss children's completed assignments and tests on a regular basis to help them see why using different study skills contributed to correct responses.

6. Point out and discuss apparent study skill errors from results of completed assignments and tests.

7. Emphasize the importance of study skills as a means to assume responsibility for one's own learning.

8. Encourage and help children in the overall planning, organizing, and evaluation of their use of study skills to complete assigned work.

As students progress through school, their continued use of study skills in school and at home allows them to become more responsible for their own learning and facilitates the proper development and use of study habits. Figure 9.4 is an easy-to-use rating scale for parents to document their perceptions of their child's study skill abilities. This may serve as a beginning point in building a school–home study skills program. This rating scale should be used in conjunction with other assessment devices discussed in this chapter. Discussions with parents about study skills development should occur after completion of the rating scale, with specific suggestions for parents to help students in the home. For additional information on this topic, the reader is referred to Hoover (1993a, 1993b).

APPLICATION ACTIVITIES

Teachers may assign the following activities for students to apply their knowledge of study skills.

1. Develop a study skills project illustrating how the learning components (acquisition, recording, location, organization, synthesis, memorization, and integration) are directly influenced by effective use of study skills.

2. Discuss specific types of difficulties students with learning problems often experience with study skill usage in the classroom.

Study Skills Home Inventory

Student: _____   Date: _____

Based on your observations and interactions with your child at home, rate each of the following study skill items as exhibited by your child using the following scale:

1 = Not mastered (infrequent use of skill);   **2** = Partially mastered (needs some improvement);   **3** = Mastered (regular and appropriate use of skill)

Study Skill	Subskills	Rating
Reading Rate	1. Uses fast-paced reading rates (skimming, scanning, rapid reading)	_____
	2. Uses normal, careful, or study-type reading rates	_____
Listening	1. Attends to listening tasks	_____
	2. Applies meaning to verbal messages	_____
Note taking/ Outlining	1. Uses headings appropriately	_____
	2. Records important information	_____
	3. Takes well-organized notes	_____
	4. Takes clear and concise notes	_____
Report Writing	1. organizes thoughts	_____
	2. Uses proper punctuation	_____
	3. Uses correct grammar	_____
Oral Presentations	1. Freely participates in oral activities	_____
	2. Speaks clearly	_____
Graphic Aids	1. Understands purposes of visual material	_____
	2. Develops own graphic aids	_____
	3. Attends to relevant elements in graphic aid	_____

Study Skill	Subskills	Rating
Test Taking	1. Organizes written answers or responses	_____
	2. Reads and understands directions	_____
	3. Identifies test-taking errors	_____
	4. Corrects previous test-taking errors	_____
	5. Identifies and uses clue words	_____
Library Usage	1. Understands and uses catalog system	_____
	2. Is able to locate library materials	_____
Reference Materials	1. Knows purposes of different reference materials	_____
	2. Uses reference materials when necessary	_____
Time Management	1. Organizes daily/weekly activities	_____
	2. Prioritizes activities	_____
	3. Completes tasks on time	_____
	4. Reorganizes time as necessary	_____
Self-Management of Behavior	1. Monitors own behavior	_____
	2. Is responsible for own behavior	_____
	3. Changes own behavior as necessary	_____

Summary Comments:

Figure 9.4. Study Skills Home Inventory.
From Teaching Study Skills to Students with Learning Problems (pp. 84–85) by J. J. Hoover, 1993, Boulder, CO: Hamilton Publications.

3. Select two study skills and present an overview of their use and purposes in the classroom.

4. Prepare and deliver a brief presentation on the importance of teaching study skills throughout school, beginning in the early elementary grades.

5. Discuss the most important factors to consider when assessing study skills.

6. Identify the strengths and weaknesses of using norm- and criterion-referenced devices for assessing study skills.

7. Develop and present a process for informally assessing study skill use in an elementary or secondary classroom.

8. Assess a student's study skills abilities using an informal assessment device, and prepare a written report of the results.

9. Select five study strategies and present an overview of the strategies and how they may be used within the classroom.

10. Develop a plan for implementing a classroom study skills program following the five guidelines presented in this section.

11. Select one study skill (e.g., listening, test taking, library usage) and develop a program for teaching the skill in different content and class activities. Include use of student study strategies as well as teaching activities in the program.

12. Create and implement a plan for helping parents to assist students at home with the development of study skills. Include at least two study skills in the plan.

Chapter 10

Transition from School to Independent Living

J. LEE WIEDERHOLT AND CAROLINE DUNN

U p to this point, the chapters in this book have focused on areas of formal education that are familiar to most professionals (i.e., language, the "3 Rs," and deportment/conduct). This chapter deals with another important aspect of education that may be less familiar to many readers but that is used frequently with students who have learning and/or behavior problems. Specifically, this chapter focuses on educational endeavors that develop students' independent living skills. The first section describes the nature of transition from school to independent living, the second section overviews commonly used assessment techniques, and the third section discusses teaching programs and activities used to foster independent living.

TRANSITION TO INDEPENDENT LIVING

Many sources note that a significant number of students leave school without having mastered the skills needed to successfully and independently manage everyday living (Edgar, 1987; Kokaska & Brolin, 1985; National Commission on Excellence in Education, 1983; Wagner, 1989; Will, 1984). Many of these individuals are unable to establish themselves in jobs, handle their money, plan nutritious meals, develop healthy relationships with others, or the like. Individuals with learning and behavior problems are especially at risk. For over a decade, follow-up and follow-along studies (Affleck, Edgar, Levine, & Kortering, 1990; Blackorby, Edgar, & Kortering, 1991; Edgar, 1987; Halpern, Close, & Nelson, 1986; L. Harris, 1986; Sittington & Frank, 1993; White, Schumaker, Warner, Alley, & Deshler, 1980) have indicated that, compared with their nondisabled peers, adults with disabilities experience (1) a higher unemployment and/or underemployment rate, (2) lower pay, (3) more restricted participation in community activities and leisure-time activities, (4) more social dissatisfaction with employment, and (5) more dependency on parents or others.

In attempting to remedy this situation, school personnel over the years have developed programs to better prepare students for adult life. Career education, vocational education, work-study programs, transition planning, and community-based training are all examples of programs designed to facilitate skill development with independent living in mind. The hope has been that participation in these programs will help students to function independently upon leaving school.

This training is especially critical in light of the fact that many students and their families have come to expect the kinds of services and security offered to them through the public school system. Moving to eligibility-based adult services after having grown accustomed to mandatory service provision is a difficult task. Efforts must be made to ensure that students acquire an awareness of resources available in the community as well as learn the functional life skills they need in order to be successful. This section provides a general orientation to the concepts of transition and independent living.

Transition

In everyday parlance, the word *transition* refers to the process of changing from one form, state, subject, or place to another. The word transition has a very specific meaning in education. It refers most frequently to the movement of students from secondary school into adult life. Less frequently, transition also refers to movement of a student from kindergarten to elementary school or from elementary school to secondary school. Increasingly, it has begun to refer to the transition of students from separate instructional programs into more inclusive instructional settings. In this chapter, however, the discussion of transition is limited primarily to students who are moving from secondary schools into adult settings.

Educational efforts in helping students in this transition are now mandated by law. The Individuals with Disabilities Education Act (IDEA) of 1990 (P.L. 101-476) requires that the Individualized Education Plans (IEPs) for students include a statement of needed transition services. Specifically, a statement of transition service and the identification of various interagency responsibilities must be part of the IEPs of all students with disabilities who are 16 years old or older. The law defines transition services as

> a coordinated set of activities for a student, designed within an outcome-oriented process, which promotes movement from school to postschool activities including postsecondary education, vocational training, integrated employment (including supported employment), continuing and adult education, adult services, independent living or community participation. [20 U.S.C. 1401 (A) (19)]

Cronin and Patton (1993) noted that a comprehensive individual transition plan should address the major areas for which students need to be prepared prior to their leaving school. This might involve teaching students specific skills needed in subsequent environments. The plan also might involve helping students establish linkages with postsecondary services. Cronin and Patton pinpointed six domains where transition services might need to be provided. These include (1) employment/education, (2) home and family, (3) leisure pursuits, (4) community involvement, (5) emotional/physical health, and (6) personal responsibility and relationships. Their book, *Life Skills Instruction for All Students with Special Needs: A Practical Guide for Integrating Real-Life Content into the Curriculum,* details how to develop and implement life skills curricula and instruction, which is a critical component of a school-to-work transition.

Independent Living

Prior to developing a transition program, one must first delineate the requirements needed for independent living. In earlier decades, most of the focus on what was required for independent living related to years in school and/or basic literacy in reading, mathematics, and so on. For example, in 1965, the U.S. Office of Education noted that 4 years of elementary school and functional literacy in math, reading, and writing, as well as a general understanding of everyday life activities, such as banking, working, maintaining a home, and so on, were indicators of the ability to function independently in society (Wiederholt, Cronin, & Stubbs, 1980).

In 1975, the Adult Performance Level (APL) study funded at The University of Texas by the U.S. Office of Education expanded and more specifically defined the concept of independent living. Northcutt (1975) described the APL study and outlined four critical aspects of adult functional independence. First, functional independence was seen as a concept meaningful only in a specific societal context. A person considered independent in one environment may be dependent in another. For example, someone who grew up on a farm in rural North Dakota might perform competently at home but may be functionally incompetent in an urban environment such as New York City. Also, the requirements for independence were believed to change as society evolves. The continued increase of interest in students' becoming computer literate is an example of a response to society's evolution.

Second, functional independence was seen as two dimensional and was described as a set of skills (reading, writing, speaking/listening/viewing, problem solving, interpersonal relationships, and computation) applied to a set of *general knowledge* areas (consumer economics, occupational knowledge, health, community resources, and government and law). Each skill related to significant competency needed in a knowledge area. For example, a patient using his or her ability to read and to follow a doctor's orders was thought of as applying an essential skill (reading) under a general knowledge area (health).

Third, persons were viewed as functionally independent only to the extent that they could meet the requirements extant at a given time. Specifically, functional independence was seen as a dynamic rather than a static state. Case in point: As people age, they typically develop more and more sophisticated levels of skills and adaptive behaviors, peak in terms of both physical and mental prowess, and then gradually become less functionally independent in their later years. Finally, functional independence was viewed as being directly related to success in adult life. More independent adults would likely also be more fiscally and interpersonally successful. Such individuals would tend to be well integrated into society at large.

Wiederholt and Larsen (1983), although in basic agreement with this model of functional independence, added a third dimension to the two-dimensional (skills and knowledge) model of the APL group. The third dimension they proposed was that of *application,* which referred to the day-to-day use of skills and knowledge. Wiederholt and Larsen noted that a person could be knowledgeable about a subject and possess an adequate level of required skills but still not choose to perform certain tasks. In other words, individuals exercise choice in the selection of ways in which they wish to perform.

The 1980s evidenced an increased and expanded interest in the matter of choice in independent living. Knowlton, Turnbull, Backus, and Turnbull (1988) argued cogently for including choice concerns in teaching skills necessary for independent living. They stated that independent living included being able to choose "how to live one's life within one's inherent capacities and means, and in a way consistent with one's personal values and preferences" (p. 46). They suggested that, in contrast to traditional thinking about independent living, the newer thinking did not put primary emphasis on the acquisition of skills so one might perform tasks; instead, emphasis was placed on skill development concurrent with expanded opportunities for making choice decisions.

Two important themes have emerged regarding making choices: self-determination and quality of life. Halloran (1993), who served as coordinator of transition programs at the Office of Special Education and Rehabilitative Services, U.S. Department of Education, has identified self-determination as one of five educational issues shaping the 1990s and considers it to be the ultimate goal of education. Deci and Ryan (1985) defined self-determination as the "capacity to choose and to have those choices be the determinants of one's actions" (p. 38). Self-determination encompasses independence, self-sufficiency, and the capacity to make informed decisions. Mithaug, Martin, Agran, and Rusch (1988) stressed that expanding students' role in directing their own affairs should be the primary goal of education for all students.

Quality of life, the second theme, is a complex construct, as reflected by the existence of numerous definitions. For example, Parmenter (1988) suggested that quality of life "represents the degree to which an individual has met his/her needs to create their own meanings so that they can establish and sustain a viable self in the social world" (p. 9). Goode (1990) stated that

> when an individual, with or without disabilities, is able to meet important needs in major life settings (work, school, home, community) while also satisfying the normative expectations that others hold for him or her in those settings, he or she is more likely to experience a high quality of life. (p. 46)

Parent (1993) identified a common point throughout these and other definitions—the significance of individual preferences and personal perceptions in determining what quality of life comprises.

Further expanding on the quality-of-life theme, Halpern (1993) proposed a taxonomy that reflects content relevant to the concept (see Table 10.1). The taxonomy comprises three broad domains, which include 15

TABLE 10.1.   Quality-of-Life Domains

Physical and Material Well-Being
• Physical and mental health
• Food, clothing, and lodging
• Financial security
• Safety from harm

Performance of Adult Roles
• Mobility and community access
• Vocation, career, employment
• Leisure and recreation
• Personal relationships and social networks
• Educational attainment
• Spiritual fulfillment
• Citizenship (e.g., voting)
• Social responsibility (e.g., not breaking laws)

Personal Fulfillment
• Happiness
• Satisfaction
• Sense of general well-being

From "Quality of Life as a Conceptual Framework for Evaluating Transition Outcomes" by A. S. Halpern, 1993, *Exceptional Children, 59,* pp. 486–498.

outcomes. Halpern explained that the outcomes for the first domain, physical and material well-being, include basic entitlements, such as safety from harm and food, clothing, and lodging, that should be available to everyone. The next level, performance of adult roles, encompasses the ways in which an individual can interact with his or her environment. Earlier discussions of independent living reflected the outcomes listed in this domain, including such skills as mobility and community access; vocation, career, and employment; and leisure and recreation. The final domain, personal fulfillment, is entirely person centered. Halpern argued that a "sense of personal fulfillment does not always correspond to the achievement of success, as commonly defined, in the various adult roles" (p. 491).

In sum, independent living is a concept that includes many components. An individual's ability to live independently requires both literacy skills and knowledge, as well as the ability to make informed choices about how one chooses to live in ways that meet personal quality-of-life needs. All of the variables need to be considered when developing transition plans. Those aspects of independent living that need to assessed in a student for transition planning are discussed in the next section.

ASSESSING INDEPENDENT LIVING SKILLS

In this section on assessing independent living skills, general assessment considerations are presented first. Next, the major types of assessments usually performed relative to independent living skills are discussed. These include standardized tests and other specific types of assessment procedures.

General Assessment Considerations

Two factors need to be considered when a student's independent living skills are assessed: the student as a whole person (functional skills, interests, values, cultural background, feelings about self and others, preferences, etc.) and the most likely next environment (work, postsecondary training, home and family management, etc.). Therefore, the student must be actively involved in the assessment process, and any academic or behavioral assessment should consider the demands of the next environment.

Student Involvement and Next Environment Considerations

Students being evaluated need to understand the purpose and results of their evaluation to the fullest extent possible. Full independence in a changing world requires the ability to continually evaluate and modify one's behavior based on the results of self-evaluation, as well as to make realistic, personally fulfilling choices. Ultimately, individuals must accept responsibility for the types of jobs they select, the people with whom they associate, the way they spend their time, their feelings about themselves, and so forth. Active involvement throughout the evaluation process affords students the optimal learning opportunity—that is, experience in directing their own affairs.

Evaluation of independent living skills requires that a student consider his or her life goals. This point is particularly important in regard to the student's self-understanding. Poor skill in math is a more serious deficit in a student who is intent on becoming an engineer than in a student who wants to be a musician. Poor money management skills are less of a concern if a student plans to live in a supervised group home than if a student plans to live alone. The key point is *congruence* between student characteristics and the most likely postschool environments. When incongruence is found, it serves as the point of intervention for either remediating the incongruence (i.e., improving the skill) or modifying the proposed career/life plan.

Table 10.2 presents some important areas that have a direct bearing on students' eventual independence. Each area is briefly defined. To achieve self-sufficiency, students must learn to consistently and realistically evaluate themselves in these areas. Students who cannot realistically self-evaluate will likely encounter problems in daily living.

Ensuring that students understand the purpose of assessment and actively participate in the evaluation process reinforces the idea that self-determination and self-evaluation are important lifelong processes. Life-skills assessment activities undertaken during elementary and secondary

TABLE 10.2. Important Areas of Independent Living Assessment

AREA	DEFINITION
Aptitudes/abilities	What one can do or has the potential to do
Daily living skills	How well one manages activities of domestication
Job-seeking skills	How successful one is at identifying and securing appropriate jobs
Interests	What one likes to do
Interpersonal skills	How one relates to others
Appearance	How one looks
Health	What physical strengths and limitations one has; prevention of health problems
Mobility	How one moves and travels within an environment
Values	What one believes in or desires
Attitudes	How one feels about self, others, and things
Expectations	What goals one has; how much power one feels one has
Work history	What work-related activities one has performed, how well, and for how long

years provide an excellent opportunity for teaching learners these lifelong processes.

Assessment in Other Areas

The results of assessments used to determine a student's abilities in academic or behavioral areas can also be used in independent living assessment. Results from techniques discussed throughout this book, such as standardized tests, teacher-made tests, checklists, Q-sorts, direct observation, role playing, and interviews, can provide information about a student's occupational or daily living capabilities.

Table 10.3 relates the subject areas of reading, writing, spelling, handwriting, mathematics, behavior, speaking, listening, and perceptual/motor to independent living areas typically assessed in adults. The possible results of deficits in these subject areas include restricted job choices, problems managing daily living, communication difficulties, problems establishing meaningful work or personal relationships, and unemployment or underemployment.

Those who assess independent living skills will want to use information already available about a student's abilities in academic and behavioral areas. The overall assessment process entails:

1. Compiling, summarizing, and integrating existing assessment information

2. Identifying problem areas or areas where more evaluation is necessary

3. Performing the required assessments

4. Assisting the student in understanding the meaning of the assessment

5. Analyzing, with the student, the implications of assessment information

TABLE 10.3. Relationship of Subject Areas to Independent Living Areas

SUBJECT AREAS	APTITUDE	INDEPENDENT LIVING AREAS								
		DAILY LIVING SKILLS	JOB-SEEKING SKILLS	INTERESTS	INTER-PERSONAL SKILLS	APPEARANCE	HEALTH	MOBILITY	VALUES	ATTITUDES
Reading	X	X	X	X	X	X	X	X		
Writing	X	X	X	X	X	X				
Spelling	X	X	X			X				
Handwriting	X		X			X				
Mathematics	X	X	X							
Behavior	X	X	X	X	X	X	X	X	X	X
Speaking	X	X	X		X	X			X	X
Listening	X	X	X	X	X	X		X	X	X
Perceptual/motor	X	X	X	X	X	X	X	X		

Standardized Tests of Independent Living

The types and formats of standardized procedures used to assess independent living skills are as varied as those used to assess academic and behavioral areas. Some tests are used to measure occupationally relevant areas, whereas others are used to measure daily living skills. Some are traditional paper-and-pencil tasks, others require extensive apparatus, and still others are behavior recording formats. Some have "right" answers and no time limits; others have no "right" answers and time limits. The general types of standardized procedures available and some representative examples are discussed in this section.

Occupations

Many factors are important to selecting an occupation (e.g., self-concept, genetic predisposition, needs, achievement orientation, personality, locus of control). Many of these are difficult to operationalize in standardized test formats. Therefore, standardized measures serve only as screening instruments and their results are only general indicators of occupations that should be included or excluded from consideration.

Individuals are matched to an occupation in three traditional ways: (1) occupational aptitude tests, (2) occupational interest tests, and (3) work-sample systems.

APTITUDE TESTING

Aptitudes are specific capacities required for an individual to perform or learn to perform a task. Each job can be analyzed to identify the major job elements and to specify the corresponding skills, knowledge, and traits necessary for successful performance. Aptitude tests are designed to measure either multiple or specific abilities.

From the beginning, aptitude tests have been plagued by low correlations between test performance and actual job performance. However, results from such tests can be useful to

1. Identify relatively strong and weak areas within an individual's abilities

2. Assist individuals to more realistically appraise their abilities

3. Broadly screen individuals into programs for which there are limited numbers of positions

Table 10.4 lists commonly used aptitude tests. One test, the *Occupational Aptitude Survey and Interest Schedule* (OASIS) (Parker, 1991), measures the aptitude of students in Grades 8 to 12. The test, normed on a national sample of 1,505 students from 13 states, can be administered to individuals, small groups, or complete classes in 30 to 40 minutes. The

TABLE 10.4. Commonly Used Aptitude Tests

TEST NAME	TARGET POPULATION
APTICOM (Vocational Research Institute, 1984)	High school students, adults
Differential Aptitude Test (Bennett, Seashore, & Wesman, 1982)	High school students
Detroit Tests of Learning Aptitude (Hammill, 1991)	School-age students
Detroit Tests of Learning Aptitude–Adult (Hammill & Bryant, 1991)	High school students, adults
General Aptitude Test Battery (United States Employment Service, 1982; Forms A/B, 1982, C/D, 1983)	High school and college students, adults
Microcomputer Evaluation and Screening Assessment (Valpar International Corporation, n.d.)	Adolescents, adults
Non-Reading Aptitude Test Battery (United States Employment Service, 1982)	High school and college students, adults
Occupational Aptitude Survey and Interest Schedule (Parker, 1991)	Junior high school and high school students
Talent Assessment Program (Talent Assessment, Inc., n.d.)	Special education high school students
Wechsler Adult Intelligence Scale–Revised (Wechsler, 1981)	High school students, adults

OASIS measures general ability, verbal aptitude, numerical aptitude, spatial aptitude, perceptual aptitude, and manual dexterity. Validity and reliability coefficients are acceptable. The numerical, spatial, and manual dexterity subtests are nonverbal. The verbal and perceptual subtests require the matching of words and phrases. Minimum aptitude scores for 120 occupations are presented in the test manuals, and scores are directly keyed to the *Dictionary of Occupational Titles* (1984), *Guide for Occupational Exploration* (1988), and *Worker Trait Group Guide* (Winefordner, 1991).

Several computerized vocational aptitude tests are now available. *APTICOM* (Vocational Research Institute, 1984) is a series of three multiple-item instruments. The aptitude battery measures general learning ability, verbal aptitude, numerical aptitude, spatial aptitude, form perception, clerical perception, motor coordination, finger dexterity, and eye–hand coordination. Tests are presented via panels mounted on *APTICOM,* a portable computerized desk-top console. Another computerized test is the *Microcomputer Evaluation and Screening Assessment* (MESA) (Valpar International Corporation, n.d.). MESA is a multiple-item computer-administered test measuring 21 factors of the Worker Qualifications Profile as defined in the U.S. Department of Labor's *Dictionary of Occupational Titles.* No reading is required on the computer terminal, and there is a high level of interaction between the student and the evaluator.

INTEREST TESTING

Interest tests seek to identify an individual's interest in activities relating to occupational fields. The matching of personal interests with job characteristics is considered an important element in job success. For instance, a person who has a high aptitude in math but dislikes the subject is not likely to succeed in an engineering job; likewise, a person who is interested in engineering but lacks the basic math skills is unlikely to complete preparatory math courses.

Interest tests generally present the test takers with a series of items in which they must choose among several activities. The following is a sample question:

> Would you rather
> > Read a book
> > Read a book to someone else
> > Write a book

Most tests have an extensive number of items covering broad areas of human activity. Scoring criteria for the items are developed by administering the item pool to groups of people with known interests (e.g., plumbers, people in business careers). Scores are then reported for general interest areas and/or specific occupational interests. A score showing a high interest in social work can be interpreted to mean that the person's responses to test items are similar to those of social workers, but not that the person necessarily likes the occupation of social worker.

Interest tests that report general interest scores are considered more suitable for junior high and high school students. Tests that report occupationally specific scores are generally considered more suitable for adults. Some tests report both general and specific occupational interests. Table 10.5 presents a list of some of the more commonly used instruments. Most general interest tests list 9 to 12 areas of interest. Although the categories differ slightly from system to system, the categories in the *Dictionary of Occupational Titles* (1984), which are listed below, are representative.

1. Artistic	7. Business Detail
2. Scientific	8. Selling
3. Nature	9. Accommodating
4. Protective	10. Humanitarian
5. Mechanical	11. Leading–Influencing
6. Industrial	12. Physical Performing

The *Occupational Interest Schedule* (Parker, 1991) was normed on the same population as the OASIS, discussed in the previous section. It also measures each of the classifications listed above. The *Interest Schedule* contains 240 items scored as *like, neutral,* or *dislike.* The test meets guidelines for sex fairness within validity constraints. Scores are directly related to the *Guide for Occupational Exploration* (1988) and the *Worker Trait Group Guide* (Winefordner, 1991).

TABLE 10.5.   Commonly Used Occupational Interest Tests

TEST NAME	TARGET POPULATION
Reading-Free Vocational Interest Inventory–Revised (Becker, 1981)	High school students who cannot read
Career Assessment Inventory (2nd ed.) (Johansson, 1982)	High school students, adults
Kuder Occupational Interest Survey (Kuder, 1985)	High school students, adults
Occupational Aptitude Survey and Interest Schedule–2 (Parker, 1991)	Junior high and high school students
Pictorial Inventory of Careers (Talent Assessment, Inc., n.d.)	Low reading or nonreading students
Project Discovery Training System (Experience Education, n.d.)	Adolescents, adults
The Self-Directed Search (Holland, 1985)	High school students, adults
Strong–Campbell Interest Inventory (Strong, Hansen, & Campbell, 1985)	High school students, adults

WORK-SAMPLE SYSTEMS

Commercial work-sample systems are designed to provide more specific information regarding work abilities than that obtained through general aptitude tests. General aptitude tests may test only a person's speed, whereas work-sample systems may examine speed, stamina, persistence, improvement, adaptability, and cooperation. Many work-sample systems employ extensive apparatus in order to simulate common work stations and tasks found in business and industry.

Work-sample systems vary greatly in the number of samples included and the types of information derived from student performance. Much of the diversity results from the fact that many available systems were developed to serve specific purposes with specific populations. Table 10.6 lists

TABLE 10.6.   Commonly Used Commercial Work Samples

SYSTEM	TARGET POPULATION
Computerized Assessment (Valpar International, 1991)	Adolescents, adults
Compute-A-Match System (Pesco International, n.d.)	Junior high, secondary, postsecondary students
Vocational Interest, Temperament, and Aptitude System (Vocational Research Institute, n.d.)	High school students, adults
Vocational Transit (Vocational Research Institute, 1989)	Individuals with developmental and head injuries
Wide Range Employability Sample Test (Jastak & Jastak, 1980)	Adolescents, adults

several of the most commonly used work-sample systems and the target population for whom each system was originally designed. Many of these systems require large expenditures of money and time and are traditionally found in sheltered workshops or rehabilitation facilities. However, with the increased emphasis on preparing secondary students for the world of work, these systems are now being used increasingly in high school special education and special needs vocational education programs.

Daily Living Skills

Occupational competence is only one aspect of the total constellation of abilities necessary for independent living success. Almost everyone knows someone who can maintain a job but cannot keep the remainder of his or her life in order—the person may feel lonely all the time, spend money foolishly, break the law, or have trouble maintaining good health. The cumulative effects of any one problem over a period of time or of simultaneous multiple problems can result in chronic dependence. The development of instruments for assessing independent living skills has increased in recent years, but the usefulness of many of these has yet to be validated. The instruments presented in Table 10.7 relate to three areas: self-care, practical knowledge, and personal/social skills. Self-care covers health, appearance, grooming, household maintenance, cooking, money management, and recreation. Practical knowledge relates to government and law,

TABLE 10.7. Representative Standardized Measures of Daily Living Skills Appropriate for School-Age Populations

SKILL	TEST NAME
Self-care	*AAMR Adaptive Behavior Scale–Residential and Community* (2nd ed.) (Nihira, Leland, & Lambert, 1993) *AAMR Adaptive Behavior Scale–School* (2nd ed.) (Lambert, Nihira, & Leland, 1993) *Social and Prevocational Information Battery–Revised* (Halpern et al., 1986) *Vineland Adaptive Behavior Scales* (Sparrow, Balla, & Cicchetti, 1985)
Practical knowledge	*Career Development Inventory* (Super et al., 1982) *Career Maturity Inventory* (Crites, 1978) *Knowledge of Occupations Test* (Baruth, 1974) *Social and Prevocational Information Battery–Revised* (Halpern et al., 1986)
Personal/social skills	*AAMR Adaptive Behavior Scale–Residential and Community* (2nd ed.) (Nihira, Leland, & Lambert, 1993) *AAMR Adaptive Behavior Scale–School* (2nd ed.) (Lambert, Nihira, & Leland, 1993) *Behavior Rating Profile* (2nd ed.) (L. Brown & Hammill, 1990) *Coopersmith Self-Esteem Inventories* (Coopersmith, 1981) *Culture-Free Self-Esteem Inventories* (2nd ed.) (Battle, 1992) *Self-Esteem Index* (L. Brown & Alexander, 1991) *Vineland Adaptive Behavior Scales* (2nd ed.) (Sparrow, Balla, & Cicchetti, 1985)

consumer economics, transportation, functional academics, community resources, first aid, occupational knowledge, and problem solving. Personal/social skills encompass friendship, dating, sexuality, family, parenting, feelings, communication, self-awareness, co-worker relationships, and adjustment to change.

Many of these standardized instruments rely on information about a student's behavior from family, teachers, counselors, peers, caretakers, or the student. The multiple observer approach is necessary because many of the competencies required in independent adult living are not observable within the school environment. Also, students may display different abilities or problems in different environments. Like standardized instruments in the occupational area, these tests may be useful as screening devices to identify potential problem students among larger groups or to identify deficits within the total group.

Other Assessment Procedures

Many times, the required information about a student cannot be obtained through standardized tests. For example, areas of interest, such as values, feelings, or day-to-day behavior, may not be amenable to standardized testing, or appropriate tests simply may not exist. In these cases, the following assessment procedures may be appropriate: simulations, observations, and paper-and-pencil formats.

Simulation Formats

Two types of simulations are role playing and locally developed work samples (different from the commercial work-sample systems discussed earlier in this chapter). Role playing can be designed to assess relating or problem solving within any content area. Key elements to successful role playing are

1. An open and relaxed classroom atmosphere.

2. A description of the activity's purpose.

3. A description of the circumstances before each role play.

4. Role-play cards with instructions for each performer.

5. Sufficient time for the role play to develop.

6. Time spent discussing the role play after completion.

The situations and role-play card content can be varied to suit the individual situation. Role reversal is a specific modification of the role-play situation in which the student is placed in a role opposite the one he or she normally plays (e.g., parent, employer). This technique permits assessment of the student's understanding of the thoughts, feelings, and actions of others.

Work samples, another simulation type of assessment, have traditionally been associated with sheltered workshops where students were asked to perform at a certain work station to determine their (1) level of skill at the task, (2) attitude toward the task, and/or (3) work habits within that setting. Some work samples, such as assembly, sorting, or clerical tasks, can easily be set up within a public school classroom, whereas others require specialized space and equipment. Although work samples sometimes seem artificial, they do permit the observation of job-related behavior in situations normally inaccessible within academic classroom settings. Sittington (1979) provided guidelines for developing school-based work samples.

Observation Strategies

Observation strategies are useful for developing information about student behavior within the regular classroom and within simulation activities. Devices used include records of targeted behavior, nonstandardized checklists, and rating scales.

Recording targeted behavior involves making set time-interval (2-minute; 5-minute) observations of a student's behavior during instruction. This technique is particularly useful in identifying visible problems in behavior that detract from the student's ability to make a positive interpersonal impression. Such problems might include not maintaining eye contact, "clock watching," passing notes, and other annoying mannerisms. Observation recording should include the stimulus and consequence of the response. Analysis of such records often reveals problems that are amenable to intervention.

Nonstandardized checklists may be used to give structure to observations. A sample checklist that may be used by a teacher, a peer, or the student to evaluate a student's performance within a job interview format is given in Table 10.8.

Rating scales are similar to checklists but are designed to provide more qualitative information regarding a student's performance. A checklist asks the rater merely to indicate that a behavior has been observed; a rating scale asks the rater to make a judgment about the behavior. Rating scales are more reliable if clear guidelines for each level of rating are given. For example, if the stimulus item is "Student initiates contact with peers," a rating scale that ranges from *never* to *always* is less precise than one that gives the following choices:

1. Never
2. Once a month
3. Once a week
4. Once a day
5. Once an hour

TABLE 10.8.   Sample Job Interview Role-Play Checklist

	GOOD	AVERAGE	IMPROVEMENT NEEDED
Appearance	_____	_____	_____
Introduction	_____	_____	_____
Ability to establish a friendly interaction with interviewer	_____	_____	_____
Brief personal description	_____	_____	_____
Explanation of disability	_____	_____	_____
Explanation of work experience as it relates to job	_____	_____	_____
Inclusion of three positive statements about self	_____	_____	_____
Attention to interviewer	_____	_____	_____
Ability to answer questions	_____	_____	_____
Ability to ask job-related questions	_____	_____	_____
Understanding of job duties	_____	_____	_____
Knowledge of company	_____	_____	_____
Body language	_____	_____	_____
Motivation	_____	_____	_____
Interest	_____	_____	_____
Apparent competence/ability to sell self	_____	_____	_____
Knowledge of next step in hiring process	_____	_____	_____

Paper-and-Pencil Assessment Formats

Intervention with certain groups of students may require that the teacher tailor assessment tools for a specific situation. Although many independent living assessment tools exist, teachers may want to design their own tools. In other circumstances, teachers may want to modify an existing instrument to make it more suitable for a particular classroom. The information in this section gives a range of options for designing tests; each format may be used in more than one assessment area. Five types of paper-and-pencil formats may be used in designing tools to assess independent living skills: incomplete sentence, forced choice, semantic differential, questionnaire, and discrepancy analysis.

INCOMPLETE SENTENCE FORMAT

In the incomplete sentence format, the student is presented with a series of sentence beginnings to complete. The stimulus sentence stems are usually developed to elicit information concerning the student's feelings about school, self, family, jobs, friends, or other areas of interest.

The biggest problems with the jobs I want are _____.

If I could be anything, I would _____.

The happiest times of my life are _____.

I've always wanted to be _____.

My friends _____.

I really hate _____.

The content of the specific responses is not as important as the general tone of the responses or the themes that emerge. Is the person angry, happy, sad, or fearful? Do there seem to be specific areas of concern that consistently arise—family, friends, self? Is the person open or restricted in responses? Obviously, such interpretations are highly subjective, and any tentative assumptions must be verified through further interactions or assessments.

FORCED-CHOICE FORMATS

The forced-choice format requires the student to choose between two items. Items are designed so that equally attractive or unattractive statements are paired. This feature allows some control over the social desirability factor.

a. I would rather have a secure job.
b. I would rather have a job with prestige.

a. It is important to take care of oneself.
b. You should always be willing to help others.

a. I would like to have a lot of friends.
b. I want to have as many good things as possible.

Such tests help clarify the relative importance of elements among a set of values, goals, and behaviors. This procedure can be used to reduce the complexity of a rank-ordering task involving a large number of variables.

SEMANTIC DIFFERENTIAL FORMAT

Like rating scales, semantic differentials ask the student to assume a general response set to a stimulus concept and then rate the concept along several dimensions. For example, a student may be asked to rate his or her feelings about school by checking the blanks closest to those feelings:

happy	___ : ___ : ___ : ___ : ___ : ___ : ___	sad
beautiful	___ : ___ : ___ : ___ : ___ : ___ : ___	ugly
dirty	___ : ___ : ___ : ___ : ___ : ___ : ___	clean
honest	___ : ___ : ___ : ___ : ___ : ___ : ___	dishonest
poor	___ : ___ : ___ : ___ : ___ : ___ : ___	rich
good	___ : ___ : ___ : ___ : ___ : ___ : ___	bad
pleasant	___ : ___ : ___ : ___ : ___ : ___ : ___	unpleasant
fair	___ : ___ : ___ : ___ : ___ : ___ : ___	unfair
healthy	___ : ___ : ___ : ___ : ___ : ___ : ___	successful

QUESTIONNAIRE FORMAT

Questionnaires are simply sets of questions asked of the students. They are useful for collecting basic information within specific areas of assessment interests (e.g., students' home environments, hobbies, interests, work experiences, awareness of jobs, or career planning). Questions are chosen that elicit the required information. A sample questionnaire used to assess the career planning of secondary students is given in Table 10.9.

DISCREPANCY ANALYSIS FORMATS

In discrepancy analysis, students rate two separate aspects of themselves (e.g., jobs, friends) and then compare the two ratings to identify dif ferences. Many times, the ratings deal with the real versus the ideal. For instance, students might be asked to rate their current personality traits and what they consider to be ideal personality traits. They could then be asked to identify the difference between their personality and the ideal as a way to find areas in which they may want to change. This technique can also be applied to current versus desired behavior, current abilities versus those required in certain jobs, or current life-style versus desired life-style. This approach has the advantage of actively involving the student in a process that can be generalized to many real-life situations.

Both standardized and other assessment procedures provide useful information for teaching independent living skills. Of course, continual assessment is necessary throughout the teaching process for measuring growth, determining the efficacy of the instructional program, and specifying directions for modifying or changing the instructional approach.

TEACHING INDEPENDENT LIVING

The independent living skills needed by individuals can be taught through school-based programs, community-based programs, and specific intervention strategies. Each of these approaches is described in this section.

TABLE 10.9.   Sample Career Planning Questionnaire

What jobs can you do now? _____

_____

What jobs do you think you might like to do in 2 years? _____

_____

What jobs do you think you might like to do 10 years from now? _____

_____

To do the jobs you want 2 years from now, what skills will you need to improve? _____

_____

To do the jobs you want 10 years from now, what abilities will you need to improve? _____

_____

_____

What are your biggest problems with the jobs you can do now?_____

_____

What problems do you have getting a job now? _____

_____

What can you do about these problems? _____

_____

_____

School-Based Programs

Career education and vocational education are examples of school-based programs. Both are found in almost every school district. Whereas some districts have implemented an extensive career education program, others give only minimal attention to this type of programming. Similarly, whereas some districts have a wide variety of vocational education programs, others have a very limited number of these programs.

Career Education

In the early days of the career education movement, professionals equated the words *career* and *occupation*. However, Super (1976), a recognized pioneer and leader in career development, pointed out that career is broader in meaning than occupation. Careers are the major positions occupied by a person throughout his or her preoccupational, occupational, and postoccupational life. Specifically, careers include work-related roles, such as that of student, employee, and pensioner, as well as complementary avocational, familial, and civic roles.

In the context of career education, the word career is conceived of as referring to the various life roles that an individual plays. Career education is therefore designed to help students select roles for their lives as well as to learn how to function in these various roles. Kokaska and Brolin (1985) defined career education in the following manner:

> Career education is a life-centered approach focusing on the individual as a productive worker in many different jobs. Individuals perform both paid and unpaid work at home, in the community, and on a job. Productive work includes that of a homemaker and a family member, citizen and volunteer, student, retiree, employee, and participant in meaningful avocational pursuits. Thus the challenge of career education is to provide learners with opportunities that will help them function adequately in these various life roles. (p. 43)

Career education is viewed as beginning at the preschool level and continuing throughout life. The Division on Career Development (DCD) of the Council for Exceptional Children stressed this point in a position paper, advocating the following career development principles (Clark, Carlson, Fisher, Cook, & D'Alonzo, 1991):

1. Education for career development and transition is for individuals with disabilities at all ages.

2. Career development is a process begun at birth and continues throughout life.

3. Early career development is essential for making satisfactory choices later.

4. Significant gaps or periods of neglect in any area of basic human development affects career development and the transition from one stage to another.

5. Career development is responsive to intervention and programming, when the programming involves direct instruction for individual needs. (pp. 115–117)

Various models of career development have emerged over the years. Clark and Kolstoe's (1990) model is particularly appropriate for individuals with learning and behavior problems (see Figure 10.1). Instruction is directed toward four key areas: (1) values, attitudes, and habits; (2) human relationships; (3) occupational information; and (4) acquisition of job and daily living skills. These four components undergird the high school, postsecondary, and adult options for education and training. Although the specific training options available to students may vary from community to community, the model advocates providing instruction in career development

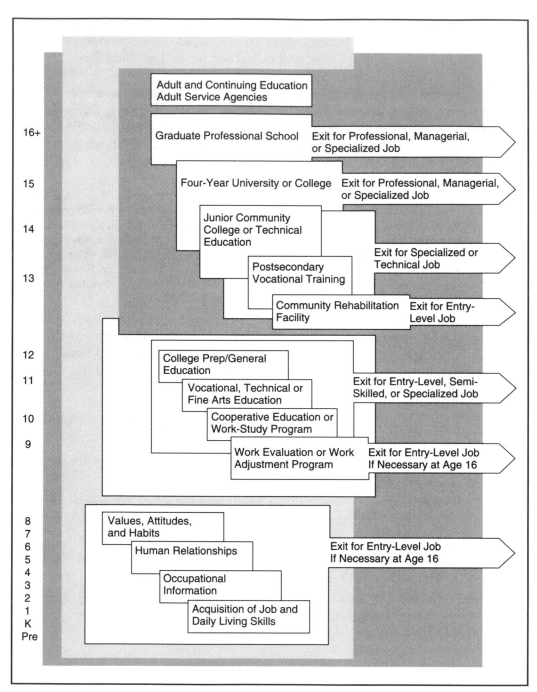

FIGURE 10.1. A school-based career development and transition education model for adolescents with handicaps.

From *Career Development and Transition Education for Adolescents with Disabilities* (p. 45) by G. M. Clark and O. P. Kolstoe, 1990, Boston: Allyn & Bacon. Copyright 1990 by Allyn & Bacon. Reprinted with permission.

and transition knowledge and skills to all students regardless of their choice of study. (For a more detailed explanation of the model, see Clark, 1981; Clark & Kolstoe, 1990; Clark & White, 1980).

In school districts with extensive career education programs, the concept of preparing students for adult independent living has been infused into day-to-day instruction. Sequential instruction with themes ranging from career awareness to career placement is conducted at various stages of students' schooling. Many students with learning and behavior problems, disabilities, or economic disadvantage profit from this educational approach.

Vocational Education

Vocational education focuses on the occupational preparation of individuals. It is concerned with career exploration, vocational assessment, training, job try-outs, and job placement (J. C. Brolin & D. E. Brolin, 1979). As such, it is a part of career education but is not as broad in its focus; it is specific to paid employment. The Vocational Act of 1963 (P.L. 88-201) defines this educational endeavor as follows:

> Vocational education means vocational or technical training or retraining which is given in schools or classes (including field or laboratory work and remedial or related academic and technical instruction incident thereto) under public supervision and control or under contract with a state board or local education agency and is conducted as part of a program designed to prepare individuals for gainful employment as semiskilled or skilled workers or technicians or subprofessionals in recognized occupations and in new and emerging occupations or to prepare individuals for enrollment in advanced technical programs, but excluding any program to prepare individuals for employment in occupations which the Commissioner determines, and specifies by regulation, to be generally considered professional or which require a baccalaureate or higher degree. (Sec. 108)

High school programs usually offer training in one or more of the "big seven" occupational areas: vocational agriculture and agribusiness, business and office occupations, marketing and distributive occupations, health occupations, trade and industrial occupations, technical occupations, and vocational home economics. Examples under each of the seven categories are included in Table 10.10.

Some of the occupations may not seem to be in keeping with the definition of vocational education (i.e., nonprofessional jobs). However, each field has varying levels of requirements for training. For example, within health occupations, a nurse would be considered a professional, whereas a nurse's aide may not. Each occupation area has supportive nonprofessional personnel.

School districts cannot usually afford to establish vocational preparation programs in each of the fields. Consequently, the characteristics of the

TABLE 10.10. The Big Seven Vocational Education Programs

Vocational Agriculture and Agribusiness Farm mechanics Fertilizers and insecticides Horticulture	*Business and Office* Accounting and computing Bookkeeping Data processing
Marketing and Distributive Retail Warehousing Wholesale	*Health* Dental Medical laboratory technology Nursing
Trade and Industrial Building trades Heating and refrigeration Manufacturing and processing	*Technical* Electronics Printing Graphics
Vocational Home Economics Industrial sewing Commercial food preparation	

student population as well as the community needs generally dictate which programs are established. For example, one would be more likely to find an extensive vocational agriculture and agribusiness education program in a rural area than in an urban one. Conversely, one would be more likely to find a strong marketing and distributive education program in an urban area than in a rural one.

The Carl Perkins Act of 1984 (P.L. 98-524) spells out the federal government's intention to encourage equal access to vocational education for students with special needs. This act also requires that every student with a disability be notified of vocational education opportunities available through the schools by the time the student reaches the ninth grade. Finally, the act ensures that students with special needs have equal access to vocational education services, such as counseling and guidance, vocational assessment, and transition assistance.

Both career education and vocational education are school-based programs that have as their specific focus the training of students for independent living. Career education begins at the preschool level and continues throughout life. It helps students to become aware of various life roles, to explore some of the career roles, and to clarify for themselves which careers they intend to incorporate into their life-style. Vocational education, while part of career education, focuses on training students for semiskilled, skilled, technical, or paraprofessional jobs.

Students with learning or behavior problems can profit from career education in that it helps them develop a better understanding of themselves and their responsibilities to themselves and others. For those who have no wish or ability to pursue higher education, vocational education offers an opportunity to prepare for post–high school employment.

Community-Based Programs

Although schools cannot bear total responsibility for the life development of students, teachers are in a good position to assess when certain critical needs are not being met. Many community-based organizations provide services related to independent living skills; the teacher who is knowledgeable about such services is able to refer students in need to the appropriate support services. All of the services and organizations described in this section may not be available in a specific community, and names and functions of organizations may differ from state to state. Consequently, the information presented in this section is intended to help identify the types of services and agencies that may be available in a specific community. To make appropriate referrals for specific students, teachers will want to determine which agencies and services exist within their local community.

Types of Services

Community-based organizations may offer a variety of services, including those described below.

Employment

Career counseling—Helps individuals set career goals and make career plans.

Employment counseling—Helps individuals find the jobs that best match their abilities, interests, and values.

Job placement—Involves an intermediary (counselor, vocational adjustment coordinator, etc.) who finds a job for an individual.

Sheltered employment—Provides noncompetitive employment to workers with disabilities and pays wages on the basis of job performance.

Supported employment—Provides competitive employment in integrated settings to workers with severe disabilities, using an on-site trainer (or job coach) to teach job-specific skills and maintain competitive production standards.

Work evaluation—Provides an assessment of a person's skill level compared with that of others doing similar work.

Housing

Cooperatives—Provide community-based housing with peer (frequently individuals without disabilities) support and with control in the hands of residents.

Foster care—Allows for the relocation of individuals who are without immediate family or whose families are dysfunctional.

Group homes—Provide semi-independent, supervised housing.

Halfway houses—Provide supervised housing with levels of independence commensurate with individuals' functional life skills.

Independent living centers (ILCs)—Typically provide information and referral services to individuals seeking accessible housing. However, some ILCs have established residential programs with control in the hands of consumers.

Residential facilities—Offer supervised housing coupled with rehabilitation programming or educational intervention alternatives to public school.

Interpersonal

Drug and alcohol abuse (chemical dependency) counseling—Helps individuals recognize and resolve drug abuse problems.

Family counseling—Helps family members work individually or together on family issues.

Genetic counseling—Provides individuals with information on the chances that they might pass on a condition to any children they might have.

Personal adjustment counseling—Helps individuals identify and solve personal problems.

Personal/social adjustment training—Helps people to improve feelings about themselves or their interactions with others.

Recreation

Adaptive recreation—Provides accessible and appropriate recreation activities for persons with handicaps.

Day activity centers—Provide daytime programming geared toward improving independent living abilities.

Support

Advocacy programs—Include those that provide legal assistance (e.g., Legal Aid and the American Civil Liberties Union), peer tutoring or mentor programs (e.g., the Association for Retarded Citizens and Big Brothers/Big Sisters), and so on.

Consumer groups—Comprise individuals with disabilities and advocates. Groups tend either to be disability specific (e.g., American Council of the Blind) or to have cross-disability representation (e.g., Coalition of Americans with Disabilities). Consumer groups advocate appropriate services and legislative support pertinent to their membership.

Self-help groups—Comprise individuals with either shared problems (e.g., job-seeking clubs, Alcoholics Anonymous, Weight Watchers) or similar characteristics (e.g., groups of diabetics, head injured individuals, epileptics).

Services for disabled students offices—Located at many community colleges, colleges, and universities, assist students with disabilities in enrolling in and attending school.

Social Security Disability Income program—Provides income support in the form of monthly checks and medical assistance in the form of Medicare.

Supplemental Security income program—Provides income support in the form of welfare checks and food stamps and medical support in the form of Medicaid.

Training

Job-seeking skills training—Teaches people how to look for jobs effectively.

On-the-job training—Allows the trainee to learn how to do a job while being paid a salary.

Personal and social adjustment training—Helps individuals develop self-care skills and adapt to altered life situations.

Rehabilitation centers—Provide extensive life/career skills programming, counseling and guidance services, and, frequently, temporary housing.

Vocational training—Teaches skills for a specific job.

Work adjustment training—Teaches good generic work habits.

Types of Organizations

A variety of community-based organizations provide services for students. Community colleges provide academic courses and vocational training. Many community colleges also offer not-for-credit parallel studies programs, which enable students with academic deficits to improve their skills in order to enroll in degree or certificate programs. In addition, community colleges often offer adult basic education and English as a second language classes. Many community colleges have counselors or advisers available to help students with disabilities become integrated into the college environment.

Community schools provide an assortment of non–college credit courses in fields ranging from human development (e.g., assertiveness skills training) to avocational skill development (e.g., classes in floral design and cake decorating). Community schools are typically affiliated with local school districts, so classes usually meet at night or on weekends in neighborhood schools.

Community-based organizations (CBOs) such as Urban Leagues and Special Education Resource Centers–Jobs for Progress offer job skills training and job placement assistance. Frequently, their vocational programs are provided with grant funding through the Job Training Partnership Act (JTPA) and are, therefore, income eligibility based. The programs encourage persons with disabilities to participate by considering them as individual wage earners (other family members' earnings are not considered in the eligibility formula). In some communities, residential schools for specific disability populations and cross-disability facilities such as Goodwill Industries have secured JTPA funding for summer youth employment programs as well as school-year job placement assistance. Some CBOs offer alternative educational programs for high school dropouts and other young adult learners, and many providing such academic programs also provide employment assistance. CBOs such as Planned Parenthood and the Teenage Parent Program provide information on sex education, birth control, and genetic counseling. When appropriate, they make referrals to other programs (e.g., health clinics or infant–parent programs). Because of the diversity of such organizations and their various locations throughout cities, counties, and states, many communities publish directories of local CBOs and make them available through public libraries.

State departments of human resources help with social problems such as hunger, child abuse, housing, and medical care for dependent children, persons with disabilities, and elderly individuals. Services may include financial assistance such as food stamps, medical assistance such as Medicaid, personal and family counseling, or assistance in finding housing, training, and so forth.

State employment agencies help employers and job applicants find each other. Free services include vocational interest and aptitude assessment, job counseling, and dissemination of information about job openings. Such agencies have responsibility for monitoring employment trends and reporting their findings to the public, as well as for overseeing unemployment claims.

State or local mental health agencies provide counseling assistance to people who are having personal problems. Services provided may include individual, group, and family counseling and drug abuse counseling.

State rehabilitation agencies provide a variety of services designed to help individuals with disabilities over age 16 go to work. Rehabilitation counselors may provide vocational interest and aptitude assessments; personal and vocational counseling; assistance to find and pay for adaptive equipment, medical procedures, and so forth; and job placement assistance. Some services are based on economic need.

Private nonprofit vocational rehabilitation facilities serve a particular need for a special population. Examples are Goodwill Industries and Lighthouses for the Blind. Depending on the facility, services may include work evaluation, adjustment-to-work training, sheltered employment, on-the-job training, personal-adjustment training/counseling, and vocational assessment/training.

To provide services most efficiently, service agencies and organizations are encouraged by the Office of Special Education and Rehabilitative Services (OSERS) to establish interagency agreements. Interagency cooperation is stressed particularly during the transitional period between school and work. Section 602(a)(20) of IDEA states that the IEP must include, "when appropriate, a statement of the interagency responsibilities or linkages before the students leave the school setting." By working together, school personnel and community-based service providers can share information about their respective roles and services, as well as avoid duplication of effort.

Specific Intervention Strategies

Various methods and materials are available for teaching independent living skills. In this section, a discussion of some general intervention issues is followed by overviews of commercially available materials and teacher-directed activities.

General Intervention Issues

Cronin and Patton (1993) delineated options for organizing the in-school remediation of skills critical to independent living (see Figure 10.2). They suggested that a realistic appraisal of the adult outcome needs of students, various restructuring movements, and current educational placements of students necessitates a continuum of options. The options encompass three types of approaches for integrating life skills content into the curriculum—infusion, augmentation, and coursework—and reflect variations in the amount of time available for addressing independent living skills content.

The infusion approach involves infusing life skills topics into the established content of existing courses. This approach is often applied to students who are in diploma-track programs and spend all of their time in general education classes. It is commonly used when elective coursework is limited by the curricular orientation. A major drawback to this approach is that the particular skills covered are dictated by the topics included in the existing course content. An example of this approach would be to include a discussion of how to treat athlete's foot when the topic of fungus is covered in a general science textbook.

The second approach, augmentation, consists of dedicating portions of existing courses to independent living topics. This is typically accomplished by adding units on life skills topics related to the subject area of the course. For example, in a consumer math course, a unit on the financial implications of dating could be added to the regular content of the course.

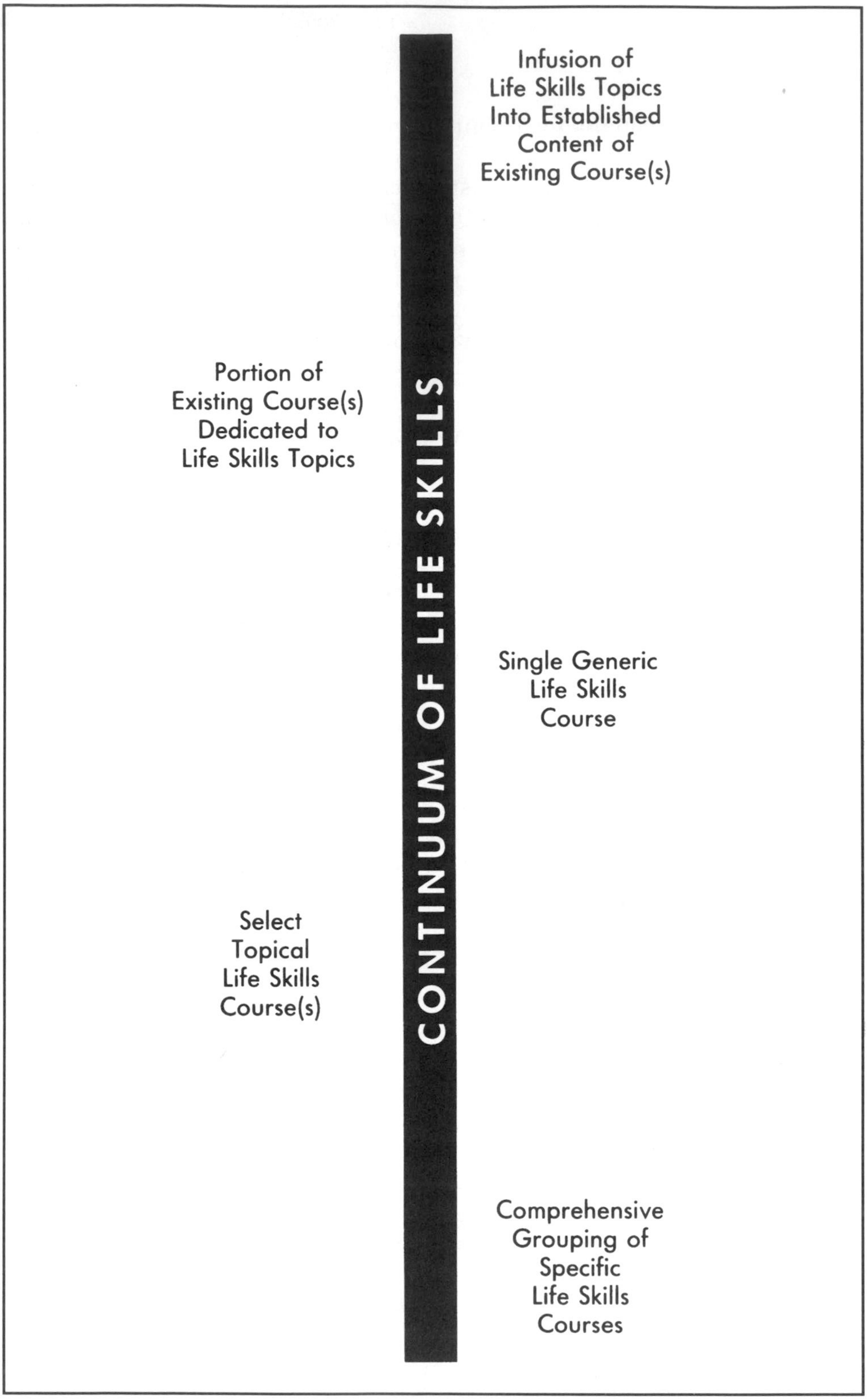

CONTINUUM OF LIFE SKILLS

Infusion of
Life Skills Topics
Into Established
Content of
Existing Course(s)

Portion of
Existing Course(s)
Dedicated to
Life Skills Topics

Single Generic
Life Skills
Course

Select
Topical
Life Skills
Course(s)

Comprehensive
Grouping of
Specific
Life Skills
Courses

FIGURE 10.2.   Options for integrating life skills content into the curriculum.

From *Life Skills Instruction for All Students with Special Needs: A Practical Guide for Integrating Real-Life Content into the Curriculum* by M. E. Cronin and J. R. Patton, 1993, Austin, TX: PRO-ED. Copyright 1993 by PRO-ED, Inc. Reprinted with permission.

This approach allows for a greater portion of the course to be dedicated to life skills content.

The coursework approach is used when the development of a distinct course or distinct set of courses addressing life skills is possible. There are several variations of this approach. One option would be the creation of a single generic course, perhaps called "Life 101," that would cover a range of topics and cut across traditional subject areas, including science, social studies, math, reading, and English. A second option involves creating a topical life skills course. Course content could be related to specific adult domains, such as employment/education or home and family, or a specific subject area, such as math (e.g., a course entitled "Math in the Real World"). Finally, a sequence of specific life skills courses could be developed. Independent living skills are related to typical subject areas, such as science, English, and math. Figure 10.3 illustrates potential courses and select sample topics.

Because of the recent concern over school-to-work transition issues, educators are beginning to provide instruction in independent living skills in community settings. The basic premise behind community-based instruction is that many learners with disabilities, particularly those with severe disabilities, will be unable to generalize skills learned in the classroom to other environments. Rather than follow traditional classroom instructional strategies, such as completing workbook exercises in consumer economics, students might engage in real-life activities, such as comparative shopping activities at a local mall. Likewise, an effort is made to place students in appropriate jobs and train them at the job site, rather than train them to perform job skills in a classroom or sheltered workshop setting.

Commercially Available Materials

The broad nature of the skills and content necessary for independent living has resulted in a proliferation of instructional materials. In the last 15 years or so, many new materials have come onto the market. Cronin and Patton (1993) wrote a comprehensive review of materials from 23 domains (e.g., general job skills, home management, self-improvement), the publishers' addresses and phone numbers, the recommended age for students, the reading level (if stated), and the type of material.

Commercial materials vary in quality of design and in breadth of coverage. Some present only curriculum outlines; others present only learning activities; still others include instructional objectives, curriculum outlines, learning activities, and pre- and post-assessment devices. Some materials are targeted toward specific concepts (e.g., functional mathematics); others address all areas (e.g., independent living curriculum). Each teacher has to consider learner characteristics and the academic curriculum in order to decide upon the appropriate materials to use.

Life Skills Course	Select Topics
Personal Finance 	maintaining a budget filing tax submitting an application for a loan using credit cards
Practical Math 	performing home repairs/maintenance estimating travel time cooking measuring dosage of prescribed medicine
Health & Hygiene 	dealing with illness administering first aid maintaining one's personal appearance handling stress
Everyday Science 	gardening identifying how things work controlling pests using science in the kitchen
Practical Communication 	using resource materials requesting information writing personal cards and notes taking phone messages
Community Awareness and Involvement 	registering to vote using community resources (e.g., library) attending neighborhood association meetings knowing one's legal rights
Occupational Development 	identifying personal interests and aptitudes preparing a career planning packet practicing interview skills identifying available jobs in the community
Interpersonal Relations 	getting along with others accepting criticism complimenting others engaging in social conversation

FIGURE 10.3. Life skills courses and select sample topics.

From *Life Skills Instruction for Students with Special Needs: A Practical Guide for Integrating Real-Life Content into the Curriculum* by M. E. Cronin and J. R. Patton, 1993, Austin, TX: PRO-ED. Copyright 1993 by PRO-ED, Inc. Reprinted with permission.

For illustrative purposes, we describe two specific materials: *Developing the Functional Use of a Telephone Book: Emphasizing Communicative, Organizational, and Problem Solving Skills* by Jorgensen and Bernhard (1993) and *Life-Centered Career Education: A Competency-Based Approach* by D. Brolin (1991). The program on using the telephone book was developed for use with adolescents who have cognitive impairments, learning disabilities, reading impairments, communication disabilities, limited English proficiency, and limited academic success. The material contains pre- and postassessments, a teaching sequence, lesson plans, handouts, activities, vocabulary lists, and parent–teacher communications. The skills taught in the program are making local calls, calling long distance, calling community services, and using pay telephones.

The life-centered career program was developed to address major critical skills that all students need to know and perform in community living and work settings. The program includes an extensive set of curriculum-based assessments, lesson plans, and staff training materials. The domains addressed included daily living skills, personal–social skills, and occupational skills. Postschool outcomes, such as integrated employment, vocation training, adult service linkages, independent living, and community participation, are addressed. There are also 10 training videotapes that include presentations, discussions, and classroom demonstrations of lesson and assessment activities, as well as a trainer guide and teacher activities book.

These two programs, the telephone program and career education, merely demonstrate the wide range of materials available. Materials may address a single independent living skill (e.g., using the telephone), or they may be more comprehensive (i.e., cover many daily, personal, and occupational skills).

Teacher-Directed Activities

When commercial materials are unavailable, either because fiscal restraints prevent acquisition of new materials or because the teacher is trying to meet an instructional need specific to a class or to one student, the teacher must develop instructional materials. Following are several general guidelines for creating instructional materials:

1. Use real-life materials whenever possible. If teaching banking, use real bank books; if teaching job applications, use real job applications.

2. Provide real-life experiences whenever possible. Allow students to learn by doing. Rather than talking about jobs, go see them. Rather than talking about calling for a job, let students make real calls. To develop independence, students must be encouraged to make decisions and enjoy (suffer) the consequences of those decisions.

3. Use both interactive and individual activities. Some skills (e.g., those relating to social situations, peers, and affect) can be mastered only by working with other people. Students' needs in other skill and content areas will be so specific and varied that individual activities will be required (e.g., job selection, leisure interests).

4. Design materials that allow you to interact with students or model behavior. Interaction allows you to develop a more trusting relationship with students and also facilitates assessment; modeling allows you to demonstrate behaviors that are hard to describe (making an assertive statement, acting on values, listening to constructive criticism).

5. Use as many community resources and resource people as possible. Many agencies and organizations have excellent community education programs that will provide speakers or equipment, arrange tours, and/or provide instructional material. By using these resources, you can broaden student experiences and acquaint students with the local community.

6. Use techniques that have been successful in other content areas for teaching independent living. For example, assigning writing may be a good method of instruction. Topics such as "What I want out of life," "My perfect job," "How I want to live in 10 years," or "The car I want" require students to do research into independent living and give them a chance to think about their goals or plans.

7. Organize curriculum presentations around concepts. Concepts are defined by specific characteristics. Each example or instance has certain observable characteristics. Therefore, any given concept is defined by referring to the observable, common characteristics of the examples collected to represent the concept. This unique group of common characteristics defines the concept and is not shared by any other concept. It follows that, when presenting examples to the learner, one must never vary or change the determined essential or defining characteristics, but must always vary the unimportant characteristics of the instances.

In fostering independent living skills, the teacher may want to make use of free materials and speakers, classroom discussions, simulations, occupational information, goal setting and plan development, support groups, and learning centers.

FREE MATERIALS AND SPEAKERS

Daily living skills and occupational knowledge involve many content-based competencies. Knowing how to care for oneself and how to manage the details of daily living relates directly to the amount of independence one has. Table 10.11 presents methods, materials, and resources that can aid independence-oriented instruction of learners with special needs. Resources are categorized by area and rated according to the most appropriate instructional arrangements. The chart is intended to stimulate thinking about sources of free instructional support within a specific community.

TABLE 10.11.   Resources for Meeting Common Student Instructional Needs in Daily Living and Occupational Knowledge

INSTRUCTIONAL NEED AREAS	RECOMMENDED STUDY ARRANGEMENT	SAMPLE ATTAINABLE MATERIALS	SAMPLE SPEAKERS/AGENCIES
Daily Living			
Health	Group or Individual	Films, brochures, books	Physicians, school nurses, state department of health
Housing	Group or Individual	Want ads, sample leases	Real estate agents, housing agencies, rental agents
Maintaining a residence	Group or Individual	How-to books, sample utility bills	Plumbers, carpenters, landscapers, housekeepers
Consumerism	Group or Individual	Budget samples, comparison shopping, contracts, credit applications, consumer guides	Bankers, credit union representatives, retailers
Recreation	Group or Individual	Recreation bulletins, club directories, films	Parks and recreation representatives, local club representatives
Transportation	Group or Individual	Bus schedules, car pool information, want ads, car financing and maintenance materials	Car salespeople, transportation systems representatives, mechanics
Occupational			
Job awareness	Group	Local job market materials, want ads	Employment counselors, personnel officers, speakers with different work backgrounds
Work habits	Group	Employment rules from organizations, lists of reasons why people lose jobs, student ratings of each other's performance	Personnel officers, business owners, supervisors
Job exploration	Individual	Products of student-performed information interviews, job analyses, or library research	Career counselors, rehabilitation counselors, workers, local employment commission
Job preparation	Individual	Training directories, vocational training facility materials, college catalogs	Vocational trainers, rehabilitation counselors
Job seeking	Group or Individual	Job applications, sample résumés, want ads, job bulletins	Personnel officers, vocational counselors, employment counselors,

CLASSROOM DISCUSSIONS

Before classroom discussions start, the group should agree upon a set of ground rules about acceptable behaviors (e.g., Everyone has a right to his or her opinion, Everyone shares in group decisions), which will serve as a contract among members of the group. The teacher then structures group activities to stimulate communication among group members. Discussion may be organized around topics selected by students or around the giving and receiving of feedback about the students themselves.

SIMULATIONS

The classroom is in many ways a simulation of a workplace, and students can learn to relate classroom expectations to work expectations. Teachers may design role-play situations to teach interpersonal skills or develop work activity simulations to provide students experience in the demands of work not normally encountered in the classroom. A good approach when using simulations is to videotape them and then allow the simulators to view the videotape prior to debriefing. The learning attained from simulations is based on the quality of the experience as well as the discussion after the simulation.

OCCUPATIONAL INFORMATION

An important development during the school years is the attainment of information about occupations, first in a general sense and then in an individual sense. Materials descriptive of occupations, field trips to representative local businesses, and guest speakers from different occupational groups can all contribute to a student's broad understanding of occupations. At the secondary level, each student will need to research his or her specific choice through reading and relating to other people. Two specific approaches that are helpful are information interviewing and job analysis. Information interviewing is a technique in which the student sets up and carries out an interview with a worker in a given occupation and then prepares a job analysis based on interview information. Job analysis is a technique that involves describing jobs in a standard way so that they can be compared. The following is a very basic outline for a job analysis:

1. *Job purpose*—a general statement about the overall purpose of the job.

2. *Job duties*—a list of the major tasks that the worker must perform.

3. *Work environment*—a description of important elements of the work setting (e.g., indoor/outdoor, people, equipment).

4. *Job qualifications*—a list of the minimum skill and credential levels necessary for successful job performance.

Job analysis helps the student identify his or her match with a particular job.

GOAL SETTING AND PLAN DEVELOPMENT

Students often need assistance in developing a goal and a correlated plan. Techniques that can assist the teacher in working with students who have problems in this area are goal differentiation, goal description, identification of steps in plan, ranking of steps in plan, and contracting.

Goal differentiation helps students to distinguish among daily detail, achievement, and personality type goals, as well as to establish the relative priority of each goal. Goal description helps students take their problem statements and convert them into positive behavioral goals:

Problem: I am too shy.

Goal: To speak more in situations where I am around strangers by December of 1995.

The identification of steps in a plan requires students to analyze the discrepancy between their goal and their current status. Students may compare their current abilities to those abilities required to attain their job goal, or their current interpersonal behavior to that of someone who displays the behavior that they would like to display. When ranking the steps, the student decides how to sequence activities to best attain a goal. Contracting is a technique used to help students commit to following through with actions they have identified in their plan. Students may contract with themselves, the teacher, parents, or peers.

SUPPORT GROUPS

Support groups are basically like classroom discussion groups, but they generally are structured to serve a more specific purpose, such as recreation or goal attainment support (e.g., to help with job seeking or losing weight). Groups may meet on regular schedules, or participants may be paired through a "buddy" system. Often, an intense group effort, in which group members may participate daily for extended periods of time, will be reinforced through a follow-along support group. Follow-along groups meet less frequently than the original group did, but they provide an ongoing catalyst for change and growth based on the initial group's cohesiveness. Participants in such groups are expected to implement or modify their plans during the period between meetings and then report their progress to the group.

LEARNING CENTERS

A good method for addressing the individual needs of students is through the development of learning centers. When content is organized into learning centers, students can access information that is specific to their needs. Learning centers typically contain reading material, listening material, games, and other activities that concentrate on a certain content area (e.g., values, jobs, community resources, budgeting).

Chapter 11

Using New Technologies with Students with Learning Problems

NETTIE R. BARTEL

Recent years have seen a remarkable increase in the use of new technologies, especially computers, at all levels of education. For the past few years, the number of computers being used in schools serving Grades 1 through 12 has been doubling every year. At a time when educational dollars have been hard to come by, millions of computers have been purchased for school use. Well over half of the special education programs in this country own computer hardware.

Many educators have seen this new technology, with its potential for individualizing instruction, as the ultimate instructional answer for students with learning problems. Furthermore, the various compensatory and adaptive technological devices that are becoming available for students with significant sensory and physical problems are making it possible to integrate more of these students into regular classrooms.

Virtually all experts expect the number and use of computers in schools to continue to increase. Therefore, classroom teachers must become informed about the fundamentals of computers, their uses and misuses, especially with students with learning problems, and some of the ethical issues involved in using computers. In this chapter, we consider each of these subjects in turn.

FUNDAMENTALS OF COMPUTERS AND RELATED TECHNOLOGY

Most teachers have had sufficient exposure to the technological revolution to recognize the basic terminology used to describe the various components of a computer system. However, as a review, we briefly describe the elements of a computer system typically found in a classroom.

Basic Computer System Components

For the computer system to do its work, a *central processing unit* (CPU) is required. The CPU is the "brain" of the computer system; it receives data, decodes it, and executes the commands contained in the data. The CPU receives input through a number of different modalities, or input devices, and directs the display, or output devices, such as monitors or printers. The CPU is frequently housed in a unit with a keyboard, with the keys arranged much as they are on a typewriter; this keyboard serves as a major input device, allowing the user to type in directions to the CPU. Other input devices might include a joystick, "mouse," or game paddles; a memory pad or board; a light pen; a finger-sensitive monitor; a disk drive; an optical disk; or a scanner or optical character reader that electronically scans a picture or "reads" text and digitizes this information so the CPU can process it. More recent input devices include notepads on which the user writes with a special pen, or voice recognition equipment which responds to the user's voice commands. When persons with disabilities use computers, special input devices are sometimes used (e.g., modified keyboards or special switches that respond to limited physical motions, such as a brow wrinkle).

When the CPU performs an operation in response to instructions received through an input device, there must be a way to show the user the result of the operation. Accordingly, every CPU needs a *display or output device* to show the results of the operations it has performed. Typically, the display is in the form of text or graphics on a monitor or cathode ray tube (CRT) or screen—either monochrome or color.

Sometimes elements of two or more computer systems are combined into a *network.* In schools, the most common type of network is one in which a minicomputer or personal computer with a powerful CPU is connected by cable to a number of terminals through which students can access the CPU and its programs. The advantages of such a system are that costs are lower (only one CPU and one set of software) and the teacher can control access to programs from one location. The configuration on a computer screen can also be sent to another computer or FAX in another location via a *modem,* another input–output device that transforms digital information from the CPU into electrical waveforms that can be transmitted over telephone lines or broadcast over the air. Recent advances have greatly increased the transmission rate by modem.

Computers in recent years have greatly increased in power, and greatly decreased in size and price. Laptop and notebook-size computers are common. Ten years ago, most computers used in schools (often Apple II's or IIe's, or Commodores) had 48K or 64K bytes of *random-access memory* (RAM). (RAM refers to the part of the CPU's capacity that is available for user use, as opposed to *read-only memory* [ROM], which is the set of permanent instructions within the CPU.) More recently purchased machines (often Apple Macintoshes or IBM or their clones) have much more RAM—typically up to 8 or 12 megabytes (8000 to 12,000 K bytes)—and correspondingly greater ROM.

Many older computers were sold with *disk drives* that use $5\frac{1}{4}$-inch diskettes, and many educational programs are still sold in this format. However, the newer computers tend to use programs marketed in $3\frac{1}{2}$-inch diskettes, and increasing numbers of educational programs are available in this format. Such diskettes have a storage capacity of 100,000 to 3,000,000 characters each. Newer computers also tend to have greatly increased storage capacities—either with a built-in hard drive of up to several billion characters of storage or with optical disk systems that can store entire encyclopedias on one compact disk.

If a permanent copy of the display produced by the CPU is required, the computer is hooked up to a *printer or plotter,* which produces a permanent, or "hard," copy of the display. Printer quality has improved in recent years, ranging from inexpensive dot matrix printers to laser printers that create high-quality images. Ink jet printers produce intermediate-quality images in either color or black and white. Speed and clarity of type are major issues to consider when one is pricing printers for classroom use.

Videodiscs were first available in 1978, but they have only recently become widely used in schools. The videodisc itself looks like a large compact disk—a shiny, metallic silver disk about the size of a long-playing (LP) record. Each side of a standard videodisc can hold 54,000 individual, high-quality pictures or frames. Each of these frames can be directly and instantaneously accessed by using settings on the videodisc player, a remote control, or a computer program. The frames themselves are displayed on a television or computer monitor. A classification system has been developed for videodiscs—from Level I which is the most basic, consisting only of a videodisc and player, to Level IV in which the player has a variety of scanning and stopping functions; has selectable audio channels; and is connected to a computer with its read, write, storage, and programming or artificial intelligence capabilities. Because of their rapid random-access audio capabilities and touch-screen possibilities, videodiscs are particularly suitable for students who cannot read, but who can use spoken instructions or audio sounds or pointing to signal the system. Self-pacing, individual pacing, group pacing, or teacher pacing may be used with videodiscs.

Several projects have demonstrated the usefulness of interactive video systems with students with learning problems. Ongoing work at the University of Utah, under the leadership of Alan Hofmeister and Ron Thorkildsen, have shown this cutting-edge technology to hold promise for students with mental retardation, learning disabilities, or other school-related problems. Current applications of interactive videodisc with problem learners include the fields of reading, mathematics, language (including sign language), and social skills training.

Peripherals and Other Assistive Devices for Persons with Disabilities

The promise of computers and related technologies for persons with disabilities is enormous. Many kinds of equipment have been designed to enable students with disabilities to perform tasks or to gain access to materials ordinarily beyond their capabilities. These aids, tools, and equipment, often termed assistive devices, help persons with disabilities function more effectively at home, school, and the workplace. The microcomputer is the most promising and most powerful of assistive devices.

In the following sections, we consider some ways in which such devices have been developed or adapted for students with specific kinds of communication, sensory, or physical disabilities. Most of the remainder of the chapter addresses issues concerning computer use with students who have mild learning and behavioral problems.

Students with Communication Problems

Students who speak poorly or are unable to speak at all present major instructional challenges. A large number of research and development efforts have yielded technological assistance in the following instructional applications with this group of students:

Evaluation and diagnosis—Devices for testing of hearing, voice, speech and language samples; use of expert systems.

Augmentative or alternative communication systems—Electronic communication boards and other devices such as "Touchtalker."

Remedial assistance—Biofeedback devices for stutterers, persons with voice disorders; establishing scenarios or contexts in which instruction can occur (e.g., simulation of a problem with which the student interacts); tutorial programs.

Instructional assistance—Software for generating instructional materials or tests; for data keeping.

Other technological innovations can help students with communication problems. A computer can be trained to recognize a discrete vocabulary or set of utterances. Voice-recognition devices are becoming increasingly sophisticated; the technology is rapidly closing in on computers that will be fully driven by voice commands. The number of potential applications for programs that run on the basis of sounds or utterances is enormous. Already available are speech training devices that transform verbal utterances of speech impaired students into visual images that can be used as the basis for speech improvement.

Steady improvement in the quality of voice synthesizers has resulted in verbal output from computers that is increasingly lifelike and easy to understand. Computers now are able to give verbal directions to students and to provide verbal feedback on their responses. Voice synthesizers are making it possible for nonverbal students to converse with nonhandicapped persons. From input provided by the student, the computer generates a verbalization.

The entire field of computer-based communication augmentation changes with each technological breakthrough. Up-to-date developments in this field can be found in the *Journal for Computer Users in Speech and Hearing* (P.O. Box 2160, Hudson, OH 44236) and the *Augmentative Communication News* (One Surf Way, Suite 215, Monterey, CA 93940).

Students with Hearing Impairments

Educational uses of technology with hearing impaired students have focused on language and related concept problems and on relevant instructional issues. Mention must be made of the recent technological success of cochlear implants, which hold the promise of restoring functional hearing in many persons who previously would have remained totally deaf.

The following are representative examples of successful computer technology applications with deaf students:

Language and concept development—Use of computer language LOGO for building concepts and logical reasons; Reading and Microcomputer Project from Texas School for the Deaf (Austin) for building vocabulary skills.

Language assessment—Computer-Assisted Evaluation (flexible blocks representing different areas of language development from California School for the Deaf (Fremont); only those that are needed are selected).

Speech and sign training—Computer-assisted training devices showing speech spectrum (pitch and nasality also represented); Dynamic Audio-Video Interaction Device for interactive video for speech reading and sign language instruction from National Institute for the Deaf/Rochester Institute of Technology (Rochester, NY).

School subjects—Math City tutorial from California School for the Deaf; interactive program for teaching beginning reading from Pennsylvania School for the Deaf (Philadelphia).

Telephone communication is now possible for deaf persons via special teletypewriter or telecommunication devices. Sensory enhancement or translation equipment can either clarify an audio or video signal or translate from one to the other so that the signal can be received or emitted by a hearing impaired student. Computer-driven telecommunication devices are becoming increasingly available in schools and libraries, making it possible for deaf students to obtain full information and reference services.

Students with Visual Impairments

Many types of sophisticated equipment are available for students with visual impairments. The purposes of these assistive aids are to give the students access to print and graphic materials and to facilitate written expression. For blind students, equipment includes text-to-braille, text-to-tactile monitors, and text-to-speech devices, as well as tactile-based and speech-based word processing technology. For partially sighted students, the technology takes the form of a variety of magnification and large-print devices. The most common of these assistive devices are briefly described below.

The Tactile Graphics Display, developed by the American Foundation for the Blind, can display alphanumeric fonts, traditional six-dot braille, computer braille, and graphics. The ULTRA (Universal Laboratory Training and Research Aid) is a flexible, portable talking laboratory computer that can be used as an instructional laboratory aid (it can be connected to a variety of laboratory equipment and take readings, converting them to speech output), talking computer terminal (it reads or describes what appears on its screen), or personal computer (it can function as a word processor and perform most of the tasks of a regular computer).

The Kurzweil Reading Machine converts printed materials in approximately 300 type styles and sizes into synthetic English speech, at a rate that can be variably controlled. The Optacon Print Reading System is a portable device that allows blind and deaf–blind students to have immediate independent access to printed materials of all kinds through translation of a visual signal (letter) into an enlarged vibrating tactile form. To assist blind students in writing, reading, note taking, and storing braille text, the VersaBraille System is available in portable form. This device may be attached to a computer modem or teletypewriter for communication with remote sources. Both VersaBraille and the Optacon were developed by Telesensory Systems.

A variety of electronic visual aids for partially sighted students have been developed. Visualtek's products have variable print size (allowing magnification of print up to 60 times), image contrast enhancement (making images sharper), and built-in lighting (to provide appropriate illumination), as well as other features. Viewscan, another computer-controlled device for the partially sighted, is a portable device for magnifying and clarifying visual images.

Students with Physical Disabilities

Computer-assisted devices are used to assist students with physical disabilities with access to educational opportunities, access to vocational skill development and employment, and recreation and daily living environmental control. Depending on the abilities of the particular student, such devices range from those that emit a low-level signal for adult attention to highly sophisticated devices for generating speech or controlling complex equipment in an employment environment. Computers may be used to turn equipment on and off (TV, lights), to activate communication aids, to control a motorized wheelchair, or to direct a robot.

Electronic page-turners permit students with severe physical disabilities to have independent access to books. Students who lack the motor coordination required for a standard keyboard can access standard computer programs using a keyboard emulator. The emulator may be in the form of an enlarged keyboard or may consist of a matrix of large squares that accept the touch of a headstick or a light-beam headpointer. An adaptive-firmware card developed for the Apple computer allows students with disabilities to run standard, unmodified software (e.g., games or educational programs) using any of 10 input routines, some of which require the use of only a single switch. Other devices and adaptations have made it possible for students with profound physical disabilities to provide computer input via switches that accept voice, muscle twitch, head or mouth stick, touch, suck, sip, puff, or eye-stare as response modalities. All of these devices permit students to have access to programs they would otherwise not be able to use.

USING COMPUTERS IN THE CLASSROOM

The preceding section provided an overview of basic computer hardware and some of the adaptations and peripherals that make it possible for students with particular cognitive, sensory, or motor problems to benefit from classroom instruction. We now consider in more explicit form the actual use of computers in a classroom that contains some students with learning or behavior problems.

Much has been written about how computers will revolutionize what happens in the classroom. Our position is that classroom teachers will continue to be central in the instructional process, and that computers provide but one more resource, in some cases a unique resource, for enabling learning to take place. Research directed toward the assessment of the effectiveness of computers in the classroom has in general led to the conclusion that computers produce good results when they are used as a *supplement* to the regular curriculum, but that mixed results are obtained when computers are used as a *substitute* for regular instruction. Overall, however, computer use has resulted in more rapid learning than has regular instruction, especially for those students who need practice in acquiring speed in reading decoding, spelling, and basic mathematics facts.

Hannaford (1993) summarized five elements that must be present in order for teachers to successfully use computers with exceptional students. Teachers need to

1. Recognize that there are technical and practical limits to what computers can do.

2. Be aware of the needs of the students who will be using the computer.

3. Give careful thought to what they want the computer to do, when, under what conditions, and to what effect.

4. Use the computer as an integrated part of an instructional, managerial, and adaptive classroom environment that is already successful. Teachers cannot expect the computer to salvage teaching when these other components are falling apart!

5. Adapt the technology to the needs of the individual student, rather than trying to get the student to adapt to the technology. (Adapted from Hannaford, 1993, p. 4)

In considering the ways in which computers can be used in a classroom, it is useful to distinguish among computer use that is directly instructional in nature (computer-assisted instruction), computer use as a tool (e.g., word processing), computer use for the management of instructional activities (computer-managed instruction), and computer use for testing and record keeping. We examine each of these in the following sections.

Computer-Assisted Instruction

Computer-assisted instruction (CAI) takes a number of forms, depending on the purpose that a teacher has in mind. This purpose depends on the kind of learning that the teacher is promoting, the student's stage of learning (acquisition, consolidation, retention, or generalization of skills), and the kind of software that is available. The following are the types of CAI that are currently in widest use.

Tutorial Programs

Tutorial programs are a mode of computer-assisted instruction in which the program does actual teaching—it assumes the role of the teacher in presenting material for the student to learn. In dialogue fashion, questions are asked of the student to assess whether the material has been mastered. If the student's responses are acceptable, new material is presented; if not, the program usually makes provisions for review or remediation of the faulty learning. This kind of program is best suited to students with good independent work habits and good reading comprehension skills.

Simulations

Simulations are designed to re-create some aspect of reality or a situation analogous to a reality that is relevant to an instructional curriculum. Simulations are especially appropriate in cases where it would not be feasible or safe to undertake the learning in the real-life situation (e.g., initial driver education training or training in first-aid techniques). The greater the similarity between the simulation and the real phenomenon that is being modeled, the more likely it is that appropriate generalization will occur. Most curricular simulation programs have been developed for the areas of science (e.g., *The Market Place,* published by MECC; *Community Aquarium,* published by Cross Educational Software), social studies (e.g., *Urbanization: The Growth of Cities,* published by Tom Snyder Productions; *War or Peace?* published by Bright Ideas Inc.), and mathematics (e.g., *Math Shop,* published by Scholastic).

Problem Solving

Teaching problem solving via computer is an area that has seen outstanding development in recent years. In fact, there are some who believe that CAI may become the educational method of choice in teaching problem solving (e.g., Emberly, 1987). Many of the problem-solving applications in CAI are in the computer language LOGO. The LOGO approach allows the student not only to solve problems but also to generate and define problems to be solved (Papert, 1980). It is particularly useful for students who are disorganized in their approach to solving problems, because it creates a set of highly motivating circumstances in which students must organize themselves in a precise manner. The skill of defining and resolving problems in a coherent manner is one that many students with learning and behavioral problems need to develop.

The range of programs is continually growing, in terms of both the types of problem-solving skills taught and the kinds of students for whom the programs are appropriate. Programs include *Castle Clobber* (published by Mindscape), which teaches logic, inference, critical thinking, and map reading to students at developmental levels of kindergarten through Grade 4, and *Decision Making and Problem Solving* (published by Wintergreen), which presents seven ways of making decisions and solving problems to students at ninth-grade through adult levels. Among the most successful problem-solving programs are the Carmen Sandiego series (*Where in the World is Carmen Sandiego?* and *Where in the USA is Carmen Sandiego?* published by Broderbund) in which students play the role of detective in order to solve crimes. To do so, they must use map skills and geographic knowledge, and organize data in a logical and orderly manner.

Programs such as *Problem Solving* (published by MECC) teach problem-solving strategies (guess and check, make a list, simplify the problem) that can be generalized to help solve problems in many areas of life, although the program itself uses problems such as estimating how many times a cue ball will bounce against the sides of a pool table of various dimensions before dropping into given pockets. Many of the best of the new problem-solving programs use an adventure or game format that is highly motivating to students, yet teaches analytic reasoning, sequencing, risk taking, perseverance, logical reasoning, prediction, strategic planning, evaluation, or critical decision making. This is one of the most exciting and promising areas of classroom programs at the present time. Again, however, we must state that the key to the successful use of these programs is the classroom teacher's ability to integrate the activity into ongoing learning experiences and to provide opportunities for generalization. In addition, students with learning problems may require additional guidance, support, and feedback to successfully use these programs.

Information/Demonstration Programs

There are basically two kinds of information/demonstration programs. One type is presequenced, and is usually used in its entirety. An example would be a demonstration of an astronomy experiment that is too dangerous or too expensive for the students or teacher to conduct themselves. The other kind is an information store or data base. Examples include *Grolier's Encyclopedia* or *Encyclopedia Britannica,* which are now available on CD-ROM. Another example is a picture/sound videodisc holding up to 54,000 still frames featuring works of art from the National Gallery of Art that can be instantaneously selected and individually viewed (*National Gallery of Art Laserguide,* published by Videodisc Publishing).

Drill and Practice

By far the most common use of CAI is drill and practice. These programs range from unimaginative exercises to those using exciting game or simulation formats. Used properly, computer-assisted drill and practice can provide an interesting and novel way for students to consolidate and integrate previously learned material. At worst, drill and practice can be "computer seatwork," with little advantage over the paper-and-pencil variety. To be avoided are programs that provide a more attractive reinforcer for an incorrect response (e.g., a loud explosion or a "naughty" sound) than for a correct response (voice synthesizer primly saying "That's right"). The best drill-and-practice programs provide feedback that helps students identify and correct their mistakes. Drill-and-practice programs are most effective with students who require immediate feedback on their responses (but teachers should avoid using only programs that reinforce after each response—this can teach students to become discouraged in other instructional situations where it is not possible to reinforce each individual response). Drill and practice can also be useful with students who benefit from repeatedly going over previously learned material.

Educational Games

Educational games are designed to be fun as well as to encourage appropriate learning. Frequently, the game strategy is similar to that of the popular commercial computer games, with an educational component built in. In general, educational games rely heavily on dazzling graphic effects; the educational aspect is not always an integral part of the game and may appear contrived. Educational games have great potential for students of low motivation, or for students who are "turned off" by traditional academic formats. In some instances, computer games can be used effectively as reinforcers for other instructional tasks successfully completed by a student.

Using Computers as Tools

Students can be taught to use computers as tools for gathering information and presenting what they know. Using computers in these ways in the classroom enhances performance and provides important rehearsal for the real-life uses of computers. The following are some of the most important ways in which computers are used as tools in the classroom.

Word Processing

Many students have great difficulty in writing. As pointed out in Chapter 4, the problem may reside in poor attitudes (resistance or reluctance to write), poor fine motor coordination (difficulty in writing legibly or rapidly), or difficulties with expression (poor conceptual development, lack of knowledge of the topic, poor language development, or poor organizational skills). Using the computer for word processing frequently improves students' self-esteem, confidence, and attitudes toward written expression, and in many cases provides an excellent alternative to writing by hand for students with motor problems.

Use of word processing can serve as an integral component of developing literacy in children using a whole language approach, where students learn to think of writing as first and foremost a communication activity. The "finished" look of writing done with a word processor and a printer results in a product that lends authenticity to the notion of students as authors and critics of written materials.

Before computer word processing is used in the classroom, students must be made aware of its advantages—ease of corrections and revisions, availability of a spelling checker, legibility, and attractiveness of the product. Researchers have found improved quantity and quality of written work as well as improved attitudes toward writing among students with mild disabilities following training in word processing. Substantial time must be invested, however, in the teaching of keyboarding skills before these benefits can be realized. Short, intensive keyboarding sessions have been found to be most effective, particularly when accompanied by specific feedback for students with learning disabilities (Neuman & Morocco, 1987; Okolo, Hinsey, & Yousefian, 1990).

On the basis of research conducted at the University of Maryland, Charles MacArthur and his associates (MacArthur, 1988) have developed a model for the implementation of a word processing program. The model consists of the following elements:

1. Emphasis on the communicative aspect of writing, including planning, drafting, revising, editing, and publishing

2. Use of the word processor as a writing and publishing tool

3. Selection or development of software appropriate to the communication task—formal written expression, classroom message center, games, newsletters, and so forth

4. Teaching students the use of appropriate strategies for successful written communication

Sitko (1986) suggested the following components for students and teachers:

Prewriting Aspects—Planning

1. Creative brainstorming (development of story)—teacher with group of students

2. Listing of elements for story—teacher with student

3. Discussion of story—student with peer

4. Development of outline—student

Writing Aspects—Writing and Revision

5. First draft of story on computer, each sentence on a separate line—student

6. First editing of story for organization, comprehensibility, and completion—student, with teacher or peer consultation

7. Second editing of story for paragraph structure—student

8. Third editing of each sentence for spelling, grammar, and punctuation—student

9. Final editing of story for quality—student

10. Printout of final product

A number of other investigators have reported successful use of word processing with students who have had difficulty in writing (Cochran-Smith, 1991; MacArthur, 1988). In general, these researchers have found that students dramatically increased the quality and quantity of their written output when taught to use computers for writing and text editing. For some students, the major impetus seems to have been the elimination of the frustration and imperfections (cross-outs, rub-outs, inserts, smudges) associated with writing by hand. Others were able to overcome debilitating spelling problems by using a spelling checker. Results with learning disabled students were especially noteworthy when the instruction was combined with brainstorming, group conferencing, or a process approach to writing. Several researchers found that the obtained gains generalized to reading, spelling, general language usage, and general attitudes toward learning.

The range and quality of software available for teaching students to use the computer as a writing tool are continually growing. For younger students, *Story Machine* (Spinnaker) or *Children's Writing and Publishing Center* (Learning Company) are useful programs; older students will make better use of *Bank Street Writer* (Scholastic), *Magic Slate* (Sunburst), or *FrEdWriter* (freeware from CUE Softswap). *Super Story Tree* (Scholastic) is an interactive Hypermedia writing program that allows students to make choices as to what will happen next in a story. Assistance in the planning stage of writing can be provided by programs such as *Bank Street PreWriter*

(Scholastic) and *Prewrite* (Mindscape). A set of language arts programs called *Quill* (Heath & Co.) provides motivating and flexible exercises that teach students to do more effective writing, revising, and editing. Programs such as *CAW: Computer Assisted Writing* (Educational Activities) provide help in the technical and conceptual aspects of report and letter writing and in creative persuasive expression. A large number of programs teach keyboarding (e.g., *Type to Learn* by Sunburst, *Muppet Learning Keys Keyboard* by Sunburst) and provide word processing capabilities (e.g., *Bank Street Writer* by Broderbund, *Dr. Peet's Talk / Writer* by Hartley, *Talking Text Writer* by Scholastic, *AppleWorks* by Claris, *Word* by Microsoft), some of them in the public domain (e.g., *MECC Keyboarding Primer, MECC Keyboarding Master, MECC Writer,* and *MECC Write Start* by MECC, St. Paul). Interested teachers would do well to consult more comprehensive listings of software (see the resources listed at the end of this chapter).

Use of Information Databases and Telecommunications

Computers equipped with modems literally make a world of information available to teachers and students. In most instances, however, meaningful use of information databases is limited to older or more capable students.

Several databases, including electronic mail and bulletin board services, focus on issues of particular interest to service providers or persons who are handicapped. These include COMPUSERVE, HANDICAPPED USER'S DATABASE, DEAFNET, SPECIALNET, and BITNET. The Council for Exceptional Children (CEC) in Reston, Virginia, provides, at nominal cost, computer search reprints on selected topics pertaining to special education. Custom computer searches are available from CEC and in most libraries. The Center for Special Education Technology in Reston, Virginia, offers a service that consists of a large number of taped messages on such topics as selecting software, small-group computing, use of games in the classroom, and teacher authoring languages for use in special education technology. These "tech tapes" can be accessed 24 hours a day by telephone. (A free list of tapes and codes may be obtained from CEC or by calling the Special Education Technology Hotline, 703-620-3660.)

To use the computer to retrieve information relevant to a particular problem, users must acquire two types of skills. One type is *technical* in nature. Students must learn to push the right keys to access the particular database they wish to use. In some instances—particularly when a complex or expensive information base is being used—the teacher or a librarian will want to be involved.

The other type of skill is *conceptual* in nature. Before a database can be accessed, the user must define the problem to be solved in a very clear and explicit manner. Most databases mandate the use of keywords to search for relevant information. The selection of appropriate keywords is a prerequisite to a successful search, and it requires that the student define and focus the topic to be searched in a very precise way. Many students find this activity quite difficult, yet it underlies successful problem solving of any kind—computer assisted or not. Using a computer only highlights the need to define a problem very specifically.

Another conceptual skill needed for the successful use of databases is the ability to sort large amounts of information (quickly, if the search is online) and to ascertain which material is relevant and important. A voluminous amount of information can be accessed on many topics, and making sense of such a quantity of material can present a major challenge. Precisely because this task mirrors real-life problem solving, it is likely to provide an excellent learning experience for students.

Recent years have seen great increases in the use of networks and bulletin boards. Their use makes it possible for students to write to real audiences in remote locations, thus improving students' motivation as well as the quality of their writing (Cohen & Riel, 1989). Networks and bulletin boards also provide students with the opportunity to make friends with people in other locations and cultures, to communicate with experts, and to carry on focused, topical discussions—important for the development of social skills and higher order thinking abilities (Steinberg, 1992).

Use of Spreadsheets, Data Management, and Desktop Publishing Programs

Although the use of spreadsheets, data management, and desktop publishing programs is beyond the capabilities of many students, it is widespread in the world of work. Thus, teaching students to use such programs will pay handsome dividends. As time goes on, more and more schools will see fit to equip students to use computers as tools for record keeping, data and budget management, and desktop publishing.

Computer-Managed Instruction and Expert Systems

Traditional Computer-Managed Instruction

A fully developed computer-managed instructional (CMI) program allows a teacher to assess entry skills of a pupil, to prescribe appropriate learning experiences (both print and nonprint), to reassess progress, to assign additional learning exercises if warranted or to "promote" a student to the next module, and to keep complete dated records on each pupil, including a record of particular areas of difficulty. Although not all CMI programs have all of these features, their basic purpose is the same—to diagnose student strengths and weaknesses in a particular content area and then to prescribe instructional activities (e.g., "Read pages 22 to 26 of your text," or "View the videotape 'Christopher Columbus'") based on the student's correct and incorrect responses.

CMI programs are not difficult for teachers to develop themselves, but it is a time-consuming process. To be effective, they should be correlated directly to the student's curriculum and should reflect precisely the learning resources and activities that are available for students (e.g., it does not make sense to have a program that prescribes reading material that is not in the local library). Used appropriately, CMI is a wonderful teaching approach for individualizing instruction, because students can proceed at their own pace and learning activities can be tailored to the particular learning needs of each student.

Authoring Languages

Unquestionably, computer-managed instruction can be extraordinarily effective for students for whom commercial programs are not appropriate. However, CMI has found limited application because of time constraints and the reluctance of many teachers to develop computer-managed instructional packages based on traditional computer languages. For this reason, a number of authoring languages have been developed. These languages facilitate CMI development by teachers. Authoring languages provide a kind of "template" into which a teacher can insert instructional text or graphics, or test questions without having to master a programming language. Among the most commonly used earlier authoring languages are *Pilot* and *Superpilot* (Apple) for the Apple series; the newer, easier, and more versatile *HyperStudio* (Roger Wagner), *HyperCard IIGS* (Apple), and *Tutortech* (Techware) are also available. More recent authoring systems that allow teachers to incorporate multimedia into their lessons include *HyperCard* for the Macintosh and *Linkway,* an equivalent language for the IBM and its clones. A number of commercially produced software packages contain authoring system components that allow teachers to modify the content, format, or response mode of a program to make it more suitable for their students.

Computer-Managed Teacher Aids

Programs are available for teachers to develop custom-made tests or instructional lessons—for example, *Quickflash* (to produce flashcards) (published by MECC), *The Lesson Planner* (Tyson Educational Systems), *Number Fact Sheets* (Gamco), *Multiple Choices* (Mindscape), *Create-a-Test* (Gamco), and *Create Lessons* (Hartley). The goal of all of these programs is to facilitate planning, instruction, and testing by the classroom teacher.

Expert Systems

The use of computers in assisting in the diagnosis of health problems by medical professionals has been adapted and is being investigated for use in special education. Derived from decision models in the field of artificial intelligence, these expert systems are able to integrate vast amounts of information and come up with a diagnostic label or proposed placement or instructional decision that represents the "best fit" with the data based on identified underlying rules. Should current research bear out the usefulness of expert systems in educational decision making, educators can look to a time when computers will help solve some of the most intractable problems faced in the areas of diagnosis, placement, and prescription of appropriate interventions.

Some educators, however, caution that the use of expert systems in special education assessment can be criticized as resting on the assumption that any existing problems reside in the student rather than in the learning environment. The implication of this criticism is that contextual indicators such as teaching style and instructional methodology must be considered, as well as student performance factors, in the use of expert systems.

Using Computers for Testing

The assessment of students through teacher-made tests in a CMI format was described briefly above. Computers can also be of assistance in more direct testing of pupils. Computers can help teachers with item banking, test assembly, test administration, test scoring, and record keeping.

Item Banking

Item banking refers to a procedure by which test items are saved and "pooled" so that they can be used in more than one test period, sometimes by more than one teacher. When a test item proves confusing to students, or obsolete, or otherwise unsatisfactory, a simple stroke of the keyboard eliminates the item from the item bank. Over time, a teacher can develop a comprehensive collection of test items from which to choose when designing a test. When item banking is combined with item performance data (e.g., proportion correct, number of examinees selecting a given item, reliability estimates, and test summary statistics), the quality of the tests that a teacher prepares can be improved greatly. Item banking also reduces the amount of time needed to prepare a test.

Test Assembly

If items are banked in a computer, the actual assembly of a test is very simple. Using a word processing and/or an editing program, the teacher simply identifies test items and adds instructions. This feature reduces the chances that errors will be introduced through faulty typing or proofreading.

Test Administration

A number of commercially produced tests are available for administration via a computer format. However, the administration of tests by computer is not limited to standardized tests; in fact, some of the greatest advantages of computer test administration become most obvious with teacher-generated tests. The format of a teacher-made test, including its spatial organization, time allowed for each item, and the use of color and graphics to highlight important information, can be easily modified when the test is administered by computer.

Modifications are particularly appropriate for many students with learning disabilities. Alterations of the presentation mode (e.g., by using a speech synthesizer) and/or the response mode (e.g., by accepting input from a joystick, switch, or keyboard emulator as well as a regular keyboard) can be made to accommodate students with particular difficulties or handicaps. Because the computer presents items in sequence, poorly organized students will not miss items. Furthermore, the motivational aspect of computers can help to keep certain students on task; the teacher can build feedback or reinforcement into the test by interspersing encouraging phrases such as "Keep trying" or "You're doing a good job" in flashing letters or graphics. A well-constructed computer-administered test can appear more like a game than a test to students who are afraid of tests.

Test Scoring and Record Keeping

Commercially prepared tests have been scored and profiled by computer for many years. However, even teacher-made tests can be computer scored and individual and group records kept, with only a minimum amount of expertise on the part of the teacher. For teachers without programming ability, the use of an authoring language can greatly facilitate test scoring and record keeping (as well as test development). An alternative is to hire a professional programmer to develop a model skeleton test into which test items and pupil names can be inserted in each new testing situation.

Using Computers for Record Keeping and in the IEP Process

Computers have wide applicability in managing virtually any kind of data or records. In fact, one of the major uses of computers is in database management or management information systems. A survey of special education administrators (Burrello, Tracy, & Glassman, 1983) showed that the most popular use of computer technology in schools was for student-data management, including student enrollment and rosters, student tracking, student program management, and assessment. Business-data management, such as handling budgets, personnel files, inventories of books and supplies, and transportation, was also frequently done by computer. Word processing and information retrieval were also popular.

Although few classroom teachers need to use computers for the scope of activities described above, computers can be helpful in record keeping and aspects of managing Individualized Education Plans at the classroom level. The previous section described how teachers can develop test item banks. Inventories of pupil activity sheets, picture files, or any other instructional files also can be organized, stored, and kept up to date by computer. IEP objectives for a given child and a record of his or her progress toward meeting those objectives can be conveniently tracked using a number of IEP programs that are now available for computers. Each child can be assigned a file using any one of a number of available database management programs. All test results are entered into the student's files as they occur, and at the touch of a keystroke a printer will print a formatted summary of the student's progress. This procedure can save a teacher much time and effort and produce attractive and accurate pupil reports. If desired, such pupil reports can be directly conveyed to the school's central office mainframe or minicomputer through a networking arrangement in which all computers in a school are interconnected.

Selecting Software for Classroom Use

A pervasive and persistent difficulty encountered by teachers who want to use computers in their classrooms is the generally low quality of available educational programs. These programs, called *software* (as opposed to *hardware,* the actual physical equipment), are available in disk form, on cassette tapes, or on cartridges. Although educational software has been significantly improved in recent years, much instructional software is technically less sophisticated and educationally less sound than it could be. Thus, teachers must develop some degree of sophistication in selecting software that is appropriate for their particular classrooms. A number of software evaluation formats have been developed to assist teachers in this task; one that we believe is both comprehensive and realistic is reproduced in Table 11.1.

Effectiveness of Computer Use in the Classroom

Computers are being found in ever-increasing numbers of elementary and secondary classrooms. Initially, many teachers viewed computers with either excitement ("Wow! This will revolutionize teaching!") or fear ("I wonder if I'll be able to learn how to use these things?" or "Will computers take away my job?"). Today, however, most teachers see computers as simply another instructional tool, albeit an important one. Both the hardware and the software are becoming increasingly sophisticated, and educators are learning how to integrate computers into classroom routines. Computers are clearly here to stay, yet educators need to know whether and

TABLE 11.1.   Modified MCE Program Evaluation Form

Directions: This evaluation form is designed to evaluate four software programs. Answer each of the questions about each program you evaluate. Use the following rating scale:

$$3 = \text{EXCELLENT}$$
$$2 = \text{ABOVE AVERAGE}$$
$$1 = \text{AVERAGE}$$
$$-1 = \text{BELOW AVERAGE}$$
$$-5 = \text{POOR}$$

After rating programs in each area, add up the total scores and place them in the appropriate spaces. Let this rating help you in your decision making in the purchase of microcomputer software.

Names of Programs Evaluated: *Type of Program Evaluated (i.e., tutorial, etc.):*

1. _____   _____

2. _____   _____

3. _____   _____

4. _____   _____

Comments on Each Program:

1. _____

_____

_____

2. _____

_____

_____

3. _____

_____

_____

4. _____

_____

_____

Program Choice (if applicable):

_____

_____

_____

_____

(continues)

TABLE 11.1. *Continued*

	PROGRAM NAMES			
	1	*2*	*3*	*4*

I. Instructional Content

1. Is the content consistent with the goals and objectives of the program?
2. Is the program one of a series in which carefully planned learning objectives have been followed?
3. Does the instructional guide provide information, suggestions, and materials to assist the teacher in successfully implementing the program?
4. Are program goals provided that are usable for Individualized Education Plans?
5. Are evaluation materials and/or criteria provided that are usable for Individualized Education Plans?
6. Are prerequisite skills, vocabulary, and concepts determined and presented?
7. Is vocabulary defined or paraphrased in text or in the prerequisite skills portion of the program principles section of the instruction?
8. Are diagnostic or prescriptive procedures built into the program?
9. Does the text follow established rules for punctuation, capitalization, grammar, and usage?
10. Are supplemental materials provided for learner and teacher?
11. Is the product designed for appropriate age and ability groups?
12. Is the program compatible with the curriculum?
13. Is the program compatible with the needs of the teacher?
14. Is the content accurate and complete?
15. Are examples provided with directions when appropriate?
16. Are redundancy and drill used effectively?
17. Is language appropriate in tone and selection?
18. Are concrete applications for concepts provided?
19. Is feedback immediate?

II. Educational Adequacy

1. Is instructional design of high quality using accepted learning theory?
2. Are learners always the target of interaction with the computer—a personalized element?
3. Are positive responses reinforced?
4. Are frames that follow incorrect responses nonpunishing?
5. Is reinforcement variable and random in context and established by behavior management principles?
6. Is branching used where the learner demonstrates need for further concept development before proceeding?
7. Are avenues of communication from the learner to the computer logical and at comprehensible levels?
8. Is evaluation of each concept appropriate and sufficient?
9. Are concepts and skills task analyzed into appropriate steps?

(continues)

TABLE 11.1. *Continued*

| | PROGRAM NAMES | | | |
	1	2	3	4
II. Educational Adequacy *(Continued)*				

10. Are color, graphics, and animation used effectively to enhance the lesson?

11. Are sound, inverse print, etc., employed for attention and reinforcement purposes and not distracting?

12. Is syllabification provided for new and/or unfamiliar words?

13. Is sentence length dependent on need and learner levels?

14. Is the learner always provided with frames that allow for progression through the program?

15. Does the program provide suitable directions for the learner?

III. Technical Adequacy

1. Will the program run to completion without being "hung up" because of unexpected responses?

2. Are the programs difficult or impossible to be inadvertently disrupted by the learner?

3. Can learners operate the programs independently?

4. Is the amount of time on each frame appropriate?

5. Is the length of each section appropriate?

6. Are words and lines spaced for ease of reading?

7. Is variation of type and organization of textual materials appropriate for a clear presentation?

8. Are inappropriate responses considered and handled appropriately?

9. Is the educational technology (i.e., microcomputer) the best available for presenting this subject matter?

10. Are backups available?

IV. Overall Evaluation Rating of Program in Its Entirety

Total for each program

Source: MCE Inc., 157 S. Kalamazoo Mall, Suite 250, Kalamazoo, MI 49007.

how computers are effective in promoting educational objectives. The following is a summary of what is known about the general effectiveness of computers with children who have learning and behavioral problems:

- Computers are best used as supplements to teacher-led instruction, rather than as substitutes for such instruction.

- Students often learn the same material more quickly from computers than from conventional instruction.

- Learning from computers is more effective when students work in pairs or in groups. Carefully planned cooperative learning from a computer can result in significant social gains, as well as cognitive and metacognitive improvement in summarizing, predicting, analyzing, questioning, and justifying.

- Drill-and-practice software usually is more beneficial for low-ability students than for high-ability students when the purpose is consolidation of skills. Both groups benefit when such software is used for review.

- Using computers is often more effective than conventional instruction with students who are unmotivated or resistant to school learning.

- Most students enjoy working with computers.

- Computers are most effective when they are used in well-managed classrooms, and are well integrated into the ongoing curriculum.

In the following sections, we more specifically consider the effects of computer use and, where possible, consider some best practices in maximizing the positive use of computers in a number of areas of school learning. For additional summaries of research on educational uses of computers, teachers are referred to the excellent reviews by Hannaford (1993), Hasselbring (1986), and Sitko (1986).

Student Self-Esteem and Attitudes Toward Learning

It is no secret that many students are "turned off" by much conventional classroom instruction. The research evidence indicates that motivation and attitude toward learning frequently improve when computers are used, especially with students who have had difficulty in school. Furthermore, considerable anecdotal information indicates that computers provide excitement and motivation for some students, resulting in improved attitudes toward learning and enhanced feelings about themselves, as evidenced in confidence, risk taking, and willingness to try.

Reading

In general, the research conducted on the effects of using computer programs to supplement classroom reading instruction has shown that student achievement can be significantly enhanced by their use. These generally positive findings have resulted in a proliferation of computer programs for teaching reading skills. Literally thousands of programs are now available. In this section, we do not review programs as such, but we identify the major types of programs teachers can expect to find and provide examples of these types. In the final section of this chapter, we have listed a number of software directories and sources that teachers will find helpful in selecting reading software.

According to Mason, Blanchard, and Daniel (1983), computer-assisted instruction in reading can be organized into three major types of programs. The first (and still most common) type of program is the simple, linear, drill-and-practice type in which the student uses the computer to practice a particular reading skill (usually word attack and decoding) that has been taught. Sometimes these programs are used for skill development and sometimes for remediation. Frequently, these programs are, in effect, electronic versions of the familiar seatwork or workbooks often used in reading instruction, with the major differences being that rate of presentation is controlled and instant feedback is given to the student. These programs can be criticized for being limited to a bottom-up approach to reading (see Chapter 3 for a discussion), with a consequent fragmentation and isolation of reading skills. Furthermore, most of these programs test, rather than teach, reading abilities. Many times, the reading level of the program instructions is more difficult than that of the skills being taught. If the capabilities and limitations of these programs are taken into account, they can provide a useful adjunct to classroom reading instruction. Examples of this type of program are numerous—they range from the *Phonics Prime Time* series published by MECC to *Construct-a-Word* and *Hint and Hunt* developed and researched by two reading researchers (Roth & Beck, 1987).

A second type of reading program is the more sophisticated tutorial, in which students are actually provided instruction in some aspect of reading. The program usually task analyzes the content and paces and branches the material to be covered based on the student's responses. Frequently, the program commences at a point commensurate with the student's entry-level skills. Programs of this type can be useful for students who are progressing at a level and pace significantly different from that of their classmates, or who need to be retaught certain reading skills. In choosing a tutorial program, teachers should consider the characteristics of a good human tutor, and use these as criteria against which to evaluate the program. Does the program take the student's entry-level skills into account? Does the program relate new learning to material previously learned by the student? Does the program have branching options, based on the progress the student is making? Examples of reading tutorial programs are *RightWriter* (published by RightSoft) and *Writing a Narrative* (available from MECC).

A third type of reading program is one in which the students "converse" with the computer as they attempt to solve problems, create stories, or predict endings. The student controls the pace and level of the interaction. An example of such a program is *The Puzzler* (published by Sunburst), in which students are presented with mystery stories that actively engage them in predicting, confirming and integrating. There is no predetermined "right" answer to the problems presented by the stories. The use of the computer program is preceded and followed by group discussions on reading strategy use led by the teacher or by another student. Another example of creative computer software is published by Scholastic in the form of a bimonthly computer-based periodical called *Microzine*. Each issue consists of four computer programs, and student and teacher guides. The programs for the most part are open-ended story games and involve individual students as well as groups. The programs tend to be highly interactive and to encourage the written and oral expression of students, and to be appropriate for students with special needs.

Spelling

Overwhelmingly, computer programs in spelling are of the drill-and-practice type (e.g., *Spelling* [Gamco], *Spelling Week by Week* [Chalksoft]). Some programs allow personalization of spelling words to be learned, based on the student's needs or errors (*Spunky Speller* [Data Command], *Speller* [MECC], or *Spellicopter* [Designware]). Computer programs can also be used to analyze students' patterns of spelling errors.

In general, the research shows that computer spelling programs can bring about gains in students' spelling achievement, especially when the programs are used as a supplement to regular spelling instruction. Students using CAI programs in spelling tend to attempt more words, and correctly spell more of the words attempted.

Some intriguing evidence indicates that the motoric element of manual tracing or writing of words helps children remember their spelling words (Cunningham & Stanovich, 1990). In this study, children learning to spell by handwriting performed better than children learning to spell by computer-based programs requiring typing.

Mathematics

Mathematics was the subject area in which the power of computer-assisted instruction was first documented. Although most computer-based mathematics programs are of the drill-and-practice type (e.g., *Early Addition, Basic Arithmetic,* and *Conquering Whole Numbers,* all published by MECC), a number of mathematics tutorials are now available (e.g., *Growgins' Fractions* [MECC] and *Introduction to Counting* [Eduware]). The discovery method of mathematics learning is used in some programs (e.g., the *Geometric Supposer* series published by Sunburst Communications). Game formats are successfully used in some programs, such as *Wizard's Revenge* (Sherston Software) or *Block It* (Electronic Courseware). A few exemplary programs engage students in higher mental processes. For example, the program *Teasers by Tobbs* (Sunburst Communications) requires students to think logically about which numerals could be used to solve addition and multiplication problems in a grid; thus, it helps students to develop and use problem-solving skills that go well beyond the bounds of mathematics problems.

Writing

Using the computer in the classroom for writing purposes addresses two objectives—teaching written expression for its own sake and teaching word processing as a tool for many purposes. Relevant programs and issues were reviewed in the previous discussion of word processing.

In summary, it is clear that the use of computers as a supplement to regular classroom instruction can have beneficial effects on students' learning. In addition to gains in achievement, improvement in attitudes toward learning can result.

RESPONSIBLE USE OF COMPUTERS

Computers moved onto the educational scene with such rapidity that many educators were left poorly prepared for the new professional skills and attitudes that their use requires. Accordingly, a number of professional organizations established committees to draft guidelines for teachers and others who use computers and other new technologies in the schools. These guidelines typically address professional skill areas and touch on pertinent legal and ethical considerations. Following is one such set of guidelines developed by the International Reading Association (IRA).[1]

Guidelines for Educators on Using Computers in the Schools

The Computer Technology and Reading Committee of the International Reading Association has compiled the following guidelines in an effort to encourage the effective use of technology in reading classrooms. The guidelines are designed to highlight important issues and provide guidance to educators as they work to make the best possible use of the many new technologies which are rapidly finding their way into schools and classrooms everywhere.

1. *About Software*   Curricular needs should be primary in the selection of reading instructional software. Above all, software designed for use in the reading classroom must be consistent with what research and practice have shown to be important in the process of learning to read or of reading to learn. The IRA believes that high quality instructional software should incorporate the following elements:

   - clearly stated and implemented instructional objectives.
   - learning to read and reading to learn activities which are consistent with established reading theory and practice.
   - lesson activities which are most effectively and efficiently done through the application of computer technology and are not merely replications of activities which could be better done with traditional means.
   - prompts and screen instructions to the student which are simple, direct and easier than the learning activity to be done.
   - prompts, screen instructions and reading texts which are at a readability level appropriate to the needs of the learner.
   - documentation and instructions which are clear and unambiguous, assuming a minimum of prior knowledge about computers for use.
   - screen displays which have clear and legible print with appropriate margins and between-line spacing.

---

1. Prepared by the 1983–1984 Computer Technology and Reading Committee: Alan E. Farstrup (Chair), Ossi Ahvenainen, Isabel Beck, Darlene Bolig, Jayne DeLawter, Shirley Feldmann, Peter Joyce, Michael Kamil, Gerald J. Kochinski, George E. Mason, Harry B. Miller, Jane D. Smith, Art Willer, Carmelita K. Williams, Linda Roberts (Consultant). Reprinted with permission of the International Reading Association.

- documentation and screen displays which are grammatically correct, factually correct, and which have been thoroughly proofed for spelling errors.
- a record keeping or information management element for the benefit of both the teacher and the learner, where appropriate.
- provisions for effective involvement and participation by the learner, coupled with rapid and extensive feedback, where appropriate.
- wherever appropriate, a learning pace which is modified by the actions of the learner or which can be adjusted by the teacher based on diagnosed needs.
- a fair, reasonable and clearly stated publisher's policy governing the replacement of defective or damaged program media such as tapes, diskettes, ROM cartridges and the like.
- a publisher's preview policy which provides pre-purchase samples or copies for review and which encourages a well-informed software acquisition process by reading educators.

2. *About Hardware* Hardware should be durable, capable of producing highly legible text displays, and safe for use in a classroom situation. Hardware should be chosen that conforms to established classroom needs. Some characteristics to be aware of include, but are not limited to, the following:

- compatibility with classroom software appropriate to the curriculum.
- proven durability in classroom situations.
- clear, unambiguous instruction manuals appropriate for use by persons having a minimum of technical experience with computers.
- sufficient memory (RAM) capability to satisfy anticipated instructional software applications.
- availability of disk, tape, ROM cartridge or other efficient and reliable data storage devices.
- screen displays which produce legible print, minimize glare, and which have the lowest possible screen radiation levels.
- a functional keyboard and the availability of other appropriate types of input devices.
- proven, accessible and reasonably priced technical support from the manufacturer or distributor.

3. *About Staff Development and Training* Staff development programs should be available which encourage teachers to become intelligent users of technology in the reading classroom. Factors to consider include, but are not limited to, the following:

- study and practice with various applications of computer technology in the reading and language arts classroom.
- training which encourages thoughtful and informed evaluation, selection and integration of effective and appropriate teaching software into the reading and language arts classroom.

4. *About Equity* All persons, regardless of sex, ethnic group, socioeconomic status, or ability, must have equality of access to the challenges and benefits of computer technology. Computer technology should be integrated into all classrooms and not be limited to scientific or mathematical applications.

5. *About Research* Research which assesses the impact of computer technology on all aspects of learning to read and reading to learn is essential. Public and private funding should be made available in support of such research. Issues which need to be part of national and international research agendas include, but are not limited to:

- the educational efficacy of computer technology in the reading and language arts classroom.
- the affective dimensions of introducing computer technology into the schools.
- the cognitive dimensions of introducing computer technology into the reading classroom.
- the application of concepts of artificial intelligence to computer software which address issues of reading diagnosis, developmental reading, remedial reading, and instructional management.
- the impact of new technology on students, reading teachers, schools, curricula, parents, and the community.

6. *About Networking and Sharing Information*   Local area and national networks or information services should be established and supported which can be accessed through the use of computers. Such services should be designed to provide an information resource on reading related topics. Such services could also be used to provide linkage and information exchange among many institutions, including professional associations such as the IRA.

7. *About Inappropriate Uses of Technology*   Computers should be used in meaningful and productive ways which relate clearly to instructional needs of students in the reading classroom. Educators must capitalize on the potential of this technology by insisting on its appropriate and meaningful use.

8. *About Legal Issues*   Unauthorized duplication and use of copyrighted computer software must not be allowed. Developers and publishers of educational software have a right to be protected from financial losses due to the unauthorized use of their products. Consumers of educational software have a concomitant right to expect fair prices, quality products and reasonable publishers' policies regarding licensing for multiple copies, replacement of damaged program media, network applications and the like. Without mutual trust and cooperation on this important issue both parties will suffer and, ultimately, so will the learner.

PROFESSIONAL RESOURCES FOR TEACHERS

Organizations/Information Centers

ABLEDATA
National Rehabilitation Information Center
4407 Eighth Street NE
Catholic University
Washington, DC 20017

Apple Computer Office of Special Education and Rehabilitation
20525 Mariani Avenue
Cupertino, CA 95014

Association for Special Education Technology (ASSET)
P.O. Box 152
Allen, TX 75002

IBM National Support Center for Persons with Disabilities
P.O. Box 2150
Atlanta, GA 30055

International Society for Technology in Education
1787 Agate Street
Eugene, OR 97403

Special Education Technology Resource Center
108 Babson Street
Mattapan, MA 02126

Technology and Media Division (TAM)
Council for Exceptional Children
1920 Association Drive
Reston, VA 22091

Books

Behrman, M. M. (Ed.). (1988). *Handbook of microcomputers in special education.* Austin, TX: PRO-ED.
Lindsay, J. D. (Ed.). (1993). *Computers and exceptional individuals* (2nd ed.). Austin, TX: PRO-ED.
Sternberg, E. R. (1991). *Computer-assisted instruction: A synthesis of theory, practice, and technology.* Hillsdale, NJ: Erlbaum.

Journals and Magazines

Bulletin of Science and Technology for the Handicapped
American Association for the Advancement of Science
1776 Massachusetts Avenue
Washington, D.C. 20036

Catalyst
Western Center for Microcomputers in Special Education
Suite 275, 1259 El Camino Real
Menlo Park, CA 94025

Classroom Computer Learning
Peter Li, Inc.
2451 East River Road
Dayton, OH 45439

Computer–Disability News
National Easter Seal Society
2023 West Ogden Avenue
Chicago, IL 60612

Computers in Education
Moorhead Publications
25 Overlead Boulevard
Suite 601
Toronto, Ontario M4H 1B1

The Computing Teacher
Journal of The International Council for Computers in Education
University of Oregon
1787 Agate Street
Eugene, OR 97403

Educational Technology
140 Sylvan Avenue
Englewood Cliffs, NJ 07632

Electronic Education
Suite 220
1311 Executive Center Drive
Tallahassee, FL 32301

Electronic Learning
Scholastic Inc.
730 Broadway
New York, NY 10003

Microzine
Scholastic
2931 East McCarty Street
P.O. Box 7502
Jefferson City, MO 65102

TAM Newsletter
Division of Technology and Media
Council for Exceptional Children
1920 Association Drive
Reston, VA 22091

T.H.E. Journal
(Technological Horizons in Education)
Information Synergy
2626 S. Pullman
Santa Ana, CA 92705

Videodisc Monitor
Future Systems
P.O. Box 26
Falls Church, VA 22046

Directories of Microcomputer Software

Educational Software Buyer's Guide
Special 1985 issue of *Compute!*
P.O. Box 914
Farmingdale, NY 11737

Educational Software Directory
Special issue of *Computers in Education*
December, 1987–January, 1988
Moorhead Publications
25 Overlead Boulevard
Suite 601
Toronto, Ontario M4H 1B1

Educational Software Preview Guide
Center for Learning Technologies
Cultural Education Center
Room 9A47
Albany, NY 12230
(educational software)

The Handicapped Source
101 Route 46, East
Pine Brook, NJ 07058
(free catalog of software suitable for handicapped populations)

International Council for Computers in Education
University of Oregon
Eugene, OR 97403

Minnesota Educational Computing Corporation (MECC)
3490 North Lexington Avenue
St. Paul, MN 55112
(listing of public domain software)

National Education Association
Educational Computer Service
4720 Montgomery Lane
Bethesda, MD 20814

SOFTSEL Product Encyclopedia
P.O. Box 546
North Oak Avenue
Inglewood, CA 90312

Software Registry—CUSH
James Fitch, Editor
Department of Speech Pathology and Audiology
University of South Alabama
Mobile, AL 36688
(communication disorders software)

Source Listing for Microcomputer Software for Special Education
LINC Resources, Inc.
1875 Morse Road
Suite 225
Columbus, OH 43229
(software and hardware directory for special education)

Special Education Software Review
3807 N. Northwood
Peoria, IL 61614

TASH: Technical Aids and Systems for the Handicapped
70 Gibson Drive, Unit 12
Markham, ON Canada L3R 4C2

Trace Center International Software/Hardware Registry
University of Wisconsin–Madison
314 Waisman Center
1500 Highland Avenue
Madison, WI 53706
(software for handicapped students)

Videodisc Compendium
Emerging Technology Consultants
Distribution Center
P.O. Box 12444
St. Paul, MN 55112

Chapter 12

Final Thoughts

DONALD D. HAMMILL AND NETTIE R. BARTEL

In this concluding chapter, we identify five areas of practice that are generic in nature and thereby applicable to most school subjects. These areas are (1) tutoring individual students, (2) involving parents in the instructional effort, (3) selecting materials and resources, (4) using direct or indirect instruction, and (5) the impact of the inclusion movement on education.

TUTORING INDIVIDUAL STUDENTS

Today, adults, high school students, and even elementary students are often employed effectively as tutors in the schools. Even though these paraprofessionals may instruct students in basic school subjects, the primary qualifications for a tutor are not necessarily academic, a fact that is reflected in the following guidelines for selecting individuals to serve as tutors. The tutor must

1. Be dependable, for missing only one or two sessions will destroy the tutoring relationship and allow the student to regress.

2. Be patient and ready to go over material a number of times before the student has finally learned it.

3. Have an understanding of the student's problems and feelings.

4. Have integrity; for example, the tutor must be truthful and never leave the student with the impression that he or she is doing much better than actually is the case.

5. Be capable of handling interpersonal relations well.

Beyond these qualifications, the tutor must be interested in helping students, accept responsibility readily, and follow directions.

Several elements must be considered before an effective tutorial program can be initiated. First, the student's problems must be assessed carefully. Second, those areas in which the tutor will work must be chosen. Third, the approach and materials to be used should be selected. Fourth, the period of time to be spent on any activity should be estimated. The tutor must know exactly what is expected, what is to be done, and how to do it. Therefore, some training should be conducted before the tutor begins the program. Left to his or her own devices without proper training and supervision, the tutor may unwittingly create problems and end up being "more trouble than he or she is worth."

Record Keeping

Each tutor should be given a notebook (preferably looseleaf) having three distinct kinds of pages. The first should be the Tutor's Lesson Plan (the

```
Name  Stanley Miller          Date Started  10/7/90
School  West Elementary       Tutor  Mrs. Clark
Grade  4                      Reading Level  Preprimer
```
Description of the Problem

Stanley has a limited sight vocabulary, poor attention and concentration, and has had almost no success in school.

9:00–9:10 Ask ~~what~~ Stanley what he thinks will happen to the Chinese brothers. Then finish the 5 Chinese Brothers.

9:10–9:20 Review the Dolch Sight Vocabulary Words that he missed yesterday. Have him put those that he still doesn't know on 3" x 5" cards.

9:20–9:30 Use SRA Lab II Rate Builder, Red 3, as a listening exercise. Help him to set a purpose for listening. Remember to keep a record of the number of answers that he gets correct.

FIGURE 12.1. Tutor's lesson plan.

teacher should complete the plan for the tutor). On this page, the activities, the procedures, and the amount of time to be devoted to each student can be listed. If special materials are required, they should be mentioned, along with an indication of where they may be obtained. A sample lesson plan is shown in Figure 12.1.

The second kind of page that should be included in the notebook is a Tutor's Log Sheet. On this page, the tutor may record any observations that seem pertinent about the progress of the child on a particular day. The availability of this sheet will foster ongoing communications between the tutor and the busy classroom teacher. An example is given in Figure 12.2.

The third kind of sheet is the Teacher's Note. On this page, the teacher can make comments, suggestions, and/or recommendations for changes in the Tutor's Lesson Plan. For an example, see Figure 12.3.

Tutor Training

The teacher must not only assess, prescribe, and gather materials, but also make sure that the tutor can and does carry out the program as specified. The teacher will usually have to provide the tutor with at least some minimal training (the tutor will have to be taught to complete the forms

| Tutor | Mrs. Clark | Student | Stanley Miller |
| Date | 10/7/90 | Grade 4 | School | West Elementary |

Stanley couldn't think what might happen but he listened and said, "Now I know!" when we came to it. We reviewed the Dolch Words and he missed 6 of them. He asked me if he could take them home. I told him I'd check with you. He answered all the questions on the rate builder correctly. This is 4 in row — he may be ready for the next color.

FIGURE 12.2. Tutor's log sheet.

| Tutor | Mrs. Clark | Student | Stanley Miller |
| Teacher | Mr. Lobb | Date | 10/7/90 |

Tell Stanley that we'll need the cards for something else later. He can take them home when we are finished. Try the next color for a listening activity. Have him select another book for the oral reading.

FIGURE 12.3. Teacher's note.

described in the previous section, to be familiarized with the basic methods and strategies used by the teacher, etc.). Of course, the experienced teacher cannot transfer to the tutor all of the skills and expertise that he or she has acquired as a result of completing a 4-year college program and several years of teaching, but the teacher can make sure that the tutor knows what to do and has the materials to do it.

Whenever possible, the tutor's training should be by example. Working with a student, the teacher should demonstrate items of importance in a tutorial lesson. For example, demonstrations for reading tutors might cover

1. Qualities of good oral reading (creating interest in a story, setting purposes, anticipating outcomes, etc.).

2. Various ways to use flashcards for drill.

3. Teaching the student to trace words correctly, if this technique is used.

4. Selecting, or helping the student to select, an appropriate book.

5. Using a positive (reinforcing) attitude in all activities.

6. Keeping comprehensive records.

7. Various materials; their location and use.

8. Physical surroundings (e.g., adequate lighting).

9. Use of a dictionary when necessary.

During the training period, rapport between the tutor and the teacher must be established. If rapport is properly fostered, the tutor will feel free to ask the teacher any question about the program. Rapport can be enhanced and maintained if, when asked a question, the teacher carefully considers a response before answering. For example, it is far better for the teacher to say, "I'm sorry; I should have told you that," than to say, "I thought that you'd use your common sense." Negative criticism can shut off communication quickly.

Problems in Tutoring

Even when tutors have received a great deal of training, problems will arise, because a tutor cannot be expected to learn everything that he or she needs to know all at once. As a result, a tutor may make gross mistakes occasionally. For example, the tutor may try to get the student to "sound out" words that are not phonetic; or to make sure that a pupil is reading, the tutor may encourage the student to whisper or to move his or her lips when reading silently. From time to time, a tutor may inadvertently threaten a student with such statements as "If you don't do this, I won't like you" or "I can't understand why you don't know this; I've told you a hundred times!" The tutor may not recognize when a student is frustrated. There are many things, some great, some small, that can go wrong in a tutoring program, so the importance of adequate preparation, planning, tutor training, and supervision cannot be stressed too often.

If possible, tutors should be paid. Although adult volunteers can fill a gap, they often leave for a paying job, especially after they get some experience and can qualify for employment in a day care center, nursery school, or private preschool. Also, they are often undependable. On the other hand, there is a wealth of untapped student talent in the school district. Students can make excellent volunteer tutors. For example, older students can work with younger pupils (cross-age tutoring), and students of the same age can, and often do, tutor each other (peer tutoring).

INVOLVING PARENTS IN SCHOOL PROGRAMS

Many teachers would like to see the parents of their students involved in school programs. Properly motivated and informed, parents can be strong partners with schools in helping students learn. Why then are parents so rarely involved?

Part of the difficulty seems to be due to fears of teachers and principals. Some of these fears are that the parents are basically not interested in their children's education; that they would not come to school if invited, especially the parents who need to come; that they would not understand the volunteer program; and that, if they did understand, they would want to control the program. According to Nicholson (1980), however, parents are interested in their children's education, know whether their children are having problems, and help their children to the best of their knowledge.

Several schools have successfully involved parents in programs (Criscuolo, 1980; Granowsky, Middleton, & Mumford, 1979). The success of such programs seems to be due to the following factors:

1. *Making parents feel welcome at school.* This may take the form of scheduling parent conferences to accommodate parents' work responsibilities, providing a resource room where parents may browse or borrow materials, or arranging for parent observation and participation in programs.

2. *Keeping parents informed about the school's programs.* Many parents may be confused about the purpose and approach of some of the school's programs. They may wonder why particular material is or is not being taught or why their child does or does not have homework. A newsletter, parent brochure, bulletin board, or parent information night can help keep parents informed, as can informal means of communication.

3. *Keeping parents informed about their children's progress.* Keeping parents informed means more than sending home grades or report cards three or four times a year. Most parents want to know where their child is in learning essential skills. Such information can be conveyed through regular progress reports, informal notes, and parent conferences, as well as the typical report card. Information about a student's progress should include specific ideas about how parents can help their children improve.

SELECTING EDUCATIONAL MATERIALS AND RESOURCES[1]

In teaching, much time is devoted to selecting the curriculum that will be used, assessing the individual needs of students, and choosing the specific

---

1. This section was written by Judy Wilson and was a chapter in earlier editions of this book.

teaching methods that will be employed. Comparatively little time is spent selecting instructional materials, in spite of the fact that at least 75%, and as much as 99%, of the students' instructional time involves the materials used in the classroom. Given that teaching is the interaction among the curriculum, the student, and the teacher, materials must be chosen carefully to ensure that they are compatible with all three elements in the triad and, in fact, serve to draw them together.

Most instructional materials are designed to meet the needs of groups of students, not one specific student. Therefore, to meet individual differences, teachers have always had to make certain accommodations in the materials used (e.g., having a student use chapters out of sequence or complete only the even-numbered questions). The further the student's needs and abilities deviate from those of the group for whom the material was originally designed, the greater this need for accommodation becomes.

For the student with learning and/or behavior problems, the variance may necessitate the use of completely different materials, a need that is often overlooked or inappropriately met by many teachers, owing to their training and orientation. Most teachers have been trained to teach a prescribed curriculum that is usually dictated by the school, to use the materials that have been selected for them by the textbook committee, and to move students through the same set of learning experiences. To satisfy the special, and often unique, requirements of the student with problems, the teacher must exchange this group orientation for an individual one in which the curricular requirements are identified in terms of the exact skills to be taught to a particular student and instructional materials are selected on the basis of curricular, student, and teacher variables.

To aid in the selection of appropriate materials, this section includes a discussion of the curriculum–student–teacher triad, the role of the triad in obtaining information about materials, and a system for analyzing materials. This section provides teachers with a frame of reference for selecting materials that are appropriate to their own curricula, students, and teaching methods.

The Curriculum–Student–Teacher Triad

The role of the curriculum–student–teacher triad in selecting material is analogous to that of the building–occupant–builder triad. The specifications for the building most certainly affect the types of materials to be used, but the selection of materials is also affected by the needs of the occupants, the desires of the builder, and what he or she knows to be effective and available.

Student Variables

The two most critical variables from the standpoint of students are their current level of functioning and their most immediate educational needs. Although consideration of individual variables will obviously be influenced by the specific nature of each student, some common areas also should be examined. These areas include the following:

1. *Needs of the student.* What skills and concepts are required of the student for immediate success?

2. *Current level of functioning.* What is the student's level of performance within the sequence of skills? What is the student's current reading level for instructional purposes?

3. *Grouping.* How well does the student work in groups of varying size (e.g., in small groups, in large groups, individually)?

4. *Programming.* What is the best way to approach the student? Can the student work independently? Is the student self-directed and motivated? Does the student require direct teaching and/or frequent reinforcement?

5. *Methods.* Have any particular methods been used successfully? Does the student react positively or negatively to particular modes of instruction (e.g., multimedia vs. print only)?

6. *Physical, social, and psychological characteristics.* Do any student characteristics (e.g., orthopedic restrictions, family problems, ethnic or cultural diversity) imply unique needs?

This list could also include such factors as ability to follow directions, both written and oral; ability to deal with material on a grade level different from the student's placement; and others.

Teacher Variables

The teacher acts as the catalyst to ensure interaction between the other two components. Because the teacher makes decisions about curricular and student variables, the teacher's desires, knowledge, and competence must be considered. Teacher variables, like those for the student, are affected by the nature of the individual, but, again, certain common areas exist:

1. *Method.* What method does the teacher want to employ? What is the teacher's philosophy toward the teaching of particular content?

2. *Approach.* What approach is required by the teacher (e.g., group instruction or individual instruction, a phonetic approach)?

3. *Time.* Does the teacher have time constraints for delivery of instruction? Does the teacher have someone else who can deliver the instruction?

4. *Training.* Has the teacher been trained to use certain materials?

5. *Education.* Has the teacher been trained in the content area?

These lists of variables are not exhaustive. Rather, they are intended to serve as guidelines for identification of relevant variables that will aid in the selection and use of materials and to ensure that the materials meet the specified needs of the curriculum, student, and teacher.

Collecting Information About Materials

Once the critical variables involved in selecting materials have been identified, the teacher is ready to obtain information on the specific materials being considered for use. The teacher will use a variety of resources to secure information on materials. Some of these resources are listed below.

1. *Colleagues.* An immediate source of information is other teachers. Not only are they within easy access, but they may have students with similar needs and therefore be able to share information on their experience with specific materials.

2. *Special resource personnel.* This category includes such people as the media/materials coordinator, librarian, and curriculum coordinator. These individuals have information on a wide variety of materials and often know or have access to information on specific aspects of the material. This information may include availability, names of others who are using the materials, evaluations of past effectiveness of the materials, and personal appraisal of the material. Resource personnel can also supply names of companies that publish the type of material under consideration.

3. *Publisher information.* The information available from publishers usually comes in at least three forms: catalogs, other sales material, and representatives or consultants. Publisher information includes bibliographic information, a physical description, and price information. Keep in mind that the information provided by publishers is slanted to facilitate the sale of the item.

4. *Media/materials resource centers.* Many school districts and/or regional centers have central collections of instructional resources. These centers may house general collections or may be directly related to special education. Such centers may have a broad array of information, including media/materials for examination and use, publishers' catalogs, retrieval systems for materials information, evaluation data on materials, facilities for adaptation and production of materials, and knowledgeable materials resource personnel. Thus, the teacher may locate information on specific products and types of products, examine actual products, use the materials with students, find out about new products, determine what others may know about the products, and gain a great deal of first-hand information about the products.

5. *College/university resources.* Most special education training programs have specific courses offered by faculty involved in media/

materials and collections of instructional media/materials. Information is generally also available from the departments of curriculum and instruction, elementary education, and secondary education.

6. *Prepared materials lists.* Lists of materials provide good resources for identifying specific information about materials. These lists may be derived from a variety of sources. In some states or school districts, approved lists of materials are identified each year. Frequently, curriculum guides include lists of materials correlated to the content of the guides. Also, in inservice and professional development workshops, lists of materials are frequently disseminated and exchanged among teachers. Materials lists may be organized in a variety of ways, such as by handicapping conditions, by difficulty or grade level, or by curriculum area. When using lists, the teacher should consider the source of the list, the organization of the list, and the fact that in most cases the list provides primarily bibliographic information about the materials, not efficacy information.

7. *Conferences.* Most conferences and conventions provide exhibits by publishers, presentations about materials by authors and/or publishers, presentations of research studies in which specific materials were used, and opportunities to discuss materials with others who have common needs. One of the more valuable types of conferences for the purpose of learning about materials is the type usually referred to as a "publisher's conference." In such a meeting, specific publishers are invited to make formal presentations about particular programs that are new to the market. Such presentations allow the teacher to gain comprehensive information about a specific material, the author, the development process, and research data.

8. *Retrieval systems.* A number of instructional materials retrieval systems have been developed by commercial companies, through federal funding, and by school systems at the local, regional, and occasionally building level. If such a system is available, the teacher should become familiar with the capabilities of the system, the techniques or procedures for use, and the data base of the system. Retrieval systems can provide a good deal of information about the physical characteristics of materials available to meet a specific need. Some systems also provide information on evaluation and availability of material. Once materials have been located, they should be carefully examined prior to final selection.

Analyzing Materials

In conducting an analysis of instructional materials, teachers should evaluate each material in terms of the following 10 informational categories. The analysis should be kept relatively short, but comprehensive.

1. *Bibliographic and price information.* This information is necessary for future reference or purchase, as well as to make determinations

that may assist in analysis. The teacher may consider such items as the following:

Title—The name of the product may help identify the content area and whether the product is part of a set or series.

Author—Is it someone known for his or her work in a specific area or someone associated with a particular approach?

Copyright—Is it current? Does the work reflect new trends and facts?

Price—Is it within the budget limitations? Is it in keeping with other materials prices and does it appear reasonable for the work's teaching value?

Publisher—Does the company have a reputation for producing a certain kind or quality of material?

2. *Instructional area and skills, scope and sequence.* Does the material cover the content area or specific components of the area? Does it address the specific skills needed? Does the material present initial instruction, remediation, and practice and/or reinforcement activities for the skills? Are the skills presented in the appropriate sequence?

3. *Component parts of the material.* Does the material have multiple pieces? Can the pieces be used independently? Can the pieces be used for other purposes? Are the pieces consumable? Can the pieces be purchased independently? Will keeping track of all components be a problem?

4. *Level of the material.* Does the publisher state the readability level of the material? Is it consistent throughout the material? Is the interest level appropriate to the content, pictures, and publisher's statements?

5. *Quality.* Is the material (paper, tape, acetate, film, etc.) of good and durable quality? Is the print clear and of appropriate size and contrast with the background color? Are the illustrations clear and relevant to content? Do they add to rather than detract from the instruction?

6. *Format.* Is the form appropriate (workbook, slide, tape, etc.)? Does it utilize the appropriate receptive and expressive modes for the content? Is the material clear and easy to follow? Is special equipment required (projector, recorder, etc.)?

7. *Support materials.* Does the material include additional components (e.g., placement tests, check-tests, resource files, objective clusters)? Are there teacher's guides and/or teacher's editions? Are there teacher training materials?

8. *Time requirements.* Are the tasks of an appropriate length? Does the material allow flexibility for scheduling? Does it allow flexibility in instructional procedures?

9. *Field test and research data.* Does the publisher offer any research to support the validity or reliability of the material? In essence, do the data support the contention that the material will do what the publisher says it will do for the type of student indicated?

10. *Method, approach, or theoretical bases.* Does the material employ a specific approach or method, or is it based on a specific theoretical concept? Is it one that meets the needs of the triad? Is it compatible with other ongoing instruction? Is the method, approach, or basic theory substantiated by any published research?

As in the case of the curriculum–student–teacher triad, these variables may change with needs; however, they should serve as basic criteria for the selection process. Selection of materials is not a simple process; it requires a great deal of effort and knowledge on the part of the trained professional responsible for the design and delivery of instruction for students with learning and behavior problems.

USING DIRECT OR INDIRECT INSTRUCTION

This section includes a brief discussion of current methodologies used in the schools, specifically direct and indirect instructional practices and their influence within a remedial and special education perspective. For convenience, the concepts of direct and indirect instruction are discussed in terms of reading, but they can be easily generalized to math, writing, and other school subjects.

Indirect Instruction

In indirect instruction, one might teach students to recall strings of digits, to walk a balance beam, or to crawl and creep properly, because such activities are thought to be in some way a part of, related to, or prerequisites for reading. A characteristic of this kind of training is that the prescribed activities do not look at all like reading.

The goal of indirect instruction is to develop hypothetical psychological processes, basic abilities, or faculties in the brain (mind) that are supposedly related to reading. For example, advocates of indirect instruction argue that, because reading is believed to involve sequencing, visual discrimination, and memory, instruction in these abilities will strengthen the student's capacity for reading. Therefore, they often recommend activities that have little apparent relationship to reading, such as bead stringing (to teach sequencing), geometric form differentiation (visual discrimination), and recalling strings of visual patterns (memory). These activities may be part of a readiness, developmental, or remedial program.

Direct Instruction

In direct instruction, one might teach a student to name letters of the alphabet, to recognize when a book is upside down, to see the main themes of paragraphs, and to comprehend the thematic as well as the phonic nature of written language, because such activities are thought to constitute important aspects of reading. The relevance that an individual attaches to any one or to any set of activities depends, of course, on how he or she conceptualizes reading. Regardless, everyone would agree that the activities just mentioned are all closely associated with reading.

Advocates of direct (on-task) teaching are frequently heard to say, "If one wants to teach Johnny to read, expose him to reading," or "One learns to read as a consequence of reading." Professionals who espouse direct instruction can be separated readily into two different (and often contending) camps—the atomistic and the holistic orientations.

Atomistic Orientation

To atomistically inclined individuals, the whole (reading) is the sum of its parts (skills). For example, the word *cat* is believed to be composed of three separate graphemes, c-a-t. Teaching students the sounds that go with the letters and having them say them fast is considered the heart and soul of atomistic education. Some atomistically inclined professionals do teach reading comprehension, but they tend to think of comprehension in terms of sequenced skills and conceive of it as being merely one of the many reading subskills. Sometimes this type of instruction is called skill centered or bottom-up.

Rather than relying on the student's natural language and interests, atomistically inclined teachers use scope-and-sequence charts composed of phonemically regular words and arbitrarily sequenced skills as guides for selecting material to be taught. Because contrived vocabularies must be used, the interest level of the reading material is usually low. Therefore, one often finds that behavior modification and management programs are used in conjunction with atomistic instruction. Invariably, atomistic instruction is curriculum- or program-centered even when individuals are being taught. Oral reading is emphasized.

Holistic Orientation

To holistically inclined individuals, the whole (reading) is never the sum of its parts (skills). These people would not break a word into its phonemic or graphemic parts for fear of destroying its meaning. The more dogmatic holistic educators would probably not even teach words in isolation, only in context. In choosing strategies, activities, and content for instruction, holistically oriented teachers rely heavily on their knowledge of the student's home environment, desires, and natural language. The approach is decidedly student centered. Silent reading for comprehension and retelling are mainstays in instruction. This type of instruction is frequently called meaning centered or top-down.

Interactional Orientation

In practice, most professionals find themselves positioned somewhere between polar opposites; that is, no one is completely atomistic or holistic in his or her instructional efforts. This has led some individuals, such as S. Jay Samuels, to postulate a third approach to instruction, the interactional. In this approach, professionals incorporate both atomistic and holistic principles into their instructional and diagnostic attempts.

Still, individuals do tend to gravitate toward one focus or the other, as can be seen when professionals talk about why they teach in this way or that way or discuss their educational philosophies.

A Special/Remedial Education Perspective

Both the direct and the indirect approaches have at one time or another been pervasive in special and remedial education in the United States. The indirect approach was paramount from around 1930 to 1975. This was the heyday of "process" and "aptitude–treatment interaction" training. In special education, the movement began with the perceptual hypotheses of Alfred Strauss and Hans Werner, among others, and was operationalized in the programs of Marianne Frostig and David Horne, William Cruickshank, Ray Barsch, Gerald Getman, and Newell Kephart. This trend continued with renewed vigor when Samuel Kirk incorporated these concepts into his idea about "psycholinguistic" training.

Indirect instruction never received the same degree of acceptance in the fields of speech or reading as it did in special education, where for years it was dominant. Since the early 1970s, however, this approach has come under attack from special education researchers (see the work of Stephen Larsen, J. Lee Wiederholt, Joe Jenkins, Thomas Lovitt, Frank Velluntino, Thomas Stephens, Lester Mann, Michael Epstein, James Kauffman, Douglas Cullinan, James Ysseldyke, Douglas Carnine, and Donald Hammill). Today, few articles supporting the benefits of indirect instruction are published in peer-reviewed journals.

Since 1975, the mainstream of special education has turned to the use of direct instruction methodologies. The proponents of atomistic instruction are pervasive today. The theories and programs of Siegfried Engelmann, Douglas Carnine, Thomas Stephens, James Kauffman, Tom Lovitt, Joe Jenkins, and Anna Gillingham, among many others, have a practical, heady appeal. However, in the early 1980s, the holistic ideas of Jean Piaget, Frank Smith, Jerome Bruner, and Ken and Yetta Goodman began to seep into the special education current, to join those long advocated by Grace Fernald.

Special issues of the *Learning Disability Quarterly* (Winter 1984), edited by Mary Poplin, and *Remedial and Special Education* (July/August 1993), edited by Russell Gersten and Joseph Dimino, are devoted to holism as a concept pertaining to remedial education. Reading these issues will provide readers with a basic understanding of the fundamental ideas underlying the approach. The reader who wishes to know more about holism and how it differs from atomistic approaches will find the articles by Iano (1986), Poplin (1988a, 1988b), and Reid (1988) to be valuable sources.

Hopefully, holistic-influenced ideas will soon stimulate the development of programs, strategies, and research. Holistic education is now the frontier of special and remedial education. Although we find this approach philosophically pleasing, it remains to be seen whether holism, either alone or as a part of interactional efforts, will prove to be preferable to purely atomistic approaches.

THE INCLUSION MOVEMENT

The goal of the inclusion movement is the full integration of people with disabilities into general educational services and society in general. Relative to school integration, the groundwork for the movement was laid during the 1950s with the publication of much research (e.g., Ainsworth, 1959; Baldwin, 1958; Thurstone, 1959) which showed that segregated special classes for students with disabilities were ineffective and possibly harmful to the very students they were intended to help.

Probably influenced by this research, M.C. Reynolds (1962) proposed that the special class and school should be augmented by the provision of a full range ("a cascade") of services and that placement of students should be in the least restrictive environment possible. Presumably, if a full range of services were available, most students could be accommodated in general classrooms and relatively few would need full-time residential schools. In 1989, Reynolds amended his cascade by deleting residential schools and special day schools for students with disabilities because he felt students could best be served in their neighborhood schools. He continued to see some value in full- and part-time special classes, resource rooms, and consultation services, and reinforced his position that the regular class was still the best placement for most students who have disabilities.

Also influenced by the early efficacy research dealing with segregated classes, Dunn (1968) incorporated its findings into a particularly powerful article that concluded with a call to *abolish* most of the special classes for students who were mildly retarded. Dunn's article was a catalyst that generated considerable controversy among professionals and stimulated another round of research on the role of the special class, the results of which supported Dunn's position (e.g., Cegelka & Tyler, 1970; Christoplos & Renz, 1969; Garrison & Hammill, 1971; Iano, 1972).

As a result of this research, advocacy from interested organizations, and "the spirit of the times," many special classes were disbanded and replaced by resource room and consultation programs. At the time, a variety of categorical resource room programs for students with mental retardation (Barksdale & Atkinson, 1971), emotional disturbance (Glavin, Quay, Annesley, & Werry, 1971), and learning disability (Bersoff, Kabler, Fiscus, & Ankney, 1972; Sabatino, 1971) were tried. Noncategorical resource programs were recommended by Hammill and Wiederholt (1972) and Wiederholt, Hammill, and Brown (1978, 1983), and prototypical programs for consulting teachers were formulated by H. S. McKenzie et al. (1970). These programs served as models for most pull-out services that became popular during the 1970s and 1980s. These new programs permitted large numbers of students with disabilities to be enrolled at least partially in general classrooms. This shift of emphasis in the direction of integrated programs was seen at the time as a major victory for those professionals and parents who were calling for least restrictive placement, mainstream education, noncategorical teacher training, elimination of labeling, and increased inclusion.

In the late 1980s, the movement toward inclusion entered a new phase. Some professionals felt that partial pull-out programs and self-contained special classes were not particularly effective and that the widespread availability of these programs was an obstacle to their total inclusion goals. They advocated that most (if not all) students with disabilities be placed in general classrooms, that general and special education teachers share the responsibility for the students' instruction, and that programs, rather than children, be labeled. This aspect of the inclusion movement is referred to as the *regular education initiative* (REI).

The REI was initiated primarily by representatives of the government (e.g., Will, 1986) and a group of professionals (e.g., M. C. Reynolds, 1989; Wang, Reynolds, & Walberg, 1986; Wang, Walberg, & Reynolds, 1992). The purpose of the effort is to significantly reduce categorical programming in the schools by totally integrating the vast majority of students with disabilities, including learning disabilities. A particularly cogent critical analysis of the REI is available in a special issue of *Remedial and Special Education* (May/June 1990) edited by Russell Gersten and John Woodward.

Even if partially successful, the REI will influence the schools in many ways. First, the numbers of students with disabilities (e.g., learning disabilities, mental retardation, behavior disorders) enrolled in general classrooms would increase dramatically while those in special classes and resource programs would decrease commensurately, an occurrence that would require teacher education and inservice programs to emphasize consultant and team teaching activities. Second, the REI might stimulate the movement toward programs in which students receive services without the necessity of being diagnosed or labeled as handicapped. If these things were to happen, teachers in regular classrooms would have a great need for the assessment and instructional methods described in this book because they would be expected to teach successfully the very students who had failed to learn in the general classroom where traditional methods had been already tried.

The success of the REI, however, is by no means a foregone conclusion. Serious questions about how the REI is to be implemented were raised by Daniel Hallahan, James Kauffman, James McKinney, Tanis Bryan, Donald Deshler, Jean Schumaker, Phillip Strain, Melvin Semmel, John Lloyd, Michael Gerber, and other prominent special educators in the January 1988 issue of the *Journal of Learning Disabilities* and by J. Lee Wiederholt and Phyllis Newcomer in the Summer 1989 issue of *Learning Disability Quarterly*. Must reading for all persons interested in this topic is Kauffman's (1989) "The Regular Education Initiative as a Reagan–Bush Education Policy: A Trickle-Down Theory of Education of the Hard-to-Teach" and Hallahan and Kauffman's (1995) *The Illusion of Full Inclusion*.

In the end, the advocates of full inclusion are unlikely to completely achieve their ultimate goal—that is, the education of *all* students with disabilities within a general education setting. Without doubt, however, their efforts will stimulate reforms that will allow many students with disabilities who are presently needlessly excluded from mainstream education programs to receive appropriate educations fully integrated with their nondisabled peers.

References

Abrams, B. J. (1992, Spring). Values clarification for students with emotional disabilities. *Teaching Exceptional Children,* pp. 28–33.

Adventures of the lollipop dragon. (1970). Chicago: Society for Visual Education.

Affleck, J., Edgar, E., Levine, P., & Kortering, L (1990). Post-school status of students classified as mildly mentally retarded, learning disabled, or nonhandicapped: Does it get better with time? *Education and Training in Mental Retardation, 26,* 142–150.

Aho, M. S. (1967). Teaching spelling to children with specific language disability. *Academic Therapy, 3*(1), 45–50.

Ainsworth, S. H. (1959). *An exploratory study of educational, social, and emotional factors in the education of mentally retarded children in Georgia public schools.* Athens: University of Georgia.

Alley, G., & Deshler, D. (1979). *Teaching the learning disabled adolescent: Strategies and methods.* Denver: Love.

Alley, G. R., Deshler, D. D., & Warner, M. M. (1979). Identification of learning disabled adolescents: A Bayesian approach. *Learning Disability Quarterly, 2*(2), 76–83.

Arena, J. (1982). *Diagnostic Spelling Potential Test.* Novato, CA: Academic Therapy Publications.

Ashlock, R. B. (1986). *Error patterns in computation: A semi-programmed approach* (4th ed.). Columbus, OH: Charles E. Merrill.

Aurich, Sister M. F. (1963). *A comparative study to determine the effectiveness of the Cuisenaire method of arithmetic instruction with children of the first grade level.* Unpublished master's thesis, the Catholic University of America, Washington, DC.

Axline, V. M. (1964). *Dibs: In search of self.* New York: Ballantine.

Baker, L. (1985). Standards for evaluating text comprehension. In D. L. Forrest-Pressley, G. E. MacKinnon, & T. G. Waller (Eds.), *Metacognition, cognition, and human performance: Vol. 1. Theoretical perspectives* (pp. 153–204). New York: Academic Press.

Baldwin, W. K. (1958). The social position of mentally handicapped children in the regular class in the public schools. *Exceptional Children, 25,* 106–108.

Bankson, N. W. (1990). *Bankson Language Test* (2nd ed.). Austin, TX: PRO-ED.

Barbe, W. B., Lucas, V. H., Wasylyk, T. M., Hackney, C. S., & Braun, L. A. (1987). *Handwriting: Basic skills and application.* Columbus, OH: Zaner-Bloser.

Barenbaum, E. M. (1983). Writing in the special class. *Topics in Learning and Learning Disabilities, 3*(3), 12–20.

Barksdale, M. W., & Atkinson, A. P. (1971). A resource room approach to instruction for the educable mentally retarded. *Focus on Exceptional Children, 3,* 12–15.

Bartel, N. R., Bryen, D. N., & Bartel, H. W. (1975). Approaches for alternative programming. In E. L. Meyen, G. A. Vergason, & R. J. Whelan (Eds.), *Alternatives for teaching exceptional children.* Denver, CO: Love.

Bartel, N. R., Grill, J. J., & Bryen, D. N. (1973). Language characteristics of black children: Implications for assessment. *Journal of School Psychology, 11,* 351–364.

Baruth, L. (1974). *Knowledge of Occupations Test.* Chesterfield, MO: Psychologists and Educators.

Battle, J. (1992) *Culture-Free Self-Esteem Inventories.* Austin, TX: PRO-ED.

Bauman, J. F. (1984). The effectiveness of a direct instruction paradigm for teaching main idea comprehension. *Reading Research Quarterly, 20,* 93–115.

Beatty, L. S., Madden, R., Gardner, E. F., & Karlsen, B. (1978). *Stanford Diagnostic Mathematics Test* (3rd ed.). San Antonio, TX: Psychological Corporation.

Becker, R. L. (1981). *Reading-free Vocational Interest Inventory–Revised.* Columbus, OH: Elbern.

Bennett, G. K., Seashore, H. G., & Wesman, A. G. (1982). *Differential Aptitude Test.* San Antonio, TX: Psychological Corporation.

Bersoff, D. N., Kabler, M., Fiscus, E., & Ankney, R. (1972). Effectiveness of special class placement for children labeled neurologically handicapped. *Journal of School Psychology, 10,* 157–163.

Bijou, S. W. (1993). *The Edmark Reading Program.* Bellevue, WA: Edmark Corporation.

Blackorby, J., Edgar, E., & Kortering, L. J. (1991). A third of our youth? A look at the problems of high school dropout among students with mild handicaps. *Journal of Special Education, 25,* 102–113.

Blake, H., & Spennato, N. A. (1980). The directed writing activity: A process with structure. *Language Arts, 57,* 317–318.

Bley, N. S., & Thornton, C. A. (1989). *Teaching mathematics to the learning disabled* (2nd ed.). Austin, TX: PRO-ED.

Bormaster, J. S., & Treat, C. L. (1994). *Building interpersonal relationships through talking, listening, communicating* (2nd ed.). Austin, TX: PRO-ED.

Botel, M. (1966). *Botel Reading Inventory.* Cleveland, OH: Modern Curriculum Press.

Brigance, A. H. (1988). *BRIGANCE prescriptive study skills: Strategies and practices.* N. Billerica, MA: Curriculum Associates.

Britton, J. (1978). The composing process and the functions of writing. In C. Copper & L. Odell (Eds.), *Research on composing points of departure.* Urbana, IL: National Council of Teachers of English.

Brolin, D. (1991). *Life-centered career education: A competency-based approach* (3rd ed.). Reston, VA: Council for Exceptional Children.

Brolin, J. C., & Brolin, D. E. (1979). Vocational education for special students. In P. Cullinan & M. H. Epstein (Eds.), *Special education for adolescents.* Columbus, OH: Charles E. Merrill.

Brown, A. L., & Palincsar, A. (1985). *Reciprocal teaching of comprehension strategies: A natural history of one program for enhancing learning* (Tech. Rep. No. 334). Urbana, IL: University of Illinois, Center for the Study of Reading.

Brown, A. L., Palincsar, A., & Armbruster, B. (1988). Instructing comprehension-fostering activities in interactive learning situations. In H. Mandl, N. Stein, & T. Trabasso (Eds.), *Learning from texts.* Hillsdale, NJ: Erlbaum.

Brown, L., & Alexander, J. A. (1991). *Self-Esteem Index.* Austin, TX: PRO-ED.

Brown, L., & Coleman, M. (1988). *Index of Personality Characteristics.* Austin, TX: PRO-ED.

Brown, L., & Hammill, D. D. (1990). *Behavior Rating Profile, second edition.* Austin, TX: PRO-ED.

Brown, L., Hammill, D. D., & Wiederholt, J. L. (1986). *Test of Reading Comprehension.* Austin, TX: PRO-ED.

Brown, V. L. (1984a). A comparison of two sight word reading programs designed for use with remedial or handicapped learners. *Remedial and Special Education, 5*(1), 46–54.

Brown, V. L. (1984b). D'Nealian Handwriting: What it is and how to teach it. *Remedial and Special Education, 5*(5), 48–52.

Brown, V. L. (1985). Direct instruction mathematics: A framework for instructional accountability. *Remedial and Special Education, 6*(2), 53–58.

Brown, V. L., Cronin, M., & McEntire, B. (1994). *Test of Mathematical Abilities, second edition.* Austin, TX: PRO-ED.

Brown, V. L., Hammill, D. D., & Wiederholt, J. L. (1995). *Test of Reading Comprehension* (3rd ed.). Austin, TX: PRO-ED.

Brueckner, L. J., & Bond, G. L. (1967). The diagnosis and treatment of learning difficulties. In E. C. Frierson & W. B. Barbe (Eds.), *Educating children with learning disabilities* (pp. 442–447). New York: Appleton-Century-Crofts.

Bruner, J. (1975). The ontogenesis of speech acts. *Journal of Child Language, 2,* 1–22.

Buffington, P. W. (1988). Paper chases. *Sky* (Delta Air Lines' magazine), *17*(8), 68–73.

Burns, H. L. (1984). Computer-assisted prewriting activities: Harmonics for invention. In R. Shostak (Eds.), *Computer in composition instruction.* Eugene, OR: International Council for Computers in Education.

Burns, P. C. (1965). Analytical testing and follow-up exercises in elementary school mathematics. *School Science and Mathematics, 65,* 34–38.

Burns, P. C., & Broman, B. L. (1983). *The language arts in childhood education* (5th ed.). Boston: Houghton Mifflin.

Burns, P. C., Broman, B. L., & Wantling, A. L. L. (1971). *The language arts in childhood education.* Boston: Houghton Mifflin.

Burrello, L. C., Tracy, M. L., & Glassman, E. J. (1983). A national status report on use of electronic technology in special education management. *Journal of Special Education, 17,* 342–353.

California Achievement Tests (5th ed.). (1992). Monterey, CA: CTB/McGraw-Hill.

Carlson, R. K. (1979). *Sparkling words: Two hundred practical and creative writing ideas.* Geneva, IL: Paladin House.

Carman, R. A., & Adams, W. R. (1972). *Study skills: A student's guide for survival.* New York: Wiley.

Carnine, D., & Silbert, J. (1990). *Direct instruction: Reading* (2nd ed.). Columbus, OH: Charles E. Merrill.

Carpenter, P., & Sandberg, S. (1985). Further psychodrama with delinquent adolescents. *Adolescence, 20,* 599–604.

Carrow-Woolfolk, E. (1974). *Carrow Elicited Language Inventory.* Chicago: Riverside.

Carrow-Woolfolk, E. (1985). *Test of Auditory Comprehension of Language.* Chicago, IL: Riverside.

Cawley, J. F., Baker-Kroczynski, S., & Urban, A. (1992). Seeking excellence in mathematics education for students with mild disabilities. *Teaching Exceptional Children, 24*(2), 40–43.

Cawley, J. F., Fitzmaurice-Hayes, A. M., & Shaw, R. A. (1988). *Mathematics for the mildly handicapped: A guide to curriculum and instruction.* Boston: Allyn & Bacon.

Cegelka, W. J., & Tyler, J. L. (1970). The efficacy of regular class placement for the mentally retarded in proper perspective. *Training School Bulletin, 67,* 33–68.

Choate, J. S., Miller, L. J., Bennett, T. Z., Poteet, J. A., Enright, B. E., & Rakes, T. A. (1987). *Assessing and programming basic curriculum skills.* Boston: Allyn & Bacon.

Chomsky, C. (1971). Write first, read later. *Childhood Education, 47*(6), 296–299.

Christie, L., McKenzie, H., & Burdett, C. (1972). The consulting teacher approach to special education: Inservice training for regular classroom teachers. *Focus on Exceptional Children, 4*(5), 1–10.

Christopolos, F., & Renz, P. (1969). A critical examination of special education programs. *Journal of Special Education, 3,* 371–379.

Clark, G. M. (1981). Career and vocational education. In G. Brown, R. L. McDowell, & J. Smith (Eds.), *Educating adolescents with behavior disorders* (pp. 25–39). New York: Merrill/Macmillan.

Clark, G. M., Carlson, B. C., Fisher, S., Cook, I. D., & D'Alonzo, B. J. (1991). *Career development for students with disabilities in elementary schools: A position statement of the Division on Career Development.* Reston, VA: Division on Career Development for Exceptional Children.

Clark, G. M., & Kolstoe, O. P. (1990). *Career development and transition education for adolescents with disabilities.* Boston: Allyn & Bacon.

Clark, G. M., & White, W. J. (1980). *Career education for the handicapped: Current perspective for teachers.* Boothwyn, PA: Education Resources Center.

Cline, R. K. J., & Kretke, G. L. (1980). An evaluation of long-term SSR in the junior high school. *Journal of Reading, 23,* 503–506.

Cochran-Smith, M. (1991). Word processing and writing in elementary classrooms. *Review of Educational Research, 61,* 107–155.

Cohen, M., & Riel, M. (1989). The effect of distant audiences on students' writing. *American Educational Research Journal, 26*(2), 143–159.

Combs, W. E. (1977). Sentence-combining practice aids reading comprehension. *The Reading Teacher, 21,* 18–24.

Comprehensive Test of Basic Skills (4th ed.). (1990). Monterey, CA: CTB/McGraw-Hill.

Connolly, A. J. (1988). *Key Math: Revised.* Circle Pines, MN: American Guidance Service.

Conoley, J. C., & Kramer, J. J. (Eds.). (1989). *The tenth mental measurements yearbook.* Lincoln: University of Nebraska Press.

Cooper, C. R., & Petrosky, A. R. (1976). A psycholinguistic view of the fluent reading process. *Journal of Reading, 20,* 184–207.

Coopersmith, S. (1981). *Coopersmith Self-Esteem Inventories.* Palo Alto, CA: Consulting Psychologists Press.

Criscuolo, N. P. (1980). Effective ways to communicate with parents about reading. *Reading Teacher, 34,* 164–166.

Crites, J. O. (1978). *Career Maturity Inventory.* Monterey, CA: CTB/Macmillan/McGraw-Hill.

Cronin, M. E., & Patton, J. R. (1993). *Life skills instruction for all students with special needs: A practical guide for integrating real-life content into the curriculum.* Austin, TX: PRO-ED.

Crowder, A. (1965). *A comparative study of two methods of teaching arithmetic in the first grade.* Unpublished doctoral dissertation, North Texas State University, Denton.

Cunningham, A. E., & Stanovich, K. E. (1990). Early spelling acquisition: Writing beats the computer. *Journal of Educational Psychology, 82*(1), 159–162.

Curtiss, S., Prutting, C. A., & Lowell, E. L. (1979). Pragmatic and semantic development in young children with impaired hearing. *Journal of Speech and Hearing Research, 22,* 534–552.

Damico, J. S. (1980). A clinical approach to discourse analysis in school age children. Miniseminar presented at the American Speech-Language-Hearing Association Convention, Detroit.

Davis, L. (1977). *My friends and me.* Circle Pines, MN: American Guidance Service.

DeBoer, A. L. (1986). *The art of consulting.* Chicago: Arcturus Books.

Deci, E. L., & Ryan, R. M. (1985). *Intrinsic motivation and self-determination in human behavior.* New York: Plenum Press.

Demos, G. (1976). *The study skills counseling evaluation.* Los Angeles: Western Psychological Services.

Denny, J. M. (1977). Techniques for individual and group art therapy. In E. Ulman & P. Dachinger (Eds.), *Art therapy in theory and practice.* New York: Schocken.

Devine, T. G. (1987). *Teaching study skills: A guide for teachers.* Boston: Allyn & Bacon.

Dictionary of Occupational Titles (4th ed.). (1984). Washington, DC: Superintendent of Documents, U.S. Government Printing Office.

Dinkmeyer, D. (1982). *Developing understanding of self and others—Revised.* Circle Pines, MN: American Guidance Service.

DiSimoni, F. (1978). *Token Test for Children.* Chicago: Riverside.

Dunn, L. M. (1968). Special education for the mildly retarded—Is much of it justifiable? *Exceptional Children, 35,* 5–22.

Dunn, L. M., & Dunn, L. M. (1981). *The Peabody Picture Vocabulary Test.* Circle Pines, MN: American Guidance Service.

DuPont, H., Gardner, O. S., & Brody, D. S. (1974). *Toward affective development.* Circle Pines, MN: American Guidance Service.

Durrell, D. D., & Catterson, J. J. (1980). *Durrell Analysis of Reading Difficulty* (3rd ed.). San Antonio, TX: Psychological Corporation.

Eanet, M. G., & Manzo, A. V. (1976). REAP—A strategy for improving reading/ writing/study skills. *Journal of Reading, 19,* 647–652.

Edgar, E. (1987). Secondary programs in special education: Are many of them justifiable? *Exceptional Children, 53,* 555–561.

Edgington, R. (1967). But he spelled them right this morning. *Academic Therapy Quarterly, 3,* 58–59.

Edwards, P. (1973). Panorama: A study technique. *Journal of Reading, 17,* 132–135.

Ehri, L. C. (1988). Sources of difficulty in learning to spell and read. In M. L. Wolraich & D. Routh (Eds.), *Advances in developmental and behavioral pediatrics.* Greenwich, CT: JAI Press.

Ehri, L. C., & Wilce, L. S. (1983). Development of word identification speed in skilled and less skilled beginning readers. *Journal of Educational Psychology, 75,* 3–18.

Ehri, L. C., & Wilce, L. S. (1985). Movement into reading: Is the first stage of printed word learning visual or phonetic? *Reading Research Quarterly, 20*(2), 163–179.

Ehri, L. C., & Wilce, L. S. (1987). Does learning to spell help beginners learn to read words? *Reading Research Quarterly, 22*(1), 47–65.

Ekwall, E. E. (1992). *Locating and correcting reading difficulties* (6th ed.). Columbus, OH: Merrill.

Ekwall, E. E., & Shanker, J. L. (1985). *Teaching reading in the elementary school.* Columbus, OH: Charles E. Merrill.

Ellis, A. (1962). *Reason and emotion in psychotherapy.* New York: Lyle Stuart.

Ellis, A. (1970). Rational-emotive therapy. In L. Hershner (Ed.), *Four psychotherapies.* New York: Appleton-Century-Crofts.

Ellis, A. (1974). *Humanistic psychotherapy.* New York: McGraw-Hill.

Ellis, A., & Grieger, R. (1977). *Handbook of rational-emotive therapy.* New York: Springer.

Ellis, A., & Harper, R. (1977). *A new guide to rational living.* New York: Harper & Row.

Emberly, J. (1987, September). The new look of educational software. *Computers in Education, 5,* pp. 27–28.

Emig, J. (1977). Writing as a mode of learning. *College Composition and Communication, 28,* 122–128.

Engelmann, S., & Silbert, J. (1983). *Expressive writing 1 & 2.* Chicago: Science Research Associates.

Estes, T. H., & Vaughan, J. L., Jr. (1985). *Reading and learning in the content classroom: Diagnostic and instructional strategies.* Boston: Allyn & Bacon.

Evans, S. S., Evans, W. H., & Mercer, C. D. (1986). *Assessment for instruction.* Boston: Allyn & Bacon.

Experience Education. (no date). *Project discovery training system.* Red Oak, IA: Author.

Fagen, S., Long, N. J., & Stevens, D. (1975). *Teaching children self-control.* Columbus, OH: Charles E. Merrill.

Fay, L. (1965). Reading study skills: Math and science. In J. A. Figurel (Ed.), *Reading and inquiry* (pp. 93–94). Newark, DE: International Reading Association.

Feingold, B. F. (1975). *Why your child is hyperactive.* New York: Random House.

Fernald, G. (1988). *Remedial techniques in basic school subjects.* Austin TX: PRO-ED.

Fitzgerald, E. (1966). *Straight language for the deaf.* Washington, DC: Volta Bureau.

Flanders, N. (1970). *Analyzing teacher behavior.* Menlo Park, CA: Addison-Wesley.

Fokes, J. (1982). *Fokes Written Language Program.* Chicago: Science Research Associates.

Fox, W., Egner, A., Paolucci, P., Perelman, P., McKenzie, H., & Garvin, J. (1973). An introduction to a regular classroom approach to special education. In E. Deno (Ed.), *Instructional alternatives for exceptional children* (pp. 22–47). Arlington, VA: Council for Exceptional Children.

Gambrell, L. B. (1978). Getting started with sustained silent reading and keeping it going. *Reading Teacher, 32,* 328–331.

Garrison, M., & Hammill, D. D. (1971). Who are the retarded? *Exceptional Children, 38,* 13–20.

Gearheart, B. R., DeRuiter, J. A., & Sileo, T. W. (1986). *Teaching mildly and moderately handicapped students.* Englewood Cliffs, NJ: Prentice-Hall.

Gearheart, B. R., Weishahn, M. W., & Gearheart, C. J. (1992). *The exceptional student in the regular classroom* (5th ed.). Columbus OH: Merrill.

Gersten, R. (1985). Direct instruction with special education students. *Journal of Special Education, 19*(1), 41–50.

Gersten, R., Woodward, J., & Darch, C. (1986). Direct instruction. *Exceptional Children, 53*(1), 17–31.

Gillingham, A. (1958). Correspondence. *Elementary English, 35,* 118–122.

Gillingham, A., & Stillman, B. (1970). *Remedial training for children with specific disability in reading, spelling, and penmanship.* Cambridge, MA: Educators Publishing Service.

Ginott, H. (1961). *Group psychotherapy with children.* New York: McGraw-Hill.

Ginsburg, H. P. (1989). *Children's arithmetic: How they learn it and how you teach it* (2nd ed.). Austin, TX: PRO-ED.

Ginsburg, H. P., & Baroody, A. J. (1990). *Test of Early Mathematics Ability, second edition.* Austin, TX: PRO-ED.

Giordano, G. (1993). *Diagnostic and remedial mathematics in special education.* Springfield, IL: Charles C. Thomas.

Glasser, W. (1965). *Reality therapy.* New York: Harper & Row.

Glasser, W. (1969). *Schools without failure.* New York: Harper & Row.

Glavin, J. N., Quay, H. C., Annesley, F. R., & Werry, J. S. (1971). An experimental resource room for behavior problem children. *Exceptional Children, 38,* 131–137.

Gleason, M., & Stults, C. (1983a). *Basic writing skills: Sentence development.* Chicago: Science Research Associates.

Gleason, M., & Stults, C. (1983b). *Basic writing skills: Capitalization and punctuation.* Chicago: Science Research Associates.

Goldman, R., & Fristoe, M. (1972). *Goldman–Fristoe Test of Articulation.* Circle Pines, MN: American Guidance Service.

Good, T. L., & Brophy, J. E. (1990). *Educational psychology: A realistic approach.* New York: Longman.

Goode, D. (1990). Thinking about and discussing quality of life. In R. Schalock & M. Begab (Eds.), *Quality of life: Perspectives and issues* (pp. 41–58). Washington, DC: American Association on Mental Retardation.

Goodman, K. S. (1969). Analysis of oral reading miscues: Applied psycholinguistics. *Reading Research Quarterly, 5,* 9–30.

Goodman, Y. M. (1972). Reading diagnosis—Qualitative or quantitative. *The Reading Teacher, 26,* 32–37.

Graham, S., & Harris, K. R. (1988). Instructional recommendations for teaching writing to exceptional students. *Exceptional Children, 54*(6), 506–512.

Graham, S., & Miller, L. (1980). Handwriting research and practice: A unified approach. *Focus on Exceptional Children, 13,* 1–16.

Granowsky, A., Middleton, F. R., & Mumford, J. H. (1979). Parents as partners in education. *Reading Teacher, 32,* 826–830.

Graves, D. (1978). *Balance the basics: Let them write.* New York: Ford Foundation.

Graves, D. H. (1975). An examination of the writing process of seven year old children. *Language Arts, 56,* 312–319.

Greenbaum, C. R. (1987). *The Spellmaster Assessment and Teaching System.* Austin, TX: PRO-ED.

Greene, H., & Petty, W. (1967). *Developing language skills in the elementary school.* Boston: Allyn & Bacon.

Grice, H. P. (1975). Logic and conversation. In P. Cole & F. Morgan (Eds.), *Syntax and semantics: Speech acts.* New York: Academic Press.

Gronlund, N. E., & Linn, R. L. (1990). *Measurement and evaluation in teaching* (6th ed.). New York: Macmillan.

Gueron, G. R., & Maier, A. S. (1983). *Informal assessment in education.* Palo Alto, CA: Mayfield.

Guide for occupational exploration. (1988). Washington, DC: U.S. Government Printing Office.

Hall, J. K. (1988). *Evaluating and improving written expression: A practical guide for teachers.* Boston: Allyn & Bacon.

Hallahan, D., & Kauffman, J. (1995). *The illusion of full inclusion.* Austin, TX: PRO-ED.

Halloran, W. D. (1993). Transition services requirement: Issues, implications, challenge. In R. C. Eaves & P. J. McLaughlin (Eds.), *Recent advances in special education and rehabilitation* (pp. 210–224). Boston: Andover Medical Publishers.

Halpern, A. (1993). Quality of life as a conceptual framework for evaluating transition outcomes. *Exceptional Children, 59,* 486–498.

Halpern, A. S., Close, D. W., & Nelson, D. J. (1986). *On my own: The impact of semi-independent living program for adults with mental retardation.* Baltimore: Paul H. Brookes.

Halpern, A., Raffeld, P., Irvin, L. K., Link, R., & Beckland, J. D. (1986). *Social and Prevocational Information Battery–Revised.* Monterey, CA: CTB/McGraw-Hill.

Hammill, D. D. (1987). *Assessing the abilities and instructional needs of students.* Austin, TX: PRO-ED.

Hammill, D. D. (1991). *Detroit Tests of Learning Aptitude, third edition.* Austin, TX: PRO-ED.

Hammill, D. D., Brown, L. L., & Bryant, B. (1992). *A consumer's guide to tests in print* (2nd ed.). Austin, TX: PRO-ED.

Hammill, D., Brown, V., Larsen, S., & Wiederholt, J. L. (1993). *Test of Adolescent and Adult Language*–third edition. Austin, TX: PRO-ED.

Hammill, D. D., & Bryant, B. (1991). *Detroit Tests of Learning Aptitude–Adult.* Austin, TX: PRO-ED.

Hammill, D. D., & Larsen, S. (1988). *The Test of Written Language–2.* Austin, TX: PRO-ED.

Hammill, D. D., Larsen, S., & McNutt, G. (1977). The effects of spelling instruction: A preliminary study. *The Elementary School Journal, 78,* 67–72.

Hammill, D. D., & Leigh, J. (1983). *Basic School Skill Inventory–Diagnostic.* Austin, TX: PRO-ED.

Hammill, D., & Newcomer, P. (1988). *The Test of Language Development–2: Intermediate.* Austin, TX: PRO-ED.

Hammill, D. D., & Wiederholt, J. L. (1972). *The resource room.* New York: Grune & Stratton.

Hanna, P. R., Hanna, J. S., Hodges, R. E., & Rudorf, E. H. (1966). *Phoneme–grapheme correspondences as cues to spelling improvement.* Washington, DC: Department of Health, Education, and Welfare.

Hanna, P. R., Hodges, R. E., & Hanna, J. S. (1971). *Spelling: Structure and strategies.* Boston: Houghton Mifflin.

Hanna, R., & Moore, J. T. (1953). Spelling—From spoken word to written symbol. *Elementary School Journal, 53,* 329–337.

Hannaford, A. E. (1993). Computers and exceptional individuals. In J. D. Lindsey (Ed.), *Computers and exceptional individuals* (2nd ed.). Austin, TX: PRO-ED.

Hansen, C. L. (1978). Writing skills. In N. G. Haring, T. C. Lovitt, M. D. Eaton, & C. L. Hansen (Eds.), *The fourth R: Research in the classroom.* Columbus, OH: Charles E. Merrill.

Harris, A. J., & Sipay, E. R. (1990). *How to increase reading ability.* New York: Longman.

Harris, K. R., Wong, B. Y. L., & Keogh, B. K. (Eds.). (1985). Cognitive-behavior modification with children: A critical review of the state-of-the-art [Special issue]. *Journal of Abnormal Child Psychology, 13,* 329–476.

Harris, L. (1986). *The ICD survey of disabled Americans: Bringing disabled Americans into the mainstream.* New York: Louis Harris and Associates.

Harris, T. L., & Herrick, V. E. (1963). Children's perception of the handwriting task. In V. E. Herrick (Ed.), *New horizons for research in handwriting* (pp. 159–184). Madison: University of Wisconsin Press.

Hasselbring, T. S. (1986). Research of the effectiveness of computer-based instruction: A review. *International Review of Education, 32,* 313–324.

Hawisher, P. (1975). *The resource room: Access to excellence.* Lancaster, SC: Region V Educational Service Center.

Haynes, J. (1963). *Cuisenaire rods and the teaching of multiplication to third grade children.* Unpublished doctoral dissertation, Florida State University, Tallahassee.

Heilman, A., Blair, T., & Rupley, W. (1981). *Principles and practices of teaching reading.* Columbus, OH: Charles E. Merrill.

Heron, T. E., & Harris, K. C. (1993). *The educational consultant: Helping professionals, parents, and mainstreamed students* (3rd ed.). Austin, TX: PRO-ED.

Hodges, R. E., & Rudorf, E. H. (1965). Searching linguistics for cues for the teaching of spelling. *Elementary English, 42,* 529–533.

Holland, J. L. (1985). *The Self-Directed Search.* Odessa, FL: Psychological Assessment Resources.

Hoover, J. J., & Collier, C. (1992). Sociocultural considerations in teaching study strategies. *Intervention in School and Clinic, 27,* 228–232.

Hoover, J. J. (1993a). Helping parents develop a home-based study skills program. *Intervention in School and Clinic, 28* 238–245.

Hoover, J. J. (1993b). *Teaching study skills to students with learning problems.* Boulder, CO: Hamilton.

Horn, E. A. (1926). *A basic writing vocabulary: 10,000 words most commonly used in writing.* University of Iowa Monographs in Education, First Series, No. 4, Iowa City, IA.

Hresko, W., Reid, K., & Hammill, D. (1990). *The Test of Early Language Development, second edition.* Austin, TX: PRO-ED.

Hudson, F., & Colson, S. (1988). *Hudson Education Skills Inventory.* Austin, TX: PRO-ED.

Iano, R. P. (1972). Shall we disband our special classes? *Journal of Special Education, 6,* 167–178.

Iano, R. P. (1986). The study and development of teaching. *Remedial and Special Education, 7*(5), 50–61.

Idol, L. (1993). *Special educator's consultation handbook* (2nd ed.). Austin, TX: PRO-ED.

Idol, L., Nevin, A., & Paolucci-Whitcomb, P. (1993). *Collaborative consultation* (2nd ed.). Austin, TX: PRO-ED.

Idol, L., & West, J. F. (1987). Consultation in special education: Training and practice (Part II). *Journal of Learning Disabilities, 20*(8), 474–494.

Idol, L., West, J. F., & Lloyd, S. (1988). Organizing and implementing specialized reading programs: A collaborative approach involving classroom, remedial, and special education teachers. *Remedial and Special Education, 9*(2), 54–62.

Idol-Maestas, L., Lloyd, S., & Lilly, M. S. (1981). Implementation of a noncategorical approach to direct service and teacher education. *Exceptional Children, 48,* 213–219.

Jastak, J. F., & Jastak, S. (1980). *Wide Range Employability Sample Test.* Wilmington, DE: Jastak Assessment Systems.

Johansson, C. B. (1982). *Career Assessment Inventory* (2nd ed). Minnetonka, MN: National Computer Systems/PAS Division.

Johnson, B., Schneider, M., & German, D. (1983). The debate over learning disability vs. reading disability: A survey of practitioners' populations and remedial methods. *Learning Disability Quarterly, 6*(3), 258–264.

Jorgensen, C. A., & Bernhard, B. A. (1993). *Developing the functional use of a telephone book: Emphasing communicative, organizational, and problem solving skills.* Austin, TX: PRO-ED.

Karlsen, B., Madden, R., & Gardner, E. F. (1984). *Stanford Diagnostic Reading Test* (3rd ed.). San Antonio, TX: Psychological Corporation.

Kauffman, J. M. (1989). The Regular Education Initiative as Reagan–Bush education policy: A trickle-down theory of education of the hard-to-teach. *The Journal of Special Education, 23,* 256–278.

Kelly, B. W., & Holmes, J. (1979). The guided lecture procedure. *Journal of Reading, 22,* 602–604.

Kessler, J. W. (1966). *Psychopathology of childhood.* Englewood Cliffs, NJ: Prentice-Hall.

Knause, W. (1974). *Rational-emotive education: A manual for elementary school teachers.* New York: Institute for Rational Living.

Knause, W. J., & McKeever, C. (1977). Rational-emotive education with learning disabled children. *Journal of Learning Disabilities, 10,* 10–14.

Knowlton, H. E., Turnbull, A. P., Backus, L., & Turnbull, R. (1988). Letting go: Consent and the "yes, but . . ." problem in transition. In B. L. Ludlow, A. P. Turnbull, & R. Luckason (Eds.), *Transition to adult life for people with mental retardation* (pp. 44–64). Baltimore: Paul H. Brookes.

Kohn, A. (1993). *Punished by rewards.* New York: Houghton Mifflin.

Kokaska, C. J., & Brolin, D. E. (1985). *Career education for handicapped individuals* (2nd ed.). Columbus, OH: Charles E. Merrill.

Kottmeyer, W. (1959). *Teacher's guide for remedial reading.* New York: McGraw-Hill.

Kottmeyer, W., & Claus, A. (1988). *Basic goals in spelling.* New York: McGraw-Hill.

Kroth, R. (1973). The behavioral Q-sort as a diagnostic tool. *Academic Therapy, 8,* 317–330.

Kuder, F. (1985). *Kuder Occupational Interest Survey, Form DD, Revised.* Monterey, CA: CTB/McGraw-Hill.

Kuska, A., Webster, E. J. D., & Elford, G. (1964). *Spelling in language arts 6.* Ontario: Thomas Nelson & Sons (Canada).

Lambert, N., Nihira, K., & Leland, H. (1993). *AAMR Adaptive Behavior Scale–School* (2nd ed.). Austin, TX: PRO-ED.

Langone, J. (1990). *Teaching students with mild and moderate learning problems.* Boston: Allyn & Bacon.

Larsen, S. C. (1987). *Assessing the writing abilities and instructional needs of students.* Austin, TX: PRO-ED.

Larsen, S., & Hammill, D. D. (1994). *The Test of Written Spelling–third edition.* Austin, TX: PRO-ED.

Lee, L., Koenigsknecht, R. A., & Mulhern, S. T. (1975). *Interactive language development teaching.* Evanston, IL: Northwestern University Press.

Lerner, J. W. (1993). *Learning disabilities: Theories, diagnosis, and teaching strategies* (6th ed.). Boston: Houghton Mifflin.

Link, D. P. (1980). *Essential learning skills and the low achieving student at the secondary level: A rating of 24 academic abilities.* Master's thesis, University of Kansas, Lawrence.

Lloyd, J. (1980). Academic instruction and cognitive behavior modification: The need for attack strategy planning. *Exceptional Education Quarterly, 1,* 53–63.

Lock, C. (1981). *Study skills.* West Lafayete, IN: Kappa Delta Pi.

Long, N. J., & Newman, R. G. (1980). Managing surface behavior of children in schools. In N. J. Long, W. C. Morse, & R. G. Newman (Eds.), *Conflict in the classroom* (4th ed.). Belmont, CA: Wadsworth.

Lovitt, T. C. (1975). Applied behavior analysis and learning disabilities. Part II: Specific research recommendations and suggestions for practitioners. *Journal of Learning Disabilities, 8,* 504–518.

MacArthur, C. A. (1988). The impact of computers on the writing process. *Exceptional Children, 54,* 536–542.

Maier, A. S. (1980). Checklist of reading abilities. In G. R. Guerin & A. S. Maier, *Informal assessment in education* (pp. 248–251). Palo Alto, CA: Mayfield.

Mandlebaum, L. H., & Wilson, R. (1989). Teaching listening skills in the special education classroom. *Academic Therapy, 24,* 449–459.

Manzo, A. V. (1985, March). Expansion modules for the ReQuest, CAT, GRP, and REAP reading/study procedures. *Journal of Reading, 20,* 498–502.

Markwardt, F. C. (1989). *Peabody Individual Achievement Test–Revised* (2nd ed.). Circle Pines, MN: American Guidance Service.

Mason, G. E., Blanchard, J. S., & Daniel, D. B. (1983). *Computer applications in reading* (2nd ed.). Newark, DE: International Reading Association.

Mastropieri, M. A., & Scruggs, T. E. (1994). *Effective instruction for special education* (2nd ed.). Austin, TX: PRO-ED.

Mastropieri, M., Scruggs, T., & Shiah, S. (1991). Mathematics instruction for learning disabled students: A review of research. *Learning Disabilities Research and Practice, 6*(2), 89–98.

Mather, N. (1992). Whole language instruction for students with learning disabilities: Caught in the cross fire. *Learning Disabilities Practice, 7,* 87–95.

McCracken, R. A., & McCracken, M. J. (1978). Modeling is the key to sustained silent reading. *Reading Teacher, 31,* 406–408.

McKenzie, H. S. (1972). Special education and consulting teachers. In F. Clark, D. Evans, & L. Hammerlynk (Eds.), *Implementing behavioral programs for schools and clinics.* Champaign, IL: Research Press.

McKenzie, H. S., Egner, A. N., Knight, M. F., Perelman, P. F., Schneider, B. M., & Gavvin, J. S. (1970). Training consultant teachers to assist elementary teachers in management and education of handicapped children. *Exceptional Children, 37,* 137–143.

McKenzie, R. G. (1991). Developing study skills through cooperative learning activities. *Intervention in School and Clinic, 26*(4), 227–229.

McLeod, T. M., & Armstrong, S. W. (1982). Learning disabilities in mathematics-skill deficits and remedial approaches at the intermediate and secondary level. *Learning Disability Quarterly, 5,* 305–311.

McLoughlin, J. A., & Lewis, R. B. (1994). *Assessing special students* (4th ed.). Columbus, OH: Charles E. Merrill.

Mecham, M. (1989). *Utah Test of Language Development.* Austin, TX: PRO-ED.

Medway, F. J. (1982). School consultation research: Past trends and future directions. *Professional Psychology, 13,* 422–430.

Medway, F. J., & Updyke, J. (1985). Meta-analysis of consultation outcome studies. *American Journal of Community Psychology, 13,* 489–504.

Meichenbaum, D. (1975). *Toward a cognitive theory of self-control* (Research Report No. 48). Waterloo: Department of Psychology, University of Waterloo, Ontario.

Meichenbaum, D. H. (1977). *Cognitive behavior modification.* New York: Plenum Press.

Meichenbaum, D. H. (1983). Teaching thinking: A cognitive-behavior approach. In *Interdisciplinary voices in learning disabilities and remedial education.* Austin, TX: PRO-ED.

Menyuk, P. (1969). *Sentences children use.* Cambridge, MA: MIT Press.

Mercer, C. D. (1987). *Students with learning disabilities.* Columbus, OH: Charles E. Merrill.

Mercer, C. D., & Mercer, A. R. (1993). *Teaching students with learning problems* (4th ed.). Columbus, OH: Charles E. Merrill.

Metropolitan Achievement Test (7th ed.). (1992). San Antonio, TX: Psychological Corporation.

Miller, J. F. (1981). *Assessing language production in children.* Boston: Allyn & Bacon.

Miller, S. K. (1985). Computers and writing. *Direct Instruction News, 4*(3), 12–13.

Miller, S. K., & Engelmann, S. (1980). *Cursive writing program.* Chicago: Science Research Associates.

Minner, S., & Beane, A. (1985, Summer). Q-sorts for special education teachers. *Teaching Exceptional Children,* 279–281.

Minton, M. J. (1980). The effect of sustained silent reading upon comprehension and attitudes of ninth graders. *Journal of Reading, 23,* 498–502.

Mithaug, D. E., Martin, J. E., Agran, M., & Rusch, F. R. (1988). *Why special education graduates fail: How to teach them to succeed.* Colorado Springs, CO: Ascent Publications.

Moffett, J. (1973). *A student-centered language arts curriculum.* Boston: Houghton Mifflin.

Moore, J. C., Jones, C. J., & Miller, D. C. (1980). What we know after a decade of sustained silent reading. *Reading Teacher, 33,* 445–450.

Moreno, J. (1934). *Who shall survive? A new approach to the problem of interrelations.* Washington, DC: Nervous & Mental Disease Publishing House.

Moreno, J. (1946). *Psychodrama.* New York: Beacon House.

Nasca, D. (1966). Comparative merits of a manipulative approach to second-grade arithmetic. *The Arithmetic Teacher, 13,* 221–226.

National Commission on Excellence in Education. (1983). *A nation at risk: The imperative for educational reform.* Washington, DC: U.S. Government Printing Office.

National Council of Teachers of Mathematics. (1989). *Curriculum and evaluation standards for school mathematics.* Reston, VA: Author.

National Council of Teachers of Mathematics. (1991). *Professional standards for teaching mathematics.* Reston, VA: Author.

Neuman, S. B., & Morocco, C. (1987). Two hands is hard for me: Keyboarding and learning disabled children. *Educational Technology, 27*(12), 36–38.

Newcomer, P. L. (1986). *The Standardized Reading Inventory.* Austin, TX: PRO-ED.

Newcomer, P. L. (1990). *Diagnostic Achievement Battery* (2nd ed.). Austin, TX: PRO-ED.

Newcomer, P. L. (1993). *Understanding and teaching emotionally disturbed children and adolescents* (2nd ed.). Austin, TX: PRO-ED.

Newcomer, P. L., Barenbaum, E. M., & Bryant, B. R. (1994). *Depression and Anxiety in Youth Scale.* Austin, TX: PRO-ED.

Newland, T. E. (1932). An analytical study of the development of illegibilities in handwriting from the lower grades to adulthood. *Journal of Educational Research, 26,* 249–258.

Nicholson, T. (1980). Why we need to talk to parents about reading. *Reading Teacher, 34,* 19–21.

Niedermeyer, F. C. (1973). Kindergarteners learn to write. *Elementary School Journal, 74,* 130–135.

Nihira, K., Leland, H., & Lambert, N. (1993) *AAMR Adaptive Behavior Scale–Residential and Community* (2nd ed.). Austin, TX: PRO-ED.

Northcutt, N. W. (1975). Functional literacy for adults. In D. M. Neilsen & H. F. Hjelm (Eds.), *Reading and career education.* Newark, DE: International Reading Association.

Okolo, C. M., Hinsey, M., & Yousefian, B. (1990). Learning disabled student's acquisition of keyboarding skills and continuing motivation under drill-and-practice and game conditions. *Learning Disabilities Research, 5,* 100–109.

Orton, S. T. (1989). *Reading, writing, and speech problems in children and selected papers.* Austin, TX: PRO-ED.

Otto, W., & Smith, R. J. (1980). *Corrective and remedial teaching* (3rd ed.). Boston: Houghton Mifflin.

Palincsar, A., & Brown, A. (1984). Reciprocal teaching of comprehension fostering and monitoring activities. *Cognition and Instruction, 1,* 117–175.

Papert, S. (1980). *Mindstorms: Children, computers, and powerful ideas.* New York: Basic Books.

Parent, W. (1993). Quality of life and consumer choice. In P. Wehman (Ed.), *The ADA mandate for social change* (pp. 19–41). Baltimore: Paul H. Brookes.

Parker, R. (1991). *Occupational Aptitude Survey and Interest Schedule* (2nd ed.). Austin, TX: PRO-ED.

Parmenter, T. (1988). An analysis of the dimensions of quality of life for people with physical disabilities. In R. I. Brown (Ed.), *Quality of life for handicapped people: A series in rehabilitation education* (pp. 7–36). London: Croom Helm.

Pauk, W. (1984). *How to study in college.* Boston: Houghton Mifflin.

PESCO International. (no date). *Compute-A-Match system.* Pleasantville, NY: Author.

Petty, W. T., & Jensen, J. M. (1980). *Developing children's language.* Boston: Allyn & Bacon.

Phelps-Gunn, T., & Phelps-Terasaki, D. (1982). *Written-language instruction.* Austin, TX: PRO-ED.

Phelps-Terasaki, D., & Phelps-Gunn, T. (1988). *Teaching competence in written language*. Austin, TX: PRO-ED.

Piaget, J. (1962). *The language and thought of the child*. New York: World.

Plattor, E. E., & Woestehoff, E. S. (1971). Toward a singular style of instruction in handwriting. *Elementary English, 48,* 1009–1011.

Polloway, E. A., Patton, J. R., & Cohen, S. B. (1981). Written language for mildly handicapped students. *Focus on Exceptional Children, 14*(3), 1–16.

Polloway, E. A., & Smith, T. E. C. (1992). *Language instruction for students with disabilities* (2nd ed.). Denver, Love.

Pooley, R. C. (1960). Dare schools set a standard in English usage? *English Journal, 49,* 179–180.

Poplin, M. (1988a). Holistic/constructivist principles of the teaching/learning process. *Journal of Learning Disabilities, 21*(7), 401–416.

Poplin, M. (1988b). The reductionist fallacy in learning disabilities: Replicating the past by reducing the present. *Journal of Learning Disabilities, 21*(7), 389–400.

Preston, R. C., & Botel, M. (1967). *Study habits checklist*. Chicago: Science Research Associates.

Proff-Witt, J. (1978). *Speed Spelling 1*. Austin, TX: PRO-ED.

Proff-Witt, J. (1979). *Speed Spelling 2*. Austin, TX: PRO-ED.

Reading Mastery Program. (1988). Blacklick, OH: SRA.

Reger, R., Schroeder, W., & Uschold, K. (1968). *Special education: Children with learning problems*. New York: Oxford University Press.

Reid, D. K. (1988). Reflections on the pragmatics of a paradigm shift. *Journal of Learning Disabilities, 21,* 417–420.

Reid, D. K., Hresko, W. P., & Hammill, D. D. (1989). *Test of Early Reading Ability* (2nd ed.). Austin, TX: PRO-ED.

Reisman, F. K. (1984). *Sequential Assessment in Mathematics Inventory (SAMI)*. San Antonio, TX: Psychological Corporation.

Reisman, F. K., & Kauffman, S. H. (1980). *Teaching mathematics to children with special needs*. Columbus, OH: Charles E. Merrill.

Reiter, S. M., Mabee, W. S., & McLaughlin, T. F. (1985). Self-monitoring: Effects for on-task and time to complete assignments. *Remedial and Special Education, 6*(1), 50–51.

Reynolds, M. C. (1962). A framework for considering some issues in special education. *Exceptional Children, 28,* 367–370.

Reynolds, M. C. (1989). An historical perspective. The delivery of special education to mildly disabled and at-risk students. *Remedial and Special Education, 10*(6), 7–11.

Reynolds, W. M. (1987). *Reynolds Adolescent Depression Scale*. Odessa, FL: Psychological Assessment Resources.

Rhodes, W. C., & Paul, J. L. (1978). *Emotionally disturbed and deviant children: New views and approaches*. Englewood Cliffs, NJ: Prentice-Hall.

Rhodes, W. C., & Tracy, M. L. (Eds.). (1972). *A study of child variance*. Ann Arbor: University of Michigan Press.

Ritter, S., & Idol-Maestas, L. (1986). Teaching middle school students to use a test-taking strategy. *Journal of Educational Research, 79*(6), 350–357.

Rivera, D. M., & Bryant, B. R. (1992). Mathematics instruction for students with special needs. *Intervention in School and Clinic, 28*(2), 71–86.

Roth, S. F., & Beck, I. L. (1987). Theoretical and instructional implications of the assessment of two microcomputer word recognition programs. *Reading Research Quarterly, 22*(2), 197–218.

Roush, D. (1984). Rational-emotive therapy and youth: Some new techniques for counselors. *Personnel and Guidance Journal, 62*, 414–417.

Ruddell, R. B. (1976). Psycholinguistic models. In H. Singer & R. Ruddell (Eds.), *Theoretical models and processes of reading.* Newark, DE: International Reading Association.

Ruedy, L. R. (1983). Handwriting instruction: It can be part of the high school curriculum. *Academic Therapy, 18*(4), 421–428.

Sabatino, D. A. (1971). An evaluation of resource rooms for children with learning disabilities. *Journal of Learning Disabilities, 4*, 84–93.

Salend, S. J. (1990). *Effective mainstreaming.* New York: Macmillan.

Salvia, J., & Ysseldyke, J. E. (1991). *Assessment in special and remedial education* (4th ed.). Boston: Houghton Mifflin.

Samuels, S. J. (1981). Some essentials of decoding. *Exceptional Education Quarterly, 4*, 11–25.

Schneider, M. F. (1989). *Children's Apperceptive Storytelling Test.* Austin, TX: PRO-ED.

Schumaker, J. B., Deshler, D. D., Nolan, S., Clark, F. L., Alley, G. R., & Warner, M. M. (1981). *Error monitoring: A learning strategy for improving academic performance of LD adolescents.* Lawrence: University of Kansas Institute for Research in Learning Disabilities.

Schumaker, J. B., Sheldon-Wildgen, J., & Sherman, J. A. (1980). *An observational study of the academic and social behaviors of learning disabled adolescents in the regular classroom.* Lawrence: University of Kansas Institute for Research in Learning Disabilities.

Schwarzwald, J., Laor, T., & Hoffman, M. (1986). Impact of sociometric method and activity content on assessment of intergroup relations in the classroom. *The British Journal of Educational Psychology, 56*, 24–31.

Serio, M. (1968). Cursive writing. *Academic Therapy, 4*, 67–70.

Shaw, H. (1971). *Spell it right!* New York: Barnes and Noble.

Shinn, T. K. (1982). Linguistic and functional spelling strategies. In D. A. Sabatino & L. Mann (Eds.), *A handbook of diagnostic and prescriptive teaching* (pp. 263–296). Austin, TX: PRO-ED.

Sieben, R. L. (1983). Medical treatment of learning problems: A critique. In *Interdisciplinary voices in learning disabilities and remedial education* (pp. 155–177). Austin, TX: PRO-ED.

Silbert, J., Carnine, D., & Stein, M. (1981). *Direct instruction mathematics.* Columbus, OH: Charles E. Merrill.

Silvaroli, J. N. (1994). *Classroom Reading Inventory* (7th ed.). Dubuque, IA: William C. Brown.

Silver Burdett Spelling. (1986). Morristown, NJ: Silver Burdett. (Series unauthored)

Silver, L. B. (1987). The "magic cure": A review of the current controversial approaches to treating learning disabilities. *Journal of Learning Disabilities, 20*, 385–397.

Simon, S. B., Howe, L. W., & Kirschenbaum, H. (1978). *Values clarification.* New York: Hart.

Simon, S. B., & O'Rourke, R. (1977). *Developing values with exceptional children.* Englewood Cliffs, NJ: Prentice-Hall.

Singer, H. (1978, May). Active comprehension: From answering to asking questions. *Reading Teacher,* p. 903.

Sitko, M. (1986). Developments in computer technology: Implications for the special student. In D. G. Bachor & C. Crealock (Eds.), *Instructional strategies for students with special needs* (pp. 407–483). Scarborough, Ontario: Prentice-Hall Canada.

Sittington, P. L. (1979). Vocational assessment and training of the handicapped. *Focus on Exceptional Children, 1,* 1–11.

Sittington, P. L., & Frank, A. R. (1993, October). *Iowa statewide follow-up study: Adult adjustment.* Des Moines: Department of Education State of Iowa.

Smith, F. (1982). *Understanding reading.* New York: Holt, Rinehart and Winston.

Smith, F. (1983). How children learn. In D. Carnine, D. Elkind, A. D. Hendrickson, D. Meichenbaum, R. L. Sieben, & F. Smith (Eds.), *Interdisciplinary voices in learning disabilities and remedial education.* Austin, TX: PRO-ED.

Smith, R. M., Neisworth, J. T., & Greer, J. G. (1978). *Evaluating educational environments.* Columbus, OH: Merrill.

Smith, T. E. C., & Dowdy, C. A. (1989). The role of study skills in the secondary curriculum. *Academic Therapy, 24*(4), 479–490.

Spache, G. D. (1981). *Diagnostic Reading Scales.* Monterey, CA: CTB/McGraw-Hill.

Spalding, R. B., & Spalding, W. T. (1986). *The writing road to reading* (3rd ed.). New York: Morrow.

Sparrow, S. S., Balla, D. A., & Cicchetti, D. V. (1985). *Vineland Adaptive Behavior Scales.* Circle Pines, MN: American Guidance Service.

Spiegel, D. L. (1992). Blending whole language and systematic direct instruction. *The Reading Teacher, 46*(1), 38–44.

Sroufe, L. A. (1975). Drug treatment of children with behavior problems. In F. D. Horowitz (Ed.), *Review of child development research* (Vol. 4). Chicago: University of Chicago Press.

Stanovich, K. E., Nathan, R. G., & Vala-Rossi, M. (1987). Developmental changes in the cognitive correlates of reading ability and the developmental lag hypothesis. *Reading Research Quarterly, 21*(3), 267–283.

Steffe, L. P. (1968). The relationship of conservation of numerousness to problem-solving abilities of first-grade children. *The Arithmetic Teacher, 15,* 47–52.

Steinberg, E. R. (1992). The potential of computer-based telecommunication for instruction. *Journal of Computer-Based Instruction, 19*(2), 42.

Stodden, R. A., & Boone, R. (1987). Assessing transition services for handicapped youth: A cooperative interagency approach. *Exceptional Children, 53*(6), 537–545.

Strong, E. K., Hansen, F. C., & Campbell, D. P. (1985) *Strong–Campbell Interest Inventory.* Palo Alto, CA: Consulting Psychologists Press.

Strong, W. (1983). *Sentence combining: A composing book.* New York: Random House.

Super, D. E. (1976). Career education and the meanings of work. In *Monographs on career education.* Washington, DC: U.S. Department of Health, Education and Welfare, U.S. Office of Education.

Super, D. E., Thompson, A. S., Linedman, R. H., Jordan, J. P., & Myers, R. A. (1982). *Career Development Inventory.* Palo Alto, CA: Consulting Psychologists Press.

Talent Assessment, Inc. (no date). *Pictorial Inventory of Careers (PIC).* Jacksonville, FL: Author.

Talent Assessment, Inc. (no date). *Talent Assessment Program (TAP).* Jacksonville, FL: Author.

Taylor, C., & Scruggs, T. (1983). Research in progress: Improving the test-taking skills of LD and BD elementary students. *Exceptional Children, 50*(3), 277.

Tharp, R. (1975). The triadic model of consultation: Current considerations. In C. A. Parker (Ed.), *Psychological consultation: Helping teachers meet special needs* (pp. 135–151). Reston, VA: Council for Exceptional Children.

Thurber, D. N. (1981). *D'Nealian handwriting.* Glenview, IL: Scott, Foresman.

Thurstone, T. G. (1959). *An evaluation on educating mentally retarded handicapped children in special classes and regular classes* (U.S. Office of Education, Cooperative Research Project No. OE-SAE 6452). Chapel Hill: University of North Carolina.

Tonjes, M. J., & Zintz, M. V. (1981). *Teaching reading/thinking/study skills in content classrooms.* Dubuque, IA: William C. Brown.

Trieschman, A. E. (1969). Understanding the stages of a typical temper tantrum. In A. E. Trieschman, J. K. Whittaker, & L. K. Brendtro (Eds.), *The other 23 hours.* Chicago: Aldine.

Troutman, A. (1980). *Diagnosis: An instruction aid: Mathematics.* Chicago: Science Research Associates.

United States Employment Service. (1982a). *General Aptitude Test Battery (GATB).* Washington, DC: U.S. Government Printing Office.

United States Employment Service. (1982b). *Non-reading Aptitude Test Battery (NATB).* Washington, DC: U.S. Government Printing Office.

Valpar International Corp. (no date). *Microcomputer Evaluation and Screening Assessment.* Tucson, AZ: Author.

Valpar International Corp. (1991). *Computerized Assessment (COMPASS).* Tucson, AZ: Author.

Van Houten, R. (1980). *How to use reprimands.* Austin, TX: PRO-ED.

Verner, Z. B., & Minturn, B. (1985). *Critical steps to effective reading and writing* (10 vols.). Chicago: Science Research Associates.

Vocational Research Institute. (1984). *APTICOM.* Philadelphia: Jewish Employment and Vocational Service.

Vocational Research Institute. (1989). *Vocational transit.* Philadelphia: Jewish Employment and Vocational Service.

Vocational Research Institute. (no date). *Vocational Interest, Temperament, and Aptitude System (VITAS).* Philadelphia: Jewish Employment and Vocational Service.

Voorhis, T. G. (1931). *The relative merits of cursive and manuscript writing.* New York: Teachers College, Columbia University.

Vygotsky, L. S. (1978). *Thought and language.* Cambridge, MA: MIT Press.

Wade, S. E. (1990). Using think alouds to assess comprehension. *The Reading Teacher, 44,* 442–451.

Wagner, M. (1989, March). *The transition experiences of youth with disabilities: A report from the National Longitudinal Transition Study.* (Available from SRI International, 333 Ravenswood Ave., Menlo Park, CA 94025).

Walker, H. M., McConnell, S., Holmes, D., Todis, B., Walker, J., & Golden, N. (1983). *Walker Social Skills Curriculum: The ACCEPTS program.* Austin, TX: PRO-ED.

Walker, H. M., Todis, B., Holmes, D., & Horton, N. (1988). *Walker Social Skills Curriculum: The ACCESS program.* Austin, TX: PRO-ED.

Wallace, E. E., Taylor, W. D., Fay, L., Kucera, H., & Gonzalez, G. (1988). *Riverside spelling.* Chicago: Riverside.

Wallace, G., Cohen, S. B., & Polloway, E. A. (1987). *Language arts: Teaching exceptional students.* Austin, TX: PRO-ED.

Wallace, G., & Hammill, D. D. (1994). *Comprehensive Receptive and Expressive Vocabulary Test.* Austin, TX: PRO-ED.

Wallace, G., & Kauffman, J. M. (1986). *Teaching students with learning and behavior problems.* Columbus, OH: Charles E. Merrill.

Wallace, G., Larsen, S. C., & Elksnin, L. K. (1992). *Educational assessment of learning problems: Testing for teaching* (2nd ed.). Boston: Allyn & Bacon.

Wallace, G., & McLoughlin, J. A. (1988). *Learning disabilities: Concepts and characteristics.* Columbus, OH: Charles E. Merrill.

Wang, M. C., Reynolds, M. C., & Walberg, H. J. (1986). Rethinking special education. *Educational Leadership, 44*(1), 26–31.

Wang, M. C., Walberg, H. J., & Reynolds, M. C. (1992). A scenario for better—not separate—special education. *Educational Leadership, 50,* 35–41.

Wasylyk, T. M., & Milone, M. N. (1984). Corrective techniques in handwriting: Cursive. In W. B. Barbe, V. H. Lucas, & T. M. Wasylyk (Eds.), *Handwriting: Basic skills for effective communication* (pp. 334–338). Columbus, OH: Zaner-Bloser.

Weber, R. M. (1968). The study of oral reading errors: A survey of the literature. *Reading Research Quarterly, 4,* 96–119.

Weber, R. M. (1970). A linguistic analysis of first-grade reading errors. *Reading Research Quarterly, 5,* 427–451.

Wechsler, D. (1981). *Wechsler Adult Intelligence Scale–Revised.* San Antonio, TX: Psychological Corporation.

Wesson, C. L., & Keefe, M. (1989). Teaching library skills to students with mild and moderate handicaps. *Teaching Exceptional Children, 21*(3), 28–31.

West, J. F., & Idol, L. (1987). School consultation: An interdisciplinary perspective on theory, models, and research. *Journal of Learning Disabilities, 21*(1), 28, 56–63.

West, J. F., Idol, L., & Cannon, G. (1988). *Collaboration in the schools: Communicating, interacting, and problem solving.* Austin, TX: PRO-ED.

White, W., Schumaker, J., Warner, M., Alley, G., & Deshler, D. (1980). *The current status of young adults identified as learning disabled during their school career* (Research Report No. 21). Lawrence: University of Kansas, Institute for Research in Learning Disabilities.

Wiederholt, J. L. (1971). Predictive validity of Frostig's constructs as measured by the Developmental Test of Visual Perception. *Dissertation Abstracts, 33,* 1556-A.

Wiederholt, J. L. (1985). *Formal Reading Inventory: A method for assessing silent reading comprehension and oral reading miscues.* Austin, TX: PRO-ED.

Wiederholt, J. L., & Bryant, B. R. (1992). *Gray Oral Reading Tests, third edition.* Austin, TX: PRO-ED.

Wiederholt, J. L., Cronin, M. E., & Stubbs, V. (1980). Measurement of functional competencies and the handicapped: Constructs, assessments, and recommendations. *Exceptional Education Quarterly, 1,* 69–74.

Wiederholt, J. L., Hammill, D. D., & Brown, V. L. (1983). *The resource teacher: A guide to effective practices.* Austin, TX: PRO-ED.

Wiederholt, J. L., Hammill, D. D., & Brown, V. L. (1983). *The resource teacher: A guide to effective practices* (2nd ed.). Austin, TX: PRO-ED.

Wiederholt, J. L., Hammill, D. D., & Brown, V. L. (1993). *The resource program: Organization and implementation.* Austin, TX: PRO-ED.

Wiederholt, J. L., & Larsen, S. C. (1983). *Test of Practical Knowledge.* Austin, TX: PRO-ED.

Wiig, E. (1982). *"Let's Talk" Inventory for Adolescents.* San Antonio, TX: Psychological Corporation.

Wiig, E. H., & Semel, E. (1984). *Language assessment and intervention for the learning disabled* (2nd ed.). Columbus, OH: Charles E. Merrill.

Wiig, E. H., & Semel, E. (1987). *Clinical Evaluation of Language Fundamentals–Revised.* San Antonio, TX: Psychological Corporation.

Wilkinson, G. S. (1994). *Wide Range Achievement Test* (3rd ed.). Wilmington, DE: Wide Range/Jastak.

Will, M. C. (1984). *OSERS programming for the transition of youth with disabilities: Bridges from school to working life.* Washington, DC: Office of Special Education and Rehabilitation Services, U.S. Department of Education.

Will, M. (1986). Educating children with learning problems: A shared responsibility. *Exceptional Children, 52,* 411–415.

Winefordner, D. (1991). *Worker trait group guide.* Bloomington, IL: McKnight Publishing.

Woltmann, A. G. (1971). The use of puppetry in therapy. In N. J. Long, W. C. Morse, & R. G. Newman (Eds.), *Conflict in the classroom* (pp. 223–227). Belmont, CA: Wadsworth.

Wong, B. Y. L. (1985). Issues in cognitive-behavioral interventions in academic'skill areas. *Journal of Abnormal Child Psychology, 13,* 425–442.

Wood, M. M. (1981). *Developmental therapy sourcebook: Vol. II. Fantasy and make-believe.* Austin, TX: PRO-ED.

Wood, M. M., & Long, N. J. (1991). *Life space intervention: Talking with children and youth in crisis.* Austin, TX: PRO-ED.

Woodcock, R. W. (1988). *Woodcock Reading Mastery Tests–Revised.* Circle Pines, MN: American Guidance Service.

Woolfolk, A. E. (1990). *Educational psychology.* Englewood Cliffs, NJ: Prentice-Hall.

Workman, E. A. (1982). *Teaching behavioral self-control to students.* Austin, TX: PRO-ED.

Zaner-Bloser Staff. (1984). *Evaluation scale.* Columbus, OH: Zaner-Bloser.

Zionts, P. (1985). *Teaching disturbed and disturbing students.* Austin, TX: PRO-ED.

Author Index

Subject Index

· ·

About the Authors

· ·

Donald D. Hammill   Before earning his doctorate degree from The University of Texas, Hammill worked in the Texas public schools for 5 years as a teacher and a speech therapist. He has served on the teaching staffs of Wichita State University and Temple University. In 1976–1977, he was president of The Council for Learning Disabilities. He is author of 60 articles published in journals having peer review. He has written eight textbooks and monographs. In addition, he has participated in the development of many diagnostic, norm-referenced assessment tests, including the *Detroit Tests of Learning Aptitude* (DTLA), the *Test of Language Development* (TOLD), and the *Test of Written Language* (TOWL). Presently Hammill's time is split between two positions. He is president of PRO-ED, Inc., a company that specializes in psychoeducational testing instruments, curricular materials, professional books, and journals in the area of special and remedial education. He is also a trustee of the Donald D. Hammill Foundation, a nonprofit agency that funds fellowships, research, and symposia in all areas pertaining to individuals with disabilities.

Nettie R. Bartel   Bartel is currently a professor of special education at Temple University. Recently she served as principal investigator of the project *Educational Aftereffects of Central Nervous System Treatment in Children Cured of Cancer,* a collaborative study with Children's Hospital of Philadelphia funded by the Office of Special Education Programs, Washington, DC. She recently conducted research on the effectiveness of various AIDS prevention strategies with different populations. Bartel holds a Ph.D. in special education from Indiana University, Bloomington. She was a public school teacher of gifted children and children with disabilities in Indiana and in Canada. Bartel's scholarly contributions include a teacher's guide on problem solving for students with learning and behavioral problems, a comprehensive series of instructional materials for AIDS education at the junior and senior high levels (available in English and Spanish) and *AIDS—A Guide for Parents.* She is the author of a number of research articles and review chapters on language development, services, interventions, public policy and social psychology of disability, and psychological and educational aftereffects of central nervous system treatment in childhood cancer survivors.

Linda Brown   A former classroom teacher and university professor, Brown is coauthor of several norm-referenced tests including the *Test of Nonverbal Intelligence,* the *Behavior Rating Profile,* the *Index of Personality Characteristics*, the *Self-Esteem Index,* and the *Test of Early Socioemotional Development.* She is also coauthor of *A Consumer's Guide to Tests in Print* and *Assessing the Socioemotional Development and Intervention Needs of Students.*

Caroline Dunn   Dunn received her Ph.D. in 1991 from The University of Texas at Austin. She has taught high school students with mild disabilities and adults with mental retardation. She is currently an assistant professor in the Department of Rehabilitation and Special Education at Auburn University. She serves on the editorial boards of the *Journal for Learning Disabilities, Intervention in School and Clinic,* and *Education and Training in Mental Retardation.* She is a member of the Council for Learning Disabilities, Council for Exceptional Children, and American Educational Research Association. She is the president-elect of the Alabama Council for Learning Disabilities.

John J. Hoover   Hoover received his Ph.D. from the University of Colorado, Boulder, specializing in curriculum/special education. He has taught exceptional learners in kindergarten through grade 12 in alternative and public school settings. He has served as a consultant and program evaluator for remedial and special education programs at numerous elementary, secondary, and postsecondary institutions nationwide. He serves on the review boards or as a consulting editor for several journals including *Intervention in School and Clinic, Teaching Exceptional Children,* and *Teacher Education* and *Special Education.* His current research interests include the classroom implementation of study skills and strategies for work with special education students. He is author or co-author of over 40 journal articles, textbook chapters, and books dealing with topics in curriculum adaptation, study skills, cognitive learning strategies, and teacher training practices. He is currently director of research and evaluation for the American Indian Science and Engineering Society (AISES) located at the University of Colorado, Boulder.

J. Lee Wiederholt   A former classroom teacher, professor, and chair of the Department of Special Education of the University of Texas, Wiederholt is vice president of PRO-ED Publishing Company, editor-in-chief of the *Journal of Learning Disabilities,* and executive director and trustee of the Donald D. Hammill Foundation. He is the author of numerous articles, books, and tests primarily in the areas of adolescents with disabilities, reading, and resource programs.